United Kingdom National Accounts

Editor:	Simon Humphries
Production team:	Alan Smith
	Helen Shanks
	Carole Rennie
	Angie Francis
	Jon Prescott
	Paul Withey
	Anna Brueton
Graphics & Design:	Richard Lloyd

London: HMSO

The Blue Book

1996

Contents

United Kingdom National Accounts 1996 © Crown copyright 1996

Contents

Contents

United Kingdom Macro-Economic Statistics Publications

Annual Publications

- UK National Accounts (Blue Book)
- UK Balance of Payments (Pink Book)
- Input/Output Balances
- Economic Trends Annual Supplement
- Share Ownership
- Public Finance Trends
- Financial Statistics Explanatory Handbook

Quarterly Publications

- UK Economic Accounts
- Consumer Trends
- Overseas trade analysed in terms of industry

Monthly Publications

- Retail Prices Index
- Producer Price Indices
- Economic Trends
- Financial Statistics
- Monthly Review of External Trade Statistics

First Releases

Annual
- Profitability of UK companies

Quarterly
- UK Balance of Payments
- UK National Accounts
- UK Output, Income & Expenditure
- GDP Preliminary estimate
- Capital Expenditure
- Stocks
- Institutional Investment
- Govt Deficit & Debt under the Treaty

Monthly
- UK Trade in goods
- Public Sector Borrowing Requirement
- Cyclical Indicators of the UK economy
- Retail Prices Index
- Producer Prices

Other publications: - Retail Prices 1914-1990 - Input/Output Tables - Labour Market Statistics - Family Spending - Sector Classification Guide

Preface

This annual publication, the ONS "Blue Book", contains estimates of the domestic and national product, income and expenditure of the United Kingdom. It covers the calendar years 1985 to 1995. The summary tables are extended to cover 1974 to 1984 on a consistent basis. Where tables cover other than 1985 to 1995, the years shown are noted in the list of contents.

This publication has been prepared by the Office for National Statistics (ONS). The collaboration of other government departments and the Bank of England is much appreciated.

Structure of the Blue Book

The tables forming the national accounts are grouped into seventeen numbered chapters, which are then presented in six sections each with its own written introduction. They form a set of inter-related economic accounts for the nation analysed by category of transaction, by industry and by sector:

Section One gives the main national and domestic aggregates which describe total economic activity.

Section Two contains analysis of these aggregates primarily by industry, and the Input-Output use matrices for 1992, 1993 and 1994.

Section Three comprises the sector transactions accounts, including a summary account for international transactions, together with national and sector balance sheets.

Section Four presents detailed information on capital formation and capital stock.

Section Five provides additional analyses, derived and complementary statistics.

Section Six supplements the tables, giving:

methodological notes bringing up to date the latest edition of *Sources and Methods*;

a glossary of the main terms used;

a table showing the revisions to the main economic aggregates since the previous Blue Book;

and an alphabetical index to items appearing in the Tables, Glossary, and Introduction.

Sources and Methods

A general description of the statistics given in the Blue Book, together with a detailed description of the definitions, sources and methods used to make the estimates is given in *United Kingdom National Accounts: Sources and Methods, Third Edition*, Studies in Official Statistics No 37 HMSO 1985. This third edition of *"Sources and Methods"* relates to the estimates published in the 1984 Blue Book - *United Kingdom National Accounts, 1984 Edition*.

Reliability of the estimates

All the value estimates are calculated as accurately as possible but they cannot always be regarded as precise to the last digit shown. Similarly, the index numbers are not necessarily accurate to the last digit shown. Some of the figures are provisional and may be revised later; this applies particularly to many of the detailed figures for 1994 and 1995. A few, generally small, series are guessed, and some of the sectoral allocations are based on fixed percentages. Further details on reliability are given in *United Kingdom National Accounts: Sources and Methods, Third Edition*.

Revisions to data

The principal revisions which have been made to the estimates contained in tables 1.1, 1.2, and 1.4 of the 1996 Blue Book are tabulated in a separate chapter within Section Six.

Quarterly estimates

Quarterly estimates of the main components of national accounts for the last few years are published in ONS First Releases and, in more detail with commentary, in *"UK Economic Accounts - The quarterly national accounts publication"*.

Long run (up to 40 years) quarterly and annual estimates consistent with the Blue Book are published in the *Economic Trends Annual Supplement*. The latest estimates are also given in summary form in the *Monthly Digest of Statistics* and the quarterly current, capital and financial accounts for each sector are published regularly in *Financial Statistics*.

A wide range of quarterly statistics are available in machine-readable form through ONS's Databank - see below.

Blue Book data in machine-readable form

Blue Book data are available in machine-readable form either on magnetic tape or on disk. The Blue Book machine-readable dataset contains **annual** series only; all series appearing in the tables with a four character identifier are included. The machine-readable dataset covers the time span given in this publication, and earlier where available.

The magnetic tape is written in IBM unlabelled EBCDIC format. The disk contains ASCII text which can be viewed on screen and read by spreadsheet packages, in particular LOTUS or SMART. Data are available on either 3.5 inch disks (at double density or high density) or 5.25 inch disks (high density only).

Further details of the annual dataset and corresponding quarterly dataset are available from the Databank Marketing Manager, Office for National Statistics , Room 56/5, Government Offices, Great George Street, London SW1P 3AQ (Telephone: 0171-270 6081 or 6386 or 6387).

Symbols and conventions used

Prices. Except where otherwise stated, all estimates of expenditure are valued at market prices.

Symbols. The following symbols are used throughout:

..   Not available.

-     Nil or less than £500,000.

£billion denotes £1,000 million.

Office for National Statistics
Great George Street
London SW1P 3AQ
August 1996

NATIONAL ACCOUNTS USER GROUP UPDATE

The first Annual General Meeting of the National Accounts User Group held on Monday 8 July 1996, in the offices of the Office for National Statistics (ONS), elected Martin Weale, Director of the National Institute of Economic and Social Research (NIESR) and one of the Chancellor's "Wise Men", as chairman of the committee. Other members of the committee elected come from a wide spectrum of users of economic statistics representing businesses, the City and academic institutions.

Tim Holt, Director of the Office for National Statistics welcoming the existence of the National Accounts User Group said "I am glad that users of our statistics are actively participating in such a group. Their contribution will help us to continue to provide the best possible service to both government and the wider community. I am sure the Group's collective knowledge and experience, in partnership with our own, will ensure we maintain and enhance the quality and relevance of our product."

Martin Weale, Director of the National Institute of Economic and Social Research and chairman of the National Accounts User Group said, "It is all too easy for economists to take statistics for granted or to fail to appreciate the very real problems faced by the ONS in compiling them. I hope the Group will provide a means for users to become better informed about the numbers they are using while at the same time providing a route for user concerns to be communicated to the ONS. It is now recognised that the ONS has a role wider than simply providing figures required by the government. The User Group should help discharge that wider role."

Dr Penelope Rowlatt, committee member of the Group and a Director of National Economic Research Associates, said "This is an excellent initiative. It will allow the users of statistics to get together with producers and the feedback should result in an even better service."

Background

The National Accounts User Group was first established through a meeting of interested National Accounts users on 29 November 1995. Further meetings to establish the Group were held in February and April.

Membership of the Group

Membership of the Group is open to all those interested in the United Kingdom's economic accounts statistics, including both government and non-government users and corporate or individual membership.

Purpose of the Group

The purpose of the Group is to develop and maintain close liaison between users and producers of economic accounts data. It provides a forum for the Office for National Statistics to obtain users' views on both existing and new products as well as the opportunity to discuss particular issues as the arise either by canvassing views of the whole group or by setting up small working sub-groups. The Group will provide opportunities to increase the users' understanding of the construction of the accounts and promote the exchange of information and expertise between users and producers.

Activities of the Group

The Group has quarterly committee meetings followed by a presentation to members of the Group. Presentations so far have been on "Treatment of the National Lottery in the National Accounts", "Chain linking the National Accounts" and "European System of Accounts". Each quarter a Newsletter is published to disseminate news of the meetings, advertise future events, convey items of statistical news and to canvas views of users on specific issues.

The Group provides an opportunity for users to make formal or informal presentations to national and international government bodies on matters of concern to statistics users. It will also organise study groups on specific points of interest (for example, the revisions policy used by national accountants).

Further information about the Group can be obtained from:

David Blunt Telephone:
Secretary of the National Accounts User Group
Office for National Statistics
Great George Street
London   SW1P 3AQ

Tel: 0171 270 5935
Fax: 0171 270 6190

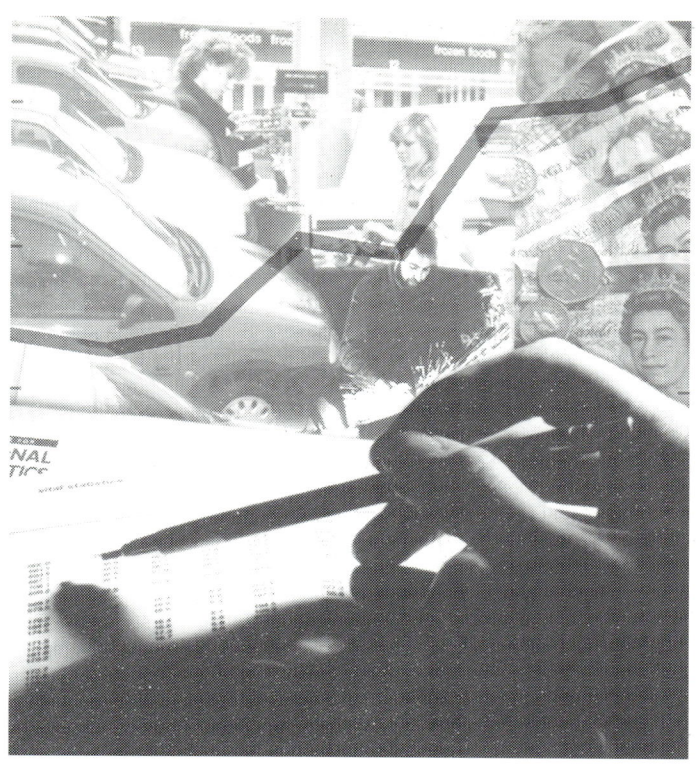

The national accounts

1

The national accounts

The national accounts at a glance

In 1995 the output of the economy as measured by **Gross domestic product** (GDP) at constant factor cost was 2.5 per cent higher than in 1994, compared with a rise of 4.0 per in 1994 over 1993.

Over the 10 years to 1995 the average rate of growth of GDP at constant factor cost has been 2.2 per cent a year.

Chart 1.1

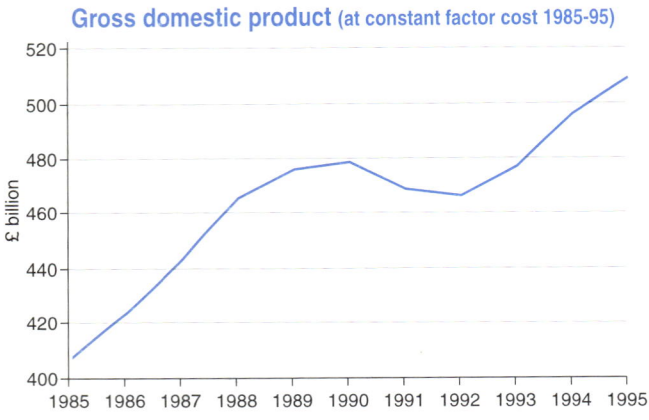

Gross domestic product (at constant factor cost 1985-95)

Money GDP (at current market prices) increased by 4.9 per cent between 1995 and 1994, compared to a 5.9 per cent increase in 1994 over 1993. Over the ten years to 1995, money GDP has risen by an average of 7.0 per cent a year.

Real National disposable income (which measures UK residents' command over resources) was 1.5 per cent higher in 1995 than in 1994. Over the ten years to 1995, it rose by an average of 2.3 per cent a year.

Chart 1.2 shows changes in the price of value-added , as reflected by the **implied GDP deflator** at constant factor cost.

Chart 1.2

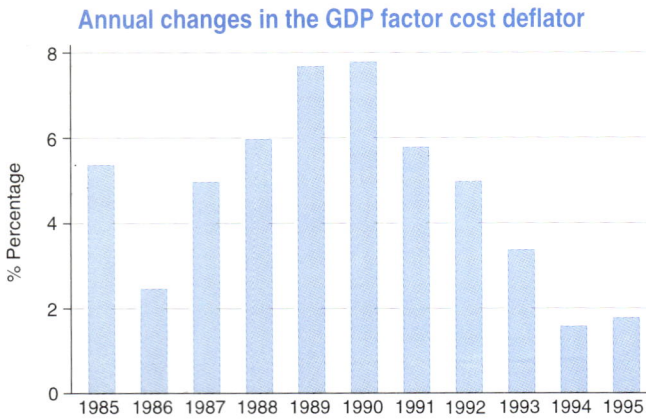

Annual changes in the GDP factor cost deflator

The annual rate of growth in the GDP deflator declined steadily from a peak of 7.8 per cent in 1990 to 1.6 per cent in 1994, but increased slightly in 1995 to 1.8 per cent.

Expenditure components of GDP:
Contributions to growth in 1995

The growth in the volume of **GDP at market prices** of 2.5 per cent in 1995 can be split amongst the various expenditure components. The table below shows what effect the changes in a component would have had if all other components had remained unchanged.

Chart 1.3 Contributions to growth in constant market price GDP from 1994 to 1995

Component	change in GDP £m	%
Consumers' expenditure	7 131	1.3
GDFCF	-115	0.0
value of physical increase in stocks	341	0.1
Exports	11 207	2.0
Imports (-)	-6 361	-1.1
Total	14 050	2.5

Total final expenditure: share by category of expenditure

Chart 1.4

GDP share by category of expenditure

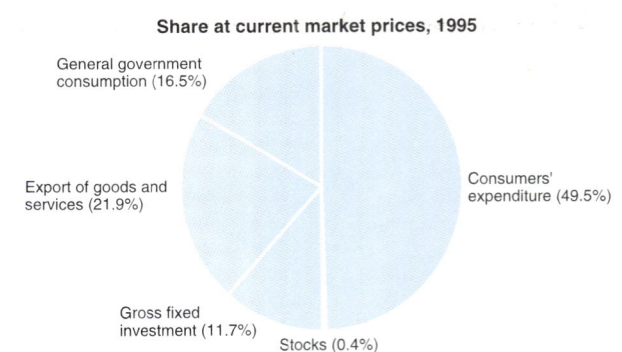

Share at current market prices, 1995

General government consumption (16.5%)

Export of goods and services (21.9%)

Gross fixed investment (11.7%)

Stocks (0.4%)

Consumers' expenditure (49.5%)

Total domestic income: share by category of income

Chart **1.5**

GDP: share by category of income

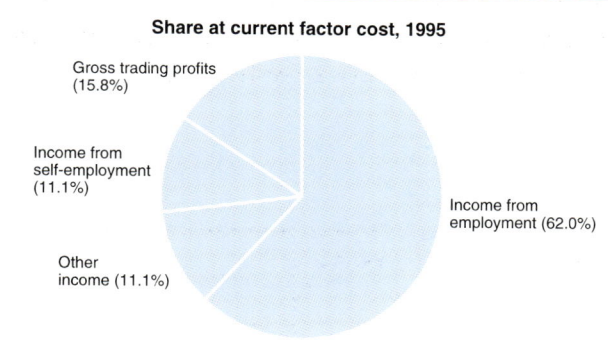

Share at current factor cost, 1995

Gross trading profits
(15.8%)

Income from
self-employment
(11.1%)

Other
income (11.1%)

Income from
employment (62.0%)

Gross domestic product by category of output

In the ten years to 1995, the average annual increase in the output of the **production sector** was 1.9 per cent a year, whereas that for the **service sector** was 2.5 per cent.

Chart **1.6**

GDP by category of output

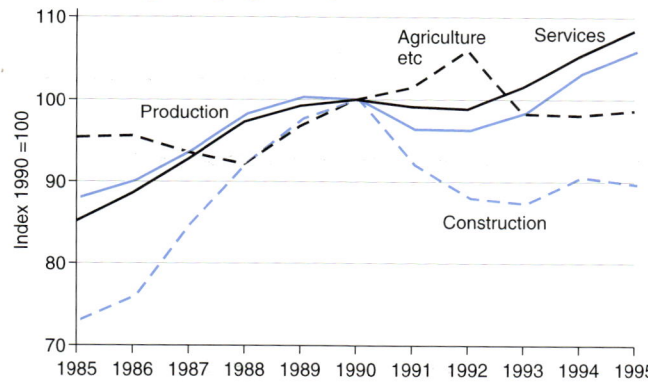

An introduction to the United Kingdom National Accounts

1. The UK National accounts are the accounts of the nation. They are compiled by the Office for National Statistics according to international standards and record and describe economic activity in the United Kingdom. As such they are used to support the formulation and monitoring of economic and social policies.

2. This introduction to section one of the national accounts is designed to give an *overview* of these accounts; to help users find their way around the tables and make the best use of the information presented. It has been divided into the following areas:

   The framework of the accounts and gross domestic product:

   　The definition of GDP:

   　　Economic activity: what production is included?
   　　What prices are measured?
   　　The rest of the world: national and domestic,
   　　The concept of net and gross.

   　The framework:

   　　The national accounts:
   　　　The production account, the income and expenditure account and the balance of payments.
   　　Features of the accounts.

   The measurement of economic activity in the whole economy:
   　　The income measure,
   　　The expenditure measure, current prices, constant prices and index numbers,
   　　Constant price series and rebasing,
   　　The output measure,
   　　Gross and real national disposable income,
   　　GDP as used by the EC, UN and OECD.

   Developments in the accounts.

   Further information.

3. Discussion of the different areas of the accounts - industrial analyses and input-output balances, the sector accounts, capital formation and capital stocks - are dealt with separately in the introductions to *sections two, three and four* respectively.

4. *Section five* - other analyses and derived statistics - provides extra analyses and details of the rates of change of gross domestic product not covered in the earlier sections of the book.

5. *Section six* - supplementary information - provides a *glossary* which explains the main terms used, *methodological notes* which bring up to date the definitions, sources and methods given in *United Kingdom National Accounts: Sources and Methods Third edition (HMSO, 1985)*, and a table summarising the *revisions* to the main aggregates since the previous edition of the Blue Book.

The framework of the national accounts and gross domestic product

6. The great wealth of data contained within this book is presented as part of a comprehensive national accounting framework. An understanding of this framework is crucial in any analysis of the figures: It helps to understand what information is available and how it has been put together, and in doing so reveals the different perspectives from which the figures can be viewed.

   *However, before going on to describe the framework it is useful to consider briefly the economy as a whole and the measurement of total domestic activity, or **Gross domestic product (GDP)**. In particular: what production is included in this measure, what prices are used to value the products of economic activity, and how are the terms 'national' and 'domestic', and 'net' and 'gross' defined?*

Economic activity: what production is included?

7. As GDP is defined as the sum of all economic activity taking place in UK territory it is important to be clear about what is defined as economic activity. In its widest sense it could cover all activities resulting in the production of goods or services and so encompass some activities which are very difficult to measure (for example cooking and cleaning and other services performed around the house by the householder).

8. In practice a *production boundary* - determined by international convention - is defined, inside which are all the economic activities taken to contribute to economic performance. These activities range from agriculture and production through service producing activities (for example financial services and hotel and catering), to the provision of health, education, public administration and defence.

9. In this approach the decision whether to include a particular activity takes into account the following:

   ● does the activity produce a useful output?

   ● is the product of the activity marketable and so have a market value?

- if the product does not have a meaningful market value can a meaningful market value be assigned? (i.e. can we impute a value)

- would exclusion (or inclusion) of the product of the activity make comparisons between countries or over time more meaningful?

10. Some activities, not directly exchanged for money, but for which a market price can be estimated or *imputed* include: provision of income in kind to employees (e.g. subsidised canteens, provision of a company car), the provision of owner occupied housing (by the owner for their own use) and the non trading use of fixed assets owned by the government and by private non profit making bodies (for example, school buildings). For the record, the productive 'domestic' activities of households are not included in GDP as estimation is so difficult; moreover inclusion by the UK alone would not help international comparisons.

What price is used to value the products of economic activity?

11. **Market prices** - that is, the prices paid by the purchaser - are the usual basis for valuing transactions in the accounts. These prices will include indirect **taxes** (for instance VAT) paid to the government and **subsidies** paid to producers by the government.

12. However it is also useful to measure GDP with these potentially distorting effects removed, that is at **factor cost**. The *factor cost adjustment* (taxes less subsidies) is subtracted to remove the effects of subsidies and indirect taxes from the market price measure (GDP_{mp}) leaving a measure at factor cost (GDP_{fc}).

i.e. $$GDP_{fc} = GDP_{mp} - taxes + subsidies$$

The rest of the world: National and Domestic

13. **Domestic Product** includes production (or income earned) from all activities taking place 'at home' or inside the domestic territory. This will *include* production by any foreign owned company in the UK but *exclude* any income earned from activities taking place outside the domestic territory.

14. For example all the profits generated by a Japanese car manufacturer operating in the UK will be *included* in GDP, even although a large part of the profits may be remitted to Japan. This is because the profits have been earned in the UK.

15. Similarly a UK company operating abroad may earn profits through its overseas subsidiary company and some of these profits are remitted to the UK. However these are *excluded* from the GDP measure as they were not earned in the UK.

16. In the same way that **profits** flow across national boundaries so do **dividend** and **interest payments**. These flows (profits, dividends

and interest) are referred to as **property income to and from abroad**. If the *net* flow into the country (i.e. inflows minus outflows) is added to GDP, the resulting measure is called **Gross national product (GNP): i.e.**

Gross *domestic* product

plus

net property income from abroad

equals

Gross *national* product

17. **National product** includes income earned by residents of the national territory, remitted to the national territory, no matter where the income is earned.

Gross domestic product: the concept of net and gross

18. The term **gross** refers to the fact that when measuring domestic production we have not allowed for an important phenomenon; **capital consumption** or **depreciation**. **Capital goods** are different from the materials and fuels used up in the production process because they are not used up in the period of account: they are instrumental in allowing that process to take place. However, over time capital goods do wear out or become obsolete and in this sense gross domestic product does not give a true picture of **value added** in the economy. In other words, in calculating value added as the difference between output and costs, we should include as a current cost that part of the capital goods used up in the production process, that is, the depreciation of the capital assets. **Net** concepts are net of this capital depreciation, for example:

Gross domestic product

minus

capital consumption

equals

Net domestic product

19. In order to account for capital consumption (depreciation) and arrive at a net measure of output it is necessary to estimate depreciation. This is difficult as depreciation cannot be measured directly by actual transactions.

20. Estimates of depreciation given in companies accounts provide poor estimates for national accounting purposes because:

- the depreciation in business accounts is based on the original (or historic) costs of the assets rather than the current cost of the capital consumed and,

- the depreciation calculation in business accounts are usually based on an assumption that the assets have a short service life. In reality the service life is usually much longer.

21. As a result it is difficult to get reliable and timely estimates of capital consumption and so gross domestic production remains the most widely used measure of economic activity.

22. **Net national product** (i.e. GNP *less* capital consumption) is also known as **Net national income**.

23. Estimates of gross national product (GNP) and net national product (NNP) are given in tables 1.1, 1.2 and 1.3.

The framework

With this introduction to gross domestic product we can go on to describe the comprehensive national accounting framework.

What is an account? What is its purpose?

24. An account displays the values of transactions carried out in the economy. By employing the accounts we can identify that the sum of resources is equal to the sum of uses. Each account requires a **balancing item** to ensure the equality of resources and uses. Normally an account is drawn up in order to reveal an economic measure (which is of interest itself) as the balancing item.

25. There are four main kinds of account: production, income and expenditure, capital and financial. The **production account** displays the transactions involved in generating income by the production of goods and services. In this case the balancing item is *value added*. For the nation's accounts the balancing item, the sum of value added, is *GDP*.

26. The **income and expenditure account** shows current income (in this case GDP) carried forward from the production account, and has as its balancing item savings, which are the difference between income and expenditure. The **capital account** shows savings carried forward from the income and expenditure account. The balancing item is the *financial surplus or deficit*. The **financial account** shows how the financial surplus or deficit brought forward from the capital account is financed by borrowing and lending. These three accounts are discussed in more detail in *Section 3: The Sector accounts* which examines the transactions *within* the economy.

The national accounts

27. Conceptually the accounts of the nation can be thought of as two main accounts. The first of these concerns production activities; the second (bringing together the income and expenditure account and the capital and financial accounts) concerns the nation's income and its disposal. They are described in turn below.

Fig 1.1 Domestic Production of goods and services

Uses	Resources
Supply	Demand
Imports	Exports
	Final consumption
	Capital formation
GDP (value added)	
Total supply	Total Demand

Domestic production (see figure 1.1)

28. The first account is the nation's **production account.** Broadly, it is a consolidation of the production accounts of every producing unit in the country (excluding sales and purchases of intermediate products). In this account GDP is the balancing item, in the same way as operating profit (or loss) might be the balancing item in a business account. (GDP is however broader than this - see below.)

29. On the right hand side are total receipts from sales (or output) of goods and services. In the national accounts these are classified into three main categories of final demand: exports, final consumption expenditure and capital formation (investment in fixed assets and stocks).

30. On the left are the overall costs of production: the nation's purchases of goods and services from the rest of the world (imports), and the value added or gross domestic product (GDP); consisting broadly of employment income (wages and salaries etc.), gross operating profits and taxes on expenditure less subsidies.

National income and expenditure (see figure 1.2)

31. The second account is more like that of a household, in which income is received from productive activity (for example in a pay packet) and spent on food, clothing, housing, etc. Any balance left over (savings) may be kept in a bank account.

32. The right hand side of the national income account refers to the nation's **income**, particularly the value added (GDP) brought down from the production account. In this context GDP is known as factor

income (ie income paid to the factors of production). Taxes on expenditure *less* subsidies (also known as the factor cost adjustment) are also included. Net income from abroad includes receipts *less* payments of factor income (interest, profits and dividends), and other transfers exchanged for payment.

33. The left hand side of the account shows how the income is spent. The expenditure may be on consumption, on investment in fixed assets and stocks or on the net acquisition of financial claims. It is an identity of the accounting framework that these claims are necessarily on the rest of the world (ie net lending to the rest of the world).

Fig1.2   National INCOME and its disposal

Uses	Resources
Expenditure	Income
Final consumption	GDP (factor income)
Capital formation	
Net lending to Rest of World	Net income from abroad
National expenditure	National disposable income

Balance of payments (see figure 1.3)

34. These two basic accounts can themselves be consolidated by putting them together and deleting common elements from both sides of the account. The result is a summary balance of payments account as shown below.

35. In balance of payments terminology, net lending to the rest of the world is equal to the "balance on current account". In the United Kingdom this is usually net borrowing rather than lending.

Fig 1.3   Balance of payments
(a consolidation of the two accounts above)

Debits	Credits
Imports	Exports
Net lending to Rest of World[1]	Net income from abroad

1 conceptually equal to the *current balance*

Accounting Principles

36. A key element in the national accounting framework is that, in principle, every transaction should have a common valuation and a common timing from the point of view of both parties involved. Otherwise the accounts would not balance.

37. These transactions are recorded at the time when the good is supplied or the service rendered, and reflect 'economic flows'. This is known as the **accruals** basis of measurement. It is not necessarily the same as the cash or receipts and payments basis, which records at the time the money changes hands. For this reason transactions are not necessarily recorded in the nations accounts at the same time as they would be in household, company or government accounts.

The features of the account

38. Although the structure used in this example is a simplification, it helps to build a basic understanding of how the more detailed accounts fit together. By looking at GDP - the sum of all economic activity taking place in the UK - as part of the production account and the income account, some basic features of the accounts and the data can be seen.

39. Some of the basic features of the **production account** are outlined below:

It provides the framework within which GDP can be estimated, particularly from the **expenditure and output approaches**;

The natural **classification** is **by industry (SIC) or type of product** (see methodological notes for further details);

The data mainly concern goods and services which (by partition into prices and quantities) can in principal be expressed in **constant** as well as **current prices**;

By elaborating the accounts, commodity flow and kind of activity accounts can be obtained. Ultimately these can provide **input/output** tables; (Further explanation of this process and the tables themselves are given in Section 2: The main analyses).

40. On the other hand although it has several elements in common with the production account, **the income account and expenditure account** has quite a different perspective:

It can be elaborated into '**sector accounts**' with the inclusion of sectorial transfer payments and financial transactions;

The **institutional sector** is the appropriate classification for the economic units concerned (ie the personal sector, the corporate sector, the government sector and the overseas sector); and

These sector accounts provide the appropriate framework for studying the **income measure of GDP**, its distribution and redistribution; consumption and saving; investment and its financing.

41. Further discussion of the **sector accounts** and the different types of transaction - be it current, capital or financial - which take place within the economy as a whole and between the different sectors can be found in *Section 3: The Sector Accounts*.

42. In addition this sector framework may be used to compile national and sectorial balance sheets showing the **stock of assets and liabilities** which may often influence the flows. More information on this aspect can be found in *Section 3: The sector accounts and Section 4: Capital formation and capital stocks*.

Summary

43. The integrated economic accounts of the United Kingdom fall into three major parts, corresponding to the three components of the model described above:

> GDP and its components;
> the sector accounts;
> the balance of payments.

44. The first two components are dealt with in this publication and the third can be found in *The UK Balance of Payments* (the Pink Book) also published by the ONS.

Measurement of economic activity in the whole economy - the three approaches to GDP

45. The output of an economy as defined by gross domestic product, can be viewed in three different but theoretically equivalent ways :

> as the total of all incomes earned in the production of goods and services;
>
> as the total of all final expenditures made either in consuming the finished goods and services produced or in adding to capital assets. (The cost of imports having been subtracted).
>
> and
>
> the sum of the value added by all activities which produce goods and services - net output.

In simple terms this is how we approach the task of estimating GDP.

46. The resulting estimates, like all statistical estimates, contain errors and omissions; we obtain the best estimate by reconciling the estimates obtained from all three approaches. The definitive estimate

of GDP (ie the published figure) is arrived at by reconciling this information through the construction of **input output balances**. This method has been used on an annual basis for GDP estimates since 1989. (For further details on annual balancing and the methods used for aligning different estimates prior to 1989, please see Section 2: The main analyses and the methodological notes).

47. For years in which no input-output balance has been struck, a residual error exists. The **residual error** shows the outstanding difference between estimates of the total of expenditure components of GDP at factor cost and the total income components of GDP after the balancing process has been carried out. This residual error is made up of two statistical discrepancies which are shown in the accounts, namely:

> the **statistical discrepancy (expenditure adjustment)**, which is the difference between the sum of the expenditure components and the definitive estimate of GDP, *plus*
>
> the **statistical discrepancy (income adjustment)**, which is the difference between the sum of the income components and the definitive estimate of GDP *(with sign reversed)*.

48. As outlined in the framework above, the different approaches to the measurement of GDP provide a breakdown into different component parts and give different perspectives on the data, which are represented in either current or constant prices, or in the case of the expenditure approach both current and constant prices.

These different approaches with each of their separate sources are described in more detail in turn below.

The income approach

49. The **income** approach, as it suggests, adds up all income earned by individuals or corporations in the production of goods and services. This is the most easily understood measure as the factors of production - land, labour and capital - receive money or factor payments - in exchange for their inputs.

50. However some types of income are not included - these are **transfer payments** like unemployment benefit, child benefit or state pensions. Although they do provide individuals with money to spend, the payments are made out of, for example, taxes and national insurance contributions. They are a *redistribution* of existing incomes and do not themselves represent any addition to current economic activity. To avoid 'double counting' these transfer payments are excluded from the calculation of GDP.

51. In the UK this measure of GDP is obtained by summing together the factor incomes: income from employment and self employment, gross trading profits and rents. As most of these incomes are subject to

tax, the figures are usually obtained from data collected for tax purposes by the Inland Revenue. However because there is some delay in providing good quality estimates by this method, other methods are used to provide initial estimates.

52. **This approach provides estimates of GDP and its 'income' component parts at current factor cost.** [*Although the income approach cannot be used to calculate constant price estimates directly (because it is not possible to separate income components into prices and quantities in the same way as for goods and services) some estimates are obtained indirectly. That is, the expenditure-based **GDP deflator at factor cost** (also known as the **index of total home costs**) is used to deflate the current factor cost estimates to provide a constant price version of the total income components of GDP (see Table 1.7).*]

53. To help illustrate the make up of the income approach an extract from table 1.4 containing figures rounded to the nearest £ billion is shown in figure 1.4 below. Paragraphs 54 to 58 give more information on some of the items included.

Fig 1.4   GDP at current factor cost

Factor incomes		£billion
	1994	**1995**
Income from employment[1]	364.9	377.9
Income from self employment[1]	64.0	67.7
Gross trading profits of companies[2]	86.5	91.0
Gross trading surplus of public corporations[3]	4.2	4.6
Gross trading surplus of general govt enterprises[4]	0.5	0.6
Rent[5]	58.6	62.8
Imputed charge for consumption of non trading capital[6]	4.4	4.7
Total domestic income	583.2	609.3
less stock appreciation[7]	-4.0	-4.9
Statistical discrepancy	0.0	-0.2
GDP at factor cost	579.2	604.3

1 From Table 4.1
2 From Table 5.1
3. From Table 6.2
4. From Tables 7.2 and 8.2
5. From Table 2.6
6. From Table 4.1, 7.2 and 8.2
7. From Table 15.4

Difference between total and sums components are due to rounding.

---

54. The estimate for **rent** includes the imputed rent for owner-occupied dwellings. An identical estimate for consumers' expenditure on rent appears in the expenditure analysis.

55. The imputed charge for **consumption of non-trading capital** is needed for completeness. Because GDP is a gross concept (see paragraph 18) for trading activities profits or surpluses are recorded gross in this sense. An imputation has to made for the consumption of capital by non trading activities. Although these activities do not give rise to trading profits or surpluses, they do use up capital assets. The same imputation is made in the expenditure analysis.

56. The **stock appreciation adjustment** is required because some income includes the value of stock appreciation (or the revaluation of stocks). No new goods or services may have been produced in the accounting period (no additions to current economic activity) but the value of the stock may change simply as the result of an increase or decrease in the price of the item in stock. For example the profits of companies include the effect of stock appreciation.

57. Where no annual input-output balance is struck, a **statistical discrepancy or income adjustment** is used to bring the income measure into line with the expenditure measure. (As with all estimates, there will be some errors and omissions in both measures. We adjust to give one 'best' estimate). (See paragraph 46 and 47).

58. As well as these adjustments within the figures for income from employment, self employment and company profits we have included an evasion adjustment. This adjustment is added to the initial estimate of income to allow for income earned but not declared to the inland revenue. (Further information can be found in the methodological notes).

59. Data on the income components can be found in tables 1.4, 2.2, 2.6, in the sector accounts and in tables 16.5, 16.12 and 16.13.

The expenditure approach

60. The **expenditure** approach measures total expenditure on finished or final goods and services produced in the domestic economy. From this total final demand for goods and services, imports are deducted to give GDP. The total is obtained from the sum of consumers' and government current expenditure on goods and services, investment (capital expenditure on fixed assets and changes in stocks), and net exports of goods and services. This approach can be represented by the following equation:

$$GDP_{mp} = C + G + I + X - M$$

Where: *C = consumers expenditure, G = local and central government consumption, I = investment or gross domestic fixed capital formation (GDFCF) and changes in stocks, X = exports and M = imports.*

61. These categories are estimated from a wide variety of sources including expenditure surveys, the government's internal accounting system, surveys of traders and the administrative documents used in the importing and exporting of some goods.

62. To avoid double counting in this approach it is important to classify expenditures as either final or intermediate. *Final goods* are the goods purchased by the ultimate consumer or user. They are final because they are no longer part of the economic flow or being traded in the market place. *Intermediate goods* on the other hand are goods which are used as inputs in the production process.

63. **Exports** include all sales to non-residents - both exports of goods and services - have to be regarded as final sales, since they are final as far as the UK economy is concerned.

64. **Imports** of goods and services are deducted because they are included directly or indirectly in final demand, but are not part of domestic production. What remains is what has been produced in the United Kingdom - gross domestic product from the expenditure side.

65. **This approach provides estimates of GDP and its component expenditure parts at current market prices and current factor cost.**

66. Figure 1.5 below illustrates the make up of GDP and GNP at market prices using figures extracted from table 1.2. The figures are rounded to the nearest £ billion. Paragraphs 67 to 69 give more information on some of the items included.

Fig 1.5 GNP by category of expenditure at current market prices

	£billion	
	1994	1995
Consumers expenditure[1]	427.3	447.2
General government final consumption[2]	144.1	149.5
Gross domestic fixed capital formation[3]	99.2	105.4
Value of physical increases in stocks and work in progress[4]	3.7	3.9
Total domestic expenditure	674.3	706.0
Exports of goods and services	176.1	197.6
Total final expenditure	805.4	903.6
less Imports of goods and services	-182.1	-203.1
statistical discrepancy	0.0	0.4
Gross domestic product	668.3	700.9
net property income from abroad	8.7	9.6
Gross national product	676.9	710.5

1 From Table 4.1
2 From Table 7.2 and 8.2
3. From Table 4.2, 5.3, 6.3, 7.3 and 8.3
4. From Table 15.4

Difference between total and sums components are due to rounding.

67. Gross domestic fixed capital formation (GDFCF) is an estimate of all expenditure, during the period of account, on fixed assets. (See paragraphs 146 to 148)

68. The **value of physical increases in stocks and work in progress** (VPI) is an estimate of the value of expenditure, by productive enterprises, on stocks not used up in the period of account. As this estimate is the difference between the levels at the start and end of the period, a negative estimate can result. (See paragraphs 150 to 151)

69. The **statistical adjustment or expenditure adjustment** is used to bring the expenditure measure into line with the income measure. (As with all estimates, there will be some errors and omissions in both measures; we adjust to give one 'best' estimate). (See paragraphs 46 to 47)

70. **Market prices** - that is, the prices paid by the purchaser - are the usual basis for valuing transactions in the accounts. These prices will include indirect **taxes** (for instance VAT) paid to the government and **subsidies** paid to producers by the government. However it is also useful to measure GDP with these potentially distorting effects removed, that is at **factor cost.**

71. The *factor cost adjustment* (taxes less subsidies) removes the effects of subsidies and indirect taxes from the market price measure leaving a measure of expenditure at factor cost. This factor cost valuation of expenditure is comparable to the other two measures of GDP.

72. Figure 1.6 below (an extract from table 1.2) shows the application of the factor cost adjustment.

Fig 1.6 National product: by category of expenditure at current prices

	£billion	
At current market prices	1994	1995
Gross domestic product	668.3	700.9
Factor cost adjustment		
Taxes on expenditure	96.1	103.6
Subsidies	7.1	7.0
Factor cost adjustment (taxes less subsidies)	89.1	96.6
At current factor cost		
Gross domestic product	579.2	604.3
net property income from abroad	8.7	9.6
Gross national product	587.9	613.8

Difference between total and sums components are due to rounding.

As you can see:

GDP at market prices

$$GDP_{mp} = C + G \text{ (local and central)} + GDFCF + \text{stocks} + (X\text{-}M)$$

and

GDP at factor cost

$$GDP_{fc} = GDP_{mp} - \text{taxes} + \text{subsidies}$$

The effects of inflation: How are changes in real output estimated?

73. When looking at the change in the economy over time the main concern is usually whether more goods and services are actually being produced now than at some time in the past. How far are the changes "real" and how far are they the result of inflation?

74. This is not as easy as making a simple comparison of the current price figures. Most national accounting data are shown in current prices which combine the effects of the changes in prices and quantities. However comparisons over time can be more useful analytically when the separate effects of movements in price and volume can be separated.

The expenditure approach at constant prices

75. As well as GDP at **current prices** the expenditure approach is used to provide information on expenditure at **constant prices**. In constant price series, the transactions are revalued for all years to a fixed price level, that is, at the average prices of a selected year (known as the *base year*).

76. Figure 1.7 below shows two series of GDP at factor cost. One series is at current prices (ie the price prevailing in that year) and the other is at constant prices (in this case the constant prices are 1990 prices). The constant price series shows the change in GDP *after* the effects of inflation have been removed.

Fig 1.7 GDP at factor cost

		£billion
	At current prices	At 1990 prices
1989	441.8	476.2
1990	478.9	478.9
1991	496.3	468.9
1992	518.1	466.5
1993	548.0	477.1
1994	579.1	496.4
1995	604.3	508.8

77. Because the constant prices are shown in 1990 prices, 1990 is called the base year. (Constant price series are discussed in more detail below).

78. How do we remove the effects of inflation to obtain this constant price series? Information obtained on price changes for particular goods and services - such as that collected for the Retail Prices Index (RPI) or the Producers Prices Index (PPI) - is used to 'deflate' the current price series.

79. Constant price versions of GDP and its main expenditure components are given in table 1.3; detail of consumers expenditure at constant prices is given in table 4.6 and 4.8.

Before going on to discuss the third measure of GDP - the output measure - which is shown at constant prices and published in index number form, it is necessary to recap and expand a little on the theory of constant prices and index numbers.

Current prices, constant prices and index numbers

80. Most of the tables are shown in **current prices**, that is the price prevailing during each period of account. Changes over time in current price series reflect both changes in price and changes in volume. For analytical purposes it is important to separate out the effects of price and volume changes. In **constant price** series, the transactions are revalued for all years to a constant price level, that is, at the average prices of the base year. In most cases the revaluation is carried out by using price indices - such as component series of the RPI and PPI - to deflate current price series at a detailed level of disaggregation.

81. Some constant price series are expressed as index numbers in which the constant price series are simply scaled proportionately to a value of 100 in the base year. These constant price index numbers are **volume indices**. They are of the 'base weighted' or 'Laspeyres' form.

Two other kinds of index are used: value indices and implied deflators.

82. An **implied deflator** series is calculated by dividing each value of a current price series by the corresponding constant price value, and multiplying by 100. The resulting price index is of the 'current weighted' or 'Paasche form'. It estimates current price levels compared with those of the base year using current year volumes.

83. **Value indices** are calculated simply by scaling current price values proportionately to a value of 100 in the base year. By definition, such a value index, if divided by the corresponding volume index and multiplied by a 100, will yield the corresponding price index.

Constant price series and rebasing

84 Over time comparisons of constant price series are complicated by changes in the *relative prices* of different goods and services and by

qualitative changes in the goods and services themselves. As time passes some goods escalate in price more rapidly than others. Others become so much improved that they become, in effect, different goods or services from those produced previously under the same name. Because of these changes, conversion to base year prices becomes more and more artificial as time passes.

85. To reduce this problem, the base year is updated periodically, in a process called **chain linking**. Each series is divided into several blocks of years, and each block of years is associated with a base year and link year. These blocks are:

Period	Base year	Link year	
1948 to 1957	1958	1958	
1958 to 1962	1963	1963	
1963 to 1968	1963	1968	Output
1968 to 1972	1970	1973	Output
1963 to 1972	1970	1973	Expenditure and income
1973 to 1977	1975	1978	
1978 to 1983	1980	1983	
1983 to 1986	1985	1986	
1986 to date	1990		

86. Within each of these blocks, all constant price figures are calculated with reference to the same base year. In the link years, figures are calculated with reference to two consecutive base years, so that a linking factor may be obtained and the whole series, as published, may be shown with reference to the latest base year. By this process, the whole period is rescaled to the same base year, but within each block the relative prices used to re-value to constant prices are those most appropriate to that period.

87. Reasonable comparisons can be made between the constant price values for any pair of years which fall within the same block. Otherwise comparisons between any two years which fall in different blocks give only a general indication of changes in the volume measured.

88. Rebasing to 1990 prices is discussed further in the methodological notes.

The Output approach

89. Third, the output approach looks at the contribution to production of each economic unit; that is the value of production less the value of the inputs used up in the production process. The sum of this **value added**, for all producers, is GDP.

90. GDP measured by this approach is presented in seasonally adjusted index number form at **constant** prices. Although the input-output balance compilation allows the calculation of this measure at **current** prices, this information is only available for those years for which the balances are produced. In this publication input output balances are given for the years 1989 to 1994.

91. In theory value added at constant prices should be estimated by deflating separately the gross inputs and the gross outputs of each economic unit and then subtracting one from the other. But, because it is hard to get reliable information from companies which would make this calculation possible on a timely basis, a simplifying assumption is made: value added is assumed to be proportional to the output produced.

92. As a result it is possible to say, broadly, if the volume of output increases by say 10 per cent, then inputs will increase by the same percentage and hence value added will also increase by 10 per cent. With this approach, which is valid in the short term, the only data required is the volume of output. This is often approximated (or proxied) by deflating the turnover or value of production. Other commonly used proxies include the quantity of goods and services provided or employment (with adjustments made for productivity). The output indicators obtained for each industry are then expressed in index number form with base year (currently 1990) equal to 100.

93. These output indicators are then combined or 'weighted together' using the value added of each industrial sector in the base year established from the input-output balance.

94. Figure 1.8 below is an extract from table 1.6 and shows GDP at constant factor cost by industry of output.

Fig 1.8   GDP at constant factor cost: by industry of output

	Weight per 1000					
	1990	1991	1992	1993	1994	1995
Agriculture hunting, forestry and fishing	19	101.5	106.0	98.2	98.0	98.6
Production						
Mining and quarrying	24	104.5	107.8	115.2	132.4	139.3
Manufacturing	232	94.6	94.0	95.3	99.3	101.5
Electricity, gas and water supply	22	105.7	107.4	111.8	113.1	116.7
Total production	278	96.3	96.2	98.3	103.2	105.9
Construction	72	92.0	87.9	87.2	90.5	89.6
Service industries						
Distribution, hotels and catering, repairs	143	99.9	103.4	104.5	103.4	104.5
Transport, storage and communication	84	98.2	99.8	104.8	112.2	118.5
Other	405	100.3	99.8	101.6	104.5	107.6
Total services	631	99.1	98.8	101.6	105.3	108.4
Gross domestic product	**1 000**	97.9	97.4	99.6	103.7	106.2

95. Tables 1.6, 2.5 and 17.2 give detailed index numbers of output at constant factor cost. Other tables on value added (2.2, 2.3, 2.4 and 2.6) are derived by apportioning, by industry or by sector, the income components of GDP.

Two other assessments of economic activity - GNDI and RNDI - are discussed in turn below.

Gross national disposable income and real national disposable income

96. In the discussions so far we have yet to consider the measure which represents the total ***disposable*** income of the country's residents.

97. Gross national product represents the ***total*** income of the country's residents and is derived from GDP by adding net property income from abroad. However there are two other areas which affect the country's residents' command over resources:

i) There are flows into and out of the country which are not concerned with economic production. These are current **transfers from abroad** and current **transfers paid abroad**. They include transactions with the European Union, overseas aid and private gifts. An estimate of **Gross national disposable income** is reached by adjusting GNP by the net amount of net income received. GNDI is shown in table 1.1.

ii) Second, disposable income is affected by the **terms of trade** effect. Some of the expenditure by UK residents is on imported goods and services; some of the income earned by residents is from exports of goods and services. If UK export prices fell relative to the price of imports, then the terms of trade effect would move against the UK; that is residents would have to sell more exports to be able to continue to buy the same amount of imports. The purchasing power of UK residents would be diminished to this extent. Similarly, if the UK export prices rose relative to prices of imports then the effect would be opposite: the purchasing power of residents would rise. An adjustment is made specifically for the terms of trade effect in calculating **Real national disposable income** (RNDI), which is the constant price version of GNDI.

98. The relationship between GNDI and RNDI is given in table 1.1. RNDI is the preferred measure of changes in the UK residents command over resources.

99. Some further details on the calculation of RNDI from the 1988 edition are given in the methodological notes.

European Community definition of Gross national product

100. The Statistical Office of the European Community (EUROSTAT) uses a slightly different definition of GDP from that used here. EUROSTAT publications use the definition of GDP at market prices based on the European system of integrated accounts (ESA). This definition is also used for statistical returns to the United Nations (UN) and to the Organisation for Economic Cooperation and Development (OECD). An estimate of this series can be obtained using published series on UK definitions as shown below in table A (previously known as table C).

A Gross national product : derivation of SNA/ESA definition data for international returns

£ million

		1985	1986	1987	1988	1989	1990	1991	1992	1993	1994	1995
Gross national product at market prices (Blue Book Table 1.1)	GIBF	359 640	389 472	427 308	475 996	519 459	552 387	575 824	602 040	633 355	676 946	710 462
less Motor vehicle excise duty paid by households (Blue Book Table 4.7)	-CDDZ	−1 482	−1 566	−1 612	−1 693	−1 793	−1 837	−1 879	−1 963	−2 301	−2 546	−2 641
plus Unremitted profits due abroad:												
in non-oil companies (Pink Book[1] Table 4.2)	HBZT	1 683	757	2 170	1 459	1 974	−202	−1 533	−1 660	2 827	1 942	3 948
in oil companies (Pink Book[1] Table 4.2)	HERX	2 079	501	1 171	843	1 682	2 171	2 067	1 840	1 227	1 636	2 180
less Unremitted profits from abroad earned by UK companies (Pink Book[1] Table 4.2)[2]	-CGQY	−4 848	−4 551	−7 332	−8 238	−9 092	−8 225	−5 971	−5 034	−9 766	−13 103	−16 052
plus unremitted earnings adjustment	XBKZ	–	–	–	52	−351	−811	−1 051	42	1 148	185	623
less unremitted profits adjustment	-XBLB	–	–	–	−522	−483	−509	−321	−327	−189	−884	−651
less Territorial coverage adjustment[3]	HDGP	–	–	−275	−284	−323	−316	−278	−310	−341	−362	−387
Gross national product at market prices[4,5]	GIYB	357 072	384 613	421 430	467 613	511 073	542 658	566 858	594 628	625 960	663 814	697 482
less Factor cost adjustment (Blue Book Table 1.2)	-CTGV	−49 442	−56 571	−62 706	−70 002	−74 198	−72 232	−79 421	−80 784	−83 133	−89 078	−96 631
plus Motor vehicle license duty paid by households (Blue Book Table 4.7)	CDDZ	1 482	1 566	1 612	1 693	1 793	1 837	1 879	1 963	2 301	2 546	2 641
Gross national product at factor cost[5]	DBHI	309 112	329 608	360 336	399 304	438 668	472 263	489 316	515 807	545 128	577 282	603 492

1 *United Kingdom Balance of Payments,* 1995 Edition (the ONS Pink Book).
2 Excluding oil companies before 1984.
3 Adjustment to compensate for balance of payments coverage of the Channel Islands and Isle of Man from 1987. These islands are not considered to be part of the UK economic territory.
4 A further adjustment is made to remove UK domestic rates from GNP at current market prices from data supplied to EUROSTAT for 1988 to 1990 for use in the "GNP as fourth EC resource" context.

5 UK National accounts record assets on finance leases on a 'user' basis. Both the SNA and ESA record such assets on an 'owner' basis. For technical reasons described in the October 1991 issue of *Economic Trends* (No.456) this results in a small change in GDP (and hence GNP). No adjustment is made in UK returns, other than that for GNP as fourth resource, to international bodies since it is not possible to carry this change through to the sector accounts.

The national accounts

Developments in the accounts

Introduction of the new international system of accounts

101. The ONS is preparing for the introduction of the latest internationally agreed system of national accounts: the 1998 Blue Book will be the first edition to incorporate the recommendations of the UN System of National Accounts 1993 (SNA93) and the requirements of the European System of Accounts 1995 (ESA95), which is consistent with the SNA93. Following the 1997 Blue Book, an ESA95 version of the accounts will be published in Autumn 1997, reworked to show as far as possible what the accounts would look like on the new basis and in the new format. This will enable users to familiarise themselves with the changes in the system and to contribute to consultations with the ONS on the changes. *If you would like to participate in consultations on the new structure and contents of the national accounts, or simply be kept informed of the outcome, please contact the editor of the Blue Book, Room 132B/1, Office for National Statistics, Great George Street, London SW1P3AQ (Tel: 0171 270 6189).*

102. At the same time as adopting the new system in 1998, the periodic change of base year for estimates of GDP at constant prices will take place. The new base year will be 1995, replacing 1990. Further developments in line with international standards include the introduction of chain-linking.

Further information

103. Further information on the national accounts can be found in the following articles and publications:

United Kingdom National Accounts: Sources and Methods, Third Edition, Studies in Official Statistics No 37 HMSO 1985

Methodological Papers:

The United Kingdom National Accounts CSO Methodological paper No.1 "The measurement of output in the estimation of GDP", August 1994[1]

A compilers guide to the 1993 SNA CSO methodological paper No.2 "A notebook to aid implementation of international guidelines in the United Kingdom system of national accounts" February 1995

The United Kingdom National Accounts CSO Methodological paper No.3 "Data sources for the quarterly account", April 1995

These methodological papers can be obtained from the ONS library (details given inside front cover).

---

[1] This paper relates to the SIC 1980 version. An updated paper, taking into account changes resulting from the move to the SIC 1992, is under preparation

Economic Trends Articles

Articles of interest are regularly published in *Economic Trends*. The following are a small selection of those that have been published in recent years.

Economic Trends No. 458 December 1991
The use of supply side estimates in the National Accounts,

Economic Trends No. 460 February 1992
Improving economic statistics

Economic Trends No. 468 October 1992
Sector allocation of dividend and interest flows; a new framework

Economic Trends No. 468 October 1992
Sources and methods in the measurement of personal sector income and expenditure

Economic Trends No. 472 February 1993
Rebasing the national accounts; the reasons and the likely effects

Economic Trends No. 479 September 1993
The UK sector accounts

Economic Trends No. 480 October 1993
Handling revisions in the National accounts

Economic Trends No. 483 January 1994
Improvements to economic statistics

Economic Trends No. 492 October 1994
Input-output balance for the United Kingdom 1991

Economic Trends No. 494 December 1994
The economy; recent developments and prospects

Economic Trends No. 498 April 1995
Quarterly national accounts in the United Kingdom; overview of UK approach

Economic Trends No. 503 September 1995
Fully reconciled UK national and sector accounts for 1991-1994

Economic Trends No. 512 June 1996
Measuring real growth - Index numbers and chain linking

Copies of articles from *Economic Trends* may be obtained from the Publications Co-ordinator, Office for National Statistics, Room 60a/3, Great George Street, London SW1P 3AQ

CHAPTER 1: National income, product and expenditure

1.1 National and domestic product

		1974	1975	1976	1977	1978	1979	1980	1981	1982	1983	1984
THE MAIN AGGREGATES (1990=100)												
GDP at current market prices ("money GDP")[1]	DJCL	15.2	19.2	22.7	26.5	30.6	36.0	42.1	46.3	50.6	55.2	59.1
GDP at current factor cost	CAON	15.8	20.0	23.5	27.0	31.2	36.2	42.0	45.7	49.8	54.5	58.6
GDP at 1990 market prices	FNAO	70.7	70.2	72.1	73.9	76.4	78.5	76.8	75.9	77.2	80.0	81.9
GDP at 1990 factor cost	DJDD	71.1	70.6	72.5	74.4	76.4	78.5	76.9	76.0	77.4	80.3	81.9
GNDI at 1990 market prices[2]	DJCR	68.8	68.9	70.6	71.7	75.2	77.7	76.4	76.2	77.5	80.9	82.9
Index of total home costs[3]	DJCM	22.2	28.3	32.4	36.4	40.9	46.1	54.6	60.1	64.3	68.0	71.6
AT CURRENT PRICES (£ million)												
At market prices												
Gross domestic product at market prices ("money GDP")[1]	CAOB	83 862	105 852	125 247	145 983	168 526	198 221	231 772	254 927	279 041	304 456	325 852
Net property income from abroad	CGOA	1 508	891	1 560	265	806	1 205	−182	1 251	1 460	2 830	4 344
Gross national product at market prices[1]	GIBF	85 370	106 743	126 807	146 248	169 332	199 426	231 590	256 178	280 501	307 286	330 196
Net transfer income from abroad	CGIO	−422	−475	−786	−1 128	−1 791	−2 210	−1 984	−1 547	−1 741	−1 593	−1 732
Gross national disposable income[1]	GIBG	84 948	106 268	126 021	145 120	167 541	197 216	229 606	254 631	278 760	305 693	328 464
At factor cost												
Gross domestic product at market prices	CAOB	83 862	105 852	125 247	145 983	168 526	198 221	231 772	254 927	279 041	304 456	325 852
Adjustment to factor cost	−CTGV	−8 267	−10 265	−12 712	−16 448	−18 981	−25 027	−30 755	−36 096	−40 656	−43 231	−45 199
Gross domestic product at factor cost	CAOM	75 595	95 587	112 535	129 535	149 545	173 194	201 017	218 831	238 385	261 225	280 653
Net property income from abroad	CGOA	1 508	891	1 560	265	806	1 205	−182	1 251	1 460	2 830	4 344
Gross national product at factor cost	GIBD	77 103	96 478	114 095	129 800	150 351	174 399	200 835	220 082	239 845	264 055	284 997
less Capital consumption	−EXCH	−9 088	−11 621	−13 976	−16 501	−19 378	−22 827	−27 952	−31 641	−33 653	−36 150	−38 758
Net national product at factor cost ("National income")	GIBE	68 156	84 857	100 312	113 595	131 285	151 958	172 883	188 382	206 209	228 066	246 239
AT 1990 PRICES (£ million)												
At market prices												
Gross domestic product at market prices	CAOO	389 674	386 867	397 610	407 002	421 073	432 849	423 490	418 026	425 252	440 888	451 131
Net property income from abroad	DIEQ	4 388	2 281	3 292	491	1 454	1 989	−273	1 741	1 899	3 427	4 837
Gross national product at market prices	GIXX	394 745	388 949	401 098	406 475	421 875	434 274	422 188	419 183	426 585	444 040	455 980
Net transfer income from abroad	DIFY	−1 228	−1 216	−1 659	−2 090	−3 231	−3 648	−2 978	−2 153	−2 265	−1 929	−1 928
Terms of trade effect	DIFZ	−12 867	−8 394	−10 160	−9 794	−6 040	−4 505	−929	−357	−434	40	−995
Real national disposable income	GIGS	376 968	377 196	387 030	393 052	411 927	425 733	418 797	417 481	424 663	443 136	453 843
At factor cost												
Gross domestic product at market prices	CAOO	389 674	386 867	397 610	407 002	421 073	432 849	423 490	418 026	425 252	440 888	451 131
Adjustment to factor cost	−DJCU	−48 387	−48 158	−50 026	−50 181	−55 223	−56 943	−55 347	−54 054	−54 846	−56 631	−59 064
Gross domestic product at factor cost	CAOP	340 683	338 138	347 129	356 101	365 920	375 974	368 216	364 055	370 493	384 351	392 067
Net property income from abroad	DIEQ	4 388	2 281	3 292	491	1 454	1 989	−273	1 741	1 899	3 427	4 837
Gross national product at factor cost	GIXY	345 588	340 152	350 503	355 589	366 701	377 380	366 889	365 190	371 804	387 483	396 917
less Capital consumption	−EXDI	−38 893	−40 752	−42 221	−43 886	−46 073	−47 244	−48 878	−50 499	−52 001	−53 515	−54 916
Net national product at factor cost ("National income")	GIXZ	306 759	301 074	308 790	311 777	320 842	330 255	319 554	315 980	320 480	333 935	341 848

1 This series is affected by the abolition of domestic rates and the introduction of the community charge - see methodological notes.
2 "Real national disposable income"
3 Expenditure-based deflator at factor cost.

Where such data can be compiled, quarterly data for series in this table are available on the ONS's Databank. This data can also be provided on paper by request. Some of these quarterly data are published regularly in the UK Economic Accounts in table A1.

1.1 National and domestic product

continued

		1985	1986	1987	1988	1989	1990	1991	1992	1993	1994	1995
THE MAIN AGGREGATES (1990=100)												
GDP at current market prices ("money GDP")[1]	DJCL	64.8	69.8	76.8	85.5	93.6	100.0	104.5	108.7	114.5	121.3	127.2
GDP at current factor cost	CAON	64.3	68.5	75.3	83.8	92.2	100.0	103.6	108.2	114.4	120.9	126.2
GDP at 1990 market prices	FNAO	84.9	88.6	92.8	97.5	99.6	100.0	98.0	97.5	99.6	103.5	106.0
GDP at 1990 factor cost	DJDD	85.2	88.6	92.7	97.3	99.4	100.0	97.9	97.4	99.6	103.7	106.2
GNDI at 1990 market prices[2]	DJCR	85.4	88.8	92.8	97.8	99.8	100.0	98.8	98.5	100.6	105.1	106.7
Index of total home costs[3]	DJCM	75.5	77.4	81.3	86.2	92.8	100.0	105.8	111.1	114.9	116.7	118.8
AT CURRENT PRICES (£ million)												
At market prices												
Gross domestic product at market prices ("money GDP")[1]	CAOB	357 344	384 843	423 381	471 430	515 957	551 118	575 674	598 916	631 158	668 255	700 890
Net property income from abroad	CGOA	2 296	4 629	3 927	4 566	3 502	1 269	150	3 124	2 197	8 691	9 572
Gross national product at market prices[1]	GIBF	359 640	389 472	427 308	475 996	519 459	552 387	575 824	602 040	633 355	676 946	710 462
Net transfer income from abroad	CGIO	−3 111	−2 157	−3 400	−3 518	−4 578	−4 896	−1 383	−5 102	−5 007	−5 027	−6 978
Gross national disposable income[1]	GIBG	356 529	387 315	423 908	472 478	514 881	547 491	574 441	596 938	628 348	671 919	703 484
At factor cost												
Gross domestic product at market prices	CAOB	357 344	384 843	423 381	471 430	515 957	551 118	575 674	598 916	631 158	668 255	700 890
Adjustment to factor cost	−CTGV	−49 442	−56 571	−62 706	−70 002	−74 198	−72 232	−79 421	−80 784	−83 133	−89 078	−96 631
Gross domestic product at factor cost	CAOM	307 902	328 272	360 675	401 428	441 759	478 886	496 253	518 132	548 025	579 177	604 259
Net property income from abroad	CGOA	2 296	4 629	3 927	4 566	3 502	1 269	150	3 124	2 197	8 691	9 572
Gross national product at factor cost	GIBD	310 198	332 901	364 602	405 994	445 261	480 155	496 403	521 256	550 222	587 868	613 831
less Capital consumption	−EXCH	−41 883	−45 085	−48 164	−52 636	−56 716	−61 261	−63 356	−62 485	−65 353	−68 289	−72 884
Net national product at factor cost ("National income")	GIBE	268 315	287 816	316 438	353 358	388 545	418 894	433 047	458 771	484 869	519 287	540 643
AT 1990 PRICES (£ million)												
At market prices												
Gross domestic product at market prices	CAOO	468 071	488 122	511 615	537 215	548 940	551 118	540 308	537 448	548 947	570 290	584 340
Net property income from abroad	DIEQ	2 458	5 179	4 290	5 029	3 620	1 269	150	3 116	2 020	7 764	7 970
Gross national product at market prices	GIXX	469 976	493 301	515 905	542 244	552 560	552 387	540 458	540 564	550 967	578 054	592 310
Net transfer income from abroad	DIFY	−3 330	−2 413	−3 715	−3 875	−4 732	−4 896	−1 379	−5 090	−4 604	−4 491	−5 810
Terms of trade effect	DIFZ	62	−4 525	−4 366	−3 053	−1 261	−	1 646	4 076	4 654	1 730	−2 249
Real national disposable income	GIGS	467 459	486 363	507 825	535 316	546 567	547 491	540 724	539 551	551 018	575 293	584 251
At factor cost												
Gross domestic product at market prices	CAOO	468 071	488 122	511 615	537 215	548 940	551 118	540 308	537 448	548 947	570 290	584 340
Adjustment to factor cost	−DJCU	−60 310	−63 908	−67 798	−71 469	−72 712	−72 232	−71 395	−70 992	−71 822	−73 913	−75 533
Gross domestic product at factor cost	CAOP	407 844	424 214	443 817	465 746	476 228	478 886	468 913	466 456	477 125	496 377	508 807
Net property income from abroad	DIEQ	2 458	5 179	4 290	5 029	3 620	1 269	150	3 116	2 020	7 764	7 970
Gross national product at factor cost	GIXY	409 714	429 393	448 107	470 775	479 848	480 155	469 063	469 572	479 145	504 141	516 777
less Capital consumption	−EXDI	−56 214	−57 112	−58 077	−59 790	−59 756	−61 261	−62 316	−62 970	−64 223	−65 620	−66 358
Net national product at factor cost ("National income")	GIXZ	353 208	372 281	390 030	410 985	420 092	418 894	406 747	406 602	414 922	438 521	450 419

See footnotes on previous page.

National income, product and expenditure

1.2 National product: by category of expenditure at current prices

£ million

		1974	1975	1976	1977	1978	1979	1980	1981	1982	1983	1984
AT CURRENT MARKET PRICES:												
Consumers' expenditure[1]	AIIK	53 256	65 590	76 225	87 165	100 524	119 212	138 564	154 274	169 372	185 611	198 820
General government final consumption	AAXI	17 151	23 652	27 698	30 179	34 127	39 607	49 984	56 512	61 641	67 204	71 201
of which: Central Government	ACHC	10 574	14 055	16 830	18 534	20 866	24 178	31 033	35 017	38 278	42 071	44 583
Local authorities	CSBA	6 577	9 597	10 868	11 645	13 261	15 429	18 951	21 495	23 363	25 133	26 618
Gross domestic fixed capital formation	DFDC	17 497	21 035	24 504	27 036	31 060	36 925	41 561	41 304	44 824	48 615	55 181
Value of physical increase in stocks and work in progress	DHBF	1 045	−1 354	901	1 824	1 804	2 162	−2 572	−2 768	−1 188	1 465	1 296
Total domestic expenditure[1]	CTGQ	88 949	108 923	129 328	146 204	167 515	197 906	227 537	249 322	274 649	302 895	326 498
Exports of goods and services	DJAD	22 879	26 863	35 090	43 298	47 476	54 898	62 616	67 432	72 694	79 880	91 632
of which: Goods	CGJP	16 282	19 185	25 080	31 683	34 981	40 471	47 149	50 668	55 331	60 700	70 265
Services	CGJZ	6 597	7 678	10 010	11 615	12 495	14 427	15 467	16 764	17 363	19 180	21 367
Total final expenditure[1]	DJAK	111 828	135 786	164 418	189 502	214 991	252 804	290 153	316 754	347 343	382 775	418 130
less Imports of goods and services[2]	−DJAG	−27 149	−28 803	−36 636	−42 382	−45 368	−54 346	−57 606	−60 388	−67 762	−77 588	−92 763
of which: Goods	−CGGL	−21 513	−22 440	−29 041	−34 005	−36 573	−43 814	−45 792	−47 416	−53 421	−62 237	−75 601
Services	−CGGZ	−5 636	−6 363	−7 595	−8 377	−8 795	−10 532	−11 814	−12 972	−14 341	−15 351	−17 162
Statistical discrepancy (expenditure adjustment)[3]	GIXM	−817	−1 131	−2 535	−1 137	−1 097	−237	−775	−1 439	−540	−731	485
Gross domestic product[1,4]	CAOB	83 862	105 852	125 247	145 983	168 526	198 221	231 772	254 927	279 041	304 456	325 852
Net property income from abroad	CGOA	1 508	891	1 560	265	806	1 205	−182	1 251	1 460	2 830	4 344
Gross national product[1,4]	GIBF	85 370	106 743	126 807	146 248	169 332	199 426	231 590	256 178	280 501	307 286	330 196
FACTOR COST ADJUSTMENT:[5]												
Taxes on expenditure[1]	AAXC	11 374	14 036	16 284	19 834	22 756	29 670	36 474	42 465	46 467	49 500	52 736
Subsidies	AAXJ	3 107	3 771	3 572	3 386	3 775	4 643	5 719	6 369	5 811	6 269	7 537
Factor cost adjustment (taxes less subsidies)	CTGV	8 267	10 265	12 712	16 448	18 981	25 027	30 755	36 096	40 656	43 231	45 199
AT CURRENT FACTOR COST:												
Consumers' expenditure	CTGX	46 941	57 871	66 668	75 240	86 864	101 751	116 962	128 529	139 956	154 127	165 553
General government final consumption	CTGY	16 448	22 686	26 537	28 610	32 258	36 925	46 392	52 335	57 012	62 872	66 806
Gross domestic capital formation	CTGZ	17 855	18 871	24 434	27 464	31 243	36 572	36 334	35 686	40 449	46 312	52 486
Total domestic expenditure	CTHA	81 244	99 428	117 639	131 314	150 365	175 248	199 688	216 550	237 417	263 311	284 845
Exports of goods and services	CTHB	22 317	26 093	34 067	41 740	45 645	52 529	59 710	64 108	69 270	76 233	88 086
Total final expenditure	CTHC	103 561	125 521	151 706	173 054	196 010	227 777	259 398	280 658	306 687	339 544	372 931
less Imports of goods and services	−DJAG	−27 149	−28 803	−36 636	−42 382	−45 368	−54 346	−57 606	−60 388	−67 762	−77 588	−92 763
Statistical discrepancy (expenditure adjustment)[3]	GIXM	−817	−1 131	−2 535	−1 137	−1 097	−237	−775	−1 439	−540	−731	485
Gross domestic product	CAOM	75 595	95 587	112 535	129 535	149 545	173 194	201 017	218 831	238 385	261 225	280 653
Net property income from abroad	CGOA	1 508	891	1 560	265	806	1 205	−182	1 251	1 460	2 830	4 344
Gross national product	GIBD	77 103	96 478	114 095	129 800	150 351	174 399	200 835	220 082	239 845	264 055	284 997
less Capital consumption	−EXCH	−9 088	−11 621	−13 976	−16 501	−19 378	−22 827	−27 952	−31 641	−33 653	−36 150	−38 758
Net national product at factor cost ("National income")	GIBE	68 156	84 857	100 312	113 595	131 285	151 958	172 883	188 382	206 209	228 066	246 239

1 This series is affected by the abolition of domestic rates and the introduction of the community charge - see methodological notes.
2 Excluding taxes on expenditure levied on imports.
3 The Statistical discrepancy (expenditure adjustment) is part of the Residual error, as shown in table 1.5.
4 Including taxes on expenditure levied on imports. See methodological notes.
5 The allocation of the factor cost adjustment between categories of final expenditure is given in Table 9.5.

Where such data can be compiled, quarterly data for series in this table are available on the ONS's Databank. This data can also be provided on paper by request. Some of these quarterly data are published regularly in the UK Economic Accounts in table A2.

1.2 National product: by category of expenditure at current prices

continued

£ million

		1985	1986	1987	1988	1989	1990	1991	1992	1993	1994	1995
AT CURRENT MARKET PRICES:												
Consumers' expenditure[1]	AIIK	217 485	241 554	265 290	299 449	327 363	347 527	365 469	383 490	406 399	427 276	447 247
General government final consumption	AAXI	75 267	80 911	87 045	93 641	101 796	112 934	124 105	131 875	138 081	144 114	149 474
of which: Central Government	ACHC	47 341	50 331	53 736	57 522	63 294	70 108	76 985	82 259	89 398	93 601	96 663
Local authorities	CSBA	27 926	30 580	33 309	36 119	38 502	42 826	47 120	49 616	48 683	50 513	52 811
Gross domestic fixed capital formation	DFDC	60 718	65 032	75 158	91 530	105 443	107 577	97 747	93 642	94 293	99 217	105 385
Value of physical increase in stocks and work in progress	DHBF	821	682	1 228	4 333	2 677	−1 800	−4 927	−1 937	329	3 732	3 851
Total domestic expenditure[1]	CTGQ	354 291	388 179	428 721	488 953	537 279	566 238	582 394	607 070	639 102	674 339	705 957
Exports of goods and services	DJAD	102 041	97 885	106 397	107 273	121 486	133 165	134 289	142 114	159 997	176 065	197 600
of which: Goods	CGJP	77 991	72 627	79 153	80 346	92 154	101 718	103 413	107 343	121 398	134 666	152 346
Services	CGJZ	24 050	25 258	27 244	26 927	29 332	31 447	30 876	34 771	38 599	41 399	45 254
Total final expenditure[1]	DJAK	456 332	486 064	535 118	596 226	658 765	699 403	716 683	749 184	799 099	850 404	903 557
less Imports of goods and services[2]	−DJAG	−98 988	−101 221	−111 737	−124 796	−142 808	−148 285	−141 009	−150 268	−167 941	−182 149	−203 086
of which: Goods	−CGGL	−81 336	−82 186	−90 735	−101 826	−116 837	−120 527	−113 697	−120 447	−134 858	−145 497	−163 974
Services	−CGGZ	−17 652	−19 035	−21 002	−22 970	−25 971	−27 758	−27 312	−29 821	−33 083	−36 652	−39 112
Statistical discrepancy (expenditure adjustment)[3]	GIXM	−	−	−	−	−	−	−	−	−	−	419
Gross domestic product[1,4]	CAOB	357 344	384 843	423 381	471 430	515 957	551 118	575 674	598 916	631 158	668 255	700 890
Net property income from abroad	CGOA	2 296	4 629	3 927	4 566	3 502	1 269	150	3 124	2 197	8 691	9 572
Gross national product[1,4]	GIBF	359 640	389 472	427 308	475 996	519 459	552 387	575 824	602 040	633 355	676 946	710 462
FACTOR COST ADJUSTMENT:[5]												
Taxes on expenditure[1]	AAXC	56 667	62 872	68 971	76 039	79 980	78 298	85 416	87 521	90 336	96 138	103 597
Subsidies	AAXJ	7 225	6 301	6 265	6 037	5 782	6 066	5 995	6 737	7 203	7 060	6 966
Factor cost adjustment (taxes *less* subsidies)	CTGV	49 442	56 571	62 706	70 002	74 198	72 232	79 421	80 784	83 133	89 078	96 631
AT CURRENT FACTOR COST:												
Consumers' expenditure	CTGX	180 811	199 811	219 293	248 042	272 596	295 939	309 096	325 936	347 877	364 311	378 182
General government final consumption	CTGY	70 851	75 955	81 715	87 941	95 711	106 130	115 937	123 167	128 792	133 906	138 747
Gross domestic capital formation	CTGZ	57 011	60 426	70 140	88 440	100 559	98 252	84 937	84 500	87 011	95 032	101 025
Total domestic expenditure	CTHA	308 673	336 192	371 148	424 423	468 866	500 321	509 970	533 603	563 680	593 249	617 954
Exports of goods and services	CTHB	98 217	93 301	101 264	101 801	115 701	126 850	127 292	134 797	152 286	168 077	188 972
Total final expenditure	CTHC	406 890	429 493	472 412	526 224	584 567	627 171	637 262	668 400	715 966	761 326	806 926
less Imports of goods and services	−DJAG	−98 988	−101 221	−111 737	−124 796	−142 808	−148 285	−141 009	−150 268	−167 941	−182 149	−203 086
Statistical discrepancy (expenditure adjustment)[3]	GIXM	−	−	−	−	−	−	−	−	−	−	419
Gross domestic product	CAOM	307 902	328 272	360 675	401 428	441 759	478 886	496 253	518 132	548 025	579 177	604 259
Net property income from abroad	CGOA	2 296	4 629	3 927	4 566	3 502	1 269	150	3 124	2 197	8 691	9 572
Gross national product	GIBD	310 198	332 901	364 602	405 994	445 261	480 155	496 403	521 256	550 222	587 868	613 831
less Capital consumption	−EXCH	−41 883	−45 085	−48 164	−52 636	−56 716	−61 261	−63 356	−62 485	−65 353	−68 289	−72 884
Net national product at factor cost ("National income")	GIBE	268 315	287 816	316 438	353 358	388 545	418 894	433 047	458 771	484 869	519 287	540 643

See footnotes on previous page.

National income, product and expenditure

1.3 Gross national product by category of expenditure at 1990 prices[1]

£ million at 1990 prices

		1974	1975	1976	1977	1978	1979	1980	1981	1982	1983	1984
AT 1990 MARKET PRICES												
Consumers' expenditure	CCBH	225 317	224 580	225 666	224 892	236 909	247 212	247 185	247 402	249 852	261 200	266 486
General government final consumption[2]	DJCZ	90 804	95 748	96 997	95 357	97 443	99 277	101 005	101 260	102 146	104 296	105 177
of which: Central Government	DJDK	56 166	59 156	60 458	59 752	60 437	61 243	63 207	63 725	64 260	65 604	66 146
Local authorities	DJDL	34 606	36 552	36 549	35 645	36 988	38 008	37 791	37 535	37 886	38 692	39 030
Gross domestic fixed capital formation	DFDM	73 173	71 720	72 921	71 618	73 777	75 840	71 764	64 888	68 404	71 845	78 270
Value of physical increase in stocks and work in progress	DHBK	3 593	–4 103	1 955	4 119	3 458	4 013	–4 064	–3 859	–1 545	1 637	1 307
Total domestic expenditure	DIEL	393 599	386 710	397 225	396 143	411 909	426 915	414 792	408 223	417 916	438 768	450 949
Exports of goods and services	DJCV	79 439	77 179	84 206	90 000	91 683	95 130	94 918	94 211	94 996	96 689	103 019
of which: Goods	CGTG	54 571	52 293	57 584	62 281	63 849	66 694	67 475	66 838	68 724	70 324	76 028
Services	CGTH	25 726	25 891	27 590	28 580	28 617	29 134	27 917	27 877	26 441	26 463	26 925
Total final expenditure	DJDA	470 741	461 473	479 851	485 669	502 752	521 191	509 274	502 130	512 372	534 409	553 528
less Imports of goods and services[3]	-DJCY	–78 997	–73 752	–77 308	–78 509	–81 840	–89 714	–86 469	–84 050	–88 146	–93 954	–103 282
of which: Goods	-CGTC	–62 017	–56 643	–60 313	–61 598	–64 409	–70 641	–66 827	–64 170	–67 771	–73 826	–82 221
Services	-CGTD	–17 198	–17 420	–17 240	–17 129	–17 641	–19 301	–20 055	–20 402	–20 849	–20 388	–21 187
Statistical discrepancy[4] (expenditure adjustment)	GIXS	–3 684	–4 001	–7 818	–3 125	–2 685	–514	–1 420	–2 394	–840	–1 075	677
Gross domestic product[5]	CAOO	389 674	386 867	397 610	407 002	421 073	432 849	423 490	418 026	425 252	440 888	451 131
Net property income from abroad	DIEQ	4 388	2 281	3 292	491	1 454	1 989	–273	1 741	1 899	3 427	4 837
Gross national product[5]	GIXX	394 745	388 949	401 098	406 475	421 875	434 274	422 188	419 183	426 585	444 040	455 980
AT 1990 FACTOR COST												
Gross domestic product at market prices[5]	CAOO	389 674	386 867	397 610	407 002	421 073	432 849	423 490	418 026	425 252	440 888	451 131
less Factor cost adjustment[6]	-DJCU	–48 387	–48 158	–50 026	–50 181	–55 223	–56 943	–55 347	–54 054	–54 846	–56 631	–59 064
Gross domestic product at factor cost	CAOP	340 683	338 138	347 129	356 101	365 920	375 974	368 216	364 055	370 493	384 351	392 067
Net property income from abroad	DIEQ	4 388	2 281	3 292	491	1 454	1 989	–273	1 741	1 899	3 427	4 837
Gross national product at factor cost	GIXY	345 588	340 152	350 503	355 589	366 701	377 380	366 889	365 190	371 804	387 483	396 917
less Capital consumption	-EXDI	–38 893	–40 752	–42 221	–43 886	–46 073	–47 244	–48 878	–50 499	–52 001	–53 515	–54 916
Net national product at factor cost ("National income")	GIXZ	306 759	301 074	308 790	311 777	320 842	330 255	319 554	315 980	320 480	333 935	341 848

1 For the years before 1986, totals differ from the sum of their components, see methodological notes.
2 An analysis of general government consumption by function is given in table 9.3.
3 Excluding taxes on expenditure levied on imports.
4 The difference between Gross domestic product and the total of its expenditure components at 1990 prices.
5 Including taxes on expenditure levied on imports. See methodological notes.
6 This represents taxes on expenditure less subsidies valued at constant rates.

Where such data can be compiled, quarterly data for series in this table are available on the ONS's Databank. This data can also be provided on paper by request. Some of these quarterly data are published regularly in the UK Economic Accounts in table A3.

1.3 Gross national product by category of expenditure at 1990 prices[1]

continued

£ million at 1990 prices

		1985	1986	1987	1988	1989	1990	1991	1992	1993	1994	1995
AT 1990 MARKET PRICES												
Consumers' expenditure	CCBH	276 742	295 622	311 234	334 591	345 406	347 527	340 037	339 652	348 015	356 914	364 045
General government final consumption[2]	DJCZ	105 097	106 824	107 858	108 612	110 139	112 934	115 845	115 732	115 992	118 207	119 701
of which: Central Government	DJDK	66 241	67 277	67 122	67 588	68 836	70 108	71 811	72 039	74 455	75 950	76 407
Local authorities	DJDL	38 856	39 547	40 736	41 024	41 303	42 826	44 034	43 693	41 537	42 257	43 294
Gross domestic fixed capital formation	DFDM	81 575	83 685	92 339	105 164	111 470	107 577	97 403	95 973	96 586	99 417	99 302
Value of physical increase in stocks and work in progress	DHBK	990	1 199	1 652	5 094	2 704	−1 800	−4 631	−1 699	312	2 917	3 258
Total domestic expenditure	DIEL	464 316	487 330	513 083	553 461	569 719	566 238	548 654	549 658	560 905	577 455	586 306
Exports of goods and services	DJCV	109 163	114 047	120 607	121 197	126 836	133 165	132 252	137 693	142 451	155 566	166 773
of which: Goods	CGTG	80 250	83 644	88 611	90 508	95 786	101 718	102 898	105 457	109 240	120 489	129 288
Services	CGTH	28 883	30 403	31 996	30 689	31 050	31 447	29 354	32 236	33 211	35 077	37 485
Total final expenditure	DJDA	573 567	601 377	633 690	674 658	696 555	699 403	680 906	687 351	703 356	733 021	753 079
less Imports of goods and services[3]	-DJCY	−105 957	−113 255	−122 075	−137 443	−147 615	−148 285	−140 598	−149 903	−154 409	−162 731	−169 092
of which: Goods	-CGTC	−84 825	−91 072	−98 128	−111 360	−120 441	−120 527	−114 101	−121 629	−126 286	−131 629	−137 153
Services	-CGTD	−21 189	−22 183	−23 947	−26 083	−27 174	−27 758	−26 497	−28 274	−28 123	−31 102	−31 939
Statistical discrepancy[4] (expenditure adjustment)	GIXS	–	–	–	–	–	–	–	–	–	–	353
Gross domestic product[5]	CAOO	468 071	488 122	511 615	537 215	548 940	551 118	540 308	537 448	548 947	570 290	584 340
Net property income from abroad	DIEQ	2 458	5 179	4 290	5 029	3 620	1 269	150	3 116	2 020	7 764	7 970
Gross national product[5]	GIXX	469 976	493 301	515 905	542 244	552 560	552 387	540 458	540 564	550 967	578 054	592 310
AT 1990 FACTOR COST												
Gross domestic product at market prices[5]	CAOO	468 071	488 122	511 615	537 215	548 940	551 118	540 308	537 448	548 947	570 290	584 340
less Factor cost adjustment[6]	-DJCU	−60 310	−63 908	−67 798	−71 469	−72 712	−72 232	−71 395	−70 992	−71 822	−73 913	−75 533
Gross domestic product at factor cost	CAOP	407 844	424 214	443 817	465 746	476 228	478 886	468 913	466 456	477 125	496 377	508 807
Net property income from abroad	DIEQ	2 458	5 179	4 290	5 029	3 620	1 269	150	3 116	2 020	7 764	7 970
Gross national product at factor cost	GIXY	409 714	429 393	448 107	470 775	479 848	480 155	469 063	469 572	479 145	504 141	516 777
less Capital consumption	-EXDI	−56 214	−57 112	−58 077	−59 790	−59 756	−61 261	−62 316	−62 970	−64 223	−65 620	−66 358
Net national product at factor cost ("National income")	GIXZ	353 208	372 281	390 030	410 985	420 092	418 894	406 747	406 602	414 922	438 521	450 419

See footnotes on previous page.

1.4 Gross domestic product at current factor cost: by category of income

£ million

		1974	1975	1976	1977	1978	1979	1980	1981	1982	1983	1984
FACTOR INCOMES												
Income from employment	DJAO	52 379	68 494	78 005	86 572	98 843	115 866	137 783	149 737	158 838	169 847	181 406
Income from self-employment[1]	CFAN	8 042	9 135	11 126	12 035	13 612	15 933	18 141	19 980	22 140	24 750	27 909
Gross trading profits of companies[1,2,3]	CIAC	11 210	11 684	14 620	19 951	22 366	29 145	27 861	27 341	31 176	39 528	43 852
Gross trading surplus of public corporations[1,3]	ADRD	2 561	3 094	4 505	5 095	5 466	5 710	6 309	7 974	9 502	10 004	8 511
Gross trading surplus of general government enterprises[1]	DJAQ	133	127	152	183	216	180	180	236	216	50	−117
Rent[4]	DIDS	5 346	6 478	7 746	8 715	10 035	11 950	14 243	16 366	17 700	18 857	19 816
Imputed charge for consumption of non-trading capital	DIDT	740	965	1 142	1 287	1 448	1 714	2 116	2 351	2 426	2 498	2 619
Total domestic income[1]	DJAU	80 411	99 977	117 296	133 838	151 986	180 498	206 633	223 985	241 998	265 534	283 996
less Stock appreciation	-DJAT	−6 109	−5 521	−6 681	−5 095	−4 228	−8 837	−6 391	−5 974	−4 276	−4 204	−4 513
Statistical discrepancy (income adjustment)[5]	GIXQ	1 293	1 131	1 920	792	1 787	1 533	775	820	663	−105	1 170
Gross domestic product at factor cost	CAOM	75 595	95 587	112 535	129 535	149 545	173 194	201 017	218 831	238 385	261 225	280 653
FACTOR INCOMES AFTER PROVIDING FOR STOCK APPRECIATION												
Income from employment	DJAO	52 379	68 494	78 005	86 572	98 843	115 866	137 783	149 737	158 838	169 847	181 406
Income from self-employment[4]	CEAP	7 337	8 524	10 430	11 452	13 165	15 157	17 422	19 354	21 778	24 200	27 584
Gross trading profits of companies[2,3,4]	CICS	6 147	7 180	9 033	15 833	18 923	21 737	22 467	22 277	27 665	35 909	39 729
Gross trading surplus of public corporations[3,4]	ADRB	2 220	2 688	4 107	4 701	5 128	5 057	6 031	7 690	9 099	9 969	8 446
Gross trading surplus of general government enterprises[4]	DJAQ	133	127	152	183	216	180	180	236	216	50	−117
Rent[4]	DIDS	5 346	6 478	7 746	8 715	10 035	11 950	14 243	16 366	17 700	18 857	19 816
Imputed charge for consumption of non-trading capital	DIDT	740	965	1 142	1 287	1 448	1 714	2 116	2 351	2 426	2 498	2 619
Statistical discrepancy (income adjustment)[5]	GIXQ	1 293	1 131	1 920	792	1 787	1 533	775	820	663	−105	1 170
Gross domestic product at factor cost	CAOM	75 595	95 587	112 535	129 535	149 545	173 194	201 017	218 831	238 385	261 225	280 653

1 Before providing for depreciation and stock appreciation.
2 Including financial institutions.
3 See footnote 1 on table 5.1 and footnote 1 on table 6.1.
4 Before providing for depreciation.
5 The Statistical discrepancy (income adjustment) is part of the Residual error, as shown in table 1.5.

Where such data can be compiled, quarterly data for series in this table are available on the ONS's Databank. This data can also be provided on paper by request. Some of these quarterly data are published regularly in the UK Economic Accounts in table A3.

1.4 Gross domestic product at current factor cost: by category of income

continued

£ million

		1985	1986	1987	1988	1989	1990	1991	1992	1993	1994	1995
FACTOR INCOMES												
Income from employment	DJAO	196 858	212 380	230 208	256 537	284 372	313 753	330 767	342 015	351 819	364 946	377 895
Income from self-employment[1]	CFAN	30 404	35 104	39 361	45 829	52 691	58 688	56 745	57 149	60 461	64 021	67 685
Gross trading profits of companies[1,2,3]	CIAC	51 146	47 339	59 453	64 377	67 195	65 703	59 455	61 856	74 820	86 468	91 027
Gross trading surplus of public corporations[1,3]	ADRD	7 262	8 213	6 993	7 554	6 528	3 801	1 809	2 361	3 454	4 230	4 634
Gross trading surplus of general government enterprises[1]	DJAQ	265	155	−75	−32	199	12	−36	206	193	490	613
Rent[4]	DIDS	21 875	23 848	26 155	29 904	33 830	38 669	45 160	52 116	55 385	58 632	62 758
Imputed charge for consumption of non-trading capital	DIDT	2 830	3 068	3 307	3 634	4 005	4 391	4 363	4 207	4 243	4 424	4 729
Total domestic income[1]	DJAU	310 640	330 107	365 402	407 803	448 820	485 017	498 263	519 910	550 375	583 211	609 341
less Stock appreciation	-DJAT	−2 738	−1 835	−4 727	−6 375	−7 061	−6 131	−2 010	−1 778	−2 350	−4 034	−4 902
Statistical discrepancy (income adjustment)[5]	GIXQ	–	–	–	–	–	–	–	–	–	–	−180
Gross domestic product at factor cost	CAOM	307 902	328 272	360 675	401 428	441 759	478 886	496 253	518 132	548 025	579 177	604 259
FACTOR INCOMES AFTER PROVIDING FOR STOCK APPRECIATION												
Income from employment	DJAO	196 858	212 380	230 208	256 537	284 372	313 753	330 767	342 015	351 819	364 946	377 895
Income from self-employment[4]	CEAP	29 929	34 932	38 870	45 079	51 888	57 993	56 351	57 110	60 448	63 645	67 265
Gross trading profits of companies[2,3,4]	CICS	48 991	45 839	55 305	59 011	60 992	60 387	57 869	60 156	72 447	82 818	86 576
Gross trading surplus of public corporations[3,4]	ADRB	7 154	8 050	6 905	7 295	6 473	3 681	1 779	2 322	3 490	4 222	4 603
Gross trading surplus of general government enterprises[4]	DJAQ	265	155	−75	−32	199	12	−36	206	193	490	613
Rent[4]	DIDS	21 875	23 848	26 155	29 904	33 830	38 669	45 160	52 116	55 385	58 632	62 758
Imputed charge for consumption of non-trading capital	DIDT	2 830	3 068	3 307	3 634	4 005	4 391	4 363	4 207	4 243	4 424	4 729
Statistical discrepancy (income adjustment)[5]	GIXQ	–	–	–	–	–	–	–	–	–	–	−180
Gross domestic product at factor cost	CAOM	307 902	328 272	360 675	401 428	441 759	478 886	496 253	518 132	548 025	579 177	604 259

See footnotes on previous page.

National income, product and expenditure

1.5 The composition of final output[1]

£ million

		1974	1975	1976	1977	1978	1979	1980	1981	1982	1983	1984
Income from employment	DJAO	52 379	68 494	78 005	86 572	98 843	115 866	137 783	149 737	158 838	169 847	181 406
Gross profits and other income[1]	GICM	21 923	25 962	32 610	42 171	48 915	55 795	62 459	68 274	78 884	91 483	98 077
Imports of goods and services	DJAG	27 149	28 803	36 636	42 382	45 368	54 346	57 606	60 388	67 762	77 588	92 763
Taxes on expenditure *less* subsidies .	CTGV	8 267	10 265	12 712	16 448	18 981	25 027	30 755	36 096	40 656	43 231	45 199
Residual error[2]	DJAS	2 110	2 262	4 455	1 929	2 884	1 770	1 550	2 259	1 203	626	685
of which:												
attributed to the expenditure analysis	-GIXM	817	1 131	2 535	1 137	1 097	237	775	1 439	540	731	−485
attributed to the income analysis	GIXQ	1 293	1 131	1 920	792	1 787	1 533	775	820	663	−105	1 170
Total final output[3]	DJAK	111 828	135 786	164 418	189 502	214 991	252 804	290 153	316 754	347 343	382 775	418 130

1 Before providing for depreciation but after providing for stock appreciation.
2 The Residual error is, by convention, the amount by which the sum of the expenditure components of GDP exceeds the sum of the income components. It is also the sum of two components: Statistical discrepancy (expenditure) with sign reversed, and the Statistical discrepancy (income) with natural sign.
3 The value, at market prices, of home produced and imported goods and services available for private and public consumption, investment and export.

1.6 Gross domestic product at constant factor cost: by industry of output[1]

1990 = 100

		1974	1975	1976	1977	1978	1979	1980	1981	1982	1983	1984
Agriculture, hunting, forestry and fishing	CKAP	70.3	64.9	59.6	67.3	72.5	71.3	79.2	81.2	88.0	83.3	100.6
Production:												
Mining and quarrying (inc oil and gas extraction)	DVZJ	88.0	99.4	93.4	90.8	90.8	109.2	110.8	115.7	124.0	125.1	117.7
Manufacturing (revised definition)	DVZK	93.4	87.0	88.6	90.3	90.8	90.6	82.8	77.7	77.6	79.2	82.2
Electricity, gas and water supply	DVZS	70.0	71.3	72.6	75.6	77.3	80.4	80.0	81.9	81.3	84.1	71.3
Total production	DVZI	79.4	75.1	77.6	81.6	83.9	87.2	81.5	78.9	80.4	83.3	83.4
Construction	DVJO	69.4	65.7	64.8	64.5	68.9	69.4	65.6	60.5	65.3	69.5	72.8
Service Industries:												
Distribution, hotels and catering; repairs	CKAQ	71.4	68.9	69.6	69.2	73.2	75.3	70.7	69.6	71.0	74.1	77.8
Transport, storage and communication	CKAR	67.7	66.8	66.4	68.3	70.8	73.6	72.3	72.4	71.7	73.8	77.4
Other	CKAS	66.8	69.3	71.7	73.0	74.7	76.6	78.2	79.1	80.4	82.8	85.4
Total services	CKCE	68.4	69.1	70.7	71.7	73.9	76.0	75.7	76.0	77.0	79.6	82.6
Gross domestic product	DJDD	71.1	70.6	72.5	74.4	76.4	78.5	76.9	76.0	77.4	80.3	81.9

1 The output analysis of Gross domestic product is naturally estimated in terms of change and expressed in index number form. It is, therefore, inappropriate to show its divergence from the estimate of Gross domestic product as a statistical discrepancy (output adjustment). Such an adjustment does, however, exist implicitly.
2 The weights are in proportion to the distribution of net output in 1990 and are used to combine the indices from 1986 onwards. For the method of calculation in earlier years see paragraph 5.19 of *United Kingdom National Accounts : Sources and Methods*, Third edition.

Where such data can be compiled, quarterly data for series in this table are available on the ONS's Databank. For the production series, data are available monthly. The data can also be provided on paper by request. Some of these quarterly data are published regularly in the UK Economic Accounts in table A2. Monthly production data are published in the Monthly Digest of Statistics, table 7.1 and Economic Trends, table 5.1.

1.5 The composition of final output[1]
continued

£ million

		1985	1986	1987	1988	1989	1990	1991	1992	1993	1994	1995
Income from employment	DJAO	196 858	212 380	230 208	256 537	284 372	313 753	330 767	342 015	351 819	364 946	377 895
Gross profits and other income[1]	GICM	111 044	115 892	130 467	144 891	157 387	165 133	165 486	176 117	196 206	214 231	226 544
Imports of goods and services	DJAG	98 988	101 221	111 737	124 796	142 808	148 285	141 009	150 268	167 941	182 149	203 086
Taxes on expenditure *less* subsidies	CTGV	49 442	56 571	62 706	70 002	74 198	72 232	79 421	80 784	83 133	89 078	96 631
Residual error[2]	DJAS	–	–	–	–	–	–	–	–	–	–	–599
of which:												
attributed to the												
expenditure analysis	-GIXM	–	–	–	–	–	–	–	–	–	–	–419
attributed to the												
income analysis	GIXQ	–	–	–	–	–	–	–	–	–	–	–180
Total final output[3]	DJAK	456 332	486 064	535 118	596 226	658 765	699 403	716 683	749 184	799 099	850 404	903 557

See footnotes on previous page.

1.6 Gross domestic product at constant factor cost: by industry of output[1]
continued

1990 = 100

	Weight per 1000[2] 1990		1985	1986	1987	1988	1989	1990	1991	1992	1993	1994	1995
Agriculture, hunting, forestry and fishing	19	CKAP	95.3	95.5	93.5	92.1	96.7	100.0	101.5	106.0	98.2	98.0	98.6
Production:													
Mining and quarrying (inc oil and gas extraction)	24	DVZJ	129.4	129.4	130.0	120.9	104.0	100.0	104.5	107.8	115.2	132.4	139.3
Manufacturing (revised definition)	232	DVZK	84.5	85.6	89.6	95.9	100.2	100.0	94.6	94.0	95.3	99.3	101.5
Electricity, gas and water supply	22	DVZS	86.5	95.1	97.6	97.7	97.3	100.0	105.7	107.4	111.8	113.1	116.7
Total production	278	DVZI	88.0	90.1	93.7	98.2	100.3	100.0	96.3	96.2	98.3	103.2	105.9
Construction	72	DVJO	73.0	76.0	84.9	92.3	97.6	100.0	92.0	87.9	87.2	90.5	89.6
Service Industries:													
Distribution, hotels and catering;													
repairs	143	CKAQ	81.0	85.5	91.8	97.8	101.2	100.0	96.1	95.2	99.9	103.4	104.5
Transport, storage and communication	84	CKAR	80.6	84.0	89.9	94.6	99.2	100.0	98.2	99.8	104.8	112.2	118.5
Other	405	CKAS	87.6	90.7	93.7	97.5	98.5	100.0	100.3	99.8	101.6	104.5	107.6
Total services	631	CKCE	85.1	88.6	92.7	97.2	99.2	100.0	99.1	98.8	101.6	105.3	108.4
Gross domestic product	1 000	DJDD	85.2	88.6	92.7	97.3	99.4	100.0	97.9	97.4	99.6	103.7	106.2

See footnotes on previous page.

National income, product and expenditure

1.7 Value, volume and price indices

1990 = 100

		1974	1975	1976	1977	1978	1979	1980	1981	1982	1983	1984
VALUE INDICES AT CURRENT PRICES												
Gross domestic product at market prices ("money GDP")[1]	DJCL	15.2	19.2	22.7	26.5	30.6	36.0	42.1	46.3	50.6	55.2	59.1
Gross domestic product at factor cost	CAON	15.8	20.0	23.5	27.0	31.2	36.2	42.0	45.7	49.8	54.5	58.6
VOLUME INDICES AT 1990 PRICES												
At market prices												
Gross domestic product	FNAO	70.7	70.2	72.1	73.9	76.4	78.5	76.8	75.9	77.2	80.0	81.9
Gross national product	GIBJ	71.4	70.4	72.6	73.5	76.3	78.6	76.4	75.8	77.2	80.3	82.6
Gross national disposable income ("RNDI")	DJCR	68.8	68.9	70.6	71.7	75.2	77.7	76.4	76.2	77.5	80.9	82.9
At factor cost												
Gross domestic product	DJDD	71.1	70.6	72.5	74.4	76.4	78.5	76.9	76.0	77.4	80.3	81.9
Gross national product	GIBH	71.9	70.8	72.9	74.0	76.3	78.5	76.4	76.0	77.4	80.6	82.7
Net national product ("National income")	GIBI	73.2	71.9	73.7	74.4	76.6	78.8	76.3	75.4	76.5	79.7	81.6
Categories of expenditure:												
At market prices												
Consumers' expenditure	GIBK	64.8	64.6	64.9	64.7	68.2	71.1	71.1	71.2	71.9	75.2	76.7
General government final consumption	GIBL	80.4	84.8	85.9	84.4	86.3	87.9	89.4	89.7	90.4	92.4	93.1
of which: Central government	GIBM	80.1	84.4	86.2	85.2	86.2	87.4	90.2	90.9	91.7	93.6	94.3
Local authorities	GIBN	80.8	85.4	85.3	83.2	86.4	88.7	88.2	87.6	88.5	90.3	91.1
Gross domestic fixed capital formation	GIBO	68.5	67.2	68.3	67.1	69.1	71.0	67.2	60.8	64.1	67.3	72.8
Total domestic expenditure	GIBP	69.5	68.3	70.2	70.0	72.8	75.4	73.3	72.1	73.8	77.5	79.6
Exports of goods and services	HHCX	59.6	57.9	63.2	67.5	68.8	71.4	71.2	70.7	71.3	72.5	77.3
of which: Goods	CGTR	53.6	51.4	56.6	61.2	62.8	65.6	66.3	65.7	67.6	69.1	74.7
Services	CGSI	81.5	82.0	87.4	90.5	90.7	92.3	88.4	88.3	83.8	83.8	85.3
Total final expenditure	GIBT	67.3	66.0	68.6	69.4	71.9	74.5	72.8	71.8	73.3	76.4	79.1
Imports of goods and services	HHCY	53.3	49.7	52.1	52.9	55.2	60.5	58.3	56.7	59.4	63.4	69.7
of which: Goods	CGTS	51.5	47.0	50.0	51.1	53.5	58.6	55.4	53.3	56.2	61.2	68.2
Services	CGSP	62.0	62.8	62.1	61.7	63.6	69.5	72.2	73.5	75.1	73.4	76.3
Factor cost adjustment	GIBX	67.0	66.7	69.3	69.5	76.5	78.8	76.6	74.8	75.9	78.4	81.8
PRICE INDICES (IMPLIED DEFLATORS)[2]												
Categories of expenditure:												
Consumers' expenditure	GIEF	23.6	29.2	33.8	38.8	42.4	48.2	56.1	62.4	67.8	71.1	74.6
General government final consumption	GIEG	18.9	24.7	28.6	31.6	35.0	39.9	49.5	55.8	60.3	64.4	67.7
Gross domestic fixed capital formation	GIEH	23.9	29.3	33.6	37.8	42.1	48.7	57.9	63.7	65.5	67.7	70.5
Total domestic expenditure	GIEI	22.6	28.2	32.6	36.9	40.7	46.4	54.9	61.1	65.7	69.0	72.4
Exports of goods and services	HDUV	28.8	34.8	41.7	48.1	51.8	57.7	66.0	71.6	76.5	82.6	88.9
Total final expenditure	GIEK	23.8	29.4	34.3	39.0	42.8	48.5	57.0	63.1	67.8	71.6	75.5
Imports of goods and services	HDWN	34.4	39.1	47.4	54.0	55.4	60.6	66.6	71.8	76.9	82.6	89.8
Gross domestic product at market prices	DJDT	21.5	27.4	31.5	35.9	40.0	45.8	54.7	61.0	65.6	69.1	72.2
HOME COSTS PER UNIT OF OUTPUT[3]												
Total home costs[4]	DJCM	22.2	28.3	32.4	36.4	40.9	46.1	54.6	60.1	64.3	68.0	71.6
Income from employment	GIED	23.6	31.1	34.5	37.3	41.4	47.2	57.4	63.1	65.7	67.8	70.6
Gross profits and other income	GIEE	18.5	22.1	27.0	34.1	38.4	42.7	48.8	53.9	61.2	68.4	72.5

1 This series is affected by the abolition of domestic rates and the introduction of the community charge - see methodological notes.
2 Implied deflators are given by dividing the estimates for each component at current market prices by the corresponding estimate at constant market prices.
3 These index numbers show how employment and trading incomes relate to the index of total home costs as explained in paragraphs 4.42-4.45 of *United Kingdom National Accounts: Sources and Methods,* 3rd edition.
4 Based on the sum of expenditure components of GDP at current and constant factor cost.

1.7 Value, volume and price indices
continued

		1985	1986	1987	1988	1989	1990	1991	1992	1993	1994	1995
VALUE INDICES AT CURRENT PRICES												
Gross domestic product at market prices ("money GDP")[1]	DJCL	64.8	69.8	76.8	85.5	93.6	100.0	104.5	108.7	114.5	121.3	127.2
Gross domestic product at factor cost	CAON	64.3	68.5	75.3	83.8	92.2	100.0	103.6	108.2	114.4	120.9	126.2
VOLUME INDICES AT 1990 PRICES												
At market prices												
Gross domestic product	FNAO	84.9	88.6	92.8	97.5	99.6	100.0	98.0	97.5	99.6	103.5	106.0
Gross national product	GIBJ	85.1	89.3	93.4	98.2	100.0	100.0	97.8	97.9	99.7	104.6	107.2
Gross national disposable income ("RNDI")	DJCR	85.4	88.8	92.8	97.8	99.8	100.0	98.8	98.5	100.6	105.1	106.7
At factor cost												
Gross domestic product	DJDD	85.2	88.6	92.7	97.3	99.4	100.0	97.9	97.4	99.6	103.7	106.2
Gross national product	GIBH	85.4	89.4	93.3	98.0	99.9	100.0	97.7	97.8	99.8	105.0	107.6
Net national product ("National income")	GIBI	84.3	88.9	93.1	98.1	100.3	100.0	97.1	97.1	99.1	104.6	107.5
Categories of expenditure:												
At market prices												
Consumers' expenditure	GIBK	79.6	85.1	89.6	96.3	99.4	100.0	97.8	97.7	100.1	102.7	104.8
General government final consumption	GIBL	93.1	94.6	95.5	96.2	97.5	100.0	102.6	102.5	102.7	104.7	106.0
of which: Central government	GIBM	94.5	96.0	95.7	96.4	98.2	100.0	102.4	102.8	106.2	108.3	109.0
Local authorities	GIBN	90.7	92.3	95.1	95.8	96.4	100.0	102.8	102.0	97.0	98.7	101.1
Gross domestic fixed capital formation	GIBO	75.8	77.8	85.8	97.8	103.6	100.0	90.5	89.2	89.8	92.4	92.3
Total domestic expenditure	GIBP	82.0	86.1	90.6	97.7	100.6	100.0	96.9	97.1	99.1	102.0	103.5
Exports of goods and services	HHCX	81.9	85.6	90.6	91.0	95.2	100.0	99.3	103.4	107.0	116.8	125.2
of which: Goods	CGTR	78.9	82.2	87.1	89.0	94.2	100.0	101.2	103.7	107.4	118.5	127.1
Services	CGSI	91.5	96.7	101.7	97.6	98.7	100.0	93.3	102.5	105.6	111.5	119.2
Total final expenditure	GIBT	82.0	86.0	90.6	96.5	99.6	100.0	97.4	98.3	100.6	104.8	107.7
Imports of goods and services	HHCY	71.5	76.4	82.3	92.7	99.5	100.0	94.8	101.1	104.1	109.7	114.0
of which: Goods	CGTS	70.4	75.5	81.4	92.4	99.9	100.0	94.7	100.9	104.8	109.2	113.8
Services	CGSP	76.3	79.9	86.3	94.0	97.9	100.0	95.5	101.9	101.3	112.0	115.1
Factor cost adjustment	GIBX	83.5	88.5	93.9	98.9	100.7	100.0	98.8	98.3	99.4	102.3	104.6
PRICE INDICES (IMPLIED DEFLATORS)[2]												
Categories of expenditure:												
Consumers' expenditure	GIEF	78.6	81.7	85.2	89.5	94.8	100.0	107.5	112.9	116.8	119.7	122.9
General government final consumption	GIEG	71.6	75.7	80.7	86.2	92.4	100.0	107.1	113.9	119.0	121.9	124.9
Gross domestic fixed capital formation	GIEH	74.4	77.7	81.4	87.0	94.6	100.0	100.4	97.6	97.6	99.8	106.1
Total domestic expenditure	GIEI	76.3	79.7	83.6	88.3	94.3	100.0	106.1	110.4	113.9	116.8	120.4
Exports of goods and services	HDUV	93.5	85.8	88.2	88.5	95.8	100.0	101.5	103.2	112.3	113.2	118.5
Total final expenditure	GIEK	79.6	80.8	84.4	88.4	94.6	100.0	105.3	109.0	113.6	116.0	120.0
Imports of goods and services	HDWN	93.4	89.4	91.5	90.8	96.7	100.0	100.3	100.2	108.8	111.9	120.1
Gross domestic product at market prices	DJDT	76.3	78.8	82.8	87.8	94.0	100.0	106.5	111.4	115.0	117.2	119.9
HOME COSTS PER UNIT OF OUTPUT[3]												
Total home costs[4]	DJCM	75.5	77.4	81.3	86.2	92.8	100.0	105.8	111.1	114.9	116.7	118.8
Income from employment	GIED	73.7	76.4	79.2	84.1	91.1	100.0	107.7	111.9	112.5	112.2	113.4
Gross profits and other income	GIEE	79.0	79.2	85.3	90.2	95.8	100.0	102.3	109.5	119.3	125.2	129.1

See footnotes on previous page.

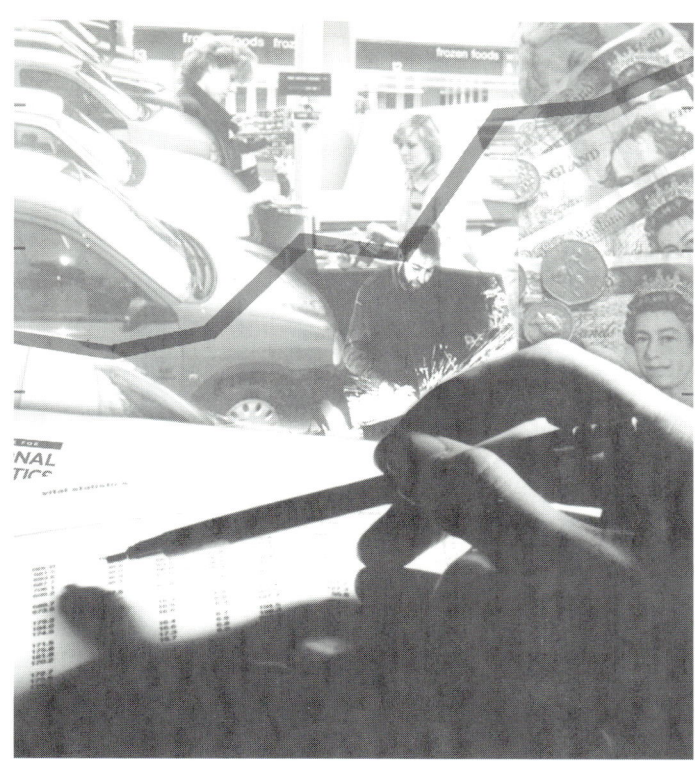

The main
analyses

2

The main analyses

Chart *2.1*

Breakdown of value added by industry

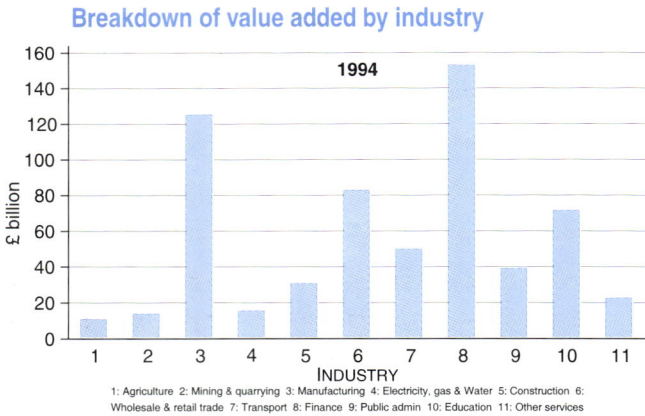

An analysis of eleven broad industrial sectors shows that in 1994 the Financial Intermediation sector produced the greatest value added, or GDP at current factor cost, at £152.10 billion.

Manufacturing, at £124.34 billion, and the Wholesaling and Retailing trades, at £82.06 billion, also featured strongly.

More details of the composition of each industry group's value added, for the latest and for earlier years, can be found in Tables 2.1, 2.2 and 2.3.

Chart *2.2*

Composition of final demand for 1994

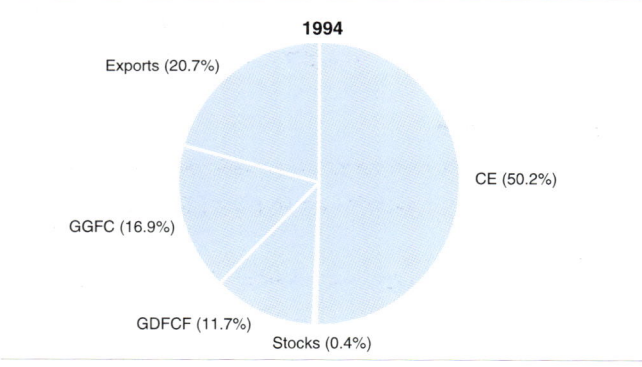

In 1994 just over half of all goods and services entering into final demand were purchased by consumers.

The next highest proportion, 20.70 per cent, went for export whilst around 16.90 per cent were used by government, both national and local. The remainder were items of capital expenditure purchased by a variety of sectors of industry.

A more detailed analysis by industry can be found in table 2.1.

Chart *2.3*

Income from employment by industry

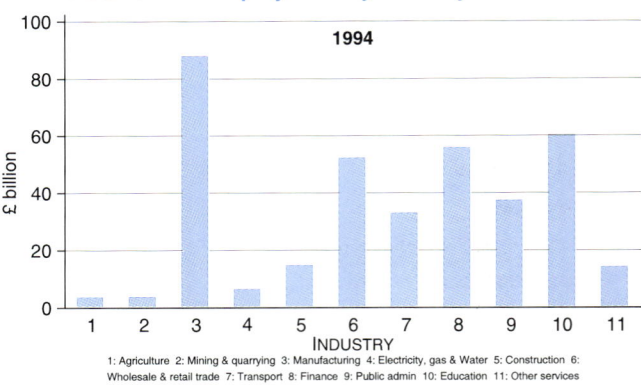

Manufacturing industries showed the greatest level of income from employment in 1994 at £87.45 billion. The next five industries in terms of total income from employment are all from the distribution and service sector, with Education at £59.73 billion, Financial Intermediation at £55.38 billion, and Wholesaling and Retailing at £51.79 billion the most prominent.

More details, together with a time series, can be found in Tables 2.2 and 2.4.

United Kingdom National Accounts 1996 © Crown copyright 1996

SECTION 2: THE MAIN ANALYSES

103. Section 2 contains the main industrial and sectoral analysis of GDP with, for example, details on the breakdown of the type of income earned within each industry, and includes the input-output "Combined" Use matrix for 1992, 1993 and 1994. This introduction gives a little more detail on the industry breakdown used and, in particular, the input-output process. Further detail can be found in the Methodological notes and the publications and articles listed under *Further information*.

The industry breakdown

104. The estimates of the analysis of GDP by industry are based on the *Standard Industrial Classification*, Revised 1992 (SIC(92)). Each economic unit (ie the individual enterprise) is classified by industry according to its *main* activity. As a result *all* of its activity - including any subsidiary activities - will be allocated to that industry. (See methodological notes).

Input-Output analysis

105. The national accounts are concerned with the composition and value of goods and services entering into *final* demand, and the factor incomes generated in the production process. The UK **input-output** balances show the *intermediate* transactions which form inputs to these processes. These balances are a central part of the process to reconcile the national accounts.

106. The input-output analyses show a balanced and complete picture of the flows of products in the economy and illustrate the relationships between producers and consumers of goods and services. Importantly they also show the interdependence between industries; what industries purchase from each other in order to produce their own output. A balance is compiled for each of the one hundred and twenty-three different industries and corresponding product groups.

107. On an annual basis, **input-output balances** are used to achieve consistency in the national accounts aggregates by linking the components of value added, output and final demand. Because each measure of GDP (income, expenditure and output) can be calculated from input-output balances, it is possible to arrive at a single agreed estimate, without statistical discrepancies. This is done by resolving imbalances between the supply and demand for goods and services and reconciling them with the corresponding value added estimates.

108. Table 2.1 - The input-output "Combined" Use matrix for the United Kingdom - gives a complete picture of the flows of products in the economy for eleven industry groups (although the underlying balances are obviously compiled at a much more detailed level).

109. Each row of the matrix shows how sales at purchasers' prices of a particular product group are distributed between intermediate industries and final demand categories. The sum of value added estimates corresponds to the income measure of GDP and is consistent with the data shown in Tables 2.2 and 2.3.

Developments

Recent developments

110. Input-output work has come a long way in the UK since the first official tables were drawn up in 1961, for the year 1954, and is now probably the fastest growing area within the national accounts.

111. Following the successful completion of the 1989 input-output balance for the 1992 Blue Book, the input-output framework and timetable is now fully integrated with the annual national accounts. Further, the 1996 Blue Book sees the publication of balances for 1992, 1993 and 1994. With this acceleration in the production of the input-output balances their importance as a tool to ensure consistency in the national accounts has increased.

Future developments

112. The next few years will see continued change. The introduction of the new ESA/SNA, which is mentioned in the introduction to Section 1, will also have implications for input-output. As an integral part of the national accounts, the input-output balances will have to be converted onto the new ESA/SNA basis. In addition constant price input-output balances will also be produced, to assist in compiling coherent estimates of volume growth in components of GDP

Further information

113. Further information on the industrial breakdown and analysis and input output can be found in the following publications and articles:

Standard Industrial Classification, Revised 1992 ((SIC(92))

Input-output balances for the United Kingdom

Input-Output Balances for the United Kingdom 1992-1994, August 1996 (consistent with Blue Book 1996)
A publication by the Government Statistical Service

Input-Output Tables for the United Kingdom are also published by HMSO for the years for which tables are available from 1954 up to 1990. The last of these published was:

Input-Output Tables for the United Kingdom 10th Edition (containing 1990 tables)
Published by HMSO 1995 ISBN 0 11 620664 0

The main analyses

Further information can be obtained from the ONS Library (details are given inside the front cover).

Economic Trends articles

Articles of interest are also published in Economic Trends. The following show those published in recent years.

Economic Trends No. 512 June 1996
'The United Kingdom's Input-Output Balances'.

Economic Trends No. 492 October 1994
Input-Output Balance for the United Kingdom 1991'

Economic Trends No. 480 October 1993
'Input-Output Balance for the United Kingdom 1990'

Economic Trends No. 467 September 1992
'Input-Output Balance for the United Kingdom 1989'

SECTION 2: THE MAIN ANALYSES
CHAPTER 2: Industrial and sector analyses

2.1 Input-Output "Combined" Use matrices for the United Kingdom for 1992 and 1993

£ million at purchasers' prices

1992	PURCHASES BY INDUSTRY GROUP[1]									
	Agriculture	Mining and quarrying	Manufact- uring	Electricity, gas and water supply	Construct- ion	Wholesale and retail trade	Transport and communi- cation	Financial intermed- iation	Public adminis- tration	Education, health and social work
SALES BY PRODUCT[1]										
Agriculture	2856	14	12600	-	4	900	46	12	19	155
Mining and quarrying	28	2465	8713	7061	1143	115	16	8	41	90
Manufacturing	4973	2293	120379	4517	15730	16233	9334	11970	13217	13636
Electricity, gas and water supply	350	280	6145	10209	338	1562	1016	1632	724	1623
Construction	201	105	552	371	19094	516	137	4772	3650	607
Wholesale and retail trade	630	178	1217	225	71	2937	1562	2000	239	409
Transport and communication	283	1516	8572	267	882	12797	11922	13842	2375	1873
Financial intermediation	1370	613	20964	1202	8927	16123	8903	46091	5305	5015
Public administration	-	-	-	-	-	-	-	-	467	-
Education, health and social work	210	21	922	59	118	308	411	1759	3980	11817
Other services	72	25	2785	83	61	324	408	908	392	1211
Total[2]	10973	7509	182849	23995	46370	51816	33754	82994	30409	36435
Sales by final buyers	14	21	1273	8	104	93	138	1409	-	10
Taxes on expenditure *less* subsidies	-938	-594	16924	2789	-109	10352	-669	2586	224	891
Value added	9738	11673	109810	13494	29796	74265	43777	130128	36774	63001
Total inputs[2]	19788	18609	310856	40285	76161	136527	76999	217117	67407	100337

£ million at purchasers' prices

1993	PURCHASES BY INDUSTRY GROUP[1]									
	Agriculture	Mining and quarrying	Manufact- uring	Electricity, gas and water supply	Construct- ion	Wholesale and retail trade	Transport and communi- cation	Financial intermed- iation	Public adminis- tration	Education, health and social work
SALES BY PRODUCT[1]										
Agriculture	2883	14	13095	-	5	924	47	11	19	135
Mining and quarrying	27	2614	9114	6597	1082	114	14	8	42	83
Manufacturing	5940	2155	127290	4168	15521	17378	10184	12616	13407	14327
Electricity, gas and water supply	334	222	6124	10100	323	1589	963	1636	698	1507
Construction	177	105	518	326	17666	508	129	5049	3927	576
Wholesale and retail trade	635	185	1266	229	75	3185	1652	2182	233	458
Transport and communication	281	1472	9127	277	906	13739	12695	14921	2436	2019
Financial intermediation	1305	610	22620	1248	9078	17322	9451	49246	5773	5411
Public administration	-	-	-	-	-	-	-	-	414	-
Education, health and social work	215	20	1021	63	124	346	458	1986	6840	20027
Other services	84	26	3043	99	69	378	448	1016	458	1335
Total[2]	11882	7424	193218	23106	44850	55484	36040	88670	34247	45878
Sales by final buyers	6	9	532	3	43	39	58	1430	-	4
Taxes on expenditure *less* subsidies	-2040	-548	17527	2692	147	10827	-421	2716	205	726
Value added	10093	12296	115672	14801	28930	78686	46321	139209	38377	66437
Total inputs[2]	19940	19180	326948	40602	73970	145036	81997	232025	72829	113045

1 Some of the industry / product group headings have been truncated. See table 2.2 for full titles.

2 Differences between totals and sums of components are due to rounding.

2.1 Input-Output "Combined" Use matrices for the United Kingdom for 1992 and 1993

continued

£ million at purchasers' prices

1992	Other services	Adjustment for financial services	Total[2]	Consumers' expenditure	General government final consumption	GDFCF	Change in stocks	Exports	Total[2]	TOTAL[2]
					FINAL DEMAND					
SALES BY PRODUCT[1]										
Agriculture	45	-	16651	7540	-	-	60	1828	9428	26079
Mining and quarrying	55	-	19735	607	-	-	62	6821	7490	27225
Manufacturing	4583	-	216864	181153	-	43675	-1017	99619	323430	540294
Electricity, gas and water supply	531	-	24410	15231	-	-	-116	60	15175	39585
Construction	401	-	30408	4806	-	45328	-926	34	49242	79650
Wholesale and retail trade	323	-	9792	36323	-	-	-	5014	41337	51129
Transport and communication	1419	-	55749	21410	-	911	-	9366	31687	87436
Financial intermediation	7277	23543	145333	74528	-	7516	-	12178	94222	239555
Public administration	-	-	467	-	67407	-	-	-	67407	67874
Education, health and social work	427	-	20031	13255	66109	-	-	1118	80482	100513
Other services	4003	-	10273	23129	5602	-	-	2147	30878	41151
Total[2]	19064	23543	549711	377982	139118	97430	-1937	138185	750778	1300490
Sales by final buyers	37	-	3107	4363	-7243	-4156	-	3929	-3107	-
Taxes on expenditure *less* subsidies	505	-	31961	1145	-	368	-	-	1513	33474
Value added	19219	-23543	518132	-	-	-	-	-	-	518132
Total inputs[2]	38825	-	1102912	383490	131875	93642	-1937	142114	749184	1852096

£ million at purchasers' prices

1993	Other services	Adjustment for financial services	Total[2]	Consumers' expenditure	General government final consumption	GDFCF	Change in stocks	Exports	Total[2]	TOTAL[2]
					FINAL DEMAND					
SALES BY PRODUCT[1]										
Agriculture	42	-	17176	7644	-	-	107	1592	9343	26519
Mining and quarrying	53	-	19748	603	-	-	-133	8802	9272	29020
Manufacturing	4966	-	227952	190697	-	45796	765	111687	348945	576897
Electricity, gas and water supply	505	-	23999	15598	-	-	-59	58	15597	39596
Construction	435	-	29417	4613	-	43654	-351	31	47947	77364
Wholesale and retail trade	322	-	10422	38318	-	-	-	5814	44132	54554
Transport and communication	1496	-	59367	22592	-	889	-	10729	34210	93577
Financial intermediation	7722	23299	153085	81228	-	7982	-	12987	102197	255282
Public administration	-	-	414	-	72829	-	-	-	72829	73243
Education, health and social work	476	-	31576	13809	66591	-	-	1231	81631	113207
Other services	4425	-	11382	24667	5543	-	--	2367	32577	43959
Total[2]	20442	23299	584538	399769	144963	98321	329	155298	798680	1383218
Sales by final buyers	16	-	2139	4752	-6882	-4708	-	4699	-2139	-
Taxes on expenditure *less* subsidies	498	-	32328	1878	-	680	-	-	2558	34886
Value added	20503	-23299	548025	-	-	-	-	-	-	548025
Total inputs[2]	41457	-	1167030	406399	138081	94293	329	159997	799099	1966129

See footnotes on previous page.

2.1 Input-Output "Combined" Use matrix for the United Kingdom for 1994
continued

£ million at purchasers' prices

1994	PURCHASES BY INDUSTRY GROUP[1]									
	Agriculture	Mining and quarrying	Manufact-uring	Electricity, gas and water supply	Construct-ion	Wholesale and retail trade	Transport and communi-cation	Financial intermed-iation	Public adminis-tration	Education, health and social work
SALES BY PRODUCT[1]										
Agriculture	2834	16	13635	-	5	1017	52	12	19	142
Mining and quarrying	26	2635	8656	7185	1012	110	15	8	44	94
Manufacturing	6165	2514	138798	4455	16620	18050	10947	13124	13577	15345
Electricity, gas and water supply	306	258	6426	9733	302	1589	1021	1675	725	1492
Construction	192	100	616	431	19033	580	157	5519	4257	595
Wholesale and retail trade	578	204	1458	270	74	3441	1776	2355	232	502
Transport and communication	261	1630	10356	269	899	14241	13829	16337	2512	2079
Financial intermediation	1236	614	25371	1272	9071	18252	10391	52701	6150	5597
Public administration	-	-	-	-	-	-	-	-	-315	-
Education, health and social work	206	19	1085	61	121	361	506	2105	8311	29865
Other services	69	27	3343	105	70	411	504	1111	594	1458
Total [2]	11873	8017	209743	23781	47206	58053	39200	94946	36736	57169
Sales by final buyers	18	26	1618	10	132	118	175	1593	-	13
Taxes on expenditure *less* subsidies	-2060	-380	18214	2641	106	12331	-1256	2642	211	652
Value added	10334	13443	124340	14983	30156	82059	49255	152100	38502	70829
Total inputs[2]	20165	21106	353916	41415	77600	152561	87374	251282	75449	128663

1 Some of the industry / product group headings have been truncated. See table 2.2 for full titles.

2 Differences between totals and sums of components are due to rounding.

2.1 Input-Output "Combined" Use matrix for the United Kingdom for 1994

continued

£ million at purchasers' prices

1993	Other services	Adjustment for financial services	Total[2]	Consumers' expenditure	General government final consumption	GDFCF	Change in stocks	Exports	Total[2]	TOTAL[2]
					FINAL DEMAND					
SALES BY PRODUCT[1]										
Agriculture	45	-	17777	7905	-	-	-202	1632	9335	27112
Mining and quarrying	55	-	19839	607	-	-	-470	9715	9852	29691
Manufacturing	5070	-	244666	199479	-	50946	3905	124100	378430	623096
Electricity, gas and water supply	490	-	24017	16039	-	-	-40	52	16051	40068
Construction	474	-	31954	4403	-	44295	538	29	49265	81219
Wholesale and retail trade	347	-	11237	40576	-	-	-	6060	46636	57873
Transport and communication	1622	-	64035	23925	-	878	-	11647	36450	100485
Financial intermediation	8450	28912	168017	86037	-	8670	1	14159	108867	276884
Public administration	-	-	315	-	75449	-	-	-	75449	75764
Education, health and social work	513	-	43153	14471	69897	-	-	1312	85680	128833
Other services	4837	-	12529	26439	5941	-	-	2616	34996	47526
Total[2]	21903	28912	637539	419881	151287	104789	3732	171322	851011	1488551
Sales by final buyers	47	-	3751	5034	-7173	-6355	-	4743	-3751	-
Taxes on expenditure *less* subsidies	536	-	33637	2361	-	783	-	-	3144	36781
Value added	22089	-28912	579177	-	-	-	-	-	-	579177
Total inputs[2]	44575	-	1254105	427276	144114	99217	3732	176065	850404	2104509

See footnotes on previous page.

2.2 Gross domestic product at current factor cost: by industry and type of income[1]

£ million

		1985	1986	1987	1988	1989	1990	1991	1992	1993	1994	1995
Agriculture, hunting, forestry and fishing:												
Income from employment	GIIB	2 160	2 261	2 399	2 634	2 825	2 990	3 181	3 448	3 266	3 321	3 387
Income from self-employment, rent and other trading income	CFLM	4 151	4 233	4 785	4 682	5 610	6 087	5 858	6 269	6 613	7 194	8 566
Total	CFLN	6 311	6 494	7 184	7 316	8 435	9 077	9 039	9 717	9 879	10 515	11 953
less Stock appreciation	-GIIE	−201	186	−64	−163	−111	−154	−74	22	215	−181	−57
Total (net)	CFLO	6 110	6 680	7 120	7 153	8 324	8 923	8 965	9 739	10 094	10 334	11 896
Mining and quarrying including oil and gas extraction:												
Income from employment[2]	CATD	3 337	4 088	3 826	3 502	3 237	3 330	3 986	4 037	3 524	3 465	3 456
Gross profits of companies, rent and income from self-employment[3]	CFLP	18 688	8 466	9 765	7 214	7 611	7 718	6 811	7 262	8 608	10 257	11 411
Gross trading surplus of public enterprises[3]	CFLQ	1 011	741	573	700	451	307	338	389	77	−305	−273
Total	CFLR	23 036	13 295	14 164	11 416	11 299	11 355	11 135	11 688	12 209	13 417	14 594
less Stock appreciation	-DGGS	60	238	−36	72	−40	−36	69	−14	87	26	−19
Total (net)[4]	CFLS	23 096	13 533	14 128	11 488	11 259	11 319	11 204	11 674	12 296	13 443	14 575
Manufacturing (revised definition):												
Income from employment[2]	CCXH	56 267	59 557	65 614	70 925	75 289	80 651	81 247	81 869	83 824	87 448	90 939
Gross profits of companies, rent and income from self-employment[3]	CFLT	20 741	22 040	24 585	29 692	34 139	33 331	26 624	28 877	32 569	38 517	42 367
Gross trading surplus of public enterprises[3]	GJFF	−123	153	441	514	31	77	90	468	544	498	794
Total	CFLU	76 885	81 750	90 640	101 131	109 459	114 059	107 961	111 214	116 937	126 463	134 100
less Stock appreciation	-GIIO	−1 124	−498	−2 017	−2 347	−2 292	−2 744	−1 066	−1 405	−1 265	−2 124	−2 442
Total (net)[4]	CFLV	75 761	81 252	88 623	98 784	107 167	111 315	106 895	109 809	115 672	124 339	131 658
Electricity, gas and water supply:												
Income from employment	CATE	3 687	3 829	4 261	4 642	4 259	4 822	5 898	5 815	6 182	6 073	6 131
Gross profits of companies, rent and income from self-employment[3]	CFLW	160	534	1 694	1 385	1 971	3 085	7 096	8 106	8 470	8 921	9 687
Gross trading surplus of public enterprises[3]	CFLX	4 380	5 134	3 944	4 427	4 354	2 737	227	−276	189	−98	3
Total	CFLY	8 227	9 497	9 899	10 454	10 584	10 644	13 221	13 645	14 841	14 896	15 821
less Stock appreciation	-DGGT	−23	−90	19	−191	−1	−61	166	−152	−39	87	−34
Total(net)	CFLZ	8 204	9 407	9 918	10 263	10 583	10 583	13 387	13 493	14 802	14 983	15 787
Construction:												
Income from employment	GIIP	9 518	10 063	11 120	12 984	14 896	16 675	15 702	15 268	13 907	14 451	14 826
Gross profits of companies, rent and income from self-employment	CFMA	9 733	10 816	13 476	17 439	20 444	18 929	15 718	14 936	15 279	16 088	17 635
Total	CFMB	19 251	20 879	24 596	30 423	35 340	35 604	31 420	30 204	29 186	30 539	32 461
less Stock appreciation	-GIIS	−827	−963	−1 438	−2 302	−2 430	−1 036	85	−408	−256	−383	−646
Total (net)	CFMC	18 424	19 916	23 158	28 121	32 910	34 568	31 505	29 796	28 930	30 156	31 815
Wholesale and retail trade; repairs; hotels and restaurants:												
Income from employment	GIIT	26 650	27 505	29 440	33 710	39 698	42 836	44 235	48 533	50 048	51 789	53 832
Gross profits, rent and other trading income	CFMD	14 654	18 873	21 092	23 635	24 391	27 581	28 887	26 466	29 831	31 673	32 589
Total	CFME	41 304	46 378	50 532	57 345	64 089	70 417	73 122	74 999	79 879	83 462	86 421
less Stock appreciation	-GIIW	−570	−761	−1 081	−1 295	−1 892	−2 144	−1 366	−733	−1 192	−1 402	−1 715
Total (net)	CFMF	40 734	45 617	49 451	56 050	62 197	68 273	71 756	74 266	78 687	82 060	84 706

1 The contribution of each industry to the gross domestic product before providing for depreciation. The industrial composition in this table is consistent with the Input-Output analyses in table 2.1.
2 Figures for separate industries are given in table 2.4.
3 Figures for companies and public corporations are affected by privatisation. For further details see methodological notes.
4 Figures for separate industries are given in table 2.3.

2.2 Gross domestic product at current factor cost: by industry and type of income[1]

continued

£ million

		1985	1986	1987	1988	1989	1990	1991	1992	1993	1994	1995
Transport, storage and communication:												
Income from employment	CCIU	16 272	17 671	18 513	21 104	24 836	27 552	28 696	29 944	31 260	32 529	33 561
Gross profits of companies, rent and income from self employment[3]	CFMG	6 795	8 303	10 623	12 373	11 670	12 033	12 662	12 627	13 857	14 917	15 648
Gross trading surplus of public enterprises[3]	GIYV	1 214	1 267	964	835	685	665	852	1 227	1 224	1 828	1 647
Total	CFMH	24 281	27 241	30 100	34 312	37 191	40 250	42 210	43 798	46 341	49 274	50 856
less Stock appreciation	−DHNM	−35	6	−63	−74	−36	−50	−20	−21	−20	−19	−21
Total(net)	CFMI	24 246	27 247	30 037	34 238	37 155	40 200	42 190	43 777	46 321	49 255	50 835
Financial intermediation, real estate, renting and business activities[5]:												
Income from employment	GIYS	28 797	31 940	34 837	40 419	43 146	49 777	52 973	52 235	53 896	55 381	57 836
Rent on dwellings[7]	CAJG	17 326	18 611	20 007	22 482	25 448	29 402	34 283	38 102	41 013	44 236	47 439
Gross trading profits, other rent[6] and other trading income	CFMK	3 666	6 475	9 845	10 601	13 097	13 042	11 827	15 268	20 820	23 560	22 068
Imputed charge for capital consumption	EZAY	–	–	–	–	51	56	55	47	61	50	55
Adjustment for financial services	GIJI	12 087	14 383	15 201	17 024	22 035	23 473	19 864	23 543	23 299	28 912	30 794
Total	CFML	61 876	71 409	79 890	90 526	103 777	115 750	119 002	129 195	139 089	152 139	158 192
less Stock appreciation	−DHKT	−6	19	−31	−42	−120	83	197	933	120	−38	32
Total (net)	CFMM	61 870	71 428	79 859	90 484	103 657	115 833	119 199	130 128	139 209	152 101	158 224
Public administration, national defence and compulsory social security:												
Income from employment	GIJK	20 531	21 517	23 169	24 653	26 690	30 209	32 799	35 368	36 927	36 943	37 730
of which:												
HM Forces	GIDJ	4 761	5 048	5 381	5 696	5 990	6 449	7 338	7 877	7 667	7 299	6 590
Civilians	GIJM	15 770	16 469	17 788	18 957	20 700	23 760	25 461	27 491	29 260	29 644	31 140
Imputed charge for capital consumption	GIJN	985	1 087	1 199	1 347	1 338	1 467	1 458	1 406	1 450	1 559	1 780
Total	CAJH	21 516	22 604	24 368	26 000	28 028	31 676	34 257	36 774	38 377	38 502	39 510
Education, health and social work:												
Income from employment	GIJO	23 999	27 079	29 931	34 191	39 955	44 004	50 196	53 496	56 237	59 727	61 839
Income from self-employment, rent and other income	CFMN	2 767	2 900	3 030	3 562	4 469	5 318	5 768	7 173	7 956	8 831	8 850
Imputed charge for capital consumption	GIJQ	1 557	1 666	1 770	1 921	2 210	2 423	2 407	2 332	2 244	2 271	2 283
Total	CFMO	28 323	31 645	34 731	39 674	46 634	51 745	58 371	63 001	66 437	70 829	72 972
Other services including sewage and refuse disposal:[8]												
Income from employment	GIYI	5 640	6 870	7 098	7 773	9 541	10 908	11 853	12 003	12 750	13 821	14 358
Gross profits of companies, rent and income from self-employment[3]	CFMQ	4 794	4 988	5 814	6 826	5 162	6 383	5 941	6 736	7 087	7 443	8 012
Gross trading surplus of public enterprises[3]	CFMR	995	1 125	1 249	1 266	908	181	150	58	177	281	274
Imputed charge for capital consumption	GIJV	288	315	338	366	406	445	443	422	488	544	611
Total	CFMS	11 717	13 298	14 499	16 231	16 017	17 917	18 387	19 219	20 502	22 089	23 255
less Stock appreciation	−DHKS	−12	28	−17	−33	−139	11	–	–	–	–	–
Total (net)	CFMT	11 705	13 326	14 482	16 198	15 878	17 928	18 387	19 219	20 502	22 089	23 255
All industries:												
Income from employment	DJAO	196 858	212 380	230 208	256 537	284 372	313 753	330 767	342 015	351 819	364 946	377 895
Gross profits and other trading income	GIJX	101 164	105 194	120 933	134 753	148 646	151 679	137 837	145 115	162 228	184 121	194 753
Rent	DIDS	21 875	23 848	26 155	29 904	33 830	38 669	45 160	52 116	55 385	58 632	62 758
Imputed charge for capital consumption	DIDT	2 830	3 068	3 307	3 634	4 005	4 391	4 363	4 207	4 243	4 424	4 729
less Stock appreciation	−DJAT	−2 738	−1 835	−4 727	−6 375	−7 061	−6 131	−2 010	−1 778	−2 350	−4 034	−4 902
less Adjustment for financial services	−GIJI	−12 087	−14 383	−15 201	−17 024	−22 035	−23 473	−19 864	−23 543	−23 299	−28 912	−30 794
Statistical discrepancy (income adjustment)	GIXQ	–	–	–	–	–	–	–	–	–	–	−180
Gross domestic product	CAOM	307 902	328 272	360 675	401 428	441 759	478 886	496 253	518 132	548 025	579 177	604 259

5 Of which: financial intermediation, insurance and pension funding:

		1989	1990	1991	1992	1993	1994	1995
Income from employment	DTCW	18 376	19 772	21 437	20 476	20 336	20 086	20 780
Gross trading profits, rent and other trading income[6]	DTCX	−8 834	−10 075	−10 570	−7 786	−4 634	−5 854	−5 262

6 Excluding adjustment for financial services.
7 Includes the imputed rent of owner-occupied dwellings, as shown at table 4.1.
8 Comprising section O, P, and Q of the SIC(92).
9 For 1992, 1993 and 1994 the type of income for each of the eleven broad industries shown are fully reconciled with the value added series in table 2.1. Between 1989 and 1991 income from employment has been mainly used as the residual to achieve reconciliation. Before 1989 the data were compiled on a different basis, which leads to step changes.
10 Components may not sum to totals due to rounding.

2.3 Gross domestic product at current factor cost: by production industries[1]

£ million

		1985	1986	1987	1988	1989	1990	1991	1992	1993	1994	1995
Mining and quarrying:												
Mining of coal and nuclear fuel	GJFH	3 765	2 946	2 608	2 827	2 458	2 162	2 538	2 488	1 463	972	967
Extraction of mineral oil and natural gas	DIEY	18 409	9 624	10 465	7 431	7 538	7 965	7 638	7 996	9 535	11 305	12 392
Other mining and quarrying[2]	DIHA	922	963	1 055	1 230	1 263	1 192	1 028	1 190	1 298	1 166	1 216
Manufacturing industries (revised definition):												
Food and beverages	DIHH	9 518	10 414	11 128	11 551	12 681	13 845	14 011	15 360	16 497	16 831	17 364
Tobacco products	DIHI	1 059	849	1 061	1 045	1 034	1 024	1 184	1 257	1 330	1 263	1 279
Textiles and leather products	DIHR	5 371	5 708	6 321	6 632	6 744	6 942	6 604	6 696	6 646	6 970	7 097
Wood and wood products	DIHP	1 151	1 236	1 461	1 689	1 712	1 704	1 544	1 538	1 448	1 526	1 546
Pulp, paper and products, printing and publishing	DIHL	7 768	8 528	9 418	10 573	11 935	12 324	12 405	13 471	13 972	14 817	16 590
Solid and nuclear fuels, oil refining	DIHM	2 030	2 471	1 988	2 426	2 629	3 121	2 800	2 579	2 573	2 416	2 932
Chemicals and man-made fibres	DIHD	7 872	8 373	9 877	10 956	11 571	11 283	11 630	12 462	12 940	13 477	15 149
Rubber and plastic products	DIHQ	2 922	3 307	3 865	4 224	4 746	5 018	5 027	5 514	5 836	6 234	7 045
Other non-metallic mineral products	DIHC	2 670	2 934	3 296	3 995	4 403	4 142	3 660	3 488	3 727	4 426	4 617
Basic metals and metal products	DIHB	9 049	9 544	10 361	11 962	12 774	12 958	11 892	11 878	12 024	13 181	14 218
Machinery and equipment	DIHE	7 295	7 491	7 743	8 651	9 501	9 937	9 161	9 183	9 382	10 663	11 015
Electrical and optical equipment	DIHF	9 698	10 055	10 881	12 563	12 642	12 987	12 918	12 499	13 494	15 316	16 322
Transport equipment	DIHG	7 390	8 227	8 756	9 651	11 828	12 988	11 178	10 781	12 331	12 994	12 321
Other manufacturing	DIHN	1 970	2 117	2 465	2 865	2 967	3 044	2 881	3 105	3 473	4 227	4 163
Electricity, gas and water supply	CFLZ	8 204	9 407	9 918	10 263	10 583	10 583	13 387	13 493	14 802	14 983	15 787
Total production industries	DIFR	107 061	104 192	112 669	120 535	129 009	133 217	131 486	134 976	142 770	152 765	162 020

1 Figures are shown after deducting of stock appreciation but before deducting
  for depreciation.
2 Includes sub-sections CB of the SIC(92).
3 Components may not sum to totals due to rounding.

2.4 Income from employment in production industries

£ million

		1985	1986	1987	1988	1989	1990	1991	1992	1993	1994	1995
Mining and quarrying:												
Mining of coal and nuclear fuel	CATF	2 060	2 615	2 502	1 933	1 920	1 807	2 169	2 107	1 265	1 175	1 227
Extraction of mineral oil and natural gas	GIAB	629	721	599	707	671	840	1 151	1 150	1 409	1 569	1 477
Other mining and quarrying[1]	GIYK	648	752	725	862	646	683	666	779	850	720	752
Manufacturing industries (revised definition):												
Food and beverages	GIYN	5 840	6 241	6 906	7 125	8 069	9 003	9 149	10 045	10 597	10 769	11 197
Tobacco products	GIYO	270	283	287	302	408	369	428	433	457	442	460
Textiles and leather products	CFNB	4 371	4 721	5 232	5 587	5 095	5 383	5 205	5 301	5 163	5 369	5 582
Wood and wood products	CFJF	996	1 067	1 193	1 330	1 041	1 011	1 002	1 087	1 042	1 090	1 134
Pulp, paper products, printing and publishing	GIAR	6 213	6 547	7 234	7 974	8 364	8 976	9 378	10 109	10 443	10 985	11 423
Solid and nuclear fuels, oil refining	GIYL	637	632	708	751	1 051	1 201	1 073	995	1 138	1 161	1 207
Chemicals and man-made fibres	GIAG	4 153	4 517	5 137	5 486	7 871	8 148	7 882	8 307	8 070	8 089	8 411
Rubber and plastic products	GIAS	2 213	2 443	2 852	3 176	3 535	3 860	4 031	4 300	4 410	4 620	4 805
Other non-metallic mineral products	GIYJ	1 799	1 845	2 111	2 417	3 093	3 075	2 846	2 738	2 757	3 116	3 240
Basic metals and metal products	DKLK	7 467	7 804	8 300	9 118	8 812	9 338	9 484	9 749	9 670	10 286	10 698
Machinery and equipment	GIAI	6 198	6 432	6 713	7 281	7 571	8 049	7 892	7 297	7 239	7 619	7 923
Electrical and optical equipment	GIAJ	7 213	7 677	8 531	9 322	8 105	8 695	9 980	9 626	10 079	10 693	11 121
Transport equipment	GIYM	7 255	7 591	8 347	8 856	10 353	11 578	10 878	9 825	10 518	10 544	10 965
Other manufacturing	CFMU	1 642	1 757	2 063	2 200	1 922	1 963	2 020	2 057	2 240	2 666	2 773
Electricity, gas and water supply	CATE	3 687	3 829	4 261	4 642	4 259	4 822	5 898	5 815	6 182	6 073	6 131
Total production industries	GIAU	63 291	67 474	73 701	79 069	82 785	88 803	91 131	91 721	93 530	96 986	100 526

1 Includes sub-section CB of the SIC(92).
2 For 1992, 1993, and 1994 the income from employment series have been fully
  reconciled with the other components of value added in line with the analyses
  in Table 2.1. Between 1989 and 1991 income from employment has been
  mainly used as the residual to achieve reconciliation. Before 1989 the data
  were compiled on a different basis, which leads to step changes.
3 Components may not sum to totals due to rounding.

2.5 Gross domestic product at constant 1990 factor cost: by industry of output[1]

1990 = 100

	Weight per 1000[2] 1990		1985	1986	1987	1988	1989	1990	1991	1992	1993	1994	1995
AGRICULTURE, HUNTING, FORESTRY AND FISHING	19	CKAP	95.3	95.5	93.5	92.1	96.7	100.0	101.5	106.0	98.2	98.0	98.6
PRODUCTION:													
Mining and quarrying:													
Mining of coal and nuclear fuel	5	DVZU	106.6	122.3	116.8	114.3	109.5	100.0	101.0	91.1	71.5	47.4	49.9
Extraction of mineral oil and natural gas	17	DVZT	136.0	135.9	137.8	124.6	102.0	100.0	106.7	114.5	130.3	161.2	170.4
Other mining and quarrying[3]	2	DVZV	100.2	99.0	101.6	108.0	107.6	100.0	95.9	93.7	93.3	93.8	93.9
Total mining and quarrying	24	DVZJ	129.4	129.4	130.0	120.9	104.0	100.0	104.5	107.8	115.2	132.4	139.3
Manufacturing:													
Food and beverages	29	DUDG	92.6	93.8	95.8	98.2	98.7	100.0	98.7	99.7	100.3	101.8	104.1
Tobacco products	2	DUDH	97.2	87.5	95.6	99.0	96.4	100.0	100.7	105.8	98.7	105.1	100.8
Textiles and leather products	14	DVZM	103.7	105.8	109.0	106.8	103.6	100.0	89.4	89.4	89.4	90.5	89.7
Wood and wood products	4	DUCP	80.8	83.8	90.9	102.0	101.4	100.0	88.7	87.2	89.3	95.5	91.2
Pulp, paper products, printing and publishing	26	DUCO	74.7	77.7	84.8	92.8	97.7	100.0	94.9	95.6	99.0	101.5	102.6
Solid and nuclear fuels, oil refining	7	DVZN	103.4	105.0	96.1	99.2	102.9	100.0	109.7	114.9	114.9	115.4	128.5
Chemicals and man-made fibres	24	DVZO	82.7	83.9	90.6	95.5	100.2	100.0	102.4	105.0	107.6	112.3	117.5
Rubber and plastic products	10	DUCQ	70.7	75.6	84.3	92.4	97.0	100.0	93.9	95.6	99.8	109.6	114.5
Other non-metallic mineral products	9	DUCR	86.8	87.8	92.9	102.4	105.1	100.0	90.3	86.0	88.9	92.7	92.1
Basic metals and metal products	27	DVZP	86.5	86.2	91.4	100.7	102.7	100.0	90.4	86.0	84.8	86.7	87.4
Machinery and equipment	21	DVZY	90.4	87.1	86.2	93.8	97.7	100.0	90.2	85.2	85.0	89.2	88.7
Electrical and optical equipment	27	DVZZ	79.5	79.8	83.9	93.0	99.7	100.0	95.3	96.0	101.2	112.0	119.2
Transport equipment	27	DUCN	76.3	79.4	82.6	88.8	101.6	100.0	93.2	90.8	87.8	92.3	93.1
Other manufacturing	6	DUCS	79.9	80.4	84.5	93.2	98.4	100.0	86.9	85.9	88.4	90.0	85.2
Total manufacturing (revised definition)	232	DVZK	84.5	85.6	89.6	95.9	100.2	100.0	94.6	94.0	95.3	99.3	101.5
Electricity, gas and water supply	22	DVZS	86.5	95.1	97.6	97.7	97.3	100.0	105.7	107.4	111.8	113.1	116.7
Total production	278	DVZI	88.0	90.1	93.7	98.2	100.3	100.0	96.3	96.2	98.3	103.2	105.9
CONSTRUCTION	72	DVJO	73.0	76.0	84.9	92.3	97.6	100.0	92.0	87.9	87.2	90.5	89.6
SERVICE INDUSTRIES:													
Wholesale and retail trade; repairs	115	CKJN	81.0	85.3	91.9	98.1	101.7	100.0	96.8	96.7	101.8	105.7	107.0
Hotels and restaurants	28	CKEP	80.7	85.9	91.3	96.1	99.1	100.0	93.5	89.3	91.7	94.2	94.3
Transport and storage	54	CKBU	83.8	85.6	92.6	96.7	100.8	100.0	97.0	99.2	103.5	110.1	114.4
Post and telecommunication	30	CKBM	75.3	81.1	85.2	90.9	96.3	100.0	100.4	100.8	107.0	116.0	125.9
Financial intermediation	72	CKKH	74.4	75.9	84.8	91.4	95.6	100.0	99.9	94.6	97.3	98.5	104.3
Real estate, renting and business activities	111	CKKI	77.4	84.3	88.4	96.3	97.9	100.0	97.9	96.4	99.1	107.5	115.0
Ownership of dwellings	62	CKBW	97.6	98.1	98.1	98.4	98.7	100.0	101.6	102.1	103.4	104.9	106.6
Public administration, national defence, social security	66	CKBX	100.2	100.2	98.8	98.3	98.5	100.0	100.9	100.5	99.1	97.6	95.7
Education	49	CKFL	94.4	96.0	98.7	101.3	101.3	100.0	100.0	100.4	97.6	99.1	100.5
Health and social work	59	CKFM	89.7	90.6	94.1	97.0	98.7	100.0	102.1	103.6	106.5	107.7	108.9
Other services[4]	37	CKKJ	81.0	85.3	93.8	99.3	99.6	100.0	99.8	100.7	108.3	115.0	122.9
Adjustment for financial services	−51	CKCA	68.3	78.1	87.3	93.0	96.9	100.0	98.5	94.3	95.8	100.2	108.0
Total services	631	CKCE	85.1	88.6	92.7	97.2	99.2	100.0	99.1	98.8	101.6	105.3	108.4
Gross domestic product	1 000	DJDD	85.2	88.6	92.7	97.3	99.4	100.0	97.9	97.4	99.6	103.7	106.2

1 The output analysis of Gross domestic product is naturally estimated in terms of change and expressed in index number form. It is, therefore, inappropriate to show its divergence from the estimate of Gross domestic product as a Statistical discrepancy (output adjustment). Such an adjustment does, however, exists implicitly.

2 The weights are in proportion to the distribution of net output in 1990 and are used to calculate the indices from 1986 onwards. For the method of calculation of earlier indices see paragraph 5.19 of United Kingdom National Accounts: Sources and Methods, Third edition.

3 Comprising sub-section CB of the SIC(92).

4 Comprising sections O, P and Q of the SIC(92).

Where such data can be compiled, quarterly data for series in this table are available on the ONS's Databank. For the production series, data are available monthly. The data can also be provided on paper by request. Some of these data are published regularly in the Economic Trends Quarterly Supplement in table A4. Monthly production data are published in the Monthly Digest of Statistics, table 7.1 and Economic Trends, table 5.1.

2.6 Gross domestic product at current factor cost: by sector of employment and type of income

£ million

		1985	1986	1987	1988	1989	1990	1991	1992	1993	1994	1995
FACTOR INCOMES ANALYSED BY SECTOR OF EMPLOYMENT												
Personal sector:												
Income from employment	GICO	18 631	21 420	24 310	28 101	33 070	36 534	39 555	41 718	44 133	47 409	50 572
of which: Income of employees of unincorporated businesses[1]	GICP	13 695	15 727	17 682	20 377	23 404	26 277	27 956	29 328	30 893	33 254	35 802
Income from self-employment[2]	CFAN	30 404	35 104	39 361	45 829	52 691	58 688	56 745	57 149	60 461	64 021	67 685
Rent[3]	DIAO	15 533	17 148	18 857	21 773	24 802	28 456	33 485	38 804	40 981	44 065	47 898
Imputed charge for capital consumption of private non-profit-making bodies	CFBM	458	485	503	524	557	585	600	604	564	587	600
less Stock appreciation	-DDAD	−475	−172	−491	−750	−803	−695	−394	−39	−13	−376	−420
Total	GICW	64 551	73 985	82 540	95 477	110 317	123 568	129 991	138 236	146 126	155 706	166 335
Industrial and commercial companies:												
Income from employment	GGAH	103 533	110 127	121 990	137 999	155 151	173 058	180 420	182 876	188 305	197 109	204 294
Gross trading profits[2,4]	AIAD	59 624	55 485	66 283	74 926	80 826	80 676	75 966	76 248	85 680	98 758	104 152
Rent[3]	CICD	2 375	2 697	3 174	3 790	4 558	5 587	6 337	7 734	8 627	8 595	8 745
less Stock appreciation	-AIAC	−2 155	−1 500	−4 148	−5 366	−6 203	−5 316	−1 586	−1 700	−2 373	−3 650	−4 451
Total	CAJN	163 377	166 809	187 299	211 349	234 332	254 005	261 137	265 158	280 239	300 812	312 740
Financial companies and institutions												
Income from employment	GIDA	13 563	15 044	16 408	19 037	20 322	23 445	24 950	24 603	25 385	26 084	27 241
Gross trading profits[2]	AIFB	−8 478	−8 146	−6 830	−10 549	−13 631	−14 973	−16 511	−14 392	−10 860	−12 290	−13 125
Rent[3]	CIIG	301	329	409	499	556	447	811	896	883	965	985
Total	GIDD	5 386	7 227	9 987	8 987	7 247	8 919	9 250	11 107	15 408	14 759	15 101
Public corporations:												
Income from employment	GISB	15 421	16 669	14 095	13 395	13 608	12 744	12 594	15 906	20 410	25 732	27 159
Gross trading surplus[2,4]	ADRD	7 262	8 213	6 993	7 554	6 528	3 801	1 809	2 361	3 454	4 230	4 634
Rent[3]	GISI	522	514	519	548	568	578	541	547	522	451	506
less Stock appreciation	-ADRC	−108	−163	−88	−259	−55	−120	−30	−39	36	−8	−31
Total	GIDI	23 097	25 233	21 519	21 238	20 649	17 003	14 914	18 775	24 422	30 405	32 268
Central government:												
Income from employment[5]:												
HM Forces	GIDJ	4 761	5 048	5 381	5 696	5 990	6 449	7 338	7 877	7 667	7 299	6 590
Civilians	GIDK	17 659	18 685	20 497	22 109	24 396	26 984	28 101	28 435	26 012	20 893	19 730
Gross trading surplus[2]	ACGG	−175	−279	−485	−459	−323	−545	−443	−186	−247	23	248
Rent[3]	GTBG	101	104	174	152	108	142	178	135	183	189	194
Imputed charge for consumption of non-trading capital	ACGL	983	1 076	1 179	1 303	1 484	1 623	1 675	1 608	1 867	1 978	2 150
Total	GIDO	23 329	24 634	26 746	28 801	31 655	34 653	36 849	37 869	35 482	30 382	28 912
Local authorities:												
Income from employment[6]	GIDP	23 290	25 387	27 527	30 200	31 835	34 539	37 809	40 600	39 907	40 420	42 309
Gross trading surplus[2]	ADAD	440	434	410	427	522	557	407	392	440	467	365
Rent[3]	ADAE	3 043	3 056	3 022	3 142	3 238	3 459	3 808	4 000	4 189	4 367	4 430
Imputed charge for consumption of non-trading capital	ADAG	1 389	1 507	1 625	1 807	1 964	2 183	2 088	1 995	1 812	1 859	1 979
Total	GIDT	28 162	30 384	32 584	35 576	37 559	40 738	44 112	46 987	46 348	47 113	49 083
All sectors:												
Income from employment	DJAO	196 858	212 380	230 208	256 537	284 372	313 753	330 767	342 015	351 819	364 946	377 895
Income from self-employment[2]	CFAN	30 404	35 104	39 361	45 829	52 691	58 688	56 745	57 149	60 461	64 021	67 685
Gross trading profits of companies[2]	CIAC	51 146	47 339	59 453	64 377	67 195	65 703	59 455	61 856	74 820	86 468	91 027
Gross trading surplus of public corporations[2]	ADRD	7 262	8 213	6 993	7 554	6 528	3 801	1 809	2 361	3 454	4 230	4 634
Gross trading surplus of general government enterprises[2]	DJAQ	265	155	−75	−32	199	12	−36	206	193	490	613
Rent[3]	DIDS	21 875	23 848	26 155	29 904	33 830	38 669	45 160	52 116	55 385	58 632	62 758
Imputed charge for consumption of non-trading capital	DIDT	2 830	3 068	3 307	3 634	4 005	4 391	4 363	4 207	4 243	4 424	4 729
less Stock appreciation	-DJAT	−2 738	−1 835	−4 727	−6 375	−7 061	−6 131	−2 010	−1 778	−2 350	−4 034	−4 902
Statistical discrepancy (income adjustment)	GIXQ	−	−	−	−	−	−	−	−	−	−	−180
Gross domestic product	CAOM	307 902	328 272	360 675	401 428	441 759	478 886	496 253	518 132	548 025	579 177	604 259

1 Wages, salaries and employers' contributions paid by unincorporated enterprises, by private non-profit-making bodies serving persons and by persons employing domestic servants.
2 Before providing for depreciation and stock appreciation.
3 Before providing for depreciation.
4 Figures for companies and public corporations are affected by privatisation. For further details see methodological notes.
5 For details see table in methodological notes.
6 Including teachers' pension increase payments. For details see table in methodological notes.

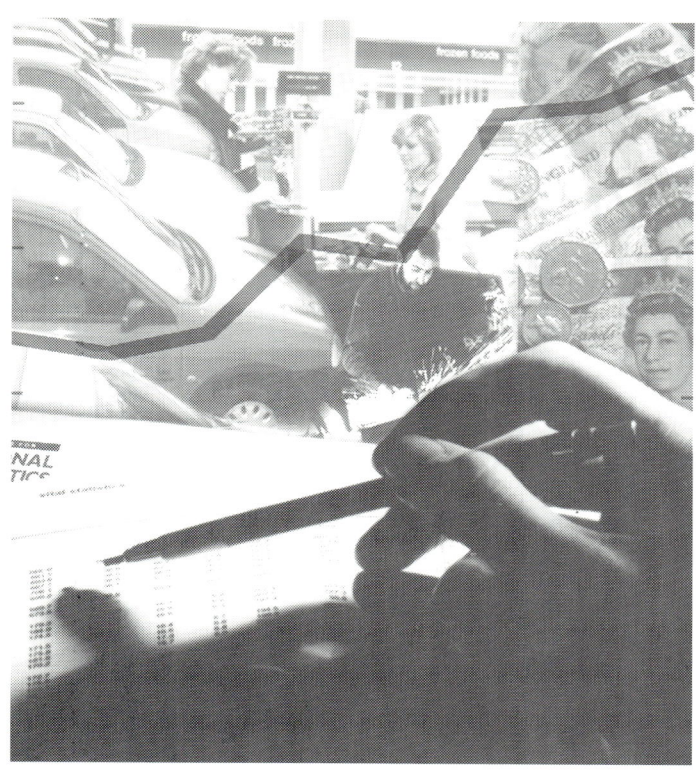

The sector accounts

SECTION 3: THE SECTOR ACCOUNTS

OVERVIEW OF THE 1995 FIGURES

The public sector financial deficit fell from £44.4 billion in 1994 to £37.8 billion in 1995. The narrowing of this deficit was mainly due to an increase in receipts of taxes on income. The deficit remains greater than the combined surplus of the personal and company sectors. The financial surplus of companies sector fell from £20.0 billion in 1994 to £8.3 billion in 1995. This fall mainly reflects higher capital expenditure and dividend and tax payments. The personal sector financial surplus rose from £22.0 billion in 1994 to £27.2 billion in 1995 reflecting a greater rise in income than in expenditure. The rise in income was related to a substantial increase in dividends and interest received from the companies sector which was related to dividend payments by the Regional Electricity companies and other privatised utilities, the National Grid Distribution and the high level of takeover and merger activity experienced during the year. The overseas sector surplus, equivalent to a deficit on the current account of the balance of payments, has remained at a similar level to 1994. The sectoral financial balances are shown in the chart 3.1 below.

Chart *3.1*

Sectoral Financial Balances

The financial transactions accounts show how, in 1995, financial institutions acted as intermediaries to channel the financial surplus of the personal sector to fund the public sector deficit. The personal sector has used its financial surplus to make large deposits with banks and building societies, and to invest in life assurance and pensions. The banks have increased lending to industrial and commercial companies, which has mainly been used to fund takeover activity, paying cash to institutional and individual shareholders for shares in the target companies. The public sector deficit has then been funded by large net issues of Treasury bills, taken up mainly by banks and building societies, and by large net issues of British government securities, taken up mainly by life assurance and pension funds.

THE SECTOR ACCOUNTS

114. The sector accounts show the relationships between different sectors of the economy and different types of transactions. They summarise the transactions of particular groups of institutions or of people in the economy, showing how income is distributed and re-distributed, and how savings are used to add to wealth through investment in physical and financial assets. This section presents chapter 3 and the subsequent chapters which deal with individual areas and subdivisions of the accounts.

115. This introduction has been divided into the following areas:

The framework of the sector accounts
    The first dimension: The institutional sectors
    The second dimension: The types of transaction
    The current, capital and financial accounts
    The balancing item
    Transactions and balances in the sector accounts

Summary analysis
    The Summary accounts of the nation
    Table B (previously Table A)
    Summary analysis by sector 1994
    Sectoral balancing items and Table C (previously Table B).

Developments
    UK company securities and money market instruments
    Revised treatment of social security contributions
    Dividend and interest payments
    Future developments
Further information

The framework of the sector accounts

116. The framework of national accounts detailed in section 1 highlights the four main kinds of accounts: production, income (and expenditure), capital and financial. The **production account** displays the transactions involved in generating income by the production of goods and services and the **income and expenditure account** shows *current income* (in this case GDP) carried forward from the production account, and has as its balancing item savings, which are the difference between income and expenditure. The **capital account** shows *savings* carried forward from the income and expenditure account. The balancing item is the financial surplus or deficit. The **financial account** shows how the *financial surplus or deficit* brought forward from the capital account is financed by borrowing and lending.

117. The production account and the national income and expenditure account are discussed in Section 1. The income and expenditure account can be elaborated to form a consistent set of sector

accounts. This is done in two dimensions, by sectors and types of transaction. A third dimension, related to capital and financial transactions, is that of asset and liability levels, the national and sector balance sheets. The sectors and types of transactions are described in turn below.

The first dimension: The institutional sectors

118. The first dimension of the breakdown of the income and expenditure account is that of the **institutional sectors**. These are groupings of economic units, brigaded broadly according to their role in the economy. Examples of these roles are: income generation, income redistribution, private consumption, collective consumption, investment, financial intermediation, etc. Most units have more than one role, but a natural and useful classification is to distinguish between persons, companies and government. The overseas sector is also identified as having a role, although it is not part of the domestic economy. It completes the picture by representing the rest of the world when the domestic sectors are involved in cross transactions. The main sectors of the UK economy are as follows:

Personal sector comprising;
Households, unincorporated businesses, life assurance and pension funds (see paragraph 120) and private and non-profit making bodies serving persons.

Corporate sector comprising;
Companies and financial institutions which is subdivided into industrial and commercial companies and financial institutions and public corporations.

General government sector comprising;
Central government and local authorities

Overseas sector (the rest of the world)

119. Definitions of these sectors are given in the appropriate chapters of Sources and Methods and, in full detail, in the *Business monitor MA23 Sector classification for the national accounts*, available from HMSO.

120. Life assurance and pension funds are regarded as the collective property of the policy holders and scheme members. The current income and expenditure of the funds (see table 4.10) is therefore included in the current account of the personal sector and the funds' current surplus forms part of personal sector saving. Given their importance as financial intermediaries and so that their financial activity can be seen, the funds are treated in the capital and financial accounts as a separate sector. The accounting framework is maintained by including an entry in the financial accounts which shows the current surplus as being invested by the personal sector in the life assurance and pension funds sector (see table 11.2).

121. The tables in chapters 3 to 10 are based on the sector classification

detailed above. In chapters 11 and 12, which deal with the financial accounts, a more detailed classification is used (see below). This classification subdivides the corporate sector further. Further information relating to the definitions and sources for information for these sectors can be found in section C of the *Financial Statistics Explanatory Handbook*.

Sector classification for the financial accounts

Personal Sector
Financial companies and institutions
    Banks and building societies
        Banks
        Building societies
    Other financial institutions (OFIs)
        Life assurance and pension funds
        Remaining financial institutions (OOFIs)
Industrial and commercial companies (ICCs)
Public sector
    General government
        Central government
        Local authorities
    Public corporations
Overseas sector

The second dimension: The types of transactions

122. The other dimension is that of the **types of transaction**. The transactions can be grouped broadly according to purpose, whether **current, capital or financial**. This is done by splitting the account as displayed in figure 1.2 and paragraphs 31 to 33 into three main parts that correspond broadly with the three types of expenditure. These are described briefly below:

Current account

123. The current account may also be known as an **income and expenditure account** or, in the case of companies, an **appropriation account**. For each sector it includes all income generated from production (i.e. factor income see paragraphs 49 to 59) together with net current transfers from or to other sectors. For the personal and general government sectors, there is also final consumption expenditure on goods and services. (Companies are not regarded as final consumers; their spending comprises a distribution of income by transfer payments to other sectors).

124. The balance on the current accounts is the amount available for investment, or adding to wealth. In the personal sector account it is called **savings** in the companies accounts it is called **undistributed income**, and the government accounts it is called the **current surplus**.

The sector accounts

Capital account

125. The capital account concerns expenditure on the acquisition of physical assets, in the form of both fixed assets and stocks. On the income side of this account are saving, brought down from the current account, and net capital transfers. Capital transfers include for example, capital grants from companies to public corporations (e.g the private sector contributions towards extension to the Jubilee Line to Docklands).

126. The balance on the capital account is known as the **financial surplus or deficit**. Conceptually this surplus or deficit, in total for the domestic sectors, represents net lending to the rest of the world (the overseas sector).

Financial account

127. The financial account elaborates the acquisition and disposal of financial assets and liabilities. Examples of financial assets are: bank deposits (which are assets of the depositors and liabilities of the banks), unit trust units (assets of the holders and liabilities of unit trusts), Treasury bills (assets of the holders and a liability of central government) and bank notes (assets of the holders and a liability of central government). The balance of all transactions in the financial account is known as **total financial transactions**. Conceptually, for each sector, the **total financial transactions** must equal the **financial surplus or deficit**.

The balancing item

128. Although in theory the **financial surplus or deficit** and the **total financial transactions** for each sector should be equal, in practice they are not, because of the (sometimes substantial) errors and omissions in the accounts. The difference between the two balances are known as the **balancing item**. The targets for balancing items and the actual figures are detailed in paragraph 134.

Transactions and balances in the sector accounts

129. A broad classification of the transactions and balances in the sector accounts is as follows:

> **GDP at market prices**
> current transfers (dividends and interest, taxes, benefits, grants, etc)
> **consumption expenditure**
> *saving*
> capital transfers
> **capital formation**
> *financial surplus or deficit*
> financial transactions
> *balancing item*

130. The transactions in **bold** type all feature in the **production** account. They constitute income and *domestic* expenditure components of

GDP. They do not have any corresponding entries in the overseas account. The transactions in ordinary type may involve the overseas sector. When the latter is included, then over all sectors total receipts equal total payments, or on a net basis the transactions add to zero. The items in *italic* type are balances in the accounts. These broad groups of transactions are further subdivided into more detailed categories.

Summary analysis

131. The current, capital and financial account can be shown together in one table with three rows, one for each account, as in figure 2.1 below. In this presentation the following conventions are adopted:

- for the domestic sectors, income is shown as positive and expenditure negative;
- the balance of payments is represented from the viewpoint of the overseas sector: so the signs are reversed, and exports means exports to UK, i.e. UK imports;
- in the production account, as is usual, demand is shown as positive and costs of production negative.

The result of these conventions is that each line contains two equal and opposite transactions.

132. This presentation highlights the relationship between the balancing items in the domestic sector accounts and the balancing items in the balance of payments account and the production account. The latter is better known as the **residual error**. The balancing items across all accounts sum to zero.

FIGURE 2.1 SUMMARY ACCOUNTS OF THE NATION 1995

Summary accounts of the nation, 1995			£bn.
	Domestic sectors	Overseas sector	Production (GDP)
GDP at market prices	700.9		-700.9
Current transfers	2.6	-2.6	
Consumption expenditure	-596.7		596.7
Exports less imports		5.5	-5.5
Balance - saving	106.9	2.9	-109.8
Capital transfers	0		
Capital expenditure	-109.2		109.2
Financial surplus	-2.3	2.9	-0.6
Financial transactions	-0.4	0.4	
Balancing item	-1.8	2.4	-0.6

United Kingdom National Accounts 1996 © Crown copyright 1996

B

Table B : Summary analysis by sector, 1995

£ million

	Personal sector	Industrial and commercial companies	Banks and building societies	Other financial institutions	Public corporations	Central government	Local authorities	Overseas sector	TOTAL
CURRENT TRANSACTIONS									
Factor incomes: D									A
Income from employment	377 895	–	–	–	–	–	–	–	377 895
Income from self-employment	67 685	–	–	–	–	–	–	–	67 685
Gross trading profits, etc	–	104 152	–13 125		4 634	248	365	–	96 274
Rent	47 898	8 745	985		506	194	4 430	–	62 758
Imputed charge for capital consumption	600	–	–		–	2 150	1 979	–	4 729
less stock appreciation	–420	–4 451	–		–31	–	–	–	–4 902
Inter-sector transfers:									
Dividends and interest:								C	
receipts	75 161	42 070	164 360		542	10 087	681	83 567 }	–
payments	–42 701	–73 857	–133 007		–2 370	–27 212	–4 182	–93 139 }	–
Taxes on income	–67 292	–17 932	–5 238		–210	90 672	–	–	–
Social security contributions	–44 251	–	–		–	44 251	–	–	–
Social security benefits	77 186	–	–		–	–78 110	–	924	–
Council tax	–8 989	–	–		–	–	8 989	–	–
Other current grants by government:									
receipts	19 304	–	–		–	3 697	57 071	9 953 }	–
payments	–	–	–		–	–72 854	–13 474	–3 697 }	–
Other current transfers: receipts	2 846	–	–		–	719	–	2 236 }	–
payments	–2 909	–358	–96		–	–	–	–2 438 }	–
Royalties and licence fees etc	–	–1 025	–		–	1 025	–	–	–
Factor cost adjustment:									B
Taxes on expenditure	–	–	–		–	103 444	153	–	103 597
Subsidies	–	–	–		–	–6 256	–710	–	–6 966
Expenditure: E									
Consumption	–447 247	–	–		–	–96 663	–52 811	–	–596 721
Exports of goods and services	–	–	–		–	–	–	–197 600	–197 600
Imports of goods and services	–	–	–		–	–	–	203 086	203 086
Balance = **Saving**[2]	54 766	57 344	13 879		3 071	–24 608	2 491	2 892	109 835
CAPITAL TRANSACTIONS									
Gross domestic fixed capital formation	–28 996	–51 559	–7 323		–5 054	–5 642	–6 811	–	–105 385
Value of physical increase in stocks and work in progress[3]	–368	–3 819	–		182	154	–	–	–3 851
Taxes on capital	–2 299	–351	–36		–	2 686	–	–	–
Other capital transfers:									
receipts	4 109	501	–		3 256	–	3 188	– }	11 054
payments	–	–368	–		–468	–9 068	–1 150	– }	–11 054
Balance = **Financial surplus or deficit**	27 212	1 748	6 520		987	–36 478	–2 282	2 892	599
FINANCIAL TRANSACTIONS[4] G				F					
Notes and coin	1 165	96	195	2	72	–1 578	–	48	–
Sterling treasury bills and government securities	–95	64	9 675	22 313	107	–32 431	–8	375	–
National savings and tax instruments	3 258	–344	–24	–	–38	–2 852	–	–	–
Issue Department's transactions in commercial bills	–	1 107	–	667	–	–2 092	–	318	–
Other government domestic transactions	–183	–2	–734	26	953	–200	140	–	–
Government overseas transactions	–	–	–260	–305	–	–153	–	718	–
Local authority debt	–12	–17	–342	297	–104	2 000	–1 770	–52	–
Public corporations' debt	–47	–	–9	45	–512	710	–36	–151	–
Deposits with banks: Sterling	12 971	6 508	–50 503	21 301	624	169	1 272	7 658	–
Foreign currency	20	–971	–42 635	13 087	12	190	28	30 269	–
Deposits with building societies: Sterling	14 204	–1 034	–14 366	1 231	–	–	–	–35	–
Foreign currency	29	58	–2 842	130	–	–	–	2 625	–
Bank lending (excluding public sector)	–6 818	–15 078	62 318	–13 226	–	–	–	–27 196	–
Other lending	–18 153	–1 990	24 009	–4 383	–3	868	–147	–201	–
Trade and retail credit	–882	–2 104	–	1 719	718	–	–	549	–
UK and overseas securities and unit trust units	–10 205	–3 011	29 526	3 708	–261	–2 484	17	–17 290	–
Other domestic instruments	34 851	–5 970	–635	–38 442	2	962	–2	9 234	–
Other overseas instruments	32	19 513	218	–12 858	146	–483	–	–6 568	–
Accruals adjustments	3 635	–653	–900	–1 346	158	338	–1 377	145	–
Total financial transactions	33 770	–3 828	12 691	–6 034	1 874	–37 036	–1 883	446	–
BALANCING ITEM	–6 558	5 576	–137		–887	558	–399	2 446	599

Table B

1 Excluding tax credits.
2 After providing for stock appreciation but before providing for additions to dividend and tax reserves.
3 A positive figure indicates a decrease in stocks.
4 For detailed analysis by sector and type of asset see table 11.1.

Where such data can be compiled, quarterly data for series in this table are available on the ONS's Databank. This data can also be provided on paper by request. Some of these quarterly data are published regularly in the UK Economic Accounts in table A20.

C

Table C: Balancing items

£ million

		1985	1986	1987	1988	1989	1990	1991	1992	1993	1994	1995
Personal sector	AAQB	−2 682	−4 321	−5 633	−4 831	−3 146	−8 777	−8 229	−4 187	905	−4 919	−6 558
Industrial and commercial companies	AAOB	7 012	1 011	7 917	8 909	2 735	8 320	3 936	6 262	4 710	4 120	5 576
Financial companies and institutions	AATA	−5 322	−2 158	6	−6 370	−2 171	−1 564	3 882	−6 453	−3 428	−4 798	−137
Public corporations	AAFY	−704	333	−98	−28	−1 147	−219	−920	−20	829	212	−887
Central government	AADB	−237	−105	35	580	133	−389	321	−726	−120	225	558
Local authorities	AAET	451	556	370	182	−626	426	501	−44	−572	91	−399
Overseas sector	AASA	1 482	4 684	−2 597	1 558	4 222	2 203	509	5 168	−2 324	5 069	2 446
Total[1]	−DJAS	−	−	−	−	−	−	−	−	−	−	599

1 *Equals*, but opposite in sign to, the residual error observed between GDP measured by the factor income approach and by the expenditure approach.

133. Figure 2.1, the summary accounts of the nation can be expanded to show the sector accounts in fuller detail as shown in Table B. In this presentation the balance of payments account is considered as the "overseas sector" and the production account as the "total" column, in both cases with arithmetic signs reversed. The *current inter-sector transfers, capital transfers* and *financial transactions* all balance out to zero. The boxes highlight a number of important economic aggregates.

Key to aggregates shown in table B:

A Income measure of GDP at factor cost (see paragraphs 49 to 59)

B Expenditure (demand) measure of GDP (see paragraphs 60 to 79)

C Net investment income from abroad

D Personal disposable income

E Consumers' expenditure

F Public sector borrowing requirement (see paragraph 143)

G Money supply (M4) (see paragraph 143)

Balancing Items

134. The sectoral balancing items are shown in Table C above. They provide a measure of the reliability of the accounts. The Office for National Statistics has targets for the size of annual balancing items and these were last published in the Central Statistical Office's 1994-95 Annual report and accounts. The main short term targets, ignoring sign, are:

● The annual overseas sector balancing item for 1995 should be less than 1 per cent of GDP at factor cost.

● The combined annual company sector balancing item for 1995 should be less than 1.25 per cent of GDP at factor cost.

● The annual public sector balancing item for 1995 should be less than 0.2 per cent of GDP at factor cost.

135. The balancing items presented in this book satisfy all the targets (both short term and long term) which are listed in the Central Statistical Office's 1994-95 annual report and accounts.

Key developments

136. There have been a number of key developments which have been introduced in this year's Blue Book. These include revised methodology for UK company securities and money market instruments in the financial account, revised treatment of social security contributions and improvements in the recording of interest and dividend payments.

UK company securities and money market instruments

137. Following a major methodological review, the figures for UK company securities have been sub- divided into three categories: quoted ordinary shares; unquoted ordinary shares; and bonds & preference shares. The new figures for the financial transaction and balance sheet figures have been compiled back to 1990 and are published for the first time in tables 11.16 and 12.13. There are also revisions in earlier years to the UK company security totals for some sectors. The revised figures for receipts and payments of interest date back to 1984 and are shown in Chapter 3.

138. The methodology has been improved in several ways. New data sources have been introduced and existing data sources enhanced following liaison with key data suppliers, in particular, the Stock Exchange and the Bank of England. Different classes of assets and liabilities have been matched more closely, as have movements in balance sheet levels and financial transactions. Some errors and omissions have been eliminated. There has been a major re-assessment of the value of shares in unquoted industrial & commercial companies and the holders of these shares. The method of allocating payments and receipts of interest has also been overhauled.

139. The figures for money market instruments were also the subject of a major review, linked in part to the review of UK company securities. One of the results is that some short term bonds and notes issued by banks and building societies have been switched from UK company securities to money market instruments in order to ensure a more consistent presentation of the data. There have also been revisions to interest, financial transactions and balance sheet levels dating back to 1986.

Revised treatment of social security contributions

140. Previously social security rent rebates (which is part of the National Insurance Fund component) was deducted on a cash basis from gross social security contributions. In this year's Blue Book the rebate element has been deducted on an accruals basis bringing it into line with the measurement of gross contributions. In the financial account improvements have also been made to the counter parting of the net accruals adjustment (total net accrued less total net cash contributions) across the various sectors.

Dividend and Interest payments

141. Dividend and interest payments and receipts (which appear in Table B and Chapters 3 to 9) have been converted onto a gross of intra-sector payments basis where possible. Previously, payments within a sector were netted out for some instruments (such as UK company dividend payments). Data have been revised back to 1984.

Future Developments

142. As mentioned in the introduction to section 1, over the next two years the Office for National Statistics will be preparing to move to the latest internationally agreed system of national accounts; the United Nations System of National Accounts 1993 (SNA93) and European System of Accounts 1995 (ESA95) which is consistent with SNA93. Further details can be found in paragraph 101.

FURTHER INFORMATION

143. In addition to the articles and publications mentioned in Section 1, further information relating to the sector accounts and in particular the financial accounts can be found in the following articles and publications:

Central Statistical Office *'Financial Statistics: Explanatory Handbook 1996 edition'*, 1995, HMSO

Office for National Statistics *'Financial Statistics'*, monthly publication, HMSO

Philip Turnbull (Central Statistical Office) *'The UK Sector Accounts'* *Economic Trends*, September 1993, HMSO

Bank of England *'Bank of England Statistical Abstract'*, 1995, Bank of England

Articles related to the Public Sector Borrowing Requirement (PSBR):

HM Treasury working paper No 61/Government Economic Service Working paper No 119 *'The Public Sector Borrowing Requirement Definition and Measurement'*, December 1993, HM Treasury

Allen Ritchie and David Lawton (HM Treasury) *'The Definition of the PSBR'* *Economic Trends*, September 1993, HMSO

HM Treasury working paper No 57 *'Central Government Funds and Accounts and the Central Government Borrowing Requirement'*, June 1990, HM Treasury

Articles related to monetary aggregates (M0, M4)

Bank of England *'The Determination of M0 and M4'* Bank of England Quarterly Bulletin pages 46 to 50, February 1994

Bank of England *'Divisia measures of money'* Bank of England Quarterly Bulletin, May 1993

CHAPTER 3: Summary sector accounts

3.1 Personal sector: current income and expenditure

£ million

		1974	1975	1976	1977	1978	1979	1980	1981	1982	1983	1984
INCOME BEFORE TAX												
Income from employment	DJAO	52 379	68 494	78 005	86 572	98 843	115 866	137 783	149 737	158 838	169 847	181 406
Income from self-employment[1]	CFAN	8 042	9 135	11 126	12 035	13 612	15 933	18 141	19 980	22 140	24 750	27 909
Rent, dividends and net interest[2]	CFAM	7 194	8 627	9 952	10 623	12 758	16 688	19 163	21 278	23 814	25 817	29 325
Social security benefits and other current grants from general government	AIIE	7 435	9 743	12 093	14 321	17 151	20 140	24 480	30 104	35 306	38 439	41 579
Other current transfers	CFBR	399	435	579	657	819	901	987	1 179	1 317	1 614	1 757
Imputed charge for capital consumption of private non-profit-making bodies	CFBM	151	188	217	242	266	308	368	403	409	417	432
Total personal income[1]	AIIA	75 600	96 622	111 972	124 450	143 449	169 836	200 922	222 681	241 824	260 884	282 408
DEDUCTIONS FROM INCOME												
UK taxes on income[2]	AIIG	10 418	15 042	17 422	18 149	19 460	21 586	25 683	28 949	31 366	33 180	34 736
Social security contributions	AIIH	5 000	6 848	8 423	9 503	10 101	11 526	13 939	15 916	18 095	20 780	22 322
Community charge/council tax	ADBH	–	–	–	–	–	–	–	–	–	–	–
Other current transfers	CFGD	534	604	665	795	1 052	1 178	1 308	1 234	1 387	1 413	1 498
Personal disposable income[3]	AIIJ	59 648	74 128	85 462	96 003	112 836	135 546	159 992	176 582	190 976	205 511	223 852
EXPENDITURE												
Consumers' expenditure	AIIK	53 256	65 590	76 225	87 165	100 524	119 212	138 564	154 274	169 372	185 611	198 820
Balance : saving[3]	AAAU	6 392	8 538	9 237	8 838	12 312	16 334	21 428	22 308	21 604	19 900	25 032
Total	AIIJ	59 648	74 128	85 462	96 003	112 836	135 546	159 992	176 582	190 976	205 511	223 852

1 Before providing for depreciation and stock appreciation.
2 Including tax credits
3 Before providing for depreciation, stock appreciation and additions to tax reserves.

3.2 Corporate sector[1]: current income and expenditure

£ million

		1974	1975	1976	1977	1978	1979	1980	1981	1982	1983	1984
INCOME												
Gross trading profits and trading surplus:												
After deducting stock appreciation[2]	GIBY	8 367	9 868	13 140	20 534	24 051	26 794	28 498	29 967	36 764	45 878	48 175
Stock appreciation	GIBZ	5 404	4 910	5 985	4 512	3 781	8 061	5 672	5 348	3 914	3 654	4 188
Total[3]	GICA	13 771	14 778	19 125	25 046	27 832	34 855	34 170	35 315	40 678	49 532	52 363
Rent	DTDN	670	754	884	1 100	1 278	1 489	1 769	2 096	2 289	2 521	2 668
Dividend and Interest Receipts:[4]	GJXL	8 101	7 910	10 408	11 390	12 401	18 153	22 547	25 744	27 589	29 425	103 877
of which: income from abroad (net of taxes paid abroad):	GICD	3 020	2 594	3 798	3 712	4 522	7 096	7 230	8 963	9 234	11 163	13 992
Total income	GICE	22 542	23 442	30 417	37 536	41 511	54 497	58 486	63 155	70 556	81 478	158 908
ALLOCATION OF INCOME												
Dividends and interest payments[4,5]												
Total	GICF	7 419	8 112	9 271	9 625	10 417	15 087	19 466	20 517	22 899	22 791	101 845
of which: profits due abroad (net of United Kingdom Tax)	CIBU	649	602	964	1 997	2 229	3 992	4 769	4 695	4 659	5 258	6 271
Current transfers	DTDO	60	65	118	277	331	582	1 208	1 424	1 669	1 973	2 566
of which: Royalties and licence fees on oil and gas production	GICJ	18	23	76	234	286	531	1 156	1 362	1 600	1 887	2 459
UK taxes on income	GICI	2 883	2 399	2 314	3 273	4 099	5 064	6 665	8 564	10 489	12 028	14 124
Balance: undistributed income after taxation[6]	GICK	11 531	12 264	17 750	22 364	24 435	29 772	26 378	27 955	30 840	39 428	40 373

1 A combination of three sectors, namely public corporations, industrial & commercial companies, financial companies & institutions. Flows between the constituent sectors are not netted out.
2 Before providing for depreciation and stock appreciation.
3 After deducting depreciation allowances but before providing for stock appreciation.
4 Since 1984 the dividends and interest matrix data includes payments and receipts on United Kingdom company securities on a gross basis i.e. including intra-sector transactions.
5 After 6 April 1973 figures are net of advance corporation tax.
6 Before providing for depreciation, stock appreciation and additions to dividend and tax reserves.

3.1 Personal sector: current income and expenditure
continued

£ million

		1985	1986	1987	1988	1989	1990	1991	1992	1993	1994	1995
INCOME BEFORE TAX												
Income from employment	DJAO	196 858	212 380	230 208	256 537	284 372	313 753	330 767	342 015	351 819	364 946	377 895
Income from self-employment[1]	CFAN	30 404	35 104	39 361	45 829	52 691	58 688	56 745	57 149	60 461	64 021	67 685
Rent, dividends and net interest[2]	CFAM	32 116	33 762	36 333	42 883	47 701	51 123	57 175	65 864	68 357	72 094	87 721
Social security benefits and other current grants from general government	AIIE	45 351	49 454	50 798	52 175	54 033	58 939	69 287	80 052	88 384	92 574	96 490
Other current transfers	CFBR	1 894	1 877	1 826	1 915	2 034	2 087	2 158	2 245	2 540	2 707	2 846
Imputed charge for capital consumption of private non-profit-making bodies	CFBM	458	485	503	524	557	585	600	604	564	587	600
Total personal income[1]	AIIA	307 081	333 062	359 029	399 863	441 388	485 175	516 732	547 929	572 125	596 929	633 237
DEDUCTIONS FROM INCOME												
UK taxes on income[2]	AIIG	37 774	40 805	43 459	48 274	53 589	61 543	63 419	65 178	63 637	68 168	74 655
Social security contributions	AIIH	24 210	26 165	27 663	30 682	33 333	34 457	36 216	36 975	39 499	41 943	44 251
Community charge/council tax	ADBH	–	–	–	–	586	8 629	8 128	7 907	8 038	8 450	8 989
Other current transfers	CFGD	1 684	1 909	2 128	2 347	2 441	2 569	2 719	2 607	2 807	2 872	2 909
Personal disposable income[3]	AIIJ	243 413	264 183	285 779	318 560	351 439	377 977	406 250	435 262	458 144	475 496	502 433
EXPENDITURE												
Consumers' expenditure	AIIK	217 485	241 554	265 290	299 449	327 363	347 527	365 469	383 490	406 399	427 276	447 247
Balance : saving[3]	AAAU	25 928	22 629	20 489	19 111	24 076	30 450	40 781	51 772	51 745	48 220	55 186
Total	AIIJ	243 413	264 183	285 779	318 560	351 439	377 977	406 250	435 262	458 144	475 496	502 433

See footnotes on previous page.

3.2 Corporate sector[1]: current income and expenditure
continued

£ million

		1985	1986	1987	1988	1989	1990	1991	1992	1993	1994	1995
INCOME												
Gross trading profits and trading surplus:												
After deducting stock appreciation[2]	GIBY	56 145	53 889	62 210	66 306	67 465	64 068	59 648	62 478	75 937	87 040	91 179
Stock appreciation	GIBZ	2 263	1 663	4 236	5 625	6 258	5 436	1 616	1 739	2 337	3 658	4 482
Total[3]	GICA	58 408	55 552	66 446	71 931	73 723	69 504	61 264	64 217	78 274	90 698	95 661
Rent	DTDN	3 198	3 540	4 102	4 837	5 682	6 612	7 689	9 177	10 032	10 011	10 236
Dividend and Interest Receipts:[4]	GJXL	113 432	111 028	116 470	137 855	197 841	227 342	210 104	184 326	162 976	173 715	206 972
of which: income from abroad (net of taxes paid abroad):	GICD	14 863	15 071	17 527	21 420	26 598	28 215	24 773	27 743	32 474	39 438	44 122
Total income	GICE	175 038	170 120	187 018	214 623	277 246	303 458	279 057	257 720	251 282	274 424	312 869
ALLOCATION OF INCOME												
Dividends and interest payments[4,5]												
Total	GICF	113 631	108 444	114 310	137 765	199 827	230 521	216 341	189 612	168 848	170 344	209 234
of which: profits due abroad (net of United Kingdom Tax)	CIBU	7 563	5 285	7 014	8 611	9 157	6 917	4 432	5 106	10 275	9 291	11 745
Current transfers	DTDO	2 489	1 099	1 335	1 055	880	976	863	926	1 385	1 412	1 479
of which: Royalties and licence fees on oil and gas production	GICJ	2 366	941	1 151	823	556	654	579	601	641	601	627
UK taxes on income	GICI	16 511	14 277	15 705	17 901	21 794	21 220	17 772	15 389	15 113	18 127	23 380
Balance: undistributed income after taxation[6]	GICK	42 407	46 300	55 668	57 902	54 745	50 741	44 081	51 793	65 936	84 541	78 776

See footnotes on previous page.

Summary sector accounts

3.3 General government: current income and expenditure

£ million

		1974	1975	1976	1977	1978	1979	1980	1981	1982	1983	1984
RECEIPTS												
Taxes on income	ACGB	12 716	16 758	18 969	20 490	22 624	25 239	31 002	36 134	40 282	43 344	46 658
Taxes on expenditure	AAXC	11 374	14 036	16 284	19 834	22 756	29 670	36 474	42 465	46 467	49 500	52 736
Social security contributions	AIIH	5 000	6 848	8 423	9 503	10 101	11 526	13 939	15 916	18 095	20 780	22 322
Community charge/council tax	ADBH	–	–	–	–	–	–	–	–	–	–	
Gross trading surplus[1]	DJAQ	133	127	152	183	216	180	180	236	216	50	–117
Rent, dividends and interest, etc.	GTAA	3 050	3 625	4 433	4 943	5 368	6 525	8 206	9 171	10 149	9 933	10 466
Miscellaneous current transfers	ACGX	57	73	118	136	151	134	169	177	187	222	217
Imputed charge for consumption of non-trading capital	AAXG	589	777	925	1 045	1 182	1 406	1 748	1 948	2 017	2 081	2 187
Total	AAXA	32 919	42 244	49 304	56 134	62 398	74 680	91 718	106 047	117 413	125 910	134 469
EXPENDITURE												
Final consumption	AAXI	17 151	23 652	27 698	30 179	34 127	39 607	49 984	56 512	61 641	67 204	71 201
Subsidies	AAXJ	3 107	3 771	3 572	3 386	3 775	4 643	5 719	6 369	5 811	6 269	7 537
Social security benefits	AUAA	6 661	8 634	10 846	12 977	15 417	18 122	21 813	27 002	31 677	32 336	34 350
Other current grants to personal sector	GTAB	774	1 109	1 247	1 344	1 734	2 018	2 667	3 102	3 629	6 103	7 229
Current grants paid abroad (net)	-HDKH	302	337	776	1 083	1 664	2 016	1 780	1 607	1 789	1 930	2 099
Debt interest	AAXL	3 490	4 127	5 293	6 288	7 097	8 679	10 888	12 719	13 952	14 208	15 670
Total current expenditure	AAXH	31 485	41 630	49 432	55 257	63 814	75 085	92 851	107 311	118 499	128 050	138 086
Balance: current surplus[1]	AAXM	1 434	614	–128	877	–1 416	–405	–1 133	–1 264	–1 086	–2 140	–3 617
Total	AAXA	32 919	42 244	49 304	56 134	62 398	74 680	91 718	106 047	117 413	125 910	134 469

1 Before providing for depreciation.

3.4 International transactions

£ million

		1974	1975	1976	1977	1978	1979	1980	1981	1982	1983	1984
UNITED KINGDOM CREDITS												
Exports of goods	CGJP	16 282	19 185	25 080	31 683	34 981	40 471	47 149	50 668	55 331	60 700	70 265
Exports of services	CGJZ	6 597	7 678	10 010	11 615	12 495	14 427	15 467	16 764	17 363	19 180	21 367
Property income from abroad net of foreign taxes	CGJS	6 211	6 564	8 389	8 816	11 181	17 506	23 681	37 529	44 397	42 449	51 621
Exports and property income from abroad	HCCS	29 090	33 427	43 479	52 114	58 657	72 404	86 297	104 961	117 091	122 329	143 253
Current transfers:												
To private sector	CGJV	357	393	537	614	774	850	935	1 117	1 248	1 528	1 652
To central government	HDKD	132	366	253	298	439	550	958	1 675	2 154	2 235	2 392
Total current credits	CGPZ	29 579	34 186	44 269	53 026	59 870	73 804	88 190	107 753	120 493	126 092	147 296
UNITED KINGDOM DEBITS												
Imports of goods	CGGL	21 513	22 440	29 041	34 005	36 573	43 814	45 792	47 416	53 421	62 237	75 601
Imports of services	CGGZ	5 636	6 363	7 595	8 377	8 795	10 532	11 814	12 972	14 341	15 351	17 162
Property income paid abroad	HCCT	4 913	5 913	7 089	8 875	10 920	17 348	25 258	39 189	46 606	44 533	53 225
less UK taxes	-DKGN	–210	–240	–260	–324	–545	–1 047	–1 394	–2 911	–3 667	–4 914	–5 948
Property income paid abroad net of UK taxes	CGGK	4 703	5 673	6 829	8 551	10 375	16 301	23 864	36 278	42 939	39 619	47 277
Imports and property income paid abroad	HCCU	31 852	34 476	43 465	50 933	55 743	70 647	81 470	96 666	110 701	117 207	140 040
Current transfers:												
From private sector	CGGV	477	531	547	659	901	1 044	1 139	1 057	1 200	1 191	1 283
From central government	CGGJ	434	703	1 029	1 381	2 103	2 566	2 738	3 282	3 943	4 165	4 491
Total current debits	CGQB	32 763	35 710	45 041	52 973	58 747	74 257	85 347	101 005	115 844	122 563	145 814
Investment and financing:												
Net investment abroad[1]	-AABI	–3 259	–1 524	–772	53	1 123	–453	2 843	6 748	4 649	3 529	1 483
Capital transfers paid abroad	AAAZ	–75	–	–	–	–	–	–	–	–	–	–
Total[2]	AIMG	–3 184	–1 524	–772	53	1 123	–453	2 843	6 748	4 649	3 529	1 482
Total debits	CGPZ	29 579	34 186	44 269	53 026	59 870	73 804	88 190	107 753	120 493	126 092	147 296

1 Equal, with opposite sign, to the overseas sector financial surplus/deficit.
2 Equal to the current balance in the Balance of payments accounts.

Where such data can be compiled, quarterly data for series in this table are available on the ONS's Databank. This data can also be provided on paper by request. Some of these quarterly data are published regularly in the UK Economic Accounts in table A18.

3.3 General government: current income and expenditure
continued

£ million

		1985	1986	1987	1988	1989	1990	1991	1992	1993	1994	1995
RECEIPTS												
Taxes on income	ACGB	51 598	51 973	55 658	61 723	70 000	76 875	75 178	73 716	73 232	80 670	90 672
Taxes on expenditure	AAXC	56 667	62 872	68 971	76 039	79 980	78 298	85 416	87 521	90 336	96 138	103 597
Social security contributions	AIIH	24 210	26 165	27 663	30 682	33 333	34 457	36 216	36 975	39 499	41 943	44 251
Community charge/council tax	ADBH	–	–	–	–	586	8 629	8 128	7 907	8 038	8 450	8 989
Gross trading surplus[1]	DJAQ	265	155	−75	−32	199	12	−36	206	193	490	613
Rent, dividends and interest, etc.	GTAA	11 695	9 792	10 080	10 132	10 802	10 621	10 210	9 975	9 999	10 598	10 823
Miscellaneous current transfers	ACGX	229	266	363	394	431	504	545	419	623	704	719
Imputed charge for consumption of non-trading capital	AAXG	2 372	2 583	2 804	3 110	3 448	3 806	3 763	3 603	3 679	3 837	4 129
Total	AAXA	147 036	153 806	165 464	182 048	198 779	213 202	219 420	220 322	225 599	242 830	263 793
EXPENDITURE												
Final consumption	AAXI	75 267	80 911	87 045	93 641	101 796	112 934	124 105	131 875	138 081	144 114	149 474
Subsidies	AAXJ	7 225	6 301	6 265	6 037	5 782	6 066	5 995	6 737	7 203	7 060	6 966
Social security benefits	AUAA	37 609	40 860	41 961	43 056	44 965	48 898	57 381	65 902	71 631	74 300	77 186
Other current grants to personal sector	GTAB	7 742	8 594	8 837	9 119	9 068	10 041	11 906	14 150	16 753	18 274	19 304
Current grants paid abroad (net)	−HDKH	3 427	2 233	3 277	3 248	4 278	4 596	1 083	4 834	4 969	5 135	7 180
Debt interest	AAXL	17 586	17 151	17 936	18 197	18 928	18 696	16 936	17 039	18 427	22 144	25 800
Total current expenditure	AAXH	148 856	156 050	165 321	173 298	184 817	201 231	217 406	240 537	257 064	271 027	285 910
Balance: current surplus[1]	AAXM	−1 820	−2 244	143	8 750	13 962	11 971	2 014	−20 215	−31 465	−28 197	−22 117
Total	AAXA	147 036	153 806	165 464	182 048	198 779	213 202	219 420	220 322	225 599	242 830	263 793

See footnotes on previous page.

3.4 International transactions
continued

		1985	1986	1987	1988	1989	1990	1991	1992	1993	1994	1995
UNITED KINGDOM CREDITS												
Exports of goods	CGJP	77 991	72 627	79 153	80 346	92 154	101 718	103 413	107 343	121 398	134 666	152 346
Exports of services	CGJZ	24 050	25 258	27 244	26 927	29 332	31 447	30 876	34 771	38 599	41 399	45 254
Property income from abroad net of foreign taxes	CGJS	52 008	47 341	48 002	56 550	73 978	79 106	76 967	68 551	74 143	77 919	93 139
Exports and property income from abroad	HCCS	154 051	145 226	154 399	163 823	195 464	212 271	211 256	210 665	234 140	253 984	290 739
Current transfers:												
To private sector	CGJV	1 775	1 732	1 666	1 715	1 750	1 800	1 900	1 957	2 211	2 322	2 438
To central government	HDKD	1 760	2 138	2 282	2 115	2 143	2 232	4 899	2 888	3 325	3 296	3 697
Total current credits	CGPZ	157 584	149 096	158 347	167 653	199 357	216 303	218 055	215 510	239 676	259 602	296 874
UNITED KINGDOM DEBITS												
Imports of goods	CGGL	81 336	82 186	90 735	101 826	116 837	120 527	113 697	120 447	134 858	145 497	163 974
Imports of services	CGGZ	17 652	19 035	21 002	22 970	25 971	27 758	27 312	29 821	33 083	36 652	39 112
Property income paid abroad	HCCT	56 773	47 139	48 115	56 127	75 931	83 924	80 959	68 968	75 563	73 150	88 835
less UK taxes	−DKGN	−7 060	−4 426	−4 041	−4 143	−5 453	−6 087	−4 142	−3 541	−3 617	−3 922	−5 268
Property income paid abroad net of UK taxes	CGGK	49 712	42 712	44 075	51 984	70 476	77 837	76 817	65 427	71 946	69 228	83 567
Imports and property income paid abroad	HCCU	148 701	143 934	155 811	176 780	213 286	226 122	217 826	215 695	239 887	251 377	286 653
Current transfers:												
From private sector	CGGV	1 459	1 656	1 789	1 985	2 050	2 100	2 200	2 225	2 249	2 214	2 236
From central government	CGGJ	5 187	4 371	5 559	5 363	6 421	6 828	5 982	7 722	8 294	8 431	10 877
Total current debits	CGQB	155 346	149 960	163 160	184 128	221 755	235 050	226 008	225 642	250 430	262 022	299 766
Investment and financing:												
Net investment abroad[1]	−AABI	2 238	−864	−4 813	−16 475	−22 398	−18 746	−7 954	−10 133	−10 756	−2 419	−2 892
Capital transfers paid abroad	AAAZ	–	–	–	–	–	–	–	–	–	–	–
Total[2]	AIMG	2 238	−864	−4 813	−16 475	−22 398	−18 746	−7 954	−10 133	−10 756	−2 419	−2 892
Total debits	CGPZ	157 584	149 096	158 347	167 653	199 357	216 303	218 055	215 510	239 676	259 602	296 874

See footnotes on previous page.

Summary sector accounts

3.5 Summary capital account[1]

£ million

		1974	1975	1976	1977	1978	1979	1980	1981	1982	1983	1984
RECEIPTS												
Saving[2]												
Personal sector	AAAU	6 392	8 538	9 237	8 838	12 312	16 334	21 428	22 308	21 604	19 900	25 032
Industrial & commercial companies	AAAQ	9 197	9 603	13 195	15 981	18 532	22 771	18 706	20 001	21 757	26 725	32 115
Financial companies and institutions	AAAM	956	1 014	1 759	3 099	2 115	3 213	3 422	2 393	2 476	5 188	2 128
Public corporations	AAAI	1 378	1 647	2 796	3 284	3 788	3 788	4 250	5 561	6 607	7 515	6 130
Central government	AAAA	846	−686	−2 279	−915	−3 008	−1 854	−2 275	−3 865	−4 177	−4 457	−5 686
Local authorities	AAAE	588	1 300	2 151	1 792	1 592	1 449	1 142	2 601	3 091	2 317	2 069
Total saving	GIGV	19 357	21 416	26 859	32 079	35 331	45 701	46 673	48 999	51 358	57 188	61 788
Capital transfers (net receipts):												
Personal sector	AAAV	−321	−302	−63	75	301	196	253	88	367	1 019	1 245
Industrial & commercial companies	AAAR	284	366	329	243	398	353	429	557	491	322	217
Financial companies and institutions	AAAN	−36	54	−28	−26	14	−107	−142	−315	−148	−61	−64
Public corporations[3]	AAAJ	213	289	377	418	500	412	472	532	473	602	568
Central government[3]	AAAB	−230	−440	−609	−685	−1 246	−946	−1 092	−904	−1 009	−1 107	−1 352
Local authorities	AAAF	15	33	−6	−25	33	92	80	42	−174	−775	−614
Total transfers[4]	AAAZ	−75	–	–	–	–	–	–	–	–	–	–
Residual error[5]	DJAS	2 110	2 262	4 455	1 929	2 884	1 770	1 550	2 259	1 203	626	685
Total	GIHN	21 392	23 678	31 314	34 008	38 215	47 471	48 223	51 258	52 561	57 813	62 473
EXPENDITURE												
Gross domestic fixed capital formation:												
Personal sector[6]	AAAW	2 805	3 816	4 390	5 505	6 279	8 261	9 399	9 840	12 046	13 927	14 998
Industrial & commercial companies	AAAS	5 797	6 780	8 019	9 753	12 897	15 287	16 447	16 434	17 329	17 704	22 304
Financial companies and institutions	AAAO	1 652	1 524	1 980	2 182	2 117	2 319	3 235	3 434	3 698	3 050	3 719
Public corporations	AAAK	2 858	3 920	4 693	4 779	5 069	5 833	6 828	6 924	7 314	8 065	7 441
Central government	AAAC	970	1 261	1 408	1 294	1 292	1 560	1 761	1 868	2 230	2 497	2 728
Local authorities	AAAG	3 415	3 734	4 014	3 523	3 406	3 665	3 891	2 804	2 207	3 372	3 991
Total	DFDC	17 497	21 035	24 504	27 036	31 060	36 925	41 561	41 304	44 824	48 615	55 181
Increase in book value of stocks and work in progress[7]:												
Personal sector	AAAX	706	366	795	938	760	1 164	479	415	420	698	513
Industrial & commercial companies	AAAT	6 157	2 960	5 985	5 647	4 969	9 277	2 794	2 531	1 845	4 316	5 370
Financial companies and institutions	AAAP	−13	9	34	−15	−10	−17	6	9	4	38	24
Public corporations	AAAL	289	841	766	299	282	610	497	344	664	371	−378
Central government	AAAD	15	−9	2	50	31	−35	43	−93	155	246	280
Total	DHHY	7 154	4 167	7 582	6 919	6 032	10 999	3 819	3 206	3 088	5 669	5 809
Net investment abroad[8]	−AABI	−3 259	−1 524	−772	53	1 123	−453	2 843	6 748	4 649	3 529	1 483
Total investment	GIHN	21 392	23 678	31 314	34 008	38 215	47 471	48 223	51 258	52 561	57 813	62 473
FINANCIAL SURPLUS OR DEFICIT												
Personal sector	AABH	2 560	4 054	3 989	2 470	5 574	7 105	11 803	12 141	9 505	6 294	10 766
Industrial & commercial companies	AABG	−2 473	229	−480	824	1 064	−1 440	−106	1 593	3 074	5 027	4 658
Financial companies and institutions	AABF	−719	−465	−283	906	22	804	39	−1 365	−1 374	2 039	−1 679
Public corporations	AABD	−1 556	−2 825	−2 286	−1 376	−1 063	−2 243	−2 603	−1 175	−898	−319	−365
Central government	AABA	−369	−2 378	−4 298	−2 944	−5 577	−4 325	−5 171	−6 544	−7 571	−8 307	−10 046
Local authorities	AABB	−2 812	−2 401	−1 869	−1 756	−1 781	−2 124	−2 669	−161	710	−1 830	−2 536
Total	GIHZ	−5 369	−3 786	−5 227	−1 876	−1 761	−2 223	1 293	4 489	3 446	2 904	798
Net investment abroad[8]	−AABI	−3 259	−1 524	−772	53	1 123	−453	2 843	6 748	4 649	3 529	1 483
less Residual error[5]	−DJAS	−2 110	−2 262	−4 455	−1 929	−2 884	−1 770	−1 550	−2 259	−1 203	−626	−685

1 Figures for companies and public corporations are affected by privatisation. For further details see methodological notes.
2 Before providing for depreciation, stock appreciation and additions to dividend and tax reserves.
3 Excluding financial transactions on writing-off debt. For details see footnote 5 to Table 6.4.
4 "Total capital transfers for the domestic sectors" *equals* capital transfers paid abroad.
5 Residual error is the difference between the totals of the expenditure and income components of gross domestic product.
6 Gross and net fixed capital formation by the personal sector excludes that by life assurance and pension funds: this is included with that of financial companies and institutions.
7 *Equal* to stock appreciation *plus* value of physical increase in stocks and work in progress.
8 Net investment abroad is *equal*, but opposite in sign, to the overseas sector's financial surplus or deficit.

Where such data can be compiled, quarterly data for series in this table are available on the ONS's Databank. This data can also be provided on paper by request. Some of these quarterly data are published regularly in the UK Economic Accounts in table A19.

3.5 Summary capital account[1]

continued

£ million

		1985	1986	1987	1988	1989	1990	1991	1992	1993	1994	1995
RECEIPTS												
Saving[2]												
Personal sector	AAAU	25 928	22 629	20 489	19 111	24 076	30 450	40 781	51 772	51 745	48 220	55 186
Industrial and commercial companies	AAAQ	35 550	35 204	43 963	47 387	43 736	40 463	39 332	41 615	54 938	66 990	61 795
Financial companies and institutions	AAAM	1 638	5 129	6 716	4 700	6 010	7 382	3 723	8 284	8 229	14 704	13 879
Public corporations	AAAI	5 219	5 967	4 989	5 815	4 999	2 896	1 026	1 894	2 769	2 847	3 102
Central government	AAAA	−3 623	−4 450	−2 303	7 186	12 376	7 354	−116	−23 333	−35 650	−31 649	−24 608
Local authorities	AAAE	1 803	2 206	2 446	1 564	1 586	4 617	2 130	3 118	4 185	3 452	2 491
Total saving	GIGV	66 515	66 685	76 300	85 763	92 783	93 162	86 876	83 350	86 216	104 564	111 845
Capital transfers (net receipts):												
Personal sector	AAAV	320	−150	−266	−1 224	−681	80	1 644	1 997	3 299	2 309	1 810
Industrial and commercial companies	AAAR	112	−289	−398	−19	−871	−774	−416	19	−1	82	−218
Financial companies and institutions	AAAN	−118	−196	−120	−140	−152	−36	−36	−36	−44	−36	−36
Public corporations[3]	AAAJ	634	456	714	805	1 230	6 438	3 189	2 856	2 812	2 789	2 788
Central government[3]	AAAB	−978	−344	−358	180	−1 039	−6 883	−5 938	−11 712	−8 147	−7 004	−6 382
Local authorities	AAAF	30	523	428	398	1 513	1 175	1 557	6 876	2 081	1 860	2 038
Total transfers[4]	AAAZ	−	−	−	−	−	−	−	−	−	−	−
Residual error[5]	DJAS	−	−	−	−	−	−	−	−	−	−	−599
Total	GIHN	66 515	66 685	76 300	85 763	92 783	93 162	86 876	83 350	86 216	104 564	111 246
EXPENDITURE												
Gross domestic fixed capital formation:												
Personal sector[6]	AAAW	16 026	18 690	22 826	30 290	29 986	28 333	25 398	23 765	25 947	27 558	28 996
Industrial and commercial companies	AAAS	28 558	29 511	36 017	43 627	52 535	54 837	49 863	47 615	47 589	46 646	51 559
Financial companies and institutions	AAAO	3 331	3 801	4 177	6 527	7 873	6 793	6 564	5 029	4 059	7 808	7 323
Public corporations	AAAK	5 931	5 521	4 561	4 580	5 467	4 955	3 779	4 727	4 895	4 915	5 054
Central government	AAAC	3 126	3 351	3 358	3 709	4 951	6 415	6 876	6 855	6 391	5 946	5 642
Local authorities	AAAG	3 746	4 158	4 219	2 797	4 631	6 244	5 267	5 651	5 412	6 344	6 811
Total	DFDC	60 718	65 032	75 158	91 530	105 443	107 577	97 747	93 642	94 293	99 217	105 385
Increase in book value of stocks and work in progress[7]:												
Personal sector	AAAX	430	519	784	1 287	1 107	671	−55	17	460	1 008	788
Industrial and commercial companies	AAAT	2 575	2 557	5 821	9 460	8 520	3 638	−3 101	−212	2 445	7 313	8 270
Financial companies and institutions	AAAP	−	−	−	−	−	−	−	−	−	−	−
Public corporations	AAAL	104	−322	−152	283	274	−134	88	53	−202	−304	−151
Central government	AAAD	450	−237	−498	−322	−163	156	156	−17	−24	−251	−154
Total	DHHY	3 559	2 517	5 955	10 708	9 738	4 331	−2 917	−159	2 679	7 766	8 753
Net investment abroad[8]	−AABI	2 238	−864	−4 813	−16 475	−22 398	−18 746	−7 954	−10 133	−10 756	−2 419	−2 892
Total investment	GIHN	66 515	66 685	76 300	85 763	92 783	93 162	86 876	83 350	86 216	104 564	111 246
FINANCIAL SURPLUS OR DEFICIT												
Personal sector	AABH	9 792	3 270	−3 387	−13 690	−7 698	1 526	17 082	29 987	28 637	21 963	27 212
Industrial and commercial companies	AABG	4 529	2 847	1 727	−5 719	−18 190	−18 786	−7 846	−5 769	4 903	13 113	1 748
Financial companies and institutions	AABF	−1 811	1 132	2 419	−1 967	−2 015	553	−2 877	3 219	4 126	6 860	6 520
Public corporations	AABD	−182	1 224	1 294	1 757	488	4 513	348	−30	888	1 025	987
Central government	AABA	−8 177	−7 908	−5 521	3 979	6 549	−6 100	−13 081	−41 883	−50 164	−44 348	−36 478
Local authorities	AABB	−1 913	−1 429	−1 345	−835	−1 532	−452	−1 580	4 343	854	−1 032	−2 282
Total	GIHZ	2 238	−864	−4 813	−16 475	−22 398	−18 746	−7 954	−10 133	−10 756	−2 419	−2 293
Net investment abroad[8]	−AABI	2 238	−864	−4 813	−16 475	−22 398	−18 746	−7 954	−10 133	−10 756	−2 419	−2 892
less Residual error[5]	−DJAS	−	−	−	−	−	−	−	−	−	−	599

See footnotes on previous page

Summary sector accounts

3.6 Summary capital account including capital consumption[1]

£ million

		1974	1975	1976	1977	1978	1979	1980	1981	1982	1983	1984
RECEIPTS:												
Saving:												
Personal sector	AAAU	6 392	8 538	9 237	8 838	12 312	16 334	21 428	22 308	21 604	19 900	25 032
Industrial & commercial companies	AAAQ	9 197	9 603	13 195	15 981	18 532	22 771	18 706	20 001	21 757	26 725	32 115
Financial companies and institutions	AAAM	956	1 014	1 759	3 099	2 115	3 213	3 422	2 393	2 476	5 188	2 128
Public corporations	AAAI	1 378	1 647	2 796	3 284	3 788	3 788	4 250	5 561	6 607	7 515	6 130
Central government	AAAA	846	−686	−2 279	−915	−3 008	−1 854	−2 275	−3 865	−4 177	−4 457	−5 686
Local authorities	AAAE	588	1 300	2 151	1 792	1 592	1 449	1 142	2 601	3 091	2 317	2 069
Total	GIGV	19 357	21 416	26 859	32 079	35 331	45 701	46 673	48 999	51 358	57 188	61 788
less **Stock appreciation:**												
Personal sector	−DDAD	−705	−611	−696	−583	−447	−776	−719	−626	−362	−550	−325
Industrial & commercial companies	−AIAC	−5 063	−4 504	−5 587	−4 118	−3 443	−7 408	−5 394	−5 064	−3 511	−3 619	−4 123
Public corporations	−ADRC	−341	−406	−398	−394	−338	−653	−278	−284	−403	−35	−65
Total	−DJAT	−6 109	−5 521	−6 681	−5 095	−4 228	−8 837	−6 391	−5 974	−4 276	−4 204	−4 513
less **Depreciation (capital consumption):**												
Personal sector	−EXFJ	−2 034	−2 534	−2 980	−3 480	−4 155	−5 008	−6 089	−6 920	−7 409	−8 201	−9 124
Industrial & commercial companies	−EXAB	−3 583	−4 624	−5 672	−6 837	−8 215	−9 641	−11 861	−13 491	−14 587	−15 764	−16 955
Financial companies and institutions	−EXAA	−227	−295	−295	−380	−487	−584	−692	−855	−987	−1 072	−1 212	−1 298
Public corporations	−EXFK	−2 120	−2 752	−3 287	−3 832	−4 332	−4 994	−6 037	−6 728	−7 012	−7 296	−7 576
Central government	−EXFL	−236	−311	−370	−425	−483	−576	−713	−806	−848	−889	−933
Local authorities	−EXFM	−888	−1 105	−1 287	−1 440	−1 609	−1 916	−2 397	−2 709	−2 725	−2 788	−2 873
Total	−EXCH	−9 088	−11 621	−13 976	−16 501	−19 378	−22 827	−27 952	−31 641	−33 653	−36 150	−38 758
Saving after providing for depreciation and stock appreciation:												
Personal sector	GIHA	3 653	5 393	5 561	4 775	7 710	10 550	14 620	14 762	13 833	11 149	15 583
Industrial & commercial companies	GIVD	551	475	1 936	5 026	6 874	5 722	1 451	1 446	3 659	7 342	11 037
Financial companies and institutions	GIVN	729	719	1 379	2 612	1 531	2 521	2 567	1 406	1 404	3 976	830
Public corporations	GIHI	−1 083	−1 511	−889	−942	−882	−1 859	−2 065	−1 451	−808	184	−1 511
Central government	GIVR	610	−997	−2 649	−1 340	−3 491	−2 430	−2 988	−4 671	−5 025	−5 346	−6 619
Local authorities	GIVS	−300	195	864	352	−17	−467	−1 255	−108	366	−471	−804
Total	GIHK	4 160	4 274	6 202	10 483	11 725	14 037	12 330	11 384	13 429	16 834	18 516
Capital transfers (net):												
Personal sector	AAAV	−321	−302	−63	75	301	196	253	88	367	1 019	1 245
Industrial & commercial companies	AAAR	284	366	329	243	398	353	429	557	491	322	217
Financial companies and institutions	AAAN	−36	54	−28	−26	14	−107	−142	−315	−148	−61	−64
Public corporations[3]	AAAJ	213	289	377	418	500	412	472	532	473	602	568
Central government[3]	AAAB	−230	−440	−609	−685	−1 246	−946	−1 092	−904	−1 009	−1 107	−1 352
Local authorities	AAAF	15	33	−6	−25	33	92	80	42	−174	−775	−614
Total transfers[4]	AAAZ	−75	–	–	–	–	–	–	–	–	–	–
Residual error[5]	DJAS	2 110	2 262	4 455	1 929	2 884	1 770	1 550	2 259	1 203	626	685
Total	GIHO	6 195	6 536	10 657	12 412	14 609	15 807	13 880	13 643	14 632	17 460	19 201
EXPENDITURE												
Net domestic fixed capital formation:												
Personal sector[6]	EXGB	771	1 282	1 410	2 025	2 124	3 253	3 310	2 920	4 637	5 726	5 874
Industrial & commercial companies	EXGC	2 214	2 156	2 347	2 916	4 682	5 646	4 586	2 943	2 742	1 940	5 349
Financial companies and institutions	EXGD	1 425	1 229	1 600	1 695	1 533	1 627	2 380	2 447	2 626	1 838	2 421
Public corporations	EXGE	738	1 168	1 406	947	737	839	791	196	302	769	−135
Central government	EXGF	734	950	1 038	869	809	984	1 048	1 062	1 382	1 608	1 795
Local authorities	EXGG	2 527	2 629	2 727	2 083	1 797	1 749	1 494	95	−518	584	1 118
Total	EXDQ	8 409	9 414	10 528	10 535	11 682	14 098	13 609	9 663	11 171	12 465	16 423
Value of physical increase in stocks and work in progress:												
Personal sector	DHHJ	1	−245	99	355	313	388	−240	−211	58	148	188
Industrial & commercial companies	FMBN	1 094	−1 544	398	1 529	1 526	1 869	−2 600	−2 533	−1 666	697	1 247
Financial companies and institutions	AAAP	−13	9	34	−15	−10	−17	6	9	4	38	24
Public corporations	DHHL	−52	435	368	−95	−56	−43	219	60	261	336	−443
Central government	AAAD	15	−9	2	50	31	−35	43	−93	155	246	280
Total	DHBF	1 045	−1 354	901	1 824	1 804	2 162	−2 572	−2 768	−1 188	1 465	1 296
Net investment abroad[8]	−AABI	−3 259	−1 524	−772	53	1 123	−453	2 843	6 748	4 649	3 529	1 483
Total net investment	GIHO	6 195	6 536	10 657	12 412	14 609	15 807	13 880	13 643	14 632	17 460	19 201
FINANCIAL SURPLUS OR DEFICIT												
Private sector	DDDS	−632	3 818	3 226	4 200	6 660	6 469	11 736	12 369	11 205	13 360	13 745
Public sector	AABE	−4 737	−7 604	−8 453	−6 076	−8 421	−8 692	−10 443	−7 880	−7 759	−10 456	−12 947
Overseas sector[8]	AABI	3 259	1 524	772	−53	−1 123	453	−2 843	−6 748	−4 649	−3 529	−1 483
Residual error[5]	DJAS	2 110	2 262	4 455	1 929	2 884	1 770	1 550	2 259	1 203	626	685

See footnotes for Table 3.5

3.6
continued
Summary capital account including capital consumption[1]

£ million

		1985	1986	1987	1988	1989	1990	1991	1992	1993	1994	1995
RECEIPTS:												
Saving:												
Personal sector	AAAU	25 928	22 629	20 489	19 111	24 076	30 450	40 781	51 772	51 745	48 220	55 186
Industrial & commercial companies	AAAQ	35 550	35 204	43 963	47 387	43 736	40 463	39 332	41 615	54 938	66 990	61 795
Financial companies and institutions	AAAM	1 638	5 129	6 716	4 700	6 010	7 382	3 723	8 284	8 229	14 704	13 879
Public corporations	AAAI	5 219	5 967	4 989	5 815	4 999	2 896	1 026	1 894	2 769	2 847	3 102
Central government	AAAA	−3 623	−4 450	−2 303	7 186	12 376	7 354	−116	−23 333	−35 650	−31 649	−24 608
Local authorities	AAAE	1 803	2 206	2 446	1 564	1 586	4 617	2 130	3 118	4 185	3 452	2 491
Total	GIGV	66 515	66 685	76 300	85 763	92 783	93 162	86 876	83 350	86 216	104 564	111 845
less **Stock appreciation:**												
Personal sector	−DDAD	−475	−172	−491	−750	−803	−695	−394	−39	−13	−376	−420
Industrial & commercial companies	−AIAC	−2 155	−1 500	−4 148	−5 366	−6 203	−5 316	−1 586	−1 700	−2 373	−3 650	−4 451
Public corporations	−ADRC	−108	−163	−88	−259	−55	−120	−30	−39	36	−8	−31
Total	−DJAT	−2 738	−1 835	−4 727	−6 375	−7 061	−6 131	−2 010	−1 778	−2 350	−4 034	−4 902
less **Depreciation (capital consumption):**												
Personal sector	−EXFJ	−10 006	−11 055	−12 356	−14 609	−15 288	−16 793	−17 493	−16 610	−17 371	−18 308	−19 097
Industrial & commercial companies	−EXAB	−20 019	−21 519	−23 601	−24 951	−27 614	−30 840	−33 204	−33 781	−35 850	−37 536	−40 451
Financial companies and institutions	−EXAA	−1 471	−1 624	−1 810	−1 994	−2 148	−2 312	−2 601	−2 524	−2 528	−2 502	−2 621
Public corporations	−EXFK	−6 300	−6 481	−5 672	−5 820	−5 750	−5 167	−3 917	−3 658	−3 633	−3 686	−3 941
Central government	−EXFL	−1 021	−1 117	−1 224	−1 342	−1 544	−1 736	−1 786	−1 820	−1 931	−2 044	−2 227
Local authorities	−EXFM	−3 066	−3 289	−3 501	−3 920	−4 373	−4 413	−4 353	−4 092	−4 040	−4 213	−4 547
Total	−EXCH	−41 883	−45 085	−48 164	−52 636	−56 716	−61 261	−63 356	−62 485	−65 353	−68 289	−72 884
Saving after providing for depreciation and stock appreciation:												
Personal sector	GIHA	15 447	11 402	7 642	3 752	7 985	12 962	22 894	35 123	34 361	29 536	35 669
Industrial & commercial companies	GIVD	13 376	12 185	16 214	17 070	9 919	4 307	4 542	6 134	16 715	25 804	16 893
Financial companies and institutions	GIVN	167	3 505	4 906	2 706	3 862	5 070	1 122	5 760	5 701	12 202	11 258
Public corporations	GIHI	−1 189	−677	−771	−264	−806	−2 391	−2 921	−1 803	−828	−847	−870
Central government	GIVR	−4 644	−5 567	−3 527	5 844	10 832	5 618	−1 902	−25 153	−37 581	−33 693	−26 835
Local authorities	GIVS	−1 263	−1 083	−1 055	−2 356	−2 787	204	−2 223	−974	145	−761	−2 056
Total	GIHK	21 894	19 765	23 409	26 752	29 005	25 770	21 512	19 087	18 513	32 241	34 059
Capital transfers (net):												
Personal sector	AAAV	320	−150	−266	−1 224	−681	80	1 644	1 997	3 299	2 309	1 810
Industrial & commercial companies	AAAR	112	−289	−398	−19	−871	−774	−416	19	−1	82	−218
Financial companies and institutions	AAAN	−118	−196	−120	−140	−152	−36	−36	−36	−44	−36	−36
Public corporations[3]	AAAJ	634	456	714	805	1 230	6 438	3 189	2 856	2 812	2 789	2 788
Central government[3]	AAAB	−978	−344	−358	180	−1 039	−6 883	−5 938	−11 712	−8 147	−7 004	−6 382
Local authorities	AAAF	30	523	428	398	1 513	1 175	1 557	6 876	2 081	1 860	2 038
Total transfers[4]	AAAZ	–	–	–	–	–	–	–	–	–	–	–
Residual error[5]	DJAS	–	–	–	–	–	–	–	–	–	–	−599
Total	GIHO	21 894	19 765	23 409	26 752	29 005	25 770	21 512	19 087	18 513	32 241	33 460
EXPENDITURE												
Net domestic fixed capital formation:												
Personal sector[6]	EXGB	6 020	7 635	10 470	15 681	14 698	11 540	7 905	7 155	8 576	9 250	10 499
Industrial & commercial companies	EXGC	8 539	7 992	12 416	18 676	24 921	23 997	16 659	13 834	11 739	9 110	10 508
Financial companies and institutions	EXGD	1 860	2 177	2 367	4 533	5 725	4 481	3 963	2 505	1 531	5 306	4 702
Public corporations	EXGE	−369	−960	−1 111	−1 240	−283	−212	−138	1 069	1 262	1 229	1 113
Central government	EXGF	2 105	2 234	2 134	2 367	3 407	4 679	5 090	5 035	4 460	3 902	3 415
Local authorities	EXGG	680	869	718	−1 123	258	1 831	914	1 559	1 372	2 131	2 264
Total	EXDQ	18 835	19 947	26 994	38 894	48 727	46 316	34 393	31 157	28 940	30 928	32 501
Value of physical increase in stocks and work in progress:												
Personal sector	DHHJ	−45	347	293	537	304	−24	−449	−22	447	632	368
Industrial & commercial companies	FMBN	420	1 057	1 673	4 094	2 317	−1 678	−4 687	−1 912	72	3 663	3 819
Financial companies and institutions	AAAP	–	–	–	–	–	–	–	–	–	–	–
Public corporations	DHHL	−4	−485	−240	24	219	−254	58	14	−166	−312	−182
Central government	AAAD	450	−237	−498	−322	−163	156	151	−17	−24	−251	−154
Total	DHBF	821	682	1 228	4 333	2 677	−1 800	−4 927	−1 937	329	3 732	3 851
Net investment abroad[8]	−AABI	2 238	−864	−4 813	−16 475	−22 398	−18 746	−7 954	−10 133	−10 756	−2 419	−2 892
Total net investment	GIHO	21 894	19 765	23 409	26 752	29 005	25 770	21 512	19 087	18 513	32 241	33 460
FINANCIAL SURPLUS OR DEFICIT												
Private sector	DDDS	12 510	7 249	759	−21 376	−27 903	−16 707	6 359	27 437	37 666	41 936	35 480
Public sector	AABE	−10 272	−8 113	−5 572	4 901	5 505	−2 039	−14 313	−37 570	−48 422	−44 355	−37 773
Overseas sector[8]	AABI	−2 238	864	4 813	16 475	22 398	18 746	7 954	10 133	10 756	2 419	2 892
Residual error[5]	DJAS	–	–	–	–	–	–	–	–	–	–	−599

See footnotes for Table 3.5

Summary sector accounts

3.7 Sector allocation of dividend and interest flows[1],[3] - 1995

£ million

	Personal sector[2]	Industrial and commercial companies	Financial Companies	Public corporations	Central government	Local authorities	Overseas sector	Total
RECEIPTS of DIVIDENDS and INTEREST:								
Sterling treasury bills	37	4	884	2	39	–	51	1 017
British government securities	11 290	172	4 258	61	1 810	12	3 771	21 374
National savings	3 212	–	–	3	–	–	–	3 215
Tax instruments	12	50	9	3	–	–	–	74
Net gvernment indebtedness to the Banking Department	–	–	–	–	–	–	–	–
Northern Ireland central government debt	15	–	–	–	–	–	–	15
Government liabilities under exchange cover scheme	–	–	–	1	19	10	–	30
Other public sector financing	–	–	–	199	–	279	–	478
Issue Department's transactions in bills	–	–	–	–	175	–	–	175
Government foreign currency debt	13	–	189	–	–	–	988	1 190
Other government overseas financing	–	–	–	–	–	–	108	108
Official reserves	–	–	–	–	1 620	–	–	1 620
Local authority debt	77	4	273	62	3 677	42	38	4 173
Public corporations debt	14	–	72	–	2 169	40	43	2 338
Deposits with banks	9 442	4 268	18 524	110	11	251	43 450	76 056
Bank sterling money market instruments	289	222	3 376	–	–	8	103	3 998
Bank foreign currency money market instruments	251	28	697	–	–	–	733	1 709
Deposits with building societies	12 053	291	255	–	–	–	257	12 856
Building society sterling money market instruments	40	40	760	–	–	–	273	1 113
Building society foreign currency money market instruments	40	4	77	–	–	–	334	455
Bank lending (excluding public sector)	–	–	70 451	–	–	–	–	70 451
Credit extended by retailers	–	420	–	–	–	–	–	420
Loans for house purchase: Building societies	–	–	17 892	–	–	–	–	17 892
Loans for house purchase: Other	133	–	12 266	–	111	17	–	12 527
Other public sector lending	–	–	–	–	105	–	–	105
Finance leasing	–	–	1 473	–	–	–	–	1 473
Other lending by financial institutions	450	–	1 962	–	–	–	–	2 412
UK unit trusts	1 591	–	11	–	–	–	–	1 602
UK company shares	27 672	12 322	7 866	9	194	–	5 167	53 230
UK company bonds	1 954	254	1 742	–	157	–	5 707	9 814
Overseas securities	5 170	125	13 883	–	–	–	–	19 178
Miscellaneous domestic instruments	60	196	87	–	–	22	579	944
Direct and other investment abroad	452	21 267	3 105	–	–	–	–	24 824
Overseas direct and other investment in the UK	–	–	–	–	–	–	11 958	11 958
Miscellaneous overseas instruments	894	2 403	4 248	92	–	–	10 007	17 644
TOTAL RECEIPTS	75 161	42 070	164 360	542	10 087	681	83 567	376 468

1 Including unremitted profits on inward and outward overseas direct investment.
2 Life assurance and pension funds are classified to the personal sector.
3 Including flows between and, where possible, within sectors.

3.7
continued

Sector allocation of dividend and interest flows[1],[3] - 1995

£ million

	Personal sector[3]	Industrial and commercial companies	Financial Companies	Public corporations	Central government	Local authorities	Overseas sector	Total
PAYMENTS of DIVIDENDS and INTEREST:								
Sterling treasury bills	–	–	–	–	1 017	–	–	1 017
British government securities	–	–	–	–	21 374	–	–	21 374
National savings	–	–	–	–	3 215	–	–	3 215
Tax instruments	–	–	–	–	74	–	–	74
Net government indebtedness to the Banking Department	–	–	–	–	–	–	–	–
Northern Ireland central government debt	–	–	–	–	15	–	–	15
Government liabilities under exchange cover scheme	–	–	–	15	11	4	–	30
Other public sector financing	–	–	279	–	199	–	–	478
Issue Department's transactions in bills	–	103	60	–	–	–	12	175
Government foreign currency debt	–	–	–	–	1 190	–	–	1 190
Other government overseas financing	–	–	–	–	108	–	–	108
Official reserves	–	–	–	–	–	–	1 620	1 620
Local authority debt	–	–	–	–	–	4 173	–	4 173
Public corporations debt	–	–	–	2 338	–	–	–	2 338
Deposits with banks	–	–	76 056	–	–	–	–	76 056
Banks sterling money market instruments	–	–	3 998	–	–	–	–	3 998
Banks foreign currency money market instruments	–	–	1 709	–	–	–	–	1 709
Deposits with building societies	–	–	12 856	–	–	–	–	12 856
Building societies sterling money market instruments	–	–	1 113	–	–	–	–	1 113
Building societies foreign currency money market instruments	–	–	455	–	–	–	–	455
Bank lending (excluding public sector)	9 691	11 665	9 236	–	–	–	39 859	70 451
Credit extended by retailers	420	–	–	–	–	–	–	420
Loans for house purchase: Building societies	17 892	–	–	–	–	–	–	17 892
Loans for house purchase: Other	12 527	–	–	–	–	–	–	12 527
Other public sector lending	5	91	–	–	–	–	9	105
Finance leasing	94	1 214	134	17	9	5	–	1 473
Other lending by financial institutions	1 632	780	–	–	–	–	–	2 412
UK unit trusts	–	–	1 602	–	–	–	–	1 602
UK company shares	–	42 361	10 869	–	–	–	–	53 230
UK company bonds	95	4 533	5 186	–	–	–	–	9 814
Overseas securities	–	–	–	–	–	–	19 178	19 178
Miscellaneous domestic instruments	22	816	106	–	–	–	–	944
Direct and other investment abroad	–	–	–	–	–	–	24 824	24 824
Overseas direct and other investment in the UK	213	9 199	2 546	–	–	–	–	11 958
Miscellaneous overseas instruments	110	3 095	6 802	–	–	–	7 637	17 644
TOTAL PAYMENTS	42 701	73 857	133 007	2 370	27 212	4 182	93 139	376 468

See footnotes on previous page.

Sector Dividends and Interest Accounts[1]

3.8 Personal sector[2]

£ million

		1985	1986	1987	1988	1989	1990	1991	1992	1993	1994	1995
RECEIPTS												
Sterling treasury bills	XAUR	2	–	–	–	–	–	4	11	7	10	37
British government securities	XANX	7 879	7 795	8 264	8 442	8 487	7 956	7 258	7 266	8 087	9 448	11 290
National savings	XAOZ	2 655	2 746	3 054	2 907	3 119	3 518	3 193	2 956	2 666	2 854	3 212
Tax instruments	XAPP	4	6	10	15	15	7	13	25	13	18	12
Northern Ireland central government debt	CTDF	2	8	6	24	25	23	16	14	14	16	15
Government foreign currency debt	XAYD	–	–	–	–	–	–	2	3	18	39	13
Local authority debt	XAON	387	258	200	208	248	172	125	96	58	81	77
Public corpoations debt	XAPJ	14	122	79	71	26	40	33	12	5	12	14
Deposits with banks	XAOH	4 879	5 102	4 637	5 998	11 211	17 312	15 124	12 812	8 210	7 640	9 442
Bank sterling money market instruments	GJRB	–	–	65	170	362	551	396	344	154	152	289
Bank foreign currency money market instruments	GJVV	–	–	9	12	60	85	81	97	124	183	251
Deposits with building societies	XAOJ	11 397	11 158	11 904	12 612	17 127	19 878	19 273	16 833	11 348	10 577	12 053
Building society sterling money market instruments	GJVW	–	–	4	10	139	362	366	303	37	40	40
Building society foreign currency money market instruments	GJVX	–	–	–	–	8	17	16	29	24	27	40
Loans for house purchase: Other	XAOT	320	313	355	406	521	507	426	325	219	158	133
Other lending by financial institutions	XALG	272	271	260	310	407	545	540	700	702	438	450
UK unit trusts	XBOF	426	434	557	690	901	1 117	1 282	1 362	1 492	1 422	1 591
UK company shares	XATP	5 799	6 997	8 677	12 298	14 970	15 897	15 895	18 641	19 203	21 065	27 672
UK company bonds	XASX	437	540	648	750	1 167	1 135	1 304	1 415	1 589	1 652	1 954
Overseas securities	XAPH	1 480	1 680	1 634	2 113	2 782	2 526	3 186	3 608	4 225	3 801	5 170
Miscellaneous domestic instruments	XAUD	320	285	278	272	310	257	138	84	64	55	60
Direct and other investment abroad	XAOL	21	216	213	186	123	70	184	180	335	187	452
Miscellaneous overseas instruments	XAOV	356	338	380	376	558	746	832	755	698	697	894
Total receipts	XAPT	36 650	38 269	41 234	47 870	62 566	72 721	69 687	67 871	59 292	60 572	75 161
PAYMENTS												
Bank lending (excluding public sector)	XANZ	5 847	6 377	6 726	7 716	11 202	13 687	11 770	10 856	8 184	8 077	9 691
Credit extended by retailers	XAOB	243	283	410	421	467	496	516	479	414	388	420
Loans for house purchase: Building societies	XAOP	12 201	12 944	14 418	15 918	20 831	24 509	23 785	21 921	17 314	17 404	17 892
Loans for house purchase: Other	XAOR	3 627	4 195	4 532	5 938	11 001	15 232	13 933	12 577	9 894	10 522	12 527
Other public sector lending	XAPF	12	4	14	13	14	6	17	9	7	1	5
Finance leasing	XAHC	31	41	57	82	107	118	138	110	107	98	94
Other lending by financial institutions	XAMA	680	825	983	981	1 148	1 373	1 348	1 231	1 147	1 258	1 632
UK company bonds	GJWZ	–	–	8	15	16	16	20	26	49	78	95
Miscellaneous domestic instruments	XASF	–	–	–	–	39	49	46	42	36	27	22
Overseas direct and other investment in the UK	HESG	8	8	30	54	81	110	127	154	178	195	213
Miscellaneous overseas instruments	XATX	105	87	86	74	144	346	310	257	104	120	110
Total payments	XAPR	22 754	24 764	27 264	31 212	45 050	55 942	52 010	47 662	37 434	38 168	42 701
Personal sector: Reconcilliation with table 4.1												
Total receipts	XAPT	36 650	38 269	41 234	47 870	62 566	72 721	69 687	67 871	59 292	60 572	75 161
less total payments	-XAPR	-22 754	-24 764	-27 264	-31 212	-45 050	-55 942	-52 010	-47 662	-37 434	-38 168	-42 701
plus tax credits[3]	DBAI	2 687	3 109	3 506	4 452	5 383	5 888	6 013	6 851	5 518	5 625	7 363
plus rent income	DIAO	15 533	17 148	18 857	21 773	24 802	28 456	33 485	38 804	40 981	44 065	47 898
Total rent, dividends and net interest	CFAM	32 116	33 762	36 333	42 883	47 701	51 123	57 175	65 864	68 357	72 094	87 721

1 See footnotes to table 3.7.
2 Life assurance and pension funds are classified to the personal sector.
3 Tax credits on UK dividend payments and unit trust distributions.

3.9 Industrial and commercial companies

£ million

		1985	1986	1987	1988	1989	1990	1991	1992	1993	1994	1995
RECEIPTS												
Sterling treasury bills	XAET	39	31	27	29	40	38	24	19	7	3	4
British government securities	XADZ	176	127	134	142	119	184	258	171	146	181	172
National savings	XAFF	21	26	39	45	51	62	55	–	–	–	–
Tax instruments	XAFX	186	182	221	166	66	48	74	131	37	89	50
Government liabilities under exchange cover scheme	XAJB	–	7	10	3	5	3	4	–	–	–	–
Other public sector financing	XAFJ	–	–	–	–	–	–	–	–	–	–	–
Local authority debt	XAEN	59	33	22	15	14	10	11	10	5	5	4
Public corporations debt	XAFP	–	–	–	–	–	–	–	–	–	–	–
Deposits with banks	XAEH	3 587	3 777	3 468	4 026	6 404	7 972	6 672	5 226	3 299	3 281	4 268
Bank sterling money market instruments	GJRP	–	–	163	301	512	606	299	243	156	158	222
Bank foreign currency money market instruments	GJUY	–	–	53	58	81	59	20	12	9	17	28
Deposits with building societies	XAEJ	173	190	176	147	144	310	399	440	303	307	291
Building society sterling money market instruments	GJVH	–	–	15	29	48	112	125	79	37	38	40
Building society foreign currency money market instruments	GJVN	–	–	–	–	–	3	4	4	2	3	4
Credit extended by retailers	XAED	183	216	347	354	394	423	516	479	414	388	420
UK company shares	XATJ	2 153	2 534	2 484	3 955	6 812	6 102	7 339	7 543	7 461	9 693	12 322
UK company bonds	XASN	91	130	149	158	239	222	190	173	177	183	254
Overseas securities	HHLL	101	91	73	100	108	95	87	107	121	119	125
Miscellaneous domestic instruments	GJWV	–	8	67	96	183	241	153	129	120	175	196
Direct and other investment abroad	HHLJ	7 340	6 662	10 159	12 529	16 190	15 564	12 294	12 158	14 271	18 133	21 267
Miscellaneous overseas instruments	XAEX	1 124	1 087	1 134	1 198	1 826	2 465	2 583	2 227	1 845	1 732	2 403
Total receipts	XAGB	15 233	15 101	18 741	23 351	33 236	34 519	31 107	29 151	28 410	34 505	42 070
PAYMENTS												
Government liabilities under exchange cover scheme	XAIR	6	4	31	29	24	30	29	6	–	–	–
Issue Department's transactions in bills	XAEL	470	471	232	347	163	372	289	364	345	145	103
Bank lending (excluding public sector)	XAEB	6 672	6 809	6 854	9 050	16 295	20 621	17 701	15 321	10 243	9 426	11 665
Other public sector lending	XAFL	76	18	80	78	85	35	110	63	56	25	91
Finance leasing	XAHD	438	586	805	1 103	1 436	1 529	1 756	1 413	1 272	1 260	1 214
Other lending by financial institutions	XAKW	336	343	349	434	707	947	973	1 062	979	744	780
UK company shares	XATD	8 231	9 994	12 019	16 609	22 979	23 434	25 232	28 259	29 078	32 235	42 361
UK company bonds	XASL	679	900	1 308	1 521	2 349	3 032	3 140	3 684	3 743	4 281	4 533
Miscellaneous domestic instruments	XAEZ	89	122	240	397	705	750	571	431	412	603	816
Overseas direct and other investment in the UK	HDVF	6 403	4 443	6 891	7 777	8 635	7 712	5 452	4 826	5 903	8 077	9 199
Miscellaneous overseas instruments	XAEV	885	842	955	1 048	1 704	2 131	2 403	2 473	2 391	2 935	3 095
Total payments	XAFZ	24 285	24 532	29 764	38 393	55 082	60 593	57 656	57 902	54 422	59 731	73 857

1 See footnotes to table 3.7.

Sector Dividends and Interest Accounts[1]

3.10 Financial Companies

£ million

		1985	1986	1987	1988	1989	1990	1991	1992	1993	1994	1995
RECEIPTS												
Sterling Treasury bills	CBTG	89	87	159	170	704	1 087	773	416	95	250	884
British government securities	GJBO	2 532	2 628	2 666	2 598	2 096	1 564	1 464	1 744	2 567	3 741	4 258
National Savings	XALB	–	–	2	4	4	4	4	–	–	–	–
Tax instruments	CBTI	44	66	89	44	6	5	9	18	5	12	9
Other public sector financing	CBTJ	57	8	–	–	–	–	–	–	–	–	–
Government foreign currency debt	CBTK	30	148	200	233	206	211	106	238	545	269	189
Local authority debt	CBTL	1 222	720	454	401	402	328	312	175	194	258	273
Public corporations debt	CBTM	327	251	238	203	130	137	108	94	91	66	72
Deposits with banks	GJXM	18 117	17 084	15 483	17 863	27 180	30 938	25 537	20 232	14 358	14 819	18 524
Bank sterling money market instruments	GJXO	–	–	1 993	2 888	4 475	5 339	4 845	3 981	2 422	2 518	3 376
Bank foreign currency money market instruments	GJXP	–	–	741	694	841	749	672	413	377	552	697
Deposites with building society	CBTN	175	143	81	115	165	247	223	245	216	269	255
Building society sterling money market instruments	GJXS	–	–	283	377	587	1 080	931	800	626	621	760
Building society foreign currency money market instruments	GJXT	–	–	–	–	5	36	37	46	72	60	77
Bank lending (excluding public sector debt)	XBGG	51 695	47 823	46 670	54 975	80 757	93 712	86 609	70 340	57 638	57 235	70 451
Loans for house purchase: Building societies	XAOP	12 201	12 944	14 418	15 918	20 831	24 509	23 785	21 921	17 314	17 404	17 892
Loans for house purchase: Other	GJXU	2 577	3 288	3 732	5 180	10 082	14 333	13 150	12 008	9 493	10 225	12 266
Finance leasing	XAJJ	552	739	1 005	1 381	1 797	1 942	2 184	1 782	1 639	1 637	1 473
Other lending by financial institutions	XASG	748	901	1 076	1 109	1 456	1 783	1 786	1 594	1 426	1 564	1 962
UK unit trusts	XBOC	8	7	7	8	6	9	12	10	9	11	11
UK company shares	GJXY	2 144	2 602	2 862	3 906	5 072	5 522	5 981	5 630	5 798	7 237	7 866
UK company bonds	GJYC	214	512	354	393	844	1 235	1 277	1 383	1 248	1 580	1 742
Overseas securities	GJYE	3 078	3 552	3 419	3 436	4 313	5 119	5 859	8 207	11 706	11 889	13 883
Miscellaneous domestic instruments	GJYG	–	2	41	102	165	198	113	76	65	53	87
Direct and other investment abroad	GJYH	383	915	566	1 126	342	–51	301	1 017	2 258	2 593	3 105
Miscellaneous overseas instruments	GJYL	1 499	1 055	877	966	1 499	2 163	2 506	2 386	4 036	3 918	4 248
Total receipts	CBTT	97 692	95 475	97 416	114 090	163 965	192 199	178 584	154 756	134 198	138 781	164 360
PAYMENTS												
Net government indebtedness to the Banking Department	CUDU	451	97	44	–	1	–	–	40	91	35	–
Other public sector financing	XAGN	17	35	85	134	248	268	230	275	192	225	279
Issue Department's transactions in bills	CBTA	529	392	205	238	96	121	180	202	152	77	60
Deposits with banks	XAHV	64 581	58 812	55 023	63 971	95 398	112 907	102 888	79 138	64 313	60 006	76 056
Bank sterling money market instruments	GJRZ	–	–	2 241	3 376	5 383	6 559	5 583	4 613	2 794	2 909	3 998
Bank foreign currency money market instruments	GJSD	–	–	803	764	1 102	1 107	990	796	863	1 260	1 709
Deposits with building societies	XAJX	11 760	11 516	12 254	13 027	17 688	20 762	20 215	17 796	12 069	11 363	12 856
Building societies sterling money market instruments	GJVD	–	1	313	435	845	1 735	1 608	1 339	842	900	1 113
Building societies foreign currency money market instruments	GJVE	–	–	–	–	82	229	247	324	277	308	455
Bank lending (excluding public sector)	CBTB	3 338	3 713	4 549	5 221	9 041	10 876	9 830	7 919	6 066	6 584	9 236
Other public sector lending	XALL	–	–	–	–	–	–	–	–	–	–	–
Finance leasing	XAHW	39	52	75	114	153	188	233	221	232	247	134
Other lending by financial institutions	XAMD	4	4	4	4	8	8	5	1	2	–	–
UK unit trusts	XBOB	434	441	564	698	907	1 126	1 294	1 372	1 501	1 433	1 602
UK company shares	GJXW	2 908	3 540	3 884	5 636	6 616	7 395	7 913	7 504	7 852	10 240	10 869
UK company bonds	GJYA	570	1 043	1 044	1 396	2 554	2 803	3 264	3 691	3 567	4 524	5 186
Miscellaneous domestic instruments	XAKX	–	2	8	40	79	140	135	93	72	82	106
Overseas direct and other investment in the UK	GJYJ	1 160	842	123	834	522	–795	–1 020	280	4 372	1 214	2 546
Miscellaneous overseas instruments	XAKT	591	529	552	886	1 387	2 553	3 804	4 872	7 756	7 083	6 802
Total payments	CBTF	86 382	81 019	81 772	96 774	142 110	167 982	157 399	130 476	113 013	108 490	133 007

1 See footnotes to table 3.7.

3.11 Public Corporations

£ million

RECEIPTS		1985	1986	1987	1988	1989	1990	1991	1992	1993	1994	1995
Sterling treasury bills	XAQF	–	4	–	32	29	8	4	–	–	3	2
British government securities	XAPZ	3	9	16	17	19	24	19	15	14	32	61
National savings	XAQL	21	15	8	9	14	13	9	9	6	2	3
Tax instruments	XAQX	31	30	4	5	3	2	1	5	1	3	3
Government liabilities under exchange cover scheme	CTCQ	111	59	15	1	16	2	2	5	6	3	1
Other public sector financing	XAQR	72	65	35	46	204	193	153	114	115	133	199
Local authority debt	CPBA	97	71	48	53	70	98	78	79	53	68	62
Deposits with banks	XAQD	43	60	59	104	135	123	56	78	69	77	110
Bank sterling money market instruments	GJQU	–	–	2	4	4	4	4	4	–	–	–
Credit extended by retailers	CPAW	60	67	63	67	73	73	–	–	–	–	–
Loans for house purchase: Other	XAGY	10	8	5	4	4	4	4	4	4	3	–
UK company shares	XATT	7	8	1	–	–	11	10	11	9	13	9
Direct and other investment abroad	HESD	2	8	1	10	1	1	1	1	–	–	–
Miscellaneous overseas instruments	HGEN	50	48	56	62	68	68	72	94	91	92	92
Total receipts	XARB	507	452	313	414	640	624	413	419	368	429	542
PAYMENTS												
Government liabilities under exchange cover scheme	CUEO	46	84	138	139	14	15	11	26	26	23	15
Public corporations debt	CPAX	2 902	2 787	2 615	2 438	2 602	1 919	1 261	1 197	1 377	2 082	2 338
Finance leasing	XAHL	16	22	21	21	19	12	14	11	10	18	17
Total payments	XAQZ	2 964	2 893	2 774	2 598	2 635	1 946	1 286	1 234	1 413	2 123	2 370

1 See footnotes to table 3.7.

3.12 Central Government

£ million

RECEIPTS		1985	1986	1987	1988	1989	1990	1991	1992	1993	1994	1995
Sterling treasury bills	XAIJ	27	28	63	22	82	77	96	134	115	39	39
British government securities	XACH	984	1 070	1 417	1 588	2 567	2 773	2 451	1 777	997	1 323	1 810
Net government indebtedness to the Banking Department	CUDU	451	97	44	–	1	–	–	40	91	35	–
Government liabilities under exchange cover scheme	XAIL	53	92	189	176	46	51	46	38	33	28	19
Issue Department's transactions in bills	XACP	1 175	1 004	519	682	289	567	559	674	575	247	175
Official reserves	HHCB	540	607	854	1 352	1 913	1 732	1 656	1 456	1 328	1 577	1 620
Local authority debt	XACR	2 677	3 188	3 663	3 948	4 410	4 622	4 650	4 491	3 981	3 807	3 677
Public corporations debt	XADL	2 000	1 936	1 911	1 878	2 177	1 649	1 037	1 008	1 218	1 924	2 169
Deposits with banks	XACL	22	17	17	19	36	35	29	24	17	12	11
Loans for house purchase: other	XATZ	242	221	141	97	113	128	164	127	116	102	111
Other public sector lending	XADH	110	39	107	102	105	47	135	75	69	34	105
UK company shares	XATR	565	686	695	412	437	562	697	460	283	227	194
UK company bonds	XASZ	340	332	542	497	452	386	491	690	453	385	157
Total receipts	XADV	9 186	9 317	10 163	10 773	12 628	12 629	12 011	10 994	9 276	9 740	10 087
PAYMENTS												
Sterling treasury bills	XACT	240	223	373	444	1 209	1 820	1 256	754	261	329	1 017
British government securities	XACF	12 813	13 027	14 080	14 650	15 221	14 282	13 475	13 512	14 584	18 417	21 374
National saving	XACX	2 697	2 787	3 103	2 965	3 188	3 597	3 261	2 965	2 672	2 856	3 215
Tax instruments	CUDP	265	284	324	230	90	62	97	179	56	122	74
Northern Ireland central government debt	CTDF	2	8	6	24	25	23	16	14	14	16	15
Government liabilities under exchange cover scheme	XAIX	121	76	35	5	27	12	10	12	18	13	11
Other public sector financing	XADF	129	73	35	46	204	193	153	114	115	133	199
Government foreign currency debt	XACN	49	205	293	318	410	518	421	845	1 345	1 068	1 190
Other government overseas financing	XADD	165	148	121	118	152	163	140	122	111	103	108
Finance leasing	XAHF	–	3	4	5	9	13	16	16	16	11	9
Miscellaneous domestic instruments	XAUF	254	218	195	176	152	88	39	7	–	–	–
Total payments	XADT	16 735	17 052	18 569	18 981	20 687	20 771	18 884	18 540	19 192	23 068	27 212
Reconciliation with table 7.2												
Total receipts	XADV	9 186	9 317	10 163	10 773	12 628	12 629	12 011	10 994	9 276	9 740	10 087
less Sterling Treasury bills	-XAIJ	–27	–28	–63	–22	–82	–77	–96	–134	–115	–39	–39
less British government securities	-XACH	–984	–1 070	–1 417	–1 588	–2 567	–2 773	–2 451	–1 777	–997	–1 323	–1 810
plus Rent	GTBG	101	104	174	152	108	142	178	135	183	189	194
plus Royalties	CTAI	2 240	925	1 127	799	522	625	543	568	600	553	574
plus Licence fees on oil and gas production	CTAG	126	16	24	24	34	29	36	33	41	48	53
plus ITC franchise payments	CUKL	–	–	–	–	–	–	–	–	350	380	398
Total rent, dividends and net interest, etc.	CTCC	10 642	9 264	10 008	10 138	10 643	10 575	10 221	9 819	9 338	9 548	9 457
Total gross payments (table 3.12)	XADT	16 735	17 052	18 569	18 981	20 687	20 771	18 884	18 540	19 192	23 068	27 212
less Sterling Treasury bills receipts	-XAIJ	–27	–28	–63	–22	–82	–77	–96	–134	–115	–39	–39
less Brtitish government securities receipts	-XACH	–984	–1 070	–1 417	–1 588	–2 567	–2 773	–2 451	–1 777	–997	–1 323	–1 810
Total net payments (table 7.2)	ACHL	15 724	15 954	17 089	17 371	18 038	17 921	16 337	16 629	18 080	21 706	25 363

1 See footnotes to table 3.7.

Sector Dividends and Interest Accounts[1]

3.13 Local Authorites

£ million

		1985	1986	1987	1988	1989	1990	1991	1992	1993	1994	1995
RECEIPTS												
Sterling treasury bills	XAGV	–	–	–	–	–	–	–	–	–	2	–
British government securities	XAGH	10	9	11	9	10	11	8	8	6	10	12
National savings	XAGX	–	–	–	–	–	–	–	–	–	–	–
Government liabilities under exchange cover scheme	XAIZ	10	10	10	1	6	7	4	7	12	10	10
Other public sector financing	XAGN	17	35	85	134	248	268	230	275	192	225	279
Local authority debt	XAYN	129	114	86	82	75	87	106	97	49	32	42
Public corporations debt	GIUL	103	80	53	37	32	26	26	30	33	41	40
Deposits with banks	XAGL	90	184	278	375	726	601	336	179	129	160	251
Bank sterling money market instruments	GJQT	–	–	18	11	13	11	10	14	8	8	8
Loans for house pruchase: Other	XAGT	478	365	299	251	281	260	189	113	62	34	17
Miscellaneous domestic instruments	XAGP	–	–	–	–	39	49	46	42	36	27	22
Total receipts	XAHJ	837	797	840	900	1 430	1 320	955	765	527	549	681
PAYMENTS												
Government liabilities under exchange cover scheme	CUES	1	4	20	8	8	6	6	6	7	5	4
Local authority debt	CEBU	4 660	4 483	4 574	4 810	5 318	5 420	5 340	5 002	4 393	4 296	4 173
Finance leasing	XAHK	28	35	43	56	73	82	27	11	2	3	5
Total payments	XAHH	4 689	4 522	4 637	4 874	5 399	5 508	5 373	5 019	4 402	4 304	4 182

1 See footnotes to table 3.7.

3.14 Overseas Sector

£ million

		1985	1986	1987	1988	1989	1990	1991	1992	1993	1994	1995
RECEIPTS												
Sterling treasury bills	XAMR	83	73	124	191	354	610	355	174	37	22	51
British government securities	XAMF	1 229	1 389	1 572	1 854	1 923	1 770	2 017	2 531	2 767	3 682	3 771
Government foreign currency debt	XAML	19	57	93	85	204	307	313	604	782	760	988
Other government overseas financing	XADD	165	148	121	118	152	163	140	122	111	103	108
Local authority debt	XAMP	89	99	101	103	99	103	58	54	53	45	38
Public corporations debt	XAMZ	458	398	334	249	237	67	57	53	30	39	43
Deposits with banks	HERP	37 843	32 588	31 081	35 586	49 706	55 926	55 134	40 587	38 231	34 017	43 450
Bank sterling money market instruments	GJRX	–	–	–	2	19	48	29	27	54	73	103
Bank foreign currency money market instruments	GJVA	–	–	–	–	120	214	217	274	353	508	733
Deposits with building societies	HHLS	15	25	93	153	252	327	320	278	202	210	257
Building society sterling money market instruments	GJVJ	–	1	11	19	71	181	186	157	142	201	273
Building society foreign currency money market instruments	GJVP	–	–	–	–	69	173	190	245	179	218	334
UK company shares	HESU	471	707	1 184	1 674	2 304	2 735	3 223	3 478	4 176	4 240	5 167
UK company bonds	XATB	167	429	667	1 134	2 217	2 873	3 162	3 740	3 892	5 083	5 707
Miscellaneous domestic instruments	XAUJ	23	47	57	143	278	282	341	242	235	402	579
Overseas direct and other investment in the UK	HHCH	7 571	5 293	7 044	8 665	9 238	7 027	4 559	5 260	10 453	9 486	11 958
Miscellaneous overseas instruments	XAMV	1 581	1 458	1 593	2 008	3 235	5 030	6 517	7 602	10 251	10 138	10 007
Total receipts	XANR	49 714	42 712	44 075	51 984	70 476	77 836	76 818	65 428	71 948	69 227	83 567
PAYMENTS												
Issue Department's transations in bills	HHMT	176	141	82	97	30	74	90	108	78	25	12
Official reserves	HHCB	540	607	854	1 352	1 913	1 732	1 656	1 456	1 328	1 577	1 620
Bank lending (excluding public sector)	HERG	35 838	30 924	28 541	32 988	44 219	48 528	47 308	36 244	33 145	33 148	39 859
Other public sector lending	XANH	22	17	13	11	6	6	8	3	6	8	9
Overseas securities	CGNV	4 659	5 323	5 126	5 649	7 203	7 740	9 132	11 922	16 052	15 809	19 178
Direct and other investment abroad	HHBY	7 746	7 801	10 939	13 851	16 656	15 584	12 780	13 356	16 864	20 913	24 824
Miscellaneous overseas instruments	HHIW	3 029	2 528	2 447	2 602	3 951	5 442	5 993	5 462	6 670	6 439	7 637
Total payments	XANP	52 010	47 341	48 002	56 550	73 978	79 106	76 967	68 551	74 143	77 919	93 139

1 See footnotes to table 3.7.

CHAPTER 4: Personal sector and its subsectors

4.1 Personal sector: income and expenditure account

£ million

		1985	1986	1987	1988	1989	1990	1991	1992	1993	1994	1995
INCOME BEFORE TAX												
Income from employment:												
Wages and salaries	CFAJ	166 774	180 754	196 689	220 328	245 482	271 602	285 254	294 900	301 638	312 309	325 756
Pay in cash and kind of HM Forces	CFAK	3 590	3 833	4 093	4 337	4 539	4 814	5 459	5 952	6 593	6 346	5 986
Total	AIJA	170 364	184 587	200 782	224 665	250 021	276 416	290 713	300 852	308 231	318 655	331 742
Employers' contributions: Social security	CEAN	12 245	13 540	14 395	16 176	18 145	19 984	21 182	21 590	23 047	23 241	24 069
Other	CFAL	14 249	14 253	15 031	15 696	16 206	17 353	18 872	19 573	20 541	23 050	22 084
Total income from employment	DJAO	196 858	212 380	230 208	256 537	284 372	313 753	330 767	342 015	351 819	364 946	377 895
Income from self-employment:												
After deducting stock appreciation	CEAP	29 929	34 932	38 870	45 079	51 888	57 993	56 351	57 110	60 448	63 645	67 265
Stock appreciation	DDAD	475	172	491	750	803	695	394	39	13	376	420
Total[1]	CFAN	30 404	35 104	39 361	45 829	52 691	58 688	56 745	57 149	60 461	64 021	67 685
Rent, dividends and net interest:												
Receipts by life assurance & pension schemes	CFBH	14 982	16 841	18 773	23 575	28 501	30 788	30 449	32 476	33 955	35 304	43 652
Imputed rent of owner-occupied dwellings	CDDF	12 880	13 993	15 281	17 272	19 633	23 257	26 652	30 208	31 825	34 613	37 639
Other receipts, net[2]	CFBJ	4 254	2 928	2 279	2 036	−433	−2 922	74	3 180	2 577	2 177	6 430
Total	CFAM	32 116	33 762	36 333	42 883	47 701	51 123	57 175	65 864	68 357	72 094	87 721
Social security benefits and other current grants from general government	AIIE	45 351	49 454	50 798	52 175	54 033	58 939	69 287	80 052	88 384	92 574	96 490
Current transfers from overseas	CGJV	1 775	1 732	1 666	1 715	1 750	1 800	1 900	1 957	2 211	2 322	2 438
Current transfers from companies	EAWU	119	145	160	200	284	287	258	288	329	385	408
Imputed charge for capital consumption of private non-profit making bodies	CFBM	458	485	503	524	557	585	600	604	564	587	600
Total personal income[1]	AIIA	307 081	333 062	359 029	399 863	441 388	485 175	516 732	547 929	572 125	596 929	633 237
DEDUCTIONS FROM INCOME												
UK taxes on income[2]	AIIG	37 774	40 805	43 459	48 274	53 589	61 543	63 419	65 178	63 637	68 168	74 655
Social security contributions[3]	AIIH	24 210	26 165	27 663	30 682	33 333	34 457	36 216	36 975	39 499	41 943	44 251
Current transfers abroad	CGGV	1 459	1 656	1 789	1 985	2 050	2 100	2 200	2 225	2 249	2 214	2 236
Community charge/council tax	ADBH	–	–	–	–	586	8 629	8 128	7 907	8 038	8 450	8 989
Miscellaneous current transfers	CIJR	225	253	339	362	391	469	519	382	558	658	673
Personal disposable income[4]	AIIJ	243 413	264 183	285 779	318 560	351 439	377 977	406 250	435 262	458 144	475 496	502 433
EXPENDITURE												
Consumers' expenditure	AIIK	217 485	241 554	265 290	299 449	327 363	347 527	365 469	383 490	406 399	427 276	447 247
Balance: saving[4]	AAAU	25 928	22 629	20 489	19 111	24 076	30 450	40 781	51 772	51 745	48 220	55 186
Total	AIIJ	243 413	264 183	285 779	318 560	351 439	377 977	406 250	435 262	458 144	475 496	502 433
MEMORANDUM ITEMS												
Saving ratio (per cent)[5]	AIIM	10.7	8.6	7.2	6.0	6.9	8.1	10.0	11.9	11.3	10.1	11.0
Real personal disposable income[6]:												
At 1990 prices	CECO	309 734	323 316	335 271	355 945	370 809	377 977	377 980	385 506	392 326	397 193	408 965
1990=100	CECQ	81.9	85.5	88.7	94.2	98.1	100.0	100.0	102.0	103.8	105.1	108.2

1 Before providing for depreciation and stock appreciation.
2 Including tax credits.
3 See table 7.2 for composition.
4 Before providing for depreciation, stock appreciation & additions to tax reserves.
5 Saving as a percentage of personal disposable income.
6 Personal disposable income revalued by the implied consumers' expenditure deflator shown in table 1.7.

Where such data can be compiled, quarterly data for series in this table are available on the ONS's Databank. This data can also be provided on paper by request. Some of these quarterly data are published regularly in the UK Economic Accounts in table A11.

4.2 Personal sector: capital account

£ million

		1985	1986	1987	1988	1989	1990	1991	1992	1993	1994	1995
RECEIPTS												
Saving[1]	AAAU	25 928	22 629	20 489	19 111	24 076	30 450	40 781	51 772	51 745	48 220	55 186
Capital transfers	AIJO	2 206	1 870	2 098	2 107	2 584	3 379	4 283	4 304	5 367	4 568	4 109
Total	CFBT	28 134	24 499	22 587	21 218	26 660	33 829	45 064	56 076	57 112	52 788	59 295
EXPENDITURE												
Gross domestic fixed capital formation:												
Dwellings[2]	DFIV	9 549	11 366	13 260	17 804	18 938	17 023	15 504	15 919	16 919	17 940	18 844
Purchases less sales of land and existing buildings	DFJM	3 033	3 718	5 430	7 267	5 202	5 542	4 835	3 460	3 908	4 346	4 348
Other	CFBU	3 444	3 606	4 136	5 219	5 846	5 768	5 059	4 386	5 120	5 272	5 804
Increase in book value of stocks and work in progress	AAAX	430	519	784	1 287	1 107	671	−55	17	460	1 008	788
Taxes on capital	GIKW	1 808	1 937	2 294	3 246	3 175	3 207	2 623	2 300	2 064	2 259	2 299
Capital transfers to public corporations	CFBX	78	83	70	85	90	92	16	7	4	–	–
Balance: financial surplus or deficit[3]	AABH	9 792	3 270	−3 387	−13 690	−7 698	1 526	17 082	29 987	28 637	21 963	27 212
Total	CFBT	28 134	24 499	22 587	21 218	26 660	33 829	45 064	56 076	57 112	52 788	59 295

1 Before providing for depreciation, stock appreciation and additions to tax reserves.
2 Excluding existing dwellings and land.
3 Including net investment abroad.

Personal sector

4.3 Personal sector: transactions in financial assets and liabilities

£ million

		1985	1986	1987	1988	1989	1990	1991	1992	1993	1994	1995
FINANCIAL SURPLUS OR DEFICIT	AABH	9 792	3 270	−3 387	−13 690	−7 698	1 526	17 082	29 987	28 637	21 963	27 212
Transactions in financial liabilities (net)												
Loans secured on dwellings from:												
Building societies	AAQG	14 627	19 434	14 923	23 720	24 002	24 185	20 928	13 696	9 559	12 478	9 171
Banks	AAJT	4 223	5 200	10 102	10 892	7 045	6 409	4 790	6 485	9 760	7 847	7 724
Local authorities	AAEO	−502	−506	−433	−329	−230	−322	−446	−358	−357	−291	−187
Other public sector	AIJT	60	54	49	144	134	−102	−436	−101	−72	−44	−23
Other	AAMO	626	2 887	4 940	5 717	2 808	3 119	1 117	−1 279	−2 791	−747	−1 448
Bank borrowing	-AAQJ	6 655	5 427	9 226	12 846	13 427	8 507	1 934	19	−1 686	3 546	6 818
Credit extended by retailers	AAPP	210	95	248	190	5	64	60	62	24	196	−109
Other loans and mortgages	-AIJX	594	622	1 239	1 107	1 344	1 079	1 380	−897	2 632	3 225	2 948
Accruals adjustment	-AAPZ	−1 930	−1 799	−846	−361	−4 295	−3 692	−2 767	−2 655	−1 104	−2 393	−3 635
Total transactions in financial liabilities	CJKU	24 563	31 414	39 448	53 926	44 240	39 247	26 560	14 972	15 965	23 817	21 259
Transactions in financial assets (net)												
Liquid assets:												
Notes and coin	AAPB	449	676	662	950	819	−136	392	1 002	930	1 071	1 165
Sterling treasury bills	DCHW	–	–	6	−2	−3	−1	15	−2	−4	−2	−4
National savings	AAPD	2 468	2 523	2 439	1 408	−1 519	783	2 168	5 019	3 020	4 596	3 275
Tax instruments	AAPE	10	43	72	29	27	31	−9	−18	−43	−34	−17
Local authority temporary debt	AAQC	30	−167	−137	−69	−72	−84	−120	294	−288	368	−118
Deposits with banks	AAQI	5 139	8 023	8 944	16 835	20 659	16 732	6 277	5 381	1 876	2 939	12 991
Deposits with building societies etc	AQVM	13 315	11 856	13 547	20 200	17 336	18 039	17 311	10 804	9 595	8 569	14 233
British government securities	AAPC	1 270	1 472	1 006	−1 958	−3 306	−1 036	1 362	−1 053	3 839	1 172	−91
Other public sector debt	AIKD	−587	−214	−699	−909	−355	−281	−7	409	−119	82	49
Company securities etc,	AIKE	−3 432	−4 893	−5 710	−14 492	−21 595	−12 154	−4 141	−221	−4 111	4 144	−9 478
Life assurance and pension funds	AAPX	18 375	19 686	21 564	23 075	27 697	27 657	28 623	27 531	29 002	27 794	33 024
Total transactions in financial assets	CJKV	37 037	39 005	41 694	45 067	39 688	49 550	51 871	49 146	43 697	50 699	55 029
NET TOTAL FINANCIAL TRANSACTIONS	AAQA	12 474	7 591	2 246	−8 859	−4 552	10 303	25 311	34 174	27 732	26 882	33 770
BALANCING ITEM	AAQB	−2 682	−4 321	−5 633	−4 831	−3 146	−8 777	−8 229	−4 187	905	−4 919	−6 558

4.4 Personal sector: income and saving after providing for depreciation and stock appreciation

£ million

		1985	1986	1987	1988	1989	1990	1991	1992	1993	1994	1995
Income from self-employment:												
Before providing for depreciation and stock appreciation	CFAN	30 404	35 104	39 361	45 829	52 691	58 688	56 745	57 149	60 461	64 021	67 685
less Stock appreciation	-DDAD	−475	−172	−491	−750	−803	−695	−394	−39	−13	−376	−420
After providing for stock appreciation	CEAP	29 929	34 932	38 870	45 079	51 888	57 993	56 351	57 110	60 448	63 645	67 265
less Depreciation[1]	-CFBY	−2 470	−2 618	−2 791	−2 963	−3 260	−3 518	−3 687	−3 580	−3 752	−3 851	−4 047
After providing for depreciation and stock appreciation	CFBZ	27 459	32 314	36 079	42 116	48 628	54 475	52 664	53 530	56 696	59 794	63 218
Total personal income:[2]												
Before providing for depreciation and stock appreciation	AIIA	307 081	333 062	359 029	399 863	441 388	485 175	516 732	547 929	572 125	596 929	633 237
After providing for stock appreciation	CFCA	306 606	332 890	358 538	399 113	440 585	484 480	516 338	547 890	572 112	596 553	632 817
less Depreciation[1]	-EXFJ	−10 006	−11 055	−12 356	−14 609	−15 288	−16 793	−17 493	−16 610	−17 371	−18 308	−19 097
After providing for depreciation and stock appreciation	CFCC	296 600	321 835	346 182	384 504	425 297	467 687	498 845	531 280	554 741	578 245	613 720
Personal saving:												
Before providing for depreciation, stock appreciation and additions to tax reserves	AAAU	25 928	22 629	20 489	19 111	24 076	30 450	40 781	51 772	51 745	48 220	55 186
After providing for stock appreciation	CFCD	25 453	22 457	19 998	18 361	23 273	29 755	40 387	51 733	51 732	47 844	54 766
After providing for depreciation and stock appreciation	GIHA	15 447	11 402	7 642	3 752	7 985	12 962	22 894	35 123	34 361	29 536	35 669
less Additions to tax reserves	-CFCE	−942	−1 147	−1 351	−1 424	−2 038	−1 319	309	651	−962	−1 983	−960
After providing for depreciation, stock appreciation and additions to tax reserves	CFCF	14 505	10 255	6 291	2 328	5 947	11 643	23 203	35 774	33 399	27 553	34 709

1 Capital consumption at current replacement cost.
2 Including tax credits.

4.5 Consumers' expenditure at current market prices: classified by commodity[1]

£ million

		1985	1986	1987	1988	1989	1990	1991	1992	1993	1994	1995
Durable goods:												
Cars, motorcycles and other vehicles	CCDT	9 853	11 502	13 460	17 456	20 035	19 034	16 977	16 470	18 063	19 728	20 825
Furniture and floor coverings	CCDU	4 193	4 687	5 260	6 196	6 386	6 422	6 415	6 695	7 357	7 969	7 750
Other durable goods	CCDV	6 120	6 783	7 703	8 736	8 993	9 220	9 476	9 903	10 587	11 212	12 297
Total	AIIL	20 166	22 972	26 423	32 388	35 414	34 676	32 868	33 068	36 007	38 909	40 872
Other goods:												
Food (household expenditure)	CCDW	30 657	32 574	34 402	36 491	39 143	41 817	44 044	45 243	46 234	47 048	48 850
Beer	CCDX	8 416	8 902	9 533	10 204	10 857	11 904	12 888	12 927	13 135	13 807	14 034
Other alcoholic drink	CCDY	7 235	7 502	7 918	8 444	8 728	9 455	10 144	10 554	11 174	11 670	12 321
Tobacco	CCDZ	7 006	7 485	7 665	7 936	8 170	8 649	9 648	10 072	10 466	11 011	11 655
Clothing other than footwear	CCEA	12 132	13 649	14 715	15 836	16 476	17 245	17 821	18 384	19 544	20 506	21 404
Footwear	CCEB	2 780	2 997	3 133	3 187	3 371	3 631	3 591	3 713	3 984	4 333	4 397
Energy products	CCEC	18 578	18 219	18 628	19 291	20 460	22 422	24 955	25 399	26 136	26 857	27 192
Other goods	CCED	23 054	25 921	28 935	32 636	36 271	39 566	41 298	43 161	45 799	47 656	48 903
Services:												
Rents, rates and water charges[2]	CCEE	27 382	29 971	32 715	36 444	40 209	38 916	42 604	48 788	52 676	57 134	61 162
Other services[3]	CCEF	60 079	71 362	81 223	96 592	108 264	119 246	125 608	132 181	141 244	148 345	156 457
Total consumers' expenditure	AIIK	217 485	241 554	265 290	299 449	327 363	347 527	365 469	383 490	406 399	427 276	447 247

1 More detailed estimates of consumers' expenditure, expressed in both current and constant prices and both unadjusted and seasonally adjusted, appear in *Consumers' Expenditure: Business Monitor MQ24* published by HMSO for the ONS. Any queries relating to consumers' expenditure should be directed to ONS consumers' expenditure section on 071-270-6207
2 Rates, sewerage and water charges are affected by the introduction of the community charge in Scotland from April 1989 and in England and Wales from April 1990. The community charge is not classified as a tax on expenditure and is not therefore part of consumers' expenditure.
3 Including the adjustments for international travel, etc. and final expenditure by private non-profit-making bodies serving persons.

Where such data can be compiled, quarterly data for series in this table are available on the ONS's Databank. This data can also be provided on paper by request. Some of these quarterly data are published regularly in the UK Economic Accounts in table A7.

4.6 Consumers' expenditure at 1990 market prices: classified by commodity[1,2]

£ million at 1990 prices

		1985	1986	1987	1988	1989	1990	1991	1992	1993	1994	1995
Durable goods:												
Cars, motorcycles and other vehicles	CCBJ	14 162	15 552	16 525	19 410	21 031	19 034	15 782	14 767	16 138	17 224	17 630
Furniture and floor coverings	CCBK	5 145	5 573	6 043	6 858	6 748	6 422	6 070	6 137	6 680	7 183	6 656
Other durable goods	CCBL	5 966	6 802	7 829	8 785	9 090	9 220	9 355	9 906	10 635	11 701	13 189
Total	CCBI	25 192	27 927	30 397	35 053	36 869	34 676	31 207	30 810	33 453	36 108	37 475
Other goods:												
Food (household expenditure)	CCBM	38 402	39 610	40 621	41 542	42 247	41 817	41 869	42 384	42 801	43 366	43 519
Beer	CCBN	11 609	11 595	11 822	11 960	11 956	11 904	11 438	10 724	10 375	10 533	10 275
Other alcoholic drink	CCBO	9 217	9 293	9 443	9 700	9 550	9 455	9 129	8 983	9 269	9 594	9 874
Tobacco	CCBP	8 990	8 771	8 706	8 729	8 730	8 649	8 437	7 969	7 562	7 432	7 368
Clothing other than footwear	CCBQ	14 207	15 618	16 582	17 234	17 096	17 245	17 387	17 906	18 936	19 832	20 678
Footwear	CCBR	3 415	3 551	3 622	3 546	3 566	3 631	3 430	3 549	3 729	4 018	4 062
Energy products	CCBS	20 191	21 420	21 871	22 482	22 335	22 422	23 151	22 889	23 021	22 720	22 209
Other goods	CCCK	28 712	31 035	33 490	36 308	38 486	39 566	38 550	38 739	40 225	41 415	41 570
Services:												
Rents, rates and water charges	CCCL	36 401	36 896	37 407	37 959	38 428	38 916	39 325	39 648	40 219	40 715	41 250
Other services[3]	CCBV	80 334	89 906	97 273	110 078	116 143	119 246	116 114	116 051	118 425	121 181	125 765
Total consumers' expenditure	CCBH	276 742	295 622	311 234	334 591	345 406	347 527	340 037	339 652	348 015	356 914	364 045

1 See footnote 1 to table 4.5.
2 For the years before 1986, totals differ from the sum of their components.
3 Including the adjustments for international travel, etc. and final expenditure by private non-profit-making bodies serving persons.

Where such data can be compiled, quarterly data for series in this table are available on the ONS's Databank. This data can also be provided on paper by request. Some of these quarterly data are published regularly in the UK Economic Accounts in table A7.

Personal sector

4.7 Consumers' expenditure at current market prices: classified by function[1]

£ million

		1985	1986	1987	1988	1989	1990	1991	1992	1993	1994	1995
Food (household expenditure):												
Bread	CCXU	1 542	1 711	1 752	1 875	1 939	1 966	1 976	2 018	2 012	1 991	2 019
Cakes and biscuits	CCXV	1 420	1 453	1 534	1 637	1 741	1 886	1 942	2 069	2 146	2 181	2 233
Other cereals	CCXW	1 203	1 391	1 506	1 646	1 821	2 019	2 292	2 295	2 415	2 522	2 786
Meat and bacon	CDCJ	7 898	8 084	8 455	8 797	9 508	9 832	9 938	10 012	10 676	10 708	10 927
Fish	CDCK	1 055	1 179	1 229	1 373	1 519	1 594	1 678	1 672	1 735	1 806	1 896
Milk, cheese and eggs	CDCL	4 385	4 519	4 737	4 955	5 210	5 505	5 803	6 144	6 225	6 082	6 186
Oils and fats	CDCM	1 041	1 011	949	985	1 031	1 036	1 048	1 087	1 069	1 056	1 074
Fruit	CDCN	1 666	1 897	2 031	2 182	2 328	2 711	2 930	2 926	2 886	3 021	3 147
Potatoes	CDCO	1 211	1 349	1 553	1 539	1 709	1 885	2 043	2 207	2 188	2 356	2 854
Vegetables	CDCP	2 328	2 560	2 753	3 022	3 229	3 497	3 823	3 873	3 983	4 019	4 427
Sugar	CDCQ	331	315	317	323	317	319	335	309	317	288	281
Confectionery	CCIH	2 691	2 790	2 956	3 161	3 328	3 573	3 886	4 085	4 252	4 623	4 405
Coffee, tea and cocoa	CDCU	1 179	1 217	1 190	1 208	1 234	1 239	1 321	1 251	1 217	1 268	1 311
Soft drinks	CDCV	1 697	1 962	2 222	2 499	2 838	3 198	3 360	3 507	3 396	3 393	3 492
Other manufactured food	CDCW	1 010	1 136	1 218	1 289	1 391	1 557	1 669	1 788	1 717	1 734	1 812
Total	CCDW	30 657	32 574	34 402	36 491	39 143	41 817	44 044	45 243	46 234	47 048	48 850
Alcoholic drink:												
Beer	CCDX	8 416	8 902	9 533	10 204	10 857	11 904	12 888	12 927	13 135	13 807	14 034
Spirits	CDCX	3 831	3 947	4 145	4 550	4 611	4 985	5 296	5 243	5 524	5 783	5 352
Wine, cider and perry	CDCY	3 404	3 555	3 773	3 894	4 117	4 470	4 848	5 311	5 650	5 887	6 969
Total	CDCZ	15 651	16 404	17 451	18 648	19 585	21 359	23 032	23 481	24 309	25 477	26 355
Tobacco:												
Cigarettes	CDDA	6 112	6 552	6 730	7 001	7 224	7 703	8 632	9 034	9 431	10 022	10 699
Other	CDDB	894	933	935	935	946	946	1 016	1 038	1 035	989	956
Total	CCDZ	7 006	7 485	7 665	7 936	8 170	8 649	9 648	10 072	10 466	11 011	11 655
Clothing and footwear:												
Men's and boys' wear	CDDC	4 108	4 687	5 021	5 318	5 444	5 635	5 835	6 013	6 361	6 596	6 845
Women's, girls' and infants' wear	CDDD	8 024	8 962	9 694	10 518	11 032	11 610	11 986	12 371	13 183	13 910	14 559
Footwear	CCEB	2 780	2 997	3 133	3 187	3 371	3 631	3 591	3 713	3 984	4 333	4 397
Total	CDDE	14 912	16 646	17 848	19 023	19 847	20 876	21 412	22 097	23 528	24 839	25 801
Housing:												
Rents, rates and water charges:												
Imputed rent of owner-occupied dwellings	CDDF	12 880	13 993	15 281	17 272	19 633	23 257	26 652	30 208	31 825	34 613	37 639
Other rents	CDDG	7 154	7 669	8 230	8 664	9 396	10 748	12 843	15 156	17 080	18 441	19 176
Rates, sewerage and water charges[2]	CDDH	7 348	8 309	9 204	10 508	11 180	4 911	3 109	3 424	3 771	4 080	4 347
Maintenance, etc by occupiers:												
Do-it-yourself goods	CDDI	2 822	3 416	3 848	4 470	4 688	4 759	5 041	5 318	5 665	6 038	6 182
Contractors' charges and insurance	CDDJ	2 395	2 968	3 193	3 823	4 272	4 640	4 938	5 164	5 535	5 415	5 245
Total	CDDK	32 599	36 355	39 756	44 737	49 169	48 315	52 583	59 270	63 876	68 587	72 589
Fuel and power:												
Electricity	CDDL	4 910	5 180	5 210	5 412	5 878	6 278	7 179	7 671	7 837	8 082	8 195
Gas	CDDM	4 034	4 385	4 465	4 562	4 454	4 864	5 804	5 684	5 718	5 747	5 909
Coal and coke	CDDN	1 016	883	829	799	750	660	736	596	592	595	530
Other	CDDO	600	417	351	291	319	448	478	429	471	461	483
Total	CDDP	10 560	10 865	10 855	11 064	11 401	12 250	14 197	14 380	14 618	14 885	15 117
Household goods and services:												
Furniture, pictures, etc.	CDDQ	2 847	3 147	3 521	4 135	4 356	4 476	4 524	4 871	5 473	5 944	5 796
Carpets and other floor coverings	CDDR	1 346	1 540	1 739	2 061	2 030	1 946	1 891	1 824	1 884	2 025	1 954
Major appliances	CDDS	3 180	3 573	4 001	4 464	4 462	4 491	4 701	4 831	5 162	5 437	5 973
Textiles and soft furnishings	CDDT	1 414	1 621	1 766	1 973	2 061	2 105	2 269	2 556	2 708	2 810	2 732
Hardware	CDDU	1 882	2 164	2 340	2 566	2 874	3 211	3 253	3 163	3 247	3 378	3 447
Cleaning materials; matches	CDDV	1 243	1 333	1 410	1 529	1 756	1 961	2 087	2 260	2 367	2 268	2 181
Household and domestic services	CDDW	2 196	2 466	2 871	3 268	3 709	3 927	4 371	4 674	5 055	5 372	5 723
Total	CDDX	14 108	15 844	17 648	19 996	21 248	22 117	23 096	24 179	25 896	27 234	27 806

1 See footnote 1 to table 4.5.
2 Rates, sewerage and water charges are affected by the introduction of the community charge in Scotland from April 1989 and in England and Wales from April 1990. The community charge is not classified as a tax on expenditure and is not therefore part of consumers' expenditure.

4.7 Consumers' expenditure at current market prices: classified by function[1]

continued

£ million

		1985	1986	1987	1988	1989	1990	1991	1992	1993	1994	1995
Transport and communication:												
Cars, motorcycles and other vehicles	CCDT	9 853	11 502	13 460	17 456	20 035	19 034	16 977	16 470	18 063	19 728	20 825
Petrol and oil	CDDY	8 018	7 354	7 773	8 227	9 059	10 172	10 758	11 019	11 518	11 972	12 075
Vehicle excise duty	CDDZ	1 482	1 566	1 612	1 693	1 793	1 837	1 879	1 963	2 301	2 546	2 641
Other running costs of vehicles	CDEA	7 142	8 352	9 577	10 762	11 654	13 137	14 160	15 174	16 863	17 433	18 330
Rail travel	CDEB	1 474	1 637	1 757	1 932	2 002	2 242	2 282	2 345	2 443	2 555	2 754
Buses and coaches	CDEC	1 971	1 992	2 074	2 181	2 338	2 464	2 566	2 635	2 785	2 808	2 938
Air travel	CDED	2 784	3 179	3 692	4 097	4 272	4 543	4 824	5 362	5 413	5 887	6 383
Other travel	CDEE	1 252	1 513	1 799	2 038	2 245	2 533	2 652	2 813	3 022	3 034	2 949
Postal services	CDEF	488	518	559	549	633	719	787	833	916	997	984
Telecommunications	CDEG	3 495	3 979	4 313	4 761	5 070	5 568	6 055	6 282	6 695	7 240	7 924
Total	CDEH	37 959	41 592	46 616	53 696	59 101	62 249	62 940	64 896	70 019	74 200	77 803
Recreation, entertainment and education:												
Radio, television and other durable goods	CDEI	2 940	3 210	3 702	4 272	4 531	4 729	4 775	5 072	5 425	5 775	6 324
Television and video hire charges, licence fees and repairs	CDEJ	2 550	2 824	2 811	2 971	3 143	3 204	3 283	3 245	3 377	3 472	3 603
Sports goods, toys, games and camping equipment	CDEK	2 053	2 203	2 441	2 659	2 992	3 443	3 367	3 613	3 851	4 043	4 239
Other recreational goods	CDEL	3 418	3 826	4 437	5 016	5 851	6 510	6 714	7 082	7 653	8 290	8 732
Betting and gaming	CDEM	2 120	2 254	2 492	2 646	2 896	3 116	3 113	3 219	3 485	3 801	5 914
Other recreational and entertainment services	CDEN	2 347	2 739	3 091	3 800	4 316	4 890	5 341	5 496	5 882	6 202	6 335
Books	CDEO	755	854	999	1 127	1 228	1 422	1 501	1 593	1 713	1 680	1 658
Newspapers and magazines	CDEP	2 309	2 450	2 659	2 787	2 978	3 286	3 336	3 428	3 608	3 721	3 721
Education	CDEQ	1 638	1 785	1 959	2 185	2 620	3 221	4 028	4 788	5 186	5 677	6 392
Total	CDER	20 130	22 145	24 591	27 463	30 555	33 821	35 458	37 536	40 180	42 661	46 918
Other goods and services:												
Pharmaceutical products and medical equipment	CDES	1 190	1 364	1 433	1 595	1 786	1 919	2 299	2 731	2 966	3 186	3 271
National health service payments and other medical expenses	CDET	1 427	1 583	1 861	2 139	2 395	2 757	3 218	3 361	3 354	3 496	3 679
Toilet articles; perfumery	CDEU	2 488	2 868	3 231	3 810	4 245	4 594	4 984	5 139	5 556	5 788	6 169
Hairdressing and beauty care	CDEV	1 300	1 444	1 603	1 743	1 848	2 014	2 126	2 205	2 275	2 295	2 352
Jewellery, silverware, watches and clocks	CDEW	1 502	1 628	1 820	2 064	2 339	2 385	2 437	2 313	2 372	2 294	2 396
Other goods	CDEX	1 978	2 194	2 551	3 040	3 473	3 971	4 010	3 965	4 093	4 160	4 175
Catering (meals and accommodation)	CDEY	13 875	16 186	17 869	23 603	27 195	29 823	30 195	32 308	34 844	36 348	38 156
Administrative costs of life assurance and pension schemes	CDEZ	3 806	4 884	5 691	6 880	7 789	9 262	10 009	9 853	10 452	10 058	10 448
Other services	CDFA	4 286	5 607	7 634	8 781	10 623	11 337	11 085	11 396	12 673	14 191	15 547
Total	CDFB	31 852	37 758	43 693	53 655	61 693	68 062	70 363	73 271	78 585	81 816	86 193
Total household and tourist expenditure in the United Kingdom	CDFC	215 434	237 668	260 525	292 709	319 912	339 515	356 773	374 425	397 711	417 758	439 087
less Expenditure by foreign tourists, etc in the United Kingdom	CDFD	−6 276	−6 455	−7 217	−7 173	−8 026	−8 878	−8 287	−9 192	−10 545	−11 102	−13 292
Household expenditure abroad	CDFE	4 440	5 651	6 702	7 605	8 668	9 052	9 047	10 450	11 433	12 894	13 632
Total household expenditure on goods and services	CDFF	213 598	236 864	260 010	293 141	320 554	339 689	357 533	375 683	398 599	419 550	439 427
Final expenditure by private non-profit making bodies	CDFG	3 887	4 690	5 280	6 308	6 809	7 838	7 936	7 807	7 800	7 726	7 820
Total consumers' expenditure	AIIK	217 485	241 554	265 290	299 449	327 363	347 527	365 469	383 490	406 399	427 276	447 247

1 See footnote 1 to table 4.5.

4.8 Consumers' expenditure at 1990 market prices: classified by function[1,2]

£ million at 1990 prices

		1985	1986	1987	1988	1989	1990	1991	1992	1993	1994	1995
Food (household expenditure):												
Bread	CCXX	2 074	2 119	2 074	2 102	2 054	1 966	1 833	1 812	1 755	1 773	1 794
Cakes and biscuits	CCXY	1 780	1 781	1 806	1 883	1 879	1 886	1 805	1 838	1 831	1 819	1 840
Other cereals	CCXZ	1 560	1 730	1 798	1 879	1 956	2 019	2 134	2 039	2 089	2 247	2 435
Meat and bacon	CCFG	9 720	9 814	10 063	10 226	10 344	9 832	9 814	9 745	10 172	10 345	10 437
Fish	CCFH	1 441	1 492	1 419	1 555	1 679	1 594	1 570	1 554	1 633	1 735	1 818
Milk, cheese and eggs	CCFI	5 685	5 659	5 682	5 669	5 595	5 505	5 536	5 586	5 440	5 215	5 062
Oils and fats	CCFJ	1 118	1 134	1 134	1 124	1 094	1 036	1 005	1 008	971	950	925
Fruit	CCFK	1 943	2 182	2 368	2 456	2 622	2 711	2 641	2 806	2 917	2 989	2 974
Potatoes	CCFL	1 882	1 729	1 838	1 844	1 848	1 885	1 917	2 054	2 077	1 994	1 980
Vegetables	CCFM	2 819	3 117	3 161	3 382	3 490	3 497	3 704	4 033	4 167	4 118	4 264
Sugar	CCFN	427	404	390	373	343	319	309	285	276	258	240
Confectionery	CCIJ	3 213	3 148	3 258	3 399	3 454	3 573	3 579	3 559	3 548	3 793	3 555
Coffee, tea and cocoa	CCFP	1 313	1 326	1 315	1 324	1 290	1 239	1 257	1 178	1 157	1 112	1 058
Soft drinks	CCFQ	2 199	2 592	2 869	2 856	3 098	3 198	3 223	3 243	3 269	3 491	3 572
Other manufactured food	CCFR	1 263	1 383	1 446	1 470	1 501	1 557	1 542	1 644	1 499	1 527	1 565
Total	CCBM	38 402	39 610	40 621	41 542	42 247	41 817	41 869	42 384	42 801	43 366	43 519
Alcoholic drink:												
Beer	CCBN	11 609	11 595	11 822	11 960	11 956	11 904	11 438	10 724	10 375	10 533	10 275
Spirits	CCFS	4 922	4 902	4 976	5 248	5 066	4 985	4 678	4 351	4 423	4 620	4 035
Wine, cider and perry	CCFT	4 296	4 391	4 467	4 452	4 484	4 470	4 451	4 632	4 846	4 974	5 839
Total	CCFU	20 822	20 888	21 265	21 660	21 506	21 359	20 567	19 707	19 644	20 127	20 149
Tobacco:												
Cigarettes	CCFV	7 923	7 700	7 648	7 690	7 716	7 703	7 533	7 128	6 783	6 738	6 734
Other	CCFW	1 067	1 071	1 058	1 039	1 014	946	904	841	779	694	634
Total	CCBP	8 990	8 771	8 706	8 729	8 730	8 649	8 437	7 969	7 562	7 432	7 368
Clothing and footwear:												
Men's and boys' wear	CCFX	4 949	5 518	5 771	5 834	5 699	5 635	5 556	5 734	6 034	6 180	6 389
Women's, girls' and infants' wear	CCFY	9 255	10 100	10 811	11 400	11 397	11 610	11 831	12 172	12 902	13 652	14 289
Footwear	CCBR	3 415	3 551	3 622	3 546	3 566	3 631	3 430	3 549	3 729	4 018	4 062
Total	FCCB	17 615	19 169	20 204	20 780	20 662	20 876	20 817	21 455	22 665	23 850	24 740
Housing:												
Rents, rates and water charges:												
Imputed rent of owner-occupied dwellings	CCFZ	20 170	20 667	21 182	21 981	22 647	23 257	23 402	23 315	23 407	23 752	24 486
Other rents	CCGA	11 512	11 470	11 408	11 078	10 880	10 748	10 970	11 367	11 795	11 892	11 660
Rates, sewerage and water charges	CCGB	4 707	4 759	4 817	4 900	4 901	4 911	4 953	4 966	5 017	5 071	5 104
Maintenance, etc by occupiers:												
Do-it-yourself goods	CCGC	3 592	4 176	4 571	5 079	5 076	4 759	4 548	4 608	4 832	5 124	5 156
Contractors' charges and insurance	CCGD	3 126	3 667	3 888	4 410	4 600	4 640	4 504	4 503	4 755	4 553	4 327
Total	CCGE	43 092	44 739	45 866	47 448	48 104	48 315	48 377	48 759	49 806	50 392	50 733
Fuel and power:												
Electricity	CCGF	6 107	6 301	6 365	6 278	6 350	6 278	6 566	6 626	6 789	6 814	6 823
Gas	CCGG	4 563	4 852	4 979	5 090	4 746	4 864	5 413	5 309	5 540	5 315	5 260
Coal and coke	CCGH	1 118	966	884	835	774	660	696	538	516	470	377
Other	CCGI	480	471	445	432	426	448	500	486	516	516	520
Total	CCGJ	11 875	12 590	12 673	12 635	12 296	12 250	13 175	12 959	13 361	13 115	12 980
Household goods and services:												
Furniture, pictures, etc.	CCGK	3 430	3 689	4 017	4 555	4 607	4 476	4 295	4 467	4 998	5 401	5 049
Carpets and other floor coverings	CCGL	1 715	1 884	2 026	2 303	2 141	1 946	1 775	1 670	1 682	1 782	1 607
Major appliances	CCGM	3 442	3 845	4 304	4 590	4 546	4 491	4 519	4 582	4 893	5 296	5 850
Textiles and soft furnishings	CCGN	1 634	1 804	1 935	2 106	2 118	2 105	2 243	2 560	2 740	2 826	2 709
Hardware	CCGO	2 381	2 634	2 743	2 880	3 061	3 211	3 022	2 864	2 897	2 980	2 977
Cleaning materials; matches	CCGP	1 588	1 664	1 718	1 776	1 912	1 961	1 835	1 819	1 818	1 762	1 674
Household and domestic services	CCGQ	3 078	3 268	3 587	3 840	4 041	3 927	4 015	4 097	4 294	4 465	4 625
Total	CCGR	17 245	18 788	20 330	22 050	22 426	22 117	21 704	22 059	23 322	24 512	24 491

1 See footnote 1 to table 4.5.
2 For the years before 1986, totals differ from the sum of their components.

4.8 Consumers' expenditure at 1990 market prices: classified by function[1,2]

continued

£ million at 1990 prices

		1985	1986	1987	1988	1989	1990	1991	1992	1993	1994	1995
Transport and communication:												
Cars, motorcycles and other vehicles	CCBJ	14 162	15 552	16 525	19 410	21 031	19 034	15 782	14 767	16 138	17 224	17 630
Petrol and oil	CCGS	8 317	8 830	9 198	9 847	10 039	10 172	9 976	9 930	9 660	9 605	9 229
Vehicle excise duty	CCGT	1 526	1 570	1 615	1 691	1 792	1 837	1 891	1 829	1 890	1 939	1 933
Other running costs of vehicles	CCGU	9 570	10 635	11 561	12 194	12 573	13 137	12 910	12 994	14 149	14 307	14 695
Rail travel	CCGV	2 061	2 198	2 242	2 305	2 176	2 242	2 112	2 078	2 021	2 007	2 053
Buses and coaches	CCGW	2 709	2 635	2 580	2 555	2 546	2 464	2 326	2 253	2 274	2 189	2 221
Air travel	CCGX	2 713	3 131	3 699	4 166	4 476	4 543	4 486	5 047	5 208	5 653	6 039
Other travel	CCGY	1 666	1 929	2 203	2 360	2 443	2 533	2 455	2 489	2 552	2 512	2 452
Postal services	CCGZ	595	634	654	623	681	719	703	708	761	803	789
Telecommunications	CCHA	4 061	4 389	4 656	5 095	5 363	5 568	5 582	5 637	5 955	6 753	7 693
Total	CCHB	47 389	51 503	54 933	60 246	63 120	62 249	58 223	57 732	60 608	62 992	64 734
Recreation, entertainment and education:												
Radio, television and other durable goods	CCHC	2 542	2 957	3 525	4 195	4 544	4 729	4 836	5 324	5 742	6 405	7 339
Television and video hire charges, licence fees and repairs	CCHD	2 908	3 145	3 093	3 197	3 271	3 204	3 117	2 991	3 036	3 126	3 165
Sports goods, toys, games and camping equipment	CCHE	2 411	2 506	2 660	2 838	3 100	3 443	3 238	3 398	3 612	3 807	4 004
Other recreational goods	CCHF	3 959	4 279	4 922	5 460	6 127	6 510	6 291	6 400	6 825	7 244	7 477
Betting and gaming	CCHG	2 858	2 924	3 092	3 121	3 166	3 116	2 933	2 914	3 089	3 273	4 937
Other recreational and entertainment services	CCHH	3 674	3 830	4 126	4 586	4 765	4 890	4 716	4 426	4 506	4 443	4 353
Books	CCHI	1 035	1 139	1 221	1 315	1 318	1 422	1 403	1 439	1 519	1 471	1 417
Newspapers and magazines	CCHJ	3 127	3 197	3 271	3 219	3 222	3 286	3 091	2 964	2 972	3 108	2 998
Education	CCHK	2 570	2 573	2 597	2 626	2 889	3 221	3 675	3 967	4 053	4 295	4 511
Total	CCHL	24 896	26 550	28 507	30 557	32 402	33 821	33 300	33 823	35 354	37 172	40 201
Other goods and services:												
Pharmaceutical products and medical equipment	CCHM	1 621	1 746	1 758	1 851	1 929	1 919	2 101	2 342	2 496	2 599	2 667
National health service payments and other medical expenses	CCHN	1 910	2 055	2 273	2 454	2 573	2 757	2 881	2 715	2 524	2 520	2 554
Toilet articles; perfumery	CCHO	3 249	3 572	3 898	4 368	4 607	4 594	4 592	4 500	4 723	4 840	4 879
Hairdressing and beauty care	CCHP	1 869	1 951	2 033	2 054	2 017	2 014	1 922	1 871	1 829	1 752	1 713
Jewellery, silverware, watches and clocks	CCHQ	1 620	1 703	1 862	2 106	2 367	2 385	2 388	2 184	2 080	1 915	1 967
Other goods	CCHR	2 489	2 615	2 931	3 310	3 649	3 971	3 798	3 661	3 711	3 739	3 645
Catering (meals and accommodation)	CCHS	19 768	21 682	22 422	27 303	29 514	29 823	27 592	27 652	28 342	28 278	29 341
Administrative costs of life assurance and pension schemes	CCHT	5 510	6 549	7 036	8 017	8 423	9 262	9 561	9 113	9 520	9 014	9 326
Other services	CCHU	5 757	6 783	8 440	9 670	10 932	11 337	10 218	10 154	10 327	10 938	11 779
Total	CCHV	43 825	48 656	52 653	61 133	66 011	68 062	65 053	64 192	65 552	65 595	67 871
Total household and tourist expenditure in the United Kingdom	CCHW	274 170	291 264	305 758	326 780	337 504	339 515	331 522	331 039	340 675	348 553	356 786
less Expenditure by foreign tourists, etc in the United Kingdom	CCHX	−8 640	−8 333	−8 789	−8 354	−8 711	−8 878	−7 639	−8 082	−8 939	−9 035	−10 360
Household expenditure abroad	CCHY	6 157	7 022	8 065	9 042	9 302	9 052	8 798	9 692	9 550	10 961	11 232
Total household expenditure on goods and services	CCHZ	271 783	289 953	305 034	327 468	338 095	339 689	332 681	332 649	341 286	350 479	357 658
Final expenditure by private non-profit making bodies	CCIA	4 959	5 669	6 200	7 123	7 311	7 838	7 356	7 003	6 729	6 435	6 387
Total consumers' expenditure	CCBH	276 742	295 622	311 234	334 591	345 406	347 527	340 037	339 652	348 015	356 914	364 045

1 See footnote 1 on table 4.5.
2 See footnote on previous page.

4.9 Households: income and expenditure

£ million

		1985	1986	1987	1988	1989	1990	1991	1992	1993	1994	1995
INCOME												
Direct money income from work and property:												
Wages and salaries including pay in cash of HM Forces	GITN	166 052	179 327	194 771	218 125	243 310	269 245	282 917	293 109	300 316	310 730	323 773
Income from self-employment[1]	GITO	25 718	30 390	34 154	39 684	44 129	48 776	47 985	49 776	54 269	57 398	60 247
Rent, dividends and interest (gross receipts)[2]	GITP	23 550	24 062	25 589	28 654	38 704	46 949	46 078	45 416	35 566	36 200	44 615
Total	GITQ	215 320	233 779	254 514	286 463	326 143	364 970	376 980	388 301	390 151	404 328	428 635
Income in kind	GITR	4 312	5 260	6 011	6 540	6 711	7 171	7 796	7 743	7 915	7 925	7 969
Pensions, social security benefits and other current transfers:												
Pensions and other benefits from life assurance and pension schemes[3]	GITS	21 433	24 729	29 080	30 242	33 957	40 192	47 979	55 899	60 812	62 452	65 925
State retirement pensions, widows' benefit, etc.	GITT	17 194	19 006	19 523	20 216	21 571	23 300	26 215	27 974	29 458	30 108	31 111
Family benefits	CSDB	4 928	4 996	5 099	5 268	5 361	5 487	6 032	7 035	7 619	7 994	8 302
Income support	CSDE	7 667	8 230	8 316	8 016	8 156	8 907	11 155	15 022	16 676	16 511	16 623
Unemployment benefit	CSDI	1 632	1 763	1 606	1 261	806	780	1 486	1 749	1 685	1 360	1 120
Other social security benefits	GITX	6 188	6 865	7 417	8 295	9 071	10 424	12 493	14 122	16 193	18 327	20 030
Other current transfers	GITY	8 959	9 352	9 399	9 667	9 688	10 213	11 567	13 153	16 096	17 640	18 939
Total	GITZ	68 001	74 941	80 440	82 965	88 610	99 303	116 927	134 954	148 539	154 392	162 050
Total household income	GIUA	287 633	313 980	340 965	375 968	421 464	471 444	501 703	530 998	546 605	566 645	598 654
less United Kingdom taxes on income[2]	-GIUB	−41 588	−44 355	−47 233	−52 165	−58 565	−67 353	−68 425	−69 333	−66 132	−70 455	−76 354
less Social security contributions (excluding employers' contributions)	-GTDR	−11 683	−12 339	−12 970	−14 187	−15 006	−14 301	−14 876	−15 236	−16 316	−18 556	−20 045
less Contributions of employees to occupational pension schemes	-GGBB	−4 810	−5 287	−6 260	−7 129	−7 900	−8 625	−9 385	−9 967	−9 814	−8 927	−8 958
Total household disposable income	GIUE	229 552	251 999	274 502	302 487	339 993	381 165	409 017	436 462	454 343	468 707	493 297
EXPENDITURE												
Expenditure on goods and services[4]	GIUF	196 912	217 987	239 038	268 989	293 132	307 170	320 872	335 622	356 322	374 879	391 340
Interest paid	GIUG	16 029	17 958	20 167	23 258	33 138	41 432	39 483	36 909	29 484	30 933	35 543
Life assurance, etc. premiums paid by individuals[5]	GIUH	9 753	13 279	16 668	14 262	17 469	20 920	28 655	32 152	37 340	33 887	35 605
Community charge/council tax	ADBH	–	–	–	–	586	8 629	8 128	7 907	8 038	8 450	8 989
Other current transfers	GIUI	3 083	3 356	3 875	4 314	4 437	4 555	4 867	4 775	5 341	5 474	5 660
Total current expenditure	GIUJ	225 777	252 580	279 748	310 823	348 762	382 706	402 005	417 365	436 525	453 623	477 137
Balance	GIUK	3 775	−581	−5 246	−8 336	−8 769	−1 541	7 012	19 097	17 818	15 084	16 160
Total	GIUE	229 552	251 999	274 502	302 487	339 993	381 165	409 017	436 462	454 343	468 707	493 297

1 After deducting interest payments, depreciation and stock appreciation.
2 Including tax credits.
3 As in table 4.10 but excluding pensions paid to overseas residents.
4 As in table 4.7 but excluding imputed rent of owner-occupied dwellings and administrative costs of life assurance and pension schemes.
5 Whether as lump sum or regular payments.

4.10 Life assurance and pension schemes: income and expenditure

£ million

		1985	1986	1987	1988	1989	1990	1991	1992	1993	1994	1995
FUNDED SCHEMES (including life assurance):												
Contributions of employers[1]	GISQ	8 737	8 386	8 753	9 090	9 951	9 399	7 910	7 118	7 339	8 861	8 109
Contributions of employees[1]	GISR	3 588	3 941	4 804	5 479	6 111	6 735	7 302	7 660	7 410	6 743	6 568
Individual premiums for life policies:												
Regular[5]	GISS	6 898	8 531	10 677	10 383	11 888	13 654	17 930	19 015	22 575	20 256	21 185
Single[5]	GIST	3 520	5 357	6 538	4 381	5 986	7 614	11 035	13 407	14 979	13 812	14 570
Rent, dividends and interest receipts	GISU	14 982	16 841	18 774	23 575	28 501	30 788	30 449	32 476	33 955	35 304	43 652
Current grants from general government	GISV	80	79	82	91	96	93	110	121	133	148	160
less Pensions and other benefits paid	-GISW	−15 431	−18 364	−22 269	−23 337	−26 615	−30 734	−35 265	−41 273	−45 184	−46 095	−48 918
less Transfers to other pension schemes (net)[2]	-GISX	−196	−237	−124	57	11	31	87	149	194	151	38
less Administrative costs, etc.[3]	-CAOY	−4 356	−5 537	−6 310	−7 500	−8 621	−9 984	−10 895	−10 850	−11 907	−11 105	−11 523
Surplus (Net increase in amount available for investment)	AALV	17 822	18 997	20 925	22 219	27 308	27 596	28 663	27 823	29 494	28 075	33 841
NOTIONALLY FUNDED SCHEMES:												
Contributions of employers	GITA	1 865	2 017	2 135	2 364	2 198	2 264	2 587	2 900	2 944	3 161	3 384
Contributions of employees	GITB	942	1 046	1 108	1 261	1 376	1 442	1 586	1 763	1 816	1 603	1 756
Other income	GITC	–	–	–	–	–	–	–	–	–	–	–
less Pensions and other benefits paid	-GITD	−2 206	−2 354	−2 464	−2 436	−3 036	−3 497	−4 046	−4 741	−5 002	−4 821	−5 819
less Transfers to other pension schemes (net)[2]	-GITE	−48	−20	−140	−333	−149	−148	−167	−214	−250	−224	−138
Surplus	AACW	553	689	639	856	389	61	−40	−292	−492	−281	−817
UNFUNDED SCHEMES:												
Contributions of employers[4]	GITG	3 647	3 850	4 142	4 242	4 057	5 690	8 375	9 555	10 258	11 028	10 591
Contributions of employees	GITH	280	300	348	389	413	448	497	544	588	581	634
less Pensions and other benefits paid[4]	-GITI	−3 889	−4 121	−4 456	−4 588	−4 426	−6 083	−8 794	−10 015	−10 766	−11 536	−11 188
less Transfers to other pension schemes (net)	-GITJ	−38	−29	−34	−43	−44	−55	−78	−84	−80	−73	−37
ALL SCHEMES:												
Contributions of employers[1]	EAFH	14 249	14 253	15 030	15 696	16 206	17 353	18 872	19 573	20 541	23 050	22 084
Contributions of employees[1]	GGBB	4 810	5 287	6 260	7 129	7 900	8 625	9 385	9 967	9 814	8 927	8 958
Individual premiums for life policies[5]	GGBD	10 418	13 888	17 215	14 764	17 874	21 268	28 965	32 422	37 554	34 068	35 755
Rent, dividends and interest receipts	GISU	14 982	16 841	18 774	23 575	28 501	30 788	30 449	32 476	33 955	35 304	43 652
Current grants from general government	GISV	80	79	82	91	96	93	110	121	133	148	160
less Pensions and other benefits paid[4]	-GGBF	−21 526	−24 839	−29 189	−30 361	−34 077	−40 314	−48 105	−56 029	−60 952	−62 452	−65 925
less Transfers to the state pension scheme	-GTDS	−282	−286	−298	−319	−182	−172	−158	−149	−136	−146	−137
less Administrative costs, etc.[3]	-CAOY	−4 356	−5 537	−6 310	−7 500	−8 621	−9 984	−10 895	−10 850	−11 907	−11 105	−11 523
Surplus	AAPX	18 375	19 686	21 564	23 075	27 697	27 657	28 623	27 531	29 002	27 794	33 024

1 See methodological notes. Including DSS rebates (from 1988).
2 Including certain transactions between the Principal Civil Service
  Pension Scheme and certain funded schemes.
3 Including tax on the investment income of life funds.
4 Including employers' liability insurance claims and employers' payments
  (less rebates from the redundancy fund) to redundant employees. Also including statutory sick pay (from 1994).
5 Including premium relief from central government to life assurance funds
  amounting in total as follows (£ million):

	1985	1986	1987	1988	1989	1990	1991	1992	1993	1994	1995
-GITM	665	609	547	502	405	348	310	270	214	181	150

5.1 All companies: current and capital accounts[1]

£ million

		1985	1986	1987	1988	1989	1990	1991	1992	1993	1994	1995
CURRENT ACCOUNT												
Income												
Gross trading profits after deducting stock appreciation[2]	CICS	48 991	45 839	55 305	59 011	60 992	60 387	57 869	60 156	72 447	82 818	86 576
Stock appreciation	AIAC	2 155	1 500	4 148	5 366	6 203	5 316	1 586	1 700	2 373	3 650	4 451
Total[3]	CIAC	51 146	47 339	59 453	64 377	67 195	65 703	59 455	61 856	74 820	86 468	91 027
Rent	CAQH	2 676	3 026	3 583	4 289	5 114	6 034	7 148	8 630	9 510	9 560	9 730
Dividend and Interest Receipts[4]:												
Total	GJCN	75 436	72 080	75 101	86 399	115 798	131 569	124 364	111 305	107 059	113 450	132 381
of which: income from abroad (net of taxes paid abroad):	CIAL	14 813	15 023	17 471	21 358	26 530	28 147	24 701	27 649	32 383	39 346	44 030
Total income	CIDB	129 258	122 445	138 137	155 065	188 107	203 306	190 967	181 791	191 389	209 478	233 138
Allocation of income												
Dividend and interest payments[4,5,6]:												
Total	GJBZ	73 178	67 055	70 480	84 125	115 789	133 426	129 728	115 776	111 886	108 385	132 815
of which: profits due abroad (net of United Kingdom Tax)	GJBX	7 563	5 285	7 014	8 611	9 157	6 917	4 432	5 106	10 275	9 291	11 745
Current transfers:	DTDK	2 484	1 093	1 335	1 055	880	976	863	926	1 385	1 412	1 479
of which: Royalties and Licence fees on oil and gas production	CIHT	2 361	935	1 151	823	556	654	579	601	641	601	627
of which: Franchise Payments to the ITC[7]	CUKL	–	–	–	–	–	–	–	–	350	380	398
United Kingdom taxes on income[8,9]:												
Advance corporation tax	CICR	3 865	4 217	4 869	5 693	6 782	7 661	7 794	8 432	8 328	7 696	8 771
Other payments	CIHQ	12 543	9 747	10 774	12 105	14 910	13 398	9 527	6 758	6 623	10 291	14 399
Total UK taxes on income	CIDC	16 408	13 964	15 643	17 798	21 692	21 059	17 321	15 190	14 951	17 987	23 170
Balance: undistributed income after taxation[10]	CIDA	37 188	40 333	50 679	52 087	49 746	47 845	43 055	49 899	63 167	81 694	75 674
CAPITAL ACCOUNT												
Receipts												
Undistributed income after taxation[10]	CIDA	37 188	40 333	50 679	52 087	49 746	47 845	43 055	49 899	63 167	81 694	75 674
Capital transfers	FMCA	591	720	511	1 019	561	513	495	453	418	473	501
Total	FMCB	37 779	41 053	51 190	53 106	50 307	48 358	43 550	50 352	63 585	82 167	76 175
Expenditure												
Gross domestic fixed capital formation	FMCC	31 889	33 312	40 194	50 154	60 408	61 630	56 427	52 644	51 648	54 454	58 882
Increase in value of stocks and work in progress	FMCD	2 575	2 557	5 821	9 460	8 520	3 638	–3 101	–212	2 445	7 313	8 270
Taxes on capital	FMCE	486	978	784	907	1 265	1 004	728	350	283	297	387
Capital transfers	CISB	111	227	245	271	319	319	219	120	180	130	368
Balance: financial surplus or deficit	GIHV	2 718	3 979	4 146	–7 686	–20 205	–18 233	–10 723	–2 550	9 029	19 973	8 268
Total	FMCB	37 779	41 053	51 190	53 106	50 307	48 358	43 550	50 352	63 585	82 167	76 175

1 Inclusion of former public corporations as from their date of privatisation causes discontinuities in the figures. See methodological notes.
2 Including United Kingdom branches and subsidiaries of non-resident parent companies, as in Table A.
3 Before providing for depreciation and stock appreciation.
4 Receipts and payments of dividends and interest exclude flows within the companies sector.
5 After 6 April 1973 figures are net of advance corporation tax.
6 Excludes payments of interest on foreign currency borrowing from overseas residents by banks and other financial institutions. See note 5.
7 Independent Television Commission (ITC) franchise payments replaced the Independent Broadcasting Authority levy from 1993. See also table 7.2.
8 Total United Kingdom taxes on company incomes, including composite rate tax on interest payments made by companies, are as follows (£ million):

		1985	1986	1987	1988	1989	1990	1991	1992	1993	1994	1995
Payments	CIIM	19 381	19 816	19 878	21 740	27 097	28 185	24 857	21 741	19 294	21 673	27 085

9 Includes payments of UK taxes on profits due abroad. These taxes are estimated to be (£ million):

		1985	1986	1987	1988	1989	1990	1991	1992	1993	1994	1995
Payments	DKGN	7 060	4 426	4 041	4 143	5 453	6 087	4 142	3 541	3 617	3 922	5 268

10 Before providing for depreciation, stock appreciation and additions to dividends and tax reserves. Depreciation is:

		1985	1986	1987	1988	1989	1990	1991	1992	1993	1994	1995
	–GIUP	–21 490	–23 143	–25 411	–26 945	–29 762	–33 152	–35 805	–36 305	–38 378	–40 038	–43 072

Where such data can be compiled, quarterly data for series in this table are available on the ONS's Databank. This data can also be provided on paper by request. Some of these quarterly data are published regularly in the UK Economic Accounts in table A12.

5.2 Industrial & commercial companies:[1] current and capital accounts

£ million

		1985	1986	1987	1988	1989	1990	1991	1992	1993	1994	1995
CURRENT ACCOUNT												
Income												
Gross trading profits after deducting stock appreciation:												
UK continental shelf companies	CIDR	18 514	8 469	9 552	7 024	6 806	7 119	6 411	6 838	8 124	9 734	10 931
Other companies	CIDS	38 955	45 516	52 583	62 536	67 817	68 241	67 969	67 710	75 183	85 374	88 770
Stock appreciation	AIAC	2 155	1 500	4 148	5 366	6 203	5 316	1 586	1 700	2 373	3 650	4 451
Total gross trading profits[2]	AIAD	59 624	55 485	66 283	74 926	80 826	80 676	75 966	76 248	85 680	98 758	104 152
Rent	CICD	2 375	2 697	3 174	3 790	4 558	5 587	6 337	7 734	8 627	8 595	8 745
Dividend and Interest Receipts:												
Total	XAGB	15 233	15 101	18 741	23 351	33 236	34 519	31 107	29 151	28 410	34 505	42 070
of which: income from abroad[3]	AIAF	8 565	7 840	11 366	13 827	18 124	18 124	14 964	14 492	16 237	19 984	23 795
Total income	AIAA	77 232	73 283	88 198	102 067	118 620	120 782	113 410	113 133	122 717	141 858	154 967
Allocation of income												
Dividend and interest payments:												
Total	XAFZ	24 285	24 532	29 764	38 393	55 082	60 593	57 656	57 902	54 422	59 731	73 857
of which: Dividends	XATD	8 231	9 994	12 019	16 609	22 979	23 434	25 232	28 259	29 078	32 235	42 361
of which: Profits due abroad (net of United Kingdom tax)[4]	HDVF	6 403	4 443	6 891	7 777	8 635	7 712	5 452	4 826	5 903	8 077	9 199
Current transfers:	DTDH	2 463	1 063	1 292	1 004	816	911	827	855	1 288	1 313	1 383
of which: Royalties and licence fees on oil and gas production	CIHT	2 361	935	1 151	823	556	654	579	601	641	601	627
of which: ITC franchise payments[5]	CUKL	–	–	–	–	–	–	–	–	350	380	398
United Kingdom taxes on income:												
Advance corporation tax	CIIB	3 299	3 594	4 155	4 837	5 841	6 546	6 611	7 362	7 060	6 375	7 404
Other payments	CIIC	11 635	8 890	9 024	10 446	13 145	12 269	8 984	5 399	5 009	7 449	10 528
Total UK taxes on income	AIAL	14 934	12 484	13 179	15 283	18 986	18 815	15 595	12 761	12 069	13 824	17 932
Balance: undistributed income after taxation (saving)[6]	AAAQ	35 550	35 204	43 963	47 387	43 736	40 463	39 332	41 615	54 938	66 990	61 795
CAPITAL ACCOUNT												
Receipts												
Saving[6]	AAAQ	35 550	35 204	43 963	47 387	43 736	40 463	39 332	41 615	54 938	66 990	61 795
Capital transfers	AIBR	591	720	511	1 019	561	513	495	453	418	473	501
Total	FMCI	36 141	35 924	44 474	48 406	44 297	40 976	39 827	42 068	55 356	67 463	62 296
Expenditure												
Gross domestic fixed capital formation	AAAS	28 558	29 511	36 017	43 627	52 535	54 837	49 863	47 615	47 589	46 646	51 559
Increase in value of stocks and work in progress	AAAT	2 575	2 557	5 821	9 460	8 520	3 638	–3 101	–212	2 445	7 313	8 270
Taxes on capital	FMCL	368	782	664	767	1 113	968	692	314	239	261	351
Capital transfers	CISB	111	227	245	271	319	319	219	120	180	130	368
Balance: financial surplus or deficit	AABG	4 529	2 847	1 727	–5 719	–18 190	–18 786	–7 846	–5 769	4 903	13 113	1 748
Total	FMCI	36 141	35 924	44 474	48 406	44 297	40 976	39 827	42 068	55 356	67 463	62 296

1 Including property companies but not banks and other financial companies and institutions. See also footnote 1 to table 5.1.
2 Before providing for depreciation and stock appreciation.
3 Net of taxes paid abroad.
4 After deducting depreciation allowances but before providing for stock appreciation.
5 Independent Television Commission (ITC) franchise payments replaced the Independent Broadcasting Authority levy from 1993. See also table 7.2.
6 Before providing for depreciation, stock appreciation and additions to dividend and tax reserves. Depreciation is:

Where such data can be compiled, quarterly data for series in this table are available on the ONS's Databank. This data can also be provided on paper by request. Some of these quarterly data are published regularly in the UK Economic Accounts in table A13.

	1985	1986	1987	1988	1989	1990	1991	1992	1993	1994	1995
–EXAB	–20 019	–21 519	–23 601	–24 951	–27 614	–30 840	–33 204	–33 781	–35 850	–37 536	–40 451

Companies

5.3 Industrial and commercial companies: transactions in financial assets and liabilities[1]

£ million

		1985	1986	1987	1988	1989	1990	1991	1992	1993	1994	1995
FINANCIAL SURPLUS OR DEFICIT	AABG	4 529	2 847	1 727	−5 719	−18 190	−18 786	−7 846	−5 769	4 903	13 113	1 748
Transactions in financial liabilities (net)												
Net unremitted profits	−AIBP	−1 119	−2 552	−3 548	−5 633	−5 207	−6 323	−5 197	−4 411	−5 775	−7 514	−7 862
Accruals adjustment	−AANZ	−446	−102	135	−1 089	−179	71	779	−1 143	60	−224	653
Import and other credit received	−AIBS	390	191	409	1 516	1 130	1 688	655	188	957	3 571	592
Borrowing from banks	−AANA	7 454	8 514	12 096	32 018	33 746	20 032	−1 391	−1 941	−11 393	−4 804	13 971
Borrowing from other sources	−AIBV	2 508	1 391	3 928	6 506	10 031	8 651	5 088	−1 001	3 596	3 227	2 543
Market capital issues:												
Ordinary shares	−AQNV	3 407	5 483	13 410	4 352	1 882	4 384	12 795	7 400	13 948	11 435	11 370
Debentures and preference shares	−AQNW	1 586	2 440	3 304	4 018	5 606	3 849	4 463	2 457	5 291	7 592	11 718
Other capital issues	−AQNZ	1 281	997	1 715	1 846	6 063	7 016	5 364	6 175	7 421	3 740	8 200
Other overseas investment	−AICA	1 581	6 382	3 112	7 926	10 970	12 170	9 999	5 229	9 459	−740	5 179
Total transactions in financial liabilities (net)	CIIO	16 642	22 744	34 561	51 460	64 042	51 538	32 555	12 953	23 564	16 283	46 364
Transactions in financial assets (net)												
Investment in UK company securities	AICC	4 189	3 256	5 080	15 028	16 284	4 241	8 284	3 326	3 856	7 019	22 487
Direct investment in overseas securities	AANU	2 183	4 977	7 275	6 739	8 323	6 097	4 921	4 081	3 108	6 557	5 790
Other investment overseas	AICD	41	660	4 373	5 944	2 032	−4 650	405	593	2 939	−1 167	2 231
Export and other credit given	AICE	549	727	740	1 332	−52	1 894	−50	319	832	1 618	−1 512
Bank deposits, notes and coin	AICF	4 366	12 686	7 192	5 786	9 909	4 641	3 445	−1 754	5 694	7 032	5 633
Other liquid assets	CIIP	461	−316	−354	−1 080	1 868	3 549	2 113	−344	941	−5	−1 272
Other financial assets:												
UK	CIIQ	−25	148	374	930	−86	−315	−133	−694	1 113	82	256
Overseas	AICJ	2 395	2 442	3 691	2 153	4 839	8 975	1 788	−4 605	5 274	4 140	8 923
Total transactions in financial assets (net)	CIIR	14 159	24 580	28 371	36 832	43 117	24 432	20 773	922	23 757	25 276	42 536
TOTAL FINANCIAL TRANSACTIONS (NET)	AAOA	−2 483	1 836	−6 190	−14 628	−20 925	−27 106	−11 782	−12 031	193	8 993	−3 828
BALANCING ITEM	AAOB	7 012	1 011	7 917	8 909	2 735	8 320	3 936	6 262	4 710	4 120	5 576

1 Inclusion of former public corporations as from their date of privatisation causes discontinuities in the figures. See methodological notes.

5.4 Financial companies and institutions: current and capital accounts

£ million

		1985	1986	1987	1988	1989	1990	1991	1992	1993	1994	1995
CURRENT ACCOUNT												
Income												
Gross trading profits[1,2]	AIFB	−8 478	−8 146	−6 830	−10 549	−13 631	−14 973	−16 511	−14 392	−10 860	−12 290	−13 125
Rent	CIIG	301	329	409	499	556	447	811	896	883	965	985
Dividends and Interest Receipts:												
Total	CBTT	97 692	95 475	97 416	114 090	163 965	192 199	178 584	154 756	134 198	138 781	164 360
of which: income from abroad[3]	AIFF	6 248	7 183	6 105	7 531	8 406	10 023	9 737	13 157	16 146	19 362	20 235
Total income	AIFA	89 515	87 658	90 995	104 040	150 890	177 673	162 884	141 260	124 221	127 456	152 220
Allocation of income												
Dividends and interest payments:[4]												
Total	CBTF	86 382	81 019	81 772	96 774	142 110	167 982	157 399	130 476	113 013	108 490	133 007
of which: profits due abroad	AIFK	1 160	842	123	834	522	−795	−1 020	280	4 372	1 214	2 546
Current transfers	DTDJ	21	30	43	51	64	65	36	71	97	99	96
United Kingdom taxes on income:												
Advance corporation tax	CIIK	566	623	714	856	941	1 115	1 183	1 070	1 268	1 321	1 367
Other payments	CIIL	908	857	1 750	1 659	1 765	1 129	543	1 359	1 614	2 842	3 871
Total UK taxes on income	AIFL	1 474	1 480	2 464	2 515	2 706	2 244	1 726	2 429	2 882	4 163	5 238
Balance: undistributed income after taxation (saving)[5]	AAAM	1 638	5 129	6 716	4 700	6 010	7 382	3 723	8 284	8 229	14 704	13 879
CAPITAL ACCOUNT												
Receipts												
Saving[5]	AAAM	1 638	5 129	6 716	4 700	6 010	7 382	3 723	8 284	8 229	14 704	13 879
Capital transfers	FMCO	–	–	–	–	–	–	–	–	–	–	–
Total	FMCP	1 638	5 129	6 716	4 700	6 010	7 382	3 723	8 284	8 229	14 704	13 879
Expenditure												
Gross domestic fixed capital formation[6]	AAAO	3 331	3 801	4 177	6 527	7 873	6 793	6 564	5 029	4 059	7 808	7 323
Increase in book value of stocks and work in progress[7]	AAAP	–	–	–	–	–	–	–	–	–	–	–
Taxes on capital	FMCS	118	196	120	140	152	36	36	36	44	36	36
Balance: financial surplus or deficit	AABF	−1 811	1 132	2 419	−1 967	−2 015	553	−2 877	3 219	4 126	6 860	6 520
Total	FMCP	1 638	5 129	6 716	4 700	6 010	7 382	3 723	8 284	8 229	14 704	13 879

1 This represents the contribution of financial companies to the gross domestic product. It is the difference between bank charges, commissions, etc., on the one hand and management expenses on the other. It excludes net receipts of interest.

2 Before providing for depreciation. Stock appreciation is estimated to be zero.

3 Net of taxes paid abroad

4 Excludes dividends and debenture interest paid by UK subsidiaries to their overseas parents.

5 Before providing for depreciation, stock appreciation and additions to dividend and tax reserves. Depreciation is:

Where such data can be compiled, quarterly data for series in this table are available on the ONS's Databank. This data can also be provided on paper by request. Some of these quarterly data are published regularly in the UK Economic Accounts in table A14.

	1985	1986	1987	1988	1989	1990	1991	1992	1993	1994	1995
−EXAA	−1 471	−1 624	−1 810	−1 994	−2 148	−2 312	−2 601	−2 524	−2 528	−2 502	−2 621

6 Including expenditure by life assurance and pension funds.

7 *Equals* value of physical increase in stocks, since financial companies have no stock appreciation.

Companies

5.5 Financial companies and institutions: transactions in financial assets and liabilities

£ million

		1985	1986	1987	1988	1989	1990	1991	1992	1993	1994	1995
FINANCIAL SURPLUS OR DEFICIT	AABF	−1 811	1 132	2 419	−1 967	−2 015	553	−2 877	3 219	4 126	6 860	6 520
Transactions in financial liabilities (net)												
Deposits with UK banks	−CJKX	39 178	88 094	71 613	58 118	75 816	68 463	−13 843	26 662	35 715	61 341	58 750
Deposits with building societies	−CJKY	13 794	12 771	14 255	20 398	21 195	22 044	21 245	12 067	10 301	10 847	15 847
Unit trust and property unit trust units	−CJLA	1 066	2 180	3 793	−521	619	23	981	−287	5 614	5 945	4 073
Net inflow to life assurance and pension funds	AALV	17 822	18 997	20 925	22 219	27 308	27 596	28 663	27 823	29 494	28 075	33 841
Capital issues:												
Market issues	−AQOB	7 800	7 904	7 705	15 169	13 574	8 483	7 574	8 803	18 621	15 793	10 718
Other issues	−AQOC	296	386	900	2 182	97	1 317	1	320	687	2 093	3 319
Other financial liabilities:												
UK	−CJLD	30	507	−524	841	−731	−3 108	−796	−2 163	−1 651	432	−83
Overseas	−CJLE	1 908	357	2 298	1 406	23 436	7 809	13 656	30 637	85 480	−57 793	41 618
Accruals adjustment	−CJLN	3 305	1 100	1 118	1 545	5 809	5 008	3 870	3 224	1 463	3 100	2 246
Total transactions in financial liabilities (net)	CJLF	85 199	132 296	122 083	121 357	167 123	137 635	61 351	107 086	185 724	69 833	170 329
Transactions in financial assets (net)												
Investment in British government securities	CJLH	5 767	3 381	−1 732	−3 379	−13 231	−7 312	1 763	19 479	32 323	18 047	21 060
Investment in local authority longer-term debt	AQYU	−1 641	−1 858	−649	−192	−423	−183	72	1 073	1 745	668	−72
Other lending	CJLL	38 171	68 553	80 180	66 602	86 240	71 321	−33 598	19 970	−17 237	56 510	53 938
Loans secured on dwellings	CJLK	19 476	27 521	29 965	40 329	33 855	33 713	26 835	18 902	16 528	19 578	15 447
Investment in UK company securities	CJLG	10 250	15 144	18 800	11 193	15 885	15 959	24 158	8 501	27 279	20 071	10 864
Investment in overseas securities	CJLJ	17 122	23 020	−6 742	11 188	37 820	18 738	29 078	28 066	84 459	−17 972	40 354
Liquid assets	CJLM	−485	−516	789	770	2 191	2 822	−408	−3 513	−7 359	6 653	10 265
Other financial assets												
UK	CJLO	466	326	601	−1 575	−666	1 484	−436	1 687	−519	−3 117	−1 802
Overseas	CJLP	−416	15	3 284	824	5 608	3 210	7 128	22 593	56 059	−18 947	26 932
Total transactions in financial assets (net)	CJLQ	88 710	135 586	124 496	125 760	167 279	139 752	54 592	116 758	193 278	81 491	176 986
TOTAL FINANCIAL TRANSACTIONS (NET)	CJLR	3 511	3 290	2 413	4 403	156	2 117	−6 759	9 672	7 554	11 658	6 657
BALANCING ITEM	AATA	−5 322	−2 158	6	−6 370	−2 171	−1 564	3 882	−6 453	−3 428	−4 798	−137

CHAPTER 6: Public corporations

6.1 Public corporations: operating account[1]

£ million

		1985	1986	1987	1988	1989	1990	1991	1992	1993	1994	1995
REVENUE												
Sales:												
Revenue sales	GIRY	51 124	45 469	36 187	35 818	36 443	32 936	27 110	28 237	35 917	44 410	47 302
Sales to own capital account	GIRZ	1 458	1 537	1 228	1 107	1 363	1 099	557	698	681	268	196
Subsidies:												
Included in gross trading surplus	ADRZ	3 112	2 135	1 887	1 575	1 649	1 223	1 719	2 577	2 255	2 795	2 604
Included in rent	ADVA	297	300	304	305	290	284	266	221	208	201	205
Total	ADRE	3 409	2 435	2 191	1 880	1 939	1 507	1 985	2 798	2 463	2 996	2 809
Total	GISA	55 991	49 441	39 606	38 805	39 745	35 542	29 652	31 733	39 061	47 674	50 307
EXPENDITURE												
Wages, salaries, etc.	GISB	15 421	16 669	14 095	13 395	13 608	12 744	12 594	15 906	20 410	25 732	27 159
Purchases of goods and services	GISC	31 407	22 214	16 943	16 624	18 382	17 433	14 471	12 634	14 148	16 643	17 558
less Value of physical increase in stocks and work in progress	-DHHL	4	485	240	−24	−219	254	−58	−14	166	312	182
Taxes on expenditure:												
Rates	GISE	938	1 019	884	948	914	833	307	322	316	306	292
ECSC levies	GTBB	9	13	12	11	12	11	10	7	1	–	–
Other	GISG	536	477	8	8	7	8	8	9	8	8	7
Balance: gross trading surplus and rent before providing for depreciation but after deducting stock appreciation[2]	GISH	7 676	8 564	7 424	7 843	7 041	4 259	2 320	2 869	4 012	4 673	5 109
Total	GISA	55 991	49 441	39 606	38 805	39 745	35 542	29 652	31 733	39 061	47 674	50 307

1 The comparability of data over time is affected by the privatisation, since 1979, of several public corporations. Further details are in the methodological notes.
2 Gross trading surplus and rent after providing for depreciation and stock appreciation is as follows (£ million):

		1985	1986	1987	1988	1989	1990	1991	1992	1993	1994	1995
	GIUM	1 376	2 083	1 752	2 023	1 291	−908	−1 597	−789	379	987	1 168

6.2 Public corporations: current account[1]

£ million

		1985	1986	1987	1988	1989	1990	1991	1992	1993	1994	1995
INCOME												
Gross trading surplus:												
After deducting stock appreciation	ADRB	7 154	8 050	6 905	7 295	6 473	3 681	1 779	2 322	3 490	4 222	4 603
Stock appreciation	ADRC	108	163	88	259	55	120	30	39	−36	8	31
Total[2]	ADRD	7 262	8 213	6 993	7 554	6 528	3 801	1 809	2 361	3 454	4 230	4 634
Rent	GISI	522	514	519	548	568	578	541	547	522	451	506
Dividend and interest receipts:												
Total	XARB	507	452	313	414	640	624	413	419	368	429	542
of which:income from abroad(net of taxes paid abroad)	HGEN	50	48	56	62	68	68	72	94	91	92	92
Total	ADRA	8 291	9 179	7 825	8 516	7 736	5 003	2 763	3 327	4 344	5 110	5 682
ALLOCATION OF INCOME												
Dividend and interest payments:												
Total	XAQZ	2 964	2 893	2 774	2 598	2 635	1 946	1 286	1 234	1 413	2 123	2 370
of which: To central government	ACGJ	2 046	2 020	2 049	2 017	2 191	1 664	1 048	1 034	1 244	1 947	2 184
of which: To local authorities	GIUL	103	80	53	37	32	26	26	30	33	41	40
Royalties and licence fees on oil and gas production	GISK	5	6	–	–	–	–	–	–	–	–	–
United Kingdom taxes on income	ADRK	103	313	62	103	102	161	451	199	162	140	210
Balance: undistributed income[2]	AAAI	5 219	5 967	4 989	5 815	4 999	2 896	1 026	1 894	2 769	2 847	3 102

1 See footnote 1 to table 6.1.
2 Before providing for depreciation and stock appreciation.

Where such data can be compiled, quarterly data for series in this table are available on the ONS's Databank. This data can also be provided on paper by request. Some of these quarterly data are published regularly in the UK Economic Accounts in table A15.

Public corporations

6.3 Public corporations: capital account[1]

£ million

		1985	1986	1987	1988	1989	1990	1991	1992	1993	1994	1995
CAPITAL RECEIPTS												
Undistributed income before providing for depreciation and stock appreciation	AAAI	5 219	5 967	4 989	5 815	4 999	2 896	1 026	1 894	2 769	2 847	3 102
Capital transfers:												
From central government	ACIJ	529	463	613	706	1 200	6 545	3 576	3 251	3 106	3 196	3 183
From local authorities	ADCF	66	22	56	29	16	16	20	41	60	57	67
From private sector	ADSE	189	180	172	218	237	266	123	43	107	8	6
Total[2]	ADSA	6 003	6 632	5 830	6 768	6 452	9 723	4 745	5 229	6 042	6 108	6 358
CAPITAL EXPENDITURE												
Gross domestic fixed capital formation:												
Mining and quarrying	EGAV	959	681	518	454	325	332	256	174	133	68	−45
Manufacturing (revised definition)	EGAW	294	311	406	426	39	40	35	384	406	336	343
Electricity, gas and water supply	EGAX	2 544	2 583	1 931	2 046	2 799	2 485	1 068	704	490	350	231
Transport, storage and communication	GISN	1 278	1 064	832	854	1 205	1 698	1 980	2 502	2 613	2 291	2 157
Financial intermediation, real estate and business activities	EGAY	134	130	224	243	360	356	403	399	268	258	267
Dwellings	DEER	280	242	253	246	256	247	211	219	236	245	243
Other[3]	GISP	442	510	397	311	483	−203	−174	345	749	1 367	1 858
Total	AAAK	5 931	5 521	4 561	4 580	5 467	4 955	3 779	4 727	4 895	4 915	5 054
Increase in book value of stocks and work in progress	AAAL	104	−322	−152	283	274	−134	88	53	−202	−304	−151
Taxes on capital	ADSB	3	61	−	−	−	−	−	−	−	−	−
Other capital transfers	ADSG	147	148	127	148	223	389	530	479	461	472	468
Total capital expenditure	ADSF	6 185	5 408	4 536	5 011	5 964	5 210	4 397	5 259	5 154	5 083	5 371
Balance: financial surplus or deficit	AABD	−182	1 224	1 294	1 757	488	4 513	348	−30	888	1 025	987
Total	ADSA	6 003	6 632	5 830	6 768	6 452	9 723	4 745	5 229	6 042	6 108	6 358

1 See footnote 1 to table 6.1.
2 Excluding notional transactions on central government debt written-off.
   See footnote 5 to table 6.4.
3 Includes National Health Service Trusts

6.4 Public corporations: transactions in financial assets and liabilities[1]

£ million

		1985	1986	1987	1988	1989	1990	1991	1992	1993	1994	1995
FINANCIAL SURPLUS OR DEFICIT	AABD	−182	1 224	1 294	1 757	488	4 513	348	−30	888	1 025	987
Transactions in financial liabilities (net)												
Accruals adjustment - taxes, etc., payable to central government[2]	-ADTB	45	−18	37	−21	88	66	−20	−54	71	28	30
Borrowing requirement:												
Loans from central government (net)	ACKD	−230	−77	−626	659	1 900	−4 305	−113	1 301	1 044	608	710
Public dividend capital, etc.	ADUK	836	157	144	147	45	5	1	1	−	−	−
Redemption of govt. guaranteed stock[3]	ACMN	−	−	−	−	−	−10	−	−	−	−	−
Other identified borrowing (net)[3]	CHAH	−468	−271	−259	−1 096	−2 655	−95	38	−508	−69	−146	−190
Transactions in short-term assets[3]	-ADUE	−189	−1 230	−222	−961	222	−129	−654	−389	−471	−144	−519
Transactions in other public sector debt (net sales)[3]	-CHAJ	−327	569	−197	−631	250	−424	−86	−1	−1 370	−1 248	−1 115
Total borrowing requirement:	ABEM	−378	−852	−1 160	−1 882	−238	−4 958	−814	404	−866	−930	−1 114
Trade creditors	CHAL	268	641	382	824	−281	1 237	−179	37	750	1 281	−1 149
Other liabilities (net)	CHAM	−86	−311	−207	−70	−111	−10	−1	−3	−4	8	−14
Total transactions in financial liabilities[5]	-ADTA	−151	−540	−948	−1 149	−542	−3 665	−1 014	384	−49	387	−2 247
Transactions in financial assets (net)												
Accruals adjustment - subsidies and local authority rates	ADTF	−38	240	233	219	439	480	180	483	−179	−141	188
Net lending to private sector	ADTG	14	62	−3	−9	267	−315	1	−8	−27	−39	−15
Net lending and investment abroad	RCZY	64	34	6	49	62	51	42	77	77	59	146
Transactions in company securities, etc. (net)	RHQP	−21	−54	−144	−87	−9	−110	−20	−10	−17	−81	−261
Trade debtors	ADTK	325	−30	339	476	361	997	52	−193	154	1 395	−433
Other assets	ADTL	27	99	13	−12	−27	−36	−1	25	2	7	2
Total transactions in financial assets	ADTE	371	351	444	636	1 093	1 067	254	374	10	1 200	−373
NET TOTAL FINANCIAL TRANSACTIONS[4]	AAFX	522	891	1 392	1 785	1 635	4 732	1 268	−10	59	813	1 874
BALANCING ITEM	AAFY	−704	333	−98	−28	−1 147	−219	−920	−20	829	212	−887

1 See footnote 1 to table 6.1.
2 Value added tax and national insurance, etc. contributions.
3 These four items comprise the public corporations' contribution to the public
   sector borrowing requirement (see table 11.13).
4 Total assets *less* total liabilities.
5 Excluding notional transactions on central government debt written off - for details see methodological notes. The amounts are as follows (£ million)

		1985	1986	1987	1988	1989	1990	1991	1992	1993	1994	1995
	CHAV	−	1 624	−	3 980	5 028	1 734	418	−	−	−	1 598

CHAPTER 7: Central government

7.1 Central government: summary account

£ million

		1985	1986	1987	1988	1989	1990	1991	1992	1993	1994	1995
CURRENT RECEIPTS												
Taxes on income	ACGB	51 598	51 973	55 658	61 723	70 000	76 875	75 178	73 716	73 232	80 670	90 672
Taxes on expenditure[1]	ACGC	43 029	47 621	52 194	57 313	60 067	73 169	85 295	87 388	90 194	95 990	103 444
Social security contributions[2]	AIIH	24 210	26 165	27 663	30 682	33 333	34 457	36 216	36 975	39 499	41 943	44 251
Gross trading surplus[3]	ACGG	−175	−279	−485	−459	−323	−545	−443	−186	−247	23	248
Rent, dividends and interest, etc.	CTCC	10 642	9 264	10 008	10 138	10 643	10 575	10 221	9 819	9 338	9 548	9 457
Miscellaneous current transfers	ACGX	229	266	363	394	431	504	545	419	623	704	719
Imputed charge for consumption of non-trading capital	ACGL	983	1 076	1 179	1 303	1 484	1 623	1 675	1 608	1 867	1 978	2 150
Total	ACGA	130 516	136 086	146 580	161 094	175 635	196 658	208 687	209 739	214 506	230 856	250 941
CURRENT EXPENDITURE												
Final consumption	ACHC	47 341	50 331	53 736	57 522	63 294	70 108	76 985	82 259	89 398	93 601	96 663
Subsidies	ACHG	5 939	5 139	5 315	5 007	4 774	5 401	5 410	6 133	6 599	6 375	6 256
Current grants to personal sector	GTAC	41 270	45 066	46 189	47 308	48 675	53 005	61 410	70 126	76 478	79 455	83 016
Current grants to local authorities[4]	ACHJ	20 438	21 813	23 277	23 452	24 200	38 273	47 578	53 091	54 632	56 233	57 071
Current grants paid abroad (net)	−HDKH	3 427	2 233	3 277	3 248	4 278	4 596	1 083	4 834	4 969	5 135	7 180
Debt interest	ACHL	15 724	15 954	17 089	17 371	18 038	17 921	16 337	16 629	18 080	21 706	25 363
Total current expenditure	ACHB	134 139	140 536	148 883	153 908	163 259	189 304	208 803	233 072	250 156	262 505	275 549
Balance: current surplus[3]	AAAA	−3 623	−4 450	−2 303	7 186	12 376	7 354	−116	−23 333	−35 650	−31 649	−24 608
Total	ACGA	130 516	136 086	146 580	161 094	175 635	196 658	208 687	209 739	214 506	230 856	250 941
CAPITAL RECEIPTS												
Current surplus[3]	AAAA	−3 623	−4 450	−2 303	7 186	12 376	7 354	−116	−23 333	−35 650	−31 649	−24 608
Taxes on capital and other capital receipts	GTAD	2 320	2 998	3 078	4 173	4 464	4 211	3 351	2 650	2 347	2 556	2 686
Total	ACIA	−1 303	−1 452	775	11 359	16 840	11 565	3 235	−20 683	−33 303	−29 093	−21 922
CAPITAL EXPENDITURE												
Gross domestic fixed capital formation	AAAC	3 126	3 351	3 358	3 709	4 951	6 415	6 876	6 855	6 391	5 946	5 642
Value of physical increase in stocks	AAAD	450	−237	−498	−322	−163	156	151	−17	−24	−251	−154
Grants and transfers to other sectors[5]	ACIG	3 298	3 342	3 436	3 993	5 503	11 094	9 289	14 362	10 494	9 560	9 068
Total capital expenditure	ACID	6 874	6 456	6 296	7 380	10 291	17 665	16 316	21 200	16 861	15 255	14 556
Balance: financial surplus or deficit	AABA	−8 177	−7 908	−5 521	3 979	6 549	−6 100	−13 081	−41 883	−50 164	−44 348	−36 478
Total	ACIA	−1 303	−1 452	775	11 359	16 840	11 565	3 235	−20 683	−33 303	−29 093	−21 922
FINANCIAL ACCOUNT												
Transactions in financial liabilities	ACJR	12 798	8 889	5 733	−3 388	−3 146	−2 506	8 077	28 794	47 549	40 273	40 073
Transactions in financial assets	ACJU	4 858	1 086	177	11	3 270	−8 217	−5 325	−12 363	−2 495	−4 300	3 037
Net total financial transactions[6]	AADA	−7 940	−7 803	−5 556	3 399	6 416	−5 711	−13 402	−41 157	−50 044	−44 573	−37 036
BALANCING ITEM	AADB	−237	−105	35	580	133	−389	321	−726	−120	225	558

1 Includes national non-domestic rates from April 1990.
2 See Table 7.2 for composition.
3 Before providing for depreciation.
4 Includes national non-domestic rates distribution from April 1990.
5 Excluding financial transactions on writing-off debt of public corporations.
6 Total assets *less* total liabilities.

Where such data can be compiled, quarterly data for series in this table are available on the ONS's Databank. This data can also be provided on paper by request. Some of these quarterly data are published regularly in the UK Economic Accounts in table A16.

7.2 Central government: current account

£ million

		1985	1986	1987	1988	1989	1990	1991	1992	1993	1994	1995
RECEIPTS												
Taxes on income:												
Income tax	GTAE	35 200	37 385	39 956	43 580	47 621	54 663	56 428	57 766	57 795	62 452	67 448
Surtax	GTAF	–	–	–	–	–	–	–	–	–	–	–
Petroleum revenue tax	GTAH	7 369	2 698	1 754	1 505	1 003	942	−105	7	380	822	820
Supplementary petroleum duty	GTAI	–	–	–	–	–	–	–	–	–	–	–
Corporation tax	GTAJ	9 015	11 827	13 865	16 548	21 273	21 136	18 742	15 871	15 057	17 396	22 404
less Overspill relief	GTAK	–	–	–	–	–	–	–	–	–	–	–
Independent Broadcasting Authority levy[6]	GTAL	14	63	83	90	103	134	113	72	–	–	–
Total taxes on income	ACGB	51 598	51 973	55 658	61 723	70 000	76 875	75 178	73 716	73 232	80 670	90 672
Taxes on expenditure:												
Customs and excise revenue:												
Beer	GTAM	1 943	1 980	1 964	2 085	2 094	2 220	2 299	2 394	2 497	2 560	2 585
Wines, cider, perry and spirits	GTAN	2 230	2 262	2 282	2 426	2 403	2 627	2 676	2 759	2 914	3 074	2 891
Tobacco	GTAO	4 378	4 640	5 075	5 020	4 991	5 541	6 121	6 055	6 359	6 839	7 402
Hydrocarbon oils[1]	GTAP	6 292	7 133	7 565	8 426	8 556	9 335	10 480	11 156	12 355	13 869	15 070
Customs/protective duties	GTAQ	1 269	1 286	1 461	1 643	1 795	1 710	1 724	1 765	2 008	1 981	2 308
EC agricultural levies	GTAR	155	224	202	172	134	127	182	178	164	153	150
Value added tax	GTAS	20 679	23 162	25 713	29 245	31 656	33 457	39 247	41 471	42 627	45 931	48 413
Car tax	GTAT	863	961	1 128	1 418	1 519	1 464	1 240	603	−4	–	–
Betting, gaming and lottery	CJQY	728	763	825	893	956	1 022	1 009	1 056	1 094	1 151	1 595
Air passenger duty	CWAA	–	–	–	–	–	–	–	–	–	33	351
Insurance premium tax	CWAD	–	–	–	–	–	–	–	–	–	116	635
Other	ACDN	24	23	22	23	22	17	9	12	–	–	–
Total customs and excise revenue	GTAW	38 561	42 434	46 237	51 351	54 126	57 520	64 987	67 449	70 014	75 707	81 400
Motor vehicle duties[2]	GTAX	2 388	2 519	2 603	2 758	2 915	2 971	2 972	3 113	3 482	3 848	3 954
National insurance surcharge	GTAY	42	–	–	–	–	–	–	–	–	–	–
Fossil fuel levy	CIQY	–	–	–	–	–	875	1 336	1 344	1 331	1 355	1 317
Gas levy	GTAZ	525	515	502	407	335	291	282	288	240	153	161
Sugar levy	GTBA	49	62	80	59	59	46	48	47	56	98	55
European coal and steel community levy	GTBB	9	13	12	11	12	11	10	7	1	–	–
Stamp duties	GTBC	1 159	1 700	2 355	2 344	2 127	1 755	1 789	1 224	1 635	1 831	1 924
National non-domestic rates	CUKY	–	–	–	–	–	9 226	13 570	13 639	13 092	12 556	12 994
Northern Ireland rates	GTBD	127	158	159	173	207	228	121	115	183	198	204
LRT levy	GTBE	159	201	170	129	175	47	–	–	–	–	–
Miscellaneous	GTBF	10	19	76	81	111	199	180	162	160	148	174
Camelot: payments to National Lottery Distribution Fund	CLCJ	..	–	–	–	–	–	–	–	–	96	1 261
Total taxes on expenditure	ACGC	43 029	47 621	52 194	57 313	60 067	73 169	85 295	87 388	90 194	95 990	103 444
Social security contributions:												
National insurance	ACGD	21 548	23 221	24 575	27 188	29 194	30 169	31 703	32 363	34 763	37 079	39 139
National health	ACGE	2 032	2 244	2 741	3 435	4 139	4 288	4 513	4 612	4 736	4 864	5 112
Redundancy Fund, etc.	ACGF	630	700	347	59	–	–	–	–	–	–	–
Total social security contributions[3]	AIIH	24 210	26 165	27 663	30 682	33 333	34 457	36 216	36 975	39 499	41 943	44 251
Gross trading surplus[4]	ACGG	−175	−279	−485	−459	−323	−545	−443	−186	−247	23	248
Rent, dividends and interest, etc:												
Rent	GTBG	101	104	174	152	108	142	178	135	183	189	194
Royalties	CTAI	2 240	925	1 127	799	522	625	543	568	600	553	574
Licence fees on oil and gas production	CTAG	126	16	24	24	34	29	36	33	41	48	53
ITC franchise payments[6]	CUKL	–	–	–	–	–	–	–	–	350	380	398
Dividends and interest, etc.:												
From local authorities	ACGI	2 678	3 192	3 683	3 956	4 418	4 628	4 656	4 497	3 988	3 812	3 681
From public corporations	ACGJ	2 046	2 020	2 049	2 017	2 191	1 664	1 048	1 034	1 244	1 947	2 184
Other	ACGK	3 451	3 007	2 951	3 190	3 370	3 487	3 760	3 552	2 932	2 619	2 373
Total rent, dividends and interest, etc	CTCC	10 642	9 264	10 008	10 138	10 643	10 575	10 221	9 819	9 338	9 548	9 457
Miscellaneous current transfers[5]	ACGX	229	266	363	394	431	504	545	419	623	704	719
Imputed charge for consumption of non-trading capital	ACGL	983	1 076	1 179	1 303	1 484	1 623	1 675	1 608	1 867	1 978	2 150
Total receipts	ACGA	130 516	136 086	146 580	161 094	175 635	196 658	208 687	209 739	214 506	230 856	250 941

1 After deducting export rebates, shipbuilders' relief and bus fuel rebates.
2 Excluding driving licences and after deducting shipbuilders' relief.
3 For an alternative breakdown see table 7.6.
4 Before providing for depreciation.
5 For details see methodological notes.
6 With effect from 1993 the IBA levy has been replaced by the series ITC franchise payments.

7.2 Central government: current account

continued

£ million

		1985	1986	1987	1988	1989	1990	1991	1992	1993	1994	1995
EXPENDITURE												
Final consumption:												
Current expenditure on goods and services[1]	GTBW	46 358	49 255	52 557	56 219	61 810	68 485	75 310	80 651	87 531	91 623	94 513
Non-trading capital consumption	ACGL	983	1 076	1 179	1 303	1 484	1 623	1 675	1 608	1 867	1 978	2 150
Total final consumption	ACHC	47 341	50 331	53 736	57 522	63 294	70 108	76 985	82 259	89 398	93 601	96 663
Subsidies[1]	ACHG	5 939	5 139	5 315	5 007	4 774	5 401	5 410	6 133	6 599	6 375	6 256
Current grants to personal sector:[1]												
Social security benefits:												
Social security funds[2,3]	GTKP	23 085	25 383	25 878	26 698	28 216	30 704	34 706	37 592	39 655	40 502	41 243
War pensions and allowances[2]	CSDD	557	572	552	570	623	677	795	947	940	1 023	1 195
Family benefits	CSDB	4 928	4 996	5 099	5 268	5 361	5 487	6 032	7 035	7 619	7 994	8 302
Supplementary benefits/Income support	CSDE	7 667	8 230	8 316	8 016	8 156	8 907	11 155	15 022	16 676	16 511	16 623
Other social security benefits	CSDC	1 372	1 679	2 116	2 504	2 609	3 123	4 693	5 306	6 741	8 270	9 823
Total social security benefits	AUAA	37 609	40 860	41 961	43 056	44 965	48 898	57 381	65 902	71 631	74 300	77 186
Other	AUAB	3 661	4 206	4 228	4 252	3 710	4 107	4 029	4 224	4 847	5 155	5 830
Total current grants to personal sector	GTAC	41 270	45 066	46 189	47 308	48 675	53 005	61 410	70 126	76 478	79 455	83 016
Current grants to local authorities[1]	ACHJ	20 438	21 813	23 277	23 452	24 200	38 273	47 578	53 091	54 632	56 233	57 071
Current grants paid abroad:[1]												
Transactions with the European Community:												
Payments to the European Community	HDLN	3 789	2 812	4 066	3 555	4 443	4 669	3 318	4 863	5 445	5 469	7 690
less Receipts	-HDIS	-1 760	-2 138	-2 282	-2 115	-2 143	-2 194	-2 789	-2 879	-3 325	-3 296	-3 697
Net	-CGII	2 029	674	1 784	1 440	2 300	2 475	529	1 984	2 120	2 173	3 993
Social security benefits paid abroad	HBVJ	349	390	426	461	538	605	712	647	794	874	924
Gulf contributions [4]	-HHQG	–	–	–	–	–	-38	-2 110	-9	–	–	–
Other	CXCW	1 049	1 169	1 067	1 347	1 440	1 554	1 952	2 212	2 055	2 088	2 263
Total current grants paid abroad	-HDKH	3 427	2 233	3 277	3 248	4 278	4 596	1 083	4 834	4 969	5 135	7 180
Debt interest												
To local authorities	CTAD	20	19	21	10	16	18	12	15	18	22	22
To public corporations	CTAE	238	182	78	110	285	242	188	148	142	176	269
To private sector and overseas	CTDA	15 466	15 753	16 990	17 251	17 737	17 661	16 137	16 466	17 920	21 508	25 072
Total	ACHL	15 724	15 954	17 089	17 371	18 038	17 921	16 337	16 629	18 080	21 706	25 363
Total current expenditure	ACHB	134 139	140 536	148 883	153 908	163 259	189 304	208 803	233 072	250 156	262 505	275 549
Balance: current surplus before providing for depreciation	AAAA	-3 623	-4 450	-2 303	7 186	12 376	7 354	-116	-23 333	-35 650	-31 649	-24 608
Total	ACGA	130 516	136 086	146 580	161 094	175 635	196 658	208 687	209 739	214 506	230 856	250 941

1 For a functional analysis see Table 7.5.
2 Excluding payments to non-residents which are shown separately in this table.
3 For a comprehensive breakdown see Table 7.6.
4 Contributions by other countries towards the UK's cost of the Gulf conflict.

7.3 Central government: capital account

£ million

		1985	1986	1987	1988	1989	1990	1991	1992	1993	1994	1995
RECEIPTS												
Current surplus before providing for depreciation	AAAA	−3 623	−4 450	−2 303	7 186	12 376	7 354	−116	−23 333	−35 650	−31 649	−24 608
Taxes on capital[1]	ACIC	2 297	2 976	3 078	4 153	4 440	4 211	3 351	2 650	2 347	2 556	2 686
Other capital receipts	ACIE	23	22	–	20	24	–	–	–	–	–	–
Total	ACIA	−1 303	−1 452	775	11 359	16 840	11 565	3 235	−20 683	−33 303	−29 093	−21 922
EXPENDITURE[2]												
Gross domestic fixed capital formation[3]	AAAC	3 126	3 351	3 358	3 709	4 951	6 415	6 876	6 855	6 391	5 946	5 642
Increase in value of stocks:												
Trading bodies, etc.[4]	DHHN	443	−237	−498	−322	−163	156	151	−17	−24	−251	−154
Emergency and strategic stocks	DHHO	7	–	–	–	–	–	–	–	–	–	–
Total increase in stocks	AAAD	450	−237	−498	−322	−163	156	151	−17	−24	−251	−154
Capital transfers:												
To private sector:												
Universities, colleges, etc.	GTDH	133	146	165	141	261	312	366	308	355	231	391
Housing associations	GTDI	926	780	753	703	1 058	1 469	1 870	1 761	2 502	1 563	1 200
Other personal sector	GTDJ	382	310	404	398	292	457	561	677	964	1 168	1 074
Company sector	GTDK	578	706	499	1 008	548	501	483	444	413	472	500
Total to private sector	ACIH	2 019	1 942	1 821	2 250	2 159	2 739	3 280	3 190	4 234	3 434	3 165
To local authorities	ACII	750	937	1 002	1 037	2 144	1 810	2 433	7 921	3 154	2 930	2 720
To public corporations	ACIJ	529	463	613	706	1 200	6 545	3 576	3 251	3 106	3 196	3 183
Total capital transfers	ACIG	3 298	3 342	3 436	3 993	5 503	11 094	9 289	14 362	10 494	9 560	9 068
Total capital expenditure	ACID	6 874	6 456	6 296	7 380	10 291	17 665	16 316	21 200	16 861	15 255	14 556
Balance: financial surplus or deficit	AABA	−8 177	−7 908	−5 521	3 979	6 549	−6 100	−13 081	−41 883	−50 164	−44 348	−36 478
Total	ACIA	−1 303	−1 452	775	11 359	16 840	11 565	3 235	−20 683	−33 303	−29 093	−21 922

1 For details see table 9.6.
2 For a functional analysis of all expenditure items see Table 7.5.
3 Net of the following sales (£million):

		1985	1986	1987	1988	1989	1990	1991	1992	1993	1994	1995
	GTDL	233	337	463	575	655	530	456	368	424	437	417

4 Includes the Intervention Board for Agricultural Produce.

7.4 Central government: transactions in financial assets and liabilities

£ million

		1985	1986	1987	1988	1989	1990	1991	1992	1993	1994	1995
FINANCIAL SURPLUS OR DEFICIT	AABA	−8 177	−7 908	−5 521	3 979	6 549	−6 100	−13 081	−41 883	−50 164	−44 348	−36 478
TRANSACTIONS IN FINANCIAL LIABILITIES (NET)												
Accruals adjustments:												
Current expenditure on goods and services	ACJC	−5	−	−9	−5	−9	238	426	−218	830	777	625
Subsidies	ACJD	−138	−124	188	238	43	−9	−502	−88	−283	−488	22
Current grants to personal sector	ACJE	3	−7	13	−15	−2	−2	−	−461	461	−	−
Debt interest	ACLE	715	376	613	291	1 288	1 501	1 235	767	406	763	1 347
Increase in value of stocks	ACLJ	−174	−341	−198	74	114	190	29	−48	−37	−218	−134
Total accruals adjustments	ACJB	401	−96	607	583	1 434	1 918	1 188	−48	1 377	834	1 860
Transactions concerning certain public sector pension schemes (net)	AACW	553	689	639	856	389	61	−40	−292	−492	−281	−817
Borrowing for finance leasing	CULP	8	9	11	12	25	36	−1	−12	−9	4	−6
Other identified financial liabilities (net)	ACJS	32	−123	404	118	140	121	−775	−94	907	1 299	374
Borrowing requirement:												
Liabilities[1]												
Notes and coin in circulation	-AACB	429	674	1 089	1 476	1 245	78	207	1 397	1 330	1 370	1 578
Market transactions:												
Sterling treasury bills	-AACC	68	253	2 186	1 335	2 936	2 149	−1 675	−4 423	−1 250	2 209	11 841
Government securities[2]	-AACD	9 555	6 876	4 609	−5 032	−18 327	−7 330	9 178	21 373	51 853	22 614	20 590
Non-marketable debt:												
National savings	-AACE	2 556	2 462	2 550	1 528	−1 547	801	2 229	5 065	2 897	4 610	3 237
Certificates of tax deposit	CTIZ	556	124	−577	−997	150	293	−24	−448	−91	−535	−385
British Gas Corporation deposits	-CTJA	−	−300	−	−	−	−	−	−	−	−	−
Temporary deposit facility	-CTJB	86	−121	204	449	−99	194	236	64	1 125	307	1 240
Ways and means advances	CTJC	−36	−48	−	−	−	−	−	−	−	−	−
Fund for the Bank for Savings repayments	CTJD	−319	−107	−	−	−	−	−	−	−	−	−
Trading fund balances with Paymaster General	CTJE	−28	−13	11	1	2	19	−30	51	98	325	−162
Net indebtedness to Bank of England Banking Department	-RRBT	122	−28	281	138	370	353	−131	−206	−6 719	4 463	−866
Northern Ireland central government debt	-AACH	−21	−13	−6	−6	−13	−3	1	−34	−10	−7	−7
Cost of exchange cover scheme on repayment of principal	-AACI	−242	−186	−147	188	87	−33	−34	−28	−46	−24	−35
British Government foreign currency bonds	HGBA	−	−	−11	−	−	−	−	−	−	−	−
Other government overseas financing	-AACM	−87	−86	−69	−73	−83	−73	−74	−99	−95	−95	−97
HMG Total $ floating rate note issues	-CTJK	1 762	2 762	−	−1 477	−	−10	1 887	5 567	1 565	1 904	59
Miscellaneous direct official borrowing from overseas	CTJL	−1	−	−	−	−	−	−	−	−	−	−
Net drawings from less repayments to IMF	AION	−	−	−	−	−	−	−	−	−	−	−
Foreign currency borrowing[3]	CTJQ	−40	−70	−152	1 026	1 256	142	−181	4 231	−2 978	−3 432	−9
Assets[1]												
Net change in official reserves	AIPA	−1 758	−2 891	−12 012	−2 761	5 440	−76	−2 679	1 407	−698	−1 045	200
Redemption of government guaranteed stock	-ACMN	−	−	−	−	−	10	−	−	−	−	−
Transactions in Building Societies deposits	-CBQM	−	−	−	−	−	−	−	−	−	−14	30
Issue Department and National Insurance Fund transactions in:												
Commercial bills and ECGD backed promissory notes	-AACK	−1 129	−522	5 735	−435	3 598	−705	−1 751	−4 517	−1 534	6 200	2 092
Public corporations debt	-ACMY	−18	−127	−38	90	147	−7	3	−	−8	2	−
Local authority, etc. debt	-ACMV	148	74	341	−31	−12	21	161	118	97	−64	−285
Deposits with banks	-AADM	201	−303	78	−376	−284	−465	382	−278	230	−371	−359
Total borrowing requirement	ABEA	11 804	8 410	4 072	−4 957	−5 134	−4 642	7 705	29 240	45 766	38 417	38 662
Total transactions in financial liabilities	ACJR	12 798	8 889	5 733	−3 388	−3 146	−2 506	8 077	28 794	47 549	40 273	40 073

1 **Assets**: increase negative/decrease positive.
  Liabilities: increase positive/decrease negative.
2 Including government guaranteed securities.
3 Including Northern Ireland central government borrowing from the European Investment Bank.

7.4 Central government: transactions in financial assets and liabilities

continued

£ million

		1985	1986	1987	1988	1989	1990	1991	1992	1993	1994	1995
TRANSACTIONS IN FINANCIAL ASSETS (NET)												
Accruals adjustments:												
Income tax	ACJW	1 288	−1 708	36	452	1 225	958	−947	234	473	610	611
Customs duties												
Value added tax	CUAI	−523	561	910	785	174	110	2 477	420	1 488	899	1 394
Car tax	CUAF	18	34	47	86	−27	−47	−20	−224	−35	–	–
Beer	CINV	8	6	−13	1	−13	−6	17	18	267	60	−61
Wines, cider, sherry and spirits	CINX	18	8	27	−10	−9	–	22	32	41	137	−133
Tobacco	CINZ	36	57	258	−2	−166	29	158	−362	−1 038	−458	−175
Hydrocarbon oils	CIOB	32	116	31	84	−5	33	112	61	105	125	−46
Customs/protective duties	CIOD	−11	14	8	−1	−3	−6	5	30	4	–	21
EC agricultural levies	CIOF	13	3	−24	8	−11	12	–	−3	−3	−4	−2
Air passenger duty	CSAV	–	–	–	–	–	–	–	–	–	24	20
Insurance premium tax	CSAW	–	–	–	–	–	–	–	–	–	115	37
National Lottery	CJQZ	..	..	..	..	..	..	..	..	..	32	20
Gas levy	CUAG	5	−9	9	−30	−6	−32	−2	7	−20	−21	−10
Northern Ireland rates	CUBN	−1	−2	–	−6	8	−5	3	−69	15	10	71
National non-domestic rates	CULD	–	–	–	–	–	−1 333	73	243	−43	230	102
National insurance surcharge	CUAH	−54	−2	–	–	–	–	–	–	–	–	–
Social security contributions	ACJY	441	55	−504	−1 295	751	213	505	−1 009	1 756	212	400
Royalties	ACJZ	−70	−242	89	37	161	−456	4	3	2	−13	1
Other interest and dividends	CUCF	−18	−3	1	4	15	−2	−92	−55	−47	−64	−52
Total accruals adjustments	CUBO	1 182	−1 112	875	113	2 094	−532	2 315	−674	2 965	1 894	2 198
Net lending:[1]												
To private sector:[1]												
Refinanced shipbuilding credits	CUBP	−82	−9	–	–	–	–	–	–	–	–	–
Other industry and trade	CUBQ	211	135	71	86	863	188	165	−72	13	21	−20
Building societies	CUBR	–	–	–	–	–	–	–	–	–	–	–
Loans secured on dwellings	AADK	69	68	60	153	137	−98	−433	−104	−74	−37	−20
Other	CUBT	−26	−12	−11	33	42	65	171	241	288	494	701
Total net lending to private sector	ACKB	172	182	120	272	1 042	155	−97	65	227	478	661
To local authorities	ABEC	4 960	5 786	5 468	4 829	2 577	762	1 230	−5 818	−1 540	−845	1 715
To public corporations[1]	ACKD	−230	−77	−626	659	1 900	−4 305	−113	1 301	1 044	608	710
To overseas sector:[1]												
Overseas governments	CUAD	−52	−69	−84	−66	−47	−51	−46	−31	−57	−53	−59
Refinanced export credits	-AACT	126	−199	–	–	–	–	–	–	–	–	–
Drawings from UK subscriptions to international lending bodies	CUAA	209	227	210	251	316	211	310	375	266	272	296
Other	CUBV	–	–	–	–	–	–	–	–	–	–	–
Total net lending to overseas sector	ACKE	283	−41	126	185	269	160	264	342	209	219	237
Total net lending	CUBX	5 185	5 850	5 088	5 945	5 788	−3 228	1 284	−4 110	−60	460	3 323
Public dividend capital, etc.[1]	ACKF	836	157	144	147	45	5	1	1	–	–	–
Company securities:[1]												
Purchases	CUBZ	1	–	2 489	38	1 580	15	–	–	6	3	3
less Sales	CUCA	−2 346	−3 809	−8 419	−6 232	−6 237	−4 477	−8 925	−7 580	−5 406	−6 657	−2 487
Net	ACKG	−2 345	−3 809	−5 930	−6 194	−4 657	−4 462	−8 925	−7 580	−5 400	−6 654	−2 484
Total transactions in financial assets	ACJU	4 858	1 086	177	11	3 270	−8 217	−5 325	−12 363	−2 495	−4 300	3 037
NET TOTAL FINANCIAL TRANSACTIONS[2]	AADA	−7 940	−7 803	−5 556	3 399	6 416	−5 711	−13 402	−41 157	−50 044	−44 573	−37 036
BALANCING ITEM	AADB	−237	−105	35	580	133	−389	321	−726	−120	225	558

1 For a functional analysis see Table 7.5.
2 Total assets less total liabilities.

7.5 Central government: analysis of total expenditure

£ million

		1985	1986	1987	1988	1989	1990	1991	1992	1993	1994	1995
General public services												
Current expenditure on goods and services:												
Wages and salaries etc[1]	GTMB	2 274	2 271	2 494	2 862	3 174	3 293	4 090	4 355	4 456	4 562	4 523
Other	GTML	596	823	651	592	1 104	1 410	921	1 026	1 083	1 500	2 119
Current grants to personal sector	GTFB	492	519	715	866	931	1 203	1 146	1 302	1 547	1 535	1 473
Current grants to local authorities	GTLN	75	86	97	95	92	162	164	162	158	116	62
Current grants abroad	GTFC	978	1 061	954	1 217	1 316	1 438	1 800	1 976	1 879	1 974	1 939
Gross domestic fixed capital formation	GTCR	368	379	349	512	687	681	730	740	766	707	697
Capital transfers to private sector	GTFD	54	66	70	73	80	91	64	60	83	61	75
Net lending to public corporations	GTFE	50	43	7	14	53	62	56	42	32	−5	12
Company securities (net)	GTFF	–	–	–	–	–	–	–	−14	–	–	–
Total	GTOD	4 887	5 248	5 337	6 231	7 437	8 340	8 971	9 649	10 004	10 450	10 900
of which: Parliament	GTFH	405	503	494	638	708	664	806	926	1 013	1 118	1 272
Finance and tax collection	GTNX	1 779	1 827	2 216	2 372	2 725	3 113	3 375	3 334	3 386	3 239	2 966
External	GTFJ	745	777	927	902	977	1 154	1 396	1 697	1 818	1 607	1 559
Other	GTOS	1 958	2 141	1 700	2 319	3 027	3 409	3 394	3 692	3 787	4 486	5 103
Defence												
Current expenditure on goods and services:												
Wages and salaries etc[1]	GTPA	6 917	7 325	7 472	7 797	8 301	9 026	10 039	10 533	10 939	10 477	9 916
Other	GTMM	10 938	11 268	11 189	11 485	12 146	13 156	14 506	12 936	12 729	12 650	12 382
Current grants to personal sector	GTPB	–	–	15	34	27	35	42	25	20	50	33
Current grants to local authorities	CTKA	10	13	17	23	21	22	19	23	21	19	20
Current grants abroad	GTFP	51	82	84	99	79	39	−2 007	169	109	49	112
of which Gulf contributions	-HHQG	–	–	–	–	–	−38	−2 110	−9	–	–	–
Gross domestic fixed capital formation	GTCS	268	356	351	356	406	619	611	711	753	726	686
Value of physical increase in stocks	GTFO	–	–	–	–	–	–	–	−11	−25	−28	−4
Capital transfers to private sector	GTFQ	21	12	–	–	–	–	1	5	6	3	5
Company securities (net)	GTLD	–	–	−190	–	–	–	–	–	–	–	–
Total	GTOE	18 205	19 056	18 938	19 794	20 980	22 897	23 211	24 391	24 552	23 946	23 150
Public order and safety												
Current expenditure on goods and services:												
Wages and salaries etc[1]	GTMC	1 000	1 102	1 301	1 433	1 548	1 759	2 124	2 321	2 304	2 272	2 278
Other	GTMN	598	852	839	980	1 141	1 301	1 752	2 208	2 249	2 485	2 334
Current grants to personal sector	GTFV	98	107	138	179	187	236	299	316	375	365	395
Current grants to local authorities	CTKB	1 828	1 781	2 334	2 133	2 565	2 876	3 177	3 514	3 722	3 859	4 149
Gross domestic fixed capital formation	GTCT	174	200	194	223	320	610	726	547	579	592	543
Capital transfers to local authorities	CTLI	–	–	26	29	54	122	156	182	169	196	182
Total	GTOF	3 698	4 042	4 832	4 977	5 815	6 904	8 234	9 088	9 398	9 769	9 881
of which: Police	GTNY	1 891	1 843	2 192	1 853	2 155	2 413	3 098	3 560	3 799	3 914	4 150
Fire	GTNZ	30	32	32	37	40	45	45	51	47	52	48
Law courts	GTOT	840	962	1 220	1 751	2 100	2 632	3 264	3 651	3 923	4 076	3 923
Prisons	GTPE	937	1 205	1 388	1 336	1 520	1 814	1 827	1 826	1 629	1 727	1 760
Education												
Current expenditure on goods and services:												
Wages and salaries etc[1]	GTMD	808	850	938	1 009	1 101	1 227	1 431	1 602	1 566	1 601	1 960
Other	GTOU	167	235	161	122	146	174	207	220	227	275	312
Education grants	CUKF	1 462	1 530	1 696	1 912	2 767	3 056	2 754	3 131	5 920	7 341	8 269
Current grants to personal sector	GTOV	373	464	399	388	338	352	522	613	905	1 030	1 158
Current grants to local authorities	CTKC	793	796	955	952	998	1 223	1 802	2 266	2 149	1 681	1 180
Gross domestic fixed capital formation	GTCU	23	30	19	25	24	25	29	33	27	43	27
Capital transfers to private sector	GTGF	208	235	245	455	570	659	569	505	776	745	881
Capital transfers to local authorities	CTNR	–	7	19	15	4	2	11	15	7	14	20
Net lending to private sector	GTGG	−3	−4	–	–	–	33	82	162	236	482	639
Total	GTOG	3 831	4 143	4 432	4 878	5 948	6 751	7 407	8 547	11 813	13 212	14 446
Health												
Current expenditure on goods and services:												
Wages and salaries etc[1]	CIKN	9 312	9 943	11 117	12 268	13 617	14 900	14 931	14 229	10 707	5 592	3 924
Other	CIKO	7 451	8 013	8 648	9 503	9 960	10 953	14 410	19 021	24 884	32 498	36 329
Current grants to personal sector	GTGK	97	99	109	127	129	206	123	93	101	115	117
Current grants to local authorities	GTLO	4	1	2	5	7	–	–	–	–	–	2
Current grants abroad	GTGL	20	26	29	31	45	39	49	58	67	65	138
Gross domestic fixed capital formation	GTCV	1 005	1 078	998	994	1 402	1 643	1 625	1 594	999	451	304
Capital transfers to private sector	GTGM	4	5	4	13	13	25	12	4	7	28	30
Company securities (net)	GTLT	–	–	–	–	−14	–	–	–	–	–	–
Total	GTOH	17 893	19 165	20 907	22 941	25 159	27 766	31 150	34 999	36 765	38 749	40 844
Social security												
Current expenditure on goods and services:												
Wages and salaries etc[1]	GTME	844	888	1 020	1 111	1 114	1 239	1 527	1 681	1 660	1 721	2 273
Other	GTMP	826	719	1 030	1 174	1 266	1 293	1 546	1 697	2 291	1 887	1 774
Current grants to personal sector	GTMX	37 614	40 864	41 968	43 062	44 964	48 914	57 396	65 926	71 658	74 330	77 226
Current grants to local authorities	CTKD	2 977	3 258	3 501	3 680	4 388	4 647	5 118	5 099	6 571	7 712	8 496
Current grants abroad	GTGS	365	405	441	478	555	620	728	661	824	899	949
Gross domestic fixed capital formation	GTCW	33	60	84	119	233	296	310	306	317	354	270
Capital transfers to private sector	GTGT	–	–	−1	−2	−3	–	–	1	3	4	1
Capital transfers to local authorities	CTLJ	–	–	1	1	1	2	2	3	2	12	27
Net lending to private sector	GTLV	–	–	–	54	48	37	26	42	48	27	47
Total	GTOI	42 659	46 194	48 044	49 677	52 566	57 048	66 653	75 416	83 374	86 946	91 063

1 Including employers' contributions to social security, superannuation, etc.

7.5 Central government: analysis of total expenditure

continued

£ million

		1985	1986	1987	1988	1989	1990	1991	1992	1993	1994	1995
Housing and community amenities												
Current expenditure on goods and services:												
Wages and salaries etc[1]	GTMF	13	13	59	51	43	51	70	89	128	150	147
Other	GTMQ	25	30	66	85	127	249	215	306	169	129	223
Subsidies	GTBX	852	849	837	924	1 027	1 484	1 482	1 373	1 305	1 101	1 188
Current grants to personal sector	GTGZ	572	800	1 263	1 102	165	146	171	117	64	35	32
Current grants to local authorities	CTKE	1 016	1 132	1 282	1 189	1 141	1 061	1 131	1 038	406	387	383
Gross domestic fixed capital formation	GTCX	26	28	33	27	31	33	33	43	93	143	124
Capital transfers to private sector	GTMZ	916	847	863	891	714	1 219	1 946	1 952	2 766	1 852	1 314
Capital transfers to local authorities	CTLK	222	293	306	380	484	659	1 119	1 303	1 546	1 144	1 110
Capital transfers to public corporations	GTHB	64	26	160	255	573	661	1 483	999	792	521	679
Net lending to private sector	AADK	69	68	60	153	137	−98	−433	−104	−74	−37	−20
Net lending to public corporations	GTHD	18	558	674	895	1 169	221	−92	36	38	36	4
Company securities (net)	GTLU	–	–	–	–	−607	−1 524	−1 391	−101	–	–	–
Total	GTOJ	3 793	4 644	5 603	5 952	5 004	4 162	5 734	7 051	7 233	5 461	5 184
of which: Housing	GTOA	2 987	2 996	3 081	3 252	3 360	4 492	5 870	5 740	5 920	4 592	3 346
Water and sewerage	GTOB	−110	441	530	736	538	−1 311	−1 319	−32	96	184	156
Other	GTOW	916	1 207	1 992	1 964	1 106	981	1 183	1 343	1 217	685	1 682
Recreational and cultural affairs												
Current expenditure on goods and services:												
Wages and salaries etc[1]	GTMG	55	93	140	102	144	170	226	271	375	346	355
Other	GTMR	147	147	142	267	275	304	317	399	405	421	339
Subsidies	GTBY	–	–	–	–	–	–	–	59	56	57	66
Current grants to personal sector	GTHM	298	290	301	293	205	223	291	398	272	394	360
Current grants to local authorities	CTKF	144	33	12	23	15	32	41	51	49	55	48
Gross domestic fixed capital formation	GTCY	33	38	59	37	129	121	170	148	240	169	219
Capital transfers to private sector	GTHN	3	1	3	6	6	9	22	10	10	29	17
Capital transfers to local authorities	CTLL	6	10	–	3	3	–	–	–	–	–	–
Capital transfers to public corporations	GTHO	–	–	–	–	–	–	–	–	–	–	–
Net lending to public corporations	GTHP	−7	−2	2	−8	3	−11	−20	−15	−4	16	13
Company securities (net)	GTOC	–	–	–	–	–	–	−68	–	–	–	–
Total	GTOK	679	610	659	723	780	848	979	1 321	1 403	1 487	1 417
Fuel and energy[2]												
Current expenditure on goods and services:												
Wages and salaries etc[1]	GTHR	197	19	–	–	1	–	–	–	–	–	–
Other	GTHS	67	285	281	167	302	237	227	244	202	175	201
Subsidies	GTHV	1 501	766	760	610	740	222	408	685	624	452	130
Current grants to personal sector	GTHW	421	593	482	159	157	103	61	48	25	37	261
Gross domestic fixed capital formation	GTCZ	50	4	–	–	–	–	–	–	–	–	–
Value of physical increase in stocks	GTHU	−1	–	–	–	–	–	–	–	–	–	–
Capital transfers to private sector	GTHX	–	–	–	–	–	–	51	35	58	90	107
Capital transfers to public corporations	GTHY	–	–	6	7	7	5 179	1 486	1 421	1 431	1 385	953
Net lending to private sector	GTHZ	−2	−2	−4	−2	−2	−3	−3	−2	–	–	–
Net lending to public corporations	GTIA	−708	−819	−1 329	72	−351	−6 046	190	1 047	295	691	1 287
Company securities (net)	GTIB	−446	−2 020	−3 566	−4 039	−2 639	−2 708	−5 474	−4 012	−1 698	−2 395	−715
Total	GTOL	1 079	−1 174	−3 370	−3 026	−1 785	−3 016	−3 054	−534	937	435	2 224
Agriculture, forestry and fishing												
Current expenditure on goods and services:												
Wages and salaries etc[1]	GTMH	188	184	238	234	256	277	341	414	403	401	343
Other	GTMS	194	216	266	244	225	308	311	419	355	403	468
Subsidies	GTIH	1 311	1 523	1 963	2 010	1 372	1 633	1 687	1 823	2 966	2 419	2 586
Current grants to personal sector	GTII	49	21	14	1	3	3	7	10	10	12	3
Current grants to local authorities	GTLP	26	27	29	30	30	32	33	33	36	17	10
Gross domestic fixed capital formation	GTDA	32	40	44	89	72	100	84	108	93	112	132
Value of physical increase in stocks	GTIG	449	−233	−493	−315	−160	161	329	175	216	−175	−181
Capital transfers to private sector	GTIJ	220	170	169	71	80	85	68	90	71	60	36
Capital transfers to local authorities	CTLM	22	11	10	16	20	15	22	17	26	21	39
Net lending to private sector	GTIK	−3	5	−3	−3	–	–	2	2	2	3	–
Company securities (net)	GTLE	–	–	−66	–	–	–	–	–	–	–	–
Total	GTOM	2 488	1 964	2 171	2 377	1 898	2 614	2 884	3 091	4 178	3 273	3 436
Mining and mineral resources, manufacturing and construction												
Current expenditure on goods and services:												
Wages and salaries etc[1]	GTMI	39	56	70	74	77	92	62	76	100	100	85
Other	GTMT	349	298	288	345	281	305	460	369	355	309	221
Subsidies	GTIQ	250	226	301	297	226	152	237	293	296	401	292
Current grants to personal sector	GTIR	86	94	35	18	9	11	56	66	68	134	68
Current grants to local authorities	GTOZ	–	–	–	–	–	–	3	7	5	38	40
Gross domestic fixed capital formation	GTDB	70	51	34	27	32	37	77	92	44	31	48
Value of physical increase in stocks	GTIP	3	−2	−4	−6	−1	−1	−1	−1	−3	−4	−3
Capital transfers to private sector	GTIS	564	697	486	971	495	432	350	288	280	354	404
Capital transfers to local authorities	CTLP	–	–	–	–	–	–	5	6	71	82	47
Capital transfers to public corporations	GTIT	233	148	76	6	10	3	–	–	23	183	157
Net lending to private sector	GTIU	130	119	75	89	860	166	165	−72	11	18	−20
Net lending to public corporations	GTIV	97	−21	66	49	699	100	−1	−2	−1	−2	−1
Public dividend capital etc	GTIW	836	157	144	147	45	5	1	1	–	–	–
Company securities (net)	GTIX	−363	−1	−385	−1 194	−1 315	−152	–	−43	–	–	–
Total	GTON	2 294	1 822	1 186	823	1 418	1 150	1 415	1 080	1 249	1 644	1 338

1 Including employers' contributions to social security, superannuation, etc.
2 Comprises identifiable expenditure only.

7.5 Central government: analysis of total expenditure
continued

£ million

		1985	1986	1987	1988	1989	1990	1991	1992	1993	1994	1995
Transport and communications												
Current expenditure on goods and services:												
Wages and salaries etc[1]	GTMJ	190	126	100	196	272	294	341	357	286	280	306
Other	GTMU	240	314	438	327	417	406	617	492	613	696	664
Subsidies	GTNP	1 047	957	956	813	736	836	1 046	1 517	1 254	1 814	1 896
Current grants to personal sector	GTJD	82	88	94	86	89	94	26	64	65	65	54
Current grants to local authorities	CTKG	143	51	4	2	2	1	1	11	22	40	92
Gross domestic fixed capital formation	GTDC	943	984	1 081	1 214	1 455	2 066	2 232	2 434	2 392	2 581	2 513
Capital transfers to private sector	GTJE	6	7	10	6	7	4	1	12	7	3	84
Capital transfers to local authorities	CTLN	218	240	255	294	312	305	456	489	487	415	360
Capital transfers to public corporations	GTNR	213	274	251	264	382	466	390	740	708	773	846
Net lending to private sector	GTJG	−9	−4	−10	−10	−10	−4	−2	−49	−1	–	–
Net lending to public corporations	GTJH	169	−56	84	−201	759	1 612	500	342	805	67	−156
Public dividend capital etc	GTJI	–	–	–	–	–	–	–	–	–	–	–
Company securities (net)	GTJJ	−1 537	−1 788	−1 723	−961	−85	−92	−1 938	−3 398	−3 708	−4 262	−1 766
Total	GTOO	1 705	1 193	1 540	2 030	4 336	5 988	3 670	3 011	2 930	2 472	4 893
Other economic affairs and services												
Current expenditure on goods and services:												
Wages and salaries etc[1]	GTMK	819	1 101	1 182	968	1 050	1 449	769	1 061	1 497	1 452	984
Other	GTMV	642	554	731	911	955	1 556	1 116	1 194	1 628	1 900	1 784
Subsidies	GTNQ	978	818	498	353	673	1 074	550	383	98	131	98
of which interest support costs	GTCF	506	315	184	151	360	406	273	134	42	31	36
Other	GTLC	472	503	314	202	313	668	277	249	56	100	62
Current grants to personal sector	GTJP	1 088	1 127	656	993	1 471	1 479	1 270	1 148	1 368	1 353	1 836
Current grants to local authorities	CTKH	21	25	21	18	33	291	381	442	403	416	250
Gross domestic fixed capital formation	GTDD	101	103	112	86	160	184	249	99	88	37	79
Value of physical increase in stocks	GTLS	−1	−2	−1	−1	−2	−4	−178	−180	−212	−44	34
Capital transfers to private sector	GTJQ	23	−98	−28	−234	197	215	196	228	167	205	211
Capital transfers to local authorities	CTLO	17	47	49	39	44	57	35	17	165	220	85
Capital transfers to public corporations	GTJR	19	15	120	174	228	236	217	91	152	334	548
Net lending to private sector	GTOX	−10	–	2	−9	9	24	66	86	5	−15	15
Net lending to public corporations	GTJT	151	220	−130	−162	−432	−243	−746	−149	−121	−195	−449
Net lending to overseas sector	-AACT	126	−199	–	–	–	–	–	–	–	–	–
Public dividend capital etc	GTJU	–	–	–	–	–	–	–	–	–	–	–
Company securities (net)	GTMW	1	–	–	–	3	14	−54	−12	6	3	−3
Total	GTOP	3 975	3 711	3 212	3 136	4 389	6 332	3 871	4 408	5 244	5 797	5 472
Other expenditure												
Non-trading capital consumption	ACGL	983	1 076	1 179	1 303	1 484	1 623	1 675	1 608	1 867	1 978	2 150
Debt interest	ACHL	15 724	15 954	17 089	17 371	18 038	17 921	16 337	16 629	18 080	21 706	25 363
Current grants to local authorities	CTJZ	13 401	14 610	15 023	15 302	14 908	27 926	35 708	40 445	41 090	41 893	42 339
of which NNDR	CIOZ	–	–	–	–	–	10 426	14 010	13 260	13 741	13 017	12 950
Current grants abroad	GTKA	2 013	659	1 769	1 423	2 283	2 460	513	1 970	2 090	2 148	4 042
Capital transfers to local authorities	CTLH	265	329	336	260	1 222	648	627	5 889	681	826	850
Net lending to local authorities	ABEC	4 960	5 786	5 468	4 829	2 577	762	1 230	−5 818	−1 540	−845	1 715
Net lending to overseas sector	GTKD	157	158	126	185	269	160	264	342	209	219	237
Total	GTOQ	37 503	38 572	40 990	40 673	40 781	51 500	56 354	61 065	62 477	67 925	76 696
Total expenditure												
Current expenditure on goods and services:												
Wages and salaries etc[1,2]	GILN	22 656	23 971	26 131	28 105	30 698	33 777	35 951	36 989	34 421	28 954	27 094
Other[3]	CUCN	22 240	23 754	24 730	26 202	28 345	31 652	36 605	40 531	47 190	55 328	59 150
Education grants	CUKF	1 462	1 530	1 696	1 912	2 767	3 056	2 754	3 131	5 920	7 341	8 269
Subsidies	ACHG	5 939	5 139	5 315	5 007	4 774	5 401	5 410	6 133	6 599	6 375	6 256
Current grants to personal sector	GTAC	41 270	45 066	46 189	47 308	48 675	53 005	61 410	70 126	76 478	79 455	83 016
Current grants to local authorities	ACHJ	20 438	21 813	23 277	23 452	24 200	38 273	47 578	53 091	54 632	56 233	57 071
Current grants abroad	-HDKH	3 427	2 233	3 277	3 248	4 278	4 596	1 083	4 834	4 969	5 135	7 180
of which Gulf contributions	-HHQG	–	–	–	–	–	−38	−2 110	−9	–	–	–
Gross domestic fixed capital formation	AAAC	3 126	3 351	3 358	3 709	4 951	6 415	6 876	6 855	6 391	5 946	5 642
Value of physical increase in stocks	AAAD	450	−237	−498	−322	−163	156	151	−17	−24	−251	−154
Capital transfers to private sector	ACIH	2 019	1 942	1 821	2 250	2 159	2 739	3 280	3 190	4 234	3 434	3 165
Capital transfers to local authorities	ACII	750	937	1 002	1 037	2 144	1 810	2 433	7 921	3 154	2 930	2 720
Capital transfers to public corporations	ACIJ	529	463	613	706	1 200	6 545	3 576	3 251	3 106	3 196	3 183
Net lending to private sector	ACKB	172	182	120	272	1 042	155	−97	65	227	478	661
Net lending to public corporations	ACKD	−230	−77	−626	659	1 900	−4 305	−113	1 301	1 044	608	710
Net lending to overseas sector	ACKE	283	−41	126	185	269	160	264	342	209	219	237
Public dividend capital etc	ACKF	836	157	144	147	45	5	1	1	–	–	–
Company securities (net)	ACKG	−2 345	−3 809	−5 930	−6 194	−4 657	−4 462	−8 925	−7 580	−5 400	−6 654	−2 484
Total	GTOR	123 022	126 374	130 745	137 683	152 627	178 978	198 237	230 164	243 150	248 727	261 716
Non-trading capital consumption	ACGL	983	1 076	1 179	1 303	1 484	1 623	1 675	1 608	1 867	1 978	2 150
Debt interest	ACHL	15 724	15 954	17 089	17 371	18 038	17 921	16 337	16 629	18 080	21 706	25 363
Net lending to local authorities	ABEC	4 960	5 786	5 468	4 829	2 577	762	1 230	−5 818	−1 540	−845	1 715
Total expenditure	GTOY	144 689	149 190	154 481	161 186	174 726	199 284	217 479	242 583	261 557	271 566	290 944

1 Including employers' contributions to social security, superannuation, etc.
2 For details of total wages and salaries and employers' contributions paid by general government see table in methodological notes.
3 Net of the following income from fees & charges, etc (£million).

	1985	1986	1987	1988	1989	1990	1991	1992	1993	1994	1995
GTCQ	2 287	1 970	2 026	2 255	2 498	2 555	2 667	2 792	2 820	2 900	2 960

7.6 Social security funds: current account and financial transactions account

£ million

		1985	1986	1987	1988	1989	1990	1991	1992	1993	1994	1995
CURRENT RECEIPTS												
Contributions from employers	CEAN	12 245	13 540	14 395	16 176	18 145	19 984	21 182	21 590	23 047	23 241	24 069
Contributions from insured persons:												
Employed persons	GTKL	10 938	12 339	12 215	13 245	13 958	13 124	13 670	13 955	14 907	17 027	18 369
Self-employed persons	GTDP	718	–	725	906	1 014	1 139	1 164	1 232	1 354	1 473	1 616
Non-employed persons	GTDQ	27	–	30	36	34	38	42	49	55	56	60
Total	GTDR	11 683	12 339	12 970	14 187	15 006	14 301	14 876	15 236	16 316	18 556	20 045
State scheme premiums	GTDS	282	286	298	319	182	172	158	149	136	146	137
Total social security contributions	AIIH	24 210	26 165	27 663	30 682	33 333	34 457	36 216	36 975	39 499	41 943	44 251
Contributions from abroad	GTKW	16	15	15	17	17	15	16	14	30	25	25
Grants from central government	GTDT	2 444	2 288	2 234	1 925	612	585	1 304	1 318	7 096	8 076	5 220
Interest	GTDU	538	577	556	684	1 026	1 025	1 096	793	288	312	471
Total current receipts	GTDV	27 208	29 045	30 468	33 308	34 988	36 082	38 632	39 100	46 913	50 356	49 967
CURRENT EXPENDITURE												
Current expenditure on goods and services	GTDW	927	797	827	873	862	1 001	1 024	1 142	1 489	1 372	1 095
Current grants to personal sector:												
National insurance fund:												
Retirement pensions	CSDG	16 273	18 013	18 535	19 182	20 587	22 269	25 191	26 788	28 270	28 896	29 926
Widows and guardians allowances	CSDH	807	839	836	877	827	873	865	1 020	1 023	1 043	1 015
Unemployment benefit	CSDI	1 632	1 763	1 606	1 261	806	780	1 486	1 749	1 685	1 360	1 120
Sickness benefit	CSDJ	293	225	170	196	227	217	263	348	308	390	336
Invalidity benefit	CSDK	2 457	2 708	2 958	3 355	3 793	4 411	5 203	6 078	6 867	7 798	7 957
Maternity benefit	CSDL	168	176	86	28	31	34	39	42	34	16	30
Death grant	CSDM	18	21	7	–	–	–	–	–	–	–	–
Injury benefit	CSDN	–	–	–	–	–	–	–	–	–	–	–
Disablement benefit	CSDO	411	452	458	460	468	512	134	–	–	–	–
Industrial death benefit	CSDP	60	66	56	61	61	62	15	–	–	–	–
Statutory sick pay	CSDQ	552	712	855	873	970	974	788	694	682	188	24
Statutory maternity pay	GTKZ	–	–	140	257	284	331	362	411	428	446	465
Payments in lieu of benefits foregone	GTKV	9	2	2	–	–	–	–	–	–	–	–
Total national insurance	ACHH	22 680	24 977	25 709	26 550	28 054	30 463	34 346	37 130	39 297	40 137	40 873
Redundancy fund benefit	GTKN	343	334	99	83	68	128	230	308	165	180	184
Maternity fund benefit	GTKO	62	72	47	1	–	–	–	–	–	–	–
Social fund benefit	GTLQ	–	–	23	64	94	113	130	154	193	185	186
Total social security funds benefits	GTKP	23 085	25 383	25 878	26 698	28 216	30 704	34 706	37 592	39 655	40 502	41 243
Current grants abroad	GTDX	336	373	409	451	519	582	676	605	770	846	892
Debt interest	GTKQ	4	–	–	–	–	–	–	–	–	–	–
Transfer to NHS	GTKR	2 016	2 228	2 725	3 422	4 141	4 286	4 490	4 393	4 495	4 595	4 800
Current balance	GTDY	840	264	629	1 864	1 250	–491	–2 264	–4 632	504	3 041	1 937
Total current expenditure	GTDV	27 208	29 045	30 468	33 308	34 988	36 082	38 632	39 100	46 913	50 356	49 967
FINANCIAL ACCOUNT												
Financial surplus or deficit	GTDY	840	264	629	1 864	1 250	–491	–2 264	–4 632	504	3 041	1 937
Transactions in financial liabilities												
Borrowing	GTKS	–37	–	–	–	–	–	–	–	–	–	–
Total financial liabilities	GTKT	803	264	629	1 864	1 250	–491	–2 264	–4 632	504	3 041	1 937
Transactions in financial assets												
Accruals adjustment	ACJY	441	55	–504	–1 295	751	213	505	–1 009	1 756	212	400
Social Fund: Net lending to persons	GTLV	–	–	–	54	48	37	26	42	48	27	47
Net investment	GTKU	362	209	1 133	3 105	451	–741	–2 795	–3 665	–1 300	2 802	1 490
Total financial assets	GTKT	803	264	629	1 864	1 250	–491	–2 264	–4 632	504	3 041	1 937

CHAPTER 8: Local authorities

8.1 Local authorities: summary account

£ million

		1985	1986	1987	1988	1989	1990	1991	1992	1993	1994	1995
CURRENT RECEIPTS												
Current grants from central government:												
National non-domestic rates distribution	CIOZ	–	–	–	–	–	10 426	14 010	13 260	13 741	13 017	12 950
Other	CUKZ	20 438	21 813	23 277	23 452	24 200	27 847	33 568	39 831	40 891	43 216	44 121
Rates	ADAB	13 638	15 251	16 777	18 726	19 913	5 129	121	133	142	148	153
Community Charge/Council Tax[1]	ADBH	–	–	–	–	586	8 629	8 128	7 907	8 038	8 450	8 989
Gross trading surplus[2]	ADAD	440	434	410	427	522	557	407	392	440	467	365
Rent, dividends and interest[3]	FNBO	3 880	3 853	3 862	4 042	4 668	4 779	4 763	4 765	4 716	4 916	5 111
Imputed charge for consumption of non-trading capital	ADAG	1 389	1 507	1 625	1 807	1 964	2 183	2 088	1 995	1 812	1 859	1 979
Total	ADAA	39 785	42 858	45 951	48 454	51 853	59 550	63 085	68 283	69 780	72 073	73 668
CURRENT EXPENDITURE												
Final consumption	CSBA	27 926	30 580	33 309	36 119	38 502	42 826	47 120	49 616	48 683	50 513	52 811
Subsidies	ADAK	1 286	1 162	950	1 030	1 008	665	585	604	604	685	710
Current grants to personal sector	ADAL	4 081	4 388	4 609	4 867	5 358	5 934	7 877	9 926	11 906	13 119	13 474
Debt interest[3]	XAHH	4 689	4 522	4 637	4 874	5 399	5 508	5 373	5 019	4 402	4 304	4 182
Total current expenditure	ADAH	37 982	40 652	43 505	46 890	50 267	54 933	60 955	65 165	65 595	68 621	71 177
Balance: current surplus[2]	AAAE	1 803	2 206	2 446	1 564	1 586	4 617	2 130	3 118	4 185	3 452	2 491
Total	ADAA	39 785	42 858	45 951	48 454	51 853	59 550	63 085	68 283	69 780	72 073	73 668
CAPITAL RECEIPTS												
Current surplus[2]	AAAE	1 803	2 206	2 446	1 564	1 586	4 617	2 130	3 118	4 185	3 452	2 491
Capital grants from central government	ACII	750	937	1 002	1 037	2 144	1 810	2 433	7 921	3 154	2 930	2 720
Miscellaneous receipts	CBGA	51	183	208	211	243	229	207	194	189	234	468
Total	ADCA	2 604	3 326	3 656	2 812	3 973	6 656	4 770	11 233	7 528	6 616	5 679
CAPITAL EXPENDITURE												
Gross domestic fixed capital formation	AAAG	3 746	4 158	4 219	2 797	4 631	6 244	5 267	5 651	5 412	6 344	6 811
Capital grants to other sectors	ADCD	771	597	782	850	874	864	1 083	1 239	1 262	1 304	1 150
Total capital expenditure	ADCC	4 517	4 755	5 001	3 647	5 505	7 108	6 350	6 890	6 674	7 648	7 961
Balance: financial surplus or deficit	AABB	−1 913	−1 429	−1 345	−835	−1 532	−452	−1 580	4 343	854	−1 032	−2 282
Total	ADCA	2 604	3 326	3 656	2 812	3 973	6 656	4 770	11 233	7 528	6 616	5 679
FINANCIAL ACCOUNT												
Transactions in financial liabilities	ADDA	1 878	1 233	1 301	931	982	1 788	1 803	−5 695	−2 561	268	479
Transactions in financial assets	ADDQ	−486	−752	−414	−86	76	910	−278	−1 308	−1 135	−855	−1 404
Net total financial transactions[4]	AAES	−2 364	−1 985	−1 715	−1 017	−906	−878	−2 081	4 387	1 426	−1 123	−1 883
BALANCING ITEM	AAET	451	556	370	182	−626	426	501	−44	−572	91	−399

1 Community charge replaced domestic rates in Scotland, from April 1989 and in England and Wales, from April 1990. This was replaced by the Council Tax in April 1993.
2 Before providing for depreciation
3 Interest receipts and payments are gross of transactions with other local authorities.
4 Total assets *less* total liabilities.

Where such data can be compiled, quarterly data for series in this table are available on the ONS's Databank. This data can also be provided on paper by request. Some of these quarterly data are published regularly in the UK Economic Accounts in table A17.

8.2 Local authorities: current account

£ million

		1985	1986	1987	1988	1989	1990	1991	1992	1993	1994	1995
RECEIPTS												
Current grants from central government[1]	ACHJ	20 438	21 813	23 277	23 452	24 200	38 273	47 578	53 091	54 632	56 233	57 071
Rates	ADAB	13 638	15 251	16 777	18 726	19 913	5 129	121	133	142	148	153
Community charge/Council tax[2]	ADBH	–	–	–	–	586	8 629	8 128	7 907	8 038	8 450	8 989
Gross trading surplus	ADAD	440	434	410	427	522	557	407	392	440	467	365
Rent	ADAE	3 043	3 056	3 022	3 142	3 238	3 459	3 808	4 000	4 189	4 367	4 430
Interest, etc.[3]	XAHJ	837	797	840	900	1 430	1 320	955	765	527	549	681
Imputed charge for consumption of non-trading capital	ADAG	1 389	1 507	1 625	1 807	1 964	2 183	2 088	1 995	1 812	1 859	1 979
Total	ADAA	39 785	42 858	45 951	48 454	51 853	59 550	63 085	68 283	69 780	72 073	73 668
EXPENDITURE												
Final consumption:												
Current expenditure on goods and services:												
General public services	CTKI	880	956	1 088	1 182	1 473	1 950	2 242	1 910	1 884	2 059	2 158
Civil defence	CTKJ	17	20	22	24	27	29	32	33	29	24	22
Public order and safety:												
Police	CTKK	3 147	3 315	3 623	4 002	4 414	4 962	5 753	6 041	6 380	6 768	7 010
Fire services	CTKL	719	761	833	908	998	1 111	1 273	1 317	1 382	1 428	1 481
Law courts	CTKN	319	371	401	449	506	590	698	735	772	796	815
Education[4]	CTKM	12 559	14 140	15 388	16 794	17 561	18 719	20 610	21 943	20 124	20 425	21 078
Social security:												
Concessionary fares	CTKO	349	297	321	340	375	399	419	431	443	450	462
Housing benefit administration	CTKP	106	156	191	222	277	379	297	389	479	516	526
Personal social services	CTKQ	2 993	3 193	3 537	3 971	4 395	5 022	5 725	6 185	6 891	7 400	8 152
Housing and community amenity:												
Housing	CTKR	131	200	248	257	233	303	363	400	376	398	405
Community development	CTKS	691	790	841	674	514	620	699	790	826	869	937
Sanitary services	CTKT	1 325	1 366	1 470	1 570	1 667	1 823	1 989	2 179	2 174	2 244	2 347
Street lighting	CTKU	191	200	203	210	219	255	252	271	271	286	295
Recreational and cultural affairs	CTKV	1 344	1 497	1 612	1 761	1 889	2 176	2 375	2 484	2 478	2 445	2 513
Agriculture (including land drainage and coast protection)	CTKW	144	152	160	169	107	55	39	45	58	60	64
Mining, manufacturing and construction:												
Consumer protection	CTKX	77	83	88	93	106	120	137	155	163	171	176
Transport and communication	CTKY	1 431	1 455	1 526	1 537	1 616	1 961	1 938	2 090	1 926	2 042	2 110
Other economic affairs and services	CTKZ	114	121	132	149	161	169	191	223	215	273	281
Total[5]	CTNA	26 537	29 073	31 684	34 312	36 538	40 643	45 032	47 621	46 871	48 654	50 832
Non-trading capital consumption	ADAG	1 389	1 507	1 625	1 807	1 964	2 183	2 088	1 995	1 812	1 859	1 979
Total final consumption[5]	CSBA	27 926	30 580	33 309	36 119	38 502	42 826	47 120	49 616	48 683	50 513	52 811
Subsidies:												
Housing	CTMO	578	538	502	537	503	129	–	–	1	–	4
Water supply	CTLB	26	24	21	21	8	–	–	–	–	–	–
Passenger transport	CTLC	487	419	238	252	264	263	286	321	336	475	514
Other economic affairs and services	CTLD	195	181	189	220	233	273	299	283	267	210	192
Current grants to personal sector:												
Education	CTNB	1 091	1 153	1 204	1 276	1 432	1 453	2 250	2 758	3 216	3 113	2 886
Rent rebates and allowances	CSBD	2 990	3 235	3 405	3 591	3 926	4 481	5 627	7 168	8 690	10 006	10 588
Debt interest:												
On loans from central government	ACGI	2 678	3 192	3 683	3 956	4 418	4 628	4 656	4 497	3 988	3 812	3 681
Other[3]	FNBM	2 011	1 330	954	918	981	880	717	522	414	492	501
Total current expenditure	ADAH	37 982	40 652	43 505	46 890	50 267	54 933	60 955	65 165	65 595	68 621	71 177
Balance: current surplus	AAAE	1 803	2 206	2 446	1 564	1 586	4 617	2 130	3 118	4 185	3 452	2 491
Total	ADAA	39 785	42 858	45 951	48 454	51 853	59 550	63 085	68 283	69 780	72 073	73 668

1 For further details, see table 7.5.
2 Community charge replaced domestic rates in Scotland, from April 1989 and in England and Wales, from April 1990. This was replaced by the Council Tax in April 1993.
3 Interest receipts and payments are gross of transactions with other local authorities.

4 Excludes expenditure of polytechnics in England from April 1989, FE and Sixth form colleges from April 1993.
5 Net of the following income from fees and charges, etc. (£ million):

		1985	1986	1987	1988	1989	1990	1991	1992	1993	1994	1995
	CTNC	2 809	3 012	3 256	3 596	3 805	4 059	4 519	4 491	4 183	4 273	4 433

8.3 Local authorities: capital account

£ million

		1985	1986	1987	1988	1989	1990	1991	1992	1993	1994	1995
RECEIPTS												
Current surplus before providing for depreciation	AAAE	1 803	2 206	2 446	1 564	1 586	4 617	2 130	3 118	4 185	3 452	2 491
Capital grants from central government[1]	ACII	750	937	1 002	1 037	2 144	1 810	2 433	7 921	3 154	2 930	2 720
Miscellaneous capital receipts	CBGA	51	183	208	211	243	229	207	194	189	234	468
Total	ADCA	2 604	3 326	3 656	2 812	3 973	6 656	4 770	11 233	7 528	6 616	5 679
EXPENDITURE												
Gross domestic fixed capital formation:												
General public services	CTLQ	321	208	203	277	518	511	468	563	267	418	508
Civil defence	CTLR	1	3	–	2	2	3	2	2	–	1	2
Public order and safety:												
Police	CTLS	91	45	101	117	183	205	187	209	231	238	301
Fire service	CTLT	59	52	58	58	74	73	59	74	74	93	89
Law courts	CTLU	20	21	36	57	62	85	52	86	83	82	74
Education	CTLV	595	638	779	597	898	1 026	901	980	932	866	1 120
Social security:												
Personal social services	CTLW	126	130	137	137	193	248	194	179	209	203	215
Housing and community amenity:												
Housing[2]	CTLX	931	1 137	1 153	244	634	1 310	824	833	818	930	982
Community development	CTLY	157	293	236	−164	−63	73	167	237	332	543	536
Water supply	CTLZ	37	40	41	40	47	69	76	107	141	148	136
Sanitary services	CTMA	168	174	186	213	208	229	211	220	233	211	217
Street lighting	CTMB	15	16	18	18	19	20	15	18	20	21	22
Recreational and cultural affairs	CTMC	368	382	340	370	534	663	601	414	431	476	407
Fuel and energy	CTMD	–	–	–	–	–	–	–	–	–	–	–
Agriculture (including land drainage and coast protection)	CTME	38	10	7	−13	17	25	38	25	−14	−22	36
Mining, manufacturing and construction	CTMF	4	1	–	1	–	–	–	–	–	–	–
Transport and communication	CTMG	766	930	897	928	1 211	1 521	1 281	1 682	1 759	1 987	1 995
Other economic affairs and services	CTMH	49	78	27	−85	94	183	191	22	−104	149	171
Total[3]	AAAG	3 746	4 158	4 219	2 797	4 631	6 244	5 267	5 651	5 412	6 344	6 811
Capital grants to personal sector												
Housing	ADCE	705	575	726	821	858	848	1 063	1 198	1 202	1 247	1 083
Capital grants to public corporations												
Transport and communication	ADCF	66	22	56	29	16	16	20	41	60	57	67
Total capital expenditure	ADCC	4 517	4 755	5 001	3 647	5 505	7 108	6 350	6 890	6 674	7 648	7 961
Balance: financial surplus or deficit	AABB	−1 913	−1 429	−1 345	−835	−1 532	−452	−1 580	4 343	854	−1 032	−2 282
Total	ADCA	2 604	3 326	3 656	2 812	3 973	6 656	4 770	11 233	7 528	6 616	5 679

1 For further details, see table 7.5.
2 Excluding houses provided for specific services (e.g. police); these appear under the service concerned.
3 Net of the following receipts from sales (£ million):

		1985	1986	1987	1988	1989	1990	1991	1992	1993	1994	1995
Council houses	CTCS	1 240	1 339	1 648	2 665	3 153	2 215	1 447	1 229	1 227	1 236	629
Other	GTEE	875	856	1 127	2 121	1 988	2 099	1 274	1 273	1 912	1 607	2 010

8.4 Local authorities: transactions in financial assets and liabilities

£ million

		1985	1986	1987	1988	1989	1990	1991	1992	1993	1994	1995
FINANCIAL SURPLUS OR DEFICIT	AABB	−1 913	−1 429	−1 345	−835	−1 532	−452	−1 580	4 343	854	−1 032	−2 282
Transactions in financial liabilities (net)												
Accruals adjustments:												
Rates	ADDC	56	302	310	210	24	−2 045	12	−23	−9	−1	1
Income tax	ADDE	31	–	29	50	133	90	−7	68	92	57	45
Social security contributions	ADDF	53	6	−66	−174	98	27	65	−131	228	28	52
National insurance surcharge	ADDG	−6	–	–	–	–	–	–	–	–	–	–
Borrowing requirement:												
Loans from central government (net)	ABEC	4 960	5 786	5 468	4 829	2 577	762	1 230	−5 818	−1 540	−845	1 715
Borrowing from other sources (net)[1]	−ABED	−2 564	−3 302	−2 139	−1 431	−1 167	344	−389	1 262	1 293	990	82
Transactions in short term assets[1]	−AMIO	−814	−1 800	−2 524	−2 726	−916	2 492	1 042	−963	−2 585	73	−1 467
Transactions in other public sector debt (net sales)[1]	−AMIV	3	−11	−69	−77	71	89	5	−2	−43	−53	44
Total borrowing requirement	ABEG	1 585	673	736	595	565	3 687	1 888	−5 521	−2 875	165	374
Other financial liabilities	ADGK	159	252	292	250	162	29	−155	−88	3	19	7
Total transactions in financial liabilities	ADDA	1 878	1 233	1 301	931	982	1 788	1 803	−5 695	−2 561	268	479
Transactions in financial assets (net)												
Accruals adjustments:												
Subsidies	ADDS	87	−94	−34	47	21	−178	−176	−110	68	−64	−2
Community charge/Council Tax	CDXW	–	–	–	–	81	145	444	−796	−566	−602	−584
National non-domestic rates	CCXN	–	–	–	–	–	1 090	−190	−132	−341	−8	−719
Other	RCZZ	43	56	39	56	74	67	83	72	36	55	26
Net lending to private sector:												
For house purchase	AAEO	−502	−506	−433	−329	−230	−322	−446	−358	−357	−291	−187
Other	AAEP	43	60	61	96	100	37	25	31	31	41	47
Net acquisition of UK company securities	ADNR	10	49	163	113	149	81	−9	−5	−1	17	17
Other financial assets	ADEE	−167	−317	−210	−69	−119	−10	−9	−10	−5	−3	−2
Total transactions in financial assets	ADDQ	−486	−752	−414	−86	76	910	−278	−1 308	−1 135	−855	−1 404
NET TOTAL FINANCIAL TRANSACTIONS[2]	AAES	−2 364	−1 985	−1 715	−1 017	−906	−878	−2 081	4 387	1 426	−1 123	−1 883
BALANCING ITEM	AAET	451	556	370	182	−626	426	501	−44	−572	91	−399

1 These three items comprise the local authorities' contribution to the public sector borrowing requirement (see table 11.13)
2 Total assets *less* total liabilities.

8.5 Housing: operating account

£ million

		1985	1986	1987	1988	1989	1990	1991	1992	1993	1994	1995
REVENUE												
Rent on dwellings:												
Paid by tenants	CTMK	2 063	2 187	2 239	2 389	2 477	2 813	3 085	2 946	2 771	2 626	2 858
Rent rebates	CTML	2 190	2 285	2 389	2 547	2 773	3 003	3 442	4 171	4 768	5 257	5 332
Rent on other properties	CTMM	108	125	130	144	173	183	192	212	229	223	229
Subsidies:												
Central government	CTMN	537	521	501	577	688	1 132	1 175	1 030	914	741	773
Local authorities	CTMO	578	538	502	537	503	129	–	–	1	–	4
Other income	CTMP	393	306	305	336	402	409	419	400	402	400	378
Total	CTMQ	5 869	5 962	6 066	6 530	7 016	7 669	8 313	8 759	9 085	9 247	9 574
EXPENDITURE												
Supervision and management	CTMR	1 084	1 172	1 251	1 401	1 551	1 631	1 741	1 855	1 950	2 036	2 130
Repairs	CTMS	1 558	1 616	1 686	1 845	1 982	2 253	2 373	2 491	2 563	2 531	2 756
Other current expenditure[1]	CTMT	184	118	107	142	245	326	391	413	383	313	258
Balance: rent before providing for interest and depreciation[2,3]	ADAE	3 043	3 056	3 022	3 142	3 238	3 459	3 808	4 000	4 189	4 367	4 430
Total	CTMQ	5 869	5 962	6 066	6 530	7 016	7 669	8 313	8 759	9 085	9 247	9 574

1 Excluding receipts and payments of interest.
2 Transferred to table 8.2.
3 Loan charges to be met from rent are as follows (£ million):

		1985	1986	1987	1988	1989	1990	1991	1992	1993	1994	1995
Debt interest (net of interest receipts)	CTMW	2 447	2 389	2 270	2 347	2 280	2 480	2 550	2 411	2 422	2 437	2 412
Repayment of principal	CTMX	449	476	520	546	583	558	544	527	525	531	540
Total	CTMY	2 896	2 865	2 790	2 893	2 863	3 038	3 094	2 938	2 947	2 968	2 952

CHAPTER 9: General government

9.1 General government: summary account

£ million

		1985	1986	1987	1988	1989	1990	1991	1992	1993	1994	1995
CURRENT RECEIPTS												
Taxes on income[1]	ACGB	51 598	51 973	55 658	61 723	70 000	76 875	75 178	73 716	73 232	80 670	90 672
Taxes on expenditure[1]	AAXC	56 667	62 872	68 971	76 039	79 980	78 298	85 416	87 521	90 336	96 138	103 597
Social security contributions[1,2]	AIIH	24 210	26 165	27 663	30 682	33 333	34 457	36 216	36 975	39 499	41 943	44 251
Community charge/council tax[1]	ADBH	–	–	–	–	586	8 629	8 128	7 907	8 038	8 450	8 989
Gross trading surplus[3]	DJAQ	265	155	–75	–32	199	12	–36	206	193	490	613
Rent, etc.[1,4]	CTGA	5 510	4 101	4 347	4 117	3 902	4 255	4 565	4 736	5 363	5 537	5 649
Interest and dividends, etc.	ATAC	6 185	5 691	5 733	6 015	6 900	6 366	5 645	5 239	4 636	5 061	5 174
Miscellaneous current transfers	ACGX	229	266	363	394	431	504	545	419	623	704	719
Imputed charge for consumption of non-trading capital	AAXG	2 372	2 583	2 804	3 110	3 448	3 806	3 763	3 603	3 679	3 837	4 129
Total	AAXA	147 036	153 806	165 464	182 048	198 779	213 202	219 420	220 322	225 599	242 830	263 793
CURRENT EXPENDITURE												
Current expenditure on goods and services	CTGD	72 895	78 328	84 241	90 531	98 348	109 128	120 342	128 272	134 402	140 277	145 345
Non-trading capital consumption	AAXG	2 372	2 583	2 804	3 110	3 448	3 806	3 763	3 603	3 679	3 837	4 129
Subsidies	AAXJ	7 225	6 301	6 265	6 037	5 782	6 066	5 995	6 737	7 203	7 060	6 966
Current grants to personal sector	AIIE	45 351	49 454	50 798	52 175	54 033	58 939	69 287	80 052	88 384	92 574	96 490
Current grants paid abroad (net)	-HDKH	3 427	2 233	3 277	3 248	4 278	4 596	1 083	4 834	4 969	5 135	7 180
Debt interest	AAXL	17 586	17 151	17 936	18 197	18 928	18 696	16 936	17 039	18 427	22 144	25 800
Total current expenditure	AAXH	148 856	156 050	165 321	173 298	184 817	201 231	217 406	240 537	257 064	271 027	285 910
Balance: current surplus[3]	AAXM	–1 820	–2 244	143	8 750	13 962	11 971	2 014	–20 215	–31 465	–28 197	–22 117
Total	AAXA	147 036	153 806	165 464	182 048	198 779	213 202	219 420	220 322	225 599	242 830	263 793
CAPITAL RECEIPTS												
Current surplus[3]	AAXM	–1 820	–2 244	143	8 750	13 962	11 971	2 014	–20 215	–31 465	–28 197	–22 117
Taxes on capital and other capital receipts[1]	GTDZ	2 371	3 181	3 286	4 384	4 707	4 440	3 558	2 844	2 536	2 790	3 154
Total	AAYA	551	937	3 429	13 134	18 669	16 411	5 572	–17 371	–28 929	–25 407	–18 963
CAPITAL EXPENDITURE												
Gross domestic fixed capital formation	AAYE	6 872	7 509	7 577	6 506	9 582	12 659	12 143	12 506	11 803	12 290	12 453
Value of physical increase in stocks	AAAD	450	–237	–498	–322	–163	–163	151	–17	–24	–251	–154
Grants and transfers to other sectors[5]	AAYG	3 319	3 002	3 216	3 806	4 233	10 148	7 939	7 680	8 602	7 934	7 498
Total capital expenditure	AAYD	10 641	10 274	10 295	9 990	13 652	22 963	20 233	20 169	20 381	19 973	19 797
Balance: financial surplus or deficit	AABC	–10 090	–9 337	–6 866	3 144	5 017	–6 552	–14 661	–37 540	–49 310	–45 380	–38 760
Total	AAYA	551	937	3 429	13 134	18 669	16 411	5 572	–17 371	–28 929	–25 407	–18 963
FINANCIAL ACCOUNT												
Transactions in financial liabilities	ABCA	9 551	4 424	1 637	–7 209	–4 993	–1 419	8 768	29 090	46 140	41 365	38 742
Transactions in financial assets	ABCD	–753	–5 364	–5 634	–4 827	517	–8 008	–6 715	–7 680	–2 478	–4 331	–177
Net total financial transactions[6]	ABCG	–10 304	–9 788	–7 271	2 382	5 510	–6 589	–15 483	–36 770	–48 618	–45 696	–38 919
BALANCING ITEM	ABCH	214	451	405	762	–493	37	822	–770	–692	316	159

1 Total revenue from taxation, social security contributions, community charge/council tax and royalties is as follows (£ million):

		1985	1986	1987	1988	1989	1990	1991	1992	1993	1994	1995
	GTEA	137 012	144 911	156 497	173 396	188 861	203 095	208 832	209 337	214 402	230 690	251 167

2 See table 7.2 for composition.
3 Before providing for depreciation.
4 Includes royalties and licence fees on oil and gas production.
5 Excludes financial transactions on writing-off debt to public corporations.
6 Total assets less total liabilities.

9.2 General government: total expenditure on goods and services at current market prices

£ million

		1985	1986	1987	1988	1989	1990	1991	1992	1993	1994	1995
CENTRAL GOVERNMENT												
Final consumption:												
Military defence:												
Pay	CIKK	6 917	7 325	7 472	7 797	8 301	9 026	10 033	10 528	10 935	10 473	9 910
Procurement	CIKL	10 905	11 245	11 158	11 450	12 095	13 097	14 454	12 899	12 698	12 627	12 371
Capital consumption	CIKM	35	38	39	41	50	55	57	60	62	65	68
Total	ACHD	17 857	18 608	18 669	19 288	20 446	22 178	24 544	23 487	23 695	23 165	22 349
National health service:												
Pay	CIKN	9 312	9 943	11 117	12 268	13 617	14 900	14 931	14 229	10 707	5 592	3 924
Procurement	CIKO	7 451	8 013	8 648	9 503	9 960	10 953	14 410	19 021	24 884	32 498	36 329
Capital consumption	CIKP	449	490	535	591	673	757	654	488	237	75	66
Total	ACHE	17 212	18 446	20 300	22 362	24 250	26 610	29 995	33 738	35 828	38 165	40 319
Other:												
Pay[1]	CIKQ	6 427	6 703	7 542	8 040	8 780	9 851	10 987	12 232	12 779	12 889	13 260
Procurement[1]	CIKR	3 884	4 496	4 924	5 249	6 290	7 602	7 741	8 611	9 608	10 203	10 450
Capital consumption[1]	CIKS	499	548	605	671	761	811	964	1 060	1 568	1 838	2 016
Education grants	CUKF	1 462	1 530	1 696	1 912	2 767	3 056	2 754	3 131	5 920	7 341	8 269
Total	ACHF	12 272	13 277	14 767	15 872	18 598	21 320	22 446	25 034	29 875	32 271	33 995
Total:												
Pay	GILN	22 656	23 971	26 131	28 105	30 698	33 777	35 951	36 989	34 421	28 954	27 094
Procurement	CUCN	22 240	23 754	24 730	26 202	28 345	31 652	36 605	40 531	47 190	55 328	59 150
Capital consumption	ACGL	983	1 076	1 179	1 303	1 484	1 623	1 675	1 608	1 867	1 978	2 150
Education grants	CUKF	1 462	1 530	1 696	1 912	2 767	3 056	2 754	3 131	5 920	7 341	8 269
Total final consumption	ACHC	47 341	50 331	53 736	57 522	63 294	70 108	76 985	82 259	89 398	93 601	96 663
Capital expenditure:												
Gross domestic fixed capital formation	AAAC	3 126	3 351	3 358	3 709	4 951	6 415	6 876	6 855	6 391	5 946	5 642
Value of physical increase in stocks	AAAD	450	−237	−498	−322	−163	156	151	−17	−24	−251	−154
Total capital expenditure	GTEB	3 576	3 114	2 860	3 387	4 788	6 571	7 027	6 838	6 367	5 695	5 488
Total expenditure	GTEC	50 917	53 445	56 596	60 909	68 082	76 679	84 012	89 097	95 765	99 296	102 151
LOCAL AUTHORITIES												
Final consumption:												
Education[2]	ADAI	13 314	14 944	16 235	17 715	18 579	19 849	21 668	22 983	21 064	21 284	22 015
Other	ADAJ	14 612	15 636	17 074	18 404	19 923	22 977	25 452	26 633	27 619	29 229	30 796
Total final consumption	CSBA	27 926	30 580	33 309	36 119	38 502	42 826	47 120	49 616	48 683	50 513	52 811
Capital expenditure:												
Gross domestic fixed capital formation												
Expenditure on fixed assets	GTED	5 861	6 353	6 994	7 583	9 772	10 558	7 988	8 153	8 551	9 187	9 450
less Sales of council housing	-CTCS	−1 240	−1 339	−1 648	−2 665	−3 153	−2 215	−1 447	−1 229	−1 227	−1 236	−629
less Other sales	-GTEE	−875	−856	−1 127	−2 121	−1 988	−2 099	−1 274	−1 273	−1 912	−1 607	−2 010
Total capital expenditure	AAAG	3 746	4 158	4 219	2 797	4 631	6 244	5 267	5 651	5 412	6 344	6 811
Total expenditure	GTEF	31 672	34 738	37 528	38 916	43 133	49 070	52 387	55 267	54 095	56 857	59 622
GENERAL GOVERNMENT												
Final consumption	AAXI	75 267	80 911	87 045	93 641	101 796	112 934	124 105	131 875	138 081	144 114	149 474
Gross domestic fixed capital formation	AAYE	6 872	7 509	7 577	6 506	9 582	12 659	12 143	12 506	11 803	12 290	12 453
Value of physical increase in stocks	AAAD	450	−237	−498	−322	−163	156	151	−17	−24	−251	−154
Total expenditure	GTEG	82 589	88 183	94 124	99 825	111 215	125 749	136 399	144 364	149 860	156 153	161 773

1 Including education elements.
2 Including school meals and milk.

9.3 General government: total expenditure on goods and services at 1990 market prices[1]

£ million

		1985	1986	1987	1988	1989	1990	1991	1992	1993	1994	1995
CENTRAL GOVERNMENT												
Final consumption:												
Military defence:												
Pay	CILF	10 340	10 197	9 874	9 560	9 361	9 026	8 875	8 714	8 172	7 567	6 999
Procurement	CILG	13 880	14 027	13 199	13 126	13 040	13 097	14 265	12 486	12 017	11 760	10 955
Capital consumption	CILH	51	52	52	52	54	55	60	63	66	68	68
Total	GTEH	24 249	24 276	23 125	22 738	22 455	22 178	23 200	21 263	20 255	19 369	18 022
National health service:												
Pay	CIKJ	15 203	15 051	15 033	14 971	14 933	14 900	13 744	11 538	7 392	3 188	1 944
Procurement	CILI	9 388	9 775	10 050	10 518	10 524	10 953	13 426	16 752	20 916	26 433	28 894
Capital consumption	CUET	632	657	682	703	726	757	691	581	312	109	98
Total	GTEI	25 144	25 483	25 765	26 192	26 183	26 610	27 861	28 871	28 620	29 675	30 936
Other:												
Pay[2]	CILJ	9 332	9 402	9 727	9 910	9 805	9 851	9 872	10 206	10 209	9 867	9 741
Procurement[2]	CILK	4 889	5 486	5 797	5 889	6 674	7 602	7 439	8 001	8 795	9 111	9 010
Capital consumption[2]	CILL	565	600	641	685	738	811	914	976	1 599	1 889	2 045
Education grants	CJPI	2 124	2 030	2 067	2 174	2 981	3 056	2 525	2 722	4 977	6 034	6 653
Total	GTEJ	16 847	17 518	18 232	18 658	20 198	21 320	20 750	21 905	25 580	26 906	27 449
Total:												
Pay	CILM	34 867	34 650	34 634	34 441	34 099	33 777	32 491	30 458	25 773	20 619	18 684
Procurement	CUCP	28 153	29 288	29 046	29 533	30 238	31 652	35 130	37 239	41 728	47 223	48 859
Capital consumption	CSBS	1 247	1 309	1 375	1 440	1 518	1 623	1 665	1 620	1 616	1 415	1 285
Education grants	CJPI	2 124	2 030	2 067	2 174	2 981	3 056	2 525	2 722	4 977	6 034	6 653
Total final consumption	DJDK	66 241	67 277	67 122	67 588	68 836	70 108	71 811	72 039	74 455	75 950	76 407
Capital expenditure:												
Gross domestic fixed capital formation	GTEL	4 040	4 236	4 109	4 297	5 194	6 415	7 100	7 574	7 365	6 846	5 993
Value of physical increase in stocks	DGAG	288	−253	−441	−210	−151	156	136	3	−48	−256	−150
Total capital expenditure	GTEM	4 682	3 983	3 668	4 087	5 043	6 571	7 236	7 577	7 317	6 590	5 843
Total expenditure	GTEN	70 972	71 260	70 790	71 675	73 879	76 679	79 047	79 616	81 772	82 540	82 250
LOCAL AUTHORITIES												
Final consumption:												
Education[3]	GTEO	19 115	19 385	19 851	20 064	19 924	19 849	20 138	19 928	17 733	17 498	17 725
Other	GTEP	19 747	20 162	20 885	20 960	21 379	22 977	23 896	23 765	23 804	24 759	25 569
Total final consumption	DJDL	38 856	39 547	40 736	41 024	41 303	42 826	44 034	43 693	41 537	42 257	43 294
Capital expenditure:												
Gross domestic fixed capital formation:												
Expenditure on fixed assets	GTER	8 103	8 473	9 041	9 027	10 412	10 558	8 221	9 216	10 325	10 490	10 235
less Sales of council housing	-GTES	−2 260	−2 163	−2 449	−3 199	−3 405	−2 215	−1 424	−1 475	−1 340	−1 167	−673
less Other sales	-GTET	−1 594	−1 383	−1 674	−2 546	−2 147	−2 099	−1 254	−1 528	−2 299	−1 661	−2 171
Total capital expenditure	GTEU	4 412	4 927	4 918	3 282	4 860	6 244	5 543	6 213	6 686	7 662	7 391
Total expenditure	GTEV	43 201	44 474	45 654	44 306	46 163	49 070	49 577	49 906	48 223	49 919	50 685
GENERAL GOVERNMENT												
Final consumption	DJCZ	105 097	106 824	107 858	108 612	110 139	112 934	115 845	115 732	115 992	118 207	119 701
Gross domestic fixed capital formation	DFDS	8 441	9 163	9 027	7 579	10 054	12 659	12 643	13 787	14 051	14 508	13 384
Value of physical increase in stocks	DGAG	288	−253	−441	−210	−151	156	136	3	−48	−256	−150
Total expenditure	GTEX	114 378	115 734	116 444	115 981	120 042	125 749	128 624	129 522	129 995	132 459	132 935

1 For the years before 1986, totals differ from the sum of their components
2 Including education elements.
3 Including school meals and milk.

General government

9.4 General government: analysis of total expenditure

£ million

		1985	1986	1987	1988	1989	1990	1991	1992	1993	1994	1995
General public services												
Current expenditure on goods and services:												
Wages and salaries etc[1]	GTEY	4 527	4 548	4 998	5 661	6 285	6 723	7 729	8 005	8 067	8 178	8 449
Other	GTEZ	−777	−498	−765	−1 025	−534	−70	−476	−714	−644	−57	351
Current grants to personal sector	GTFB	492	519	715	866	931	1 203	1 146	1 302	1 547	1 535	1 473
Current grants abroad	GTFC	978	1 061	954	1 217	1 316	1 438	1 800	1 976	1 879	1 974	1 939
Gross domestic fixed capital formation	GTFA	689	587	552	789	1 205	1 192	1 198	1 303	1 033	1 125	1 205
Capital transfers to private sector	GTFD	54	66	70	73	80	91	64	60	83	61	75
Net lending to public corporations	GTFE	50	43	7	14	53	62	56	42	32	−5	12
Company securities (net)	GTFF	–	–	–	–	–	–	–	−14	–	–	–
Total	GTFG	6 013	6 326	6 531	7 595	9 336	10 639	11 517	11 960	11 997	12 811	13 504
of which: Parliament	GTFH	405	503	494	638	708	664	806	926	1 013	1 118	1 272
Finance and tax collection	GTFI	1 980	2 061	2 477	2 624	3 144	3 707	3 992	3 966	4 045	4 023	3 745
External	GTFJ	745	777	927	902	977	1 154	1 396	1 697	1 818	1 607	1 559
Other	GTFK	2 883	2 985	2 633	3 431	4 507	5 114	5 323	5 371	5 121	6 063	6 928
Defence												
Current expenditure on goods and services:												
Wages and salaries etc[1]	GTFL	6 925	7 335	7 484	7 811	8 316	9 043	10 057	10 551	10 956	10 491	9 929
Other	GTFM	10 947	11 278	11 199	11 495	12 158	13 168	14 520	12 951	12 741	12 660	12 391
Current grants to personal sector	GTPB	–	–	15	34	27	35	42	25	20	50	33
Current grants abroad	GTFP	51	82	84	99	79	39	−2 007	169	109	49	112
of which Gulf contributions	−HHQG	–	–	–	–	–	−38	−2 110	−9	–	–	–
Gross domestic fixed capital formation	GTFN	269	359	351	358	408	622	613	713	753	727	688
Value of physical increase in stocks	GTFO	–	–	–	–	–	–	–	−11	−25	−28	−4
Capital transfers to private sector	GTFQ	21	12	–	–	–	–	1	5	6	3	5
Company securities (net)	GTLD	–	–	−190	–	–	–	–	–	–	–	–
Total	GTFR	18 213	19 066	18 943	19 797	20 988	22 907	23 226	24 403	24 560	23 952	23 154
Public order and safety												
Current expenditure on goods and services:												
Wages and salaries etc[1]	GTFS	4 670	5 058	5 618	6 165	6 722	7 600	8 598	9 424	9 765	9 955	10 372
Other	GTFT	1 113	1 343	1 379	1 607	1 885	2 123	3 002	3 198	3 322	3 794	3 546
Current grants to personal sector	GTFV	98	107	138	179	187	236	299	316	375	365	395
Gross domestic fixed capital formation	GTFU	344	318	389	455	639	973	1 024	916	967	1 005	1 007
Total	GTFW	6 225	6 826	7 524	8 406	9 433	10 932	12 923	13 854	14 429	15 119	15 320
of which: Police	GTFX	3 557	3 691	3 852	4 254	4 695	5 291	6 468	6 946	7 402	7 773	7 999
Fire	GTFY	808	845	923	1 003	1 112	1 229	1 377	1 442	1 503	1 573	1 618
Law courts	GTFZ	1 030	1 219	1 509	1 973	2 295	2 690	3 251	3 640	3 895	4 046	3 943
Prisons	GTGA	830	1 071	1 240	1 176	1 331	1 722	1 827	1 826	1 629	1 727	1 760
Education												
Current expenditure on goods and services:												
Wages and salaries etc[1]	GTGB	10 581	11 927	13 043	14 325	14 663	15 353	16 775	18 520	17 098	17 206	17 724
Other	GTGC	4 415	4 828	5 140	5 512	6 912	7 823	8 227	8 376	10 739	12 436	13 895
Current grants to personal sector	GTGE	1 464	1 617	1 603	1 664	1 770	1 805	2 772	3 371	4 121	4 143	4 044
Gross domestic fixed capital formation	GTGD	618	668	798	622	922	1 051	930	1 013	959	909	1 147
Capital transfers to private sector	GTGF	208	235	245	455	570	659	569	505	776	745	881
Net lending to private sector	GTGG	−3	−4	–	–	–	33	82	162	236	482	639
Total	GTGH	17 283	19 271	20 829	22 578	24 837	26 724	29 355	31 947	33 929	35 921	38 330
Health												
Current expenditure on goods and services:												
Wages and salaries etc[1]	CIKN	9 312	9 943	11 117	12 268	13 617	14 900	14 931	14 229	10 707	5 592	3 924
Other	CIKO	7 451	8 013	8 648	9 503	9 960	10 953	14 410	19 021	24 884	32 498	36 329
Current grants to personal sector	GTGK	97	99	109	127	129	206	123	93	101	115	117
Current grants abroad	GTGL	20	26	29	31	45	39	49	58	67	65	138
Gross domestic fixed capital formation	GTCV	1 005	1 078	998	994	1 402	1 643	1 625	1 594	999	451	304
Capital transfers to private sector	GTGM	4	5	4	13	13	25	12	4	7	28	30
Company securities (net)	GTLT	–	–	–	–	−14	–	–	–	–	–	–
Total	GTGN	17 889	19 164	20 905	22 936	25 152	27 766	31 150	34 999	36 765	38 749	40 842
Social security												
Current expenditure on goods and services:												
Wages and salaries etc[1]	GTGO	3 058	3 314	3 747	4 135	4 459	5 030	5 615	6 120	6 371	6 460	7 639
Other	GTGP	2 060	1 939	2 352	2 683	2 968	3 302	3 899	4 263	5 393	5 514	5 548
Current grants to personal sector	GTGR	40 604	44 099	45 373	46 653	48 890	53 395	63 023	73 094	80 348	84 336	87 814
Current grants abroad	GTGS	365	405	441	478	555	620	728	661	824	899	949
Gross domestic fixed capital formation	GTGQ	159	190	221	256	426	544	504	485	526	557	485
Capital transfers to private sector	GTGT	–	–	−1	−2	−3	–	–	1	3	4	1
Net lending to private sector	GTLV	–	–	–	54	48	37	26	42	48	27	47
Total	GTGU	46 246	49 947	52 133	54 257	57 343	62 928	73 795	84 666	93 513	97 797	102 483

1 Including employers' contributions to social security, superannuation, etc.

9.4 General government: analysis of total expenditure

continued

£ million

		1985	1986	1987	1988	1989	1990	1991	1992	1993	1994	1995
Housing and community amenities												
Current expenditure on goods and services:												
Wages and salaries etc[1]	GTGV	1 311	1 456	1 575	1 484	1 225	1 217	1 224	1 233	1 226	1 184	1 257
Other	GTGW	1 065	1 143	1 312	1 363	1 578	2 084	2 364	2 802	2 718	2 892	3 097
Subsidies	GTGY	1 456	1 411	1 360	1 482	1 538	1 613	1 482	1 373	1 306	1 101	1 192
Current grants to personal sector	GTGZ	572	800	1 263	1 102	165	146	171	117	64	35	32
Gross domestic fixed capital formation	GTGX	1 334	1 688	1 667	378	876	1 734	1 326	1 458	1 637	1 996	2 017
Capital transfers to private sector	GTHA	1 621	1 422	1 589	1 712	1 572	2 067	3 009	3 150	3 968	3 099	2 397
Capital transfers to public corporations	GTHB	64	26	160	255	573	661	1 483	999	792	521	679
Net lending to private sector	GTHC	−433	−438	−373	−176	−93	−420	−879	−462	−431	−328	−207
Net lending to public corporations	GTHD	18	558	674	895	1 169	221	−92	36	38	36	4
Company securities (net)	GTLU	–	–	–	–	−607	−1 524	−1 391	−101	–	–	–
Total	GTHE	7 008	8 066	9 227	8 495	7 996	7 799	8 697	10 605	11 318	10 536	10 468
of which: Housing	GTHF	4 192	4 222	4 491	3 929	4 251	5 289	5 960	6 073	6 542	5 712	4 607
Water and sewerage	GTHG	−98	457	547	793	586	−1 246	−1 253	69	230	327	290
Other	GTHH	2 914	3 387	4 189	3 773	3 159	3 756	3 990	4 463	4 546	4 497	5 571
Recreational and cultural affairs												
Current expenditure on goods and services:												
Wages and salaries etc[1]	GTHI	904	1 017	1 117	1 149	1 232	1 343	1 347	1 239	1 278	1 365	1 432
Other	GTHJ	642	720	777	981	1 076	1 307	1 571	1 915	1 980	1 847	1 775
Subsidies	GTBY	–	–	–	–	–	–	–	59	56	57	66
Current grants to personal sector	GTHM	298	290	301	293	205	223	291	398	272	394	360
Gross domestic fixed capital formation	GTHK	401	420	399	407	663	784	771	562	671	645	626
Capital transfers to private sector	GTHN	3	1	3	6	6	9	22	10	10	29	17
Capital transfers to public corporations	GTHO	–	–	–	–	–	–	–	–	–	–	–
Net lending to public corporations	GTHP	−7	−2	2	−8	3	−11	−20	−15	−4	16	13
Company securities (net)	GTOC	–	–	–	–	–	–	−68	–	–	–	–
Total	GTHQ	2 241	2 446	2 599	2 828	3 185	3 655	3 914	4 168	4 263	4 353	4 289
Fuel and energy[2]												
Current expenditure on goods and services:												
Wages and salaries etc[1]	GTHR	197	19	–	–	1	–	–	–	–	–	–
Other	GTHS	67	285	281	167	302	237	227	244	202	175	201
Subsidies	GTHV	1 501	766	760	610	740	222	408	685	624	452	130
Current grants to personal sector	GTHW	421	593	482	159	157	103	61	48	25	37	261
Gross domestic fixed capital formation	GTHT	50	4	–	–	–	–	–	–	–	–	–
Value of physical increase in stocks	GTHU	−1	–	–	–	–	–	–	–	–	–	–
Capital transfers to private sector	GTHX	–	–	–	–	–	–	51	35	58	90	107
Capital transfers to public corporations	GTHY	–	–	6	7	7	5 179	1 486	1 421	1 431	1 385	953
Net lending to private sector	GTHZ	−2	−2	−4	−2	−2	−3	−3	−1	–	–	–
Net lending to public corporations	GTIA	−708	−819	−1 329	72	−351	−6 046	190	1 047	295	691	1 287
Company securities (net)	GTIB	−446	−2 020	−3 566	−4 039	−2 639	−2 708	−5 474	−4 012	−1 698	−2 395	−715
Total	GTIC	1 079	−1 174	−3 370	−3 026	−1 785	−3 016	−3 054	−534	937	435	2 224
Agriculture, forestry and fishing												
Current expenditure on goods and services:												
Wages and salaries etc[1]	GTID	199	192	247	242	263	284	348	421	410	407	349
Other	GTIE	327	360	417	405	325	356	343	457	406	457	526
Subsidies	GTIH	1 311	1 523	1 963	2 010	1 372	1 633	1 687	1 823	2 966	2 419	2 586
Current grants to personal sector	GTII	49	21	14	1	3	3	7	10	10	12	3
Gross domestic fixed capital formation	GTIF	70	50	51	76	89	125	122	133	79	90	168
Value of physical increase in stocks	GTIG	449	−233	−493	−315	−160	161	329	175	216	−175	−181
Capital transfers to private sector	GTIJ	220	170	169	71	80	85	68	90	71	60	36
Net lending to private sector	GTIK	−3	5	−3	−3	–	–	2	2	2	3	–
Company securities (net)	GTLE	–	–	−66	–	–	–	–	–	–	–	–
Total	GTIL	2 622	2 088	2 299	2 487	1 972	2 647	2 906	3 111	4 160	3 273	3 487
Mining and mineral resources, manufacturing and construction												
Current expenditure on goods and services:												
Wages and salaries etc[1]	GTIM	94	112	132	142	152	177	157	184	214	216	209
Other	GTIN	371	325	314	370	312	340	502	416	404	364	273
Subsidies	GTIQ	250	226	301	297	226	152	237	293	296	401	292
Current grants to personal sector	GTIR	86	94	35	18	9	11	56	66	68	134	68
Gross domestic fixed capital formation	GTIO	74	52	34	28	32	37	77	92	44	31	48
Value of physical increase in stocks	GTIP	3	−2	−4	−6	−1	−1	–	−1	−3	−4	−3
Capital transfers to private sector	GTIS	564	697	486	971	495	432	350	288	280	354	404
Capital transfers to public corporations	GTIT	233	148	76	6	10	3	–	–	23	183	157
Net lending to private sector	GTIU	130	119	75	89	860	166	165	−72	11	18	−20
Net lending to public corporations	GTIV	97	−21	66	49	699	100	−1	−2	−1	−2	−1
Public dividend capital etc	GTIW	836	157	144	147	45	5	1	1	–	–	–
Company securities (net)	GTIX	−363	−1	−385	−1 194	−1 315	−152	–	−43	–	–	–
Total	GTIY	2 375	1 906	1 274	917	1 524	1 270	1 544	1 222	1 336	1 695	1 427

1 Including employers' contributions to social security, superannuation, etc.
2 Comprises identifiable expenditure only.

9.4 General government: analysis of total expenditure
continued

£ million

		1985	1986	1987	1988	1989	1990	1991	1992	1993	1994	1995
Transport and communications												
Current expenditure on goods and services:												
Wages and salaries etc[1]	GTIZ	656	540	545	664	710	765	849	852	762	743	794
Other	GTJA	1 205	1 355	1 519	1 396	1 595	1 896	2 047	2 087	2 063	2 275	2 286
Subsidies	GTJC	1 534	1 376	1 194	1 065	1 000	1 099	1 332	1 838	1 590	2 289	2 410
Current grants to personal sector	GTJD	82	88	94	86	89	94	26	64	65	65	54
Gross domestic fixed capital formation	GTJB	1 709	1 914	1 978	2 142	2 666	3 587	3 513	4 116	4 151	4 568	4 508
Capital transfers to private sector	GTJE	6	7	10	6	7	4	1	12	7	3	84
Capital transfers to public corporations	GTJF	279	296	307	293	398	482	410	781	768	830	913
Net lending to private sector	GTJG	−9	−4	−10	−10	−10	−4	−2	−49	−1	–	–
Net lending to public corporations	GTJH	169	−56	84	−201	759	1 612	500	342	805	67	−156
Public dividend capital etc	GTJI	–	–	–	–	–	–	–	–	–	–	–
Company securities (net)	GTJJ	−1 537	−1 788	−1 723	−961	−85	−92	−1 938	−3 398	−3 708	−4 262	−1 766
Total	GTJK	4 094	3 728	3 998	4 480	7 129	9 443	6 738	6 645	6 502	6 578	9 127
Other economic affairs and services												
Current expenditure on goods and services:												
Wages and salaries etc[1]	GTJL	918	1 205	1 295	1 093	1 185	1 588	922	1 243	1 690	1 602	1 140
Other	GTJM	657	571	750	935	981	1 586	1 154	1 235	1 650	2 023	1 909
Subsidies	GTJO	1 173	999	687	573	906	1 347	849	666	365	341	290
Current grants to personal sector	GTJP	1 088	1 127	656	993	1 471	1 479	1 270	1 148	1 368	1 353	1 836
Gross domestic fixed capital formation	GTJN	150	181	139	1	254	367	440	121	−16	186	250
Value of physical increase in stocks	GTLS	−1	−2	−1	−1	−2	−4	−178	−180	−212	−44	34
Capital transfers to private sector	GTJQ	23	−98	−28	−234	197	215	196	228	167	205	211
Capital transfers to public corporations	GTJR	19	15	120	174	228	236	217	91	152	334	548
Net lending to private sector	GTKC	33	60	63	87	109	61	91	117	36	26	62
Net lending to public corporations	GTJT	151	220	−130	−162	−432	−243	−746	−149	−121	−195	−449
Net lending to overseas sector	-AACT	126	−199	–	–	–	–	–	–	–	–	–
Public dividend capital etc	GTJU	–	–	–	–	–	–	–	–	–	–	–
Company securities (net)	GTJV	11	49	163	113	152	95	−63	−17	5	20	14
Total	GTJW	4 348	4 128	3 714	3 572	5 049	6 727	4 152	4 503	5 084	5 851	5 845
Other expenditure												
Non-trading capital consumption	AAXG	2 372	2 583	2 804	3 110	3 448	3 806	3 763	3 603	3 679	3 837	4 129
Debt interest	AAXL	17 586	17 151	17 936	18 197	18 928	18 696	16 936	17 039	18 427	22 144	25 800
Current grants	GTKA	2 013	659	1 769	1 423	2 283	2 460	513	1 970	2 090	2 148	4 042
Net lending to overseas sector	GTKD	157	158	126	185	269	160	264	342	209	219	237
Total	GTKE	22 128	20 551	22 635	22 915	24 928	25 122	21 476	22 954	24 405	28 348	34 208
Total expenditure												
Current expenditure on goods and services:												
Wages and salaries etc[1,2]	GTKF	43 352	46 666	50 918	55 139	58 830	64 023	68 552	72 021	68 544	63 399	63 218
Other	GTKG	29 543	31 662	33 323	35 392	39 518	45 105	51 790	56 251	65 858	76 878	82 127
Subsidies	AAXJ	7 225	6 301	6 265	6 037	5 782	6 066	5 995	6 737	7 203	7 060	6 966
Current grants to personal sector	AIIE	45 351	49 454	50 798	52 175	54 033	58 939	69 287	80 052	88 384	92 574	96 490
Current grants abroad	-HDKH	3 427	2 233	3 277	3 248	4 278	4 596	1 083	4 834	4 969	5 135	7 180
of which Gulf contributions	-HHQG	–	–	–	–	–	−38	−2 110	−9	–	–	–
Gross domestic fixed capital formation	AAYE	6 872	7 509	7 577	6 506	9 582	12 659	12 143	12 506	11 803	12 290	12 453
Value of physical increase in stock	AAAD	450	−237	−498	−322	−163	156	151	−17	−24	−251	−154
Capital transfers to private sector	GTKH	2 724	2 517	2 547	3 071	3 017	3 587	4 343	4 388	5 436	4 681	4 248
Capital transfers to public corporations	GTKI	595	485	669	735	1 216	6 561	3 596	3 292	3 166	3 253	3 250
Net lending to private sector	GTKJ	−287	−264	−252	39	912	−130	−518	−262	−99	228	521
Net lending to public corporations	ACKD	−230	−77	−626	659	1 900	−4 305	−113	1 301	1 044	608	710
Net lending to overseas sector	ACKE	283	−41	126	185	269	160	264	342	209	219	237
Public dividend capital etc	ACKF	836	157	144	147	45	5	1	1	–	–	–
Company securities (net)	GTLF	−2 335	−3 760	−5 767	−6 081	−4 508	−4 381	−8 934	−7 585	−5 401	−6 637	−2 467
Total	GTKK	137 806	142 605	148 501	156 930	174 711	193 041	207 640	233 861	251 092	259 437	274 779
Non-trading capital consumption	AAXG	2 372	2 583	2 804	3 110	3 448	3 806	3 763	3 603	3 679	3 837	4 129
Debt interest	AAXL	17 586	17 151	17 936	18 197	18 928	18 696	16 936	17 039	18 427	22 144	25 800
Total expenditure	ABAB	157 764	162 339	169 241	178 237	197 087	215 543	228 339	254 503	273 198	285 418	304 708

1 Including employers' contributions to social security, superannuation, etc.
2 For details of total wages and salaries and employers' contributions paid by
  general government see table in methodological notes.

9.5 Taxes on expenditure and subsidies: allocation by sector and by type of expenditure[1]

£ million

		1985	1986	1987	1988	1989	1990	1991	1992	1993	1994	1995
PERSONAL SECTOR												
Taxes on expenditure												
Current expenditure												
Durable goods:												
Cars, motorcycles and other vehicles	CTHH	1 567	1 852	2 104	2 826	3 195	3 022	2 826	2 448	2 383	2 819	2 992
Furniture and floor coverings	CTHK	560	587	660	780	800	799	893	970	1 067	1 156	1 128
Other durable goods	CTHL	916	1 004	1 141	1 291	1 340	1 361	1 529	1 639	1 763	1 854	2 046
Total durable goods	CTHM	3 043	3 443	3 905	4 897	5 335	5 182	5 248	5 057	5 213	5 829	6 166
Other goods:												
Food (household expenditure)	CTHN	1 057	1 185	1 262	1 332	1 401	1 500	1 765	1 824	1 923	2 112	1 996
Alcoholic drink: Beer	CTHO	3 002	3 101	3 154	3 349	3 434	3 684	4 128	4 283	4 416	4 578	4 636
Spirits	CTHP	1 895	1 930	1 963	2 129	2 139	2 357	2 531	2 602	2 746	2 890	2 705
Wines, cider and perry	CTHQ	1 106	1 135	1 196	1 261	1 291	1 415	1 547	1 665	1 764	1 850	1 953
Tobacco	CTHS	5 283	5 605	6 064	6 047	6 050	6 659	7 503	7 542	7 906	8 464	9 124
Clothing and footwear	CTHT	1 832	2 023	2 177	2 326	2 436	2 537	2 852	3 029	3 242	3 404	3 566
Energy products: Fuel and power	CTHU	284	290	281	231	185	162	162	167	143	1 061	1 568
Petrol and oil	CTHV	3 970	4 274	4 456	4 907	5 075	5 574	6 324	6 717	7 337	8 093	8 655
Other goods	CTHW	2 615	2 935	3 280	3 720	4 148	4 494	5 179	5 559	5 903	6 141	6 346
Total other goods	GIWD	21 044	22 478	23 833	25 302	26 159	28 382	31 991	33 388	35 380	38 593	40 549
Services: Rates[2]	CTHY	5 761	6 587	7 358	8 465	8 914	2 372	135	124	129	135	139
Vehicle excise duty	CDDZ	1 482	1 566	1 612	1 693	1 793	1 837	1 879	1 963	2 301	2 546	2 641
Other services	CTIA	5 545	6 448	7 429	8 560	9 666	10 463	11 830	12 642	13 556	14 246	15 348
Total services	GIWE	12 788	14 601	16 399	18 718	20 373	14 672	13 844	14 729	15 986	16 927	18 128
Total taxes on consumers' expenditure	CTIB	36 875	40 522	44 137	48 917	51 867	48 236	51 083	53 174	56 579	61 349	64 843
Taxes on capital formation	GIWF	1 294	1 547	1 946	2 766	2 701	2 492	2 401	1 700	1 931	2 107	2 194
Total taxes on personal sector	GIWZ	38 169	42 069	46 083	51 683	54 568	50 728	53 484	54 874	58 510	63 456	67 037
GENERAL GOVERNMENT												
Taxes on expenditure												
Current expenditure	GIWI	3 694	4 011	4 268	4 529	4 866	5 437	6 615	7 118	7 646	8 517	8 874
Capital formation	GIWJ	247	269	292	348	515	872	743	890	765	1 172	922
Total taxes on general government	GIWK	3 941	4 280	4 560	4 877	5 381	6 309	7 358	8 008	8 411	9 689	9 796
COMPANIES AND PUBLIC CORPORATIONS												
Non refundable taxes on expenditure												
Intermediate expenditure	GIWN	12 261	14 046	15 409	16 447	16 931	18 476	21 564	21 689	20 063	19 907	23 421
Capital formation	GIWO	1 330	1 466	1 782	1 910	1 861	1 465	1 690	1 460	1 628	1 218	1 381
Total taxes on companies and public corps	GIWP	13 591	15 512	17 191	18 357	18 792	19 941	23 254	23 149	21 691	21 125	24 802
OVERSEAS SECTOR												
Taxes on UK exports of goods and services	GIWS	966	1 011	1 137	1 122	1 239	1 320	1 320	1 490	1 724	1 868	1 962
TOTAL ALL SECTORS												
Taxes on expenditure												
Current expenditure	GIWV	53 796	59 590	64 951	71 015	74 903	73 469	80 582	83 471	86 012	91 641	99 100
Capital formation	GIWW	2 871	3 282	4 020	5 024	5 077	4 829	4 834	4 050	4 324	4 497	4 497
Total taxes on expenditure	AAXC	56 667	62 872	68 971	76 039	79 980	78 298	85 416	87 521	90 336	96 138	103 597
Subsidies	AAXJ	7 225	6 301	6 265	6 037	5 782	6 066	5 995	6 737	7 203	7 060	6 966
Total taxes *less* subsidies	CTGV	49 442	56 571	62 706	70 002	74 198	72 232	79 421	80 784	83 133	89 078	96 631
Allocation of taxes *less* subsidies by type of final expenditure												
Consumers' expenditure	CTIL	36 674	41 743	45 997	51 407	54 767	51 588	56 373	57 554	58 522	62 965	69 065
General government final consumption	GIAY	4 416	4 956	5 330	5 700	6 085	6 804	8 168	8 708	9 289	10 208	10 727
Gross domestic capital formation	GIAZ	4 528	5 288	6 246	7 423	7 561	7 525	7 883	7 205	7 611	7 917	8 211
Exports of goods and services	GIBA	3 824	4 584	5 133	5 472	5 785	6 315	6 997	7 317	7 711	7 988	8 628

1 Up to the 1988 edition of the ONS Blue Book, Table 9.5 showed taxes on expenditure and subsidies broken down by sector and by type of expenditure. It did not prove practicable to provide the usual table in the 1989 edition of the ONS Blue Book. A table was subsequently published in the November issue of Economic Trends showing the usual breakdown of taxes on expenditure but subsidies were shown only in total pending a review of the basis of their sectoral breakdown. It has been decided that there is no satisfactory basis for a sectoral breakdown of subsidies which are therefore only shown in total.

2 This series is affected by the abolition of domestic rates and the introduction of community charge - see methodological notes.

9.6 Taxes on income and capital, other revenue: allocation by sector, type of income[1], and property

£ million

		1985	1986	1987	1988	1989	1990	1991	1992	1993	1994	1995
TAXES ON INCOME AND SOCIAL SECURITY, ETC CONTRIBUTIONS												
Taxes on income (payments):												
Personal sector	AIIG	37 774	40 805	43 459	48 274	53 589	61 543	63 419	65 178	63 637	68 168	74 655
less Tax credits	−DBAI	−2 687	−3 109	−3 506	−4 452	−5 383	−5 888	−6 013	−6 851	−5 518	−5 625	−7 363
Companies[2]	DAAB	9 348	9 538	11 602	13 655	16 239	14 972	13 179	11 649	11 334	14 065	17 902
Public corporations	ADRK	103	313	62	103	102	161	451	199	162	140	210
Non-residents	DKGN	7 060	4 426	4 041	4 143	5 453	6 087	4 142	3 541	3 617	3 922	5 268
Social security contributions	AIIH	24 210	26 165	27 663	30 682	33 333	34 457	36 216	36 975	39 499	41 943	44 251
Community charge/council tax	ADBH	−	−	−	−	586	8 629	8 128	7 907	8 038	8 450	8 989
Royalties	CTAI	2 240	925	1 127	799	522	625	543	568	600	553	574
ITC franchise payments	CUKL	−	−	−	−	−	−	−	−	350	380	398
Total	GIKF	78 048	79 063	84 448	93 204	104 441	120 586	120 065	119 166	121 719	131 996	144 884
Income tax:												
Deducted from												
Wages, salaries and forces' pay[3]	GIKG	31 436	34 013	36 356	38 643	43 415	48 504	50 279	51 510	52 449	56 353	60 409
Dividends, interest, rent and trading incomes[3]	GIKH	7 021	6 369	6 780	8 305	8 887	11 418	10 745	10 161	8 059	8 189	8 589
Social security benefits	GIKI	1 107	1 206	1 213	1 143	1 127	1 273	1 300	1 250	1 250	1 250	1 250
Life assurance premiums relieved at source	GIKJ	−636	−590	−508	−477	−385	−308	−268	−234	−168	−138	−133
Mortgage interest relieved at source	GIKK	−3 728	−3 613	−3 885	−4 034	−5 423	−6 224	−5 628	−4 921	−3 795	−3 202	−2 667
Surtax	GTAF	−		−		−		−		−		−
Petroleum revenue tax	GTAH	7 369	2 698	1 754	1 505	1 003	942	−105	7	380	822	820
Supplementary petroleum duty	GTAI	−		−		−		−		−		−
Corporation tax	GTAJ	9 015	11 827	13 865	16 548	21 273	21 136	18 742	15 871	15 057	17 396	22 404
less Overspill relief	GTAK	−										−
Independent Broadcasting Authority levy	GTAL	14	63	83	90	103	134	113	72	−		−
Social security contributions:												
Employers[4]	CEAN	12 245	13 540	14 395	16 176	18 145	19 984	21 182	21 590	23 047	23 241	24 069
Employees[4]	GIKT	11 220	12 625	12 513	13 564	14 140	13 296	13 828	14 104	15 043	17 173	18 506
Self-employed and non-employed persons	GIKU	745	−	755	942	1 048	1 177	1 206	1 281	1 409	1 529	1 676
Community charge/council tax	ADBH	−	−	−	−	586	8 629	8 128	7 907	8 038	8 450	8 989
Royalties	CTAI	2 240	925	1 127	799	522	625	543	568	600	553	574
ITC franchise payments	CUKL	−	−	−	−	−	−	−	−	350	380	398
Total	GIKF	78 048	79 063	84 448	93 204	104 441	120 586	120 065	119 166	121 719	131 996	144 884
TAXES ON CAPITAL												
Personal sector	GIKW	1 808	1 937	2 294	3 246	3 175	3 207	2 623	2 300	2 064	2 259	2 299
Companies[2]	FMCE	486	978	784	907	1 265	1 004	728	350	283	297	387
Public corporations	ADSB	3	61	−	−	−	−	−	−	−	−	−
Total	ACIC	2 297	2 976	3 078	4 153	4 440	4 211	3 351	2 650	2 347	2 556	2 686
Death duties:												
Land and buildings	GILA	209	228	277	337	423	423	359	313	269	286	276
Government and local authority debt	GILB	72	76	75	65	59	63	59	56	69	81	78
Company and overseas securities	GILC	309	355	396	389	376	434	441	441	497	594	598
Other assets	GTNW	215	235	260	261	280	355	361	375	398	456	464
Total	GILF	805	894	1 008	1 052	1 138	1 275	1 220	1 185	1 233	1 417	1 416
Tax on other capital transfers[5]	GILG	49	60	50	38	33	40	43	42	35	26	31
Taxes on capital gains	GILH	1 375	1 957	1 990	3 046	3 258	2 890	2 087	1 423	1 078	1 112	1 238
Development land tax	GILJ	68	65	30	17	11	6	1	−	1	1	1
Special tax on banking deposits	ACCL	−	−	−	−	−	−	−	−	−	−	..
Total	ACIC	2 297	2 976	3 078	4 153	4 440	4 211	3 351	2 650	2 347	2 556	2 686

1 In the case of taxpayers receiving income of more than one type the allocation of tax can only be arbitrary. The allocation procedure is described in paragraphs 11.25-29 of *United Kingdom National Accounts: Sources and Methods,* Third edition.
2 Including financial institutions.
3 From April 1979, before life assurance premium relief and, from April 1983, before most mortgage interest relief. See methodological notes.
4 Including payments in lieu of graduated contributions and state scheme premiums.
5 This consists of capital transfer tax paid on lifetime transfers and distributions from trusts.

CHAPTER 10: International transactions

10.1 United Kingdom transactions with the rest of the world[1]

£ million

		1985	1986	1987	1988	1989	1990	1991	1992	1993	1994	1995
UK CURRENT RECEIPTS (= payments by the RoW[2])												
Exports of goods and services to RoW												
Goods (f.o.b)	CGJP	77 991	72 627	79 153	80 346	92 154	101 718	103 413	107 343	121 398	134 666	152 346
Services: General government	CGJR	483	511	521	550	445	425	457	441	540	543	481
Sea transport	CGJW	2 986	2 859	2 932	3 276	3 522	3 444	3 351	3 525	3 913	4 246	4 550
Civil aviation	CGJO	3 078	2 786	3 159	3 292	3 869	4 474	4 039	4 512	5 144	5 461	5 931
Travel	CGKA	5 442	5 553	6 260	6 184	6 945	7 785	7 168	8 076	9 487	9 920	11 906
Financial and other services	HHDE	12 061	13 549	14 372	13 625	14 551	15 319	15 861	18 217	19 515	21 229	22 386
Total goods and services	DJAD	102 041	97 885	106 397	107 273	121 486	133 165	134 289	142 114	159 997	176 065	197 600
Property and entrepreneurial income from RoW (net of foreign taxes)												
Earnings on direct investment	HHBY	7 746	7 801	10 939	13 851	16 656	15 584	12 780	13 356	16 864	20 913	24 824
Earnings on portfolio investment	CGNV	4 659	5 323	5 126	5 649	7 203	7 740	9 132	11 922	16 052	15 809	19 178
Interest on:												
UK bank lending	HERG	35 838	30 924	28 541	32 988	44 219	48 528	47 308	36 244	33 145	33 148	39 859
Other external assets of private sector and public corporations	HHIW	3 029	2 528	2 447	2 602	3 951	5 442	5 993	5 462	6 670	6 439	7 637
Official reserves	HHCB	540	607	854	1 352	1 913	1 732	1 656	1 456	1 328	1 577	1 620
Other external assets of central government	HERI	197	158	95	107	36	80	98	111	84	33	21
Total income from RoW	CGJS	52 008	47 341	48 002	56 550	73 978	79 106	76 967	68 551	74 143	77 919	93 139
Current transfers from RoW												
To central government from EC	HDKD	1 760	2 138	2 282	2 115	2 143	2 232	4 899	2 888	3 325	3 296	3 697
To private sector	CGJV	1 775	1 732	1 666	1 715	1 750	1 800	1 900	1 957	2 211	2 322	2 438
Total current transfers from RoW	HCBG	3 535	3 870	3 948	3 830	3 893	4 032	6 799	4 845	5 536	5 618	6 135
Total UK current receipts	CGPZ	157 584	149 096	158 347	167 653	199 357	216 303	218 055	215 510	239 676	259 602	296 874
UK CURRENT PAYMENTS (= receipts by the RoW[2])												
Imports of goods and services from RoW												
Goods (f.o.b.)	CGGL	81 336	82 186	90 735	101 826	116 837	120 527	113 697	120 447	134 858	145 497	163 974
Services: General government	CGGI	1 781	1 920	2 141	2 351	2 699	2 784	2 808	2 546	2 332	2 523	2 501
Sea transport	CGGW	3 515	3 323	3 219	3 517	3 779	3 756	3 634	3 821	4 225	4 561	4 715
Civil aviation	CGGG	2 877	3 194	3 775	4 203	4 397	4 769	4 423	5 048	5 413	6 125	6 272
Travel	CGHA	4 871	6 083	7 280	8 216	9 357	9 916	9 834	11 283	12 972	14 500	15 609
Financial and other services	HBVH	4 608	4 515	4 587	4 683	5 739	6 533	6 613	7 123	8 141	8 943	10 015
Total goods and services	DJAG	98 988	101 221	111 737	124 796	142 808	148 285	141 009	150 268	167 941	182 149	203 086
Property and entrepreneurial income paid to RoW (net of UK taxes)												
Earnings on direct investment	HHCH	7 571	5 293	7 044	8 665	9 238	7 027	4 559	5 260	10 453	9 486	11 958
Earnings on portfolio investment	HERN	1 908	2 575	3 459	4 627	6 597	7 766	8 660	10 130	11 583	13 937	16 120
Interest on:												
Borrowing by UK banks	HERP	37 843	32 588	31 081	35 586	49 706	55 926	55 134	40 587	38 231	34 017	43 450
Other external liabilities of UK, private sector and public corporations	HHOQ	2 088	1 965	2 170	2 718	4 267	6 088	7 713	8 686	11 264	11 523	11 736
External liabilities of central government	HERR	303	292	320	388	670	1 030	751	764	415	265	303
Total income paid to RoW	CGGK	49 712	42 712	44 075	51 984	70 476	77 837	76 817	65 427	71 946	69 228	83 567
Current transfers to RoW												
From central government												
To European Communities	HDLN	3 789	2 812	4 066	3 555	4 443	4 669	3 318	4 863	5 445	5 469	7 690
Bilateral aid	CGEG	614	656	570	756	837	856	1 058	1 086	967	1 080	1 030
Other	HHAB	784	903	923	1 052	1 141	1 303	1 606	1 773	1 882	1 882	2 157
From private sector	CGGV	1 459	1 656	1 789	1 985	2 050	2 100	2 200	2 225	2 249	2 214	2 236
Total transfers to RoW	HCBH	6 646	6 027	7 348	7 348	8 471	8 928	8 182	9 947	10 543	10 645	13 113
Total UK current payments	CGQB	155 346	149 960	163 160	184 128	221 755	235 050	226 008	225 642	250 430	262 022	299 766
BALANCE: surplus/deficit on current account[3]	AIMG	2 238	−864	−4 813	−16 475	−22 398	−18 746	−7 954	−10 133	−10 756	−2 419	−2 892
Capital transfers from the RoW (net)	AAAZ	–	–	–	–	–	–	–	–	–	–	–
Financial surplus/deficit of the UK	-AABI	2 238	−864	−4 813	−16 475	−22 398	−18 746	−7 954	−10 133	−10 756	−2 419	−2 892
Financial transactions of the UK												
Transactions (net) in external financial liabilities of the UK[4]	HEQW	46 897	87 874	90 132	72 412	108 844	96 958	26 128	86 565	168 691	32 497	124 491
Transactions (net) in external financial assets of the UK[4]	-HEPZ	50 617	91 693	82 722	57 495	90 668	80 415	18 683	81 600	155 611	35 147	124 045
Other (net)[5]	HHON	–	–	–	–	–	–	–	–	–	–	–
Total financial transactions of the UK (net)[6]	-AARZ	3 720	3 820	−7 410	−14 917	−18 176	−16 543	−7 445	−4 965	−13 080	2 650	−446
BALANCING ITEM[7]	-AASA	−1 482	−4 684	2 597	−1 558	−4 222	−2 203	−509	−5 168	2 324	−5 069	−2 446

1 Differences between totals and sums of components are due to rounding.
2 RoW = Rest of the world
3 *Equal* to the current balance in balance of payments accounts.
4 Increase (+) , decrease (-).
5 See footnote 4 to Table 10.2.
6 Total assets *less* total liabilities and other. Increase in net assets (+).
7 *Equal* but opposite in sign to the balancing item in balance of payments accounts (unidentified acquisition by RoW of assets in the UK) shown as negative.

10.2 United Kingdom financial transactions with the rest of the world (Financial account of the United Kingdom with the rest of the world)[1]

£ million

		1985	1986	1987	1988	1989	1990	1991	1992	1993	1994	1995
TRANSACTIONS IN FINANCIAL LIABILITIES OF THE UK (NET)[2]												
Direct investment in the UK by overseas residents	HHBU	4 504	5 837	9 449	12 006	18 567	18 514	9 058	9 184	10 298	6 823	20 480
Portfolio investment in the UK by overseas residents:												
General government securities	HEZW	3 114	3 144	4 472	1 206	−1 701	23	7 245	8 361	16 343	5 711	−305
Public corporations' securities	HEZX	−10	−4	−113	−56	−409	19	−	−	−	−	−
UK companies' securities	HEZV	6 572	8 842	17 874	19 453	16 757	11 721	9 779	16 255	29 123	26 899	17 165
Total portfolio investment	HEYR	9 676	11 982	22 233	20 603	14 647	11 763	17 024	24 616	45 466	32 609	16 859
Borrowing etc from overseas residents by UK banks:												
Foreign currency	HCAF	24 894	59 811	43 668	19 570	33 369	34 318	−13 590	18 598	22 842	41 237	28 797
Sterling	HEPD	4 148	5 317	8 784	13 724	12 152	12 658	−9 412	2 610	390	6 342	7 542
Borrowing from overseas by UK residents other than banks and general government:												
Transactions with banks abroad	HETN	2 682	3 786	2 447	3 724	6 205	10 264	13 697	9 558	12 262	−1 507	18 781
Other liabilities	HETQ	967	871	1 627	1 823	21 178	8 757	11 707	23 372	80 296	−53 507	30 316
Other external liabilities of general government	HEUR	24	271	1 923	964	2 727	684	−2 357	−1 375	−2 864	500	1 715
Total transactions in financial liabilities of the UK (net)	HEQW	46 897	87 874	90 132	72 412	108 844	96 958	26 128	86 565	168 691	32 497	124 491
of which:												
General government	HEYT	3 138	3 415	6 395	2 170	1 026	707	4 888	6 986	13 479	6 211	1 410
Public corporations	HEYU	−51	−28	−247	−277	−2 075	−81	−56	−469	−27	−110	−153
UK private sector	HEYV	43 810	84 488	83 983	70 521	109 892	96 333	21 297	80 046	155 239	26 396	123 234
TRANSACTIONS IN FINANCIAL ASSETS OF THE UK (NET)[2]												
Direct investment overseas by UK residents	−HHBV	8 430	11 649	19 147	20 863	21 503	10 490	9 056	10 850	17 026	18 363	25 546
Portfolio investment in overseas securities by UK residents:												
UK banks	−HHAL	10 120	7 603	−295	1 162	6 447	5 917	8 520	12 928	35 637	14 178	23 780
Other UK financial institutions	−HHAM	6 204	14 045	−6 152	9 100	31 219	11 912	20 960	13 747	49 060	−32 993	17 145
Other UK residents	−HHAN	430	640	1 123	947	−1 142	−623	−323	671	131	847	−598
Total portfolio investment	−CGOS	16 754	22 288	−5 324	11 209	36 524	17 206	29 157	27 346	84 828	−17 968	40 327
Lending etc to overseas residents by UK banks:												
Foreign currency	−HEZZ	20 209	47 288	45 909	14 176	26 217	35 980	−27 729	16 066	−12 939	49 967	24 145
Sterling	−HCAD	1 815	5 822	4 613	4 609	2 909	3 805	−4 840	10 767	8 263	−308	2 733
Deposits and lending overseas by UK residents other than banks and general government:												
Transactions with banks abroad	−HESZ	1 305	3 094	5 291	4 026	9 466	8 491	4 661	6 151	8 812	10 902	11 096
Other assets	−HETE	−384	−1 848	278	−1 036	−1 384	3 342	4 805	11 145	48 314	−27 473	19 761
Official reserves	−AIPA	1 758	2 891	12 012	2 761	−5 440	76	2 679	−1 407	698	1 045	−200
Other external assets of central government	−HEUJ	730	509	796	887	873	1 025	894	682	609	619	637
Total transactions in financial assets of the UK (net)	−HEPZ	50 617	91 693	82 722	57 495	90 668	80 415	18 683	81 600	155 611	35 147	124 045
of which:												
General government	−HCDN	2 488	3 401	12 808	3 648	−4 567	1 101	3 573	−725	1 307	1 664	437
Public corporations	−HEYO	−370	121	21	33	59	48	38	73	76	74	146
UK private sector	−HCDG	48 500	88 171	69 892	53 814	95 176	79 266	15 073	82 251	154 228	33 409	123 461
OTHER[3]												
EEA loss on forward commitments	HCHF	−	−	−	−	−	−	−	−	−	−	−
Allocation of Special Drawing Rights to the UK by the IMF	HBUN	−	−	−	−	−	−	−	−	−	−	−
Gold subscription to IMF	HBWO	−	−	−	−	−	−	−	−	−	−	−
TOTAL FINANCIAL TRANSACTIONS OF THE UK (NET)[4]	−AARZ	3 720	3 820	−7 410	−14 917	−18 176	−16 543	−7 445	−4 965	−13 080	2 650	−446

1 Differences between totals and sums of components are due to rounding.
2 Increase (+), decrease (-).
3 Comprising the counterparts of other transactions contributing occasionally to the UK balance of payments but not regarded as giving rise to external assets or liabilities (these are: EEA loss on forward commitments, allocation of special drawing rights and gold subscription to IMF).
4 Total assets *less* total liabilities and other. Increase in net assets (+).

11.1 Sector summary, 1991

£ million

	Private sector					Public sector			Overseas sector
		Companies and financial institutions							
	Personal sector	Industrial and commercial companies	Banks and building societies	Life assurance and pension funds	Other financial institutions	Public corporations	Central government	Local authorities	Overseas sector
CURRENT TRANSACTIONS									
Factor incomes:before deducting stock appreciation									
Income from employment	330 767	–		–		–	–	–	–
Gross profits and other trading income	56 745	75 966		–16 511		1 809	–443	407	–
Rent	33 485	6 337		811		541	178	3 808	–
Imputed charge for capital consumption	600	–		–		–	1 675	2 088	–
Inter-sector transfers:									
Dividends and interest (receipts)	69 687	31 107		178 584		413	12 011	955	76 818
(payments)	–52 010	–57 656		–157 399		–1 286	–18 884	–5 373	–76 967
Taxes on income	–57 406	–15 595		–1 726		–451	75 178	–	–
Social security contributions	–36 216	–		–		–	36 216	–	–
Social security benefits	57 381	–		–		–	–58 093	–	712
Community charge/Council Tax	–8 128	–		–		–	–	8 128	–
Other current grants by government (net receipts)	11 906	–		–		–	–51 978	39 701	371
Other current transfers (net receipts)	–561	–248		–36		–	545	–	300
Royalties and licence fees etc	–	–579		–		–	579	–	–
Factor cost adjustment (Taxes on expenditure *less* subsidies)	–	–		–		–	79 885	–464	–
Expenditure (at market prices)									
Consumption	–365 469	–		–		–	–76 985	–47 120	–
Net exports of goods and services	–	–		–		–	–	–	6 720
Balance = **Saving before deducting stock appreciation**[1]	40 781	39 332		3 723		1 026	–116	2 130	7 954
CAPITAL TRANSACTIONS									
Gross domestic fixed capital formation	–25 398	–49 863		–6 564		–3 779	–6 876	–5 267	–
Increase in book value of stocks and work in progress	55	3 101		–		–88	–151	–	–
Capital transfers (net receipts)	1 644	–416		–36		3 189	–5 938	1 557	–
Balance: **Financial surplus or deficit**[2]	17 082	–7 846		–2 877		348	–13 081	–1 580	7 954
FINANCIAL TRANSACTIONS[3]									
Notes and coin	392	39	–166	–	4	–111	–207	–	49
Sterling treasury bills	15	–5	631	71	–717	–33	1 675	3	–1 640
British government securities	1 362	487	–1 324	–	3 086	–48	–9 178	–9	5 624
National savings	2 168	35	2	2	–	22	–2 229	–	–
Tax instruments	–9	–110	49	–	–5	51	24	–	–
Net government indebtedness to Banking Dept	–	–	–131	–	–	–	131	–	–
Northern Ireland central government debt	–	–	1	–	–	–	–1	–	–
Government liabilities under exchange cover scheme	–	–15	–	–	–	–11	34	–8	–
Other public sector financing: Non-marketable debt	–	–	–	–	–	206	–206	–	–
Short-term assets	–37	29	–981	–	–9	–	–	998	–
Issue Department's transactions in bills	–	–1 000	–	–	–522	–	1 751	–	–229
Government foreign currency debt	–	–	36	37	33	–	–1 706	–	1 600
Other government overseas financing	–	–	–	–	–	–	74	–	–74
Official reserves	–	–	–	–	–	–	2 679	–	–2 679
Local authority debt: Sterling securities	–120	–57	7	–273	118	8	–161	478	–
Foreign currency	–	–	–	–	–	–	–	59	–59
Temporary	–85	–	7	36	36	–	–	6	–
Other sterling debt	203	–3	–21	1	13	–9	1 230	–1 376	–38
Public corporations debt: Foreign currency	–	–	–	–	–2	50	–	–	–48
Sterling	–125	–	10	162	37	35	–115	1	–5
Deposits with banks: Sterling	6 458	4 852	2 043	–8 042	4 982	678	–444	–2 072	–8 455
Foreign currency	–65	–1 357	–2 194	–	5 935	–24	62	–33	–2 324
Sterling money market instruments	–142	–185	2 220	–134	–930	–	–	65	–894
Foreign currency money market instruments	26	96	9 333	383	247	–	–	–	–10 085
Deposits with building societies: Sterling	17 251	1 389	–19 773	705	–	–	–	–	428
Sterling money market instruments	49	348	–1 362	438	258	–	–	–	269
Foreign currency	11	26	–1 695	100	84	–	–	–	1 474
Bank lending (excl public sector): Foreign currency	371	1 673	–18 779	–	–10 994	–	–	–	27 729
Sterling	–2 305	718	–47	599	–4 034	–	–	–	5 069
Credit extended by retailers	–60	60	–	–	–	–	–	–	–
Identified trade credit: Domestic	–606	–596	–	–	971	231	–	–	–
Import and export	–	–169	–	–	106	3	–	–	60
Loans secured on dwellings: Building societies	–20 928	–	20 928	–	–	–	–	–	–
Other	–5 025	–	4 790	–315	1 432	–3	–433	–446	–
Other public sector lending	–171	–194	–	–	–	4	540	25	–204
Other lending by financial institutions: Finance leasing	9	22	–154	–	–25	–8	1	155	–
Other forms of lending	262	–620	1 118	1 228	–1 988	–	–	–	–
Unit trust units	1 016	–	–	1 388	–2 404	–	–	–	–
United Kingdom company securities	–5 539	–14 338	1 526	18 938	–3 881	–20	–8 925	–9	12 248
Overseas securities	–431	4 921	8 567	14 097	6 414	–	–	–	–33 568
Life assurance and pension funds	28 623	–	–	–28 663	–	–	40	–	–
Miscellaneous domestic instruments	669	–4 440	591	–226	–264	9	203	–9	3 467
Direct and other investment abroad	32	5 850	–842	–98	–637	–4	–	–	–4 301
Overseas direct and other investment in the UK	–725	–3 868	–196	4	–101	–	–	–	4 886
Miscellaneous overseas instruments	–	–4 591	–2	458	–5 220	42	632	–	8 681
Accruals adjustments	2 767	–779	–495	716	–4 091	200	1 127	91	464
Total financial transactions	25 311	–11 782	3 697	1 612	–12 068	1 268	–13 402	–2 081	7 445
BALANCING ITEM[2]	–8 229	3 936		3 882		–920	321	501	509

1 Before providing for depreciation, stock appreciation & additions to tax reserves.

2 The entries in this row *sum*, with changed sign, to the residual error in table 1.4

3 Acquisition of assets or reduction in liabilities is shown **positive**; sale of assets or increase in liabilities **negative**

11.1 Sector summary, 1992
continued

£ million

		Private sector					Public sector			
			Companies and financial institutions							
	Personal sector	Industrial and commercial companies	Banks and building societies	Life assurance and pension funds	Other financial institutions	Public corporations	Central government	Local authorities	Overseas sector
CURRENT TRANSACTIONS									
Factor incomes:before deducting stock appreciation									
Income from employment	342 015	–		–		–	–	–	–
Gross profits and other trading income	57 149	76 248		–14 392		2 361	–186	392	–
Rent	38 804	7 734		896		547	135	4 000	–
Imputed charge for capital consumption	604	–		–		–	1 608	1 995	–
Inter-sector transfers:									
Dividends and interest (receipts)	67 871	29 151		154 756		419	10 994	765	65 428
(payments)	–47 662	–57 902		–130 476		–1 234	–18 540	–5 019	–68 551
Taxes on income	–58 327	–12 761		–2 429		–199	73 716	–	–
Social security contributions	–36 975	–		–		–	36 975	–	–
Social security benefits	65 902	–		–		–	–66 549	–	647
Community charge/Council Tax	–7 907	–		–		–	–	7 907	–
Other current grants by government (net receipts)	14 150	–		–		–	–61 502	43 165	4 187
Other current transfers (net receipts)	–362	–254		–71		–	419	–	268
Royalties and licence fees etc	–	–601		–		–	601	–	–
Factor cost adjustment (Taxes on expenditure *less* subsidies)	–	–		–		–	81 255	–471	–
Expenditure (at market prices)									
Consumption	–383 490	–		–		–	–82 259	–49 616	–
Net exports of goods and services	–	–		–		–	–	–	8 154
Balance = **Saving before deducting stock appreciation**[1]	51 772	41 615		8 284		1 894	–23 333	3 118	10 133
CAPITAL TRANSACTIONS									
Gross domestic fixed capital formation	–23 765	–47 615		–5 029		–4 727	–6 855	–5 651	–
Increase in book value of stocks and work in progress	–17	212		–		–53	17	–	–
Capital transfers (net receipts)	1 997	19		–36		2 856	–11 712	6 876	–
Balance: **Financial surplus or deficit**[2]	29 987	–5 769		3 219		–30	–41 883	4 343	10 133
FINANCIAL TRANSACTIONS[3]									
Notes and coin	1 002	79	402	–	3	–148	–1 397	–	59
Sterling treasury bills	–2	–8	–2 888	–11	–318	30	4 423	–5	–1 221
British government securities	–1 053	–718	1 971	13 948	3 559	–21	–21 373	2	3 685
National savings	5 019	–	–	–	–	46	–5 065	–	–
Tax instruments	–18	–338	–96	–	3	1	448	–	–
Net government indebtedness to Banking Dept	–	–	–206	–	–	–	206	–	–
Northern Ireland central government debt	–35	–	1	–	–	–	34	–	–
Government liabilities under exchange cover scheme	–	14	–	–	–	–27	28	–15	–
Other public sector financing: Non-marketable debt	–	–	–	–	–	115	–115	–	–
Short-term assets	–117	–4	–677	–	36	–	–	762	–
Issue Department's transactions in bills	–	–2 339	–	–	–322	–	4 517	–	–1 856
Government foreign currency debt	–	–	4 761	79	181	–	–9 798	–	4 777
Other government overseas financing	–	–	–	–	–	–	99	–	–99
Official reserves	–	–	–	–	–	–	–1 407	–	1 407
Local authority debt: Sterling securities	294	–20	129	–431	–100	–44	–118	290	–
Foreign currency	–	–	–	–	1	–	–	71	–72
Temporary	–22	–	–11	19	18	–	–	–4	–
Other sterling debt	450	6	1 064	–16	–2	22	–5 818	4 214	80
Public corporations debt: Foreign currency	–	–	–	–	–	430	–	–	–430
Sterling	16	–	–65	–74	23	–1 197	1 302	5	–10
Deposits with banks: Sterling	5 481	–242	–8 466	1 523	–2 078	369	221	186	3 006
Foreign currency	8	–1 466	–30 731	–	7 447	20	57	20	24 645
Sterling money market instruments	–85	–47	1 187	161	–749	–	–	–5	–462
Foreign currency money market instruments	–23	–78	4 692	517	–165	–	–	–	–4 943
Deposits with building societies: Sterling	10 810	958	–13 163	1 214	73	–	–	–	108
Sterling money market instruments	–7	–218	–133	393	–196	–	–	–	161
Foreign currency	1	–	–352	69	28	–	–	–	254
Bank lending (excl public sector): Foreign currency	323	1 705	13 177	–	861	–	–	–	–16 066
Sterling	–342	2 575	8 319	652	–2 294	–	–	–	–8 910
Credit extended by retailers	–62	62	–	–	–	–	–	–	–
Identified trade credit: Domestic	102	–65	–	–	193	–230	–	–	–
Import and export	–	134	–	–	–49	29	–	–	–114
Loans secured on dwellings: Building societies	–13 696	–	13 696	–	–	–	–	–	–
Other	–4 747	–	6 485	–107	–1 172	3	–104	–358	–
Other public sector lending	–241	52	–	–	–	–11	549	31	–380
Other lending by financial institutions: Finance leasing	81	977	121	–	–1 272	–7	12	88	–
Other forms of lending	811	–1 539	787	636	–695	–	–	–	–
Unit trust units	–316	–	–	711	–395	–	–	–	–
United Kingdom company securities	–257	–12 706	–1 540	5 984	–5 066	–10	–7 580	–5	21 180
Overseas securities	140	4 081	13 630	1 345	13 091	–	–	–	–32 287
Life assurance and pension funds	27 531	–	–	–27 823	–	–	292	–	–
Miscellaneous domestic instruments	742	801	1 429	2 711	–4 776	10	–127	–10	–780
Direct and other investment abroad	32	5 122	624	280	–242	–4	–	–	–5 812
Overseas direct and other investment in the UK	–301	–2 519	12	–	–70	–	–	–	2 878
Miscellaneous overseas instruments	–	–7 433	35	44	–8 678	77	183	–	15 772
Accruals adjustments	2 655	1 143	374	–167	–3 431	537	–626	–880	395
Total financial transactions	34 174	–12 031	14 568	1 657	–6 553	–10	–41 157	4 387	4 965
BALANCING ITEM[2]	–4 187	6 262		–6 453		–20	–726	–44	5 168

1 Before providing for depreciation, stock appreciation & additions to tax reserves.

2 The entries in this row *sum*, with changed sign, to the residual error in table 1.4

3 Acquisition of assets or reduction in liabilities is shown **positive;** sale of assets or increase in liabilities **negative**

11.1 Sector summary, 1993
continued

£ million

	Personal sector	Industrial and commercial companies	Banks and building societies	Life assurance and pension funds	Other financial institutions	Public corporations	Central government	Local authorities	Overseas sector
		Private sector				Public sector			
		Companies and financial institutions							
CURRENT TRANSACTIONS									
Factor incomes:before deducting stock appreciation									
Income from employment	351 819	–	–	–	–	–	–	–	–
Gross profits and other trading income	60 461	85 680	–10 860			3 454	–247	440	–
Rent	40 981	8 627	883			522	183	4 189	–
Imputed charge for capital consumption	564	–	–			–	1 867	1 812	–
Inter-sector transfers:									
Dividends and interest (receipts)	59 292	28 410	134 198			368	9 276	527	71 948
(payments)	–37 434	–54 422	–113 013			–1 413	–19 192	–4 402	–74 143
Taxes on income	–58 119	–12 069	–2 882			–162	73 232	–	–
Social security contributions	–39 499	–	–			–	39 499	–	–
Social security benefits	71 631	–	–			–	–72 425	–	794
Community charge/Council Tax	–8 038	–	–			–	–	8 038	–
Other current grants by government (net receipts)	16 753	–	–			–	–63 654	42 726	4 175
Other current transfers (net receipts)	–267	–297	–97			–	623	–	38
Royalties and licence fees etc	–	–991	–			–	991	–	–
Factor cost adjustment (Taxes on expenditure *less* subsidies)	–	–	–			–	83 595	–462	–
Expenditure (at market prices)									
Consumption	–406 399	–	–			–	–89 398	–48 683	–
Net exports of goods and services	–	–	–			–	–	–	7 944
Balance = **Saving before deducting stock appreciation**[1]	51 745	54 938	8 229			2 769	–35 650	4 185	10 756
CAPITAL TRANSACTIONS									
Gross domestic fixed capital formation	–25 947	–47 589	–4 059			–4 895	–6 391	–5 412	–
Increase in book value of stocks and work in progress	–460	–2 445	–			202	24	–	–
Capital transfers (net receipts)	3 299	–1	–44			2 812	–8 147	2 081	–
Balance: **Financial surplus or deficit**[2]	28 637	4 903	4 126			888	–50 164	854	10 756
FINANCIAL TRANSACTIONS[3]									
Notes and coin	930	101	157	–	2	87	–1 330	–	53
Sterling treasury bills	–4	–196	–751	45	–30	112	1 250	13	–439
British government securities	3 839	481	10 485	11 406	10 434	43	–51 853	27	15 138
National savings	3 020	–	–	–	–	–123	–2 897	–	–
Tax instruments	–43	–18	–9	–	–10	–11	91	–	–
Net government indebtedness to Banking Dept	–	–	–6 719	–	–	–	6 719	–	–
Northern Ireland central government debt	–8	–	–2	–	–	–	10	–	–
Government liabilities under exchange cover scheme	–	–18	–	–	–	–4	46	–24	–
Other public sector financing: Non-marketable debt	–	–	–	–	–	1 223	–1 223	–	–
Short-term assets	–343	1	–413	–	–77	–	–	832	–
Issue Department's transactions in bills	–	–1 310	–	–	–797	–	1 534	–	573
Government foreign currency debt	–	–	387	–58	–222	–	1 413	–	–1 520
Other government overseas financing	–	–	–	–	–	–	95	–	–95
Official reserves	–	–	–	–	–	–	698	–	–698
Local authority debt: Sterling securities	–288	–100	–247	75	128	33	–97	496	–
Foreign currency	–	–	–	–	–1	–	–	84	–83
Temporary	–196	–	97	119	–13	–	–	–7	–
Other sterling debt	127	3	1 543	–	–	6	–1 540	–302	163
Public corporations debt: Foreign currency	–	–	–	–	–	18	–	–	–18
Sterling	–42	–	–62	6	38	–989	1 052	3	–6
Deposits with banks: Sterling	1 920	4 991	–15 407	1 320	5 258	503	–206	1 755	–134
Foreign currency	–67	843	–44 217	–	3 926	–32	–24	–1	39 572
Sterling money market instruments	98	–159	–871	–821	799	–	–	–1	955
Foreign currency money market instruments	–75	–82	13 555	997	–254	–	–	–	–14 141
Deposits with building societies: Sterling	9 707	747	–11 830	–257	752	–	–	–	881
Sterling money market instruments	–95	64	818	–402	–1 112	–	–	–	727
Foreign currency	–17	–37	1 806	12	–88	–	–	–	–1 676
Bank lending (excl public sector): Foreign currency	536	5 687	–7 228	–	–11 934	–	–	–	12 939
Sterling	1 150	7 016	6 198	–59	–5 469	–	–	–	–8 836
Credit extended by retailers	–24	24	–	–	–	–	–	–	–
Identified trade credit: Domestic	298	156	–	–	142	–596	–	–	–
Import and export	–	–305	–	–	47	3	–	–	255
Loans secured on dwellings: Building societies	–9 559	–	9 559	–	–	–	–	–	–
Other	–6 540	–	9 760	–622	–2 169	2	–74	–357	–
Other public sector lending	–288	–15	–	–	–	–29	266	31	35
Other lending by financial institutions: Finance leasing	31	70	158	–	–264	–1	9	–3	–
Other forms of lending	–1 390	–768	664	184	1 310	–	–	–	–
Unit trust units	5 937	–	–	2 792	–8 729	–	–	–	–
United Kingdom company securities	–10 211	–22 804	–469	9 810	–1 370	–17	–5 400	–1	30 462
Overseas securities	–59	3 108	36 458	4 570	43 431	–	–	–	–87 508
Life assurance and pension funds	29 002	–	–	–29 494	–	–	492	–	–
Miscellaneous domestic instruments	–290	–1 756	2 564	826	–1 676	5	–642	–5	974
Direct and other investment abroad	32	10 383	697	17	2 217	–1	–	–	–13 345
Overseas direct and other investment in the UK	–460	–2 590	–1 206	–	–782	–	–	–	5 038
Miscellaneous overseas instruments	–	–3 264	–10	1 146	–31 547	77	–21	–	33 619
Accruals adjustments	1 104	–60	771	–462	–1 772	–250	1 588	–1 114	195
Total financial transactions	27 732	193	6 236	1 150	168	59	–50 044	1 426	13 080
BALANCING ITEM[2]	905	4 710	–3 428			829	–120	–572	–2 324

1 Before providing for depreciation, stock appreciation & additions to tax reserves.

2 The entries in this row *sum*, with changed sign, to the residual error in table 1.4

3 Acquisition of assets or reduction in liabilities is shown **positive;** sale of assets or increase in liabilities **negative**

Sector financial accounts

11.1 Sector summary, 1994

continued

£ million

| | | Private sector | | | | | Public sector | | | |
| | | | Companies and financial institutions | | | | | | | |
	Personal sector	Industrial and commercial companies	Banks and building societies	Life assurance and pension funds	Other financial institutions	Public corpora-tions	Central govern-ment	Local authori-ties	Overseas sector
CURRENT TRANSACTIONS									
Factor incomes: before deducting stock appreciation									
Income from employment	364 946	–		–		–	–	467	–
Gross profits and other trading income	64 021	98 758		−12 290		4 230	23	467	–
Rent	44 065	8 595		965		451	189	4 367	–
Imputed charge for capital consumption	587	–		–		–	1 978	1 859	–
Inter-sector transfers:									
Dividends and interest (receipts)	60 572	34 505		138 781		429	9 740	549	69 227
(payments)	−38 168	−59 731		−108 490		−2 123	−23 068	−4 304	−77 919
Taxes on income	−62 543	−13 824		−4 163		−140	80 670	–	–
Social security contributions	−41 943					–	41 943	–	–
Social security benefits	74 300	–		–		–	−75 174	–	874
Community charge/Council Tax	−8 450					–	–	8 450	
Other current grants by government (net receipts)	18 274	–		–		–	−65 649	43 114	4 261
Other current transfers (net receipts)	−165	−332		−99		–	704	–	−108
Royalties and licence fees etc	–	−981		–		–	981	–	–
Factor cost adjustment (Taxes on expenditure *less* subsidies)	–					–	89 615	−537	–
Expenditure (at market prices)									
Consumption	−427 276	–		–		–	−93 601	−50 513	–
Net exports of goods and services	–	–		–		–	–	–	6 084
Balance = **Saving before deducting stock appreciation**[1]	48 220	66 990		14 704		2 847	−31 649	3 452	2 419
CAPITAL TRANSACTIONS									
Gross domestic fixed capital formation	−27 558	−46 646		−7 808		−4 915	−5 946	−6 344	–
Increase in book value of stocks and work in progress	−1 008	−7 313		–		304	251		–
Capital transfers (net receipts)	2 309	82		−36		2 789	−7 004	1 860	–
Balance: **Financial surplus or deficit**[2]	21 963	13 113		6 860		1 025	−44 348	−1 032	2 419
FINANCIAL TRANSACTIONS[3]									
Notes and coin	1 071	75	−1	–	2	122	−1 370	–	101
Sterling treasury bills	−2	54	2 488	74	−67	−142	−2 209	11	−207
British government securities	1 172	−113	1 891	16 143	13	517	−22 614	28	2 963
National savings	4 596	–	–	–	–	14	−4 610	–	–
Tax instruments	−34	−457	−44	–	–	–	535	–	–
Net government indebtedness to Banking Dept	–	–	4 463	–	–	–	−4 463	–	–
Northern Ireland central government debt	−7	–	–	–	–	–	7	–	–
Government liabilities under exchange cover scheme	–	–	–	–	–	–	24	−24	–
Other public sector financing: Non-marketable debt	–	–	–	–	–	632	−632	–	–
Short-term assets	−238	–	−732	–	23	241	14	692	–
Issue Department's transactions in bills	–	4 035	–	–	1 122	–	−6 200	–	1 043
Government foreign currency debt	–	–	−4 098	−37	−162	–	1 528	–	2 769
Other government overseas financing	–	–	–	–	–	–	95	–	−95
Official reserves	–	–	–	–	–	–	1 045	–	−1 045
Local authority debt: Sterling securities	368	58	68	−269	−61	91	64	−319	–
Foreign currency	–	–	–	–	50	–	–	43	−93
Temporary	−54	–	36	293	13	–	–	−288	–
Other sterling debt	104	–	229	47	–	14	−845	443	8
Public corporations debt: Foreign currency	–	–	–	–	–	116	–	–	−116
Sterling	39	–	−37	−36	−6	−578	606	14	−2
Deposits with banks: Sterling	2 644	5 250	−14 554	−66	1 612	−155	424	−763	5 608
Foreign currency	26	1 221	−48 089	–	6 476	58	−53	−4	40 365
Sterling money market instruments	238	372	−4 597	662	2 392	–	–	2	931
Foreign currency money market instruments	31	114	−7 120	1 332	611	–	–	–	5 032
Deposits with building societies: Sterling	8 434	361	−9 985	701	161	–	–	–	328
Sterling money market instruments	143	110	−2 282	−388	1 125	–	–	–	1 292
Foreign currency	−8	−18	−564	305	80	–	–	–	205
Bank lending (excl public sector): Foreign currency	−113	1 634	56 019	–	−7 573	–	–	–	−49 967
Sterling	−3 433	−865	10 762	−323	−5 406	–	–	–	−735
Credit extended by retailers	−196	196	–	–	–	–	–	–	–
Identified trade credit: Domestic	560	−1 689	–	–	1 015	114	–	–	–
Import and export	–	−460	–	–	−190	−8	–	–	658
Loans secured on dwellings: Building societies	−12 478	–	12 478	–	–	–	–	–	–
Other	−6 765	–	7 847	−693	−54	−7	−37	−291	–
Other public sector lending	−494	−30	–	–	–	−32	921	41	−406
Other lending by financial institutions: Finance leasing	−4	−5	276	–	−233	−11	−4	−19	–
Other forms of lending	−2 004	138	1 337	−593	1 122	–	–	–	–
Unit trust units	6 261	–	–	1 593	−7 854	–	–	–	–
United Kingdom company securities	−3 164	−15 748	3 972	10 065	−11 852	−81	−6 654	17	23 445
Overseas securities	191	6 557	15 360	−1 188	−32 144	–	281	–	11 224
Life assurance and pension funds	27 794	–	–	−28 075	–	–	–	–	–
Miscellaneous domestic instruments	251	−3 248	554	264	19	3	−534	−3	2 694
Direct and other investment abroad	32	10 253	288	−96	1 204	15	–	–	−11 696
Overseas direct and other investment in the UK	−472	−4 468	−316	–	1 402	–	–	–	3 854
Miscellaneous overseas instruments	–	5 442	13	−465	37 006	59	−952	–	−41 103
Accruals adjustments	2 393	224	−246	−238	−2 616	−169	1 060	−703	295
Total financial transactions	26 882	8 993	25 416	−988	−12 770	813	−44 573	−1 123	−2 650
BALANCING ITEM[2]	−4 919	4 120		−4 798		212	225	91	5 069

1 Before providing for depreciation, stock appreciation & additions to tax reserves.

2 The entries in this row *sum*, with changed sign, to the residual error in table 1.4

3 Acquisition of assets or reduction in liabilities is shown **positive**; sale of assets or increase in liabilities **negative**

11.1 Sector summary, 1995
continued

£ million

	Personal sector	Industrial and commercial companies	Banks and building societies	Life assurance and pension funds	Other financial institutions	Public corpora- tions	Central govern- ment	Local authori- ties	Overseas sector
		Private sector — Companies and financial institutions				Public sector			
CURRENT TRANSACTIONS									
Factor incomes: before deducting stock appreciation									
Income from employment	377 895	–	–		–	–	–	–	–
Gross profits and other trading income	67 685	104 152	-13 125			4 634	248	365	–
Rent	47 898	8 745	985			506	194	4 430	–
Imputed charge for capital consumption	600	–	–			–	2 150	1 979	–
Inter-sector transfers:									
Dividends and interest (receipts)	75 161	42 070	164 360			542	10 087	681	83 567
(payments)	-42 701	-73 857	-133 007			-2 370	-27 212	-4 182	-93 139
Taxes on income	-67 292	-17 932	-5 238			-210	90 672	–	–
Social security contributions	-44 251	–	–			–	44 251	–	–
Social security benefits	77 186	–	–			–	-78 110	–	924
Community charge/Council Tax	-8 989	–	–			–	–	8 989	–
Other current grants by government (net receipts)	19 304	–	–			–	-69 157	43 597	6 256
Other current transfers (net receipts)	-63	-358	-96			–	719	–	-202
Royalties and licence fees etc	–	-1 025	–			–	1 025	–	–
Factor cost adjustment (Taxes on expenditure *less* subsidies)	–	–	–			–	97 188	-557	–
Expenditure (at market prices)									
Consumption	-447 247	–	–			–	-96 663	-52 811	–
Net exports of goods and services	–	–	–			–	–	–	5 486
Balance = **Saving before deducting stock appreciation[1]**	55 186	61 795	13 879			3 102	-24 608	2 491	2 892
CAPITAL TRANSACTIONS									
Gross domestic fixed capital formation	-28 996	-51 559	-7 323			-5 054	-5 642	-6 811	–
Increase in book value of stocks and work in progress	-788	-8 270	–			151	154	–	–
Capital transfers (net receipts)	1 810	-218	-36			2 788	-6 382	2 038	–
Balance: **Financial surplus or deficit[2]**	27 212	1 748	6 520			987	-36 478	-2 282	2 892
FINANCIAL TRANSACTIONS[3]									
Notes and coin	1 165	96	195	–	2	72	-1 578	–	48
Sterling treasury bills	-4	4	9 505	802	624	100	-11 841	-24	834
British government securities	-91	60	170	17 738	3 149	7	-20 590	16	-459
National savings	3 275	–	–	–	–	-38	-3 237	–	–
Tax instruments	-17	-344	-24	–	–	–	385	–	–
Net government indebtedness to Banking Dept	–	–	-866	–	–	–	866	–	–
Northern Ireland central government debt	-10	–	3	–	–	–	7	–	–
Government liabilities under exchange cover scheme	–	–	–	–	–	-8	35	-27	–
Other public sector financing: Non-marketable debt	–	–	–	–	–	1 078	-1 078	–	–
Short-term assets	-173	-2	129	–	26	-117	-30	167	–
Issue Department's transactions in bills	–	1 107	–	–	667	–	-2 092	–	318
Government foreign currency debt	–	–	-260	-1	-304	–	-50	–	615
Other government overseas financing	–	–	–	–	–	–	97	–	-97
Official reserves	–	–	–	–	–	–	-200	–	200
Local authority debt: Sterling securities	-118	-16	-215	152	90	-108	285	-70	–
Foreign currency	–	–	–	–	3	–	–	84	-87
Temporary	42	–	-16	66	-14	–	–	-78	–
Other sterling debt	64	-1	-111	-1	1	4	1 715	-1 706	35
Public corporations debt: Foreign currency	–	–	–	–	–	144	–	–	-144
Sterling	-47	–	-9	-29	74	-656	710	-36	-7
Deposits with banks: Sterling	13 100	5 980	-50 455	7 066	14 800	624	169	1 276	7 440
Foreign currency	-92	-1 155	-25 453	–	11 460	12	190	28	15 010
Sterling money market instruments	-129	528	-48	968	-1 533	–	–	-4	218
Foreign currency money market instruments	112	184	-17 182	213	1 414	–	–	–	15 259
Deposits with building societies: Sterling	14 176	-784	-14 472	675	179	–	–	–	226
Sterling money market instruments	28	-250	106	536	-159	–	–	–	-261
Foreign currency	29	58	-2 842	-17	147	–	–	–	2 625
Bank lending (excl public sector): Foreign currency	-22	-340	29 964	–	-5 457	–	–	–	-24 145
Sterling	-6 796	-14 738	32 354	325	-8 094	–	–	–	-3 051
Credit extended by retailers	109	-109	–	–	–	–	–	–	–
Identified trade credit: Domestic	-991	-1 379	–	–	1 654	716	–	–	–
Import and export	–	-616	–	–	65	2	–	–	549
Loans secured on dwellings: Building societies	-9 171	–	9 171	–	–	–	–	–	–
Other	-6 066	–	7 724	-212	-1 236	-3	-20	-187	–
Other public sector lending	-701	-15	–	–	–	-12	882	47	-201
Other lending by financial institutions: Finance leasing	-78	-976	349	–	694	12	6	-7	–
Other forms of lending	-2 137	-999	6 765	489	-4 118	–	–	–	–
Unit trust units	3 947	–	–	2 474	-6 421	–	–	–	–
United Kingdom company securities	-13 740	-8 801	4 611	-911	-6 873	-261	-2 484	17	28 442
Overseas securities	-412	5 790	24 915	3 629	11 810	–	–	–	-45 732
Life assurance and pension funds	33 024	–	–	-33 841	–	–	817	–	–
Miscellaneous domestic instruments	2 051	-294	-179	315	-3 261	2	145	-2	1 223
Direct and other investment abroad	32	15 759	195	116	3 231	–	–	–	-19 333
Overseas direct and other investment in the UK	-224	-5 676	-456	–	-1 655	–	–	–	8 011
Miscellaneous overseas instruments	–	3 754	23	637	-16 842	146	-483	–	12 765
Accruals adjustments	3 635	-653	-900	-59	-1 287	158	338	-1 377	145
Total financial transactions	33 770	-3 828	12 691	1 130	-7 164	1 874	-37 036	-1 883	446
BALANCING ITEM[2]	-6 558	5 576	-137			-887	558	-399	2 446

1 Before providing for depreciation, stock appreciation & additions to tax reserves.

2 The entries in this row *sum*, with changed sign, to the residual error in table 1.4

3 Acquisition of assets or reduction in liabilities is shown **positive**; sale of assets or increase in liabilities **negative**

11.2 Personal sector[1]

£ million

		1985	1986	1987	1988	1989	1990	1991	1992	1993	1994	1995
FINANCIAL SURPLUS OR DEFICIT	AABH	9 792	3 270	−3 387	−13 690	−7 698	1 526	17 082	29 987	28 637	21 963	27 212
Notes and coin	AAPB	449	676	662	950	819	−136	392	1 002	930	1 071	1 165
Sterling treasury bills	DCHW	−	−	6	−2	−3	−1	15	−2	−4	−2	−4
British government securities	AAPC	1 270	1 472	1 006	−1 958	−3 306	−1 036	1 362	−1 053	3 839	1 172	−91
National savings	AAPD	2 468	2 523	2 439	1 408	−1 519	783	2 168	5 019	3 020	4 596	3 275
Tax instruments	AAPE	10	43	72	29	27	31	−9	−18	−43	−34	−17
Northern Ireland central government debt	AAPF	−21	−6	−6	−1	−13	−4	−	−35	−8	−7	−10
Other public sector financing: short term assets	AAQK	−	−31	5	−3	−34	37	−37	−117	−343	−238	−173
Local authority debt: Temporary	AAQC	30	−167	−137	−69	−72	−84	−120	294	−288	368	−118
Sterling securities	RZAU	−118	306	146	−81	117	−48	−85	−22	−196	−54	42
Other sterling debt	RZAV	−455	−496	−796	−797	−480	−168	203	450	127	104	64
Public corporations debt	AAPH	7	−18	−43	−30	21	−61	−125	16	−42	39	−47
Deposits with banks: Sterling	RRCX	4 894	7 949	8 471	16 509	21 810	15 934	6 458	5 481	1 920	2 644	13 100
Foreign currency	RRCY	245	−61	334	244	349	701	−65	8	−67	26	−92
Sterling money market instruments	RRDC	−	139	35	22	−1 498	106	−142	−85	98	238	−129
Foreign currency money market instruments	RRHM	−	−4	104	60	−2	−9	26	−23	−75	31	112
Deposits with building societies: Sterling	RRTR	13 314	11 847	13 525	20 160	17 167	17 933	17 251	10 810	9 707	8 434	14 176
Sterling money market instruments	RRHC	1	9	22	40	158	100	49	−7	−95	143	28
Foreign currency money market instruments	RRDN	−	−	−	−	11	6	11	1	−17	−8	29
Bank lending:[2] Foreign currency	AAPN	−632	−38	−128	−377	−341	−340	371	323	536	−113	−22
Sterling	AAPO	−6 023	−5 389	−9 098	−12 469	−13 086	−8 167	−2 305	−342	1 150	−3 433	−6 796
Credit extended by retailers	−AAPP	−210	−95	−248	−190	−5	−64	−60	−62	−24	−196	109
Identified trade credit: Domestic	RREY	−278	22	−75	−677	−446	−192	−606	102	298	560	−991
Loans secured on dwellings: Building societies	−AAQG	−14 627	−19 434	−14 923	−23 720	−24 002	−24 185	−20 928	−13 696	−9 559	−12 478	−9 171
Other	AAQH	−4 407	−7 635	−14 658	−16 424	−9 757	−9 104	−5 025	−4 747	−6 540	−6 765	−6 066
Other public sector lending	AAPS	26	12	11	−33	−42	−65	−171	−241	−288	−494	−701
Other lending by financial institutions: Finance leasing	AQOU	−147	−60	−77	−122	−202	−142	9	81	31	−4	−78
Other forms of lending	AQOT	−631	−853	−898	−580	−1 034	−528	262	811	−1 390	−2 004	−2 137
Unit trust units	−AALS	983	2 092	3 342	−472	628	−22	1 016	−316	5 937	6 261	3 947
United Kingdom company securities	RYWA	−5 086	−8 072	−10 879	−16 098	−22 196	−11 205	−5 539	−257	−10 211	−3 164	−13 740
Overseas securities	AAPW	534	799	1 135	888	−862	−553	−431	140	−59	191	−412
Life assurance and pension funds	AAPX	18 375	19 686	21 564	23 075	27 697	27 657	28 623	27 531	29 002	27 794	33 024
Miscellaneous domestic instruments	AAPY	650	753	930	1 914	2 378	767	669	742	−290	251	2 051
Direct and other investment abroad	−AAQN	13	15	20	30	32	32	32	32	32	32	32
Overseas direct and other investment in the United Kingdom	AAQL	−90	−192	−463	−446	−1 161	−1 362	−725	−301	−460	−472	−224
Accruals adjustment	AAPZ	1 930	1 799	846	361	4 295	3 692	2 767	2 655	1 104	2 393	3 635
TOTAL FINANCIAL TRANSACTIONS	AAQA	12 474	7 591	2 246	−8 859	−4 552	10 303	25 311	34 174	27 732	26 882	33 770
BALANCING ITEM	AAQB	−2 682	−4 321	−5 633	−4 831	−3 146	−8 777	−8 229	−4 187	905	−4 919	−6 558

See footnotes on page 84.

11.3 Industrial and commercial companies[1,2]

£ million

		1985	1986	1987	1988	1989	1990	1991	1992	1993	1994	1995
FINANCIAL SURPLUS OR DEFICIT	**AABG**	4 529	2 847	1 727	−5 719	−18 190	−18 786	−7 846	−5 769	4 903	13 113	1 748
Notes and coin	**AANB**	45	67	44	86	74	28	39	79	101	75	96
Sterling treasury bills	**AANC**	−41	57	–	–	–	–	−5	−8	−196	54	4
British government securities	**AAOC**	−410	−210	250	−355	−140	866	487	−718	481	−113	60
National savings	**AAOD**	25	81	94	73	2	31	35	–	–	–	–
Tax instruments	**AANE**	419	−562	−380	−397	134	255	−110	−338	−18	−457	−344
Northern Ireland central government debt	**AAOE**	4	−4	5	−5	–	–	–	–	–	–	–
Government liabilities under exchange cover scheme	**ABHK**	−10	−18	−31	15	−6	−11	−15	14	−18	–	–
Other public sector financing:												
Non-marketable debt	**AAOV**	–	–	−29	–	–	−10	–	–	–	–	–
Short-term assets	**AAOQ**	7	−40	−7	−69	−1	90	29	−4	1	–	−2
Issue Department's transactions in commercial bills	**AANF**	−541	−647	3 133	−481	2 147	−372	−1 000	−2 339	−1 310	4 035	1 107
Local authority debt:												
Temporary	**AAOF**	−26	−74	−72	−44	42	130	−57	−20	−100	58	−16
Other sterling	**ADKX**	8	−6	−13	−21	−13	−14	−3	6	3	–	−1
Public corporations debt	**AAOH**	–	–	–	–	–	–	–	–	–	–	–
Deposits with banks:												
Sterling	**RRBH**	2 869	8 266	6 584	4 017	7 350	2 075	4 852	−242	4 991	5 250	5 980
Foreign currency	**RRHI**	1 066	3 213	−447	183	2 021	4 275	−1 357	−1 466	843	1 221	−1 155
Sterling money market instruments	**RRDB**	169	715	1 355	1 295	467	−1 184	−185	−47	−159	372	528
Foreign currency money market instruments	**RRHL**	217	425	−344	205	−3	−553	96	−78	−82	114	184
Deposits with building societies:												
Sterling	**RRCR**	494	362	−309	−476	1 332	1 555	1 389	958	747	361	−784
Sterling money market instruments	**RRHB**	–	30	63	119	475	700	348	−218	64	110	−250
Foreign currency money market instruments	**RRDL**	–	–	–	–	23	12	26	–	−37	−18	58
Bank lending:												
Foreign currency	**AANN**	−2 374	−945	−2 886	−8 310	−8 178	−1 959	1 673	1 705	5 687	1 634	−340
Sterling	**AANO**	−4 539	−6 922	−12 343	−23 227	−27 715	−17 701	718	2 575	7 016	−865	−14 738
Credit extended by retailers	**AANP**	171	68	248	190	5	64	60	62	24	196	−109
Identified trade credit:												
Domestic	**AAOI**	−202	314	−168	−632	−1 248	−259	−596	−65	156	−1 689	−1 379
Import and export	**AAOJ**	190	154	251	258	61	401	−169	134	−305	−460	−616
Other public sector lending	**AANR**	−195	−262	−140	−182	−843	−253	−194	52	−15	−30	−15
Other lending by financial institutions:												
Finance leasing	**AQOS**	−1 837	−683	−733	−1 358	−2 615	−1 555	22	977	70	−5	−976
Other forms of lending	**AQOR**	−303	−160	−587	−1 067	−2 297	−1 412	−620	−1 539	−768	138	−999
United Kingdom company securities	**AANT**	−2 085	−5 664	−13 349	4 812	2 733	−11 008	−14 338	−12 706	−22 804	−15 748	−8 801
Overseas securities	**AANU**	2 183	4 977	7 275	6 739	8 323	6 097	4 921	4 081	3 108	6 557	5 790
Miscellaneous domestic instruments	**AANV**	−207	−70	−2 019	−2 889	−4 342	−5 801	−4 440	801	−1 756	−3 248	−294
Direct and other investment abroad	**AANW**	4 614	4 401	11 273	13 586	10 883	3 469	5 850	5 122	10 383	10 253	15 759
Overseas direct and other investment in the United Kingdom	**AANX**	−3 286	−3 144	−5 204	−6 924	−9 082	−6 624	−3 868	−2 519	−2 590	−4 468	−5 676
Miscellaneous overseas instruments	**AANY**	646	−1 985	2 431	−858	−693	1 633	−4 591	−7 433	−3 264	5 442	3 754
Accruals adjustment	**AANZ**	446	102	−135	1 089	179	−71	−779	1 143	−60	224	−653
TOTAL FINANCIAL TRANSACTIONS	**AAOA**	−2 483	1 836	−6 190	−14 628	−20 925	−27 106	−11 782	−12 031	193	8 993	−3 828
BALANCING ITEM	**AAOB**	7 012	1 011	7 917	8 909	2 735	8 320	3 936	6 262	4 710	4 120	5 576

1 Acquisition of assets or reduction in liabilities is shown **positive;** sale of assets or increase in liabilities **negative.**

2 Inclusion of former public corporations as from their date of privatisation causes discontinuities in the f gures. See methodological notes.

Where such data can be compiled, quarterly data for series in this table are available on the ONS's Databank. This data can also be provided on paper by request. Some of these quarterly data are published regularly in the UK Economic Accounts in table A22.

Sector financial accounts

11.4 Financial companies and institutions[1]

£ million

		1985	1986	1987	1988	1989	1990	1991	1992	1993	1994	1995
FINANCIAL SURPLUS OR DEFICIT	**AABF**	−1 811	1 132	2 419	−1 967	−2 015	553	−2 877	3 219	4 126	6 860	6 520
Notes and coin	AQRA	−131	−26	328	394	320	−21	−162	405	159	1	197
Sterling treasury bills	AQRB	98	14	792	1 169	1 669	1 667	−15	−3 217	−736	2 495	10 931
British government securities	AQXQ	5 771	3 384	−1 727	−3 379	−13 231	−7 313	1 762	19 478	32 325	18 047	21 057
National savings	AAMD	−2	14	14	6	3	11	4	−	−	−	−
Tax instruments	AQRC	163	485	−311	−692	34	61	44	−93	−19	−44	−24
Net government indebtedness to												
Banking Department	-RRBT	122	−28	281	138	370	353	−131	−206	−6 719	4 463	−866
Northern Ireland central government debt	AQRD	−4	−3	−5	−	−	1	1	1	−2	−	3
Other public sector financing:												
Non-marketable debt	AQRE	−319	−107	−	−	−	−	−	−	−	−	−
Short-term assets	AQRF	−145	−645	−603	−1 006	−978	1 213	−990	−641	−490	−709	155
Issue Department's transactions in bills	AQRG	−937	199	1 508	−148	1 078	−139	−522	−322	−797	1 122	667
Government foreign currency debt	AQRH	1 400	1 550	395	−1 771	−62	207	106	5 021	107	−4 297	−565
Local authority debt:												
Temporary	AQRI	−416	−868	−315	−245	−205	751	−148	−402	−44	−262	27
Foreign currency	AQRJ	−5	−2	141	−104	−4	−	−	1	−1	50	3
Sterling debt	AQRK	−290	−286	−128	−67	−24	−74	79	26	203	342	36
Other sterling debt	AQRL	−1 346	−1 570	−662	−21	−395	−109	−7	1 046	1 543	276	−111
Public corporations debt:												
Foreign currency	AQRM	174	−98	−224	−628	−2	−38	−2	−	−	−	−
Sterling	AQRN	−847	−402	96	93	−205	163	209	−116	−18	−79	36
Deposits with banks:												
Sterling	RCHP	−12 998	−23 766	−25 551	−36 583	−39 589	−30 142	−1 017	−9 021	−8 829	−13 008	−28 589
Foreign currency	RCHX	−33 457	−50 319	−31 234	−14 419	−39 081	−42 180	3 741	−23 284	−40 291	−41 613	−13 993
Sterling money market instruments	RCIF	154	−1 121	−1 823	−2 172	−803	1 151	1 156	599	−893	−1 543	−613
Foreign currency money market instruments	RCJM	7 123	−12 888	−13 005	−4 944	3 657	2 708	9 963	5 044	14 298	−5 177	−15 555
Deposits with building societies:												
Sterling	RCJR	−13 794	−12 712	−14 128	−20 161	−18 589	−19 887	−19 068	−11 876	−11 335	−9 123	−13 618
Sterling money market instruments	RCJZ	−	−59	−127	−237	−1 045	−1 356	−666	64	−696	−1 545	483
Foreign currency money market instruments	RRDY	−	−	−	−	−1 561	−801	−1 511	−255	1 730	−179	−2 712
Bank lending:												
Foreign currency	AQRR	23 215	48 271	48 923	22 863	34 736	38 279	−29 773	14 038	−19 162	48 446	24 507
Sterling	AQRS	12 726	18 059	27 148	40 499	44 083	29 479	−3 482	6 677	670	5 033	24 585
Identified trade credit:												
Domestic	RREV	421	340	306	1 654	1 060	693	971	193	142	1 015	1 654
Import and export	RREU	143	−264	42	20	71	190	106	−49	47	−190	65
Loans secured on dwellings:												
Building societies	AAQG	14 627	19 434	14 923	23 720	24 002	24 185	20 928	13 696	9 559	12 478	9 171
Other	AQRT	4 849	8 087	15 042	16 609	9 853	9 528	5 907	5 206	6 969	7 100	6 276
Other public sector lending	AQRU	−	−	−	−	−390	339	−	−	−	−	−
Other lending by financial institutions:												
Finance leasing	RYZV	2 233	1 011	1 116	1 741	3 012	1 762	−179	−1 151	−106	43	1 043
Other forms of lending	RYZU	934	1 013	1 485	1 647	3 331	1 940	358	728	2 158	1 866	3 136
Unit trust units	AALS	−983	−2 092	−3 342	472	−628	22	−1 016	316	−5 937	−6 261	−3 947
United Kingdom company securities	AQRW	2 154	6 854	10 195	−6 158	2 214	6 159	16 583	−622	7 971	2 185	−3 173
Overseas securities	CJLJ	17 122	23 020	−6 742	11 188	37 820	18 738	29 078	28 066	84 459	−17 972	40 354
Life assurance and pension funds	-AALV	−17 822	−18 997	−20 925	−22 219	−27 308	−27 596	−28 663	−27 823	−29 494	−28 075	−33 841
Miscellaneous domestic instruments	AQRX	−650	−1 014	704	−709	651	1 970	101	−636	1 714	837	−3 125
Direct and other investment abroad	AQRY	709	712	869	−418	1 075	−207	−1 577	662	2 931	1 396	3 542
Overseas direct and other investment in												
the United Kingdom	AQRZ	−309	−945	−646	−1 173	−2 903	−386	−293	−58	−1 988	1 086	−2 111
Miscellaneous overseas instruments	AQSA	−2 867	155	721	989	−16 071	−4 196	−4 764	−8 599	−30 411	36 554	−16 182
Accruals adjustment	CJLN	−3 305	−1 100	−1 118	−1 545	−5 809	−5 008	−3 870	−3 224	−1 463	−3 100	−2 246
TOTAL FINANCIAL TRANSACTIONS	**CJLR**	3 511	3 290	2 413	4 403	156	2 117	−6 759	9 672	7 554	11 658	6 657
BALANCING ITEM	**AATA**	−5 322	−2 158	6	−6 370	−2 171	−1 564	3 882	−6 453	−3 428	−4 798	−137

1 Acquisition of assets or reduction in liabilities is shown **positive;** sale of assets or increase in liabilities **negative.**

Where such data can be compiled, quarterly data for series in this table are available on the ONS's Databank. This data can also be provided on paper by request. Some of these quarterly data are published regularly in the UK Economic Accounts in table A23.

11.5 Banks[1]

£ million

		1985	1986	1987	1988	1989	1990	1991	1992	1993	1994	1995
FINANCIAL SURPLUS OR DEFICIT[2]		..	..	..	..	..	..	..	..	..	..	..
Notes and coin	AAJB	−164	−51	264	270	263	−52	−199	289	157	3	246
Sterling treasury bills	AAJC	114	16	505	1 243	430	879	495	−1 905	−548	2 515	6 696
British government securities	AAJD	268	1 306	−906	−2 361	−1 904	−1 027	−281	1 059	9 037	1 131	1 602
Tax instruments	AAJE	100	136	99	−313	78	46	79	−97	−39	−8	−24
Net government indebtedness to Banking Department	-RRBT	122	−28	281	138	370	353	−131	−206	−6 719	4 463	−866
Northern Ireland central government debt	AAKI	2	1	−5	–	–	1	1	1	−2	–	3
Other public sector financing:												
Non-marketable debt	AAKJ	−319	−107	–	–	–	–	–	–	–	–	–
Issue Department's transactions in bills	-AAKQ	−316	−1	942	650	199	–	–	–	–	–	–
Government foreign currency debt	AAJH	211	293	−281	166	−44	48	36	4 548	599	−4 161	−218
Local authority debt:												
Temporary	AAJI	−5	−397	−189	−255	−342	17	−29	7	−40	167	−94
Foreign currency	AAJJ	−8	–	140	−108	−5	–	–	–	–	–	–
Sterling securities	AAJK	−206	−176	−5	−25	−24	−6	−10	−2	10	30	–
Other sterling debt	AAJL	−1 157	−1 384	−530	211	−201	−231	−32	1 158	1 491	194	−96
Public corporations debt:												
Foreign currency	AAJM	199	−99	−224	−630	–	−38	–	–	–	–	–
Sterling	AAJN	−847	−422	45	106	−185	107	10	−65	−62	−37	−9
Deposits with banks:												
Sterling	RRHG	−18 992	−27 326	−38 863	−46 263	−52 635	−40 590	−213	−9 824	−16 934	−13 216	−49 662
Foreign currency	RCFT	−34 436	−55 623	−39 185	−16 770	−44 861	−48 355	−2 194	−31 102	−44 382	−48 404	−26 145
Sterling money market instruments	RRHR	−180	−2 391	−7 027	−7 212	−4 561	−3 323	48	2 160	−860	−5 622	−2 178
Foreign currency money market instruments	RRHK	7 114	−12 810	−13 522	−5 240	2 572	2 461	9 333	4 498	13 226	−7 686	−17 749
Deposits with building societies:												
Sterling	RRBG	−25	552	259	119	347	607	−26	217	−26	518	−1 104
Sterling money market instruments	RRHH	67	−127	146	284	169	1 188	−446	71	1 501	103	400
Foreign currency money market instruments	RJZO	–	–	–	–	–	62	78	−91	55	46	−18
Bank lending (excluding public sector):												
Foreign currency	AAJR	24 191	54 988	55 644	23 966	41 970	37 387	−18 779	13 177	−7 228	56 019	29 964
Sterling	AAJS	16 645	26 918	36 751	49 715	55 759	39 469	286	8 477	7 348	10 739	32 325
Loans secured on dwellings	AAJT	4 223	5 200	10 102	10 892	7 045	6 409	4 790	6 485	9 760	7 847	7 724
Other public sector lending	AAKD	–	–	–	–	–	–	–	–	–	–	–
Other lending by financial institutions:												
Finance leasing	AQOO	78	−72	−74	−127	−91	−24	−154	121	158	276	349
United Kingdom company securities	AAJU	−4 330	3 318	−1 804	−5 976	−571	18	1 507	−1 795	−771	2 349	4 375
Overseas securities	AAJV	10 815	8 483	−555	1 829	7 054	6 169	8 567	13 599	36 128	15 005	24 419
Miscellaneous domestic instruments	AAKE	–	61	367	−123	19	−177	−79	57	144	118	−93
Direct and other investment abroad	AAJX	508	792	−388	−548	201	377	−842	624	697	288	195
Overseas direct and other investment in the United Kingdom	AAJY	−318	−146	−53	−334	−117	−240	−196	12	−1 206	−316	−456
Miscellaneous overseas instruments	AAKF	–	60	1	−39	−4	−11	−2	35	−10	13	23
Accruals adjustment	AAJZ	−228	27	−31	−21	−126	−208	135	108	102	−95	−201
TOTAL FINANCIAL TRANSACTIONS	AAKA	3 126	991	1 904	3 244	10 805	1 316	1 752	11 616	1 586	22 279	9 408
BALANCING ITEM[2]		..	..	..	..	..	..	..	..	..	..	..

1 Acquisition of assets or reduction in liabilities is shown **positive;** sale of assets or increase in liabilities **negative.**

2 Not available : See methodological notes.

11.6 Building societies

£ million

		1985	1986	1987	1988	1989	1990	1991	1992	1993	1994	1995
FINANCIAL SURPLUS OR DEFICIT[2]		..	..	..	..	..	..	..	..	..	..	..
Notes and coin	AHJM	31	23	62	120	53	24	33	113	–	–4	–51
Sterling treasury bills	AHJQ	–8	6	55	10	846	301	136	–983	–203	–27	2 809
British government securities	AHJT	91	–1 523	–1 189	560	–2 618	–651	–1 043	912	1 448	760	–1 432
National savings	CJHE	–	6	6	5	1	6	2	–	–	–	–
Tax instruments	AHJX	63	349	–410	–379	–40	16	–30	1	30	–36	–
Northern Ireland central government debt	-DXKC	–6	–4	–	–	–	–	–	–	–	–	–
Other public sector financing:												
Short-term assets	AQSB	–	–109	–39	–759	–739	587	–981	–677	–413	–732	129
Government foreign currency debt	HRVO	–	–	–	–	–	–	–	213	–212	63	–42
Local authority debt:												
Temporary	AHJR	–222	–307	48	–1	4	349	36	122	–207	–99	–121
Sterling securities	AHJH	–48	–78	–60	–30	–10	17	17	–9	87	6	–16
Other sterling debt	AHJI	–134	–212	–213	–223	–129	153	11	–94	52	35	–15
Deposits with banks:												
Sterling	RRTW	2 746	–7	2 415	1 353	1 300	1 911	2 256	1 358	1 527	–1 338	–793
Foreign currency	VTOA	–	–	–	–	–	–	–	371	165	315	692
Sterling money market instruments	RRDA	438	1 017	3 493	3 304	993	2 060	2 172	–973	–11	1 025	2 130
Foreign currency money market instruments	RCLY	–	–	–	–	–	–	–	194	329	566	567
Deposits with building societies:												
Sterling	RRTX	–13 965	–13 648	–14 714	–20 658	–19 506	–21 136	–19 747	–13 380	–11 804	–10 503	–13 368
Sterling money market instruments	RHKL	–66	37	–529	–521	–2 368	–5 257	–916	–204	–683	–2 385	–294
Foreign currency	RYWG	–	–	–	–	–1 825	–1 023	–1 773	–261	1 751	–610	–2 824
Bank lending:												
Sterling	-AHKQ	187	383	–504	–391	922	358	–333	–158	–1 150	23	29
Loans secured on dwellings	AAQG	14 627	19 434	14 923	23 720	24 002	24 185	20 928	13 696	9 559	12 478	9 171
Other lending by financial institutions:												
Other forms of lending	AQSC	84	114	419	917	2 358	2 094	1 118	787	664	1 337	6 765
United Kingdom company securities	AQSD	–1 116	–3 641	–374	–2 951	–1 257	–666	19	255	302	1 623	236
Overseas securities	RYWJ	5	–4	–3	–	–	–	–	31	330	355	496
Miscellaneous domestic instruments	AQSE	64	297	256	557	1 863	950	670	1 372	2 420	436	–86
Accruals adjustments	AQSG	–995	1 404	–274	–659	–1 535	–1 480	–630	266	669	–151	–699
TOTAL FINANCIAL TRANSACTIONS	AQSH	1 776	3 537	3 368	3 974	2 315	2 798	1 945	2 952	4 650	3 137	3 283
BALANCING ITEM[2]		..	..	..	..	..	..	..	..	..	..	..

1 Acquisition of assets or reduction in liabilities is shown **positive;** sale of
  assets or increase in liabilities **negative**.
2 Not available : See methodological notes.

11.7 Life assurance and pension funds[1]

£ million

		1985	1986	1987	1988	1989	1990	1991	1992	1993	1994	1995
FINANCIAL SURPLUS OR DEFICIT[2]		..	..	..	..	..	..	..	..	..	..	..
Sterling treasury bills	ACQS	−26	−9	−1	7	−2	53	71	−11	45	74	802
British government securities	ACON	4 969	2 142	−1 710	−1 476	−5 854	−4 021	−	13 948	11 406	16 143	17 738
National savings	CJGF	−2	8	8	1	2	5	2	−	−	−	−
Government foreign currency debt	AQTG	−	3	−8	−1	−1	−	37	79	−58	−37	−1
Local authority debt:												
Temporary	CJGG	−229	−83	231	72	4	280	−273	−431	75	−269	152
Sterling securities	CJGH	−29	−28	−59	−12	18	−87	36	19	119	293	66
Other sterling debt	CJGI	13	27	84	−8	−48	−20	1	−16	−	47	−1
Public corporations debt:												
Sterling	CJGJ	13	2	46	−26	−1	66	162	−74	6	−36	−29
Deposits with banks:												
Sterling	AQTB	367	2 828	5 289	2 611	4 945	6 312	−8 042	1 523	1 320	−66	7 066
Sterling money market instruments	RHZZ	−81	−92	703	1 299	469	488	−134	161	−821	662	968
Foreign currency money market instruments	RHZY	−30	−1	−4	10	886	172	383	517	997	1 332	213
Deposits with building societies:												
Sterling	AHJY	196	384	327	378	570	642	705	1 214	−257	701	675
Sterling money market instruments	RJZN	−	−	−	−	292	1 073	438	393	−402	−388	536
Foreign currency money market instruments	RJAB	−	−	−	−	155	87	100	69	12	305	−17
Bank lending:												
Sterling	AQTF	12	−295	−531	−169	−217	4	599	652	−59	−323	325
Loans secured on dwellings	CJGP	173	177	558	324	−350	−57	−315	−107	−622	−693	−212
Other lending by financial institutions:												
Other forms of lending	CJGQ	74	248	215	310	797	360	1 228	636	184	−593	489
Unit trust units	CJGR	1 286	2 782	2 436	1 942	2 872	157	1 388	711	2 792	1 593	2 474
United Kingdom company securities	CJGS	6 810	7 580	12 131	6 680	6 182	13 430	18 938	5 984	9 810	10 065	−911
Overseas securities	CJGT	3 948	3 862	944	6 482	14 473	9 126	14 097	1 345	4 570	−1 188	3 629
Life assurance and pension funds	−AALV	−17 822	−18 997	−20 925	−22 219	−27 308	−27 596	−28 663	−27 823	−29 494	−28 075	−33 841
Miscellaneous domestic instruments	CJGV	−77	−968	−151	395	1 314	−1 071	−226	2 711	826	264	315
Direct and other investment abroad	CJGW	−150	−6	80	−90	105	606	−98	280	17	−96	116
Overseas direct and other investment in												
the United Kingdom	CJGX	1	4	−32	32	1	−4	4	−	−	−	−
Miscellaneous overseas instruments	CJGY	187	551	69	322	674	173	458	44	1 146	−465	637
Accruals adjustments	RRES	−3	145	1 017	1 790	−581	−42	716	−167	−462	−238	−59
TOTAL FINANCIAL TRANSACTIONS	CJGZ	−400	264	717	−1 346	−603	136	1 612	1 657	1 150	−988	1 130
BALANCING ITEM[2]		..	..	..	..	..	..	..	..	..	..	..

1 Acquisition of assets or reduction in liabilities is shown **positive;** sale of
  assets or increase in liablilities **negative.**
2 Not available: See methodological notes.

11.8 Financial institutions excluding banks, building societies and life assurance and pension funds[1]

£ million

		1985	1986	1987	1988	1989	1990	1991	1992	1993	1994	1995
FINANCIAL SURPLUS OR DEFICIT[2]		..	..	..	..	..	..	..	..	..	..	..
Notes and coin	AQTH	2	2	2	4	4	7	4	3	2	2	2
Sterling treasury bills	ACQT	18	1	233	−91	395	434	−717	−318	−30	−67	624
British government securities	ACOO	443	1 459	2 078	−102	−2 855	−1 614	3 086	3 559	10 434	13	3 149
Tax instruments	AQTI	−	−	−	−	−4	−1	−5	3	−10	−	−
Other public sector financing:												
Short-term assets	AQTK	−145	−536	−564	−247	−239	626	−9	36	−77	23	26
Issue Department's transactions in bills	-AAMZ	−621	200	566	−798	879	−139	−522	−322	−797	1 122	667
Government foreign currency debt	AQTL	1 189	1 254	684	−1 936	−17	159	33	181	−222	−162	−304
Local authority debt:												
Temporary	CJHK	40	−81	−405	−61	129	105	118	−100	128	−61	90
Foreign currency	AAMF	3	−2	1	4	1	−	−	1	−1	50	3
Sterling securities	CJHM	−7	−4	−4	−	−8	2	36	18	−13	13	−14
Other sterling debt	CJHN	−68	−1	−3	−1	−17	−11	13	−2	−	−	1
Public corporations debt:												
Foreign currency	AABK	−25	1	−	2	−2	−	−2	−	−	−	−
Sterling	CJHP	−13	18	5	13	−19	−10	37	23	38	−6	74
Deposits with banks:[3]												
Sterling	RRTU	2 881	739	5 608	5 716	6 801	2 225	4 982	−2 078	5 258	1 612	14 800
Foreign currency	RRTV	979	5 304	7 951	2 351	5 780	6 175	5 935	7 447	3 926	6 476	11 460
Sterling money market instruments	RRHF	−23	345	1 008	437	2 296	1 926	−930	−749	799	2 392	−1 533
Foreign currency money market instruments	RRHO	39	−77	521	286	199	75	247	−165	−254	611	1 414
Deposits with building societies:												
Sterling	RJBK	−	−	−	−	−	−	−	73	752	161	179
Sterling money market instruments	ASLA	−1	31	256	−	862	1 640	258	−196	−1 112	1 125	−159
Foreign currency money market instruments	RRDM	−	−	−	−	109	73	84	28	−88	80	147
Bank lending:[3]												
Foreign currency	AQTP	−976	−6 717	−6 721	−1 103	−7 234	892	−10 994	861	−11 934	−7 573	−5 457
Sterling	AQTQ	−4 118	−8 947	−8 568	−8 656	−12 381	−10 352	−4 034	−2 294	−5 469	−5 406	−8 094
Identified trade credit:												
Domestic	RREV	421	340	306	1 654	1 060	693	971	193	142	1 015	1 654
Import and export	RREU	143	−264	42	20	71	190	106	−49	47	−190	65
Loans secured on dwellings	CJHX	453	2 710	4 382	5 393	3 158	3 176	1 432	−1 172	−2 169	−54	−1 236
Other public sector lending	AQPF	−	−	−	−	−390	339	−	−	−	−	−
Other lending by financial institutions:												
Finance leasing	AQOQ	2 155	1 083	1 190	1 868	3 103	1 786	−25	−1 272	−264	−233	694
Other forms of lending	AQOP	776	651	851	420	176	−514	−1 988	−695	1 310	1 122	−4 118
Unit trust units	CJIA	−2 269	−4 874	−5 778	−1 470	−3 500	−135	−2 404	−395	−8 729	−7 854	−6 421
United Kingdom company securities	CJIB	790	−403	242	−3 911	−2 140	−6 623	−3 881	−5 066	−1 370	−11 852	−6 873
Overseas securities	CJIC	2 354	10 679	−7 128	2 877	16 293	3 443	6 414	13 091	43 431	−32 144	11 810
Miscellaneous domestic instruments	CJID	−637	−404	232	−1 538	−2 545	2 268	−264	−4 776	−1 676	19	−3 261
Direct and other investment abroad	CJIE	351	−74	1 177	220	769	−1 190	−637	−242	2 217	1 204	3 231
Overseas direct and other investment in the United Kingdom	CJIF	8	−803	−561	−871	−2 787	−142	−101	−70	−782	1 402	−1 655
Miscellaneous overseas instruments	CJIG	−3 054	−456	651	706	−16 741	−4 358	−5 220	−8 678	−31 547	37 006	−16 842
Accruals adjustments	AQTR	−2 079	−2 676	−1 830	−2 655	−3 567	−3 278	−4 091	−3 431	−1 772	−2 616	−1 287
TOTAL FINANCIAL TRANSACTIONS	CJII	−991	−1 502	−3 576	−1 469	−12 361	−2 133	−12 068	−6 553	168	−12 770	−7 164
BALANCING ITEM[2]		..	..	..	..	..	..	..	..	..	..	..

1 Acquisition of assets or reduction in liabilities is shown **positive;** sale of assets or increase in liabilities **negative.**
2 Not available: see methodological notes.
3 Residual to total reported by banks for other financial institutions after deducting figures reported by life assurance and pension funds.

11.9 Public corporations[1,2]

£ million

		1985	1986	1987	1988	1989	1990	1991	1992	1993	1994	1995
FINANCIAL SURPLUS OR DEFICIT	**AABD**	−182	1 224	1 294	1 757	488	4 513	348	−30	888	1 025	987
Notes and coins	**AAIA**	57	−95	18	−3	−27	229	−111	−148	87	122	72
Sterling treasury bills	**AAFB**	10	−10	–	120	6	−92	−33	30	112	−142	100
British government securities	**AAFC**	–	132	29	−4	−10	63	−48	−21	43	517	7
National savings	**AAGB**	67	−156	2	39	−33	−25	22	46	−123	14	−38
Tax instruments	**AAFD**	−36	158	42	63	−45	−54	51	1	−11	–	–
Government liabilities under exchange cover scheme	**AAFE**	−223	−162	−108	179	103	−12	−11	−27	−4	–	−8
Other public sector financing:												
Non-marketable debt	**AAFF**	22	−482	244	450	−97	223	206	115	1 223	632	1 078
Short-term assets	**AAIP**	−12	127	−25	–	–	–	–	–	–	241	−117
Local authority debt:												
Temporary	**AAFG**	209	−109	−130	−32	−38	83	8	−44	33	91	−108
Sterling securities	**AAFH**	1	–	–	–	–	–	–	–	–	–	–
Other sterling debt	**ADKU**	−3	−7	−8	−2	−6	−3	−9	22	6	14	4
Public corporations debt:												
Foreign currency	**AAFJ**	−233	115	459	924	2 111	140	50	430	18	116	144
Sterling	**AAFK**	318	238	390	−813	−1 504	4 277	35	−1 197	−989	−578	−656
Deposits with banks:												
Sterling	**RCFK**	165	887	284	980	−180	98	678	369	503	−155	624
Foreign currency	**AAFN**	42	9	−36	−26	−42	31	−24	20	−32	58	12
Sterling money market instruments	**RRHQ**	−6	207	−1	7	–	–	–	–	–	–	–
Credit extended by retailers	**AAFO**	39	27	–	–	–	–	–	–	–	–	–
Identified trade credit:												
Domestic	**AAFP**	57	−671	−43	−348	642	−240	231	−230	−596	114	716
Import and export	**AAFQ**	−11	43	−34	−32	−60	−24	3	29	3	−8	2
Loans secured on dwellings	**AAFR**	−9	−14	−11	−9	−3	−4	−3	3	2	−7	−3
Other public sector lending	**AAFS**	23	76	8	–	270	−311	4	−11	−29	−32	−12
Other lending by financial institutions:												
Finance leasing	**AQOV**	−81	−6	−3	1	−8	–	−8	−7	−1	−11	12
Other forms of lending	**AQOW**	–	–	–	–	–	–	–	–	–	–	–
United Kingdom company securities	**RHQP**	−21	−54	−144	−87	−9	−110	−20	−10	−17	−81	−261
Miscellaneous domestic instruments	**AAHY**	166	346	257	89	152	1	9	10	5	3	2
Direct and other investment abroad	**RZCF**	–	–	–	–	–	−3	−4	−4	−1	15	–
Miscellaneous overseas instruments	**RCZY**	64	34	6	49	62	51	42	77	77	59	146
Accruals adjustment	**AAFW**	−83	258	196	240	351	414	200	537	−250	−169	158
TOTAL FINANCIAL TRANSACTIONS	**AAFX**	522	891	1 392	1 785	1 635	4 732	1 268	−10	59	813	1 874
BALANCING ITEM	**AAFY**	−704	333	−98	−28	−1 147	−219	−920	−20	829	212	−887

1 Acquisition of assets or reduction in liabilities is shown **positive;** sale of assets or increase in liabilities **negative.**

2 The comparability of data over time is affected by the privatisation of former public corporations. See methodological notes.

Where such data can be compiled, quarterly data for series in this table are available on the ONS's Databank. This data can also be provided on paper by request. Some of these quarterly data are published regularly in the UK Economic Accounts in table A24.

11.10 Central government[1]

£ million

		1985	1986	1987	1988	1989	1990	1991	1992	1993	1994	1995
FINANCIAL SURPLUS OR DEFICIT	**AABA**	−8 177	−7 908	−5 521	3 979	6 549	−6 100	−13 081	−41 883	−50 164	−44 348	−36 478
Notes and coin	**AACB**	−429	−674	−1 089	−1 476	−1 245	−78	−207	−1 397	−1 330	−1 370	−1 578
Sterling treasury bills	**AACC**	−68	−253	−2 186	−1 335	−2 936	−2 149	1 675	4 423	1 250	−2 209	−11 841
British government securities	**AACD**	−9 555	−6 876	−4 609	5 032	18 327	7 330	−9 178	−21 373	−51 853	−22 614	−20 590
National savings	**AACE**	−2 556	−2 462	−2 550	−1 528	1 547	−801	−2 229	−5 065	−2 897	−4 610	−3 237
Tax instruments	**AACF**	−556	−124	577	997	−150	−293	24	448	91	535	385
Net government indebtedness to Banking Department	**RRBT**	−122	28	−281	−138	−370	−353	131	206	6 719	−4 463	866
Northern Ireland central government debt	**AACH**	21	13	6	6	13	3	−1	34	10	7	7
Government liabilities under exchange cover scheme	**AACI**	242	186	147	−188	−87	33	34	28	46	24	35
Other public sector financing: Non-marketable debt	**AADP**	297	589	−215	−450	97	−213	−206	−115	−1 223	−632	−1 078
Short-term assets	**CBQM**	−	−	−	−	−	−	−	−	−	14	−30
Issue department's transactions in commercial bills	**AACK**	1 129	522	−5 735	435	−3 598	705	1 751	4 517	1 534	−6 200	−2 092
Government foreign currency debt	**AACL**	−1 721	−2 692	163	451	−1 256	−132	−1 706	−9 798	1 413	1 528	−50
Other government overseas financing	**AACM**	87	86	69	73	83	73	74	99	95	95	97
Official reserves	**−AIPA**	1 758	2 891	12 012	2 761	−5 440	76	2 679	−1 407	698	1 045	−200
Local authority debt: Temporary	**AADD**	−28	75	−187	−76	143	−20	−161	−118	−97	64	285
Sterling securities	**AADC**	−120	−149	−154	107	−131	−1	−	−	−	−	−
Other sterling debt	**ABEC**	4 960	5 786	5 468	4 829	2 577	762	1 230	−5 818	−1 540	−845	1 715
Public corporations debt	**AACP**	624	207	−444	716	1 798	−4 303	−115	1 302	1 052	606	710
Deposits with banks: Sterling	**RYNG**	−63	312	−155	476	286	441	−444	221	−206	424	169
Foreign currency	**AACR**	−138	−9	77	−100	−2	24	62	57	−24	−53	190
Identified trade credit: Domestic	**AACA**	2	−5	−20	3	−8	−2	−	−	−	−	−
Import and export	**−AACT**	126	−199	−	−	−	−	−	−	−	−	−
Loans secured on dwellings	**AADK**	69	68	60	153	137	−98	−433	−104	−74	−37	−20
Other public sector lending	**AADL**	232	521	−87	373	969	607	540	549	266	921	882
Other lending by financial institutions: Finance leasing	**−CULP**	−8	−9	−11	−12	−25	−36	1	12	9	−4	6
United Kingdom company securities	**AADI**	−2 345	−3 809	−5 930	−6 194	−4 657	−4 462	−8 925	−7 580	−5 400	−6 654	−2 484
Overseas securities	**−AADJ**	−	−	−	−	−	−	−	−	−	−	−
Life assurance and pension funds	**−AACW**	−553	−689	−639	−856	−389	−61	40	292	492	281	817
Miscellaneous domestic instruments	**AACX**	−5	34	14	56	100	186	203	−127	−642	−534	145
Miscellaneous overseas instruments	**AACY**	−1	−155	−125	−246	−27	−499	632	183	−21	−952	−483
Accruals adjustment	**AACZ**	781	−1 016	268	−470	660	−2 450	1 127	−626	1 588	1 060	338
TOTAL FINANCIAL TRANSACTIONS	**AADA**	−7 940	−7 803	−5 556	3 399	6 416	−5 711	−13 402	−41 157	−50 044	−44 573	−37 036
BALANCING ITEM	**AADB**	−237	−105	35	580	133	−389	321	−726	−120	225	558

1 Acquisition of assets or reduction in liabilities is shown **positive;** sale of assets or increase in liabilities **negative.**

Where such data can be compiled, quarterly data for series in this table are available on the ONS's Databank. This data can also be provided on paper by request. Some of these quarterly data are published regularly in the UK Economic Accounts in table A25.

11.11 Local authorities[1]

£ million

		1985	1986	1987	1988	1989	1990	1991	1992	1993	1994	1995
FINANCIAL SURPLUS OR DEFICIT	AABB	−1 913	−1 429	−1 345	−835	−1 532	−452	−1 580	4 343	854	−1 032	−2 282
Sterling treasury bills	AAEB	14	−14	–	1	9	−8	3	−5	13	11	−24
British government securities	AAEC	4	7	22	27	4	−9	−9	2	27	28	16
National savings	AAED	−2	–	1	2	–	1	–	–	–	–	–
Government liabilities under exchange cover scheme	AAEE	−9	−6	−8	−6	−10	−10	−8	−15	−24	−24	−27
Other public sector financing:												
Short-term assets	AAEY	138	601	611	1 078	1 013	−1 340	998	762	832	692	167
Local authority debt:												
Temporary	AAEF	233	1 144	843	466	130	−860	478	290	496	−319	−70
Foreign currency	AAEG	−83	−100	−248	112	67	64	59	71	84	43	84
Sterling securities	AAEH	627	229	137	41	38	123	6	−4	−7	−288	−78
Other sterling debt	AAEI	−3 164	−3 751	−4 053	−4 011	−1 635	−423	−1 376	4 214	−302	443	−1 706
Public corporations debt	AAEJ	−19	18	46	47	−84	−73	1	5	3	14	−36
Deposits with banks:												
Sterling	RCFA	664	1 103	1 849	1 729	−99	−1 146	−2 072	186	1 755	−763	1 276
Foreign currency	AAEM	8	16	−3	8	21	3	−33	20	−1	−4	28
Sterling money-market instruments	RRHP	4	80	67	−89	−19	−9	65	−5	−1	2	−4
Identified trade credit:												
Domestic	RRBI	–	–	–	–	–	–	–	–	–	–	–
Loans secured on dwellings	AAEO	−502	−506	−433	−329	−230	−322	−446	−358	−357	−291	−187
Other public sector lending	AAEP	43	60	61	96	100	37	25	31	31	41	47
Other lending by financial institutions:												
Finance leasing	AQON	−160	−253	−292	−250	−162	−29	155	88	−3	−19	−7
United Kingdom company securities	ADNR	10	49	163	113	149	81	−9	−5	−1	17	17
Miscellaneous domestic instruments	AAEQ	−166	−316	−210	−69	−119	−10	−9	−10	−5	−3	−2
Accruals adjustment	AAER	−4	−346	−268	17	−79	3 052	91	−880	−1 114	−703	−1 377
TOTAL FINANCIAL TRANSACTIONS	AAES	−2 364	−1 985	−1 715	−1 017	−906	−878	−2 081	4 387	1 426	−1 123	−1 883
BALANCING ITEM	AAET	451	556	370	182	−626	426	501	−44	−572	91	−399

1 Acquisition of assets or reduction in liabilities is shown **positive**; sale of assets or increase in liabilities **negative.**

Where such data can be compiled, quarterly data for series in this table are available on the ONS's Databank. This data can also be provided on paper by request. Some of these quarterly data are published regularly in the UK Economic Accounts in table A26.

Sector financial accounts

11.12 Public sector[1,2]

£ million

		1985	1986	1987	1988	1989	1990	1991	1992	1993	1994	1995
FINANCIAL SURPLUS OR DEFICIT	**AABE**	−10 272	−8 113	−5 572	4 901	5 505	−2 039	−14 313	−37 570	−48 422	−44 355	−37 773
Notes and coin	**AAGE**	−372	−769	−1 071	−1 479	−1 272	151	−318	−1 545	−1 243	−1 248	−1 506
Sterling treasury bills	**AAGF**	−44	−277	−2 186	−1 214	−2 921	−2 249	1 645	4 448	1 375	−2 340	−11 765
British government securities	**AAGG**	−9 551	−6 737	−4 558	5 055	18 321	7 384	−9 235	−21 392	−51 783	−22 069	−20 567
National savings	**AAGH**	−2 491	−2 618	−2 547	−1 487	1 514	−825	−2 207	−5 019	−3 020	−4 596	−3 275
Tax instruments	**AAGI**	−592	34	619	1 060	−195	−347	75	449	80	535	385
Net government indebtedness to Banking Department	**RRBT**	−122	28	−281	−138	−370	−353	131	206	6 719	−4 463	866
Northern Ireland central government debt	**AACH**	21	13	6	6	13	3	−1	34	10	7	7
Government liabilities under exchange cover scheme	**−ABHK**	10	18	31	−15	6	11	15	−14	18	–	–
Other public sector financing:												
Non-marketable debt	**AAGL**	319	107	29	–	–	10	–	–	–	–	–
Short-term assets	**AAHV**	126	728	586	1 078	1 013	−1 340	998	762	832	947	20
Issue Department's transactions in commercial bills	**AACK**	1 129	522	−5 735	435	−3 598	705	1 751	4 517	1 534	−6 200	−2 092
Government foreign currency debt	**AACL**	−1 721	−2 692	163	451	−1 256	−132	−1 706	−9 798	1 413	1 528	−50
Other government overseas financing	**AACM**	87	86	69	73	83	73	74	99	95	95	97
Official reserves	**−AIPA**	1 758	2 891	12 012	2 761	−5 440	76	2 679	−1 407	698	1 045	−200
Local authority debt[4]:												
Temporary	**AAHF**	414	1 110	526	358	235	−797	325	128	432	−164	107
Foreign currency	**AAHG**	−83	−100	−248	112	67	64	59	71	84	43	84
Sterling securities	**AAHH**	508	80	−17	148	−93	122	6	−4	−7	−288	−78
Other sterling debt	**AAHI**	1 793	2 028	1 407	816	936	336	−155	−1 582	−1 836	−388	13
Public corporations debt:												
Foreign currency	**AAHJ**	−233	115	459	924	2 111	140	50	430	18	116	144
Sterling	**AAHK**	923	463	−8	−50	210	−99	−79	110	66	42	18
Deposits with banks:												
Sterling	**RCHK**	766	2 302	1 978	3 185	7	−607	−1 838	776	2 052	−494	2 069
Foreign currency	**AAHN**	−88	16	38	−118	−23	58	5	97	−57	1	230
Sterling money market instruments	**RCIB**	−2	287	66	−82	−19	−9	65	−5	−1	2	−4
Credit extended by retailers	**AAFO**	39	27	–	–	–	–	–	–	–	–	–
Identified trade credit:												
Domestic	**AAHO**	59	−676	−63	−345	634	−242	231	−230	−596	114	716
Import and export	**AAHP**	115	−156	−34	−32	−60	−24	3	29	3	−8	2
Loans secured on dwellings	**AAGW**	−442	−452	−384	−185	−96	−424	−882	−459	−429	−335	−210
Other public sector lending	**AAGX**	298	657	−18	469	1 339	333	569	569	268	930	917
Other lending by financial institutions:												
Finance leasing	**AQOY**	−249	−268	−306	−261	−195	−65	148	93	5	−34	11
Other forms of lending	**AQOW**	–	–	–	–	–	–	–	–	–	–	–
United Kingdom company securities	**AAHR**	−2 356	−3 814	−5 911	−6 168	−4 517	−4 491	−8 954	−7 595	−5 418	−6 718	−2 728
Overseas securities	**−AADJ**	–	–	–	–	–	–	–	–	–	–	–
Life assurance and pension funds	**−AACW**	−553	−689	−639	−856	−389	−61	40	292	492	281	817
Miscellaneous domestic instruments	**DDEK**	−5	64	61	76	133	177	203	−127	−642	−534	145
Direct and other investment abroad	**RZCF**	–	–	–	–	–	−3	−4	−4	−1	15	–
Miscellaneous overseas instruments	**AAHB**	63	−121	−119	−197	35	−448	674	260	56	−893	−337
Accruals adjustment	**AAHC**	694	−1 104	196	−213	932	1 016	1 418	−969	224	188	−881
TOTAL FINANCIAL TRANSACTIONS	**AAHD**	−9 782	−8 897	−5 879	4 167	7 145	−1 857	−14 215	−36 780	−48 559	−44 883	−37 045
BALANCING ITEM	**AAHE**	−490	784	307	734	−1 640	−182	−98	−790	137	528	−728

1 Acquisition of assets or reduction in liabilities is shown **positive;** sale of assets or increase in liabilities **negative.**
2 The comparability of data over time is affected by the privatisation of former public corporations. See methodological notes.

11.13 Public sector[1]: transactions in financial assets and liabilities

£ million

		1985	1986	1987	1988	1989	1990	1991	1992	1993	1994	1995
FINANCIAL SURPLUS OR DEFICIT:												
General government	AABC	−10 090	−9 337	−6 866	3 144	5 017	−6 552	−14 661	−37 540	−49 310	−45 380	−38 760
Public corporations	AABD	−182	1 224	1 294	1 757	488	4 513	348	−30	888	1 025	987
Total	AABE	−10 272	−8 113	−5 572	4 901	5 505	−2 039	−14 313	−37 570	−48 422	−44 355	−37 773
Transactions in financial liabilities (net)												
Accruals adjustments	DDEL	580	194	917	648	1 777	56	1 238	−188	1 759	946	1 988
Transactions concerning certain public sector pension schemes	AACW	553	689	639	856	389	61	−40	−292	−492	−281	−817
Other financial liabilities (net)	DDEM	214	207	579	872	−252	1 348	−955	−60	1 653	2 588	−789
Public sector borrowing requirement:												
Central government	ABEA	11 804	8 410	4 072	−4 957	−5 134	−4 642	7 705	29 240	45 766	38 417	38 662
Local authorities	AAZK	−3 375	−5 113	−4 732	−4 234	−2 012	2 925	658	297	−1 335	1 010	−1 341
Public corporations	AAZL	−984	−932	−678	−2 688	−2 183	−658	−702	−898	−1 910	−1 538	−1 824
Total	ABEN	7 445	2 365	−1 338	−11 879	−9 329	−2 375	7 661	28 639	42 521	37 889	35 497
Total transactions in financial liabilities	AAZC	8 792	3 455	797	−9 503	−7 415	−910	7 904	28 099	45 441	41 142	35 879
Transactions in financial assets (net)												
Accruals adjustments	DDEO	1 274	−910	1 113	435	2 709	1 072	2 656	−1 157	1 983	1 134	1 107
Net lending, etc. to the private sector and overseas:												
Net lending to the private sector:												
General government	DDEP	−287	−264	−252	39	912	−130	−518	−262	−99	228	521
Public corporations	ADTG	14	62	−3	−9	267	−315	1	−8	−27	−39	−15
Net lending to overseas governments	CUAD	−52	−69	−84	−66	−47	−51	−46	−31	−57	−53	−59
Drawings from United Kingdom subscriptions to international lending bodies	CUAA	209	227	210	251	316	211	310	375	266	272	296
Other net lending and investment abroad:												
General government	CUAE	126	−193	–	–	–	–	–	–	–	–	–
Public corporations	RCZY	64	34	6	49	62	51	42	77	77	59	146
Cash expenditure on company securities, etc. (net):												
Central government	AACV	−2 345	−3 809	−5 930	−6 194	−4 657	−4 462	−8 925	−7 580	−5 400	−6 654	−2 484
Local authorities	ADNR	10	49	163	113	149	81	−9	−5	−1	17	17
Public corporations	RHQP	−21	−54	−144	−87	−9	−110	−20	−10	−17	−81	−261
Total net lending	ABKG	−2 282	−4 017	−6 034	−5 904	−3 007	−4 725	−9 165	−7 444	−5 258	−6 251	−1 839
Other financial assets	DDES	18	−515	−161	133	28	886	198	−80	157	1 376	−434
Total transactions in financial assets	AAZH	−990	−5 442	−5 082	−5 336	−270	−2 767	−6 311	−8 681	−3 118	−3 741	−1 166
NET TOTAL FINANCIAL TRANSACTIONS[2]	AAHD	−9 782	−8 897	−5 879	4 167	7 145	−1 857	−14 215	−36 780	−48 559	−44 883	−37 045
BALANCING ITEM	AAHE	−490	784	307	734	−1 640	−182	−98	−790	137	528	−728

1 The comparability of data over time is affected by the privatisation of former public corporations. See methodological notes.
2 Total assets *less* total liabilities.

Sector financial accounts

11.14 Financing of the public sector borrowing requirement

£ million

		1985	1986	1987	1988	1989	1990	1991	1992	1993	1994	1995
NON-BANK, NON-BUILDING SOCIETY PRIVATE SECTOR												
Notes and coin	AQUP	496	745	708	1 040	897	−101	435	1 084	1 033	1 148	1 263
Sterling treasury bills	AQUQ	−49	49	238	−86	390	486	−636	−339	−185	59	1 426
British government securities	AQUR	6 272	4 863	1 624	−3 891	−12 155	−5 805	4 935	15 736	26 160	17 215	20 856
National savings	AQUS	2 491	2 612	2 541	1 482	−1 515	819	2 205	5 019	3 020	4 596	3 275
Tax instruments	AQUT	429	−519	−308	−368	157	285	−124	−353	−71	−491	−361
Northern Ireland central government debt	AQUU	−17	−10	−1	−6	−13	−4	–	−35	−8	−7	−10
Government liabilities under exchange cover scheme	ABHK	−10	−18	−31	15	−6	−11	−15	14	−18	–	–
Other public sector financing:												
Non-marketable debt	AQUV	–	–	−29	–	–	−10	–	–	–	–	–
Short-term assets	AQUW	−138	−607	−566	−319	−274	753	−17	−85	−419	−215	−149
Issue Department's transactions in bills	ABGQ	−1 162	−447	3 699	−1 279	3 026	−511	−1 522	−2 661	−2 107	5 157	1 774
Government foreign currency debt	ACMM	1 189	1 257	676	−1 937	−18	159	70	260	−280	−199	−305
Local authority debt	AQVC	−838	−609	−1 027	−1 018	−327	85	−131	197	−146	549	268
Public corporations debt	AQVF	−18	3	8	−41	−1	−5	72	−35	2	−3	−2
Total	AQVG	8 645	7 319	7 532	−6 408	−9 839	−3 860	5 272	18 802	26 981	27 809	28 035
of which:												
Other financial institutions	AQVH	5 525	4 373	1 184	−4 656	−7 635	−4 166	2 108	16 596	21 045	17 142	23 045
Industrial and commercial companies	ABGD	−520	−1 356	2 994	−1 198	2 239	993	−600	−3 328	−1 056	3 652	904
Personal sector	ABGE	3 640	4 302	3 354	−554	−4 443	−687	3 764	5 534	6 992	7 015	4 086
BANKS AND BUILDING SOCIETIES												
Notes and coin	AQSI	−133	−28	326	390	316	−28	−166	402	157	−1	195
Sterling treasury bills	AQSJ	106	22	560	1 253	1 276	1 180	631	−2 888	−751	2 488	9 505
British government securities	AQSK	359	−217	−2 095	−1 801	−4 522	−1 678	−1 324	1 971	10 485	1 891	170
National savings	CJHE	–	6	6	5	1	6	2	–	–	–	–
Tax instruments	AQSL	163	485	−311	−692	38	62	49	−96	−9	−44	−24
Net government indebtedness to Banking Department	-RRBT	122	−28	281	138	370	353	−131	−206	−6 719	4 463	−866
Northern Ireland central government debt	AQSM	−4	−3	−5	–	–	1	1	1	−2	–	3
Other public sector financing:												
Non-marketable debt	AAKJ	−319	−107	–	–	–	–	–	–	–	–	–
Short-term assets	AQSB	–	−109	−39	−759	−739	587	−981	−677	−413	−732	129
Issue Department's transactions in bills	-AAKQ	−316	−1	942	650	199	–	–	–	–	–	–
Government foreign currency debt	RHYT	211	293	−281	166	−44	48	36	4 761	387	−4 098	−260
Local authority debt	AQVI	−1 780	−2 554	−809	−431	−707	299	−7	1 182	1 393	333	−342
Public corporations debt	AQVJ	−648	−521	−179	−524	−185	69	10	−65	−62	−37	−9
Deposits with banks	-AAGS	−676	−2 605	−2 082	−2 985	35	558	1 768	−868	−1 994	491	−2 295
Total	AQVK	−2 915	−5 367	−3 686	−4 590	−3 962	1 457	−112	3 517	2 472	4 754	6 206
OVERSEAS SECTOR												
Notes and coin	AASD	9	52	37	49	59	−22	49	59	53	101	48
Sterling treasury bills	AARB	−13	206	1 388	47	1 255	583	−1 640	−1 221	−439	−207	834
British government securities	AARC	2 920	2 091	5 029	637	−1 644	99	5 624	3 685	15 138	2 963	−459
Other public sector financing:												
Short-term assets	-AASH	12	−12	19	–	–	–	–	–	–	–	–
Issue Department's transactions in bills	AASK	349	−74	1 094	194	373	−194	−229	−1 856	573	1 043	318
Government foreign currency debt	AARD	321	1 142	−558	1 320	1 318	−75	1 600	4 777	−1 520	2 769	615
Other government overseas financing	-AACM	−87	−86	−69	−73	−83	−73	−74	−99	−95	−95	−97
Official reserves	AIPA	−1 758	−2 891	−12 012	−2 761	5 440	−76	−2 679	1 407	−698	−1 045	200
Local authority debt	AASN	−14	45	168	15	−111	−109	−97	8	80	−85	−52
Public corporations debt	AASM	−24	−60	−280	−309	−2 135	−105	−53	−440	−24	−118	−151
Total	ABGH	1 715	413	−5 184	−881	4 472	28	2 501	6 320	13 068	5 326	1 256
PUBLIC SECTOR BORROWING REQUIREMENT	ABEN	7 445	2 365	−1 338	−11 879	−9 329	−2 375	7 661	28 639	42 521	37 889	35 497

11.15 Overseas sector[1]

£ million

		1985	1986	1987	1988	1989	1990	1991	1992	1993	1994	1995
FINANCIAL SURPLUS OR DEFICIT[2]	AABI	−2 238	864	4 813	16 475	22 398	18 746	7 954	10 133	10 756	2 419	2 892
Notes and coin	AASD	9	52	37	49	59	−22	49	59	53	101	48
Sterling treasury bills	AARB	−13	206	1 388	47	1 255	583	−1 640	−1 221	−439	−207	834
British government securities	AARC	2 920	2 091	5 029	637	−1 644	99	5 624	3 685	15 138	2 963	−459
Other public sector financing:												
Short-term assets	−AASH	12	−12	19	–	–	–	–	–	–	–	–
Issue departments transactions in												
ECGD promissory notes	AASK	349	−74	1 094	194	373	−194	−229	−1 856	573	1 043	318
Government foreign currency debt	AARD	321	1 142	−558	1 320	1 318	−75	1 600	4 777	−1 520	2 769	615
Other government overseas financing	−AACM	−87	−86	−69	−73	−83	−73	−74	−99	−95	−95	−97
Official reserves	AIPA	−1 758	−2 891	−12 012	−2 761	5 440	−76	−2 679	1 407	−698	−1 045	200
Local authority debt:												
Temporary	RJBL	−2	−1	−2	–	–	–	–	–	–	–	–
Foreign currency	AARH	88	102	107	−8	−63	−64	−59	−72	−83	−93	−87
Other sterling debt	ADKZ	–	44	64	23	−48	−45	−38	80	163	8	35
Sterling securities	AARI	−100	−100	−1	–	–	–	–	–	–	–	–
Public corporations debt:												
Foreign currency	AARJ	59	−17	−235	−296	−2 109	−102	−48	−430	−18	−116	−144
Sterling	AARK	−83	−43	−45	−13	−26	−3	−5	−10	−6	−2	−7
Deposits with banks:												
Sterling	RRHJ	4 469	5 249	8 518	12 872	10 422	12 740	−8 455	3 006	−134	5 608	7 440
Foreign currency	RRTT	32 234	47 151	31 309	14 110	36 734	37 146	−2 324	24 645	39 572	40 365	15 010
Sterling money market instruments	RRDD	−321	−20	367	937	1 853	−64	−894	−462	955	931	218
Foreign currency money market instruments	RRHN	−7 340	12 467	13 245	4 679	−3 652	−2 146	−10 085	−4 943	−14 141	5 032	15 259
Deposits with building societies:												
Sterling	RRTS	−14	503	912	477	90	399	428	108	881	328	226
Sterling money market instruments	RRHD	−1	20	42	78	412	556	269	161	727	1 292	−261
Foreign currency	RRDR	–	–	–	–	1 527	783	1 474	254	−1 676	205	2 625
Bank lending:												
Foreign currency	AARQ	−20 209	−47 288	−45 909	−14 176	−26 217	−35 980	27 729	−16 066	12 939	−49 967	−24 145
Sterling	AARR	−2 164	−5 748	−5 707	−4 803	−3 282	−3 611	5 069	−8 910	−8 836	−735	−3 051
Identified trade credit	AASB	−448	266	−259	−246	−72	−567	60	−114	255	658	549
Other public sector lending	AART	−129	−407	147	−254	−64	−354	−204	−380	35	−406	−201
United Kingdom company securities	AARU	7 373	10 696	19 944	23 612	21 766	20 545	12 248	21 180	30 462	23 445	28 442
Overseas securities	AARV	−19 839	−28 796	−1 668	−18 815	−45 281	−24 282	−33 568	−32 287	−87 508	11 224	−45 732
Miscellaneous domestic instruments	AASC	212	267	324	1 608	1 180	2 887	3 467	−780	974	2 694	1 223
Direct and other investment abroad	AARW	−5 336	−5 128	−12 162	−13 198	−11 990	−3 291	−4 301	−5 812	−13 345	−11 696	−19 333
Overseas direct and other investment in												
the United Kingdom	AARX	3 685	4 281	6 313	8 543	13 146	8 372	4 886	2 878	5 038	3 854	8 011
Miscellaneous overseas instruments[3]	AARY	2 158	1 951	−3 033	66	16 729	3 011	8 681	15 772	33 619	−41 103	12 765
Accruals adjustments	RCZX	235	303	211	308	403	371	464	395	195	295	145
TOTAL FINANCIAL TRANSACTIONS	AARZ	−3 720	−3 820	7 410	14 917	18 176	16 543	7 445	4 965	13 080	−2 650	446
BALANCING ITEM	AASA	1 482	4 684	−2 597	1 558	4 222	2 203	509	5 168	−2 324	5 069	2 446

1 Acquisition of assets or reduction in liabilities by the overseas sector is shown **positive;** sale of assets or increase in liabilities **negative.**

2 *Equals,* apart from the change in sign, the current balance in the balance of payments account, *plus* capital transfers abroad.

3 Residual in this table; includes all timing and coverage adjustments to basis used in the capital account of the balance of payments.

Where such data can be compiled, quarterly data for series in this table are available on the ONS's Databank. This data can also be provided on paper by request. Some of these quarterly data are published regularly in the UK Economic Accounts in table A27.

11.16 United Kingdom Company Securities: further detail
Flows

£ million

		1990	1991	1992	1993	1994	1995
Quoted Ordinary Shares							
Liabilities							
Banks	DYXM	−1 198	−1 088	−546	−1 036	−526	−925
Other Financial Institutions	DYXZ	−544	−895	−1 295	−3 985	−5 400	−907
Industrial and Commercial Companies	DYYF	−4 555	−12 898	−7 615	−15 946	−11 950	−10 962
Assets							
Central Government	DYWX	−3 690	−7 212	−6 858	−4 563	−3 654	−2 380
Local Authorities	DYXA	46	−14	−17	−17	−1	−5
Public Corporations	DYXD	−	−	−	−	−	2
Banks	DYXJ	−55	65	54	15	167	228
Life Assurance and Pension Funds	DYXT	12 942	15 204	3 344	7 096	8 531	−2 298
Remaining Financial Institutions	DYXW	974	340	−1 121	7 745	6 583	4 902
Industrial and Commercial Companies	DYYC	3 928	7 480	2 213	1 571	2 912	16 844
Personal sector	DYYI	−10 810	−4 820	1 095	−8 396	−1 013	−10 407
Overseas sector	DYYL	2 962	3 838	10 746	17 516	4 351	5 908
Unquoted Ordinary Shares							
Liabilities							
Public Corporations	DYXH	−35	−5	−12	−16	−18	−22
Banks	DYXN	−282	−261	−116	−197	−109	−148
Other Financial Institutions	DYYA	−2 865	−1 670	−1 445	−1 973	−3 300	−5 659
Industrial and Commercial Companies	DYYG	−5 249	−3 870	−5 058	−4 534	−2 147	−7 168
Financial Assets							
Central Government	DYWY	−280	−155	−126	−	−724	−104
Local Authorities	DYXB	35	5	12	16	18	22
Public Corporations	DYXE	−75	−15	2	−1	−63	−241
Banks	DYXK	1 507	1 646	1 116	969	1 454	3 013
Building Societies	DYXQ	39	157	149	968	465	−170
Life Assurance and Pension Funds	DYXU	−18	472	169	158	104	−397
Remaining Financial Institutions	DYXX	−1 050	504	83	−328	−589	−773
Industrial and Commercial Companies	DYYD	−8	310	1 035	1 449	3 766	4 511
Personal sector	DYYJ	−595	−919	−1 469	−1 725	−2 220	−3 186
Overseas sector	DYYM	8 876	3 801	5 660	5 214	3 363	10 322
Bonds and Preference Shares							
Liabilities							
Banks	DYXO	−1 188	−852	−3 507	−4 654	−1 237	−2 064
Building Societies	DYXS	−705	−138	−50	−948	837	444
Other Financial Institutions	DYYB	−3 018	−2 671	−2 164	−6 515	−8 151	−4 778
Industrial and Commercial Companies	DYYH	−5 445	−5 854	−3 359	−6 180	−8 670	−13 158
Personal sector	−RYVW	−	−	−83	−290	−131	−347
Assets							
Central Government	DYWZ	−492	−1 558	−596	−837	−2 276	−
Public Corporations	DYXF	−	−	−	−	−	−
Banks	DYXL	1 234	1 997	1 204	4 132	2 600	4 271
Building Societies	RHRH	−	−	156	282	321	−38
Life Assurance and Pension Funds	DYXV	506	3 262	2 471	2 556	1 430	1 784
Remaining Financial Institutions	DYXY	−120	511	876	3 686	−995	342
Industrial and Commercial Companies	DYYE	321	494	78	836	341	1 132
Personal sector	DYYK	200	200	200	200	200	200
Overseas sector	DYYN	8 707	4 609	4 774	7 732	15 731	12 212

CHAPTER 12: National and sector balance sheets

12.1 National balance sheet[1]

£ billion at end year

		1985	1986	1987	1988	1989	1990	1991	1992	1993	1994	1995
Tangible assets												
Residential buildings	ALLA	626.6	735.7	895.1	1 202.5	1 291.1	1 270.6	1 267.2	1 195.6	1 214.9	1 200.8	1 217.7
Agricultural land, buildings & forestry	ALLB	36.4	34.7	34.6	40.1	46.5	40.2	36.6	32.8	38.2	41.1	40.8
Commercial buildings	ALLC	163.9	173.5	214.6	278.7	327.6	305.1	298.0	284.1	291.9	277.6	265.2
Industrial buildings	ALLD	25.9	25.2	28.0	35.5	41.0	37.6	36.5	33.9	35.3	33.6	32.1
Other buildings	ALLE	100.9	103.1	108.1	129.6	149.4	141.6	136.8	124.8	134.4	136.1	134.5
Civil engineering works	ALLF	157.6	167.9	187.2	216.8	227.2	229.7	227.7	212.6	223.1	234.7	254.2
Plant and machinery	ALLG	239.1	253.4	268.8	284.7	312.4	335.0	353.2	373.1	395.0	419.0	441.1
Ships, aircraft and railway rolling stock	ALLH	8.9	7.5	6.5	6.3	6.8	6.3	6.0	6.3	6.4	6.9	7.2
Road vehicles	ALLI	18.1	19.7	20.2	25.6	27.2	27.4	26.6	27.0	27.1	29.5	30.4
Stocks and work in progress	ALLJ	88.8	92.7	98.9	109.9	119.9	118.1	115.1	117.3	117.4	125.3	134.1
Total tangible assets[2]	ALLK	1 466.2	1 613.4	1 862.0	2 329.7	2 549.1	2 511.6	2 503.7	2 407.5	2 483.7	2 504.6	2 557.3
Intangible non-financial assets												
Non-marketable tenancy rights	ALLL	108.0	117.1	138.0	167.4	178.9	185.9	179.4	171.4	188.4	157.3	150.5
External assets of the UK:												
Other public sector financing: Short-term assets	REUY	0.2	0.2	–	–	–	–	–	–	–	–	–
Issue Department transactions in bills, etc	REVL	1.9	2.0	0.9	0.7	0.3	0.5	0.7	2.6	2.0	1.0	0.6
Official reserves	APDD	13.2	17.4	27.0	28.7	26.3	22.5	26.0	28.3	29.7	30.7	31.8
Bank lending (excl public sector): Foreign currency	RHHU	346.7	409.3	390.6	408.5	478.8	452.3	420.6	516.2	503.8	545.6	619.7
Sterling	AMXG	23.1	28.9	34.6	39.4	42.8	46.2	39.9	48.5	57.3	57.9	61.8
Identified trade credit: Import and export	REYR	0.8	0.4	0.5	0.8	0.9	1.6	1.6	1.7	1.7	1.5	1.0
Other public sector lending	RMEF	3.8	3.9	4.1	4.2	4.5	4.7	4.9	5.3	5.5	5.7	5.9
Overseas securities	APYY	99.4	140.1	112.9	145.6	215.2	189.6	240.9	303.0	438.4	401.6	481.9
Direct and other investment abroad	REYL	69.6	80.9	85.5	104.4	124.0	119.7	125.3	148.4	169.2	179.5	213.8
Miscellaneous instruments	REWM	34.9	37.8	39.2	42.3	64.2	74.3	89.4	122.9	180.4	165.4	200.5
Total external assets[2]	APWB	593.6	720.8	695.1	774.6	957.0	911.3	949.3	1 176.8	1 388.0	1 388.9	1 617.0
External liabilities of the UK:												
Notes and coin	APME	0.3	0.3	0.4	0.4	0.5	0.5	0.5	0.6	0.6	0.7	0.8
Sterling Treasury bills	ACQJ	0.6	0.8	2.2	2.2	3.4	3.9	2.3	1.1	0.7	0.5	1.3
British government securities	HEWD	11.6	13.7	18.1	18.8	16.1	16.2	22.7	28.8	48.7	44.2	46.3
Government foreign currency debt	REUR	0.6	1.7	0.9	1.7	3.9	3.6	5.3	12.8	10.8	13.9	15.2
Other government overseas financing	REUU	3.2	3.2	2.7	2.7	2.9	2.4	2.4	2.8	2.8	2.6	2.6
Local authority debt: Temporary	RMHO	–	–	–	–	–	–	–	–	–	–	–
Foreign currency	RDYX	0.6	0.7	0.8	0.7	0.8	0.7	0.7	0.6	0.5	0.4	0.4
Sterling securities	HCCK	0.1	–	–	–	–	–	–	–	–	–	–
Other Sterling debt	ADKL	–	0.6	0.6	0.6	0.6	0.6	0.5	0.6	0.7	0.7	0.8
Public corporations debt: Foreign currency	REZX	3.7	3.8	3.0	2.6	1.0	0.6	0.6	0.1	0.1	0.3	0.2
Sterling	REXG	0.2	0.2	0.1	0.1	0.1	–	–	–	–	–	–
Deposits with banks: Sterling other	RRGZ	33.4	38.7	47.0	59.8	70.0	82.6	72.5	74.0	74.0	79.6	87.2
Foreign currency other	RMFF	330.3	389.4	363.4	379.0	461.9	444.7	436.5	546.3	582.0	623.0	699.7
Sterling money market instruments	RMFL	0.5	0.7	1.2	2.2	3.4	3.2	2.4	2.5	3.9	4.5	5.1
Foreign currency money market instruments	RMFR	51.8	55.6	54.4	62.6	70.5	57.0	49.5	54.6	41.9	44.9	60.5
Deposits with building societies:												
Sterling other	RMFW	0.1	0.6	1.5	1.9	2.0	2.4	2.7	3.0	3.9	4.2	4.5
Sterling money market instruments	RMGB	0.1	0.1	0.1	0.2	0.9	1.4	1.7	1.9	2.6	4.1	3.6
Foreign currency money market instruments	RMGE	–	–	–	–	1.5	2.6	4.1	5.6	3.9	4.1	6.1
Identified trade credit: Import and export	RDYR	0.6	0.4	0.4	0.5	0.5	0.5	0.6	0.7	1.1	1.4	1.7
Other public sector lending	AIRH	0.7	0.5	0.7	0.7	0.9	0.7	0.7	0.7	0.9	0.7	0.8
United Kingdom company securities	REYY	20.1	32.8	48.6	66.3	89.1	87.4	102.9	135.1	184.5	190.7	228.7
Overseas direct and other investment in the UK	REYM	44.3	51.7	62.6	76.8	99.8	113.2	120.7	122.7	127.9	129.6	150.4
Miscellaneous instruments	REWH	19.9	25.1	24.7	30.3	65.0	78.3	106.8	157.4	256.5	201.8	248.4
Accruals adjustments	RMHK	1.6	1.9	2.1	2.4	2.8	3.2	3.7	4.2	4.4	4.7	4.8
Total external liabilities[2]	APMB	524.1	622.7	635.4	712.6	897.7	905.8	939.8	1 156.3	1 352.5	1 356.8	1 568.9
Net external financial wealth	-APMA	69.5	98.1	59.7	62.0	59.3	5.5	9.5	20.5	35.5	32.1	48.0
Total net wealth[2]	RDYZ	1 643.7	1 828.6	2 059.7	2 559.1	2 787.3	2 703.0	2 692.6	2 599.4	2 707.6	2 694.0	2 755.8

1 For scope of updates see methodological notes.
2 Differences between totals and sums of components are due to rounding.

Balance sheets

12.2 Personal sector[1]

£ billion at end year

		1985	1986	1987	1988	1989	1990	1991	1992	1993	1994	1995
Tangible assets:												
Residential buildings	ALLN	557.7	652.5	796.4	1 084.6	1 172.5	1 158.7	1 157.5	1 091.3	1 115.9	1 113.1	1 127.5
Agricultural land, buildings & forestry	ALLO	30.0	28.6	29.4	34.2	39.9	34.5	31.5	28.2	32.9	35.4	35.1
Commercial, industrial and other buildings	ALLP	36.9	40.9	48.7	57.2	59.4	56.8	52.2	49.8	49.6	50.2	47.6
Civil engineering works	ALLQ	0.5	0.7	1.3	1.7	1.7	1.9	1.7	1.4	1.5	1.4	1.6
Plant and machinery	ALLR	14.0	14.9	15.9	17.1	18.9	20.4	21.0	21.6	23.5	25.0	24.0
Vehicles, including ships, aircraft, etc	ALLS	4.3	4.2	4.1	5.1	5.4	5.4	5.1	4.9	5.3	5.6	5.7
Stocks and work in progress	ALLT	8.2	8.8	9.6	10.9	12.2	13.0	11.9	11.9	12.2	13.3	14.2
Total tangible assets[2]	ALLU	651.6	750.6	905.4	1 210.8	1 310.0	1 290.7	1 280.9	1 209.1	1 240.9	1 244.0	1 255.7
Intangible non-financial assets												
Non-marketable tenancy rights	ALLL	108.0	117.1	138.0	167.4	178.9	185.9	179.4	171.4	188.4	157.3	150.5
Financial assets:												
Notes and coin	AQHA	10.4	11.4	12.0	12.9	13.7	13.6	14.0	15.0	15.9	17.0	18.2
Sterling Treasury bills	DCHX	–	–	–	–	–	–	–	–	–	–	–
British government securities	RDBR	15.7	18.6	17.3	12.5	9.5	9.5	11.5	19.1	19.3	11.8	14.8
National savings	REYC	30.4	32.6	34.9	36.3	34.8	35.6	37.7	43.5	46.6	51.2	54.4
Tax instruments	ACSB	0.1	0.2	0.3	0.3	0.3	0.3	0.3	0.3	0.3	0.2	0.2
Northern Ireland central government debt	REYH	0.3	0.2	0.2	0.2	0.2	0.2	0.2	0.1	0.1	0.1	0.1
Local authority debt: Temporary	ADHJ	0.2	0.2	0.1	0.1	0.1	0.1	0.1	0.1	0.1	0.1	0.1
Sterling securities	AQHF	–	0.1	–	0.1	–	0.1	–	0.1	–	0.1	0.1
Other Sterling debt	ADKK	0.9	0.7	0.5	0.3	0.2	0.1	0.1	0.1	0.1	0.1	0.1
Public corporations debt: Sterling other	REVA	0.2	–	–	–	–	–	–	–	–	–	–
Deposits with banks: Sterling other	RRGY	61.5	67.4	75.6	91.9	138.4	153.5	159.2	163.7	165.8	166.9	194.0
Foreign currency other	RMFE	2.2	2.5	2.3	2.5	3.0	3.2	2.8	3.5	3.4	3.4	3.4
Sterling money market instruments	RMFK	–	–	0.1	0.1	0.4	0.5	0.3	0.3	0.5	0.7	0.6
Foreign currency money market instruments	RMFQ	–	0.1	0.1	0.2	0.2	0.1	0.2	0.2	0.1	0.1	0.2
Deposits with building societies:												
Sterling other	RMFV	104.0	115.1	129.4	149.5	141.9	159.7	177.1	188.2	197.9	207.6	208.1
Sterling money market instruments	RMGA	–	0.1	0.1	0.1	0.2	0.3	0.3	0.2	0.1	0.2	0.2
Foreign currency market instruments	RMJZ	..	–	–	–	–	–	–	–	–	–	–
Identified trade credit: Domestic	ALDJ	25.3	27.2	29.7	32.3	37.9	42.0	46.4	49.2	49.2	49.0	47.8
Unit trust units	AKUI	9.7	14.8	16.7	17.8	25.5	18.2	20.0	23.7	39.4	43.5	53.9
United Kingdom company securities	REYX	65.1	92.5	113.6	119.1	146.0	168.6	200.8	222.6	273.7	285.0	334.6
Overseas securities	AQHG	8.1	10.3	9.9	11.4	12.4	11.5	12.7	14.2	16.4	16.8	18.7
Life assurance and pension funds	AMWV	290.8	358.2	390.2	453.8	565.4	528.0	611.0	694.8	882.8	832.2	971.0
Direct and other investment abroad	AQHH	0.4	0.5	0.5	0.5	0.6	0.5	0.7	0.8	0.8	0.8	0.8
Miscellaneous instruments	REWG	7.4	8.3	9.5	11.1	13.5	15.3	16.0	18.3	18.3	18.1	20.4
Accruals adjustments	ALDN	12.5	12.2	14.1	16.2	20.5	24.4	28.7	29.6	30.0	32.4	34.9
Total financial assets[2]	ALDO	645.3	773.0	857.0	969.3	1 164.7	1 185.2	1 340.2	1 487.8	1 760.8	1 737.4	1 976.7
Financial liabilities:												
Other public sector financing: Short-term assets	ADNH	–	–	–	–	0.1	–	0.1	0.1	–	–	–
Bank lending (excl public sector): Foreign currency	RHHT	1.0	1.0	0.9	1.3	1.8	1.9	1.6	1.0	0.5	0.6	0.6
Sterling	AMXF	39.1	44.0	52.4	64.9	78.1	85.5	85.6	82.5	77.7	80.0	85.9
Credit extended by retailers	RRAQ	4.3	3.9	2.2	2.4	2.4	2.4	2.5	2.5	2.6	2.6	2.5
Identified trade credit: Domestic	AQHR	21.8	23.2	25.2	26.6	28.5	30.5	32.5	34.0	34.0	34.0	34.0
Loans secured on dwellings: Building societies	AHKV	97.2	116.6	131.6	155.3	152.6	176.7	197.2	211.4	219.6	231.2	223.2
Other	REEH	30.0	37.1	51.3	67.6	104.2	118.1	123.0	127.6	137.6	144.4	166.9
Other public sector lending	REUH	0.2	0.2	0.2	0.2	0.2	0.2	0.4	0.6	0.9	1.4	2.1
Lending by financial institutions: Finance leasing	ASLM	0.5	0.6	0.7	0.8	1.0	1.2	1.1	1.1	1.0	1.0	1.1
Other	RMIS	..	0.8	0.9	1.0	1.2	1.5	1.8	1.5	1.7	1.6	1.6
United Kingdom company securities	RJYY	..	–	–	–	–	0.2	0.3	0.5	1.2	1.2	1.7
Overseas direct and other investment in the UK	ALDW	1.9	2.6	3.7	5.3	6.3	7.2	7.8	7.2	7.6	8.5	8.7
Miscellaneous instruments	REWL	9.3	10.0	13.9	15.0	16.4	17.5	17.6	17.4	18.6	20.3	22.6
Accruals adjustment	ALDX	3.5	1.1	1.3	1.4	2.1	2.5	3.7	2.6	2.4	2.1	1.6
Total financial liabilities[2]	ALDY	208.9	241.3	284.3	341.8	394.6	445.2	475.3	489.9	505.4	528.8	552.6
Net financial wealth[2]	ALDZ	436.4	531.7	572.7	627.5	770.1	740.0	864.9	997.9	1 255.4	1 208.6	1 424.1
Total net wealth[2]	ALLV	1 196.0	1 399.4	1 616.1	2 005.7	2 259.0	2 216.6	2 325.2	2 378.4	2 684.7	2 609.9	2 830.3

1 For scope of updates see Methodological notes.
2 Differences between totals and sums of totals are due to rounding.

12.3 Industrial and commercial companies[1]

£ billion at end year

		1985	1986	1987	1988	1989	1990	1991	1992	1993	1994	1995
Tangible assets:												
Residential buildings	ALLX	7.7	10.1	13.6	18.6	17.3	15.4	15.3	15.1	12.6	11.3	12.1
Agricultural land, buildings & forestry	ALLY	1.9	1.8	1.9	2.2	2.4	2.1	1.9	1.7	2.0	2.1	2.1
Commercial, industrial and other buildings	ALLZ	133.0	132.8	154.8	209.1	266.6	243.6	245.0	232.0	242.6	215.0	200.4
Civil engineering works	ALMA	16.1	30.3	31.5	34.7	73.0	80.9	83.8	79.6	82.7	80.9	84.0
Plant and machinery	ALMB	155.5	169.3	181.1	192.6	213.5	255.4	277.6	294.8	312.1	331.2	350.6
Vehicles, including ships, aircraft etc.	ALMC	13.6	13.3	13.9	17.3	18.4	17.7	16.5	17.1	18.3	20.6	21.3
Stocks and work in progress	ALMD	74.5	77.2	83.3	93.2	102.7	100.3	100.3	100.3	102.4	109.9	118.1
Total tangible assets[2]	ALME	402.3	434.8	480.1	567.7	693.9	715.4	740.4	740.6	772.7	771.0	788.6
Financial assets:												
Notes and coin	APSD	1.1	1.2	1.3	1.4	1.5	1.5	1.6	1.6	1.7	1.8	1.9
Sterling Treasury bills	ACQI	0.2	0.2	0.2	0.2	0.2	0.2	0.2	0.2	–	0.1	0.1
British government securities	AIEI	1.6	1.4	1.6	1.3	1.1	2.0	2.5	1.7	2.2	2.1	2.0
National savings	AQJI	0.3	0.3	0.5	0.6	0.6	0.6	0.7	–	–	–	–
Tax instruments	ACSA	2.6	2.6	2.2	1.8	1.9	2.2	2.1	1.8	1.7	1.3	0.9
Northern Ireland central government debt	RCTD	–	–	–	–	–	–	–	–	–	–	–
Government liabilities under exchange cover scheme	REXE	–	–	–	–	–	–	–	–	–	–	–
Local authority debt: Temporary	ADHI	0.3	0.2	0.1	0.1	0.1	0.2	0.2	0.2	0.1	0.1	0.1
Sterling securities	AQJK	–	–	–	–	–	–	–	–	–	–	–
Other Sterling debt	ADKJ	0.1	0.1	0.1	–	–	–	–	–	–	–	–
Public corporations debt: Sterling	RCTW	–	–	–	–	–	–	–	–	–	–	–
Deposits with banks: Sterling other	RRGX	27.8	34.8	41.9	46.1	53.4	56.8	61.1	59.6	67.0	71.0	77.0
Foreign currency other	RMFD	9.5	10.7	8.7	8.8	11.9	14.4	12.1	12.7	13.6	14.6	14.2
Sterling money market instruments	RMFJ	0.7	1.7	2.4	3.7	4.0	2.8	2.7	2.7	2.6	2.9	3.5
Foreign currency money market instruments	RMFP	1.0	1.3	0.8	1.0	1.0	0.3	0.4	0.4	0.3	0.4	0.6
Deposits with building societies: Sterling other	RMFU	1.6	2.1	2.0	1.5	2.5	4.1	5.5	3.9	4.7	5.1	4.0
Sterling money market instruments	RMFZ	0.1	0.2	0.2	0.3	0.6	0.8	1.2	0.5	0.6	0.7	0.4
Foreign currency money market instruments	RMJY	..	–	–	–	–	–	0.1	0.1	0.1	–	0.1
Credit extended by retailers	ALCH	4.1	3.9	2.2	2.4	2.4	2.4	2.5	2.5	2.6	2.6	2.5
Identified trade credit: Domestic	RCTX	71.1	72.6	79.5	83.3	83.3	83.3	83.3	83.3	83.3	83.3	83.3
Import and export	RHHK	0.2	0.2	0.3	0.6	0.6	1.1	1.0	1.2	1.1	1.1	0.5
United Kingdom company securities	REYW	31.3	44.7	52.1	60.4	70.1	34.3	38.6	39.2	42.0	44.7	50.3
Overseas securities	AQBF	1.9	1.9	2.0	2.6	2.7	2.1	1.2	2.0	2.2	2.8	2.7
Direct and other investment abroad	REYK	60.0	67.3	72.4	91.5	107.3	108.9	112.0	131.5	141.6	152.4	181.1
Miscellaneous instruments	REWF	7.1	7.8	11.7	12.3	13.1	14.0	15.7	16.0	21.6	21.8	24.7
Accruals adjustments	ALCM	5.8	6.9	7.7	8.8	9.9	9.7	11.7	13.0	14.5	16.1	16.7
Total financial assets[2]	ALCN	228.4	262.0	289.9	328.8	368.5	341.9	356.3	374.2	403.6	425.2	466.8
Financial liabilities:												
Other public sector financing: Short-term assets	ADNF	–	–	–	0.1	0.1	–	–	–	–	–	–
Issue Department transactions in bills, etc	REWZ	5.4	5.8	2.9	3.5	1.5	1.9	2.8	5.0	6.3	2.5	1.5
Bank lending (excl public sector): Foreign currency	RHHS	16.2	17.7	17.7	26.0	37.6	35.0	33.5	37.0	31.0	28.7	30.2
Sterling	AMXE	47.7	54.9	66.9	89.4	117.7	134.4	130.9	125.9	116.9	113.0	124.9
Identified trade credit: Domestic	RDLG	72.5	74.4	81.1	86.4	90.3	92.8	94.7	96.1	96.8	98.3	98.6
Import and export	REYQ	0.5	0.3	0.3	0.3	0.3	0.3	0.3	0.5	0.8	1.2	1.5
Other public sector lending	REVT	1.3	3.0	3.1	3.2	4.3	4.6	5.0	5.0	5.0	5.0	4.9
Lending by financial institutions: Finance leasing	AMWU	7.4	8.1	8.9	10.2	12.9	14.4	14.4	13.4	13.4	13.2	14.2
Other	RMAQ	1.7	2.6	3.0	3.9	5.7	6.9	7.6	8.3	8.9	8.6	8.3
United Kingdom company securities	REZD	239.4	321.8	377.1	419.9	524.9	495.2	603.6	691.0	861.7	825.0	959.8
Overseas direct and other investment in the UK	AQBP	37.5	42.5	48.1	58.9	77.3	87.3	92.6	95.0	95.3	96.7	112.2
Miscellaneous instruments	REWK	18.1	22.4	23.2	29.4	38.9	41.5	49.6	58.0	76.1	78.1	83.8
Accruals adjustments	ALCW	11.1	11.8	13.2	14.3	15.3	15.4	17.7	17.5	18.1	20.7	21.8
Total financial liabilities[2]	ALCX	458.8	565.2	645.6	745.6	926.9	929.6	1 052.7	1 152.8	1 330.3	1 291.1	1 461.6
Net financial wealth[2]	ALCY	−230.4	−303.2	−355.6	−416.8	−558.4	−587.8	−696.4	−778.5	−926.7	−865.9	−994.8
Total net wealth[2]	ALMF	171.9	131.6	124.5	150.9	135.5	127.6	44.0	−37.9	−154.0	−94.9	−206.2

1 For scope of updates see Methodological notes.
2 Differences betweens totals and sums of components are due to rounding.

Balance sheets

12.4 Financial companies and institutions[1]

£ billion at end year

		1985	1986	1987	1988	1989	1990	1991	1992	1993	1994	1995
Tangible assets												
Residential buildings	CXAU	0.6	0.9	1.2	1.0	1.2	3.6	6.6	6.1	4.0	1.9	1.8
Agricultural land, buildings & forestry	CXAV	0.6	0.5	0.6	0.6	0.7	0.6	0.6	0.5	0.6	0.7	0.7
Commercial, industrial and other buildings	CXAW	43.0	46.4	57.4	75.5	83.1	80.0	74.5	67.5	73.9	78.6	77.6
Civil engineering works	CXAZ	–	–	–	–	–	–	–	–	–	–	–
Plant and machinery	CXBA	6.6	7.1	8.0	8.9	10.3	11.5	15.0	15.9	17.2	19.1	21.3
Vehicles, including ships, aircraft, etc	CXBB	3.1	4.0	4.2	5.1	5.8	5.9	6.2	5.7	4.2	4.2	4.2
Stocks and work in progress	CXBD	–	–	–	–	–	–	–	–	–	–	–
Total tangible assets[2]	CXBE	53.9	58.9	71.4	91.1	101.1	101.6	102.9	95.7	99.9	104.5	105.6
Financial assets:												
Notes and coin	RERT	3.1	2.8	3.2	3.8	4.2	4.3	4.3	5.0	5.3	5.5	5.8
Sterling Treasury bills	RERU	0.6	0.6	1.4	2.7	4.3	6.0	6.0	2.8	2.0	4.5	15.4
British government securities	RERV	88.1	91.4	95.6	93.4	81.0	71.9	75.7	97.1	150.8	153.5	187.5
National savings	RERW	–	0.1	0.1	0.1	0.1	0.1	0.1	–	–	–	–
Tax instruments	RERX	0.7	1.2	0.9	0.2	0.2	0.3	0.3	0.3	0.2	0.2	0.2
Net government indebtedness to Banking Dept	RRGO	0.6	0.7	1.0	1.1	1.4	1.8	1.7	1.5	-5.0	-0.8	-1.6
Northern Ireland central government debt	RERY	–	–	–	–	–	–	–	–	–	–	–
Other public sector financing: Non-marketable debt	RERZ	0.1	–	–	–	–	–	–	–	–	–	–
Government foreign currency debt	REAG	2.1	3.4	2.9	1.2	1.2	1.2	1.3	6.9	7.0	2.5	2.0
Local authority debt: Temporary	RESB	2.6	1.8	2.0	1.8	1.4	2.1	1.8	1.4	1.4	1.2	1.1
Foreign currency	REXL	–	–	–	–	–	–	–	–	–	0.1	0.1
Sterling securities	RESC	0.7	0.5	0.4	0.3	0.3	0.1	0.1	0.1	0.1	0.4	0.5
Other Sterling debt	RESD	6.1	4.8	3.3	2.6	1.8	1.6	1.5	2.8	4.5	5.1	5.2
Public corporations debt: Foreign currency	REBX	1.4	1.5	0.9	0.1	–	–	–	–	–	–	–
Sterling	RESE	1.4	1.0	1.0	1.1	1.1	0.9	1.3	2.1	1.7	1.3	1.1
Deposits with banks: Sterling other	RMGL	82.5	91.5	113.2	134.6	169.1	188.4	171.0	182.1	180.5	189.5	212.2
Foreign currency other	RMGM	97.5	117.2	106.5	106.5	111.5	109.7	97.0	122.3	132.3	150.6	161.3
Sterling money market instruments	RMGN	13.8	17.0	25.3	31.2	33.9	45.6	45.8	44.1	42.7	51.6	56.6
Foreign currency money market instruments	RMGO	12.7	14.4	10.5	9.1	11.2	12.5	14.2	16.3	14.6	16.4	20.3
Deposits with building societies:												
Sterling other	RMGP	1.0	0.8	1.0	1.2	1.5	4.6	5.3	7.7	8.2	9.6	8.5
Sterling money market instruments	RMGQ	1.3	2.6	3.5	3.9	7.2	11.1	11.5	10.7	10.7	11.6	11.8
Foreign currency money market instruments	RJZD	..	–	–	–	0.3	0.5	0.8	1.4	1.4	1.9	2.0
Bank lending (excl public sector): Foreign currency	RHHW	381.3	452.6	436.3	464.0	557.5	523.3	480.7	582.5	575.9	623.1	723.5
Sterling	REYE	133.4	153.6	189.0	239.6	297.7	335.9	328.1	329.3	330.0	334.3	366.3
Identified trade credit: Domestic	RDEZ	0.9	1.1	1.4	2.0	2.3	2.8	2.7	3.1	3.8	4.7	5.3
Import and export	REYN	0.4	0.1	0.2	0.2	0.3	0.5	0.6	0.5	0.6	0.4	0.4
Loans secured on dwellings: Building societies	AHKV	97.2	116.6	131.6	155.3	152.6	176.7	197.2	211.4	219.6	231.2	223.2
Other	RESJ	24.6	32.2	46.7	63.1	99.8	114.2	120.1	125.1	135.5	142.6	165.4
Lending by financial institutions: Finance leasing	REBZ	10.1	11.4	11.8	13.8	17.1	19.1	19.5	18.2	17.9	17.8	18.7
Other	RMAS	2.2	3.9	4.5	5.4	7.4	8.4	9.4	9.8	10.6	10.3	10.0
Unit trust units	RCWO	9.6	15.8	17.8	21.7	29.6	25.7	32.3	36.9	51.3	43.6	52.9
United Kingdom company securities	RESK	167.2	216.9	241.3	267.1	340.8	314.8	382.2	448.0	592.3	549.3	650.8
Overseas securities	RESM	89.3	127.8	101.0	131.6	200.1	175.9	227.1	286.8	419.8	381.9	460.5
Direct and other investment abroad	RESN	9.0	12.9	12.4	12.3	16.1	10.3	12.5	16.1	26.8	26.4	31.9
Miscellaneous instruments	RESP	45.0	47.3	51.1	57.0	80.4	89.1	102.2	137.1	194.6	183.8	219.4
Accruals adjustments	RESO	2.9	0.6	0.7	0.8	0.9	1.2	1.9	1.8	2.0	1.9	1.9
Total financial assets[2]	RESQ	1 289.5	1 546.1	1 618.6	1 828.5	2 234.6	2 260.8	2 356.5	2 711.0	3 138.9	3 156.0	3 620.3
Financial liabilities:												
Notes and coin	APTD	1.1	1.1	1.3	1.4	1.6	1.7	1.8	2.1	2.2	2.5	2.6
Other public sector financing: Short-term assets	RESR	0.2	–	1.7	3.0	4.0	2.1	3.1	3.7	4.4	5.0	4.4
Issue Department transactions in bills, etc	REST	3.9	4.0	2.1	2.2	0.9	1.1	1.7	2.2	3.0	1.6	0.9
Deposits with banks: Sterling other	RRGW	208.4	237.3	284.6	342.4	441.0	490.0	470.0	486.8	496.0	515.6	584.9
Foreign currency other	RMFC	439.8	520.0	481.2	497.0	588.5	572.3	548.7	685.2	731.7	792.0	879.1
Sterling money market instruments	RMFI	15.0	19.5	29.3	37.3	41.8	52.2	51.4	49.7	49.8	59.8	66.0
Foreign currency money market instruments	RMFO	65.5	71.5	65.8	72.8	82.9	70.0	64.3	71.6	57.0	61.8	81.7
Deposits with building societies:												
Sterling other	RMFT	106.7	118.5	133.9	154.1	148.0	170.8	190.6	202.9	214.7	226.5	225.1
Sterling money market instruments	RMFY	1.5	2.9	3.8	4.5	8.8	13.6	14.7	13.3	14.0	16.7	16.0
Foreign currency money market instruments	RMGD	–	–	–	–	1.8	3.2	4.9	7.1	5.4	6.0	8.2
Bank lending (excl public sector): Foreign currency	RHHR	17.4	24.6	27.0	28.2	39.4	34.1	25.0	28.3	40.6	48.1	73.0
Sterling	RESU	23.5	25.8	35.2	45.9	59.2	69.8	71.6	72.4	78.0	83.4	93.7
Identified trade credit: Domestic	AQJH	0.3	0.3	0.3	0.3	0.3	0.3	0.3	0.3	0.3	0.3	0.3
Other public sector lending	RESV	0.1	0.2	–	–	–	–	–	–	–	–	–
Lending by financial institutions: Finance leasing	RKWG	1.3	1.6	0.9	1.1	1.3	1.7	2.2	2.0	1.9	1.7	1.6
Other	RMAP	–	–	–	–	0.1	0.1	–	–	–	–	–
Unit trust units	RDNQ	19.3	30.5	34.5	39.5	55.2	44.0	52.3	60.6	90.7	87.1	106.8
United Kingdom company securities	RESW	61.6	81.4	92.4	105.6	135.4	124.2	137.6	169.2	243.0	250.9	305.8
Life assurance and pension funds	ALDK	283.2	349.9	381.3	444.1	555.2	517.7	600.8	685.0	873.4	823.1	962.7
Overseas direct and other investment in the UK	RESX	5.0	6.7	10.8	12.6	16.2	18.7	20.3	20.6	25.0	24.3	29.5
Miscellaneous instruments	REBW	16.1	17.4	19.6	22.8	51.3	62.1	83.7	130.0	214.7	159.1	203.2
Accruals adjustments	RESY	21.9	21.0	22.4	24.5	30.3	35.1	40.2	42.6	44.2	47.2	49.0
Total financial liabilities[2]	RESZ	1 291.7	1 534.2	1 628.2	1 839.4	2 263.3	2 285.0	2 385.4	2 735.4	3 189.9	3 213.0	3 694.5
Net financial wealth[2]	RETA	-2.3	11.9	-9.6	-10.9	-28.8	-24.2	-28.9	-24.4	-51.0	-57.1	-74.2
Total net wealth[2]	RETB	51.6	70.8	61.8	80.2	72.3	77.4	74.0	71.3	48.9	47.4	31.4

1 For scope of updates see Methodological notes.
2 Differences between totals and sums of components are due to rounding.

12.5 Banks[1]

£ billion at end year

		1985	1986	1987	1988	1989	1990	1991	1992	1993	1994	1995
Tangible assets:												
Residential buildings	ALMG	0.1	0.2	0.3	0.2	0.4	1.3	2.1	1.9	1.3	0.7	0.6
Agricultural land, buildings & forestry	ALMH	–	–	–	–	–	–	–	–	–	–	–
Commercial, industrial and other buildings	ALMI	5.4	5.4	6.8	8.1	9.7	10.0	9.7	9.6	9.1	9.0	7.7
Civil engineering works	ALMJ	–	–	–	–	–	–	–	–	–	–	–
Plant and machinery	ALMK	2.8	3.2	3.6	4.2	4.9	5.0	5.3	5.5	5.6	5.7	5.9
Vehicles, including ships, aircraft etc.	ALML	0.2	0.2	0.2	0.3	0.4	0.4	0.4	0.5	0.5	0.6	0.5
Stocks and work in progress	ALMM	–	–	–	–	–	–	–	–	–	–	–
Total tangible assets[2]	ALMN	8.5	9.0	10.9	12.8	15.4	16.7	17.5	17.5	16.5	16.0	14.7
Financial assets:												
Notes and coin	APSQ	2.6	2.6	3.0	3.4	3.9	4.0	3.9	4.5	4.7	5.0	5.4
Sterling Treasury bills	ACQE	0.5	0.5	1.0	2.3	2.8	3.7	4.2	2.2	1.7	4.2	11.1
British government securities	RCAO	7.5	8.8	8.4	6.0	5.9	4.2	3.9	4.9	14.0	15.9	18.4
Tax instruments	ACRX	0.2	0.3	0.4	0.1	0.2	0.2	0.3	0.2	0.2	0.2	0.2
Net government indebtedness to Banking Dept	RRGO	0.6	0.7	1.0	1.1	1.4	1.8	1.7	1.5	–5.0	–0.8	–1.6
Northern Ireland central government debt	REYG	–	–	–	–	–	–	–	–	–	–	–
Other public sector financing: Non-marketable debt	APHZ	0.1	–	–	–	–	–	–	–	–	–	–
Issue Department transactions in bills, etc	RMAV	–	–	–	–	–	–	–	–	–	–	–
Government foreign currency debt	REXO	0.9	0.9	0.3	0.4	0.4	0.4	0.4	5.4	5.9	1.7	1.6
Local authority debt: Temporary	APHF	1.5	1.1	0.9	0.6	0.2	0.3	0.2	0.2	0.2	0.4	0.3
Foreign currency	REZS	–	–	–	–	–	–	–	–	–	–	–
Sterling securities	APHK	0.2	0.1	0.1	–	–	–	–	–	–	–	–
Other Sterling debt	ADKH	4.3	2.8	2.0	1.5	1.0	0.5	0.7	1.9	3.5	3.8	4.0
Public corporations debt: Foreign currency	APQS	1.4	1.5	0.9	0.1	–	–	–	–	–	–	–
Sterling	RMEK	1.1	0.7	0.7	0.8	0.5	0.4	0.4	0.8	0.8	0.4	0.4
Deposits with banks: Sterling other	RRGV	51.8	64.3	70.1	81.3	100.2	108.6	91.5	100.4	90.7	98.6	99.6
Foreign currency other	RRGT	90.2	101.6	86.1	83.8	80.0	76.1	77.1	89.7	96.1	106.2	94.1
Sterling money market instruments	RMFH	12.1	13.5	16.6	17.6	19.0	26.3	25.3	25.5	24.7	29.5	32.6
Foreign currency money market instruments	RMFN	12.6	13.1	9.3	7.4	8.7	10.5	11.4	12.0	9.2	8.2	10.5
Deposits with building societies:												
Sterling other	RCOB	0.2	0.8	1.0	1.2	1.5	2.1	2.1	2.3	2.3	2.9	1.4
Sterling money market instruments	RMFX	1.1	1.0	1.1	1.4	1.9	3.0	2.6	5.1	6.6	6.0	6.3
Foreign currency money market instruments	RMJR	..	–	–	–	–	0.1	0.1	0.7	0.7	0.8	0.8
Bank lending (excl public sector): Foreign currency	RHHW	381.3	452.6	436.3	464.0	557.5	523.3	480.7	582.5	575.9	623.1	723.5
Sterling	RHHY	133.4	153.6	189.0	239.6	297.7	335.9	328.1	329.3	330.0	334.3	366.3
Loans secured on dwellings: Other	AKGF	21.1	25.9	36.0	45.3	79.2	85.7	90.4	96.4	108.5	115.9	139.9
Lending by financial institutions: Finance leasing	ASLF	1.3	1.4	0.6	0.5	0.6	0.7	0.8	0.9	1.0	1.1	1.4
United Kingdom company securities	REYU	9.5	11.6	12.3	16.0	20.6	23.1	26.6	27.5	33.2	39.5	47.6
Overseas securities	APHO	28.1	34.4	28.9	31.2	41.9	44.3	53.5	75.7	111.8	122.9	149.7
Direct and other investment abroad	APHP	0.9	3.5	3.8	2.2	2.1	1.9	1.2	2.5	3.4	4.5	5.1
Miscellaneous instruments	REWD	–	0.1	0.5	0.3	0.3	0.2	0.1	0.2	0.3	0.4	0.4
Accruals adjustments	APSS	–	–	–	–	0.1	–	–	–	–0.1	–0.1	–0.1
Total financial assets[2]	APHB	764.4	897.3	910.6	1 008.2	1 227.8	1 257.3	1 207.4	1 372.3	1 420.2	1 524.6	1 718.5
Financial liabilities:												
Notes and coin	APTD	1.1	1.1	1.3	1.4	1.6	1.7	1.8	2.1	2.2	2.5	2.6
Issue Department transactions in bills, etc	AEDQ	1.8	1.8	0.8	0.2	–	–	–	–	–	–	–
Deposits with banks: Sterling other	RRGW	208.4	237.3	284.6	342.4	441.0	490.0	470.0	486.8	496.0	515.6	584.9
Foreign currency other	RMFC	439.8	520.0	481.2	497.0	588.5	572.3	548.7	685.2	731.7	792.0	879.1
Sterling money market instruments	RMFI	15.0	19.5	29.3	37.3	41.8	52.2	51.4	49.7	49.8	59.8	66.0
Foreign currency money market instruments	RMFO	65.5	71.5	65.8	72.8	82.9	70.0	64.3	71.6	57.0	61.8	81.7
Bank lending (excl public sector): Sterling	RCAN	2.4	0.1	–	0.1	0.1	0.1	0.1	0.1	0.1	–	–
Other public sector lending	APTG	–	–	–	–	–	–	–	–	–	–	–
Lending by financial institutions: Finance leasing	ASLG	0.3	0.4	0.4	0.5	0.7	0.8	1.1	1.0	0.9	0.8	0.8
United Kingdom company securities	REZA	21.1	26.6	29.9	34.5	48.0	29.9	32.8	39.6	55.6	56.7	60.3
Overseas direct and other investment in the UK	APTJ	3.5	4.3	6.1	6.8	6.9	9.4	10.7	10.7	13.0	13.9	16.0
Miscellaneous instruments	RKWF	–	–	–	–	–	–	–	–	–	–	–
Accruals adjustments	APTK	0.3	0.3	0.4	0.5	0.6	0.8	0.6	0.5	0.3	0.4	0.4
Total financial liabilities[2]	APTB	759.2	882.9	899.9	993.5	1 212.2	1 227.2	1 181.5	1 347.1	1 406.7	1 503.5	1 691.9
Net financial wealth[2]	APHA	5.2	14.4	10.6	14.7	15.6	30.1	25.9	25.2	13.5	21.1	26.7
Total net wealth[2]	ALMO	13.7	23.4	21.5	27.5	31.0	46.8	43.4	42.7	30.0	37.1	41.4

1 For scope of updates see Methodological notes.
2 Differences between totals and sums of components are due to rounding.

Balance sheets

12.6 Building societies[1]

£ billion at end year

		1985	1986	1987	1988	1989	1990	1991	1992	1993	1994	1995
Tangible assets:												
Residential buildings		..	..	..	..	..	..	..	..	..	..	..
Agricultural land, buildings & forestry		..	..	..	..	..	..	..	..	..	..	..
Commercial, industrial and other buildings		..	..	..	..	..	..	..	..	..	..	..
Civil engineering works		..	..	..	..	..	..	..	..	..	..	..
Plant and machinery		..	..	..	..	..	..	..	..	..	..	..
Vehicles, including ships, aircraft etc.		..	..	..	..	..	..	..	..	..	..	..
Stocks and work in progress		..	..	..	..	..	..	..	..	..	..	..
Total tangible assets[2]		..	..	..	..	..	..	..	..	..	..	..
Financial assets:												
Notes and coin	AHIM	0.1	0.1	0.2	0.3	0.3	0.3	0.3	0.5	0.5	0.5	0.4
Sterling Treasury bills	AHIQ	–	–	0.1	0.1	0.9	1.2	1.3	0.3	0.1	0.1	2.7
British government securities	RDEW	11.0	9.5	8.3	8.8	4.4	3.8	2.7	3.3	5.1	8.0	7.0
National savings	AROD	–	–	–	–	–	–	–	–	–	–	–
Tax instruments	AGKV	0.5	0.8	0.4	0.1	–	–	–	–	–	–	–
Northern Ireland central government debt	REDH	–	–	–	–	–	–	–	–	–	–	–
Government foreign currency debt	HRVP	–	–	–	–	–	–	–	0.2	–	0.1	–
Local authority debt: Temporary	ADHW	0.4	0.1	0.1	0.1	0.1	0.5	0.5	0.6	0.4	0.3	0.2
Sterling securities	RECB	0.2	0.2	0.1	–	–	–	–	–	–	–	–
Other Sterling debt	RECV	1.3	1.1	0.6	0.4	0.1	0.3	0.3	0.2	0.3	0.5	0.4
Deposits with banks: Sterling other	AHIN	6.9	6.9	9.3	10.5	11.5	13.2	15.9	16.8	18.3	17.4	15.8
Foreign currency other	RHQZ	..	–	–	–	–	–	–	0.4	0.5	0.9	1.5
Sterling money market instruments	RMJV	..	2.5	5.9	9.3	8.3	10.4	12.5	11.6	11.6	12.9	14.8
Foreign currency money market instruments	RMHC	..	–	–	–	–	–	–	0.2	0.5	1.1	1.4
Deposits with building societies:												
Sterling money market instruments	RMKD	..	1.2	1.8	1.9	1.9	2.1	2.3	3.0	3.0	2.9	3.2
Foreign currency money market instruments	RMJS	..	–	–	–	–	–	–	–	–	0.1	0.1
Loans secured on dwellings: Building societies	AHKV	97.2	116.6	131.6	155.3	152.6	176.7	197.2	211.4	219.6	231.2	223.2
Lending by financial institutions: Other	AUAJ	0.2	0.3	0.5	0.8	1.8	2.7	3.2	2.8	3.2	2.7	3.0
UK company securities	RMHI	–	–	0.2	0.5	0.6	0.8	1.2	3.3	4.5	3.9	3.3
Overseas securities	RJYP	..	–	–	–	–	–	–	–	0.4	1.1	1.6
Miscellaneous instruments	REBV	2.5	3.1	3.8	5.2	6.7	8.9	9.1	10.9	12.9	14.1	13.2
Total financial assets[2]	ARNQ	121.5	142.4	162.8	193.1	189.3	220.8	246.7	265.5	280.9	297.7	291.9
Financial liabilities:												
Other public sector financing: Short-term assets	REVH	0.2	–	1.1	1.9	2.4	1.8	2.8	3.6	4.1	4.9	4.3
Deposits with building societies:												
Sterling other	RMFT	106.7	118.5	133.9	154.1	148.0	170.8	190.6	202.9	214.7	226.5	225.1
Sterling money market instruments	RMFY	1.5	2.9	3.8	4.5	8.8	13.6	14.7	13.3	14.0	16.7	16.0
Foreign currency money market instruments	RMGD	–	–	–	–	1.8	3.2	4.9	7.1	5.4	6.0	8.2
Bank lending (excl public sector): Sterling	AHKY	1.1	–	2.6	3.0	2.0	1.7	2.0	2.1	3.3	3.2	2.8
Other public sector lending	AHIC	–	–	–	–	–	–	–	–	–	–	–
United Kingdom company securities	REZB	1.8	5.4	6.0	9.2	6.6	7.3	7.5	10.4	11.4	9.2	9.6
Accruals adjustments	ARNY	4.5	3.1	3.4	4.0	5.6	7.1	7.7	6.2	5.6	5.7	6.1
Total financial liabilities[2]	ARNS	115.9	130.0	150.8	176.8	175.3	205.5	230.1	245.7	258.4	272.3	272.2
Net financial wealth[2]	ARNU	5.7	12.5	12.0	16.3	14.0	15.3	16.6	19.8	22.5	25.4	19.7
Total net wealth[2]		..	..	..	..	..	..	..	..	..	..	..

1 For scope of updates see Methodological notes.
2 Differences between totals and sums of components are due to rounding.

12.7 Life assurance and pension funds[1]

£ billion at end year

		1985	1986	1987	1988	1989	1990	1991	1992	1993	1994	1995
Tangible assets:												
Residential buildings		..	..	..	..	..	..	..	..	..	..	..
Agricultural land,buildings & forestry		..	..	..	..	..	..	..	..	..	..	..
Commercial buildings		..	..	..	..	..	..	..	..	..	..	..
Industrial buildings		..	..	..	..	..	..	..	..	..	..	..
Other buildings		..	..	..	..	..	..	..	..	..	..	..
Civil engineering works		..	..	..	..	..	..	..	..	..	..	..
Plant and machinery		..	..	..	..	..	..	..	..	..	..	..
Ships,aircraft and railway rolling stock		..	..	..	..	..	..	..	..	..	..	..
Road vehicles		..	..	..	..	..	..	..	..	..	..	..
Stocks and work in progress		..	..	..	..	..	..	..	..	..	..	..
Total tangible assets[2]		..	..	..	..	..	..	..	..	..	..	..
Financial assets:												
Sterling Treasury bills	RMEM	–	–	–	–	–	0.1	0.1	0.1	0.2	0.2	1.0
British government securities	RRIO	60.1	63.4	68.7	69.1	64.4	59.1	60.6	76.2	106.9	106.8	133.9
National savings	AROE	–	–	0.1	0.1	0.1	0.1	0.1	–	–	–	–
Government foreign currency debt	ASKC	–	–	–	–	–	–	0.1	0.1	0.3	0.1	0.1
Local authority debt: Temporary	RRIM	–	–	0.8	0.8	0.8	1.1	0.8	0.4	0.5	0.2	0.4
Sterling securities	RRIQ	0.2	0.2	0.3	0.2	0.2	0.1	0.1	0.1	0.1	0.3	0.4
Other Sterling debt	RRIS	0.5	0.9	0.7	0.7	0.7	0.8	0.5	0.6	0.8	0.7	0.8
Public corporations debt: Sterling	ASKG	0.1	0.1	0.1	0.1	0.3	0.1	0.5	0.7	0.4	0.4	0.4
Deposits with banks: Sterling other	RRGK	7.7	10.5	15.8	18.4	23.4	29.7	21.7	23.2	24.5	24.4	31.5
Sterling money market instruments	RMJW	..	0.4	0.9	2.1	2.6	3.1	3.0	2.8	2.0	2.6	3.8
Foreign currency money market instruments	ASKJ	–	–	–	–	0.9	0.9	1.3	2.2	3.3	4.4	4.6
Deposits with building societies:												
Sterling other	RMDM	0.8	–	–	–	–	2.5	3.2	4.3	4.1	4.8	5.2
Sterling money market instruments	RMJU	..	–	–	–	1.5	2.6	3.1	0.7	0.3	0.1	0.4
Foreign currency money market instruments	RMJT	..	–	–	–	0.2	0.2	0.3	0.4	0.4	0.7	0.7
Loans secured on dwellings	ASKK	2.5	2.7	3.3	3.6	3.2	3.2	2.9	2.8	2.1	1.5	1.2
Lending by financial institutions: Other	ASKM	0.5	2.7	3.0	3.3	4.1	3.9	5.2	5.8	6.0	5.4	5.9
Unit trust units	RRJK	9.3	15.4	17.3	21.3	29.3	25.2	31.8	36.5	50.7	43.0	52.3
United Kingdom company securities	ASKO	132.0	170.3	188.4	207.1	261.4	237.4	296.1	349.3	452.7	405.4	475.4
Overseas securities	ASKP	38.7	53.4	45.2	63.9	100.5	82.4	108.5	121.2	160.4	147.7	178.2
Direct and other investment abroad	ASKQ	4.5	5.1	4.9	5.2	6.6	1.7	2.2	2.5	2.5	2.0	1.9
Miscellaneous instruments	AMVA	5.8	3.5	2.9	3.4	2.6	1.9	1.4	2.2	2.2	2.0	2.0
Accruals adjustment	RMIR	..	–	–	–	–	0.2	0.8	0.5	0.7	0.6	0.5
Total financial assets[2]	ASKW	265.5	328.9	352.3	399.3	502.9	456.3	544.2	632.4	820.9	753.2	900.4
Financial liabilities:												
Bank lending (excl public sector): Sterling	ASKN	1.3	1.6	2.1	2.3	2.5	2.5	1.9	1.2	1.3	1.6	1.3
Life assurance and pension funds	ALDK	283.2	349.9	381.3	444.1	555.2	517.7	600.8	685.0	873.4	823.1	962.7
Miscellaneous instruments	AMVB	0.1	–	0.2	0.2	0.1	0.1	0.1	–	–	0.1	0.1
Accruals adjustments	RMIO	–	–	–1.0	–2.4	–2.0	–2.2	–2.3	–2.4	–1.8	–1.7	–1.7
Total financial liabilities[2]	AMVC	286.9	351.6	382.6	444.2	555.8	518.2	600.5	683.8	873.0	823.1	962.5
Net financial wealth[2]	AMVD	–21.4	–22.7	–30.3	–44.8	–52.9	–61.8	–56.2	–51.4	–52.1	–70.0	–62.0
Total net wealth[2]		..	..	..	..	..	..	..	..	..	..	..

1 For scope of updates see Methodological notes.
2 Differences between totals and sums of components are due to rounding.

Balance sheets

12.8 Financial institutions (excluding banks, building societies and life assurance and pension funds)[1]

£ billion at end year

		1985	1986	1987	1988	1989	1990	1991	1992	1993	1994	1995
Tangible assets												
Residential buildings		..	..	..	..	..	..	..	..	..	..	..
Agricultural land, buildings & forestry		..	..	..	..	..	..	..	..	..	..	..
Commercial buildings		..	..	..	..	..	..	..	..	..	..	..
Industrial buildings		..	..	..	..	..	..	..	..	..	..	..
Other buildings		..	..	..	..	..	..	..	..	..	..	..
Civil engineering works		..	..	..	..	..	..	..	..	..	..	..
Plant and machinery		..	..	..	..	..	..	..	..	..	..	..
Ships, aircraft and railway rolling stock		..	..	..	..	..	..	..	..	..	..	..
Road vehicles		..	..	..	..	..	..	..	..	..	..	..
Stocks and work in progress		..	..	..	..	..	..	..	..	..	..	..
Total tangible assets[2]		..	..	..	..	..	..	..	..	..	..	..
Financial assets:												
Notes and coin	ARNG	0.1	0.1	0.1	0.1	0.1	0.1	0.1	0.1	0.1	0.1	0.1
Sterling Treasury bills	RMEL	–	0.1	0.3	0.3	0.6	1.1	0.4	0.1	0.1	–	0.6
British government securities	RMEN	9.5	9.6	10.2	9.5	6.2	4.8	8.4	12.7	24.8	22.8	28.3
Tax instruments	ARNE	–	–	–	–	–	–	–	–	–	–	–
Northern Ireland central government debt	RCWA	–	–	–	–	–	–	–	–	–	–	–
Other public sector financing: Non-marketable debt	REVE	–	–	–	–	–	–	–	–	–	–	–
Government foreign currency debt	RMAX	1.2	2.5	2.6	0.8	0.8	0.8	0.8	1.1	0.8	0.7	0.4
Local authority debt: Temporary	RRIN	0.8	0.7	0.2	0.2	0.2	0.2	0.3	0.1	0.3	0.3	0.3
Foreign currency	AMWZ	–	–	–	–	–	–	–	–	–	0.1	0.1
Sterling securities	RRIR	–	–	–	–	–	–	–	–	–	–	0.1
Other Sterling debt	RRIT	–	–	–	–	–	–	–	–	–	–	–
Public corporations debt: Foreign currency	REXM	–	–	–	–	–	–	–	–	–	–	–
Sterling	AMVQ	0.2	0.2	0.2	0.2	0.3	0.4	0.4	0.6	0.4	0.5	0.3
Deposits with banks: Sterling other	RRGP	16.1	9.8	18.0	24.3	34.1	36.9	42.0	41.7	47.0	49.0	65.3
Foreign currency other	RMFG	7.4	15.6	20.4	22.7	31.5	33.6	19.9	32.2	35.6	43.6	65.6
Sterling money market instruments	RMFM	0.1	0.7	1.9	2.3	3.9	5.8	4.9	4.2	4.5	6.6	5.5
Foreign currency money market instruments	RMFS	0.1	1.3	1.2	1.6	1.6	1.1	1.5	1.9	1.6	2.6	3.8
Deposits with building societies:												
Sterling other	RMIP	–	–	–	–	–	–	–	1.1	1.9	1.9	1.9
Sterling money market instruments	RMGC	0.2	0.3	0.5	0.7	1.9	3.4	3.6	2.0	0.8	2.5	1.9
Foreign currency money market instruments	RMJX	..	–	–	–	0.1	0.2	0.3	0.4	0.3	0.4	0.5
Identified trade credit: Domestic	RDEZ	0.9	1.1	1.4	2.0	2.3	2.8	2.7	3.1	3.8	4.7	5.3
Import and export	REYN	0.4	0.1	0.2	0.2	0.3	0.5	0.6	0.5	0.6	0.4	0.4
Loans secured on dwellings: Other	AMVX	1.0	3.5	7.5	14.2	17.4	25.4	26.8	25.9	24.9	25.3	24.2
Lending by financial institutions: Finance leasing	REVQ	8.9	10.0	11.3	13.2	16.5	18.4	18.7	17.3	17.0	16.6	17.3
Other	RMDN	1.5	0.9	1.0	1.3	1.5	1.8	1.1	1.2	1.4	2.2	1.1
Unit trust units	RRJL	0.3	0.4	0.5	0.3	0.3	0.5	0.4	0.4	0.6	0.7	0.6
United Kingdom company securities	AMWA	25.7	34.9	40.4	43.6	58.2	53.5	58.3	68.0	101.8	100.6	124.5
Overseas securities	AMWB	22.5	40.0	26.9	36.5	57.7	49.3	65.0	89.9	147.2	110.3	131.1
Direct and other investment abroad	AMWC	3.6	4.3	3.7	4.9	7.4	6.7	9.2	11.2	20.9	19.9	24.9
Miscellaneous instruments	AMWE	36.8	40.7	43.8	48.1	70.7	78.2	91.7	123.8	179.1	167.3	203.8
Accruals adjustments	APSP	0.5	0.6	0.6	0.7	0.9	1.0	1.2	1.3	1.4	1.5	1.5
Total financial assets[2]	AMWF	138.0	177.6	193.0	227.9	314.5	326.4	358.2	440.7	616.9	580.5	709.5
Financial liabilities:												
Other public sector financing: Short-term assets	RMHP	–	–	0.6	1.1	1.6	0.3	0.3	0.1	0.2	0.1	0.1
Issue Department transactions in bills, etc	RCND	2.1	2.2	1.3	2.0	0.9	1.1	1.7	2.2	3.0	1.6	0.9
Bank lending (excl public sector): Foreign currency	RHHR	17.4	24.6	27.0	28.2	39.4	34.1	25.0	28.3	40.6	48.1	73.0
Sterling	AMWI	18.6	24.1	30.4	40.5	54.6	65.6	67.7	68.9	73.4	78.6	89.5
Identified trade credit: Domestic	AQJH	0.3	0.3	0.3	0.3	0.3	0.3	0.3	0.3	0.3	0.3	0.3
Other public sector lending	RECX	0.1	0.1	–	–	–	–	–	–	–	–	–
Lending by financial institutions: Finance leasing	REWS	1.0	1.2	0.4	0.5	0.7	0.8	1.1	1.0	0.9	0.8	0.8
Other	RMAP	–	–	–	–	0.1	0.1	–	–	–	–	–
Unit trust units	RDNQ	19.3	30.5	34.5	39.5	55.2	44.0	52.3	60.6	90.7	87.1	106.8
United Kingdom company securities	REZC	38.7	49.3	56.5	61.9	80.7	87.0	97.3	119.2	176.0	185.0	235.9
Overseas direct and other investment in the UK	AMWO	1.5	2.4	4.8	5.8	9.3	9.3	9.6	9.8	12.0	10.5	13.5
Miscellaneous instruments	AMWP	16.1	17.3	19.4	22.6	51.2	62.0	83.6	129.9	214.6	159.0	203.0
Accruals adjustments	ARNZ	14.7	17.6	19.6	22.4	26.1	29.5	34.2	38.3	40.1	42.8	44.1
Total financial liabilities[2]	AMWQ	129.7	169.8	194.8	224.9	320.0	334.1	373.3	458.7	651.8	614.1	768.0
Net financial wealth[2]	AMWR	8.2	7.7	–1.9	3.0	–5.5	–7.8	–15.1	–17.9	–34.9	–33.6	–58.5
Total net wealth[2]		..	..	..	..	..	..	..	..	..	..	..

1 For scope of updates see Methodological notes.
2 Differences between totals and sums of components are due to rounding.

12.9 Public corporations[1]

£ billion at end year

		1985	1986	1987	1988	1989	1990	1991	1992	1993	1994	1995
Tangible assets:												
Residential buildings	ALMY	3.4	3.9	4.9	6.0	6.1	5.7	5.2	4.7	4.8	4.9	5.1
Agricultural land, buildings & forestry	ALMZ	0.5	0.5	0.5	0.6	0.7	0.6	0.5	0.5	0.6	0.6	0.6
Commercial, industrial and other buildings	ALNA	10.5	9.5	11.0	11.2	14.9	12.8	12.9	13.9	15.5	22.2	26.1
Civil engineering works	ALNB	55.6	43.8	48.5	51.6	16.4	13.1	11.5	13.7	14.9	16.0	15.2
Plant and machinery	ALNC	52.1	50.2	51.0	52.4	54.4	30.8	22.0	22.2	22.4	23.1	24.0
Vehicles, including ships, aircraft etc.	ALND	4.7	4.5	3.4	3.3	3.3	3.4	3.4	4.0	4.0	4.3	4.7
Stocks and work in progress	ALNE	4.6	5.4	5.2	5.4	4.7	4.3	2.3	4.5	2.1	1.8	1.7
Total tangible assets[2]	ALNF	131.4	117.8	124.5	130.5	100.5	70.7	57.8	63.5	64.3	72.9	77.4
Financial assets:												
Notes and coin	APFD	0.6	0.6	0.6	0.6	0.5	0.8	0.7	0.5	0.6	0.7	0.8
Sterling Treasury bills	APFJ	–	–	–	0.1	0.1	–	–	–	0.1	–	0.1
British government securities	APFK	–	0.1	0.2	0.2	0.2	0.2	0.2	0.2	0.2	0.7	0.7
National savings	REXI	0.3	0.1	0.1	0.2	0.1	0.1	0.1	0.2	–	0.1	–
Tax instruments	APFH	0.4	–	0.1	0.1	0.1	–	0.1	0.1	0.1	0.1	0.1
Government liabilities under exchange cover scheme	REXD	–	–	–	–	–	–	–	–	–	–	–
Other public sector financing: Non-marketable debt	REVS	0.6	0.1	0.3	0.8	0.7	0.9	1.1	1.2	2.4	3.1	4.2
Short-term assets	REVG	0.2	0.2	–	–	–	–	–	–	–	0.2	0.1
Local authority debt: Temporary	APFG	0.5	0.4	0.2	0.2	0.2	0.2	0.2	0.2	0.2	0.3	0.2
Sterling securities	APFL	–	–	–	–	–	–	–	–	–	–	–
Other Sterling debt	ADKG	0.7	0.7	0.7	0.7	0.7	0.7	0.7	0.7	0.7	0.7	0.7
Deposits with banks: Sterling other	RRGU	0.7	0.9	1.2	1.9	1.5	1.2	1.1	1.9	1.7	1.8	2.4
Foreign currency other	RRGS	0.2	0.2	0.1	0.1	0.1	0.1	0.1	0.1	0.1	0.2	0.2
Sterling money market instruments	RCBV	–	–	–	–	–	–	–	–	–	–	–
Credit extended by retailers	AQKI	0.3	–	–	–	–	–	–	–	–	–	–
Identified trade credit: Domestic	RDBN	6.9	5.8	6.1	5.8	5.0	4.6	3.3	2.9	3.3	4.2	3.8
Loans secured on dwellings: Other	AKFY	0.1	0.1	0.1	0.1	0.1	–	–	–	–	–	–
Other public sector lending	APFT	0.3	0.4	0.3	0.3	0.3	0.3	0.3	0.2	0.2	0.1	0.1
United Kingdom company securities	REYT	0.2	0.5	0.5	0.4	0.4	0.3	0.3	0.3	0.3	0.2	0.1
Direct and other investment abroad	RYXX	0.2	0.2	0.2	–	–	–	–	–	–	–	–
Miscellaneous instruments	REWC	0.9	1.0	1.0	1.0	1.1	1.1	1.2	1.3	1.3	1.4	1.5
Accruals adjustments	APFY	2.5	2.7	2.9	3.2	3.6	4.0	4.3	4.8	4.6	4.5	4.6
Total financial assets[2]	APFB	15.6	13.9	14.7	15.6	14.7	14.7	13.6	14.6	16.0	18.4	19.8
Financial liabilities:												
Public corporations debt: Foreign currency	REZW	5.1	5.4	3.9	2.7	1.0	0.7	0.6	0.2	0.1	0.3	0.2
Sterling	REVB	25.2	23.3	22.7	26.0	27.9	23.2	23.5	25.6	26.2	26.4	26.9
Identified trade credit: Domestic	RDPD	7.2	6.7	8.3	7.8	6.9	6.3	5.3	5.1	5.5	5.5	4.3
Import and export	HGIO	0.1	0.1	0.1	0.2	0.2	0.2	0.2	0.2	0.2	0.2	0.2
Lending by financial institutions: Finance leasing	ASLL	0.3	0.3	0.3	0.3	0.3	0.3	0.2	0.3	0.3	0.3	0.3
Other	REUW	0.5	0.5	0.5	0.5	0.5	–	–	–	–	–	–
United Kingdom company securities	REYZ	0.2	0.3	0.5	0.5	0.5	0.5	0.5	0.4	0.4	0.4	0.4
Miscellaneous instruments	ALGE	0.8	0.5	0.3	0.2	0.1	0.1	0.1	–	–	–	–
Accruals adjustments	APQQ	1.0	0.9	1.0	1.1	0.6	0.7	0.7	0.6	0.6	0.7	0.8
Total financial liabilities[2]	APQB	40.4	37.8	37.5	39.2	37.9	32.0	31.1	32.4	33.3	33.9	33.1
Net financial wealth[2]	APFA	−24.8	−23.9	−22.9	−23.6	−23.3	−17.2	−17.4	−17.8	−17.2	−15.5	−13.3
Total net wealth[2]	ALNG	106.6	93.9	101.6	106.9	77.2	53.5	40.4	45.7	47.1	57.4	64.1

1 For scope of updates see Methodological notes.
2 Differences between totals and sums of components are due to rounding.

Balance sheets

12.10 Central government[1]

£ billion at end year

		1985	1986	1987	1988	1989	1990	1991	1992	1993	1994	1995
Tangible assets:												
Residential buildings	ALNH	1.7	2.1	2.5	3.0	3.1	2.8	2.5	2.3	2.4	2.5	2.5
Agricultural land, buildings & forestry	ALNI	2.1	2.2	1.1	1.2	1.2	1.0	0.9	0.8	0.9	1.0	1.0
Commercial, industrial and other buildings	ALNJ	20.6	22.5	23.7	28.0	25.6	23.5	21.6	19.9	20.4	21.6	21.5
Civil engineering works	ALNK	29.8	30.8	33.5	38.7	42.3	43.6	42.0	39.8	40.6	46.2	53.8
Plant and machinery	ALNL	6.3	7.0	7.7	8.3	9.4	10.6	11.4	12.4	13.6	14.2	14.7
Vehicles, including ships, aircraft etc.	ALNM	0.3	0.3	0.2	0.3	0.4	0.4	0.5	0.6	0.8	0.9	0.7
Stocks and work in progress	ALNN	1.5	1.3	0.8	0.4	0.3	0.4	0.6	0.6	0.6	0.3	0.1
Total tangible assets[2]	ALNO	62.3	66.2	69.5	79.9	82.3	82.3	79.5	76.4	79.3	86.7	94.3
Financial assets:												
Other public sector financing: short term assets	CSWK	..	–	–	–	–	–	–	–	0.1	0.1	–
Issue Department transactions in bills, etc	REVJ	11.2	11.7	6.0	6.4	2.8	3.5	5.3	9.7	11.3	5.1	3.0
Official reserves	APDD	13.2	17.4	27.0	28.7	26.3	22.5	26.0	28.3	29.7	30.7	31.8
Local authority debt: Temporary	APDH	0.6	0.5	0.4	0.4	0.5	0.5	0.4	0.3	0.2	0.3	0.6
Sterling securities	APDZ	–	–	–	–	–	–	–	–	–	–	–
Other Sterling debt	APDP	27.2	33.0	38.5	43.3	45.9	48.0	47.9	42.0	40.5	39.7	41.4
Public corporations debt: Sterling	REZY	23.4	22.0	21.4	24.6	26.6	22.3	22.1	23.4	24.5	25.1	25.8
Deposits with banks: Sterling other	RRGL	0.8	1.1	0.9	1.5	1.8	2.1	1.7	1.9	1.7	2.1	5.9
Foreign currency other	RRGQ	0.1	0.1	0.1	–	–	0.1	0.1	0.2	0.2	0.1	0.3
Identified trade credit: Domestic	APDV	–	0.2	0.5	0.6	0.8	1.0	1.2	1.3	1.3	1.3	1.3
Import and export	XBJN	0.2	–	–	–	–	–	–	–	–	–	–
Loans secured on dwellings: Other	AKHJ	1.7	1.8	1.8	2.0	2.1	2.0	1.6	1.5	1.4	1.4	1.3
Other public sector lending	REVO	5.0	6.7	7.0	7.4	8.7	9.2	10.0	10.6	11.1	11.8	12.8
United Kingdom company securities	REYP	17.1	15.8	13.4	12.2	13.5	14.0	16.4	15.2	12.7	6.7	2.3
Overseas securities	APDN	–	–	–	–	–	–	–	–	–	–	–
Miscellaneous instruments	RDCB	0.1	0.1	0.1	0.1	0.1	0.1	0.1	0.1	0.1	0.1	0.1
Accruals adjustments	APDW	17.9	16.7	17.6	17.7	19.7	18.9	20.9	20.4	22.2	25.7	27.9
Total financial assets[2]	APDB	118.3	126.9	134.7	144.9	148.8	144.1	153.7	155.0	157.0	150.2	154.5
Financial liabilities:												
Notes and coin	APOE	14.5	15.1	16.2	17.7	18.9	19.0	19.2	20.6	22.0	23.3	24.9
Sterling Treasury bills	ACQC	1.4	1.7	3.9	5.2	8.1	10.2	8.6	4.2	2.9	5.1	17.0
British government securities	RYXY	117.1	125.4	132.9	126.2	108.0	99.8	112.6	147.0	221.3	212.5	251.6
National savings	REYD	31.0	33.1	35.6	37.2	35.6	36.4	38.6	43.7	46.6	51.2	54.5
Tax instruments	ACRV	3.9	4.0	3.4	2.4	2.6	2.9	2.9	2.4	2.3	1.8	1.4
Net government indebtedness to Banking Dept	RRGO	0.6	0.7	1.0	1.1	1.4	1.8	1.7	1.5	−5.0	−0.8	−1.6
Northern Ireland central government debt	REYI	0.3	0.3	0.2	0.2	0.2	0.2	0.2	0.1	0.1	0.1	0.1
Government liabilities under exchange cover scheme	REXB	–	–	–	–	–	–	–	–	–	–	–
Other public sector financing: Non-marketable debt	REVF	0.7	0.1	0.3	0.8	0.7	0.9	1.1	1.2	2.4	3.1	4.2
Government foreign currency debt	REUQ	2.7	5.1	3.7	2.9	5.1	4.8	6.6	19.7	17.8	16.4	17.2
Other government overseas financing	REUU	3.2	3.2	2.7	2.7	2.9	2.4	2.4	2.8	2.8	2.6	2.6
Identified trade credit: Domestic	APOR	0.9	0.9	0.4	0.6	1.0	1.4	1.8	2.0	2.0	2.0	2.0
Other public sector lending	AIRH	0.7	0.5	0.7	0.7	0.9	0.7	0.7	0.7	0.9	0.7	0.8
Lending by financial institutions: Finance leasing	ASLD	–	–	–	0.1	0.1	0.1	0.1	0.1	0.1	0.1	0.1
Life assurance and pension funds	REUP	7.6	8.3	8.9	9.8	10.2	10.2	10.2	9.9	9.4	9.1	8.3
Miscellaneous instruments	REWI	1.7	1.8	1.9	2.1	2.0	2.3	1.5	1.6	2.3	3.8	4.1
Accruals adjustments	APOT	3.1	3.3	3.9	4.2	5.7	7.3	8.6	9.2	10.3	11.5	13.3
Total financial liabilities[2]	APOB	189.3	203.4	216.0	213.7	203.2	200.3	216.8	266.8	338.2	342.7	400.4
Net financial wealth[2]	APDA	−71.0	−76.5	−81.3	−68.8	−54.4	−56.2	−63.1	−111.8	−181.2	−192.5	−245.9
Total net wealth[2]	ALNP	−8.7	−10.3	−11.8	11.1	27.9	26.1	16.4	−35.4	−101.9	−105.8	−151.6

1 For scope of updates see Methodological notes.
2 Differences between totals and sums of components are due to rounding.

12.11 Local authorities[1]

£ billion at end year

		1985	1986	1987	1988	1989	1990	1991	1992	1993	1994	1995
Tangible assets:												
Residential buildings	ALNQ	55.5	66.2	76.5	89.3	90.9	84.4	80.1	76.1	75.2	67.1	68.8
Agricultural land, buildings & forestry	ALNR	1.3	1.1	1.1	1.3	1.6	1.4	1.3	1.1	1.3	1.4	1.4
Commercial, industrial and other buildings	ALNS	46.7	49.7	55.1	62.8	68.4	67.6	65.2	59.9	59.7	59.9	58.8
Civil engineering works	ALNT	55.6	62.3	72.4	90.1	93.8	90.2	88.7	78.1	83.5	90.2	99.4
Plant and machinery	ALNU	4.4	4.8	5.1	5.4	5.9	6.3	6.2	6.2	6.2	6.4	6.5
Vehicles, including ships, aircraft etc.	ALNV	1.0	0.9	0.8	0.9	0.9	0.9	0.9	0.9	0.9	0.8	0.8
Stocks and work in progress	ALNW	–	–	–	–	–	–	–	–	–	–	–
Total tangible assets[2]	ALNX	164.5	185.0	211.0	249.8	261.5	250.8	242.4	222.3	226.8	225.8	235.7
Financial assets:												
Sterling Treasury bills	ADNG	–	–	–	–	–	–	–	–	–	–	–
British government securities	APEI	0.1	0.1	0.1	0.1	0.1	0.1	0.1	0.1	0.1	0.1	0.2
National savings	APSL	–	–	–	–	–	–	–	–	–	–	–
Government liabilities under exchange cover scheme	REXC	–	–	–	–	–	–	–	–	–	–	–
Other public sector financing: Short-term assets	REUJ	0.2	0.1	1.8	3.1	4.2	2.2	3.2	3.8	4.3	4.6	4.3
Public corporations debt: Sterling	ADND	0.1	0.1	0.1	0.2	0.1	–	–	–	–	–	–
Deposits with banks: Sterling other	RRGN	1.7	3.0	4.8	6.6	6.7	5.4	3.4	3.6	5.3	4.6	6.2
Foreign currency other	RRGR	–	–	–	–	0.1	–	–	–	–	–	0.1
Sterling money market instruments	RCBE	–	0.1	0.2	0.1	0.1	0.1	0.1	0.1	0.1	0.1	0.1
Identified trade credit: Domestic	APEQ	3.2	3.4	3.6	3.6	3.6	3.6	3.6	3.6	3.6	3.6	3.6
Loans secured on dwellings: Other	APEN	3.6	3.1	2.7	2.4	2.1	1.8	1.4	1.0	0.7	0.4	0.2
Other public sector lending	REUI	0.1	0.2	0.1	0.1	0.1	0.1	0.1	0.1	0.1	0.1	0.1
United Kingdom company securities	REYS	0.3	0.3	0.5	0.6	0.7	0.8	0.7	0.7	0.8	0.8	0.8
Miscellaneous instruments	APQT	0.8	0.5	0.3	0.2	0.1	0.1	0.1	–	–	–	–
Accruals adjustments	APER	0.3	0.3	0.4	0.4	0.6	1.9	2.2	1.4	0.5	–	–1.3
Total financial assets[2]	APEB	10.5	11.4	14.7	17.4	18.4	16.1	14.9	14.5	15.7	14.5	14.2
Financial liabilities:												
Other public sector financing: Non-marketable debt	AROH	–	–	–	–	–	–	–	–	–	–	–
Local authority debt: Temporary	RMAC	4.2	3.0	2.8	2.5	2.1	3.1	2.7	2.2	2.0	2.0	2.1
Foreign currency	REZU	0.6	0.7	0.8	0.7	0.8	0.7	0.7	0.6	0.5	0.5	0.5
Sterling securities	RDUA	0.8	0.6	0.4	0.4	0.3	0.1	0.1	0.2	0.2	0.5	0.5
Other Sterling debt	REZR	35.0	39.8	43.7	47.6	49.3	51.1	50.8	46.3	46.6	46.4	48.2
Identified trade credit: Domestic	APPK	4.6	4.9	5.5	5.9	5.9	5.9	5.9	5.9	5.9	5.9	5.9
Lending by financial institutions: Finance leasing	ASLE	0.5	0.8	1.1	1.3	1.5	1.5	1.4	1.3	1.3	1.5	1.5
Miscellaneous instruments	AQKJ	0.3	0.3	0.3	0.3	0.3	0.3	0.3	0.3	0.3	0.3	0.3
Accruals adjustments	APPL	2.9	3.3	3.7	4.0	4.1	2.4	2.6	2.7	2.6	3.0	3.1
Total financial liabilities[2]	APPB	48.9	53.4	58.3	62.8	64.5	65.3	64.6	59.4	59.5	60.0	62.1
Net financial wealth[2]	APEA	–38.4	–42.0	–43.6	–45.4	–46.1	–49.2	–49.6	–44.9	–43.8	–45.5	–47.9
Total net wealth[2]	ALNY	126.1	143.0	167.4	204.4	215.4	201.6	192.8	177.4	183.0	180.3	187.8

1 For scope of updates see Methodological notes.
2 Differences between totals and sums of components are due to rounding.

Balance sheets

12.12 Public sector[1]

£ billion at end year

		1985	1986	1987	1988	1989	1990	1991	1992	1993	1994	1995
Tangible assets												
Residential buildings	CXBF	60.6	72.2	83.9	98.3	100.1	92.9	87.8	83.1	82.4	74.5	76.3
Agricultural land, buildings & forestry	CXBG	3.9	3.8	2.7	3.1	3.5	3.0	2.7	2.4	2.8	3.0	3.0
Commercial, industrial and other buildings	CXBH	77.8	81.7	89.8	102.0	108.9	103.9	99.7	93.7	95.6	103.6	106.4
Civil engineering works	CXBI	141.0	136.9	154.4	180.4	152.5	146.9	142.2	131.6	139.0	152.4	168.4
Plant and machinery	CXBJ	62.8	62.0	63.8	66.1	69.7	47.7	39.6	40.8	42.2	43.7	45.2
Vehicles, including ships, aircraft, etc	CXBK	6.0	5.7	4.4	4.5	4.6	4.7	4.8	5.6	5.6	6.0	6.2
Stocks and work in progress	CXBM	6.1	6.7	6.0	5.8	5.0	4.8	2.9	5.1	2.7	2.1	1.8
Total tangible assets[2]	CXBN	358.2	369.0	405.0	460.2	444.3	403.9	379.7	362.3	370.3	385.3	407.3
Financial assets:												
Notes and coin	RETC	0.6	0.6	0.6	0.6	0.5	0.8	0.7	0.5	0.6	0.7	0.8
Sterling Treasury bills	RETD	–	–	–	0.1	0.1	–	–	–	0.2	–	0.1
British government securities	RETE	0.1	0.3	0.3	0.3	0.3	0.3	0.3	0.2	0.3	0.9	0.9
National savings	RECC	0.3	0.1	0.1	0.2	0.1	0.1	0.1	0.2	–	0.1	–
Tax instruments	APFH	0.4	–	0.1	0.1	0.1	–	0.1	0.1	0.1	0.1	0.1
Government liabilities under exchange cover scheme	RECD	–	–	–	–	–	–	–	–	–	–	–
Other public sector financing: Non-marketable debt	REVS	0.6	0.1	0.3	0.8	0.7	0.9	1.1	1.2	2.4	3.1	4.2
Short-term assets	RETF	0.5	0.3	1.8	3.1	4.2	2.2	3.2	3.8	4.4	5.0	4.4
Issue Department transactions in bills, etc	RETG	11.2	11.7	6.0	6.4	2.8	3.5	5.3	9.7	11.3	5.1	3.0
Official reserves	APDD	13.2	17.4	27.0	28.7	26.3	22.5	26.0	28.3	29.7	30.7	31.8
Local authority debt: Temporary	RETH	1.1	0.9	0.6	0.6	0.6	0.7	0.7	0.5	0.5	0.6	0.8
Sterling securities	RETI	–	–	–	–	–	–	–	–	–	–	–
Other Sterling debt	RETJ	27.9	33.7	39.2	44.0	46.6	48.7	48.6	42.7	41.2	40.4	42.1
Public corporations debt: Sterling	RETK	23.5	22.0	21.5	24.8	26.6	22.3	22.2	23.5	24.5	25.1	25.8
Deposits with banks: Sterling other	RMGI	3.2	4.9	6.9	10.0	10.1	8.8	6.2	7.3	8.7	8.5	14.5
Foreign currency other	RMGJ	0.3	0.3	0.3	0.2	0.2	0.2	0.2	0.4	0.3	0.3	0.6
Sterling money market instruments	RMGK	0.1	0.1	0.2	0.1	0.1	0.1	0.2	0.2	0.2	0.2	0.2
Credit extended by retailers	AQKI	0.3	–	–	–	–	–	–	–	–	–	–
Identified trade credit: Domestic	RETP	10.1	9.4	10.2	10.0	9.4	9.2	8.1	7.8	8.2	9.1	8.7
Import and export	REAH	0.2	–	–	–	–	–	–	–	–	–	–
Loans secured on dwellings: Other	RETQ	5.4	5.0	4.6	4.4	4.3	3.8	3.0	2.5	2.1	1.7	1.5
Other public sector lending	RETR	5.4	7.3	7.4	7.8	9.1	9.6	10.3	10.9	11.4	12.1	13.0
United Kingdom company securities	RETS	17.5	16.6	14.4	13.1	14.6	15.0	17.4	16.2	13.8	7.8	3.3
Overseas securities	APDN	–	–	–	–	–	–	–	–	–	–	–
Direct and other investment abroad	RYXX	0.2	0.2	0.2	–	–	–	–	–	–	–	–
Miscellaneous instruments	RETT	1.8	1.5	1.3	1.3	1.2	1.3	1.3	1.4	1.4	1.5	1.6
Accruals adjustments	RETU	20.6	19.8	20.9	21.3	23.9	24.9	27.4	26.6	27.4	30.1	31.3
Total financial assets[2]	RETV	144.4	152.2	164.0	177.9	181.9	174.9	182.2	184.1	188.7	183.0	188.6
Financial liabilities:												
Notes and coin	APOE	14.5	15.1	16.2	17.7	18.9	19.0	19.2	20.6	22.0	23.3	24.9
Sterling Treasury bills	ACQC	1.4	1.7	3.9	5.2	8.1	10.2	8.6	4.2	2.9	5.1	17.0
British government securities	RYXY	117.1	125.4	132.9	126.2	108.0	99.8	112.6	147.0	221.3	212.5	251.6
National savings	REYD	31.0	33.1	35.6	37.2	35.6	36.4	38.6	43.7	46.6	51.2	54.5
Tax instruments	ACRV	3.9	4.0	3.4	2.4	2.6	2.9	2.9	2.4	2.3	1.8	1.4
Net government indebtedness to Banking Dept	RRGO	0.6	0.7	1.0	1.1	1.4	1.8	1.7	1.5	-5.0	-0.8	-1.6
Northern Ireland central government debt	RETW	0.3	0.3	0.2	0.2	0.2	0.2	0.2	0.1	0.1	0.1	0.1
Government liabilities under exchange cover scheme	REXB	–	–	–	–	–	–	–	–	–	–	–
Other public sector financing: Non-marketable debt	RETX	0.7	0.1	0.3	0.8	0.7	0.9	1.1	1.2	2.4	3.1	4.2
Government foreign currency debt	REUQ	2.7	5.1	3.7	2.9	5.1	4.8	6.6	19.7	17.8	16.4	17.2
Other government overseas financing	REUU	3.2	3.2	2.7	2.7	2.9	2.4	2.4	2.8	2.8	2.6	2.6
Local authority debt: Temporary	RMAC	4.2	3.0	2.8	2.5	2.1	3.1	2.7	2.2	2.0	2.0	2.1
Foreign currency	REZU	0.6	0.7	0.8	0.7	0.8	0.7	0.7	0.6	0.5	0.5	0.5
Sterling securities	RDUA	0.8	0.6	0.4	0.4	0.3	0.1	0.1	0.2	0.2	0.5	0.5
Other Sterling debt	REZR	35.0	39.8	43.7	47.6	49.3	51.1	50.8	46.3	46.6	46.4	48.2
Public corporations debt: Foreign currency	REZW	5.1	5.4	3.9	2.7	1.0	0.7	0.6	0.2	0.1	0.3	0.2
Sterling	RETY	25.2	23.3	22.7	26.0	27.9	23.2	23.5	25.6	26.2	26.4	26.9
Bank lending (excl public sector): Foreign currency	RKWH	–	–	–	–	–	–	–	–	–	..	..
Sterling	RETZ	1.1	0.7	0.7	0.8	0.5	0.4	0.4	0.4	0.4	..	..
Identified trade credit: Domestic	REUA	12.8	12.4	14.2	14.3	13.8	13.6	13.0	13.1	13.4	13.4	12.3
Import and export	REXH	0.1	0.1	0.1	0.2	0.2	0.2	0.2	0.2	0.2	0.2	0.2
Other public sector lending	REUB	0.7	0.5	0.7	0.7	0.9	0.7	0.7	0.7	0.9	0.7	0.8
Lending by financial institutions: Finance leasing	ASLN	0.9	1.1	1.4	1.7	1.8	1.9	1.7	1.6	1.6	1.9	1.9
Other	REUW	0.5	0.5	0.5	0.5	0.5	–	–	–	–	–	–
United Kingdom company securities	REYZ	0.2	0.3	0.5	0.5	0.5	0.5	0.5	0.4	0.4	0.4	0.4
Life assurance and pension funds	REUP	7.6	8.3	8.9	9.8	10.2	10.2	10.2	9.9	9.4	9.1	8.3
Miscellaneous instruments	REUC	2.8	2.5	2.4	2.6	2.4	2.7	1.8	2.0	2.6	4.1	4.4
Accruals adjustments	REUD	7.0	7.5	8.6	9.2	10.4	10.4	11.9	12.5	13.6	15.3	17.2
Total financial liabilities[2]	REUE	278.6	294.5	311.8	315.6	305.6	297.5	312.4	358.6	431.0	436.6	495.6
Net financial wealth[2]	REUF	-134.2	-142.3	-147.8	-137.7	-123.7	-122.6	-130.2	-174.5	-242.3	-253.6	-307.0
Total net wealth[2]	REUG	224.0	226.7	257.2	322.5	320.6	281.3	249.5	187.8	128.0	131.7	100.3

1 For scope of updates see Methodological notes.
2 Differences between totals and sums of components are due to rounding.

12.13 United Kingdom Company Securities: further detail
Levels

£ billion

		1990	1991	1992	1993	1994	1995
Quoted Ordinary Shares							
Liabilities							
Banks	RSAI	12.9	17.3	21.3	31.0	28.7	31.0
Other Financial Institutions	RSAV	55.6	62.4	77.4	122.5	109.1	147.9
Industrial and Commercial Companies	RSBB	381.2	456.9	522.2	650.0	620.5	720.4
Total liabilities	RJZG	449.6	536.6	620.9	803.6	758.3	899.3
Assets							
Central Government	RRZT	8.9	10.5	10.7	9.4	5.3	0.9
Local Authorities	RRZW	0.3	0.3	0.3	0.4	0.4	0.4
Public Corporations	RRZZ	–	–	–	–	–	–
Banks	RSAF	1.6	1.8	2.1	2.5	3.4	4.6
Life Assurance and Pension Funds	RSAP	221.7	273.1	322.0	414.2	375.9	442.2
Remaining Financial Institutions	RSAS	43.4	47.4	53.2	77.0	72.6	94.7
Industrial and Commercial Companies	RSAY	14.9	15.2	12.3	7.9	11.7	11.4
Personal sector	RSBE	103.5	121.5	132.0	163.7	168.9	199.6
Overseas sector	RSBH	55.3	66.7	88.3	128.5	120.0	145.5
Total assets	RJZK	449.6	536.6	620.9	803.6	758.3	899.3
Unquoted Ordinary Shares							
Liabilities							
Public Corporations	RSAD	0.5	0.5	0.4	0.4	0.4	0.4
Banks	RSAJ	6.7	8.0	8.1	8.4	8.5	8.7
Other Financial Institutions	RSAW	7.0	8.7	10.5	12.7	30.6	39.6
Industrial and Commercial Companies	RSBC	84.8	104.1	120.8	153.1	147.8	172.7
Total liabilities	RJZM	99.0	121.2	139.9	174.5	187.4	221.4
Assets							
Central Government	RRZU	0.1	0.1	0.1	0.1	0.1	0.1
Local Authorities	RRZX	0.5	0.5	0.4	0.4	0.4	0.4
Public Corporations	RSAA	0.3	0.2	0.2	0.3	0.2	0.1
Banks	RSAG	7.6	8.2	9.2	10.8	15.1	19.9
Building Societies	RSAM	0.8	1.2	1.9	2.9	1.9	1.6
Life Assurance and Pension Funds	RSAQ	1.5	2.4	2.4	3.4	2.7	2.7
Remaining Financial Institutions	RSAT	6.0	6.9	8.7	13.5	17.9	21.9
Industrial and Commercial Companies	RSAZ	16.8	20.6	24.2	30.6	29.6	34.5
Personal sector	RSBF	61.6	77.2	88.3	107.4	113.4	132.1
Overseas sector	RJYS	3.8	3.8	4.5	5.2	6.1	8.0
Total assets	RKWP	99.0	121.2	139.9	174.5	187.4	221.4
Bonds and Preference Shares							
Liabilities							
Banks	RSAK	10.4	7.6	10.2	16.3	19.5	20.7
Building Societies	RSAO	7.3	7.5	10.4	11.4	9.2	9.6
Other Financial Institutions	RSAX	24.4	26.2	31.2	40.8	45.3	48.4
Industrial and Commercial Companies	RSBD	29.2	42.6	48.0	58.6	56.7	66.7
Personal sector	RJYX	0.2	0.3	0.5	1.2	1.2	1.7
Total liabilities	RKWQ	71.5	84.2	100.4	128.1	131.9	147.0
Assets							
Central Government	RRZV	5.0	5.8	4.4	3.2	1.4	1.4
Public Corporations	RSAB	–	–	–	–	–	–
Banks	RSAH	13.9	16.6	16.2	19.9	21.0	23.0
Building Societies	RJYV	–	–	1.3	1.6	1.9	1.7
Life Assurance and Pension Funds	RSAR	14.3	20.6	24.9	35.1	26.8	30.6
Remaining Financial Institutions	RSAU	4.1	3.9	6.1	11.4	10.1	7.9
Industrial and Commercial Companies	RSBA	2.5	2.7	2.7	3.5	3.4	4.3
Personal sector	RSBG	3.4	2.1	2.3	2.5	2.7	2.9
Overseas sector	RSBJ	28.3	32.5	42.3	50.8	64.6	75.2
Total assets	RYCM	71.5	84.2	100.4	128.1	131.9	147.0

1 Differences between totals and sums of totals are due to rounding

Capital formation
and capital stocks

4

Capital formation and capital stocks

Capital formation and capital stock at a glance

Chart *4.1*

Gross domestic fixed capital formation
(at constant 1990 prices)

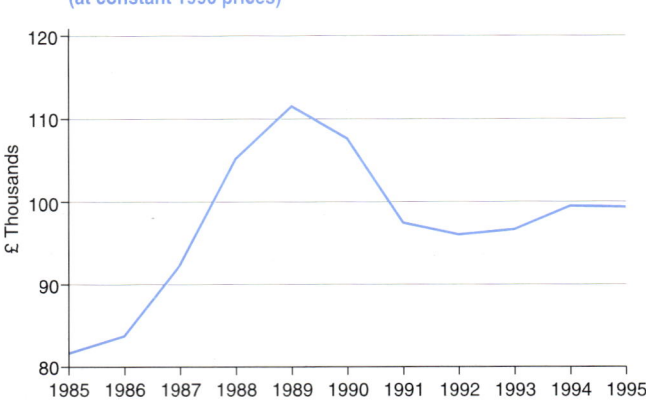

In real terms gross domestic fixed capital formation in 1995 was little changed from the level in 1994. This follows growth in fixed investment in both 1993 and 1994 although investment remains much subdued from its record 1989 level when it stood over 12 per cent higher than in 1995. Investment in plant and machinery grew in 1995 when compared with 1994 whilst investment fell in all the other main categories.

Chart *4.2*

Gross domestic fixed capital Formation
(at constant 1990 market prices)

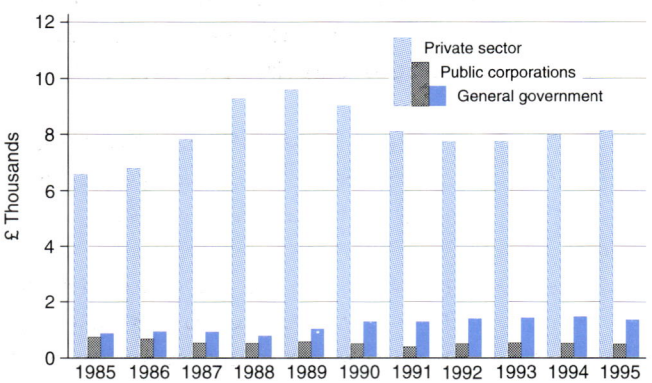

Over the last decade the proportion of private sector gross fixed capital formation has also changed very little, remaining at around 80-85 per cent of the total. Private sector investment in 1995 at around 82 per cent edged closer to its share of total investment in the early 1990s after remaining at around 80 per cent during the years 1992-94.

Chart *4.3*

Capital formation by asset 1995

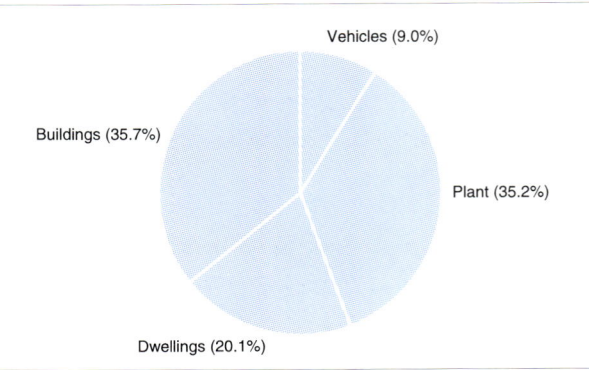

Construction industry products (dwellings and new buildings and works) are an important element of fixed investment accounting for some 56 per cent of the total in 1995. Plant and machinery makes up another 35 per cent of the assets purchased with the remainder being vehicles. The contribution each asset type makes to the total has been relatively stable during the 1990s with each asset type varying by not more than 2 per cent.

Chart *4.4*

Value of the physical increase
(in stocks and work in progress)

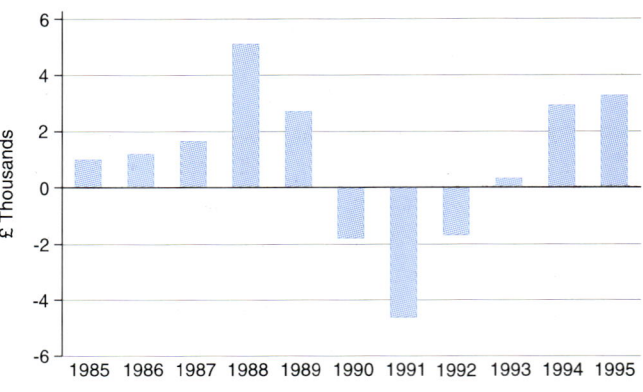

Stockbuilding continued, in real terms, during 1995, after three years of destocking in the early 1990s. Whilst the level of stockbuilding was not inconsiderable, at over £3 billion , it was much lower than the level seen in 1988 of over £5 billion.

United Kingdom National Accounts 1996 © Crown copyright 1996

SECTION 4: CAPITAL FORMATION AND CAPITAL STOCK

144. This section encompasses Chapters 13 through to 15 covering gross domestic fixed capital formation, capital stock and stockbuilding respectively.

145. All of these items involve the United Kingdom's capital account and so contribute to the nation's wealth. Capital formation is investment in tangible assets and consists of gross domestic fixed capital formation and the acquisition of stocks and work in progress. Capital stock however represents the total assets currently in use in the economy and is measured both before and after depreciation. Each of these areas is described in more detail below:

Capital formation

146. **Capital formation** - gross domestic fixed capital formation and the acquisition of stocks and work in progress - is used within the expenditure approach to GDP. It appears on the resources side of the domestic production of goods and services accounts making it a component of final demand (See Section 1 paragraphs 29, 33 and 60).

Gross Domestic Fixed Capital Formation

147. **Gross domestic fixed capital formation** (GDFCF) is defined as expenditure on fixed assets (buildings, vehicles, plant and machinery and dwellings) which either replace existing assets that are no longer productive or increase the availability of productive assets. The expenditure is said to be gross as it takes no account of capital consumption (depreciation) and domestic because the assets must reside within the domestic economy. Assets held by consumers, such as vehicles and consumer durables, are not included in capital formation as they are considered to be consumed when purchased and therefore form part of current expenditure.

148. The amount by which expenditure on GDFCF exceeds the wearing away or depreciation of existing assets represents the addition to the nation's wealth. This concept is known as **net domestic capital formation**. However fixed capital formation is shown gross because of the difficulty in measuring capital consumption (depreciation) and the fact that GDFCF is important in itself (since the replacement of assets can, to an extent, be postponed).

149. The tables in chapter 13 show GDFCF analysed in 3 ways: by industry, by type of asset and by institutional sector. Some tables are cross classified (for example table 13.1 gives an analysis by broad sector and type of asset) and most of the information is shown in current and constant market prices.

150. Information on capital consumption (discussed further below) and net domestic fixed capital formation are shown in chapter 14.

Stocks and Work in Progress

151. **Stocks and work in progress** are goods that are held by trading enterprises and are destined either to be used within the production process or to be sold. They include: materials and fuel in excess of the amount used; work in progress and unsold finished goods. Stockbuilding is the value of the physical increase or decrease in these stocks that contributes to capital formation however, unlike other types of expenditure on goods, the value of the physical increase is not an economic transaction and cannot be measured directly.

152. Tables 15.2 and 15.3 show an analysis of the value the physical increase of stocks and work in progress by industry at current and constant market prices.

153. **Stock appreciation**, associated with stocks and work in progress, is used within the income approach to GDP (See Figure 1.4). It is defined as the part of the change in the value of stocks and work in progress during the year which arises from increases or decreases in the price at which the stocks are valued. It is similar to a holding gain or loss which stems simply from ownership of the asset rather than any productive process. It is included in the income approach to GDP because companies include these holding gains in their profits. As GDP is a measure of economic activity a stock appreciation adjustment is required to remove these holding gains.

Capital Stock

154. **Capital stock** estimates were first made to enable the compilation of **capital consumption**. This is necessary as capital consumption cannot be measured directly and estimates of capital consumption are required to move gross domestic product to a net basis.

155. Capital stock estimates are an essential element in assessments of efficiency with which capital is used. Their principal use is in the derivation of rate of return on investment in fixed capital..

156. **Gross capital stock** shows the value of assets in place at their full replacement cost ie the cost to replace them now. **Net capital stock** is the gross capital stock less accrued capital consumption. Gross capital stock is the measure usually used to measure the production potential of the current stock of fixed capital.

157. By convention capital consumption and capital stock estimates are derived using the perpetual inventory approach. This makes use of estimates of investment in fixed assets and the convention employed by accountants for estimating depreciation: that is that the use of an asset may be recorded as being in some way spread over a predefined life. Capital consumption is calculated using a straight line depreciation assumption.

158. Estimates of net capital stock by sector and type of asset are shown in table 14.7. Gross capital stock (at 1990 replacement cost) is analysed by industry in table 14.8 and by type of asset in table 14.9.

CHAPTER 13: Gross domestic fixed capital formation at market prices

13.1 Analysis by broad sector and type of asset at current market prices

£ million

		1985	1986	1987	1988	1989	1990	1991	1992	1993	1994	1995
Private sector:												
Vehicles, ships and aircraft	DFMT	5 522	5 445	7 044	8 059	9 298	9 223	7 785	7 675	8 880	10 219	9 901
Plant and machinery	DFMU	19 766	20 632	23 131	27 406	31 641	31 568	31 329	30 140	30 573	33 459	36 859
Dwellings[1]	DFDF	9 683	11 526	13 439	18 013	19 142	17 212	15 681	16 108	17 120	18 147	19 064
Other new buildings and works	DFHU	7 793	8 601	12 053	15 828	20 334	23 263	20 110	17 456	14 447	13 700	15 914
Purchases *less* sales of land and existing buildings[2]	DFHV	5 151	5 798	7 353	11 138	9 979	8 697	6 920	5 030	6 575	6 487	6 140
Total	DFDG	47 915	52 002	63 020	80 444	90 394	89 963	81 825	76 409	77 595	82 012	87 878
Public corporations:												
Vehicles, ships and aircraft	DEEP	657	487	458	466	585	616	535	630	735	644	529
Plant and machinery	DEEQ	2 672	2 443	2 278	2 381	2 575	2 734	1 272	1 602	1 909	2 098	2 497
Dwellings[1]	DEER	280	242	253	246	256	247	211	219	236	245	243
Other new buildings and works	DEES	2 703	2 757	2 473	2 764	3 222	2 203	2 425	2 745	2 584	2 463	2 335
Purchases *less* sales of land and existing buildings[2]	DEET	−381	−408	−901	−1 277	−1 171	−845	−664	−469	−569	−535	−550
Total	AAAK	5 931	5 521	4 561	4 580	5 467	4 955	3 779	4 727	4 895	4 915	5 054
General government:												
Vehicles, ships and aircraft	DFFX	260	290	303	324	441	427	327	405	385	457	397
Plant and machinery	DFFY	1 432	1 615	1 664	1 717	2 166	2 460	2 076	2 112	2 083	1 779	1 728
Dwellings[1]	DFHW	2 256	2 372	2 663	2 668	3 590	3 980	2 609	2 407	2 618	2 732	2 530
Other new buildings and works	DFHX	4 722	5 156	5 348	6 202	7 812	9 389	9 224	9 197	9 248	9 467	9 906
Purchases *less* sales of land and existing buildings[2]	DFHY	−1 798	−1 924	−2 401	−4 405	−4 427	−3 597	−2 093	−1 615	−2 531	−2 145	−2 108
Total	AAYE	6 872	7 509	7 577	6 506	9 582	12 659	12 143	12 506	11 803	12 290	12 453
Total	DFDC	60 718	65 032	75 158	91 530	105 443	107 577	97 747	93 642	94 293	99 217	105 385

1 Excluding existing buildings and land.
2 The value of land and existing buildings which pass from one sector to another nets out over all sectors. The total figures refer to costs of transferring the ownership of such assets.

Where such data can be compiled, quarterly data for series in this table are available on the ONS's Databank. This data can also be provided on paper by request. Some of these quarterly data are published regularly in the UK Economic Accounts in table A8.

13.2 Analysis by type of asset at current market prices

£ million

		1985	1986	1987	1988	1989	1990	1991	1992	1993	1994	1995
Buses and coaches	DFKA	122	125	166	199	179	164	139	116	149	157	148
Other road vehicles	DFKB	4 970	5 329	6 754	7 677	8 603	8 013	6 532	6 807	7 559	8 446	9 179
Railway rolling stock	DFKC	106	95	126	187	242	377	363	504	591	521	419
Ships	GGBU	332	162	239	116	122	234	500	119	363	461	659
Aircraft	GGBV	909	511	520	670	1 178	1 478	1 113	1 164	1 338	1 735	422
Plant and machinery[1]	DFCX	23 870	24 690	27 073	31 504	36 382	36 762	34 677	33 854	34 565	37 336	41 084
Dwellings	DFDK	12 219	14 140	16 355	20 927	22 988	21 439	18 501	18 734	19 974	21 124	21 837
Other new buildings and works	DFJL	15 218	16 514	19 874	24 794	31 368	34 855	31 759	29 398	26 279	25 630	28 155
Transfer costs of land and buildings[2]	DFBH	2 972	3 466	4 051	5 456	4 381	4 255	4 163	2 946	3 475	3 807	3 482
Total	DFDC	60 718	65 032	75 158	91 530	105 443	107 577	97 747	93 642	94 293	99 217	105 385

1 Including changes in the stock of breeding animals.
2 The value of land and existing buildings which pass from one sector to another nets out over all sectors. The total figures refer to the costs of transferring the ownership of such assets.

Where such data can be compiled, quarterly data for series in this table are available on the ONS's Databank. This data can also be provided on paper by request. Some of these quarterly data are published regularly in the UK Economic Accounts in table A8.

13.3 Analysis by broad sector and type of asset at 1990 market prices[1]

£ million at 1990 prices

		1985	1986	1987	1988	1989	1990	1991	1992	1993	1994	1995
Private sector:												
Vehicles, ships and aircraft	DFMV	8 217	7 502	8 926	9 463	10 122	9 223	7 196	6 847	7 726	8 704	8 192
Plant and machinery	DFHZ	22 499	23 055	24 930	29 456	33 021	31 568	30 689	29 087	28 152	30 262	31 440
Dwellings[2]	DFDP	14 899	16 681	18 036	21 741	20 653	17 212	15 083	15 524	16 448	17 025	17 144
Other new buildings and works	DFIB	10 791	11 266	15 273	18 449	21 169	23 263	21 114	19 730	17 754	16 833	17 743
Purchases *less* sales of land and existing buildings[3]	DFIC	9 397	9 373	10 927	13 372	10 780	8 697	6 814	6 037	7 188	6 942	6 577
Total	DFDQ	65 820	67 877	78 092	92 481	95 745	89 963	80 896	77 225	77 268	79 766	81 096
Public corporations:												
Vehicles, ships and aircraft	DEEU	872	605	546	528	625	616	508	573	665	560	439
Plant and machinery	DEEV	3 084	2 759	2 455	2 533	2 676	2 734	1 238	1 487	1 686	1 797	2 052
Dwellings[2]	DEEW	385	322	327	294	275	247	213	235	266	265	244
Other new buildings and works	DEEX	3 627	3 618	3 225	3 285	3 358	2 203	2 559	3 219	3 277	3 102	2 676
Purchases *less* sales of land and existing buildings[3]	DFMW	−696	−659	−1 333	−1 536	−1 263	−845	−654	−553	−627	−581	−589
Total	DFCZ	7 277	6 645	5 220	5 104	5 671	4 955	3 864	4 961	5 267	5 143	4 822
General government:												
Vehicles, ships and aircraft	DFFU	370	386	374	381	484	427	304	367	336	377	315
Plant and machinery	DFFV	1 515	1 698	1 701	1 781	2 228	2 460	2 028	2 028	1 911	1 586	1 482
Dwellings[2]	DFID	3 104	3 167	3 444	3 212	3 861	3 980	2 623	2 576	2 947	2 974	2 559
Other new buildings and works	DFIE	6 650	7 029	7 105	7 488	8 279	9 389	9 751	10 728	11 634	11 887	11 302
Purchases *less* sales of land and existing buildings[3]	DFIF	−3 280	−3 117	−3 597	−5 283	−4 798	−3 597	−2 063	−1 912	−2 777	−2 316	−2 274
Total	DFDS	8 441	9 163	9 027	7 579	10 054	12 659	12 643	13 787	14 051	14 508	13 384
Total	DFDM	81 575	83 685	92 339	105 164	111 470	107 577	97 403	95 973	96 586	99 417	99 302

1 For the years before 1986, totals differ from the sum of their components.
2 Excluding existing buildings and land.
3 The value of land and existing buildings which pass from one sector to another nets out over all sectors. The total figures refer to the costs of transferring the ownership of such assets.

Where such data can be compiled, quarterly data for series in this table are available on the ONS's Databank. This data can also be provided on paper by request. Some of these quarterly data are published regularly in the UK Economic Accounts in table A8.

13.4 Analysis by type of asset at 1990 market prices[1]

£ million at 1990 prices

		1985	1986	1987	1988	1989	1990	1991	1992	1993	1994	1995
Buses and coaches	DFKF	170	163	193	233	190	164	151	124	131	146	135
Other road vehicles	DFKG	7 527	7 454	8 672	9 083	9 422	8 013	5 963	6 029	6 567	7 141	7 584
Railway rolling stock, ships and aircraft	DFKH	1 617	876	981	1 056	1 619	2 089	1 894	1 634	2 029	2 354	1 227
Plant and machinery[2]	DFCY	27 081	27 512	29 086	33 770	37 925	36 762	33 955	32 602	31 749	33 645	34 974
Dwellings	DFDV	18 424	20 170	21 807	25 247	24 789	21 439	17 919	18 335	19 661	20 264	19 947
Other new buildings and works	DFKE	21 073	21 913	25 603	29 222	32 806	34 855	33 424	33 677	32 665	31 822	31 721
Transfer costs of land and buildings[3]	DFDW	5 422	5 597	5 997	6 553	4 719	4 255	4 097	3 572	3 784	4 045	3 714
Total	DFDM	81 575	83 685	92 339	105 164	111 470	107 577	97 403	95 973	96 586	99 417	99 302

1 For the years before 1986, totals differ from the sum of their components.
2 Including changes in the stock of breeding animals.
3 The value of land and existing buildings which pass from one sector to another nets out over all sectors. The total figures refer to the costs of transferring the ownership of such assets.

Where such data can be compiled, quarterly data for series in this table are available on the ONS's Databank. This data can also be provided on paper by request. Some of these quarterly data are published regularly in the UK Economic Accounts in table A8.

Gross domestic fixed capital formation

13.5 Analysis by type of asset and sector at current market prices

£ million

		1985	1986	1987	1988	1989	1990	1991	1992	1993	1994	1995
Vehicles, ships and aircraft												
Personal sector	DFIG	1 033	1 090	1 274	1 586	1 685	1 586	1 324	1 171	1 465	1 662	1 639
Industrial and commercial companies	GGAV	4 221	3 905	5 053	5 400	6 289	6 319	5 234	5 454	6 775	7 852	7 136
Financial companies and institutions[1]	GGBR	268	450	717	1 073	1 324	1 318	1 227	1 050	640	705	1 126
Public corporations	DEEP	657	487	458	466	585	616	535	630	735	644	529
Central government: Trading	DFQF	7	13	5	3	9	11	9	6	10	8	4
Non-trading	DFIL	61	53	62	87	147	118	108	197	197	220	150
Local authorities: Trading	DFIK	8	11	17	39	49	47	35	28	20	49	52
Non-trading	DFIM	184	213	219	195	236	251	175	174	158	180	191
Total	DFEJ	6 439	6 222	7 805	8 849	10 324	10 266	8 647	8 710	10 000	11 320	10 827
Plant and machinery												
Personal sector	DFIN	1 425	1 513	1 656	2 209	2 350	2 250	2 068	1 725	2 226	2 273	2 591
Industrial and commercial companies	GGAW	17 216	17 755	19 635	22 943	26 305	26 575	26 603	26 601	26 265	28 495	31 454
Financial companies and institutions[1]	GGBS	1 125	1 364	1 840	2 254	2 986	2 743	2 658	1 814	2 082	2 691	2 814
Public corporations	DEEQ	2 672	2 443	2 278	2 381	2 575	2 734	1 272	1 602	1 909	2 098	2 497
Central government: Trading	DFIQ	28	31	32	35	39	40	10	3	–	–	–
Non-trading	DFIR	699	910	924	940	1 269	1 604	1 600	1 627	1 588	1 249	1 207
Local authorities: Trading	DFIS	21	21	28	152	150	151	66	53	44	48	38
Non-trading	DFIT	684	653	680	590	708	665	400	429	451	482	483
Total	DFCX	23 870	24 690	27 073	31 504	36 382	36 762	34 677	33 854	34 565	37 336	41 084
Dwellings[2]												
Personal sector	DFIV	9 549	11 366	13 260	17 804	18 938	17 023	15 504	15 919	16 919	17 940	18 844
Industrial and commercial companies	GGAX	134	160	179	209	204	189	177	189	201	207	220
Financial companies and institutions[1]	DFIX	–	–	–	–	–	–	–	–	–	–	–
Public corporations	DEER	280	242	253	246	256	247	211	219	236	245	243
Central government: Non-trading	DFIZ	50	64	79	85	125	252	210	218	368	244	138
Local authorities: Trading	DFJA	2 194	2 307	2 583	2 583	3 464	3 728	2 398	2 186	2 240	2 481	2 385
Non-trading	DFJB	12	1	1	–	1	–	1	3	10	7	7
Total	DFDK	12 219	14 140	16 355	20 927	22 988	21 439	18 501	18 734	19 974	21 124	21 837
Other new buildings and works												
Personal sector	DFJD	986	1 003	1 206	1 424	1 811	1 932	1 667	1 490	1 429	1 337	1 574
Industrial and commercial companies	GGAY	5 590	6 242	9 124	12 019	15 556	18 013	16 269	14 467	12 005	11 087	12 817
Financial companies and institutions[1]	GGBT	1 217	1 356	1 723	2 385	2 967	3 318	2 174	1 499	1 013	1 276	1 523
Public corporations	DEES	2 703	2 757	2 473	2 764	3 222	2 203	2 425	2 745	2 584	2 463	2 335
Central government: Trading	DFJH	62	22	17	13	17	32	18	13	5	14	9
Non-trading	DFJI	2 292	2 403	2 437	2 790	3 574	4 465	4 915	4 627	4 136	4 095	4 061
Local authorities: Trading	DFJJ	189	230	205	450	524	585	509	431	421	531	553
Non-trading	DFJK	2 179	2 501	2 689	2 949	3 697	4 307	3 782	4 126	4 686	4 827	5 283
Total	DFJL	15 218	16 514	19 874	24 794	31 368	34 855	31 759	29 398	26 279	25 630	28 155
Purchases less sales of land and existing buildings												
Personal sector	DFJM	3 033	3 718	5 430	7 267	5 202	5 542	4 835	3 460	3 908	4 346	4 348
Property companies	DFJN	29	163	300	800	1 500	900	–99	–46	650	68	82
Other non-financial companies	DFJO	1 368	1 286	1 726	2 256	2 681	2 841	1 679	950	1 693	–1 063	–150
Financial companies and institutions[1]	DFJP	721	631	–103	815	596	–586	505	666	324	3 136	1 860
Public corporations	DEET	–381	–408	–901	–1 277	–1 171	–845	–664	–469	–569	–535	–550
Central government: Trading	DFJR	22	17	53	41	53	41	19	30	–5	–11	–32
Non-trading	DFJS	–95	–162	–251	–285	–282	–148	–13	134	92	127	105
Local authorities: Trading	DFJT	–1 401	–1 356	–1 718	–2 982	–3 335	–2 820	–1 773	–1 503	–1 723	–1 680	–1 582
Non-trading	DFJU	–324	–423	–485	–1 179	–863	–670	–326	–276	–895	–581	–599
Total	DFBH	2 972	3 466	4 051	5 456	4 381	4 255	4 163	2 946	3 475	3 807	3 482
All fixed assets												
Personal sector	AAAW	16 026	18 690	22 826	30 290	29 986	28 333	25 398	23 765	25 947	27 558	28 996
Industrial and commercial companies	AAAS	28 558	29 511	36 017	43 627	52 535	54 837	49 863	47 615	47 589	46 646	51 559
Financial companies and institutions[1]	AAAO	3 331	3 801	4 177	6 527	7 873	6 793	6 564	5 029	4 059	7 808	7 323
Public corporations	AAAK	5 931	5 521	4 561	4 580	5 467	4 955	3 779	4 727	4 895	4 915	5 054
Central government: Trading	DFJW	119	83	107	92	118	124	56	52	10	11	–19
Non-trading	DFJX	3 007	3 268	3 251	3 617	4 833	6 291	6 820	6 803	6 381	5 935	5 661
Local authorities: Trading	DFJY	1 011	1 213	1 115	242	852	1 691	1 235	1 195	1 002	1 429	1 446
Non-trading	DFJZ	2 735	2 945	3 104	2 555	3 779	4 553	4 032	4 456	4 410	4 915	5 365
Total	DFDC	60 718	65 032	75 158	91 530	105 443	107 577	97 747	93 642	94 293	99 217	105 385

1 Including expenditure by life assurance and pension funds.
2 Excluding existing buildings and land.

Where such data can be compiled, quarterly data for series in this table are available on the ONS's Databank. This data can also be provided on paper by request. Some of these quarterly data are published regularly in the UK Economic Accounts in table A8.

13.6 Analysis by industry group at current market prices[1]

£ million

		1985	1986	1987	1988	1989	1990	1991	1992	1993	1994	1995
Agriculture, hunting, forestry and fishing[1,2]	DFKI	1 181	1 196	1 265	1 420	1 485	1 368	1 063	1 070	1 167	930	933
Mining and quarrying including oil and gas extraction	DFTO	3 968	3 636	3 226	3 536	4 055	4 700	5 958	5 743	4 904	3 817	4 463
Manufacturing (revised definition)	DFDD	10 283	10 105	11 040	12 415	14 248	14 227	13 183	12 433	12 410	13 534	15 237
Electricity, gas and water supply	DFTP	2 660	2 792	2 798	3 119	3 943	4 742	5 608	6 365	5 910	5 225	4 802
Construction	DFKK	626	609	763	1 142	1 111	965	585	563	650	727	770
Wholesale and retail trade; repairs; hotels and restaurants	DFDJ	5 739	6 269	7 687	9 456	9 468	9 136	8 352	8 225	7 936	8 263	10 642
Transport, storage and communication	DFDI	5 867	5 683	6 840	7 875	9 604	9 453	9 279	9 175	10 667	12 559	10 483
Financial intermediation, real estate, renting and business activities	DFEL	7 133	8 197	11 534	15 532	20 372	21 170	15 360	12 675	10 746	12 192	15 061
Other services[3]	DFKP	8 070	8 939	9 599	10 652	13 788	16 122	15 695	15 713	16 454	17 039	17 675
Dwellings	DFDK	12 219	14 140	16 355	20 927	22 988	21 439	18 501	18 734	19 974	21 124	21 837
Transfer costs of land and buildings	DFBH	2 972	3 466	4 051	5 456	4 381	4 255	4 163	2 946	3 475	3 807	3 482
Total	DFDC	60 718	65 032	75 158	91 530	105 443	107 577	97 747	93 642	94 293	99 217	105 385

1 For a more detailed analysis, see table 13.8.
2 Including changes in the stock of breeding animals.
3 Comprising sections L, M, N, O, P and Q of SIC(92).

13.7 Analysis by industry group at 1990 market prices[1]

£ million at 1990 prices

		1985	1986	1987	1988	1989	1990	1991	1992	1993	1994	1995
Agriculture, hunting, forestry and fishing[2]	DFKR	1 493	1 461	1 491	1 587	1 537	1 368	1 049	1 074	1 161	909	856
Mining and quarrying including oil and gas extraction	DFTM	5 101	4 513	3 898	4 047	4 252	4 700	6 101	6 383	5 565	4 254	4 509
Manufacturing (revised definition)	DFDN	12 710	12 097	12 641	13 846	14 984	14 227	12 803	11 828	11 230	11 997	12 638
Electricity, gas and water supply	DFTN	3 334	3 404	3 304	3 490	4 094	4 742	5 612	6 561	6 115	5 341	4 434
Construction	DFKT	829	771	907	1 287	1 180	965	568	557	598	654	661
Wholesale and retail trade; repairs; hotels and restaurants	DFDU	7 400	7 681	9 056	10 638	9 923	9 136	8 331	8 490	8 095	8 304	9 973
Transport, storage and communication	DFDT	7 248	6 767	7 811	8 768	10 100	9 453	9 108	9 002	10 357	11 738	9 278
Financial intermediation, real estate, renting and business activities	DFEO	8 728	9 770	13 523	17 331	21 387	21 170	15 637	12 831	11 333	12 787	14 923
Other services[3]	DFKY	10 657	11 454	11 904	12 370	14 505	16 122	16 178	17 340	18 687	19 124	18 369
Dwellings	DFDV	18 424	20 170	21 807	25 247	24 789	21 439	17 919	18 335	19 661	20 264	19 947
Transfer costs of land and buildings	DFDW	5 422	5 597	5 997	6 553	4 719	4 255	4 097	3 572	3 784	4 045	3 714
Total	DFDM	81 575	83 685	92 339	105 164	111 470	107 577	97 403	95 973	96 586	99 417	99 302

1 For the years before 1986, totals differ from the sum of their components.
2 Including changes in the stock of breeding animals.
3 See footnote 3 on table 13.6.

Gross domestic fixed capital formation

13.8 Analysis by industry and type of asset at current market prices

£ million

			1985	1986	1987	1988	1989	1990	1991	1992	1993	1994	1995
VEHICLES, SHIPS AND AIRCRAFT													
Agriculture and hunting		DFKZ				140	161	211	141	164	170	166	152
Forestry	DCGD	DFLA	81	142	142	5	11	13	11	8	10	8	4
Fishing		DFLB				2	2	–	–	2	2	2	23
Extraction of mineral oil and natural gas		DFLD				3	−26	−30	–	−23	−19	17	15
Other mining and quarrying[1]	DFTS	DFTQ	33	42	63	49	63	42	22	13	12	18	17
Manufacturing (revised definition)[2,3]:													
Solid and nuclear fuels, oil refining	SAQZ		6	4	6	5	8	4	2	3	–	1	3
Chemicals and man-made fibres		DFLK				72	80	90	78	102	69	66	
Other non-metallic mineral products	DCGF	SAUP	174	124	143	6	8	6	7	21	49	58	247
Basic metals and metal products		GIEN				60	73	69	85	41	71	77	
Machinery and equipment		DFLM				87	104	100	71	83	80	86	
Electrical and optical equipment	DCGG	DFLN	193	199	195	79	125	82	69	69	73	53	171
Transport equipment		SARQ				12	63	66	11	34	20	31	
Food, beverages and tobacco products		SAPP				135	135	133	126	102	140	127	
Textiles and leather products		SAQQ				43	44	35	33	36	34	36	
Pulp, paper products, printing and publishing	DCGH	DFLV	313	352	380	113	117	101	65	89	135	107	382
Other manufacturing[6]		SASQ				99	114	102	75	110	104	110	
Total	GGBW		684	679	724	711	871	789	622	694	775	752	803
Electricity		DFLF				58	88	92	79	66	65	37	37
Gas	DFTT	DFLG	91	110	112	29	34	42	33	86	46	−14	80
Water		DFLH				36	38	28	23	23	23	15	18
Construction	DFMX		267	264	306	421	429	351	218	139	261	392	331
Motor vehicle sales, repair and maintenance		DFTR				168	172	142	107	78	95	150	
Wholesale trade[2]	DCGI	DFMA	1 233	1 235	1 277	897	673	576	485	441	556	612	1 309
Retail trade		DFMB				350	255	317	309	265	390	317	
Hotels and restaurants		DFMC				72	107	96	82	49	81	56	
Rail transport		DFMD				159	208	242	293	516	435	393	
Other land transport[4]		DFME				1 163	1 251	943	777	809	1 315	1 610	
Water transport[2]		DFMF				104	134	252	491	136	380	440	
Air transport	DCGJ	DFMG	2 149	1 647	2 266	208	335	388	350	637	1 081	1 610	2 871
Other transport services		DFMH				265	256	229	155	206	185	203	
Post and telecommunications		DFMI				245	400	453	391	381	307	282	
Financial intermediation, real estate, renting and business activities[2]	DCGK		1 264	1 461	2 270	3 037	3 849	4 040	3 154	3 145	2 867	3 179	4 295
Public administration, etc.		DFMM				147	196	168	128	207	219	266	
Roads		DFMN				23	34	46	27	27	27	36	
Education		DFMO				39	47	51	43	42	38	39	
Health and social work	DCGL	DFGD	637	642	645	132	129	126	120	125	122	113	872
Sewage and refuse disposal		DFMQ				70	96	116	80	60	46	56	
Other services[5]		DFMR				316	511	543	506	414	511	565	
Total	DFEJ		6 439	6 222	7 805	8 849	10 324	10 266	8 647	8 710	10 000	11 320	10 827

1 Comprising subsections CA10, CA12 and section CB of the SIC(92).
2 For the classification of leased assets, see methodological notes.
3 Differences between the totals and the sum of constituent parts of manufacturing are due to rounding.
4 Includes transport via pipelines.
5 Comprising groups 91, 92 and 93 of section O and sections P and Q of the Standard Industrial Classification Revised 1992.
6 Comprising sub-sections DD, DH and DN of the SIC(92).

13.8 Analysis by industry and type of asset at current market prices
continued

£ million

			1985	1986	1987	1988	1989	1990	1991	1992	1993	1994	1995
PLANT AND MACHINERY													
Agriculture and hunting		DFMY				634	645	461	375	478	565	376	359
Forestry	DCFU	DFMZ	546	587	588	118	109	108	78	18	8	8	8
Fishing		DFNA				–	2	1	1	1	1	–	1
Extraction of mineral oil and natural gas	DFTU	DFNC	1 945	1 882	1 527	539	821	1 010	1 195	1 409	1 177	714	1 055
Other mining and quarrying[1]		DFUD				981	961	844	526	221	180	184	184
Manufacturing (revised definition)[2,3]:													
Solid and nuclear fuels, oil refining	SAYZ		612	721	665	800	762	800	814	633	474	301	367
Chemicals and man-made fibres		GIEQ				1 405	1 743	1 861	1 916	1 731	1 625	1 522	
Other non-metallic mineral products	DCFW	SASS	2 270	1 862	2 219	173	246	221	148	515	555	623	3 438
Basic metals and metal products		GIEO				836	990	1 370	722	513	703	899	
Machinery and equipment		GIES				689	801	816	700	647	583	692	
Electrical and optical equipment	DCFX	GIET	2 750	2 689	2 681	1 121	1 256	1 148	988	1 031	1 011	1 205	4 212
Transport equipment		SAZA				1 113	1 504	1 635	1 691	1 471	1 251	1 374	
Food, beverages and tobacco products		SAYX				1 302	1 398	1 429	1 494	1 502	1 719	1 825	
Textiles and leather products		SAYY				462	410	348	294	339	374	447	
Pulp, paper products printing and publishing	DCFY	GIFB	2 762	2 951	3 395	1 386	1 397	1 022	1 279	1 096	1 189	1 451	4 807
Other manufacturing[6]		SAZB				839	909	881	704	807	836	926	
Total	GGBX		8 392	8 223	8 960	10 126	11 417	11 531	10 750	10 285	10 320	11 265	12 824
Electricity		DFNE				1 317	1 914	2 144	2 225	2 408	2 457	2 385	2 317
Gas	DFTV	DFNF	1 437	1 427	1 532	308	351	368	437	493	415	341	428
Water		DFNI				145	96	282	399	536	455	349	395
Construction	DFNJ		294	300	354	594	544	438	255	304	350	310	356
Motor vehicle sales, repair and maintenance		DFTW				229	285	281	249	497	312	286	
Wholesale trade[2]		DFNK				1 387	1 393	1 463	1 168	1 138	1 210	1 419	
Retail trade	DCFZ	DFNL	2 804	2 936	3 285	1 929	1 911	1 722	1 738	1 663	1 796	2 045	5 546
Hotels and restaurants		DFNM				698	740	713	690	638	645	665	
Rail transport		DFNN				77	108	92	88	94	43	208	
Other land transport[4]		DFNO				232	230	284	456	445	527	402	
Water transport[2]	DCGA	DFNP	2 785	3 150	3 570	21	26	46	−23	13	24	47	5 391
Air transport		DFNQ				26	19	21	19	1	12	7	
Other transport services		DFNR				205	238	241	453	447	358	392	
Post and telecommunications		DFNS				3 642	4 355	4 080	3 332	2 942	3 500	4 553	
Financial intermediation, real estate, renting and business activities[2]	DCGB		3 561	3 843	4 712	5 644	6 833	6 678	6 403	5 960	5 605	6 548	7 082
Public administration, etc.		DFNW				962	1 173	1 318	1 243	1 292	1 464	1 317	
Roads		DFNX				73	81	90	56	57	47	52	
Education	DCGC	DFNY	2 106	2 342	2 545	366	459	424	414	369	413	436	5 138
Health and social work		DFGC				252	435	547	601	912	1 107	1 392	
Sewage and refuse disposal		DFNZ				123	129	126	500	592	510	501	
Other services[5]		DFOA				876	1 107	1 449	1 049	641	1 064	1 134	
Total	DFCX		23 870	24 690	27 073	31 504	36 382	36 762	34 677	33 854	34 565	37 336	41 084

See footnotes on previous page.

Gross domestic fixed capital formation

13.8 Analysis by industry and type of asset at current market prices
continued

£ million

			1985	1986	1987	1988	1989	1990	1991	1992	1993	1994	1995
NEW BUILDINGS AND WORKS													
Agriculture and hunting	DCFL	DFOB				480	520	542	441	391	400	359	373
Forestry		DFOC	554	467	535	41	34	32	15	8	11	10	12
Fishing		DFOD				–	1	–	1	–	–	1	1
Extraction of mineral oil and natural gas	DFTY	DFOF	1 990	1 712	1 636	1 664	1 914	2 587	4 038	4 031	3 475	2 813	3 178
Other mining and quarrying[1]		DFTX				300	322	247	177	92	79	71	14
Manufacturing (revised definition)[2,3]:													
Solid and nuclear fuels, oil refining	SAZJ		95	114	169	134	136	153	135	115	82	131	123
Chemicals and man-made fibres		GIFG				216	281	254	309	284	264	285	
Other non-metalic mineral products	DCFN	SAQD	245	248	279	21	37	31	21	39	54	69	359
Basic metals and metal products		GIFE				54	84	98	64	42	99	58	
Machinery and equipment		GIFI				65	139	189	139	66	54	87	
Electrical and optical equipment	DCFO	GIFJ	421	411	358	171	248	163	144	108	85	157	579
Transport equipment		SAZK				186	288	281	435	199	119	124	
Food, beverages and tobacco		SAZH				323	322	352	321	342	354	332	
Textiles and leather products		SAZI				54	50	47	33	41	30	42	
Pulp, paper and products printing and publishing	DCFP	GIFR	449	429	550	234	218	202	128	102	104	167	549
Other manufacturing[6]		SAZL				120	157	137	82	111	70	65	
Total	GGBY		1 207	1 203	1 356	1 578	1 960	1 907	1 811	1 454	1 315	1 517	1 610
Electricity		DFOH				244	295	367	811	1 150	758	527	228
Gas	DFTZ	DFOI	1 132	1 255	1 154	427	447	547	671	678	515	480	364
Water		DFOJ				555	680	872	930	925	1 176	1 105	935
Construction	DFOK		65	45	103	127	138	176	112	120	39	25	83
Motor vehicle sales, repair and maintenance		DFUA				204	279	281	215	69	215	184	
Wholesale trade[2]		DFOL				609	676	669	424	451	378	319	
Retail trade	DCFQ	DFOM	1 702	2 098	3 125	1 877	1 776	1 692	1 967	1 834	1 623	1 525	3 787
Hotels and restaurants		DFON				1 036	1 201	1 184	918	1 102	635	685	
Rail transport		DFOO				644	836	1 030	1 220	1 400	1 253	760	
Other land transport[4]		DFOP				272	390	462	339	369	465	623	
Water transport[2]	DCFR	DFOQ	933	886	1 004	8	20	31	33	27	30	28	2 221
Air transport		DFOR				4	4	4	4	4	4	4	
Other transport services		DFOS				396	452	479	710	575	612	831	
Post and telecommunications		DFOT				204	342	176	191	173	136	166	
Financial intermediation, real estate, renting and business activities[2]	DCFS		2 308	2 893	4 552	6 851	9 690	10 452	5 803	3 570	2 274	2 465	3 684
Public administration, etc.		DFOX				1 232	1 746	2 179	2 273	2 212	2 482	2 622	
Roads		DFOY				2 027	2 467	3 178	3 075	3 544	3 597	3 899	
Education		DFOZ				982	1 251	1 398	1 346	1 426	1 563	1 384	
Health and social work	DCFT	DFGB	5 327	5 955	6 409	1 268	1 472	1 550	1 555	1 331	871	756	11 665
Sewage and refuse disposal		DFPA				834	978	1 005	897	1 020	846	950	
Other services[5]		DFPB				930	1 477	1 808	1 782	1 442	1 527	1 521	
Total expenditure on other new buildings and works	DFJL		15 218	16 514	19 874	24 794	31 368	34 855	31 759	29 398	26 279	25 630	28 155
Dwellings	DFDK		12 219	14 140	16 355	20 927	22 988	21 439	18 501	18 734	19 974	21 124	21 837
Total expenditure on new buildings and works	DFPD		27 437	30 654	36 229	45 721	54 356	56 294	50 260	48 132	46 253	46 754	49 992

See footnotes on previous page.

13.8 Analysis by industry and type of asset at current market prices
continued

£ million

			1985	1986	1987	1988	1989	1990	1991	1992	1993	1994	1995
ALL FIXED ASSETS													
Agriculture and hunting		DFPE				1 254	1 326	1 214	957	1 033	1 135	901	884
Forestry	DFKI	DFPF	1 181	1 196	1 265	164	154	153	104	34	29	26	24
Fishing		DFPG				2	5	1	2	3	3	3	25
Extraction of mineral oil and natural gas	DFTO	DFDE	3 968	3 636	3 226	2 206	2 709	3 567	5 233	5 417	4 633	3 544	4 248
Other mining and quarrying[1]		DFUB				1 330	1 346	1 133	725	326	271	273	215
Manufacturing (revised definition)[2,3]:													
Solid and nuclear fuels, oil refining	SAZE		713	839	840	939	906	957	951	751	556	433	493
Chemical and man-made fibres		GIFW				1 693	2 104	2 205	2 303	2 117	1 958	1 873	
Other non-metallic mineral products	DFRL	GIFV	2 689	2 234	2 641	200	291	258	176	580	658	750	4 044
Basic metals and metal products		GIFU				950	1 147	1 537	871	600	873	1 034	
Machinery and equipment		GIFY				841	1 044	1 105	910	796	717	865	
Electrical and optical equipment	DFRM	GIFZ	3 364	3 299	3 234	1 371	1 630	1 393	1 201	1 208	1 169	1 415	4 962
Transport equipment		SAZF				1 311	1 855	1 982	2 137	1 704	1 390	1 529	
Food, beverages and tobacco		SAZC				1 760	1 855	1 914	1 941	1 946	2 213	2 284	
Textile and leather products		SAZD				559	504	430	360	416	438	525	
Pulp, paper and products printing and publishing	DFRN	GIGH	3 524	3 732	4 325	1 733	1 732	1 325	1 472	1 287	1 428	1 725	5 738
Other manufacturing[6]		SAZG				1 058	1 180	1 120	861	1 028	1 010	1 101	
Total	DFDD		10 283	10 105	11 040	12 415	14 248	14 227	13 183	12 433	12 410	13 534	15 237
Electricity		DFPK				1 619	2 297	2 603	3 115	3 624	3 280	2 949	2 582
Gas	DFTP	DFPL	2 660	2 792	2 798	764	832	957	1 141	1 257	976	807	872
Water		DFPM				736	814	1 182	1 352	1 484	1 654	1 469	1 348
Construction	DFKK		626	609	763	1 142	1 111	965	585	563	650	727	770
Motor vehicle sales, repair and maintenance		DFUC				601	736	704	571	644	622	620	
Wholesale trade[2]		DFPN				2 893	2 742	2 708	2 077	2 030	2 144	2 350	
Retail trade	DFDJ	DFPO	5 739	6 269	7 687	4 156	3 942	3 731	4 014	3 762	3 809	3 887	10 642
Hotels and restaurants		DFPP				1 806	2 048	1 993	1 690	1 789	1 361	1 406	
Rail transport		DFPQ				880	1 152	1 364	1 601	2 010	1 731	1 361	
Other land transport[4]		DFPR				1 667	1 871	1 689	1 572	1 623	2 307	2 635	
Water transport[2]	DFDI	DFPS	5 867	5 683	6 840	133	180	329	501	176	434	515	10 483
Air transport		DFPT				238	358	413	373	642	1 097	1 621	
Other transports services		DFPU				866	946	949	1 318	1 228	1 155	1 426	
Post and telecommunications		DFKM				4 091	5 097	4 709	3 914	3 496	3 943	5 001	
Financial intermediation, real estate, renting and business activities[2]	DFEL		7 133	8 197	11 534	15 532	20 372	21 170	15 360	12 675	10 746	12 192	15 061
Public administration, etc.		DFPY				2 341	3 115	3 665	3 644	3 711	4 165	4 205	
Roads		DFPZ				2 123	2 582	3 314	3 158	3 628	3 671	3 987	
Education	DFKP	DFQA	8 070	8 939	9 599	1 387	1 757	1 873	1 803	1 837	2 014	1 859	17 675
Health and social work		DFQB				1 652	2 036	2 223	2 276	2 368	2 100	2 261	
Sewage and refuse disposal		DFQC				1 027	1 203	1 247	1 477	1 672	1 402	1 507	
Other services[5]		DFQD				2 122	3 095	3 800	3 337	2 497	3 102	3 220	
Dwellings	DFDK		12 219	14 140	16 355	20 927	22 988	21 439	18 501	18 734	19 974	21 124	21 837
Total expenditure on equipment, new buildings and works	DFQE		57 746	61 566	71 107	86 074	101 062	103 322	93 584	90 696	90 818	95 410	101 903
Transfer costs of land and buildings	DFBH		2 972	3 466	4 051	5 456	4 381	4 255	4 163	2 946	3 475	3 807	3 482
Total	DFDC		60 718	65 032	75 158	91 530	105 443	107 577	97 747	93 642	94 293	99 217	105 385

See footnotes on previous page.

CHAPTER 14: Capital consumption and stock of fixed capital

14.1 Capital consumption by industry group at current prices[1]

£ million

		1985	1986	1987	1988	1989	1990	1991	1992	1993	1994	1995
Agriculture, hunting, forestry and fishing	EXEX	1 358	1 394	1 432	1 471	1 578	1 629	1 604	1 525	1 549	1 568	1 594
Mining and quarrying	EZAK	3 078	3 179	3 235	3 380	3 634	3 783	3 743	3 682	3 830	3 996	4 320
Manufacturing (revised definition)	EXCL	9 370	9 800	10 365	10 728	11 685	12 515	12 917	13 122	13 719	14 095	14 910
Electricity, gas and water supply	EZAL	2 970	3 150	3 272	3 403	3 598	3 798	3 834	3 865	3 988	4 119	4 514
Construction	EXCM	698	720	756	787	850	910	945	919	938	939	979
Wholesale and retail trade; repairs; hotels and restaurants	EXCN	2 915	3 202	3 498	3 766	4 167	4 522	4 790	4 797	4 992	5 148	5 516
Transport and storage	EXCP	3 733	3 999	3 608	3 437	3 534	3 729	3 633	3 573	3 733	3 940	4 221
Post and telecommunications	EXCQ	1 969	2 057	2 270	2 427	2 668	2 943	3 075	3 237	3 501	3 656	3 923
Financial intermediation, real estate, renting and business activities	EXCR	2 950	3 349	3 838	4 406	5 106	5 913	6 657	6 738	7 161	7 525	8 212
Other services[2]	EXCS	3 504	3 821	4 142	4 537	5 178	5 729	5 847	5 822	6 051	6 413	7 085
Dwellings	EXCT	6 368	6 948	7 697	8 838	10 337	11 535	12 144	12 259	12 415	13 085	14 128
Transfer costs of land and buildings	EXCU	2 972	3 466	4 051	5 456	4 381	4 255	4 163	2 946	3 475	3 807	3 482
Total	EXCH	41 883	45 085	48 164	52 636	56 716	61 261	63 356	62 485	65 353	68 289	72 884

1 Differences between totals and sums of components are due to rounding.
2 Comprising sections L, M, N, O, P and Q of the SIC (92).

14.2 Capital consumption by industry group at 1990 prices[1]

£ million at 1990 prices

		1985	1986	1987	1988	1989	1990	1991	1992	1993	1994	1995
Agriculture, hunting, forestry and fishing	EXCW	1 677	1 658	1 645	1 637	1 635	1 629	1 614	1 578	1 552	1 518	1 451
Mining and quarrying	EZAO	3 791	3 873	3 899	3 861	3 808	3 783	3 836	3 993	4 152	4 226	4 262
Manufacturing (revised definition)	EXCZ	11 393	11 566	11 753	11 965	12 235	12 515	12 630	12 637	12 483	12 443	12 431
Electricity, gas and water supply	EZAQ	3 664	3 682	3 703	3 718	3 749	3 798	3 796	3 898	4 006	4 081	4 127
Construction	EXDA	903	889	880	886	904	910	904	876	851	834	818
Wholesale and retail trade; repairs; hotels and restaurants	EXDB	3 820	3 954	4 085	4 243	4 404	4 522	4 642	4 701	4 761	4 824	4 915
Transport and storage	EXDC	5 050	4 967	4 255	3 874	3 754	3 729	3 508	3 483	3 530	3 647	3 717
Post and telecommunications	EXDD	2 272	2 365	2 475	2 612	2 777	2 943	2 970	3 023	3 065	3 129	3 207
Financial intermediation, real estate, renting and business activities	EXDE	3 401	3 639	3 953	4 456	5 154	5 913	6 506	6 858	7 114	7 346	7 632
Other services[2]	EXDF	4 723	4 906	5 087	5 265	5 477	5 729	5 938	6 172	6 400	6 668	6 933
Dwellings	EXDG	9 716	10 016	10 345	10 720	11 140	11 535	11 875	12 179	12 489	12 815	13 145
Transfer costs of land and buildings	EXDH	5 422	5 597	5 997	6 553	4 719	4 255	4 097	3 572	3 820	4 089	3 720
Total	EXDI	56 214	57 112	58 077	59 790	59 756	61 261	62 316	62 970	64 223	65 620	66 358

See Table 14.1 for footnotes

14.3 Capital consumption by sector at current replacement cost[1]

£ million

		1985	1986	1987	1988	1989	1990	1991	1992	1993	1994	1995
Dwellings												
Personal sector	EXEY	4 700	5 179	5 821	6 757	7 966	9 286	9 876	10 069	10 275	10 824	11 664
Industrial and commercial companies	EXEZ	167	177	192	213	238	257	267	268	267	272	282
Public corporations	EXFA	134	141	148	163	183	200	199	190	184	194	211
Central government	EXFB	34	36	38	42	48	53	55	54	54	60	66
Local authorities	EXFC	1 333	1 415	1 498	1 663	1 903	1 739	1 747	1 680	1 635	1 735	1 904
Total	EXCT	6 368	6 948	7 697	8 838	10 337	11 535	12 144	12 259	12 415	13 085	14 128
Other fixed assets[2]												
Personal sector	EXFD	5 306	5 876	6 535	7 852	7 322	7 507	7 617	6 541	7 096	7 483	7 433
Industrial and commercial companies	EXFE	19 852	21 342	23 409	24 738	27 376	30 583	32 937	33 513	35 583	37 264	40 169
Financial companies and institutions	EXFF	1 471	1 624	1 810	1 994	2 148	2 312	2 601	2 524	2 528	2 502	2 621
Public corporations	EXFG	6 166	6 340	5 524	5 657	5 567	4 967	3 719	3 468	3 450	3 493	3 730
Central government	EXFH	987	1 081	1 186	1 300	1 496	1 683	1 732	1 766	1 877	1 985	2 161
Local authorities	EXFI	1 733	1 874	2 003	2 257	2 470	2 674	2 606	2 412	2 405	2 478	2 643
Total	EXHR	35 515	38 137	40 467	43 798	46 379	49 726	51 210	50 224	52 938	55 205	58 757
All fixed assets												
Personal sector	EXFJ	10 006	11 055	12 356	14 609	15 288	16 793	17 493	16 610	17 371	18 308	19 097
Industrial and commercial companies	EXAB	20 019	21 519	23 601	24 951	27 614	30 840	33 204	33 781	35 850	37 536	40 451
Financial companies and institutions	EXAA	1 471	1 624	1 810	1 994	2 148	2 312	2 601	2 524	2 528	2 502	2 621
Public corporations	EXFK	6 300	6 481	5 672	5 820	5 750	5 167	3 917	3 658	3 633	3 686	3 941
Central government	EXFL	1 021	1 117	1 224	1 342	1 544	1 736	1 786	1 820	1 931	2 044	2 227
Local authorities	EXFM	3 066	3 289	3 501	3 920	4 373	4 413	4 353	4 092	4 040	4 213	4 547
Total	EXCH	41 883	45 085	48 164	52 636	56 716	61 261	63 356	62 485	65 353	68 289	72 884

1 Differences between totals and sums of components are due to rounding.
2 Including transfer costs of land and buildings. They are wholly written off in the
year incurred.

Stock of fixed capital

14.4 Net domestic fixed capital formation[1] by industry group[2] at current prices

£ million

		1985	1986	1987	1988	1989	1990	1991	1992	1993	1994	1995
Agriculture, hunting, forestry and fishing	DHHZ	−177	−198	−167	−51	−93	−261	−541	−455	−382	−638	−661
Mining and quarrying	EZAC	890	457	−9	156	421	917	2 215	2 061	1 074	−179	143
Manufacturing (revised definition)	DHIC	913	305	675	1 687	2 563	1 712	266	−689	−1 309	−561	327
Electricity, gas and water supply	EZAE	−310	−358	−474	−284	345	944	1 774	2 500	1 922	1 106	288
Construction	EXDJ	−72	−111	7	355	261	55	−360	−356	−288	−212	−209
Wholesale and retail trade; repairs; hotels and restaurants	EXDK	2 824	3 067	4 189	5 690	5 301	4 614	3 562	3 428	2 944	3 115	5 126
Transport, storage and communication	EYJD	165	−373	962	2 011	3 402	2 781	2 571	2 365	3 433	4 963	2 339
Financial intermediation, real estate, renting and business activities	EXDN	4 183	4 848	7 696	11 126	15 266	15 257	8 703	5 937	3 585	4 667	6 849
Other services[3]	EXDO	4 566	5 118	5 457	6 115	8 610	10 393	9 848	9 891	10 403	10 626	10 590
Dwellings	EXDP	5 851	7 192	8 658	12 089	12 651	9 904	6 357	6 475	7 559	8 039	7 709
Total	EXDQ	18 835	19 947	26 994	38 894	48 727	46 316	34 393	31 157	28 940	30 928	32 501

1 Gross domestic fixed capital formation *less* capital consumption.
2 Differences between totals and sums of components are due to rounding.
3 Comprising sections L, M, N, O, P and Q of the SIC (92).

14.5 Net domestic fixed capital formation[1] by industry group at 1990 prices[2]

£ million at 1990 prices

		1985	1986	1987	1988	1989	1990	1991	1992	1993	1994	1995
Agriculture, hunting, forestry and fishing	EXDR	−184	−197	−154	−50	−98	−261	−565	−504	−391	−609	−595
Mining and quarrying	EZAG	1 310	640	−1	186	444	917	2 265	2 390	1 413	28	247
Manufacturing (revised definition)	EXDU	1 317	531	888	1 881	2 749	1 712	173	−809	−1 253	−446	207
Electricity, gas and water supply	EZAI	−330	−278	−399	−228	345	944	1 816	2 663	2 109	1 260	307
Construction	EXDV	−74	−118	27	401	276	55	−336	−319	−253	−180	−157
Wholesale and retail trade; repairs; hotels and restaurants	EXDW	3 580	3 727	4 971	6 395	5 519	4 614	3 689	3 789	3 334	3 480	5 058
Transport, storage and communication	EZAB	−74	−565	1 081	2 282	3 569	2 781	2 630	2 496	3 762	4 962	2 354
Financial intermediation, real estate, renting and business activities	EXDZ	5 327	6 131	9 570	12 875	16 233	15 257	9 131	5 973	4 219	5 441	7 291
Other services[3]	EXEA	5 934	6 548	6 817	7 105	9 028	10 393	10 240	11 168	12 287	12 456	11 436
Dwellings	EXEB	8 708	10 154	11 462	14 527	13 649	9 904	6 044	6 156	7 172	7 449	6 802
Total	EXEC	25 361	26 573	34 262	45 374	51 714	46 316	35 087	33 003	32 363	33 797	32 944

1 Gross domestic fixed capital formation *less* capital consumption.
2 Differences between totals and sums of components are due to rounding.
3 Comprising sections L, M, N, O, P and Q of the SIC (92).

14.6 Net domestic fixed capital formation[1] by sector at current prices[2]

£ million

		1985	1986	1987	1988	1989	1990	1991	1992	1993	1994	1995
Dwellings[3]												
Personal sector	EXFO	4 849	6 187	7 439	11 047	10 972	7 737	5 628	5 850	6 644	7 116	7 180
Industrial and commercial companies	EXFP	−33	−17	−13	−4	−34	−68	−90	−79	−66	−65	−62
Public corporations	EXFQ	146	101	105	83	73	47	12	29	52	51	32
Central government	EXFR	16	28	41	43	77	199	155	164	314	184	72
Local authorities	EXFS	873	893	1 086	920	1 562	1 989	652	509	615	753	488
Total	EXDP	5 851	7 192	8 658	12 089	12 651	9 904	6 357	6 475	7 559	8 039	7 709
Other fixed assets												
Personal sector	EXFU	1 171	1 448	3 031	4 634	3 726	3 803	2 277	1 305	1 932	2 135	3 319
Industrial and commercial companies	EXFV	8 572	8 009	12 429	18 680	24 955	24 065	16 749	13 913	11 805	9 175	10 570
Financial companies and institutions	EXFW	1 860	2 177	2 367	4 533	5 725	4 481	3 963	2 505	1 531	5 306	4 702
Public corporations	EXFX	−515	−1 061	−1 216	−1 323	−356	−259	−151	1 040	1 209	1 177	1 081
Central government	EXFY	2 089	2 206	2 093	2 324	3 330	4 480	4 934	4 871	4 146	3 717	3 343
Local authorities	EXFZ	−193	−24	−368	−2 043	−1 304	−158	262	1 050	757	1 378	1 776
Total	EXGA	12 984	12 755	18 336	26 805	36 076	36 412	28 036	24 684	21 381	22 888	24 791
All fixed assets												
Personal sector	EXGB	6 020	7 635	10 470	15 681	14 698	11 540	7 905	7 155	8 576	9 250	10 499
Industrial and commercial companies	EXGC	8 539	7 992	12 416	18 676	24 921	23 997	16 659	13 834	11 739	9 110	10 508
Financial companies and institutions	EXGD	1 860	2 177	2 367	4 533	5 725	4 481	3 963	2 505	1 531	5 306	4 702
Public corporations	EXGE	−369	−960	−1 111	−1 240	−283	−212	−138	1 069	1 262	1 229	1 113
Central government	EXGF	2 105	2 234	2 134	2 367	3 407	4 679	5 090	5 035	4 460	3 902	3 415
Local authorities	EXGG	680	869	718	−1 123	258	1 831	914	1 559	1 372	2 131	2 264
Total	EXDQ	18 835	19 947	26 994	38 894	48 727	46 316	34 393	31 157	28 940	30 928	32 501

1 Gross domestic fixed capital formation *less* capital consumption.
2 Differences between totals and sums of components are due to rounding.
3 Excluding existing land and buildings.

Stock of fixed capital

14.7 Net capital stock by sector[1] and type of asset at current replacement cost[2]

£ billion

		1985	1986	1987	1988	1989	1990	1991	1992	1993	1994	1995
Vehicles, ships and aircraft												
Personal sector	EXGH	5.7	6.2	6.6	7.4	8.2	8.7	9.1	8.6	8.6	8.5	8.4
Industrial and commercial companies	EXGI	20.5	21.5	24.8	27.2	30.8	34.0	35.6	35.2	36.7	38.4	40.2
Financial companies and institutions	EXGJ	1.2	1.3	1.6	2.0	2.6	3.3	3.8	3.9	3.8	3.7	4.1
Public corporations	EXGK	5.6	5.7	4.6	4.5	4.2	4.3	4.4	4.6	4.8	5.1	5.4
Central government	EXGL	0.3	0.4	0.4	0.4	0.5	0.6	0.7	0.8	0.9	1.0	1.0
Local authorities	EXGM	0.9	1.0	1.1	1.1	1.2	1.3	1.3	1.3	1.1	1.1	1.1
Total	EXGN	34.2	36.0	39.1	42.6	47.5	52.2	54.9	54.3	56.0	57.7	60.2
Plant and machinery												
Personal sector	EXGO	14.0	14.9	15.9	17.1	18.9	20.4	21.0	21.6	23.5	25.0	24.0
Industrial and commercial companies	EXGP	155.5	169.3	181.1	192.6	213.5	255.4	277.6	294.8	312.1	331.2	350.6
Financial companies and institutions	EXGQ	6.6	7.1	8.0	8.9	10.3	11.5	15.0	15.9	17.2	19.1	21.3
Public corporations	EXGR	52.1	50.2	51.0	52.4	54.4	30.8	22.0	22.2	22.4	23.1	24.0
Central government	EXGS	6.3	7.0	7.7	8.3	9.4	10.6	11.4	12.4	13.6	14.2	14.7
Local authorities	EXGT	4.4	4.8	5.1	5.4	5.9	6.3	6.2	6.2	6.2	6.4	6.5
Total	EXGU	239.1	253.4	268.8	284.7	312.4	335.0	353.1	373.3	394.9	419.0	441.0
Dwellings												
Personal sector	EXGV	245.2	271.5	309.6	364.4	416.9	467.3	475.2	473.3	482.3	507.4	561.3
Industrial and commercial companies	EXGW	6.1	6.6	7.3	8.2	9.1	9.5	9.5	9.3	9.2	9.5	10.3
Financial companies and institutions	EXGX	–	–	–	–	–	–	–	–	–	–	–
Public corporations	EXGY	11.3	11.8	12.5	13.8	15.2	15.7	15.1	14.3	14.4	15.3	16.9
Central government	EXGZ	2.7	2.8	3.0	3.4	3.8	4.1	4.1	4.0	4.3	4.8	5.4
Local authorities	EXHA	83.9	87.0	92.5	102.0	112.3	96.6	92.5	87.7	87.3	92.5	101.8
Total	EXHB	349.2	379.7	424.9	491.8	557.3	593.2	596.3	588.6	597.6	629.5	695.7
Other buildings and works												
Personal sector	EXHC	26.4	28.0	30.2	34.2	38.1	39.2	36.4	34.0	33.7	36.2	40.5
Industrial and commercial companies	EXHD	112.1	135.4	149.4	173.2	228.5	240.9	221.2	211.6	213.3	232.4	262.7
Financial companies and institutions	EXHE	20.4	22.4	25.3	30.0	34.6	37.0	35.2	32.8	32.2	34.9	39.5
Public corporations	EXHF	68.6	61.1	63.9	72.1	47.5	46.1	39.6	37.7	38.0	42.2	48.0
Central government	EXHG	55.3	58.3	63.5	73.9	83.0	86.2	83.0	79.6	80.6	88.9	101.3
Local authorities	EXHH	79.0	82.4	89.2	102.8	114.9	117.5	109.6	103.3	103.6	113.0	128.3
Total	EXHI	361.8	387.6	421.5	486.2	546.6	566.9	524.9	499.0	501.5	547.6	620.4
All fixed assets												
Personal sector	EXHJ	291.4	320.6	362.3	423.1	482.1	535.6	541.7	537.5	548.1	577.0	634.3
Industrial and commercial companies	EXHK	294.3	332.8	362.6	401.2	481.9	539.8	543.9	550.9	571.4	611.5	663.7
Financial companies and institutions	EXHL	28.0	30.8	34.9	40.9	47.5	51.8	54.0	52.7	53.1	57.7	64.8
Public corporations	EXHM	137.6	128.8	132.0	142.8	121.3	96.9	81.1	78.8	79.7	85.7	94.3
Central government	EXHN	64.7	68.5	74.6	86.0	96.7	101.5	99.1	96.8	99.4	108.9	122.4
Local authorities	EXHO	168.2	175.2	187.9	211.3	234.3	221.7	209.6	198.4	198.3	212.9	237.8
Total	EXHP	984.3	1 056.7	1 154.3	1 305.3	1 463.8	1 547.3	1 529.3	1 515.2	1 549.9	1 653.8	1 817.3

1 Differences between totals and sums of the components are due to rounding.
2 For an account of the principles of valuation, see paragraphs 12.104-124 of *United Kingdom National Accounts: Sources and Methods,* Third edition. Figures relate to end of year.

14.8 Gross capital stock by industry at 1990 replacement cost[1]

£ billion at 1990 prices

		1985	1986	1987	1988	1989	1990	1991	1992	1993	1994	1995
Agriculture, hunting, forestry and fishing	EXED	37.7	37.8	37.9	38.0	38.2	38.1	35.5	35.0	34.6	34.0	32.9
Mining and quarrying	EZAS	60.8	62.9	62.9	64.0	64.0	65.0	66.8	69.7	71.8	72.6	73.6
Manufacturing (revised definition)	EXEG	353.9	359.3	364.6	371.2	379.0	385.6	390.0	389.3	387.8	388.4	389.3
Electricity, gas and water supply	EZAV	141.5	143.2	145.5	147.8	152.0	156.0	157.8	161.7	165.1	167.6	169.0
Construction	EXEH	20.0	20.0	20.1	20.7	21.1	21.3	20.8	20.5	20.3	20.0	19.8
Wholesale and retail trade; repairs; hotels and restaurants	EXEI	113.6	119.0	125.6	133.7	141.1	147.6	155.5	161.4	166.8	172.3	179.4
Transport and storage	EXEJ	94.4	93.6	92.6	92.7	93.1	92.8	97.0	100.1	102.6	106.4	107.1
Post and telecommunications	EXEK	50.4	51.6	54.4	57.2	60.6	64.2	64.0	64.6	65.3	66.9	69.2
Financial intermediation, real estate, renting, and business activities	EXEL	119.7	126.5	136.5	153.4	174.5	195.2	210.8	221.6	229.3	238.2	248.6
Other services[2]	EXEM	300.4	309.8	319.5	329.6	341.6	355.2	375.6	390.2	405.7	421.8	437.0
Dwellings	EXEO	790.1	807.5	826.5	848.7	870.4	888.8	903.6	918.7	935.2	952.1	968.7
Total[3]	EXEP	2 082.5	2 131.0	2 186.1	2 257.0	2 335.6	2 409.8	2 477.4	2 532.9	2 584.4	2 640.1	2 694.7

1 For an account of the principles of valuation, see paragraphs 12.104-124 of *United Kingdom National Accounts: Sources and Methods,* Third edition. Figures relate to end of year.
2 Comprising sections L,M,N,O,P & Q of the SIC (92).
3 Differences between totals and sums of components are due to rounding.

14.9 Gross capital stock by type of asset at 1990 replacement cost[1]

£ billion at 1990 prices

		1985	1986	1987	1988	1989	1990	1991	1992	1993	1994	1995
Road vehicles	EXEQ	74.0	74.6	76.0	78.1	81.0	82.6	82.0	81.9	81.7	81.7	81.7
Railway rolling stock, ships and aircraft	EXER	18.4	17.5	17.0	16.5	16.1	15.8	15.9	16.6	16.4	17.2	17.1
Plant and machinery	EXES	489.6	504.9	520.3	544.4	572.6	598.9	617.9	629.6	639.5	652.5	666.2
Dwellings	EXEO	790.1	807.5	826.5	848.7	870.4	888.8	903.6	918.7	935.2	952.1	968.7
Other buildings and works	EXEU	710.4	726.5	746.1	769.2	795.5	823.7	858.0	886.0	911.7	936.6	961.0
Total gross capital stock[2]	EXEP	2 082.5	2 131.0	2 186.1	2 257.0	2 335.6	2 409.8	2 477.4	2 532.9	2 584.4	2 640.1	2 694.7

1 For an account of the principles of valuation, see paragraphs 12.104-124 of *United Kingdom National Accounts: Sources and Methods,* Third edition. Figures relate to end of year.
2 Differences between totals and sums of components are due to rounding.

CHAPTER 15: Change in the book value of stocks at market prices

15.1 Change in the book value of stocks by industry at market prices

£ million

		1985	1986	1987	1988	1989	1990	1991	1992	1993	1994	1995	Value of stocks at end of 1995
Agriculture, hunting, forestry and fishing	DHIE	−41	−147	−119	26	23	113	4	8	−185	184	8	3 584
Mining and quarrying	DGFS	−382	−358	−12	−64	242	−80	142	83	−164	−253	−119	384
Manufacturing (revised definition):													
Food, beverages and tobacco:													
Materials and fuel	DHIQ	−27	−27	−60	40	58	89	51	157	−81	126	204	4 145
Work in progress	DHIR	18	37	59	−34	96	181	126	97	−69	44	−27	1 075
Finished goods	DHIS	−31	35	18	117	56	174	−58	173	134	41	238	3 235
Textiles and leather products:													
Materials and fuel	DHIT	41	−11	120	47	−25	−61	−81	26	25	136	64	1 140
Work in progress	DHIU	63	–	75	5	5	−18	−49	3	17	45	43	730
Finished goods	DHIV	86	39	111	105	32	57	−29	7	47	158	156	1 727
Solid and nuclear fuel, oil refining:													
Materials and fuel	DGFT	−81	−224	−44	−49	41	78	−115	14	40	−30	9	452
Work in progress	DGFU	−38	−177	−11	10	64	80	−59	47	−32	−29	−2	254
Finished goods	DGFV	−140	−283	60	−63	102	92	−97	27	−21	−4	14	428
Chemicals and man-made fibres:													
Materials and fuel	DHIK	4	−49	94	139	70	47	−70	−6	−3	93	67	1 797
Work in progress	DHIL	34	−28	65	20	78	11	9	28	51	−46	67	1 301
Finished goods	DHIM	115	−117	195	143	175	43	−154	46	−18	128	258	2 614
Basic metals and metal products:													
Materials and fuel	DHIH	−15	11	94	144	101	−91	−223	−52	24	152	173	1 616
Work in progress	DHII	20	−84	109	167	44	−97	−159	−62	−66	99	253	1 309
Finished goods	DHIJ	14	25	12	99	73	14	−56	−29	−13	38	165	1 238
Machinery, electrical and optical equipment, transport equipment:													
Materials and fuel	DHIN	165	−49	161	439	296	190	−307	−16	198	430	681	6 807
Work in progress	DHIO	−66	522	94	835	130	−515	−507	−760	−597	843	1 411	13 617
Finished goods	DHIP	347	189	–	546	613	398	−672	131	94	502	586	7 224
Other manufacturing:													
Materials and fuel	DHIW	−36	66	260	257	78	−39	−201	−1	−3	371	405	3 307
Work in progress	DHIX	41	42	107	84	87	25	−52	16	62	82	126	1 602
Finished goods	DHIY	128	40	197	210	315	203	13	17	−33	195	399	3 800
Total[1]	DHIZ	648	−48	1 713	3 256	2 483	859	−2 688	−135	−241	3 377	5 285	59 418
of which:													
Materials and fuel	DHJA	51	−285	623	1 015	617	213	−945	124	203	1 278	1 602	19 264
Work in progress	DHJB	72	310	497	1 087	501	−335	−691	−632	−635	1 039	1 870	19 888
Finished goods	DHJC	519	−73	593	1 153	1 364	980	−1 051	373	191	1 060	1 813	20 266
Electricity, gas and water supply	DGGD	396	62	−112	228	113	−67	11	14	−214	−619	−221	1 684
Construction	DHJD	1 268	1 250	2 030	3 304	2 757	1 298	−156	−412	29	766	885	13 397
Wholesale and retail trade; repairing etc.	DGFW	1 108	2 156	2 776	3 859	3 580	1 675	−449	1 140	3 395	3 930	3 277	50 328
Other industries	DHJG	112	−161	177	421	703	377	67	−840	82	626	−207	6 697
Central government[2]	AAAD	450	−237	−498	−322	−163	156	151	−17	−24	−251	−154	149
Total	DHHY	3 559	2 517	5 955	10 708	9 738	4 331	−2 917	−159	2 679	7 766	8 753	135 641
less **Stock appreciation**	-DJAT	−2 738	−1 835	−4 727	−6 375	−7 061	−6 131	−2 010	−1 778	−2 350	−4 034	−4 902	
Value of physical increase at current prices	DHBF	821	682	1 228	4 333	2 677	−1 800	−4 927	−1 937	329	3 732	3 851	

1 Differences between totals and the sum of constituent parts of manufacturing are due to rounding.
2 Excluding stocks of Forestry Commission, Northern Ireland forestry and the Atomic Energy Authority, which are in the appropriate industries above.

15.2 Value of the physical increase by industry at current market prices

£ million

		1985	1986	1987	1988	1989	1990	1991	1992	1993	1994	1995
Agriculture, hunting, forestry and fishing	DHFB	−242	39	−183	−137	−88	−41	−71	30	30	3	−49
Mining and quarrying	DGGW	−314	−115	−34	24	214	−103	172	74	−73	−210	−135
Manufacturing (revised definition):												
Food, beverages and tobacco:												
Materials and fuel	DHFN	14	−6	−47	−11	−32	46	−13	75	−126	−33	4
Work in progress	DHFO	−108	−4	27	−88	94	81	19	67	−93	25	−45
Finished goods	DHFP	−101	−50	−21	22	−12	19	−198	67	31	−40	145
Textiles and leather products:												
Materials and fuel	DHFQ	51	−36	75	18	−75	−30	−89	15	16	56	−27
Work in progress	DHFR	41	−27	35	−38	−30	−57	−76	−14	8	21	24
Finished goods	DHFS	40	−4	72	45	−13	2	−88	−26	29	108	109
Solid and nuclear fuel, oil refining:												
Materials and fuel	DGGG	78	115	−12	10	−54	−29	−46	−2	71	−34	−33
Work in progress	DGGR	10	−22	−20	51	41	55	−42	34	−47	−33	−8
Finished goods	DGGH	−141	−171	47	−53	39	3	−80	15	−49	−17	14
Chemicals and man-made fibres:												
Materials and fuels	DHFH	14	62	13	102	16	−53	4	−63	−5	−35	−20
Work in progress	DHFI	7	−10	10	−18	48	−26	2	−11	52	−71	38
Finished goods	DHFJ	27	−48	35	31	115	−128	−105	2	−94	−5	179
Basic metals and metal products:												
Materials and fuels	DHFE	6	5	22	−18	65	−34	−187	−88	1	−6	98
Work in progress	DHFF	25	−106	34	58	−11	−142	−158	−92	−103	−2	175
Finished goods	DHFG	11	−8	−42	−2	17	−28	−65	−57	−50	−56	85
Machinery, electrical and optical equipment, transport equipment:												
Materials and fuels	DHFK	80	−144	−81	92	68	−51	−387	−134	53	209	441
Work in progress	DHFL	−629	15	−413	191	−532	−1 362	−1 070	−1 246	−958	596	942
Finished goods	DHFM	94	−43	−271	245	267	−29	−838	17	−134	356	364
Other manufacturing:												
Materials and fuel	DHFT	−24	−10	104	136	−37	−119	−149	−39	−30	119	145
Work in progress	DHFU	−4	−7	44	23	22	−59	−109	−13	34	30	32
Finished goods	DHFV	16	−59	52	81	170	26	−92	−52	−118	58	183
Total[1]	DHBA	−493	−555	−335	873	164	−1 913	−3 769	−1 544	−1 510	1 244	2 843
of which:												
Materials and fuel	DHCO	217	−11	77	327	−46	−266	−870	−235	−19	275	607
Work in progress	DHDE	−657	−159	−284	177	−368	−1 511	−1 434	−1 275	−1 107	565	1 156
Finished goods	DHCT	−55	−384	−126	368	581	−136	−1 467	−34	−388	404	1 080
Electricity, gas and water supply	DGGE	373	−28	−93	37	113	−129	177	−136	−253	−533	−255
Construction	DHFX	441	287	593	1 003	328	263	−69	−821	−227	664	239
Wholesale and retail trade; repairing etc.	DGGX	281	1 272	1 721	2 545	1 723	−420	−1 759	446	2 244	2 562	1 562
Other industries	DHGA	325	19	57	310	386	388	241	35	143	254	−196
Central government[2]	AAAD	450	−237	−498	−322	−163	156	151	−17	−24	−251	−154
Total	DHBF	821	682	1 228	4 333	2 677	−1 800	−4 927	−1 937	329	3 732	3 851

1 Differences between totals and the sum of constituent parts of manufacturing are due to rounding.
2 Excluding stocks of Forestry Commission, Northern Ireland forestry and the Atomic Energy Authority, which are in the appropriate industries above.

Stocks and work in progress

15.3 Value of the physical increase by industry at 1990 market prices[1]

£ million at 1990 prices

		1985	1986	1987	1988	1989	1990	1991	1992	1993	1994	1995	Value of stocks held at end of 1995
Agriculture, hunting, forestry and fishing	DHJJ	−266	48	−206	−143	−86	−41	−71	51	27	17	−46	**3 543**
Mining and quarrying	DGGV	−174	−95	12	17	215	−103	170	66	−45	−231	−168	437
Manufacturing (revised definition):													
Food, beverages and tobacco:													
Materials and fuel	DHJV	3	−7	−51	−14	−33	46	−14	69	−103	−41	−8	3 395
Work in progress	DHJW	−40	−4	29	−87	106	81	21	64	−70	25	−30	879
Finished goods	DHJX	−121	−62	−22	26	−17	19	−181	58	34	−33	114	2 594
Textiles and leather products:													
Materials and fuel	DHJY	54	−40	80	13	−73	−30	−88	15	16	56	−21	985
Work in progress	DHJZ	32	−31	41	−39	−30	−57	−71	−13	9	18	21	623
Finished goods	DHKA	46	−3	86	51	−13	2	−82	−22	26	96	94	1 469
Solid and nuclear fuel, oil refining:													
Materials and fuel	DGGI	34	87	−15	13	−57	−29	−46	9	74	−35	−39	464
Work in progress	DGGJ	28	−33	−21	58	47	55	−45	33	−44	−38	−8	293
Finished goods	DGGK	−130	−174	45	−62	44	3	−79	10	−41	−19	17	506
Chemicals and man-made fibres:													
Materials and fuels	DHJP	14	68	18	108	19	−53	−	−64	−5	−31	−18	1 573
Work in progress	DHJQ	8	−11	12	−21	50	−26	2	−10	45	−63	32	1 127
Finished goods	DHJR	21	−59	39	31	120	−128	−99	−	−96	−14	160	2 249
Basic metals and metal products:													
Materials and fuel	DHJM	2	9	22	−20	60	−34	−193	−90	2	−11	82	1 394
Work in progress	DHJN	33	−130	42	70	−11	−142	−156	−90	−99	−1	149	1 098
Finished goods	DHJO	−5	−9	−51	1	20	−28	−60	−58	−47	−58	73	1 024
Machinery, electrical and optical equipment, transport equipment:													
Materials and fuel	DHJS	96	−175	−93	106	72	−51	−375	−114	64	217	394	6 016
Work in progress	DHJT	−847	17	−495	243	−554	−1 362	−1 008	−1 100	−853	535	816	11 373
Finished goods	DHJU	137	−45	−371	261	286	−29	−757	9	−84	298	343	6 222
Other manufacturing:													
Materials and fuel	DHKB	−29	−7	115	142	−37	−119	−147	−38	−26	119	132	2 770
Work in progress	DHKC	−9	−8	52	24	23	−59	−101	−9	32	28	29	1 316
Finished goods	DHKD	10	−67	54	86	180	26	−87	−43	−112	49	164	3 122
Total[2]	DHBH	−612	−686	−486	991	199	−1 913	−3 565	−1 382	−1 281	1 102	2 499	50 495
of which:													
Materials and fuel	DHCU	172	−66	74	349	−51	−266	−861	−211	20	277	523	16 598
Work in progress	DHCW	−796	−199	−342	249	−370	−1 511	−1 358	−1 124	−981	504	1 012	16 710
Finished goods	DHCX	−45	−420	−221	393	620	−136	−1 346	−47	−320	321	964	17 187
Electricity, gas and water supply	DGGF	321	195	−132	104	−62	−129	200	−100	−270	−584	−296	1 742
Construction	DHKF	589	385	803	1 208	347	263	−61	−868	−138	382	188	11 048
Wholesale and retail trade; repairing etc.	DGGQ	340	1 532	1 980	2 734	1 841	−420	−1 687	444	2 064	2 255	1 363	42 370
Other industries	DHKI	320	73	122	393	401	387	246	87	1	233	−132	5 242
Central government[3]	DGAG	288	−253	−441	−210	−151	156	136	3	−48	−256	−150	859
Total	DHBK	990	1 199	1 652	5 094	2 704	−1 800	−4 631	−1 699	312	2 917	3 258	115 735

1 For the years before 1986, totals differ from the sum of their components.
2 Differences between totals and the sum of constituent parts of manufacturing are due to rounding.
3 Excluding stocks of Forestry Commission, Northern Ireland forestry and the Atomic Energy Authority, which are in the appropriate industries above.

15.4 Changes in stocks and work in progress by sector[1]

£ million

		1985	1986	1987	1988	1989	1990	1991	1992	1993	1994	1995
Value of physical increase in stocks and work in progress												
Personal sector[2]	DHHJ	−45	347	293	537	304	−24	−449	−22	447	632	368
Industrial and commercial companies	FMBN	420	1 057	1 673	4 094	2 317	−1 678	−4 687	−1 912	72	3 663	3 819
Financial companies and institutions	AAAP	–	–	–	–	–	–	–	–	–	–	–
Public corporations	DHHL	−4	−485	−240	24	219	−254	58	14	−166	−312	−182
Central government:												
Trading bodies	DHHN	443	−237	−498	−322	−163	156	151	−17	−24	−251	−154
Emergency and strategic stocks	DHHO	7	–	–	–	–	–	–	–	–	–	–
Total	AAAD	450	−237	−498	−322	−163	156	151	−17	−24	−251	−154
Total	DHBF	821	682	1 228	4 333	2 677	−1 800	−4 927	−1 937	329	3 732	3 851
Stock appreciation												
Personal sector[2]	DDAD	475	172	491	750	803	695	394	39	13	376	420
Industrial and commercial companies	AIAC	2 155	1 500	4 148	5 366	6 203	5 316	1 586	1 700	2 373	3 650	4 451
Public corporations	ADRC	108	163	88	259	55	120	30	39	−36	8	31
Total	DJAT	2 738	1 835	4 727	6 375	7 061	6 131	2 010	1 778	2 350	4 034	4 902
Increase in book value of stocks and work in progress												
Personal sector[2]	AAAX	430	519	784	1 287	1 107	671	−55	17	460	1 008	788
Industrial and commercial companies	AAAT	2 575	2 557	5 821	9 460	8 520	3 638	−3 101	−212	2 445	7 313	8 270
Financial companies and institutions	AAAP	–	–	–	–	–	–	–	–	–	–	–
Public corporations	AAAL	104	−322	−152	283	274	−134	88	53	−202	−304	−151
Central government:												
Trading bodies	DHHN	443	−237	−498	−322	−163	156	151	−17	−24	−251	−154
Emergency and strategic stocks	DHHO	7	–	–	–	–	–	–	–	–	–	–
Total	AAAD	450	−237	−498	−322	−163	156	151	−17	−24	−251	−154
Total	DHHY	3 559	2 517	5 955	10 708	9 738	4 331	−2 917	−159	2 679	7 766	8 753

1 The book value of stocks and work in progress held at the end of 1995 by each
of the sectors was as follows:

	£ million
Personal sector	14254
Companies and financial institutions	119691
Public corporations	1547
Central government	149

2 Stocks held for business purposes by professional persons, farmers and other
sole traders and partnerships.

Other analyses and derived statistics

5

Section 5 : Other analyses and derived statistics

Section 5 supports the first 4 sections by providing additional analyses, derived and complementary statistics. In more detail;

Tables 16.1 to 16.7 show the percentage distributions of each of the 3 measure of GDP, together with personal income and its disposal and other key aggregates.

Tables 16.8 to 16.13 detail growth rates for GDP, output per person employed, personal disposable income and personal disposable income per capita. These tables show up to 40 years of data.

Table 17.1 analyses population and employment.

Table 17.2 shows index numbers of production analysed by type of market.

CHAPTER 16: Percentage distributions and growth rates

16.1 Composition of total expenditure[1]

Percentage

	Average 1974-1984	1985	1986	1987	1988	1989	1990	1991	1992	1993	1994	1995
TOTAL DOMESTIC EXPENDITURE:												
By type of expenditure												
Consumers' expenditure	60.5	61.4	62.2	61.9	61.2	60.9	61.4	62.8	63.2	63.6	63.4	63.4
General government final consumption	21.3	21.2	20.8	20.3	19.2	18.9	19.9	21.3	21.7	21.6	21.4	21.2
Gross domestic fixed capital formation	18.0	17.1	16.8	17.5	18.7	19.6	19.0	16.8	15.4	14.8	14.7	14.9
VPI stocks[2]	0.2	0.2	0.2	0.3	0.9	0.5	−0.3	−0.8	−0.3	0.1	0.6	0.5
Total domestic expenditure	100.0	100.0	100.0	100.0	100.0	100.0	100.0	100.0	100.0	100.0	100.0	100.0
TOTAL FINAL EXPENDITURE:												
By type of expenditure												
Consumers' expenditure	47.6	47.7	49.7	49.6	50.2	49.7	49.7	51.0	51.2	50.9	50.2	49.5
General government final consumption	16.8	16.5	16.6	16.3	15.7	15.5	16.1	17.3	17.6	17.3	16.9	16.5
Gross domestic fixed capital formation	14.1	13.3	13.4	14.0	15.4	16.0	15.4	13.6	12.5	11.8	11.7	11.7
VPI stocks[2]	0.2	0.2	0.1	0.2	0.7	0.4	−0.3	−0.7	−0.3	–	0.4	0.4
Total domestic expenditure	78.7	77.6	79.9	80.1	82.0	81.6	81.0	81.3	81.0	80.0	79.3	78.1
Exports of goods and services	21.3	22.4	20.1	19.9	18.0	18.4	19.0	18.7	19.0	20.0	20.7	21.9
Total final expenditure	100.0	100.0	100.0	100.0	100.0	100.0	100.0	100.0	100.0	100.0	100.0	100.0
By sector and type of expenditure												
Private sector:												
Consumers' expenditure	47.6	47.7	49.7	49.6	50.2	49.7	49.7	51.0	51.2	50.9	50.2	49.5
Gross domestic fixed capital formation	9.5	10.5	10.7	11.8	13.5	13.7	12.9	11.4	10.2	9.7	9.6	9.7
VPI stocks[2]	0.1	0.1	0.3	0.4	0.8	0.4	−0.2	−0.7	−0.3	0.1	0.5	0.5
Total	57.1	58.2	60.7	61.7	64.5	63.8	62.3	61.7	61.1	60.6	60.4	59.7
Public corporations:												
Gross domestic fixed capital formation	2.4	1.3	1.1	0.9	0.8	0.8	0.7	0.5	0.6	0.6	0.6	0.6
VPI stocks[2]	0.1	–	−0.1	–	–	–	–	–	–	–	–	–
Total	2.4	1.3	1.0	0.8	0.8	0.9	0.7	0.5	0.6	0.6	0.5	0.5
General government:												
Final consumption	16.8	16.5	16.6	16.3	15.7	15.5	16.1	17.3	17.6	17.3	16.9	16.5
Gross domestic fixed capital formation	2.3	1.5	1.5	1.4	1.1	1.5	1.8	1.7	1.7	1.5	1.4	1.4
VPI stocks[2]	–	0.1	–	−0.1	−0.1	–	–	–	–	–	–	–
Total	19.1	18.1	18.1	17.6	16.7	16.9	18.0	19.0	19.3	18.8	18.4	17.9
Overseas sector:												
Exports of goods and services	21.3	22.4	20.1	19.9	18.0	18.4	19.0	18.7	19.0	20.0	20.7	21.9
Total final expenditure	100.0	100.0	100.0	100.0	100.0	100.0	100.0	100.0	100.0	100.0	100.0	100.0

1 Based on tables 1.2, 13.1 and 15.4.
2 Value of physical increase in stocks and work in progress.

16.2 Cost composition of total final output[1]

Percentage

	Average 1974-1984	1985	1986	1987	1988	1989	1990	1991	1992	1993	1994	1995
Income from self-employment[2]	6.2	6.6	7.2	7.3	7.6	7.9	8.3	7.9	7.6	7.6	7.5	7.4
Gross trading profits of industrial and commercial companies[2]	9.1	12.6	11.1	11.6	11.7	11.3	10.8	10.4	10.0	10.4	11.2	11.0
Gross trading profits of financial companies and institutions[2,3]	−1.5	−1.9	−1.7	−1.3	−1.8	−2.1	−2.1	−2.3	−1.9	−1.4	−1.4	−1.5
Gross trading surplus of public corporations[2]	2.3	1.6	1.7	1.3	1.2	1.0	0.5	0.2	0.3	0.4	0.5	0.5
Gross trading surplus of general government enterprises[2]	0.1	0.1	–	–	–	–	–	–	–	–	0.1	0.1
Rent	4.8	4.8	4.9	4.9	5.0	5.1	5.5	6.3	7.0	6.9	6.9	6.9
Non-trading capital consumption	0.7	0.6	0.6	0.6	0.6	0.6	0.6	0.6	0.6	0.5	0.5	0.5
Gross profits and other trading income[2]	21.7	24.3	23.8	24.4	24.3	23.9	23.6	23.1	23.5	24.6	25.2	25.1
Income from employment	46.4	43.1	43.7	43.0	43.0	43.2	44.9	46.2	45.7	44.0	42.9	41.8
Imports of goods and services	21.2	21.7	20.8	20.9	20.9	21.7	21.2	19.7	20.1	21.0	21.4	22.5
Taxes on expenditure *less* subsidies	9.6	10.8	11.6	11.7	11.7	11.3	10.3	11.1	10.8	10.4	10.5	10.7
Residual error	1.0	–	–	–	–	–	–	–	–	–	–	−0.1
Total final output[4]	100.0	100.0	100.0	100.0	100.0	100.0	100.0	100.0	100.0	100.0	100.0	100.0

1 Based on tables 1.4, 1.5, 5.4 and 5.7.
2 Before providing for depreciation but after providing for stock appreciation.
3 The gross trading profits of financial companies and institutions comprise the difference between bank charges, commissions etc. on the one hand and management expenses on the other.
4 The value, at market prices, of home produced and imported goods and services available for private and public consumption, investment and export.

16.3 Shares in total domestic income, in domestic product and in gross national product at market prices[1,2]

Percentage

	Average 1974-1984	1985	1986	1987	1988	1989	1990	1991	1992	1993	1994	1995
FACTOR INCOMES												
Before providing for stock appreciation												
Income from self-employment	9.2	9.8	10.6	10.8	11.2	11.7	12.1	11.4	11.0	11.0	11.0	11.1
Gross trading profits of industrial and commercial companies	15.9	19.2	16.8	18.1	18.4	18.0	16.6	15.2	14.7	15.6	16.9	17.1
Gross trading profits of financial companies[3]	−2.1	−2.7	−2.5	−1.9	−2.6	−3.0	−3.1	−3.3	−2.8	−2.0	−2.1	−2.2
Gross trading surplus of public corporations	3.5	2.3	2.5	1.9	1.9	1.5	0.8	0.4	0.5	0.6	0.7	0.8
Gross trading surplus of general government enterprises	0.1	0.1	–	–	–	–	–	–	–	–	0.1	0.1
Rent	6.8	7.0	7.2	7.2	7.3	7.5	8.0	9.1	10.0	10.1	10.1	10.3
Non-trading capital consumption	1.0	0.9	0.9	0.9	0.9	0.9	0.9	0.9	0.8	0.8	0.8	0.8
Gross profits and other trading income	34.4	36.6	35.7	37.0	37.1	36.6	35.3	33.6	34.2	36.1	37.4	38.0
Income from employment	65.6	63.4	64.3	63.0	62.9	63.4	64.7	66.4	65.8	63.9	62.6	62.0
Total domestic income at factor cost	100.0	100.0	100.0	100.0	100.0	100.0	100.0	100.0	100.0	100.0	100.0	100.0
After providing for stock appreciation												
Income from self-employment	9.1	9.7	10.6	10.8	11.2	11.7	12.1	11.4	11.0	11.0	11.0	11.1
Gross trading profits of industrial and commercial companies	13.2	18.7	16.4	17.2	17.3	16.9	15.7	15.0	14.4	15.2	16.4	16.5
Gross trading profits of financial companies[3]	−2.1	−2.8	−2.5	−1.9	−2.6	−3.1	−3.1	−3.3	−2.8	−2.0	−2.1	−2.2
Gross trading surplus of public corporations	3.3	2.3	2.5	1.9	1.8	1.5	0.8	0.4	0.4	0.6	0.7	0.8
Gross trading surplus of general government enterprises	0.1	0.1	–	–	–	–	–	–	–	–	0.1	0.1
Rent	7.0	7.1	7.3	7.3	7.4	7.7	8.1	9.1	10.1	10.1	10.1	10.4
Non-trading capital consumption	1.0	0.9	0.9	0.9	0.9	0.9	0.9	0.9	0.8	0.8	0.8	0.8
Gross profits and other trading income	31.6	36.1	35.3	36.2	36.1	35.6	34.5	33.3	34.0	35.8	37.0	37.5
Income from employment	67.6	63.9	64.7	63.8	63.9	64.4	65.5	66.7	66.0	64.2	63.0	62.5
Statistical discrepancy (income adjustment)	0.8	–	–	–	–	–	–	–	–	–	–	–
Gross domestic product at factor cost	100.0	100.0	100.0	100.0	100.0	100.0	100.0	100.0	100.0	100.0	100.0	100.0
After providing for stock appreciation and capital consumption												
Income from self-employment	9.5	10.3	11.4	11.5	12.1	12.6	13.0	12.2	11.7	11.7	11.7	11.9
Net trading profits and rent of industrial and commercial companies	9.5	15.0	12.4	13.3	13.9	13.4	12.0	11.0	10.6	11.6	13.0	12.8
Net trading profits and rent of financial companies[3]	−2.8	−3.6	−3.3	−2.6	−3.5	−4.0	−4.0	−4.2	−3.5	−2.6	−2.7	−2.8
Net trading surplus and rent of public corporations	0.7	0.5	0.7	0.6	0.6	0.3	−0.2	−0.4	−0.2	0.1	0.2	0.2
Net trading surplus and rent of general government	1.1	0.6	0.5	0.4	0.3	0.3	0.3	0.4	0.4	0.5	0.5	0.5
Rent income of personal sector	3.2	3.2	3.2	3.1	3.1	3.5	3.8	4.7	5.8	5.8	5.9	6.3
Net profits and other trading income	22.1	26.0	25.0	26.3	26.4	26.1	24.9	23.6	24.9	27.1	28.6	28.9
Wages and salaries[4]	67.5	64.0	65.2	64.2	64.4	64.9	66.2	67.2	66.0	63.9	62.4	62.4
Employers' contributions[5]	10.4	10.0	9.8	9.4	9.1	8.9	8.9	9.3	9.0	9.0	9.1	8.7
Income from employment[6]	77.9	74.0	75.0	73.7	73.6	73.9	75.1	76.4	75.1	72.9	71.4	71.1
Net domestic product at factor cost	100.0	100.0	100.0	100.0	100.0	100.0	100.0	100.0	100.0	100.0	100.0	100.0
INCOME AFTER CURRENT TRANSFERS, TAXES ON INCOME, SOCIAL SECURITY CONTRIBUTIONS AND COMMUNITY CHARGE/COUNCIL TAX												
Personal sector:												
Disposable income	68.0	67.7	67.8	66.9	66.9	67.7	68.4	70.6	72.3	72.3	70.2	70.7
Companies' undistributed income:												
Industrial and commercial companies[7]	9.6	9.9	9.0	10.3	10.0	8.4	7.3	6.8	6.9	8.7	9.9	8.7
Financial companies[3,7]	1.3	0.5	1.3	1.6	1.0	1.2	1.3	0.6	1.4	1.3	2.2	2.0
Public corporations:												
Undistributed income[7]	2.0	1.5	1.5	1.2	1.2	1.0	0.5	0.2	0.3	0.4	0.4	0.4
General government:												
Taxes on income, social security contributions and community charge/council tax	20.5	21.1	20.1	19.5	19.4	20.0	21.7	20.8	19.7	19.1	19.4	20.3
Taxes on expenditure less subsidies	12.2	13.7	14.5	14.7	14.7	14.3	13.1	13.8	13.4	13.1	13.2	13.6
Other income less current transfers[7]	−11.5	−14.4	−14.4	−13.8	−12.6	−12.0	−12.2	−12.6	−14.6	−15.4	−15.4	−15.9
Total	21.1	20.4	20.2	20.4	21.5	22.3	22.6	21.9	18.5	16.8	17.1	17.9
Current transfers paid abroad (net)	0.7	0.9	0.6	0.8	0.7	0.9	0.9	0.2	0.8	0.8	0.7	1.0
less Stock appreciation	−3.4	−0.8	−0.5	−1.1	−1.3	−1.4	−1.1	−0.3	−0.3	−0.4	−0.6	−0.7
Statistical discrepancy (income adjustment)	0.7	–	–	–	–	–	–	–	–	–	–	–
Gross national product at market prices	100.0	100.0	100.0	100.0	100.0	100.0	100.0	100.0	100.0	100.0	100.0	100.0

1 Based on tables 1.4, 2.6, 3.1, 3.3, 4.4, 5.4, 5.6, 5.7, 5.8, 6.2 and 14.3
2 Net domestic product is *equal* to Gross domestic product *less* Capital consumption at current replacement cost.
3 Including financial institutions. See also footnote 3 to table 16.2.
4 Including forces pay.
5 Employers' contributions to national insurance etc. and pension funds.
6 Expenditure on motor vehicles and consumer durables by households is treated as current rather than capital expenditure in the national accounts and no allowance is made for depreciation of these items.
7 Before providing for depreciation and stock appreciation.

16.4 Value added analysed by industry[1,2]

Percentage

	1985	1986	1987	1988	1989	1990	1991	1992	1993	1994	1995
Agriculture, hunting, forestry and fishing	2.0	2.0	2.0	1.8	1.9	1.9	1.8	1.9	1.8	1.8	2.0
Mining of coal and nuclear fuel	1.2	0.9	0.7	0.7	0.6	0.5	0.5	0.5	0.3	0.2	0.2
Extraction of mineral oil and natural gas	6.0	2.9	2.9	1.9	1.7	1.7	1.5	1.5	1.7	2.0	2.1
Other mining and quarrying[3]	0.3	0.3	0.3	0.3	0.3	0.2	0.2	0.2	0.2	0.2	0.2
Manufacturing (revised definition)	24.6	24.8	24.6	24.6	24.3	23.2	21.5	21.2	21.1	21.5	21.8
Electricity, gas and water supply	2.7	2.9	2.7	2.6	2.4	2.2	2.7	2.6	2.7	2.6	2.6
Construction	6.0	6.1	6.4	7.0	7.4	7.2	6.3	5.8	5.3	5.2	5.3
Wholesale and retail trade; repairs; hotels and restaurants	13.2	13.9	13.7	14.0	14.1	14.3	14.5	14.3	14.4	14.2	14.0
Transport, storage and communication	7.9	8.3	8.3	8.5	8.4	8.4	8.5	8.4	8.5	8.5	8.4
Financial intermediation, real estate, renting and business activities	20.1	21.8	22.1	22.5	23.5	24.2	24.0	25.1	25.4	26.3	26.2
Public administration, national defence and compulsory social security	7.0	6.9	6.8	6.5	6.3	6.6	6.9	7.1	7.0	6.6	6.5
Education, health and social work	9.2	9.6	9.6	9.9	10.6	10.8	11.8	12.2	12.1	12.2	12.1
Other services[4]	3.8	4.1	4.0	4.0	3.6	3.7	3.7	3.7	3.7	3.8	3.8
Adjustment for financial services[5]	−3.9	−4.4	−4.2	−4.2	−5.0	−4.9	−4.0	−4.5	−4.3	−5.0	−5.1
Statistical discrepancy (income adjustment)	–	–	–	–	–	–	–	–	–	–	–
Gross domestic product at factor cost	100.0	100.0	100.0	100.0	100.0	100.0	100.0	100.0	100.0	100.0	100.0

1 Based on tables 2.2 and 2.3.
2 Before providing for depreciation but after deducting stock appreciation.
3 Comprising sub-sections CA10, CA12 and sections CB of the SIC (92)
4 Comprising sections O, P and Q of the SIC (92)
5 The contribution of the Financial intermediation, real estate, etc. industries is measured before deducting these industries' net receipts of interest. This is offset in the aggregate gross domestic product by the item "Adjustment for financial services" *equal* to the net interest receipts.

16.5 Composition of total personal income and its disposal[1]

Percentage

	Average 1974-1984	1985	1986	1987	1988	1989	1990	1991	1992	1993	1994	1995
INCOME BEFORE TAX												
Wages and salaries[2]	58.9	55.5	55.4	55.9	56.2	56.6	57.0	56.3	54.9	53.9	53.4	52.4
Employers' contributions[3]	9.0	8.6	8.3	8.2	8.0	7.8	7.7	7.8	7.5	7.6	7.8	7.3
Income from self-employment[4]	9.6	9.9	10.5	11.0	11.5	11.9	12.1	11.0	10.4	10.6	10.7	10.7
Rent, dividends and net interest, etc.[5]	9.7	10.6	10.3	10.3	10.9	11.0	10.7	11.2	12.2	12.1	12.2	14.0
Current transfers from overseas	0.5	0.6	0.5	0.5	0.4	0.4	0.4	0.4	0.4	0.4	0.4	0.4
Social Security benefits and other current grants from general government	12.3	14.8	14.8	14.1	13.0	12.2	12.1	13.4	14.6	15.4	15.5	15.2
Total personal income[4]	100.0	100.0	100.0	100.0	100.0	100.0	100.0	100.0	100.0	100.0	100.0	100.0
United Kingdom taxes on income	13.6	12.3	12.3	12.1	12.1	12.1	12.7	12.3	11.9	11.1	11.4	11.8
Social security contributions	7.3	7.9	7.9	7.7	7.7	7.6	7.1	7.0	6.7	6.9	7.0	7.0
Community charge/council tax	–	–	–	–	–	0.1	1.8	1.6	1.4	1.4	1.4	1.4
Other current transfers[6]	0.6	0.5	0.6	0.6	0.6	0.6	0.5	0.5	0.5	0.5	0.5	0.5
Personal disposable income[7]	78.5	79.3	79.3	79.6	79.7	79.6	77.9	78.6	79.4	80.1	79.7	79.3
Total personal income[4]	100.0	100.0	100.0	100.0	100.0	100.0	100.0	100.0	100.0	100.0	100.0	100.0
Consumers' expenditure	88.8	89.3	91.4	92.8	94.0	93.1	91.9	90.0	88.1	88.7	89.9	89.0
Saving	11.2	10.7	8.6	7.2	6.0	6.9	8.1	10.0	11.9	11.3	10.1	11.0
Personal disposable income[7]	100.0	100.0	100.0	100.0	100.0	100.0	100.0	100.0	100.0	100.0	100.0	100.0

1 Based on table 4.1.
2 Including forces' pay.
3 Employers' contributions to social security and pension funds.
4 Before providing for depreciation and stock appreciation.
5 Including current transfers from companies, and the imputed charge for capital consumption of private non-profit-making bodies.
6 Including current transfers to overseas and other miscellaneous current transfers.
7 Before providing for depreciation, stock appreciation and additions to tax reserves.
8 Differences between totals and sums of components are due to rounding.

175

Percentage distributions and growth rates

16.6 Annual increases in categories of expenditure at 1990 prices[1]

Percentage increase over previous year

	1985	1986	1987	1988	1989	1990	1991	1992	1993	1994	1995
Consumers' expenditure	3.8	6.8	5.3	7.5	3.2	0.6	−2.2	−0.1	2.5	2.6	2.0
General government final consumption:											
Central government	0.1	1.6	−0.2	0.7	1.8	1.8	2.4	0.3	3.4	2.0	0.6
Local authorities	−0.4	1.8	3.0	0.7	0.7	3.7	2.8	−0.8	−4.9	1.7	2.5
Total	−0.1	1.6	1.0	0.7	1.4	2.5	2.6	−0.1	0.2	1.9	1.3
Gross domestic fixed capital formation:											
Private sector	9.8	3.1	15.0	18.4	3.5	−6.0	−10.1	−4.5	0.1	3.2	1.7
Public corporations	−23.7	−8.7	−21.4	−2.2	11.1	−12.6	−22.0	28.4	6.2	−2.4	−6.2
General government	0.4	8.6	−1.5	−16.0	32.7	25.9	−0.1	9.0	1.9	3.3	−7.7
Total	4.2	2.6	10.3	13.9	6.0	−3.5	−9.5	−1.5	0.6	2.9	−0.1
Exports of goods and services	6.0	4.5	5.8	0.5	4.7	5.0	−0.7	4.1	3.5	9.2	7.2
Total final expenditure at market prices[2]	3.6	4.8	5.4	6.5	3.2	0.4	−2.6	0.9	2.3	4.2	2.7
Imports of goods and services	2.6	6.9	7.8	12.6	7.4	0.5	−5.2	6.6	3.0	5.4	3.9
Adjustment to factor cost	2.1	6.0	6.1	5.4	1.7	−0.7	−1.2	−0.6	1.2	2.9	2.2
Gross domestic product at factor cost	4.0	4.0	4.6	4.9	2.3	0.6	−2.1	−0.5	2.3	4.0	2.5

1 Based on tables 1.3 and 13.2.
2 Including value of physical increase in stocks and work in progress.

16.7 Some aggregates related to the gross national product at factor cost[1]

Percentage of GNP at factor cost

	Average 1974-1984	1985	1986	1987	1988	1989	1990	1991	1992	1993	1994	1995
Taxes on income	16.1	16.6	15.6	15.3	15.2	15.7	16.0	15.1	14.1	13.3	13.7	14.8
Taxes on expenditure[2]	16.8	18.3	18.9	18.9	18.7	18.0	16.3	17.2	16.8	16.4	16.4	16.9
Taxes on capital	0.7	0.7	0.9	0.8	1.0	1.0	0.9	0.7	0.5	0.4	0.4	0.4
Total taxes	33.6	35.6	35.4	35.0	35.0	34.7	33.2	33.0	31.4	30.2	30.5	32.1
Social security contributions[3]	7.2	7.8	7.9	7.6	7.6	7.5	7.2	7.3	7.1	7.2	7.1	7.2
Community charge/council tax	–	–	–	–	–	0.1	1.8	1.6	1.5	1.5	1.4	1.5
Subsidies	2.9	2.3	1.9	1.7	1.5	1.3	1.3	1.2	1.3	1.3	1.2	1.1
Total investment at home and abroad	20.9	20.6	19.5	19.6	19.6	19.3	18.1	17.1	15.6	15.2	17.1	17.3

1 Based on tables 1.2, 3.5 and 9.6.
2 Including local authority rates and National Insurance surcharge.
3 Including both employers' and employees' contributions.

16.8 Rates of change of gross domestic product at current market prices ("money GDP")[1]

Initial year	Terminal year																				
	1954	1955	1956	1957	1958	1959	1960	1961	1962	1963	1964	1965	1966	1967	1968	1969	1970	1971	1972	1973	1974
1953	5.8	6.9	7.1	6.7	6.2	6.2	6.3	6.2	6.1	6.1	6.4	6.5	6.5	6.4	6.6	6.6	6.8	7.1	7.3	7.7	7.9
1954		7.9	7.7	7.0	6.3	6.2	6.4	6.3	6.1	6.1	6.5	6.6	6.6	6.5	6.6	6.7	6.9	7.1	7.4	7.8	8.0
1955			7.6	6.6	5.8	5.8	6.0	6.0	5.9	5.9	6.3	6.4	6.4	6.3	6.5	6.6	6.8	7.1	7.4	7.8	8.0
1956				5.6	4.9	5.3	5.7	5.7	5.6	5.7	6.1	6.3	6.3	6.2	6.4	6.5	6.7	7.1	7.4	7.8	8.1
1957					4.3	5.1	5.7	5.8	5.6	5.7	6.2	6.4	6.4	6.3	6.5	6.6	6.8	7.2	7.5	7.9	8.2
1958						6.0	6.4	6.3	6.0	6.0	6.5	6.7	6.7	6.5	6.7	6.8	7.1	7.4	7.7	8.2	8.5
1959							6.9	6.4	6.0	6.0	6.7	6.9	6.8	6.6	6.8	6.9	7.2	7.5	7.8	8.3	8.6
1960								6.0	5.5	5.7	6.6	6.8	6.8	6.6	6.8	6.9	7.2	7.6	7.9	8.4	8.8
1961									5.0	5.6	6.8	7.1	6.9	6.7	6.9	7.0	7.3	7.7	8.1	8.7	9.0
1962										6.2	7.7	7.7	7.4	7.0	7.2	7.3	7.6	8.0	8.4	9.0	9.3
1963											9.3	8.5	7.9	7.2	7.4	7.5	7.8	8.3	8.7	9.3	9.6
1964												7.8	7.1	6.5	7.0	7.1	7.6	8.1	8.6	9.3	9.6
1965													6.5	5.9	6.7	7.0	7.5	8.2	8.7	9.5	9.8
1966														5.3	6.9	7.1	7.8	8.5	9.1	9.9	10.3
1967															8.4	8.0	8.6	9.3	9.9	10.7	11.0
1968																7.6	8.7	9.6	10.2	11.1	11.4
1969																	9.8	10.7	11.1	12.0	12.2
1970																		11.5	11.8	12.8	12.8
1971																			12.0	13.4	13.2
1972																				14.8	13.9
1973																					12.9

Initial year	Terminal year																				
	1975	1976	1977	1978	1979	1980	1981	1982	1983	1984	1985	1986	1987	1988	1989	1990	1991	1992	1993	1994	1995
1953	8.7	9.1	9.4	9.6	9.9	10.2	10.2	10.2	10.1	10.0	10.0	9.9	9.9	10.0	10.0	9.9	9.7	9.6	9.5	9.4	9.3
1954	8.8	9.2	9.6	9.8	10.1	10.4	10.3	10.3	10.3	10.2	10.1	10.1	10.1	10.1	10.1	10.0	9.8	9.7	9.6	9.5	9.4
1955	8.9	9.3	9.6	9.9	10.2	10.5	10.4	10.4	10.4	10.2	10.2	10.1	10.1	10.2	10.1	10.0	9.9	9.7	9.6	9.5	9.4
1956	9.0	9.4	9.7	10.0	10.3	10.6	10.6	10.5	10.5	10.3	10.3	10.2	10.2	10.2	10.2	10.1	10.0	9.8	9.7	9.6	9.4
1957	9.1	9.6	9.9	10.2	10.5	10.8	10.8	10.7	10.6	10.5	10.5	10.4	10.4	10.4	10.4	10.3	10.1	9.9	9.8	9.7	9.5
1958	9.4	9.9	10.3	10.5	10.8	11.1	11.1	11.0	10.9	10.8	10.7	10.6	10.6	10.6	10.6	10.5	10.3	10.1	9.9	9.8	9.7
1959	9.7	10.1	10.5	10.8	11.1	11.4	11.3	11.2	11.1	11.0	10.9	10.8	10.8	10.8	10.7	10.6	10.4	10.2	10.1	9.9	9.8
1960	9.8	10.4	10.7	11.0	11.3	11.6	11.5	11.4	11.3	11.1	11.1	10.9	10.9	10.9	10.9	10.7	10.5	10.3	10.2	10.0	9.9
1961	10.1	10.7	11.0	11.3	11.6	11.9	11.8	11.7	11.6	11.4	11.3	11.1	11.1	11.1	11.0	10.9	10.7	10.5	10.3	10.2	10.0
1962	10.5	11.1	11.4	11.7	12.0	12.3	12.2	12.0	11.9	11.7	11.6	11.4	11.3	11.3	11.3	11.1	10.9	10.6	10.5	10.3	10.2
1963	10.9	11.5	11.8	12.0	12.4	12.7	12.5	12.3	12.2	11.9	11.8	11.6	11.6	11.6	11.5	11.3	11.1	10.8	10.6	10.5	10.3
1964	11.0	11.6	12.0	12.2	12.6	12.9	12.7	12.5	12.3	12.1	11.9	11.7	11.7	11.7	11.6	11.4	11.1	10.9	10.7	10.5	10.3
1965	11.4	12.0	12.4	12.6	13.0	13.2	13.0	12.8	12.6	12.3	12.2	11.9	11.9	11.8	11.7	11.5	11.2	11.0	10.8	10.6	10.4
1966	11.9	12.6	12.9	13.1	13.5	13.7	13.5	13.2	13.0	12.6	12.5	12.2	12.1	12.1	12.0	11.7	11.4	11.1	10.9	10.7	10.5
1967	12.8	13.4	13.7	13.9	14.2	14.4	14.1	13.8	13.5	13.1	12.9	12.6	12.5	12.4	12.3	12.0	11.7	11.4	11.2	11.0	10.7
1968	13.4	14.0	14.3	14.4	14.7	14.9	14.5	14.1	13.8	13.4	13.1	12.8	12.7	12.6	12.5	12.2	11.8	11.5	11.3	11.0	10.8
1969	14.4	15.0	15.2	15.2	15.4	15.6	15.1	14.7	14.3	13.8	13.5	13.1	13.0	12.9	12.7	12.4	12.0	11.7	11.4	11.2	10.9
1970	15.4	15.9	16.0	15.9	16.1	16.2	15.6	15.1	14.6	14.0	13.7	13.4	13.2	13.1	12.9	12.6	12.2	11.8	11.5	11.2	11.0
1971	16.4	16.7	16.7	16.5	16.7	16.7	16.0	15.4	14.9	14.2	13.9	13.5	13.3	13.1	12.9	12.6	12.2	11.8	11.5	11.2	11.0
1972	17.9	18.0	17.7	17.3	17.4	17.3	16.5	15.7	15.1	14.4	14.1	13.6	13.3	13.2	13.0	12.6	12.2	11.8	11.5	11.2	10.9
1973	19.4	19.0	18.4	17.8	17.8	17.7	16.7	15.8	15.2	14.4	14.0	13.5	13.2	13.1	12.9	12.5	12.1	11.6	11.3	11.0	10.7
1974	26.2	22.2	20.3	19.1	18.8	18.5	17.2	16.2	15.4	14.5	14.1	13.5	13.3	13.1	12.9	12.5	12.0	11.5	11.2	10.9	10.6
1975		18.3	17.4	16.8	17.0	17.0	15.8	14.9	14.1	13.3	12.9	12.5	12.2	12.2	12.0	11.6	11.2	10.7	10.4	10.2	9.9
1976			16.6	16.0	16.5	16.6	15.3	14.3	13.5	12.7	12.4	11.9	11.7	11.7	11.5	11.2	10.7	10.3	10.0	9.7	9.5
1977				15.4	16.0	16.5	16.7	15.0	13.8	13.0	12.2	11.8	11.4	11.2	11.2	11.1	10.8	10.3	9.9	9.6	9.4	9.1
1978					17.6	17.3	14.8	13.4	12.6	11.6	11.3	10.9	10.8	10.8	10.7	10.4	9.9	9.5	9.2	9.0	8.7
1979						16.9	13.4	12.1	11.3	10.5	10.3	9.9	10.0	10.1	10.0	9.7	9.3	8.9	8.6	8.4	8.2
1980							10.0	9.7	9.5	8.9	9.0	8.8	9.0	9.3	9.3	9.0	8.6	8.2	8.0	7.9	7.7
1981								9.5	9.3	8.5	8.8	8.6	8.8	9.2	9.2	8.9	8.5	8.1	7.8	7.7	7.5
1982									9.1	8.1	8.6	8.4	8.7	9.1	9.2	8.9	8.4	7.9	7.7	7.5	7.3
1983										7.0	8.3	8.1	8.6	9.1	9.2	8.8	8.3	7.8	7.6	7.4	7.2
1984											9.7	8.7	9.1	9.6	9.7	9.2	8.5	7.9	7.6	7.4	7.2
1985												7.7	8.8	9.7	9.6	9.1	8.3	7.7	7.4	7.2	7.0
1986													10.0	10.7	10.3	9.4	8.4	7.6	7.3	7.1	6.9
1987														11.3	10.4	9.2	8.0	7.2	6.9	6.7	6.5
1988															9.4	8.1	6.9	6.2	6.0	6.0	5.8
1989																6.8	5.6	5.1	5.2	5.3	5.2
1990																	4.5	4.2	4.6	4.9	4.9
1991																		4.0	4.7	5.1	5.0
1992																			5.4	5.6	5.4
1993																				5.9	5.4
1994																					4.9

1 This series is affected by the abolition of domestic rates and the introduction of community charge - see methodological notes.

16.9 Rates of change of gross domestic product at current factor cost

Percentage change, at annual rate

Terminal year

Initial year	1954	1955	1956	1957	1958	1959	1960	1961	1962	1963	1964	1965	1966	1967	1968	1969	1970	1971	1972	1973	1974
1953	6.1	6.8	7.1	6.8	6.3	6.2	6.4	6.4	6.2	6.2	6.4	6.5	6.4	6.3	6.4	6.4	6.6	7.0	7.3	7.7	8.0
1954		7.6	7.6	7.0	6.3	6.2	6.4	6.4	6.2	6.2	6.4	6.5	6.5	6.4	6.4	6.4	6.6	7.0	7.3	7.8	8.1
1955			7.6	6.7	5.9	5.9	6.2	6.2	6.0	6.0	6.3	6.4	6.4	6.3	6.4	6.3	6.6	7.0	7.3	7.8	8.2
1956				5.8	5.1	5.3	5.9	5.9	5.7	5.8	6.2	6.3	6.2	6.1	6.3	6.2	6.5	6.9	7.3	7.8	8.2
1957					4.3	5.1	5.9	5.9	5.7	5.8	6.2	6.3	6.3	6.2	6.3	6.3	6.6	7.0	7.4	7.9	8.3
1958						5.9	6.7	6.5	6.0	6.1	6.5	6.6	6.5	6.4	6.5	6.5	6.8	7.2	7.6	8.2	8.6
1959							7.5	6.8	6.1	6.1	6.6	6.8	6.6	6.4	6.6	6.5	6.8	7.3	7.8	8.3	8.8
1960								6.1	5.4	5.7	6.4	6.6	6.5	6.3	6.5	6.4	6.8	7.3	7.8	8.4	8.9
1961									4.7	5.4	6.6	6.7	6.6	6.3	6.5	6.5	6.8	7.4	8.0	8.6	9.1
1962										6.2	7.5	7.4	7.0	6.6	6.8	6.7	7.1	7.8	8.3	9.0	9.5
1963											8.8	8.0	7.3	6.8	6.9	6.8	7.2	7.9	8.5	9.2	9.8
1964												7.3	6.6	6.1	6.5	6.4	7.0	7.8	8.5	9.3	9.9
1965													5.9	5.5	6.2	6.2	6.9	7.9	8.7	9.5	10.1
1966														5.1	6.4	6.3	7.2	8.3	9.1	10.1	10.7
1967															7.7	6.9	7.9	9.2	9.9	10.9	11.5
1968																6.1	8.0	9.7	10.5	11.6	12.2
1969																	10.0	11.5	12.0	13.0	13.4
1970																		12.9	13.1	14.0	14.3
1971																			13.2	14.6	14.7
1972																				16.0	15.5
1973																					15.1

Terminal year

Initial year	1975	1976	1977	1978	1979	1980	1981	1982	1983	1984	1985	1986	1987	1988	1989	1990	1991	1992	1993	1994	1995
1953	8.8	9.2	9.4	9.7	9.9	10.1	10.1	10.0	10.0	9.9	9.9	9.8	9.8	9.9	9.9	9.8	9.7	9.5	9.4	9.3	9.2
1954	8.9	9.3	9.6	9.8	10.0	10.3	10.2	10.2	10.2	10.1	10.0	9.9	9.9	10.0	10.0	9.9	9.8	9.6	9.5	9.4	9.3
1955	9.0	9.4	9.7	9.9	10.1	10.4	10.3	10.3	10.2	10.1	10.1	10.0	10.0	10.1	10.1	10.0	9.8	9.7	9.6	9.5	9.3
1956	9.1	9.5	9.8	10.0	10.3	10.5	10.4	10.4	10.3	10.2	10.2	10.1	10.1	10.1	10.1	10.1	9.9	9.7	9.6	9.5	9.4
1957	9.3	9.7	10.0	10.2	10.5	10.7	10.6	10.6	10.5	10.4	10.4	10.2	10.2	10.3	10.3	10.2	10.0	9.8	9.7	9.6	9.5
1958	9.6	10.0	10.3	10.5	10.8	11.0	10.9	10.8	10.8	10.6	10.6	10.5	10.4	10.5	10.5	10.4	10.2	10.0	9.9	9.8	9.6
1959	9.8	10.3	10.5	10.8	11.0	11.3	11.1	11.0	11.0	10.8	10.8	10.6	10.6	10.6	10.6	10.5	10.3	10.1	10.0	9.9	9.7
1960	10.0	10.4	10.7	11.0	11.2	11.4	11.3	11.2	11.1	11.0	10.9	10.8	10.7	10.8	10.7	10.6	10.4	10.2	10.1	10.0	9.8
1961	10.2	10.7	11.0	11.3	11.5	11.7	11.6	11.5	11.4	11.2	11.1	11.0	10.9	10.9	10.9	10.8	10.6	10.4	10.2	10.1	9.9
1962	10.7	11.2	11.4	11.7	11.9	12.1	12.0	11.8	11.7	11.5	11.4	11.2	11.2	11.2	11.1	11.0	10.8	10.6	10.4	10.2	10.1
1963	11.1	11.6	11.8	12.0	12.3	12.5	12.3	12.1	12.0	11.8	11.7	11.4	11.4	11.4	11.3	11.2	10.9	10.7	10.5	10.4	10.2
1964	11.3	11.8	12.0	12.3	12.5	12.7	12.5	12.3	12.2	11.9	11.8	11.6	11.5	11.5	11.4	11.3	11.0	10.8	10.6	10.4	10.2
1965	11.7	12.2	12.5	12.7	12.9	13.1	12.8	12.6	12.4	12.2	12.0	11.8	11.7	11.7	11.6	11.5	11.2	10.9	10.7	10.5	10.3
1966	12.3	12.9	13.1	13.3	13.5	13.6	13.3	13.0	12.8	12.5	12.4	12.1	12.0	11.9	11.9	11.7	11.4	11.1	10.9	10.7	10.5
1967	13.3	13.8	13.9	14.0	14.2	14.3	13.9	13.6	13.3	13.0	12.8	12.5	12.3	12.3	12.2	12.0	11.6	11.4	11.1	10.9	10.7
1968	14.1	14.6	14.6	14.7	14.8	14.9	14.4	14.0	13.7	13.3	13.1	12.7	12.6	12.5	12.4	12.2	11.8	11.5	11.3	11.1	11.0
1969	15.5	15.8	15.7	15.7	15.7	15.7	15.1	14.7	14.3	13.8	13.6	13.1	13.0	12.9	12.7	12.5	12.1	11.7	11.5	11.3	11.0
1970	16.6	16.8	16.6	16.4	16.4	16.3	15.6	15.1	14.6	14.1	13.8	13.3	13.1	13.0	12.9	12.6	12.2	11.8	11.6	11.3	11.0
1971	17.6	17.6	17.2	16.9	16.8	16.7	15.9	15.2	14.8	14.2	13.9	13.4	13.1	13.0	12.9	12.6	12.2	11.8	11.5	11.2	10.9
1972	19.1	18.7	18.0	17.6	17.3	17.2	16.2	15.5	14.9	14.3	13.9	13.4	13.1	13.0	12.8	12.6	12.1	11.7	11.7	11.1	10.8
1973	20.6	19.6	18.5	17.9	17.5	17.3	16.2	15.4	14.8	14.1	13.7	13.2	12.9	12.8	12.6	12.4	11.9	11.5	11.2	10.9	10.6
1974	26.4	22.0	19.7	18.6	18.0	17.7	16.4	15.4	14.8	14.0	13.6	13.0	12.8	12.7	12.5	12.2	11.7	11.3	11.0	10.7	10.4
1975		17.7	16.4	16.1	16.0	16.0	14.8	13.9	13.4	12.7	12.4	11.9	11.7	11.7	11.6	11.3	10.8	10.5	10.2	9.9	9.7
1976			15.1	15.3	15.5	15.6	14.2	13.3	12.8	12.1	11.8	11.3	11.2	11.2	11.1	10.9	10.4	10.0	9.8	9.5	9.2
1977				15.4	15.6	15.8	14.0	13.0	12.4	11.7	11.4	10.9	10.8	10.8	10.8	10.6	10.1	9.7	9.4	9.2	8.9
1978					15.8	15.9	13.5	12.4	11.8	11.1	10.9	10.3	10.3	10.4	10.3	10.2	9.7	9.3	9.0	8.8	8.6
1979						16.1	12.4	11.2	10.8	10.1	10.1	9.6	9.6	9.8	9.8	9.7	9.2	8.8	8.6	8.4	8.1
1980							8.9	8.9	9.1	8.7	8.9	8.5	8.7	9.0	9.1	9.1	8.6	8.2	8.0	7.9	7.6
1981								8.9	9.3	8.6	8.9	8.4	8.7	9.1	9.2	9.1	8.5	8.2	8.0	7.8	7.5
1982									9.6	8.5	8.9	8.3	8.6	9.1	9.2	9.1	8.5	8.1	7.9	7.7	7.4
1983										7.4	8.6	7.9	8.4	9.0	9.2	9.0	8.4	7.9	7.7	7.5	7.2
1984											9.7	8.2	8.7	9.4	9.5	9.3	8.5	8.0	7.7	7.5	7.2
1985												6.6	8.2	9.2	9.4	9.2	8.3	7.7	7.5	7.3	7.0
1986													9.9	10.6	10.4	9.9	8.6	7.9	7.6	7.4	7.0
1987														11.3	10.7	9.9	8.3	7.5	7.2	7.0	6.7
1988															10.0	9.2	7.3	6.6	6.4	6.3	6.0
1989																8.4	6.0	5.5	5.5	5.6	5.4
1990																	3.6	4.0	4.6	4.9	4.8
1991																		4.4	5.1	5.3	5.0
1992																			5.8	5.7	5.3
1993																				5.7	5.0
1994																					4.3

16.10 Rates of change of gross domestic product at constant factor cost

Percentage change, at annual rate

Initial year	Terminal year 1954	1955	1956	1957	1958	1959	1960	1961	1962	1963	1964	1965	1966	1967	1968	1969	1970	1971	1972	1973	1974
1953	4.2	3.9	3.0	2.7	2.1	2.4	2.9	2.9	2.7	2.8	3.1	3.1	3.0	2.9	3.0	3.0	2.9	2.9	2.9	3.1	2.9
1954		3.6	2.4	2.2	1.6	2.1	2.7	2.7	2.5	2.7	3.0	3.0	2.9	2.8	2.9	2.9	2.8	2.8	2.8	3.0	2.8
1955			1.3	1.5	0.9	1.7	2.5	2.5	2.4	2.6	2.9	2.9	2.8	2.8	2.9	2.9	2.8	2.7	2.7	3.0	2.8
1956				1.7	0.8	1.9	2.8	2.8	2.6	2.8	3.1	3.1	3.0	2.9	3.0	3.0	2.9	2.8	2.8	3.1	2.8
1957					-0.1	1.9	3.2	3.0	2.7	2.9	3.3	3.3	3.1	3.0	3.1	3.1	3.0	2.9	2.9	3.2	2.9
1958						4.1	4.8	4.1	3.5	3.6	3.9	3.9	3.7	3.5	3.4	3.5	3.4	3.3	3.1	3.4	3.1
1959							5.6	4.1	3.2	3.4	3.9	3.7	3.4	3.3	3.4	3.3	3.2	3.1	3.0	3.4	3.0
1960								2.7	2.1	2.7	3.4	3.3	3.1	3.0	3.1	3.1	3.0	2.8	2.8	3.2	2.8
1961									1.5	2.7	3.7	3.5	3.2	3.0	3.2	3.1	3.0	2.9	2.8	3.2	2.9
1962										4.0	4.8	4.1	3.6	3.3	3.5	3.3	3.2	3.0	3.0	3.4	3.0
1963											5.6	4.2	3.4	3.1	3.4	3.2	3.1	2.9	2.9	3.3	2.9
1964												2.9	2.4	2.3	2.8	2.8	2.6	2.5	2.5	3.1	2.6
1965													1.9	2.1	2.8	2.7	2.6	2.4	2.5	3.1	2.6
1966														2.2	3.3	3.0	2.8	2.5	2.6	3.3	2.7
1967															4.4	3.4	3.0	2.6	2.7	3.5	2.7
1968																2.5	2.2	2.1	2.2	3.3	2.5
1969																	2.0	1.8	2.2	3.5	2.5
1970																		1.7	2.2	4.0	2.6
1971																			2.8	5.1	2.9
1972																				7.5	2.9
1973																					-1.5

Initial year	Terminal year 1975	1976	1977	1978	1979	1980	1981	1982	1983	1984	1985	1986	1987	1988	1989	1990	1991	1992	1993	1994	1995
1953	2.7	2.7	2.7	2.7	2.7	2.5	2.4	2.4	2.4	2.4	2.4	2.5	2.6	2.6	2.6	2.6	2.4	2.4	2.4	2.4	2.4
1954	2.6	2.6	2.6	2.6	2.6	2.4	2.3	2.3	2.3	2.3	2.4	2.4	2.5	2.6	2.6	2.5	2.4	2.3	2.3	2.3	2.3
1955	2.6	2.6	2.6	2.6	2.6	2.4	2.3	2.2	2.3	2.3	2.3	2.4	2.5	2.5	2.5	2.5	2.3	2.3	2.3	2.3	2.3
1956	2.6	2.6	2.6	2.6	2.6	2.4	2.3	2.3	2.3	2.3	2.4	2.4	2.5	2.6	2.6	2.5	2.4	2.3	2.3	2.3	2.3
1957	2.7	2.7	2.7	2.7	2.7	2.5	2.3	2.3	2.4	2.3	2.4	2.5	2.5	2.6	2.6	2.5	2.4	2.3	2.3	2.4	2.4
1958	2.9	2.9	2.8	2.8	2.8	2.6	2.4	2.4	2.5	2.4	2.5	2.6	2.6	2.7	2.7	2.6	2.5	2.4	2.4	2.4	2.4
1959	2.8	2.8	2.8	2.8	2.8	2.5	2.4	2.4	2.4	2.4	2.4	2.5	2.6	2.7	2.6	2.6	2.4	2.3	2.3	2.4	2.4
1960	2.6	2.6	2.6	2.6	2.6	2.4	2.2	2.2	2.3	2.2	2.3	2.4	2.5	2.6	2.5	2.5	2.3	2.2	2.2	2.3	2.3
1961	2.6	2.6	2.6	2.6	2.6	2.4	2.2	2.2	2.2	2.2	2.3	2.4	2.5	2.5	2.5	2.5	2.3	2.2	2.2	2.3	2.3
1962	2.7	2.7	2.7	2.7	2.7	2.4	2.2	2.2	2.3	2.3	2.3	2.4	2.5	2.6	2.6	2.5	2.3	2.2	2.2	2.3	2.3
1963	2.6	2.6	2.6	2.6	2.6	2.3	2.1	2.1	2.2	2.2	2.3	2.3	2.4	2.5	2.5	2.4	2.3	2.2	2.2	2.2	2.3
1964	2.3	2.3	2.4	2.4	2.4	2.1	1.9	1.9	2.0	2.0	2.1	2.2	2.3	2.4	2.4	2.3	2.2	2.1	2.1	2.1	2.2
1965	2.2	2.3	2.3	2.3	2.4	2.1	1.9	1.9	2.0	2.0	2.1	2.2	2.3	2.4	2.4	2.3	2.1	2.0	2.0	2.1	2.1
1966	2.3	2.3	2.3	2.4	2.4	2.1	1.9	1.9	2.0	2.0	2.1	2.2	2.3	2.4	2.4	2.3	2.1	2.0	2.0	2.1	2.1
1967	2.3	2.3	2.4	2.4	2.4	2.1	1.8	1.8	2.0	2.0	2.1	2.2	2.3	2.4	2.4	2.3	2.1	2.0	2.0	2.1	2.1
1968	2.0	2.1	2.1	2.2	2.3	1.9	1.6	1.7	1.8	1.8	1.9	2.1	2.2	2.3	2.3	2.2	2.0	1.9	2.0	2.0	2.0
1969	1.9	2.0	2.1	2.2	2.2	1.8	1.6	1.6	1.7	1.8	1.9	2.0	2.2	2.3	2.3	2.2	2.0	1.9	1.9	2.0	2.0
1970	1.9	2.0	2.1	2.2	2.3	1.8	1.5	1.6	1.7	1.7	1.9	2.0	2.2	2.3	2.3	2.2	2.0	1.9	1.9	2.0	2.0
1971	2.0	2.1	2.2	2.3	2.3	1.8	1.5	1.5	1.7	1.8	1.9	2.1	2.2	2.4	2.4	2.3	2.0	1.9	1.9	2.0	2.0
1972	1.7	1.9	2.1	2.2	2.3	1.7	1.4	1.4	1.6	1.7	1.8	2.0	2.2	2.3	2.3	2.2	2.0	1.9	1.9	2.0	2.0
1973	-1.1	0.1	0.7	1.1	1.4	0.9	0.6	0.8	1.1	1.1	1.4	1.6	1.8	2.0	2.0	1.9	1.7	1.6	1.6	1.7	1.8
1974	-0.7	0.9	1.5	1.8	2.0	1.3	1.0	1.1	1.3	1.4	1.6	1.8	2.1	2.3	2.3	2.2	1.9	1.8	1.8	1.9	1.9
1975		2.7	2.6	2.7	2.7	1.7	1.2	1.3	1.6	1.7	1.9	2.1	2.3	2.5	2.5	2.3	2.1	1.9	1.9	2.0	2.1
1976			2.6	2.7	2.7	1.5	1.0	1.1	1.5	1.5	1.8	2.0	2.3	2.5	2.5	2.3	2.0	1.9	1.9	2.0	2.0
1977				2.8	2.8	1.1	0.6	0.8	1.3	1.4	1.7	2.0	2.2	2.5	2.5	2.3	2.0	1.8	1.8	2.0	2.0
1978					2.7	0.3	-0.2	0.3	1.0	1.2	1.6	1.9	2.2	2.4	2.4	2.3	1.9	1.7	1.8	1.9	2.0
1979						-2.1	-1.6	-0.5	0.6	0.8	1.4	1.7	2.1	2.4	2.4	2.2	1.9	1.7	1.7	1.9	1.9
1980							-1.1	0.3	1.4	1.6	2.1	2.4	2.7	3.0	2.9	2.7	2.2	2.0	2.0	2.2	2.2
1981								1.8	2.7	2.5	2.9	3.1	3.4	3.6	3.4	3.1	2.6	2.3	2.3	2.4	2.4
1982									3.7	2.9	3.3	3.4	3.7	3.9	3.7	3.3	2.7	2.3	2.3	2.5	2.5
1983										2.0	3.0	3.3	3.7	3.9	3.6	3.2	2.5	2.2	2.2	2.4	2.4
1984											4.0	4.0	4.2	4.4	4.0	3.4	2.6	2.2	2.2	2.4	2.4
1985												4.0	4.3	4.5	4.0	3.3	2.4	1.9	2.0	2.2	2.2
1986													4.6	4.8	3.9	3.1	2.0	1.6	1.7	2.0	2.0
1987														4.9	3.6	2.6	1.4	1.0	1.2	1.6	1.7
1988															2.3	1.4	0.2	0.0	0.5	1.1	1.3
1989																0.6	-0.8	-0.7	0.0	0.8	1.1
1990																	-2.1	-1.3	-0.1	0.9	1.2
1991																		-0.5	0.9	1.9	2.1
1992																			2.3	3.2	2.9
1993																				4.0	3.3
1994																					2.5

Percentage distributions and growth rates

16.11 Rates of change of output per person employed Based on output data[1]

Percentage change, at annual rate

Initial year	Terminal year 1961	1962	1963	1964	1965	1966	1967	1968	1969	1970	1971	1972	1973	1974	1975	1976	1977	1978	1979	1980	1981
1960	1.7	1.3	2.1	2.6	2.5	2.3	2.5	2.8	2.8	2.7	2.7	2.7	2.9	2.6	2.4	2.4	2.4	2.4	2.4	2.2	2.2
1961		0.9	2.4	3.0	2.7	2.5	2.6	3.0	2.9	2.8	2.9	2.8	3.0	2.6	2.4	2.5	2.5	2.5	2.4	2.2	2.2
1962			3.8	4.0	3.3	2.8	3.0	3.3	3.2	3.1	3.1	3.0	3.2	2.8	2.5	2.6	2.6	2.6	2.5	2.3	2.3
1963				4.2	3.0	2.5	2.8	3.2	3.1	3.0	3.0	2.9	3.1	2.7	2.4	2.5	2.5	2.5	2.4	2.2	2.2
1964					1.9	1.7	2.3	2.9	2.9	2.8	2.8	2.8	3.0	2.5	2.3	2.4	2.4	2.4	2.3	2.1	2.1
1965						1.5	2.5	3.3	3.1	3.0	3.0	2.9	3.2	2.6	2.3	2.4	2.4	2.4	2.3	2.1	2.1
1966							3.6	4.2	3.7	3.3	3.3	3.1	3.4	2.8	2.4	2.5	2.5	2.5	2.4	2.1	2.1
1967								4.9	3.7	3.2	3.2	3.0	3.4	2.6	2.3	2.4	2.4	2.4	2.3	2.0	2.0
1968									2.5	2.4	2.6	2.6	3.1	2.3	1.9	2.1	2.1	2.1	2.1	1.8	1.8
1969										2.3	2.7	2.6	3.2	2.2	1.8	2.0	2.1	2.1	2.0	1.7	1.7
1970											3.0	2.7	3.5	2.2	1.7	2.0	2.1	2.0	2.0	1.6	1.7
1971												2.4	3.8	1.9	1.4	1.8	1.9	1.9	1.9	1.5	1.6
1972													5.3	1.7	1.0	1.7	1.8	1.8	1.8	1.4	1.5
1973														-1.8	-1.0	0.5	1.0	1.2	1.2	0.8	1.0
1974															-0.3	1.6	1.9	1.9	1.8	1.3	1.4
1975																3.5	3.0	2.6	2.3	1.6	1.7
1976																	2.4	2.2	1.9	1.1	1.3
1977																		2.0	1.7	0.7	1.1
1978																			1.5	0.0	0.8
1979																				-1.4	0.4
1980																					2.3

Initial year	Terminal year 1982	1983	1984	1985	1986	1987	1988	1989	1990	1991	1992	1993	1994	1995
1960	2.3	2.3	2.2	2.3	2.3	2.3	2.3	2.2	2.1	2.1	2.1	2.1	2.1	2.1
1961	2.3	2.4	2.3	2.3	2.3	2.3	2.3	2.2	2.1	2.1	2.1	2.1	2.2	2.1
1962	2.4	2.4	2.3	2.3	2.4	2.4	2.4	2.2	2.2	2.1	2.1	2.2	2.2	2.2
1963	2.3	2.4	2.2	2.3	2.3	2.3	2.3	2.2	2.1	2.1	2.1	2.1	2.1	2.1
1964	2.2	2.3	2.2	2.2	2.2	2.3	2.2	2.1	2.0	2.0	2.0	2.0	2.1	2.1
1965	2.2	2.3	2.2	2.2	2.3	2.3	2.2	2.1	2.0	2.0	2.0	2.0	2.1	2.1
1966	2.2	2.3	2.2	2.2	2.3	2.3	2.3	2.1	2.1	2.0	2.0	2.1	2.1	2.1
1967	2.1	2.3	2.1	2.2	2.2	2.3	2.2	2.1	2.0	1.9	1.9	2.0	2.0	2.0
1968	1.9	2.1	2.0	2.0	2.1	2.1	2.1	1.9	1.9	1.8	1.8	1.9	1.9	1.9
1969	1.9	2.1	1.9	2.0	2.1	2.1	2.1	1.9	1.8	1.8	1.8	1.9	1.9	1.9
1970	1.9	2.0	1.9	1.9	2.1	2.1	2.0	1.9	1.8	1.8	1.8	1.8	1.9	1.9
1971	1.8	2.0	1.8	1.9	2.0	2.0	2.0	1.8	1.7	1.7	1.7	1.8	1.9	1.8
1972	1.7	1.9	1.8	1.8	2.0	2.0	2.0	1.8	1.7	1.7	1.7	1.8	1.8	1.8
1973	1.3	1.6	1.4	1.6	1.7	1.8	1.7	1.6	1.5	1.5	1.5	1.6	1.7	1.7
1974	1.7	2.0	1.8	1.9	2.0	2.0	2.0	1.8	1.7	1.7	1.7	1.8	1.8	1.8
1975	2.0	2.3	2.0	2.1	2.2	2.2	2.2	2.0	1.8	1.8	1.8	1.9	2.0	1.9
1976	1.7	2.1	1.8	1.9	2.1	2.1	2.1	1.8	1.7	1.7	1.7	1.8	1.9	1.9
1977	1.6	2.0	1.7	1.9	2.1	2.1	2.0	1.8	1.7	1.6	1.6	1.7	1.8	1.8
1978	1.5	2.1	1.7	1.8	2.1	2.1	2.0	1.8	1.6	1.6	1.6	1.7	1.8	1.8
1979	1.5	2.2	1.7	1.9	2.1	2.2	2.1	1.8	1.7	1.6	1.6	1.7	1.9	1.8
1980	3.1	3.4	2.5	2.6	2.8	2.7	2.6	2.2	2.0	1.9	1.9	2.0	2.1	2.1
1981	3.8	4.0	2.6	2.7	2.8	2.8	2.6	2.2	1.9	1.8	1.8	2.0	2.1	2.1
1982		4.2	2.0	2.3	2.6	2.6	2.4	1.9	1.7	1.6	1.6	1.8	1.9	1.9
1983			-0.2	1.3	2.1	2.2	2.0	1.6	1.3	1.3	1.4	1.6	1.7	1.7
1984				2.9	3.2	3.0	2.6	1.9	1.6	1.5	1.6	1.8	1.9	1.9
1985					3.6	3.1	2.5	1.7	1.4	1.3	1.4	1.6	1.8	1.8
1986						2.5	1.9	1.1	0.8	1.0	1.3	1.6	1.6	
1987							1.4	0.4	0.2	0.4	0.7	1.2	1.5	1.5
1988								-0.7	-0.3	0.0	0.5	1.1	1.5	1.5
1989									0.0	0.4	1.0	1.6	1.9	1.9
1990										0.8	1.4	2.1	2.4	2.3
1991											2.1	2.7	3.0	2.6
1992												3.4	3.4	2.8
1993													3.4	2.6
1994														1.7

1 This table is based on the ratio of GDP (see table 1.1) to the employed labour force (see Table 17.1: Workforce in employment less Work related government training programmes).

16.12
Rates of change of personal disposable income at constant prices
Total

Percentage change, at annual rate

Initial year	Terminal year																				
	1954	1955	1956	1957	1958	1959	1960	1961	1962	1963	1964	1965	1966	1967	1968	1969	1970	1971	1972	1973	1974
1953	3.2	4.0	3.4	3.0	2.7	3.1	3.6	3.7	3.4	3.5	3.5	3.4	3.3	3.2	3.1	2.9	3.0	2.9	3.2	3.3	3.1
1954		4.7	3.6	2.9	2.6	3.1	3.7	3.7	3.4	3.5	3.6	3.4	3.3	3.2	3.1	2.9	3.0	2.9	3.2	3.3	3.1
1955			2.4	2.0	1.9	2.7	3.5	3.6	3.2	3.3	3.4	3.3	3.2	3.0	2.9	2.8	2.9	2.8	3.1	3.3	3.0
1956				1.6	1.6	2.8	3.7	3.8	3.4	3.5	3.6	3.4	3.2	3.1	3.0	2.8	2.9	2.8	3.1	3.3	3.1
1957					1.7	3.4	4.4	4.4	3.7	3.8	3.8	3.6	3.4	3.2	3.1	2.9	3.0	2.9	3.2	3.4	3.2
1958						5.1	5.9	5.3	4.2	4.2	4.2	3.9	3.7	3.4	3.2	3.0	3.1	3.0	3.3	3.5	3.3
1959							6.6	5.4	3.9	4.0	4.0	3.7	3.4	3.2	3.0	2.8	2.9	2.8	3.2	3.4	3.1
1960								4.2	2.7	3.1	3.4	3.1	2.9	2.7	2.6	2.4	2.6	2.4	2.9	3.2	2.9
1961									1.2	2.6	3.1	2.8	2.7	2.5	2.4	2.2	2.4	2.3	2.8	3.1	2.8
1962										4.0	4.1	3.4	3.1	2.7	2.6	2.3	2.5	2.4	3.0	3.3	2.9
1963											4.2	3.1	2.8	2.4	2.3	2.1	2.3	2.2	2.8	3.2	2.8
1964												1.9	2.0	1.8	1.8	1.6	2.0	1.9	2.7	3.1	2.7
1965													2.1	1.8	1.8	1.6	2.0	1.9	2.8	3.2	2.8
1966														1.5	1.6	1.4	2.0	1.8	2.9	3.4	2.9
1967															1.8	1.3	2.2	1.9	3.2	3.7	3.1
1968																0.9	2.4	2.0	3.5	4.1	3.3
1969																	3.8	2.5	4.4	4.9	3.8
1970																		1.2	4.7	5.3	3.8
1971																			8.4	7.4	4.6
1972																				6.5	2.8
1973																					-0.8

Initial year	Terminal year																				
	1975	1976	1977	1978	1979	1980	1981	1982	1983	1984	1985	1986	1987	1988	1989	1990	1991	1992	1993	1994	1995
1953	3.0	2.9	2.7	2.8	2.9	2.9	2.8	2.6	2.6	2.7	2.7	2.8	2.8	2.9	2.9	2.9	2.8	2.8	2.8	2.7	2.7
1954	3.0	2.9	2.6	2.8	2.9	2.9	2.7	2.6	2.6	2.7	2.7	2.7	2.8	2.9	2.9	2.9	2.8	2.8	2.7	2.7	2.7
1955	2.9	2.8	2.5	2.7	2.9	2.8	2.7	2.6	2.6	2.6	2.6	2.7	2.7	2.8	2.8	2.8	2.7	2.7	2.7	2.7	2.7
1956	2.9	2.8	2.5	2.8	2.9	2.8	2.7	2.6	2.6	2.6	2.6	2.7	2.7	2.8	2.9	2.8	2.8	2.7	2.7	2.7	2.7
1957	3.0	2.8	2.6	2.8	2.9	2.9	2.7	2.6	2.6	2.6	2.7	2.7	2.8	2.9	2.9	2.9	2.8	2.8	2.7	2.7	2.7
1958	3.1	2.9	2.6	2.9	3.0	2.9	2.8	2.6	2.6	2.7	2.7	2.8	2.8	2.9	2.9	2.9	2.8	2.8	2.8	2.7	2.7
1959	3.0	2.8	2.5	2.8	2.9	2.8	2.7	2.5	2.5	2.6	2.6	2.7	2.7	2.8	2.9	2.8	2.7	2.7	2.7	2.7	2.7
1960	2.7	2.5	2.3	2.5	2.7	2.6	2.5	2.3	2.4	2.4	2.4	2.5	2.6	2.7	2.7	2.7	2.6	2.6	2.6	2.5	2.6
1961	2.6	2.4	2.1	2.4	2.6	2.6	2.4	2.3	2.3	2.3	2.4	2.5	2.5	2.6	2.7	2.7	2.6	2.6	2.5	2.5	2.5
1962	2.8	2.5	2.2	2.5	2.7	2.6	2.5	2.3	2.3	2.4	2.4	2.5	2.6	2.7	2.7	2.7	2.6	2.6	2.6	2.5	2.5
1963	2.7	2.4	2.1	2.4	2.6	2.6	2.4	2.2	2.2	2.3	2.4	2.4	2.5	2.6	2.7	2.7	2.6	2.6	2.5	2.5	2.5
1964	2.5	2.3	1.9	2.3	2.5	2.5	2.3	2.1	2.1	2.2	2.3	2.4	2.4	2.6	2.6	2.6	2.5	2.5	2.5	2.4	2.4
1965	2.6	2.3	1.9	2.3	2.6	2.5	2.3	2.1	2.2	2.2	2.3	2.4	2.4	2.6	2.7	2.6	2.5	2.5	2.5	2.4	2.5
1966	2.6	2.3	1.9	2.4	2.6	2.5	2.3	2.1	2.2	2.2	2.3	2.4	2.5	2.6	2.7	2.7	2.6	2.5	2.5	2.5	2.5
1967	2.8	2.4	2.0	2.4	2.7	2.6	2.4	2.2	2.2	2.3	2.3	2.4	2.5	2.7	2.7	2.7	2.6	2.6	2.5	2.5	2.5
1968	2.9	2.5	2.0	2.5	2.8	2.7	2.4	2.2	2.2	2.3	2.4	2.5	2.6	2.7	2.8	2.8	2.6	2.6	2.6	2.5	2.5
1969	3.2	2.7	2.1	2.7	3.0	2.8	2.5	2.3	2.3	2.4	2.5	2.6	2.6	2.8	2.9	2.8	2.7	2.7	2.6	2.6	2.6
1970	3.1	2.5	1.9	2.5	2.9	2.7	2.4	2.2	2.2	2.3	2.4	2.5	2.6	2.8	2.8	2.8	2.7	2.6	2.6	2.5	2.6
1971	3.6	2.8	2.0	2.7	3.1	2.9	2.5	2.3	2.3	2.4	2.5	2.6	2.7	2.9	2.9	2.9	2.7	2.7	2.7	2.6	2.6
1972	2.1	1.5	0.7	1.8	2.4	2.3	1.9	1.7	1.8	1.9	2.0	2.2	2.3	2.5	2.6	2.6	2.4	2.4	2.4	2.3	2.4
1973	-0.1	-0.2	-0.7	0.9	1.7	1.7	1.4	1.1	1.3	1.5	1.7	1.9	2.0	2.3	2.4	2.4	2.2	2.2	2.2	2.1	2.2
1974	0.6	0.1	-0.6	1.3	2.2	2.1	1.7	1.4	1.5	1.7	1.9	2.1	2.2	2.5	2.6	2.6	2.4	2.4	2.3	2.3	2.3
1975		-0.3	-1.2	1.6	2.6	2.4	1.8	1.5	1.6	1.9	2.0	2.2	2.3	2.6	2.7	2.7	2.5	2.5	2.4	2.4	2.4
1976			-2.1	2.5	3.6	3.1	2.3	1.8	1.9	2.2	2.3	2.5	2.6	2.9	3.0	2.9	2.7	2.7	2.6	2.5	2.6
1977				7.4	6.5	4.8	3.4	2.6	2.6	2.8	2.8	3.0	3.1	3.4	3.4	-3.3	3.1	3.0	2.9	2.8	2.8
1978					5.7	3.6	2.1	1.5	1.7	2.0	2.2	2.5	2.6	3.0	3.1	3.0	2.7	2.7	2.6	2.5	2.6
1979						1.5	0.4	0.1	0.7	1.3	1.6	2.0	2.2	2.7	2.8	2.7	2.5	2.5	2.4	2.3	2.4
1980							-0.8	-0.6	0.4	1.3	1.6	2.1	2.3	2.8	3.0	2.8	2.6	2.5	2.5	2.4	2.4
1981								-0.5	1.1	1.9	2.3	2.7	2.9	3.3	3.4	3.3	2.9	2.8	2.8	2.6	2.7
1982									2.7	3.2	3.2	3.5	3.5	4.0	4.0	3.7	3.3	3.2	3.1	2.9	2.9
1983										3.7	3.5	3.8	3.8	4.2	4.2	3.9	3.4	3.2	3.1	2.9	2.9
1984											3.2	3.8	3.8	4.4	4.3	3.9	3.4	3.2	3.0	2.8	2.9
1985												4.4	4.0	4.7	4.6	4.1	3.4	3.2	3.0	2.8	2.8
1986													3.7	4.9	4.7	4.0	3.2	3.0	2.8	2.6	2.6
1987														6.2	5.2	4.1	3.0	2.8	2.7	2.5	2.5
1988															4.2	3.0	2.0	2.0	2.0	1.8	2.0
1989																1.9	1.0	1.3	1.4	1.4	1.6
1990																	0.0	1.0	1.2	1.2	1.6
1991																		2.0	1.9	1.7	2.0
1992																			1.8	1.5	2.0
1993																				1.2	2.1
1994																					3.0

Percentage distributions and growth rates

16.13 Rates of change of personal disposable income at constant prices
Per capita

Percentage change, at annual rate

Initial year	Terminal year 1954	1955	1956	1957	1958	1959	1960	1961	1962	1963	1964	1965	1966	1967	1968	1969	1970	1971	1972	1973	1974
1953	2.9	3.6	3.0	2.6	2.3	2.7	3.1	3.1	2.8	2.9	2.9	2.8	2.7	2.6	2.5	2.3	2.4	2.3	2.6	2.8	2.6
1954		4.3	3.1	2.5	2.1	2.6	3.1	3.2	2.8	2.9	2.9	2.8	2.7	2.5	2.4	2.3	2.4	2.3	2.6	2.8	2.6
1955			1.9	1.5	1.4	2.2	2.9	3.0	2.6	2.7	2.8	2.6	2.5	2.4	2.3	2.2	2.3	2.2	2.5	2.7	2.5
1956				1.2	1.2	2.3	3.2	3.2	2.7	2.8	2.9	2.7	2.6	2.4	2.3	2.2	2.3	2.2	2.5	2.7	2.5
1957					1.2	2.9	3.8	3.7	3.0	3.0	3.1	2.9	2.7	2.6	2.4	2.3	2.4	2.2	2.6	2.8	2.6
1958						4.6	5.2	4.5	3.4	3.4	3.4	3.1	2.9	2.7	2.6	2.4	2.5	2.3	2.7	3.0	2.7
1959							5.7	4.5	3.1	3.1	3.2	2.9	2.7	2.5	2.3	2.2	2.3	2.1	2.6	2.8	2.6
1960								3.3	1.7	2.3	2.6	2.3	2.2	2.0	1.9	1.8	1.9	1.8	2.3	2.6	2.4
1961									0.2	1.8	2.4	2.1	2.0	1.8	1.7	1.6	1.8	1.7	2.2	2.6	2.3
1962										3.4	3.4	2.7	2.4	2.1	2.0	1.8	2.0	1.8	2.4	2.8	2.5
1963											3.5	2.4	2.1	1.8	1.7	1.5	1.8	1.6	2.3	2.7	2.4
1964												1.3	1.4	1.3	1.3	1.1	1.5	1.4	2.2	2.6	2.3
1965													1.6	1.3	1.3	1.1	1.5	1.4	2.3	2.8	2.4
1966														0.9	1.1	0.9	1.5	1.4	2.4	3.0	2.5
1967															1.3	0.9	1.7	1.5	2.8	3.3	2.7
1968																0.5	2.0	1.5	3.1	3.7	3.0
1969																	3.5	2.1	4.0	4.6	3.5
1970																		0.7	4.3	5.0	3.5
1971																			8.0	7.1	4.4
1972																				6.3	2.7
1973																					-0.8

Initial year	Terminal year 1975	1976	1977	1978	1979	1980	1981	1982	1983	1984	1985	1986	1987	1988	1989	1990	1991	1992	1993	1994	1995
1953	2.5	2.4	2.2	2.4	2.5	2.5	2.4	2.3	2.3	2.3	2.3	2.4	2.4	2.5	2.6	2.5	2.5	2.4	2.4	2.4	2.4
1954	2.5	2.4	2.2	2.4	2.5	2.5	2.3	2.2	2.3	2.3	2.3	2.4	2.4	2.5	2.5	2.5	2.4	2.4	2.4	2.4	2.4
1955	2.4	2.3	2.1	2.3	2.4	2.4	2.3	2.2	2.2	2.2	2.3	2.3	2.3	2.5	2.5	2.5	2.4	2.4	2.3	2.3	2.3
1956	2.4	2.3	2.1	2.3	2.5	2.4	2.3	2.2	2.2	2.2	2.3	2.3	2.4	2.5	2.5	2.5	2.4	2.4	2.4	2.3	2.3
1957	2.5	2.4	2.1	2.4	2.5	2.5	2.3	2.2	2.2	2.3	2.3	2.4	2.4	2.5	2.6	2.5	2.4	2.4	2.4	2.3	2.4
1958	2.6	2.4	2.2	2.4	2.6	2.5	2.4	2.3	2.3	2.3	2.3	2.4	2.4	2.6	2.6	2.6	2.5	2.5	2.4	2.4	2.4
1959	2.5	2.3	2.1	2.3	2.5	2.4	2.3	2.2	2.2	2.2	2.3	2.3	2.4	2.5	2.5	2.5	2.4	2.4	2.4	2.3	2.3
1960	2.3	2.1	1.8	2.1	2.3	2.3	2.1	2.0	2.0	2.1	2.1	2.2	2.2	2.4	2.4	2.4	2.3	2.3	2.3	2.2	2.2
1961	2.2	2.0	1.8	2.1	2.3	2.2	2.1	1.9	2.0	2.0	2.1	2.2	2.2	2.3	2.4	2.4	2.3	2.3	2.2	2.2	2.2
1962	2.3	2.1	1.9	2.2	2.4	2.3	2.2	2.0	2.1	2.1	2.2	2.2	2.3	2.4	2.5	2.4	2.3	2.3	2.3	2.2	2.3
1963	2.2	2.0	1.8	2.1	2.3	2.3	2.1	2.0	2.0	2.1	2.1	2.2	2.2	2.4	2.4	2.4	2.3	2.3	2.3	2.2	2.2
1964	2.1	1.9	1.6	2.0	2.3	2.2	2.0	1.9	1.9	2.0	2.0	2.1	2.2	2.3	2.4	2.4	2.3	2.2	2.2	2.2	2.2
1965	2.2	2.0	1.6	2.1	2.3	2.3	2.1	1.9	2.0	2.0	2.1	2.2	2.2	2.4	2.5	2.4	2.3	2.3	2.2	2.2	2.2
1966	2.3	2.0	1.7	2.1	2.4	2.3	2.1	1.9	2.0	2.1	2.1	2.2	2.3	2.4	2.5	2.5	2.3	2.3	2.3	2.2	2.2
1967	2.5	2.2	1.7	2.2	2.5	2.4	2.2	2.0	2.0	2.1	2.2	2.3	2.3	2.5	2.6	2.5	2.4	2.4	2.3	2.3	2.3
1968	2.6	2.3	1.8	2.3	2.6	2.5	2.2	2.1	2.1	2.2	2.2	2.3	2.4	2.6	2.6	2.6	2.4	2.4	2.4	2.3	2.3
1969	3.0	2.5	1.9	2.5	2.8	2.7	2.4	2.2	2.2	2.3	2.3	2.4	2.5	2.7	2.7	2.7	2.5	2.5	2.4	2.4	2.4
1970	2.9	2.4	1.7	2.4	2.8	2.6	2.3	2.1	2.1	2.2	2.3	2.4	2.4	2.6	2.7	2.6	2.5	2.5	2.4	2.3	2.4
1971	3.5	2.7	1.9	2.7	3.0	2.8	2.5	2.2	2.2	2.3	2.4	2.5	2.5	2.7	2.8	2.7	2.6	2.5	2.5	2.4	2.4
1972	2.0	1.4	0.7	1.8	2.3	2.2	1.9	1.6	1.7	1.9	1.9	2.1	2.2	2.4	2.5	2.5	2.3	2.3	2.2	2.2	2.2
1973	-0.1	-0.2	-0.6	0.9	1.7	1.6	1.3	1.1	1.3	1.5	1.6	1.8	1.9	2.2	2.3	2.2	2.1	2.1	2.0	2.0	2.0
1974	0.6	0.2	-0.6	1.3	2.2	2.0	1.6	1.4	1.5	1.7	1.8	2.0	2.1	2.4	2.5	2.4	2.3	2.2	2.2	2.1	2.1
1975		-0.3	-1.2	1.6	2.6	2.3	1.8	1.5	1.6	1.8	1.9	2.1	2.2	2.5	2.6	2.5	2.4	2.3	2.3	2.2	2.2
1976			-2.0	2.6	3.6	3.0	2.2	1.8	1.9	2.1	2.2	2.4	2.5	2.8	2.8	2.8	2.5	2.5	2.4	2.3	2.3
1977				7.4	6.5	4.7	3.3	2.6	2.6	2.7	2.7	2.9	2.9	3.2	3.3	3.1	2.9	2.8	2.7	2.6	2.6
1978					5.6	3.5	2.0	1.4	1.6	1.9	2.1	2.3	2.5	2.8	2.9	2.8	2.5	2.5	2.4	2.3	2.3
1979						1.4	0.3	0.0	0.7	1.2	1.5	1.9	2.1	2.5	2.6	2.5	2.3	2.2	2.2	2.1	2.1
1980							-0.8	-0.6	0.4	1.2	1.5	2.0	2.2	2.6	2.8	2.7	2.4	2.3	2.2	2.1	2.2
1981								-0.4	1.1	1.9	2.1	2.5	2.7	3.1	3.2	3.0	2.7	2.6	2.5	2.4	2.4
1982									2.6	3.1	3.0	3.3	3.3	3.7	3.8	3.5	3.0	2.9	2.8	2.6	2.6
1983										3.5	3.2	3.5	3.5	4.0	4.0	3.6	3.1	2.9	2.8	2.6	2.6
1984											2.9	3.5	3.5	4.1	4.0	3.6	3.0	2.9	2.7	2.5	2.5
1985												4.2	3.8	4.5	4.3	3.8	3.1	2.9	2.7	2.5	2.5
1986													3.4	4.6	4.4	3.7	2.9	2.7	2.5	2.3	2.3
1987														5.9	4.9	3.8	2.7	2.5	2.3	2.1	2.2
1988															3.9	2.7	1.7	1.7	1.6	1.5	1.6
1989																1.6	0.6	0.9	1.1	1.0	1.3
1990																	-0.4	0.6	0.9	0.9	1.2
1991																		1.6	1.5	1.3	1.6
1992																			1.4	1.1	1.6
1993																				0.8	1.7
1994																					2.6

CHAPTER 17: Production, population and employment

17.1 Population and employment[1]
Mid-year estimates

Thousands

		1985	1986	1987	1988	1989	1990	1991	1992	1993	1994	1995
Home population[2]	DYAY	56 685	56 852	57 009	57 158	57 358	57 561	57 808	58 006	58 191	58 395	58 613
Workforce	DYDB	27 891	27 969	28 172	28 492	28 700	28 775	28 584	28 454	28 249	28 096	28 002
less Unemployed[3]	−BCAB	−3 179	−3 229	−2 905	−2 341	−1 743	−1 556	−2 241	−2 678	−2 865	−2 586	−2 255
Workforce in employment	DYDA	24 712	24 739	25 266	26 151	26 957	27 220	26 343	25 776	25 384	25 511	25 747
of which:												
Employees in employment	BCAD	21 423	21 387	21 584	22 258	22 661	22 920	22 270	21 931	21 613	21 660	21 933
Self-employed	BCAG	2 787	2 804	3 052	3 235	3 526	3 573	3 422	3 230	3 189	3 298	3 351
HM Forces	BCAH	326	322	319	316	308	303	297	290	271	250	230
Work related government training programmes[4]	DYCZ	176	226	311	343	462	423	353	325	312	302	232
Analysis of workforce in employment by sector												
Central government:												
HM Forces	BCAH	326	322	319	316	308	303	297	290	271	250	230
Civilians	DYBF	2 034	2 015	1 993	2 007	2 006	1 997	1 881	1 721	1 370	935	827
Local authorities[5]	DYBG	2 958	3 010	3 062	3 081	2 940	2 967	2 947	2 897	2 680	2 642	2 644
Public corporations[5]	DYBH	1 251	1 187	985	912	832	786	724	874	1 158	1 467	1 531
Private sector	DYBI	17 967	17 980	18 596	19 492	20 409	20 743	20 141	19 669	19 594	19 915	20 283
Work related government training programmes[6]	DYCZ	176	226	311	343	462	423	353	325	312	302	232
Total	DYDA	24 712	24 739	25 266	26 151	26 957	27 220	26 343	25 776	25 384	25 511	25 747
Analysis of employees in employment by industry[7]												
Agriculture, hunting, forestry and fishing	CGZF	357	345	337	329	316	314	306	309	326	317	314
Mining of coal and nuclear fuel	CGZG	216	178	145	121	103	90	81	63	36	18	14
Extraction of mineral oil and natural gas	CGZH	31	31	32	34	36	36	37	34	29	27	29
Other mining and quarrying[8]	CGZI	42	37	34	33	35	36	31	29	27	27	26
Manufacturing	CGZJ	4 988	4 868	4 799	4 839	4 828	4 709	4 299	4 084	3 906	3 890	3 943
Electricity, gas and water supply	CGZK	270	262	257	257	252	241	230	216	205	192	170
Construction	CGZL	1 055	1 027	1 049	1 091	1 129	1 143	1 053	951	865	871	838
Wholesale and retail trade; repairs; hotels and restaurants	CGZM	4 367	4 364	4 374	4 554	4 785	4 912	4 825	4 803	4 747	4 836	4 937
Transport and storage	CGZN	880	858	845	862	892	921	909	900	888	890	890
Post and telecommunications	CGZO	451	443	444	462	471	471	464	455	430	419	404
Financial intermediation, real estate, renting and business activities	CGZP	2 754	2 841	2 958	3 163	3 333	3 480	3 419	3 396	3 445	3 452	3 606
Public administration, national defence and compulsory social security	CGZQ	1 478	1 473	1 492	1 477	1 401	1 442	1 462	1 464	1 460	1 430	1 380
Education, health and social work	CGZR	3 664	3 777	3 924	4 121	4 155	4 200	4 244	4 288	4 284	4 314	4 371
Other services[9]	CGZS	870	883	894	915	925	925	910	939	965	977	1 011
Total	BCAD	21 423	21 387	21 584	22 258	22 661	22 920	22 270	21 931	21 613	21 660	21 933

1 Total employment figures are consistent with those published in the ONS *Labour Market Trends*.
2 Source: Population estimates unit, ONS. 1995 figure is a projection.
3 Unadjusted claimant unemployed.
4 Programme participants who receive training in the context of the workplace but do not have contracts of employment (those with contracts of employment are included among the employees in employment).
5 See methodological notes for details of changes in coverage.
6 Trainees cannot be split between those in public sector workplaces and and those in private sector workplaces.
7 From this Blue Book this category is based on the Standard Industrial Classification 1992 basis.
8 Comprising sub-section 11 of sub-section C of SIC (92).
9 Comprising sections O, P and Q of the SIC (92).

17.2 Index numbers of production at constant factor cost: analysis by type of market[1]

1990=100

	Weight per 1000[2] 1990		1986	1987	1988	1989	1990	1991	1992	1993	1994	1995
Durable goods industries:												
Cars, etc.	25	NAAB	81.9	89.5	100.8	107.6	100.0	88.7	90.0	90.4	97.9	106.1
Other durables	27	NAAC	81.4	86.2	97.1	99.1	100.0	92.4	88.1	90.6	97.6	96.5
Total	52	NAAA	81.6	87.8	98.9	103.2	100.0	90.6	89.0	90.5	97.8	101.2
Non durable goods industries:												
Clothing and footwear	26	NAAE	111.6	112.5	107.8	103.4	100.0	89.2	89.6	88.9	91.0	89.4
Food, drink and tobacco[3]	101	NAAF	93.1	96.2	98.0	98.5	100.0	98.6	100.1	99.9	101.9	103.7
Other non durables	94	NAAG	80.5	86.3	93.8	98.8	100.0	95.0	96.7	99.9	103.7	107.6
Total	221	NAAD	89.9	93.9	97.4	99.2	100.0	96.0	97.4	98.6	101.4	103.7
Investment goods industries:												
Electrical	36	NAAI	73.2	78.5	91.7	100.9	100.0	99.7	105.2	115.9	136.6	151.2
Transport	58	NAAJ	78.3	79.6	82.9	100.2	100.0	94.2	89.5	86.6	85.8	82.2
Other	114	NAAK	86.5	87.0	94.2	98.3	100.0	90.7	86.1	86.4	88.1	88.7
Total	208	NAAH	81.9	83.5	90.6	99.3	100.0	93.2	90.4	91.6	95.9	97.8
Intermediate goods industries:												
Fuels	167	NAAM	113.1	113.2	108.9	101.0	100.0	106.4	110.1	116.2	125.8	132.7
Materials	351	NAAN	84.6	90.1	96.6	100.7	100.0	94.4	93.5	94.8	98.9	100.1
Total	518	NAAL	93.8	97.6	100.6	100.8	100.0	98.2	98.8	101.7	107.5	110.6

1 The indices are consistent with indices of production (Mining and quarrying manufacturing and electricity, gas and water supply) in table 2.5.
2 These sum to the total of 1000 for the production industries.
3 This does not include certain activities classified to intermediate goods industries : materials.

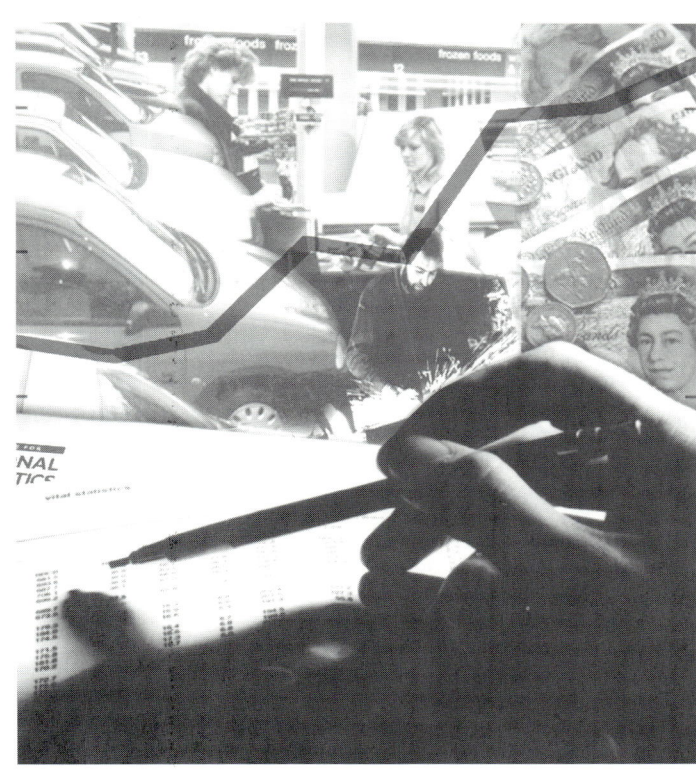

Supplementary information

SECTION SIX: SUPPLEMENTARY INFORMATION

Glossary of terms

Fuller explanations are given in **United Kingdom National Accounts: Sources and Methods**, Third Edition (HMSO 1985)

A

Accruals basis of accounting. Transactions are recorded when the expenditure is incurred (as opposed to the cash basis of accounting on which transactions are recorded when money passes).

Additions to dividend reserves. The excess of accruals of dividends over actual payments during the year.

Additions to tax reserves. The excess of accruals of tax over the actual payments of tax in the year.

Adjustment for financial services. This item reflects the treatment of interest as non-trading (or transfer) income in the national accounts. It equals the net receipts of interest by financial companies and institutions. By convention, in the industrial analysis of the income components of Gross domestic product (table 2.2), the contribution of the *financial intermediation, real estate, renting and business activities* industry is shown including these net receipts of interest. The adjustment is shown to reconcile with GDP, which does not include such non-trading income.

B

Blue Book. The name given to this and other issues of the annual publication **United Kingdom National Accounts** (formerly called National Income and Expenditure).

C

Capital consumption. The amount of fixed capital resources used up in the process of production during the year. Capital consumption is not an identifiable set of transactions: it is an imputed transaction which can be measured only by a system of conventions.

Capital goods. Fixed assets.

Capital transfers. *Transfers* which directly affect or are based upon the level of capital investment or wealth of the recipient or payer. Mainly capital grants by the central government to other sectors and receipts by the central government from taxes on capital.

Central government. All departments, offices, establishments and other bodies for whose activities a Minister of the Crown, or other responsible person is accountable to Parliament.

Companies and financial institutions. Industrial and commercial companies, and financial companies and institutions.

Consumers' expenditure. Personal expenditure consisting of household expenditure on goods and services (including income in kind, imputed rent of owner-occupied dwellings and administrative costs of life assurance and superannuation schemes) and final expenditure by non-profit-making bodies. Excluded are interest payments, all business expenditure and the purchase of land and buildings.

Corporate enterprises. Companies, financial institutions and public corporations.

Current grants paid abroad by central government, net. Grants to overseas governments under the economic aid programme; military aid to overseas governments; subscriptions and contributions to international organisations, war pensions and national insurance benefits paid to persons abroad, less transfers received from the European Union.

Current grants to local authorities. Includes revenue support grant, general grants, and grants towards specific services paid by central government to local authorities. From 1st April 1990 this includes central government distribution to local authorities from the national non-domestic rates pool. Capital grants are excluded.

Current surplus. The balancing item in the current accounts of central government and local authorities.

Current transfers. *Transfers* intended to finance production or consumption, but not investment, and which are made out of the current income of the donor and regarded as current income by the recipient.

Current transfers to central government from overseas governments. Receipts by the UK government from overseas governments and institutions e.g. receipts from the European Union budget and the European Coal and Steel Community and payments towards the cost of the Gulf War in 1990 and 1991.

Current transfers to charities from companies. Identified contributions made by companies for charitable purposes to non-profit-making bodies in the personal sector.

D

Debt interest. *Interest* paid by central government and local authorities on their borrowing.

Depreciation. See *Capital consumption*.

Dividends. The portion of a company's profits that the board of directors decide to distribute to holders of preference and ordinary shares in the company.

Domestic product. See *Gross domestic product*.

E

Employers' social security contributions. Employers' contributions to the national insurance scheme, to the national health service, to the Redundancy Fund and to the Maternity Pay Fund. Payments of the national insurance surcharge are not included but are classified as taxes on expenditure.

Employers' contributions - other. Employers' contributions to superannuation and other pension funds which are, in the case of unfunded schemes, proxied by pensions and gratuities actually paid to retired employees, principally payments to former central government employees and to retired police and firemen. Also includes compensation payments by employers to injured employees or to their dependants and redundancy payments made by employers which are not covered by rebates from the Redundancy Fund.

Exports of goods and services. Sales by UK residents to the rest of the world. Covers goods and services provided by general government, public corporations, and the private sector.

F

Factor cost. Equivalent to a *market price* valuation *less* taxes on expenditure *plus* subsidies.

Final consumption of central government and local authorities. Current expenditure by the central government (including the National Insurance Fund) and local authorities, constituting a direct demand for goods and services, including the services of government employees, *plus* an imputed charge for the consumption of non-trading capital *less* fees and charges for sales of goods and services.

Final expenditure by private non-profit-making bodies serving persons. Similar to *final consumption of central government and local authorities*, this constitutes current expenditure by private non-profit-making bodies on goods and services including the services of their employees *plus* an imputed charge for consumption of non-trading capital *less* any fees or charges made for services rendered and goods supplied.

Financial companies and institutions. Those productive enterprises which provide financial services and act as financial intermediaries.

Financial surplus or deficit. Equals saving before providing for depreciation, stock appreciation, and addition to reserves, *plus* net receipts of capital transfers *less* gross domestic fixed capital formation *less* the increase in the book value of stocks and work in progress.

Fixed assets. Produced assets that are themselves used repeatedly or continuously in a production process for more than one year.

G

GDP deflator. See *Total home costs per unit of output*.

General government. Central government and local authorities.

General government final consumption. See *Final consumption of central government and local authorities*.

Grants paid to personal sector by central government. Social security fund's benefits, supplementary benefits, family benefits, war pensions, etc, rebates to employers paid from the Redundancy Fund and grants to non-profit-making bodies serving persons.

Grants paid to personal sector by local authorities. Scholarships and other education awards and rent rebates and allowances granted to tenants under the 1972 Housing Finance Act and the housing benefit scheme.

Gross domestic fixed capital formation. Expenditure on fixed assets (buildings, vehicles, plant and machinery, etc.) either for replacing or adding to the stock of existing fixed assets. Expenditure on maintenance and repairs is excluded.

Gross domestic product. Domestic product measures total economic activity taking place on UK territory. Equals the sum of all incomes (whether individual or corporate, etc) earned in the UK from the production of goods and services; also equals the total of final expenditures on the goods and services produced in the UK *less* their import content; and further equals the sum of the value added by all activities which produce goods and services on UK territory. Termed 'gross' when the aggregate is measured before providing for capital consumption and 'net' after deduction of capital consumption. Measured at market prices or at factor cost expressed in either current prices (to give value of activity) or constant prices (relating to a specific base year (currently 1990) to give volume of activity).

Gross national disposable income at constant market prices. Can be derived from Gross domestic product at constant market prices by adding an adjustment for the effect of changes in terms of trade, for net property income from abroad and for net current transfers abroad. Further details are given in Table 1.1 and in paragraphs 75 to 77 of the 'Introduction to the UK National Accounts' in Section One. Also known as 'real national disposable income'.

Gross national disposable income at current market prices. Equal to gross national product at market prices less net current transfers paid abroad.

Gross national product. Income of residents of the UK, before providing for capital consumption. Equal to gross domestic product *plus* UK residents' income from economic activity abroad and from property held abroad *less* the corresponding income in the UK of non-residents. Measured at market prices or at factor cost.

Gross trading profits of companies and financial institutions. Trading profits, before deduction of tax or interest payments and before providing for depreciation and stock appreciation, of companies, co-operative societies and financial institutions operating in the UK including UK branches and subsidiaries of non-resident companies.

Gross trading surplus of general government enterprises. The surpluses of the trading departments of central government and of local authority undertakings engaged in providing passenger transport, export credit, harbours, docks, etc. and before making any provision for interest payments and before providing for depreciation and stock appreciation.

Gross trading surplus of public corporations. The trading surpluses before deduction of tax or interest payments and before providing for depreciation and stock appreciation of the nationalised industries and certain other public bodies engaged in providing trading activities (see public corporations).

H

Households. A sub-sector of the personal sector, representing households and individuals considered as final consumers. In practice it is not always possible to separate the transactions of unincorporated businesses from the purely personal transactions of their proprietors.

Household disposable income. Total household income from work and property (in cash or kind) together with pensions, social security benefits and other transfers, reduced by taxes on income, national insurance contributions and employees' contributions to occupational pension schemes. Excludes imputed rent of owner-occupied dwellings.

I

Imports of goods and services. Purchases from abroad by UK residents. Covers goods and services received by general government, public corporations, and the private sector.

Imputation. The process of having to invent a transaction where, although no money has changed hands, there has been a flow of goods of services. Imputation is confined to a very small number of cases where a reasonably satisfactory basis for the assumed valuation is available.

Imputed charge for consumption of non-trading capital. The imputed income of general government and private non-profit-making bodies from owned non-trading fixed capital assets. Derived from the estimates of capital consumption shown in Chapter 14.

Income from abroad of corporate enterprises. Rent, interest, profits and dividends accruing to UK companies and public corporations from overseas, after deducting depreciation allowances and taxes on income paid to overseas governments, but before providing for stock appreciation.

Income from employment. Wages and salaries in cash and in kind, pay of HM Forces and employers' contributions to national insurance, etc. and other pension schemes.

Income from self-employment. Income of persons from unincorporated businesses, mainly farmers, professional people (not those who receive salaries), shopkeepers and other sole traders and partnerships. Measured after deducting all business operating expenses but before deducting income tax, interest payments, and before providing for depreciation and stock appreciation.

Index of total home costs. Measures, conceptually, the price of domestic value added. This deflator is derived from the total of the expenditure components of GDP at factor cost.

Industrial and commercial companies. All corporate bodies other than public corporations, banks, and other financial companies and institutions. Includes Property companies.

Input-output balances. These show a balanced and complete picture of the flows of goods and services in the economy for a specific year. Their primary purpose is to reconcile all of the components of GDP. Further details are given in the introduction to section two.

Interest. The amount that a debtor becomes liable to pay a creditor, under the terms of a financial instrument agreed between them, over a given period of time without reducing the amount of principal outstanding.

Intermediate consumption. Consists of the value of goods and services which are transformed or entirely consumed as inputs into production in the period of account.

L

Local authorities. Public authorities of limited geographical scope, having power to raise funds by certain forms of taxation. Include county, borough, district and parish councils, and joint boards and committees formed by two or more councils.

M

Market prices. The prices which purchasers pay for the goods and services they acquire or use. Excludes deductible VAT (that is, includes non-deductible VAT).

N

National income (net national product at factor cost). The total income of residents of the UK after providing for capital consumption. Equal to the gross national product at factor cost less capital consumption.

National insurance, etc. contributions and benefits. See *Social Security contributions and benefits*.

Net domestic fixed capital formation. Equal to gross domestic fixed capital formation *less* capital consumption.

Net investment abroad. Net increase in the value of overseas assets acquired by UK residents *less* the net increase in the value of assets in the UK acquired by non-residents. Overseas assets include investment in physical assets, financial assets and gold and foreign currency reserves. Net investment abroad is equal to the current balance in the balance of payments account, after capital transfers paid abroad have been deducted.

Net national product. See *National income*.

Net property income from abroad. Income from rent, interest, profits and dividends received by UK residents from overseas *less* income paid to overseas residents from activity in the UK. Profits are after deducting depreciation allowances but before providing for stock appreciation.

O

Overseas sector. The accounts for this sector describe the economic relationships of residents of the UK with the rest of the world and cover essentially the transactions shown in balance of payments accounts. The sector is defined by its transactions with, claims on or liabilities to, UK residents.

P

Pay in cash and kind of HM Forces. Pay and cash allowances of, and the cost of issues of clothing to, 'effective' members of the armed forces and auxiliary services, excluding those on release leave but including those serving in government departments.

Personal saving. The residual difference between total personal income and total current personal expenditure. Saving, as defined, includes increases in the funds of life assurance companies and superannuation schemes. Measured before providing for depreciation and stock appreciation.

Personal sector. Consists mainly of households and individuals resident in the UK. Includes individuals living in hostels and other institutions as well as those living in private households. Also includes unincorporated private businesses, life assurance and pension funds (in parts of the national accounts only), private non-profit-making bodies serving persons, and private trusts.

Private non-profit-making bodies serving persons. Universities including former polytechnics, further education colleges, grant maintained schools and other non-profit making educational establishments, churches, charities, clubs and societies, trades unions, friendly societies, and private housing associations.

Private sector. Personal sector *plus* companies and financial institutions.

Profits due abroad, net of United Kingdom tax. Profits earned in the UK by foreign-owned branches and subsidiaries.

Property income from abroad. Rent, interest, profits and dividends received from overseas by UK residents, net of foreign taxes. Profits are before providing for stock appreciation but after deducting depreciation allowances.

Property income paid abroad. Rent, interest, profits and dividends paid to overseas residents. The estimates are shown both before and after deducting UK taxes. Profits are before providing for stock appreciation but after deducting depreciation allowances.

Public corporations. Public trading bodies, including the nationalised industries, which have a substantial degree of financial independence from the public authority which created them, including the powers to borrow and maintain reserves. Also includes National Health Service trust hospitals. A list of the corporations is given in the methodological notes.

Public sector. Comprises central and local government and public corporations.

Purchaser's price. This is the price actually paid by the purchaser, excluding any deductible VAT, in order to take delivery of a good or service at the time and place required by the purchaser. It includes transport charges paid separately by the purchaser to take delivery.

R

Real national disposable income. See *Gross national disposable income at constant market prices*.

Rent. Gross receipts from ownership of land and buildings less actual expenditure by the owners on repairs, maintenance and insurance. An imputed income is included for owner-occupied dwellings and farm houses provided rent free by employers and houses owned by general government. Imputed income from owner-occupied trading property is included in trading income and is not part of rent.

Rent and non-trading income of corporate enterprises. Principal components are public debt interest, interest paid to financial companies and rent from property owned and let.

Rent, dividends and interest received by general government. Major components are rent income in respect of houses owned by local authorities and interest received by the central government on loans to public corporations. Interest received by the central government from local authorities, and interest received by one part of the central government from another are excluded.

Rent, dividends and net interest received by personal sector. Total receipts of rent and of dividends, including co-operative society dividends, together with receipts *less* payments of interest. The receipts of life assurance and superannuation funds, including industrial assurance funds, are regarded as the income of the policy holders and members of the schemes and are included in the receipts of the personal sector. (See reconciliation in table 3.8).

Residual error. Two estimates of the total gross domestic product are built up from largely independent data on incomes and on final expenditures. These estimates are reconciled in those years for which input-output analysis is available (1989 to 1994) and for the years 1985 to 1988 - see methodological notes on section one: the national accounts. Residual error - the difference between the income and expenditure totals in those years for which the two estimates have not been reconciled - is presented as though it were an item (positive or negative) of income. This is purely for convenience of presentation and does not imply that the estimates of expenditure are necessarily superior in accuracy to the estimates of income. Residual error is arithmetically also the difference between the Statistical discrepancy (income adjustment) and the Statistical discrepancy (expenditure adjustment). Residual error is not attributed to any of the sectors; it is however treated as a form of saving in the summary capital account.

S

Saving (or undistributed income). The residual difference between current income and current expenditure in each sector.

Sector. A group of entities similar to one another in general characteristics affecting economic behaviour. The following sectors are distinguished - personal sector; industrial and commercial companies; financial companies and institutions; (which is further sectorised in parts of the accounts); public corporations; central government; local authorities; and overseas sector.

Social security fund's benefits. Comprise payments from the social security fund to persons in the form of retirement pensions, widows' benefits, guardians' allowances, death grant, and benefits to cover unemployment, sickness, invalidity, maternity, injury, disablement, and industrial death. Includes imputed benefits in respect of Statutory Sick Pay (whereby employers pay their employees sickness benefit in return for a deduction from the contributions they pay).

Social security contributions. Contributions by employers, employees and self-employed persons to the national insurance scheme, the national health service, the Redundancy Fund, and the Maternity Pay Fund. Includes imputed contributions in respect of Statutory Sick Pay (whereby employers pay their employees sickness contributions return for a deduction from the contributions they pay).

Stock appreciation. The part of the change in the value of stocks and work in progress during the year which arises from increases in the price at which stocks and work in progress are valued. Estimates of stock appreciation are related to estimates of the value of stocks, and are highly uncertain.

Statistical discrepancy (expenditure and income adjustments) - explicit adjustments to compensate for deviation between the sum of expenditure or of income components and GDP.

Subsidies. Payments made by the central government or local authorities to a producer or trader with the object of reducing his selling price below the factor cost of production. The financing of certain losses on public trading services and the deficit on local authorities housing revenue account are included as well as payments made to nationalised transport undertakings.

T

Tax credits. Tax credits on dividends received by the personal sector.

Taxes. Compulsory, unrequited payments made to general government.

Taxes on expenditure. 'Indirect' taxes which relate to the volume of production of, or trade in, particular goods and services (as distinct from taxes related to the income or capital resources of particular individuals, companies, etc.) levied by Central government *plus* rates -and payments in lieu of rates - levied by local authorities. From April 1990, domestic rates were replaced in England and Wales by the Community Charge and non-domestic rates became a central government tax. The Community charge is not a tax on expenditure while non-domestic rates levied by central government remain part of taxes on expenditure. Also included is the national insurance surcharge.

Taxes on income. Taxes related to the income of particular individuals, companies etc. Included are receipts from income tax, surtax, corporation tax, petroleum revenue tax, profits tax and excess profits taxes.

Total domestic expenditure at market prices. Expenditure by UK residents on consumption and investment.

Total final expenditure at market prices. Equal to total domestic expenditure at market prices plus exports of goods and services.

Total final output. The value at market prices of home produced and imported goods and services available for private and public consumption, investment and export. Equal to total final expenditure at market prices.

Total home costs per unit of output. Derived by dividing the estimate of the gross domestic product at current factor cost based on expenditure data by the corresponding estimate at constant factor cost. Also known as the implied 'gdp factor cost deflator'.

Transfers. Payments made by one sector to another without any goods or services being received directly in return by the payer. They represent a distribution of the national income without adding to its total. A distinction is made between *current transfers* and *capital transfers*, depending upon the purpose for which, the basis on which, and the frequency with which the transfer is made.

Transfers abroad (net) by personal sector. Net transfers abroad by persons including legacies and migrants funds.

U

Undistributed income. See savings.

United Kingdom taxes on property income paid abroad. This comprises corporation tax, income tax, petroleum revenue tax, profits tax and excess profits taxes paid on profits earned in the UK by foreign-owned branches and subsidiaries, and income tax deducted from dividends and interest paid to non-residents from their portfolio investments in UK securities.

V

Value added. Gross value added is defined as the value of output less the value of intermediate consumption. Net value added is defined as the value of output *less* the values of both intermediate consumption and consumption of value added.

Value of physical increase in stocks and work in progress. The increase in the quantity of stocks and works in progress held by trading enterprises or by the central government for strategic purposes, valued at average prices of the year. Calculation of the value of the physical increase in stocks is related to the calculation of stock appreciation. Considerable uncertainty attaches to the division of the change in value of stocks between these two elements.

W

Wages and salaries. Earnings of civilian wage earners and salaried employees, other than employers social contributions before deduction of income tax, surtax or insurance contributions *including* income in kind *less* expenses of employment. The figures include directors' fees.

METHODOLOGICAL NOTES

General principles

This section is designed to bring up to date the description of definitions, sources and methods given in *United Kingdom National Accounts: Sources and Methods Third edition* (Studies in Official Statistics No 37, HMSO, 1985). Where there has been a change, the relevant paragraph in *Sources and Methods* (SM) is indicated.

Industrial classification

The tables which contain industrial analyses are based on the *Standard Industrial Classification, Revised 1992* (SIC(92)), described in articles in the October 1992 and February 1993 issues of *Economic Trends* (Nos 468, 472).

Historical series for these tables are calculated by re-grouping data on the previous industrial classification or by applying a correlator to the data. Consistent series on the new classification will extend for the same time period as series on the previous classification.

Revisions

The principal revisions which have been made to the estimates contained in last year's National Accounts Blue Book (*United Kingdom National Accounts 1995 Edition*) are given following these Notes.

The years prior to 1984 have not been reopened to incorporate revisions. There have been no revisions to GDP prior to 1991.

SECTION ONE: The national accounts

Chapter 1: National income, product and expenditure

Table 1.1: National and domestic product

From the 1992 edition, changes were made to the presentation of estimates of national and domestic product. References to different measures of GDP were dropped and the accounts now focus on a single GDP estimate. This estimate, without suffix, is the equivalent of the former average estimate, known as GDP(A), and fulfils the same role as the best central estimate of the level of this key economic aggregate and of changes over time. Table 1.1 shows estimates of GDP along with derived estimates, such as Gross national product (GNP) and National disposable income, and associated index numbers.

The 1992 edition of the Blue Book was the first in which an input-output analysis contributed to the determination of the best central estimate of GDP. In this 1996 edition, the estimates of GDP in 1989 to 1994 have been derived from input-output analysis of economic flows which describe supply, intermediate and final demand and value added. (See notes, introduction to section two and table 2.1).

For years prior to this innovation, estimates of GDP have been derived along other routes. Basically, the level of GDP is derived from the aggregates of the two broadly independent analyses of GDP based on its income and expenditure components. Account is taken also of the changes in volume and value added derived from the output analysis of GDP, which is compiled only in index number format. The methodology was refined from the 1988 Blue Book and further modifications were introduced in the 1992 edition for the years from 1985 onwards.

These new procedures using input-output analysis replace other methods used to reconcile the different measures of GDP in the 1989, 1990 and 1991 editions of the Blue Book.

All of the methods used to reconcile these different measures of GDP are explained below.

(i) Estimates of GDP: years up to 1985

In concept, the sums of income, expenditure and output components of GDP should be the same. But, as a result of measurement and other errors, there inevitably are differences. For each of the base years (that is 1958, 1963, 1970, 1975, 1980 and 1985), the level of GDP is estimated as the unweighted arithmetic average of the sums of the income and expenditure components of GDP. In this way, the growth in GDP between any two base years is determined entirely by its income and expenditure components. The contribution of the aggregate derived from output components is constrained to influence estimates of growth in, and levels of, GDP only in the periods between the base years. A technical note describing the estimation was published in the October 1988 issue of *Economic Trends* (No.420).

ii) GDP: 1985 to 1988

For the years 1985 to 1988, a better reconciliation has been achieved between the broadly independent estimates of income and expenditure components at current prices than hitherto, reflecting better understanding of the basic sources and the use of information from the 1989 and 1990 input-output tables. The discrepancies remaining between the sums of income and expenditure components at the initial reconciliation were comparatively small and well within the margins of error of the aggregates. It was therefore decided to distribute the discrepancy, or residual error as it is conventionally known, equally between the income and expenditure aggregates. This process eliminates the residual error in those years. The following table shows the aggregate series before this final distribution and the amount distributed.

Adjustments made to reconcile income and expenditure components

	Aggregates at initial reconciliation		Residual error distribution		£million Reconciled
	Income	Expenditure	Income	Expenditure	estimate
1985	307,924	307,881	-22	+21	307,902
1986	328,380	328,163	-108	+109	328,272
1987	360,599	360,751	+76	-76	360,675
1988	401,355	401,501	+73	-73	401,428

Given the improved coherence between the income and expenditure data, GDP at current prices could thus be set for the years 1986 to 1988, as in the base year 1985, at this reconciled estimate of the aggregate of the sums of the income and expenditure components. GDP at constant prices has been estimated as the sum of expenditure components, including the residual error distribution, at constant prices. This sum, of course, equals the total of income, including the residual error distribution, components deflated using the implied GDP deflator.

iii) GDP: 1989 to 1994

As noted above, the levels of GDP in 1989 to 1994 and its income and expenditure components are derived from the balanced input-output tables for those years.

iv) GDP: 1995

For the latest year, 1995, the expenditure and income components are less firm at this stage than those on which the reconciled estimates for 1985 to 1994 are based. For this reason the aggregate output indicators have also been used in the estimates of GDP for these years. GDP is estimated, for 1995, on the basis of the average of the growth rates shown by the total of the expenditure, income and output components applied to the level of GDP in 1994.

Real national disposable income

From the 1988 edition, Real national disposable income is calculated by a slightly simplified formula, as follows (SM4.41):

$$RNDI = TDE + a + NIA/p$$

where:
TDE	is Total domestic expenditure at constant prices;
a	is an adjustment equal to the statistical discrepancy (expenditure adjustment) at constant prices;
NIA	is Net investment abroad (at current prices); and
p	is the import price index.

Table 1.7 now contains all the remaining index numbers previously shown in Table 1.1.

Individual measures of GDP

As explained in the notes to Table 1.1, with effect from the 1992 Blue Book references to four different measures of GDP (reached by the expenditure, income and output approaches or as an average of those three measures) have been dropped in favour of the use of a single measure of GDP. It is regarded as the best central estimate both of the level and of changes over time.

The former expenditure and income measures are linked to the single measure through a statistical discrepancy term shown explicitly in the tables in Section 1. This enables easy reconstruction of the former measures (for example, GDP less statistical discrepancy (expenditure adjustment) equals the expenditure measure of GDP).

Tables showing the measures dropped from the current presentation are available from NAGDP Branch, Office for National Statistics.

Constant price series: rebasing to 1990 prices

Constant price series are estimates of the volume of economic activity expressed in the average prices of a selected base year. In order to keep abreast of the changing structure of prices in the economy, a new base year has, from time to time, to be introduced. From the 1993 Blue Book, constant price series are expressed in 1990 (rather than, as formerly, 1985) prices and index numbers take 1990 = 100. The relative prices in the base year of goods and services determine their weights in aggregate measures, such as Gross domestic product. Therefore choice of base year can affect the derived change over time in aggregate production. Because the constant price series used are of the chain linked form (see Introduction paragraphs 69 and 70), rebasing to 1990 prices will affect the growth rates only for comparisons involving the period from 1986 onwards.

Articles explaining rebasing, were published in the March 1988, January 1989 and February 1993 issues of *Economic Trends* (Nos. 413, 423 and 472).

Measures at market prices: effects of introducing the Community Charge and Council Tax.

GDP estimates for years from 1989 are affected by the abolition of domestic rates and the introduction of the Community Charge in Scotland from April 1989 and in England and Wales from April 1990. In the national accounts, domestic rates are classified as a tax on expenditure on housing services, and are therefore included in Consumers' expenditure at market prices (SM 6.506, 6.593, 9.27, 10.17). However, the Community Charge is classified as a transfer and is not part of Consumers' expenditure. It is treated as a deduction from income in calculating Personal disposable income.

Estimates of Consumers' expenditure and of GDP at current market prices from 1989 are therefore marginally lower than they would have been if the Community Charge had not replaced domestic rates. GDP at current factor cost is unaffected. Estimates at constant 1990 prices of Consumers' expenditure and GDP are also unaffected. A fuller description of the treatment of domestic rates and the Community Charge, and the impact of the switch from one to the other, appeared in the August 1989 issue of Economic Trends (No 430).

The Community Charge was replaced by the Council Tax in April 1993. This is treated identically in the national accounts, so there is no discontinuity in GDP estimates as a result of its introduction. A technical note on the treatment of Council Tax in the national accounts appeared in the January 1993 edition of *Economic Trends* (No. 471).

Table 1.2: Gross national product by category of expenditure

The estimates of Gross domestic product and Gross national product at market prices are defined to include taxes on expenditure levied on

D

Taxes on expenditure levied on imports

£ million

		1985	1986	1987	1988	1989	1990	1991	1992	1993	1994	1995
At current prices	CWCW	2 931	3 142	3 383	3 538	3 603	3 831	4 043	4 181	4 543	4 981	5 177
At 1990 prices	CWCX	3 080	3 211	3 388	3 516	3 605	3 831	3 732	3 858	3 961	4 272	4 213

imports. The main identifiable taxes are shown in total in the table above. Included are customs duties and agricultural levies paid on imports and excise duties paid on imported alcoholic beverages and tobacco products. Value added tax on imports is not included, nor is the imported element of car tax.

From the 1992 Blue Book, the estimates of Gross national product and of National income are derived from the definitive estimate of Gross domestic product. The Statistical discrepancy (expenditure adjustment) is defined as Gross domestic product *less* total expenditure components of Gross domestic product.

Table 1.3: Gross national product by category of expenditure at 1990 prices

For the years before 1986, sub-totals and totals may not equal the sums of their components. This arises from the methods used to produce constant price estimates at 1990 prices. The nature of the differences is illustrated in the following table which shows the difference between the expenditure measure of Gross domestic product at 1990 factor cost and the sum of its components.

Gross domestic product at 1990 factor cost

	Total (1)	Sum of components (2)	£million Difference (1)less(2) as percentage of (1)
1971	314,928	315,154	-0.1
1972	319,760	321,285	-0.5
1973	346,356	349,133	-0.8
1974	344,367	346,198	-0.5
1975	342,139	341,783	0.1
1976	354,947	355,095	-
1977	359,226	358,735	0.1
1978	368,605	367,414	0.3
1979	376,488	376,217	0.1
1980	369,635	367,572	0.6
1981	366,448	364,451	0.5
1982	371,332	370,322	0.3
1983	385,426	385,653	-0.1
1984	391,390	392,370	-0.3
1985	407,844	407,646	-

The estimates for some years (particularly the mid-1970's) are subject to wider margins of error than others. This is because price indices are used in calculating many of the components of the constant price aggregates, by revaluing data expressed at current prices. The problems associated with this revaluation become more acute when the rate of change of prices is relatively large, or itself changes rapidly.

Table 1.4: Gross domestic product by category of income

From the 1992 Blue Book, the definitive estimate of Gross domestic product at factor cost is included. The Statistical discrepancy (income adjustment) is defined as Gross domestic product *less* total income components of Gross domestic product.

The allowances for evasion (see SM 3.32-36) have been revised since **Sources and Methods** was published. As a percentage of GDP, the total allowance now rises from two per cent in the early 1970's to three per cent in the mid 1970's before falling to one and a half per cent in 1981 and to one and a quarter per cent from 1982. The evasion adjustment increased to one and a half per cent in 1992.

Rent. Further methodological changes were introduced in this Blue Book. They are described in the section on Rent in Table 4.7

Table 1.6: Gross domestic product at constant factor cost: by industry of output

The line for total services was first introduced in the 1986 Blue Book (SM 4.14). See also note for Table 2.5.

Table 1.7: Volume, value and price indices

Table 1.7 now includes the index numbers formerly given in Table 1.1. They are, following rebasing, given in the form 1990=100.

Constant price estimates of GDP are compiled for both the expenditure and output approaches. Direct constant price estimates cannot be made on the income components because volume changes in factor incomes, particularly profits, cannot be satisfactorily distinguished from price changes. A constant price version of the total income components of GDP is obtained indirectly as follows. *First*, an implied deflator for the total of the expenditure components of GDP is calculated. *Second*, the values of current price income components of GDP are divided by the corresponding values of this implied deflator to give an estimate of constant price GDP analysed by income. The deflator used is that derived from the total of the expenditure components of GDP at factor cost. It is known as the *Index of total home costs*, because it measures, conceptually, the price of domestic value added.

SECTION TWO: The main analyses.

Chapter 2: Industrial and sector analyses.

The estimates of the analysis of GDP by industry are based on classifying each economic unit (individual, enterprise etc) by industry, based on its main activity, and allocating all its activity to that industry. Subsidiary activities of these units are therefore included with the main activity. From the 1993 Blue Book, this general principle has been extended to treatment of Rent income, which is now allocated by industry according to the main activity of each rent-receiving unit. Also from the 1993 Blue Book, the subdivision of total GDP by industry at Table 2.2 is derived from data for economic units which are classified by industry according to ONS's business register. Previously, it was based on summing industry-specific estimates for each income component, and thus on the industry classifications in the various data sources for these components.

Table 2.1: Input-output balances for 1992, 1993 and 1994

Input-output balances have become a central part of the process to reconcile the national accounts in recent years. The input-output framework makes it possible to agree a definitive level of GDP at current prices without statistical discrepancies using all the components of income, expenditure and output.

In the 1992 and 1993 editions, a single input-output balance was presented for 1989 and 1990 respectively. Input-output balances were advanced a year in 1994 and this edition contains balances for 1992, 1993 and 1994.

Table 2.1 shows a complete picture of the flows of products in the economy for eleven industry groups for 1992, 1993 and 1994. The underlying input-output balances are compiled at a much more detailed level: the reconciliation process balances supply and demand for one hundred and twenty-three product groups. This detailed analysis for 1992, 1993 and 1994 is available from the ONS Databank in machine-readable form - see Preface.

Each row of the matrix shows how sales at purchasers' prices (domestic production and imports) of a specific product group are distributed between intermediate industries and final demand categories purchasing that product. The columns are completed by the addition of three rows to arrive at total inputs. Sales by final buyers cover purchases of goods and services from the categories of final demand. Taxes on expenditure represent those taxes paid directly to government less any subsidies received. Value added, the last entry for each industry group, represents the sum of gross trading profits and income from employment etc. for that industry. The sum of the value added estimates in this row corresponds conceptually to the output measure of GDP.

The taxes on expenditure less subsidies as identified in Table 2.1 do not represent all of the taxes included in the national accounts' factor cost adjustment. Import duties and some taxes on expenditure (mainly VAT) are already included in the value of purchases in the main body of the table.

General government is shown as purchasing the output of its own services. The purchases of the various functional divisions of general government are included in the appropriate industry group, for example public administration, education or health.

The balances for 1992, 1993 and 1994 are based on data collected using the new SIC(92) industrial classification. This, along with the availability of firmer data, has contributed to changes to the 1993 balance published in the 1995 Blue Book.

Table 2.5: Gross domestic product at constant factor cost: by industry of output

From the 1993 Blue Book, the aggregate is derived from constant price estimates of output at 1990 prices (SM 5.18-19). The weight assigned to each component series is determined by the value added contribution made by the corresponding activity towards total Gross domestic product in 1990.

The weights in Table 2.5 are entirely consistent with the corresponding figures in the 1993 edition for total net income in 1990 in Tables 2.2 and 2.4 except that the weight for **financial intermediation, real estate, renting and business activities** is calculated before subtracting the adjustment for financial services and a separate negative weight is shown for the financial services adjustment (SM 5.45-50). In the 1994 edition the estimate of the adjustment for financial services in 1990 was revised, but the weights were not changed.

The line for total services was first introduced in the 1986 Blue Book (SM 4.58). By convention, it includes contributions from Ownership of dwellings and from the Adjustment for financial services.

An examination of the output, expenditure and income measures of GDP before rebasing suggested that the growth in the output measure of GDP was over-stated by around half a per cent between 1987 and 1989. This was described in more detail in the 1992 Blue Book. In the rebased figures this over-statement has largely disappeared.

Small differences in growth for the measure of GDP were also evident for 1991 and 1992, with the initial output-based estimate falling by more than the income and expenditure measures in 1991 and falling less in 1992.

The output measure is based, essentially, on gross output indicators. It is thought that, during the decline in economic activity such indicators are likely initially to overstate the fall in constant price net output. To allow for this a number of adjustments have been made to annual output growth rates.

These concentrate on what are considered to be the weakest of the services output estimates. These were as follows:-

1991 :- An upwards adjustment of 0.4% has been applied to the following sections where employment and VAT data are being used as an annual output proxy.

This adjustment has been imposed throughout the whole of the following sections:-

Construction
Hotels and restaurants
Education
Health and social work

This adjustment has been applied to part of the following sections:-

Transport, storage and communication, Other community, social and personal service activities

For financial intermediation and for real estate, renting and business activities quarterly estimates of turnover are used as an indicator of output. An upward adjustment of 0.8% was made for the whole of financial intermediation and part of real estate, renting and business activities.

For wholesale an upwards adjustment of 1.4% was applied because the gross output indicators are felt to poorly reflect changes in margins during recessions.

1992 :- A downward adjustment of 0.4% has been applied to the following industries where there may be some inadequacies in the deflators used. (The exception being wholesale and retail where part was adjusted by 0.4%, the rest was adjusted by 1.4%.)

This adjustment has been applied to the whole of the following sections.

Agriculture, hunting and forestry
Fishing
Construction
Hotels and restaurants
Transport, storage and communication
Education
Health and social work
Other community, social and personal service activities

This adjustment has been applied to part of the following section:-

Real estate, renting and business activities

For the 1992 financial intermediation and for real estate, renting and business services, due to possible inadequacies in the deflators, a downward adjustment of 0.9% was applied.

The effects of these adjustments are to reduce the decline in GDP from -2.4% to -2.2% in 1991, increase the decline from negligible to -0.4% in

1992 and to increase growth in 1993 by 0.2% to 2.2%. These results are more in line with the declines shown by expenditure and income methods.

All adjustments are thought to be within the likely error range of the data and within the level of accuracy of those results indicated generally by the Office for National Statistics.

The analyses of GDP by category of output at table 2.5, reflect estimates based on the 1992 Standard Industrial Classification (SIC 92).

Table 2.6: Gross domestic product by sector and type of income

The estimate of company sector rent income is, from the 1985 Blue Book, based on data from Inland Revenue tax records. Similarly, the estimates of personal sector income from rent make more use of Inland Revenue tax data and the results of their Surveys of Personal Incomes. For subsequent years, where complete Inland Revenue data are not yet available, the estimates are derived from consumers' expenditure on private rents for dwellings and from available information on trends in rental income from portfolios of commercial property (SM Appendix).

SECTION THREE: The sector accounts.

General

Assets on finance leases

Assets on finance leases are recorded on a 'user' basis, with the lessees (users) regarded as undertaking capital formation with loans from the lessors (owners). The rental payments to the lessors are regarded as a mixture of loan repayments and finance charges. This treatment, which accords with SSAP 21, allocates the assets to the sector or industry using them to generate value added from productive activity. Assets on operating leases are recorded on an 'owner' basis.

Prior to the 1991 Blue Book, assets on finance leases were recorded on an 'owner' basis, with the lessors regarded as undertaking the capital formation and receiving rent payments from the lessees.

Details about the effects of the change, and a description of the estimates, were published in the October 1991 issue of *Economic Trends*. (No. 456)

Chapter 3: Summary sector accounts.

Table 3.3: General government current account

The heading 'National insurance etc contributions' has been replaced with 'Social security contributions'. This is now consistent with international terminology (SM 9.30).

'Final consumption' includes from the 1993 Blue Book, current payments (other than scholarship or maintenance grants) by central government to private sector educational institutions - see notes at Table 7.2 on final consumption.

'Social Security benefits' includes Redundancy Fund and Maternity Fund benefits (see Table 7.6) and non-contributory benefits such as war

pensions and supplementary benefits (see Table 7.2) as well as National Insurance benefits. The coverage of *'other current grants to persons'* has been correspondingly reduced (SM 9.90).

Table 3.4: International transactions

The figures in table 3.4 are compatible with those in **United Kingdom Balance of Payments**, 1996 Edition (The ONS Pink Book), which gives detailed figures from 1985 to 1995 and summary figures for earlier years. It also includes detailed notes and definitions which expand on and update the methodology described in Chapter Fifteen of **Sources and Methods**.

The principal change in presentation introduced since **Sources and Methods** was published is in the way the Balance of Payments accounts are classified into groups (SM 15.2). The entries previously included under **'official financing'** have been integrated with **'investment and other capital transactions'** under new headings covering **'transactions in UK external assets'** and **'transactions in UK external liabilities'**. Within the accounts, oil companies' direct investment has now been included with other direct investment entries (SM 15.31, 15.91-92).

Table 3.5: Summary capital account and
Table 3.6: Summary capital account including capital consumption

These two tables are, from the 1987 Blue Book, a re-presentation, without definitional or methodological change, of the material previously in Table 1.11: **Summary capital account** and Table 13.1: **Financial surplus or deficit: summary analysis by sector**.

Tables 3.7 to 3.14: Sector allocation of dividend and interest flows

Table 3.7 was introduced in the 1993 Blue Book. It shows sectoral receipts and payments of dividends and interest, broken down by financial instruments, in the latest year. This follows the introduction for the 1992 Blue Book of a new framework for estimating these flows, which yield this extra detail. For more information see the article *Sector allocation of dividend and interest flows - a new framework* in the October 1992 issue of *Economic Trends* (No 468).

Tables 3.8 to 3.14 show dividend and interest payments and receipts for each sector. The 1996 edition includes the presentation of dividends and interest paid on United Kingdom company securities on a gross basis i.e. including intra sector transactions.

Chapter 4: Personal sector and its subsectors.

Table 4.1: Income and expenditure account

Income from employment: Wages and salaries and **Income from employment Employers contributions: Other**. See notes at Table 4.10 on employers' and employees' contributions.

Imputed rent for owner occupied dwellings (Table 4.1). Further methodological changes were introduced this Blue Book. They are described in the section on Rent in Table 4.1.

Wages and salaries (Table 4.1). In the 1992 Blue Book the estimates for

the value of private use of company cars and fuel for periods since 1984 were reviewed in the light of the revised tax scales introduced by the Inland Revenue in recent years (SM 6.72). The revisions to the estimates for the value of company car benefits were also included in the consumers' expenditure.

Social security benefits and social security contributions (Tables 4.1 and 4.9). **'Social Security'** has been adopted, from the 1986 Blue Book, in place of the previous usage **'National insurance, etc'**. This is to align with the conventions of international organisations (SM 6.20-21).

Income from self employment. From the 1987 Blue Book, Inland Revenue estimates of self-employment income have been adjusted to take account of non-allowable business expenses (SM 6.91ff).

From the 1992 Blue Book estimates for years since 1984 include income (net of allowable expenses) from furnished lettings. The coverage of income from farming has been improved from the 1992 edition to include (from 1984) estimates of earnings from non-agricultural activity carried out on farm premises and from agriculture undertaken at other establishments (SM 6.92-93).

Current transfers from overseas; current transfers abroad. Up until the 1984 Blue Book, current transfers received from overseas were deducted from transfers abroad and the net balance was treated as a deduction from personal income. From the 1985 Blue Book, transfers to and from overseas have been separately identified. Current transfers from overseas are included in total personal income, and current transfers abroad are treated as a deduction from personal income (SM 6.29).

The definition of current transfers abroad was revised in the 1985 Blue Book to include occupational pensions paid by the UK government. Previously these transfers were part of current grants paid abroad by central government (SM 6.29).

Miscellaneous current transfers. This item, which was introduced in the 1985 Blue Book, includes certain compulsory fees and fines paid by the personal sector to central government, for example, fees for passports and driving licences. These fees and fines were formerly treated as a tax on expenditure and were part of consumers' expenditure. They were reclassified from the 1985 Blue Book to a new category of receipts by central government, excluded from consumers' expenditure and treated as a deduction from personal income. The change does not affect personal sector saving (SM 6.30-33, 6.506).

Community Charge and Council Tax. see note about treatment on page 150.

Consumers' expenditure: Social Security benefits and other current grants from general government. The treatment of the Community Programme Scheme (which was wound up in 1988) was amended from the 1986 Blue Book. It was assumed that approximately one-half of the scheme was operated by private non-profit-making bodies (PNPMBs) serving persons. Accordingly, approximately one-half of the cost of the scheme was re-classified from subsidies to current grants to the personal sector, and the expenditure on wages and salaries, etc by PNPMBs was included in consumers' expenditure as final expenditure by PNPMBs. See also notes on Central government (Chapter 7, entry on 'subsidies') (SM 6.20-21).

Table 4.3: Personal sector transactions in financial assets and liabilities.
First published in the 1987 Blue Book, this is a regrouping of the figures shown in Table 11.2.

For the methodology used in this table, see *Financial Statistics Explanatory Handbook* 1991 edition, sections on Table 9.2 *'Sources and Uses of Funds'.*

Tables 4.5 - 4.8: Consumers' expenditure (SM 6.514 ff).
Food. From the 1989 edition, the estimates of expenditure on food reflect an improvement in the method by which household results from the National Food Survey are grossed up for the population at large. The estimates also reflect a review of the methodology for several items, the changes to *soft drinks* being the most notable.

From the 1991 edition, revised constant price estimates of food, with the exception only of soft drinks and confectionery, have been obtained by deflating the corresponding current price estimates using an appropriate component of the retail prices index. The constant price estimates were previously based on the product of the weight consumed and the price per unit weight in the base year (then 1985); this did not allow for changes in quality over time. The change, introduced from 1986, resulted in substantial upward revisions except in 1986; for that year previous estimates at current and constant prices were judged to be overstated in relation to retail sales and other evidence, and the estimates adjusted downwards.

In Tables 4.7 and 4.8, the *'food'* headings from the 1989 edition have been changed as follows: *confectionery* is now shown separately from *preserves*; the latter is now subsumed within *other manufactured food.* From the 1991 edition, *bread and cereals* has been broken down into three separate items: *bread, cakes and biscuits,* and *other cereals* (SM 6.560-564).

Alcohol: From the 1994 edition a more accurate methodology for alcoholic drink has been introduced. Estimates for alcoholic drink, in both current and constant prices, are based on volume of sales and average prices of individual types of alcoholic beverages for both the "off" and "on" trades. This information is obtained from a continuous survey of retail outlets. The volume data extracted from this survey are grossed up to align with annual clearance figures from HM Customs & Excise.

Housing: rents, rates and water charges. From the 1993 Blue Book,

the estimates of rent (including imputed rent), rates and water charges reflect different means of calculation to those described in *Sources and Methods. Rents* at current prices up to 1990 are grossed up by reference to the estimated rateable value by tenure type; from 1991, the grossing ratios are derived from the estimated numbers of occupied dwellings by tenure type. A change to the method for calculating *owner-occupiers imputed rent* is introduced in this Blue Book for years subsequent to 1990. In accordance with a European Union Council Decision under the GNP Directive, a new benchmark establishing the value of imputed rents has been set for Q1 1991. This is based on an econometric regression model which uses certain characteristics of dwellings to link owner-occupied to rented properties. This benchmark is then projected forward using numbers of owner-occupied dwellings and broadly comparable paid rents data. From 1991, the path of constant price rents is based on the estimated number of occupied dwellings adjusted by a quality factor to represent overall improvements in the housing stock.

As from the second quarter of 1990, current price *domestic rates* and rates rebates apply only to payments in Northern Ireland, with the constant price path being determined by domestic rateable values in the province. Because domestic rates were paid in England and Wales up to the first quarter of 1990, the constant price series at 1990 prices must reflect that payment also. This is based on domestic rateable values up to that year. From the second quarter of 1990 onwards, the number of occupied dwellings in England and Wales, adjusted for quality provides the path. *Sewerage and water charges* at current prices for England and Wales use data provided by the Office of Water Services from 1990; corresponding data is obtained from the Scottish Office. The constant price estimates are based on the movements in domestic rateable values up to 1990. Thereafter, the appropriate Retail Prices Index component is used to deflate the current price series. (SM 6.588-594).

Housing: maintenance etc by occupiers. From the 1993 Blue Book, estimates of *DIY* goods reflect several changes. The estimates incorporate the results of the extended commodity breakdown available from the 1990 Retailing Inquiry; this has provided a better split between DIY and hardware goods. DIY estimates now include expenditure on lighting previously included under hardware. Finally, the 1990 Wholesaling Inquiry has provided a firmer basis for the inclusion of direct sales from wholesalers to consumers. Estimates of **contractors' charges and insurance** have been reviewed. In particular, *contractors' charges financed by insurance* claims now make use of data provided by the Association of British Insurers. This has also resulted in an improvement to the estimates of the administrative costs of structural insurance (SM 6.554-559; 6.596-599).

Fuel and power: coal and coke; other fuel. From the 1990 Blue Book, more accurate national average prices for house coal and coke have been introduced. Similarly an improvement has occurred with respect to gas oil prices where scheduled prices have been replaced by national average domestic gas oil prices, from returns submitted by the oil companies (SM 6.580-581).

Supplementary information

Household goods and services. From the 1991 Blue Book, estimates of contents insurance within **household and domestic services** have been reviewed to better reflect the administrative costs of providing the service (SM 6.600). From the 1993 edition, estimates of expenditure on **hardware** goods reflect the same changes as those affecting DIY goods; see Housing: maintenance etc by occupiers (SM6.554-599).

Transport and communication. From the 1996 Blue Book, a new, direct method has been introduced to estimate Consumers' Expenditure on new motor vehicles. Previously Consumers' Expenditure on new cars was taken as the residual after subtracting capital formation from the value of total new car registrations. It is now possible, using information on the V55 Registration Document to measure directly the number of vehicles sold to private individuals. These are valued using trade information and taking account of on the road costs. The method has been applied back to 1993.

From the 1990 edition, estimates of **petrol and oil** reflect two changes: a review of the proportion of total diesel oil expenditure associated with consumers; and the use of better-weighted average quarterly prices for all grades of petrol, including unleaded petrol (SM 6.582).

The 1990 edition also reflects revisions to expenditure on motor vehicle repairs, subsumed within **other running costs of vehicles**. These result from the addition of repairs financed specifically by insurance claims; these had previously been omitted because the Family Expenditure Survey does not record expenditure on repairs where the insurance company settles directly with the repairer (SM 6.603). Further improvements to expenditure on repairs occur in the 1991 edition along with better researched and deflated estimates of motor insurance, also subsumed within **other running costs of vehicles** (SM 6.603-607).

From the 1989 edition, consumers' expenditure on **air travel** reflects an improvement in the estimates of international travel by UK residents, based on data from the International Passenger Survey. In particular the estimates now cover the full cost of overseas journeys rather than payments only for flights immediately to and from the UK (SM 6.612-614).

From the 1990 edition, expenditure on sea travel (within **other travel**) includes expenditure on board ship as well as on fares paid to or from British ports by UK residents (SM 6.616-617).

From the 1991 edition, expenditure on taxis (within **other travel**) are now based on information from the National Travel Survey; previous estimates, obtained from the Family Expenditure Survey, were thought to be understated (SM 6.615)

Recreation, entertainment and education: television and video hire charges, licence fees and repairs. From the 1990 edition, estimates of video hire charges include video cassettes as well as the equipment. Estimates have been supplied by the British Videogram Association; such hire charges were previously assumed to be covered by the Retailing Inquiries. Revised estimates of expenditure on TV licences have been supplied by the NTVLRO from the 1990 Blue Book; these replace those previously supplied by the Post Office. The same edition also reflects improved estimates of spending on cinema admissions (subsumed within **other recreational and entertainment services**); the revisions are now based on annual and quarterly inquiries to cinema exhibitors since 1987 (SM 6.630).

Recreation, entertainment and education. From the 1991 Blue Book, estimates of spending on **books** have been adjusted upwards to reflect expenditure by students and other purchases not covered by the Family Expenditure Survey. Use has also been made of a more representative index of book prices, compiled by the Publishers' Association, to obtain constant price estimates after 1985 (SM 6.585). From the same Blue Book, expenditure at constant prices on **education** provided by local authority and private colleges have been calculated using an improved price index; the index used takes account of the costs of wages and salaries and of goods and services procured for education (SM 6.631-633).

From the 1995 Blue Book estimates of *betting and gaming* included expenditure on the National Lottery based on data from OFLOT. The constant price estimates have been obtained using the Retail Prices Index as the deflator. As with all other forms of gambling, consumers' expenditure on the National Lottery is the cost to persons taking part in this activity, i.e. the amount staked less the amount returned in the form of winnings. (SM 6.505).

Other goods and services: pharmaceutical products and medical equipment. From the 1990 Blue Book, estimates of spending on non-NHS spectacles have been revised following an improvement in the methodology; better use is being made of Family Expenditure Survey results together with a specific price index for spectacles which is available within the RPI (SM 6.638-639).

Catering (meals and accommodation). From the 1988 Blue Book, expenditure on accommodation now includes specific estimates for residential and nursing home care for the elderly, etc., and on board and lodging by others living outside households. Estimates of such non-household expenditure were previously based on an allowance related to data from the Family Expenditure Survey. From the 1991 edition, estimates of expenditure on **catering** reflect several changes. Estimates now explicitly allow for spending on private entertainment (e.g. parties, weddings, receptions, etc) and for students living in university or college accommodation; the former is based on Family Expenditure Survey (FES) data; the latter is derived from Department for Education and Employment (DfEE) sponsored surveys of student expenditure together with DfEE estimates of student numbers. Adjustments to the catering estimates have also been made in relation to juvenile expenditure, taking account of survey evidence, and for food in kind associated with the armed forces. From the 1993 edition, estimates of expenditure by those living in residential and nursing homes are benchmarked on a 1993 survey of such establishments. New estimates of expenditure by military personnel living in barracks have also been obtained, using Ministry of Defence survey data relating to 1992 and earlier years (SM 6.635-637).

Administrative costs of life assurance and pension schemes. From the 1991 edition, constant price estimates have been obtained using a deflator more closely related to an index of costs in the industry; previously, the expenses of the service being purchased were revalued at constant prices using the general consumers' expenditure deflator (SM 6.641).

Other services. From the 1985 Blue Book, certain fees and fines payable direct to the central government by consumers (e.g. driving licences, passport fees, court fines) have been excluded from this item and appear as ***Miscellaneous current transfers*** in Table 4.1 (SM 6.604, 6.648). From the 1991 edition, estimates of expenditure on undertaking (within ***other services***) have been adjusted upwards in line with information about the average cost per funeral from the National Association of Funeral Directors (SM 6.644). From the 1993 edition, estimates of expenditure on financial services (within ***other services***) have been reviewed in the light of better researched data on bank and unit trust charges (SM 6.645).

Final expenditure by private non-profit-making bodies (PNPMBs). See entry on Consumers' expenditure: Social security benefits and other current grants from central government in notes for Table 4.1, above. From the 1993 edition, central government current payments (other than scholarships or maintenance grants) to private sector educational institutions (universities, polytechnics (from April 1989) and grant maintained schools (from April 1990) are now regarded as central government final consumption. The institutions themselves remain classified as PNPMBs but their final consumption is lower than that shown in previous editions by the amount that has been attributed to central government final consumption - see the entry for final consumption for Table 7.2 Central Government Current Account, below. From the 1993 Blue Book, estimates of final expenditure by PNPMBs incorporate the results of a 1993 survey of charities (SM 6.513, 6.656-657).

Other improvements. From the 1991 edition, a number of changes have been incorporated in the estimates to make good small deficiencies in the coverage of certain retail sales. Among other retailers, these include adjustments to take account of certain goods sold by petrol filling and motorway service stations. From the 1993 edition, use was made of the 1990 Wholesaling Inquiry to improve estimates of direct sales from wholesalers to consumers; such sales are not covered by the annual Retailing Inquiries.

Table 4.10: Life assurance and pension schemes
From the 1992 Blue Book the estimates for life assurance and insurance-invested pension schemes for years from 1986 are mainly sourced from income and expenditure data compiled within ONS, although some parts of the analysis continue to draw on information obtained from the Association of British Insurers (SM 6.117-118).

Contributions of employers (Funded Schemes and All Schemes). In this table the series include transfers into personal pension schemes from the National Insurance Fund. They represent repayments of amounts originally paid by employers and employees as contributions to the State Earnings-related Pension Scheme, together with incentive payments made by the Department of Social Security to employees contracting out of the earnings-related element of the state scheme. For the purposes of Table 4.1 an increase in personal disposable income results because the amounts are netted off current social security contributions; they do not affect the assessments of ***wages and salaries*** or ***employers' contributions: other*** (SM 6.116-125). ***Contributions of employees (Funded Schemes and All Schemes)***. See above.

Chapter 5: Companies.
Table 5.1 shows data for total companies.

Table 5.2 shows current and capital accounts for industrial and commercial companies.

Table 5.3 shows transactions in financial asset and liabilities for industrial and commercial companies.

Table 5.4 shows current and capital accounts for financial companies and institutions.

Table 5.5 shows transactions in financial assets and liabilities for financial companies and institutions.

Securities dealers, first set up in response to the deregulation of UK securities markets ('Big Bang') of October 1986, are classified as financial institutions (SM 2.17).

Gross trading profits (Tables 5.1, 5.2 and 5.4). From the 1985 Blue Book the gross trading profits of industrial and commercial companies reflect the reclassification of the Independent Broadcasting Association levy as a tax on income. In 1993 the levy was replaced by franchise payments to the Independent Television Commission, which is classified as a payment made out of gross trading profits.

Net interest received under the fixed-rate shipbuilding and export credit schemes was also reclassified as a subsidy from the 1985 Blue Book, when it was treated as a subsidy to industrial and commercial companies. From the 1986 Blue Book, it is treated as a subsidy to financial companies. For further details see notes on Table 7.2 (SM 7.65).

From the 1987 Blue Book, agricultural companies' profits are based on Inland Revenue data (SM 7.62 (ii)).

From the 1987 Blue Book, launch aid, provided by central government for specific development projects by industrial and commercial companies, is classified as lending. It was formerly classified as a subsidy (SM 7.62). See also notes for Table 7.4.

From the 1987 Blue Book, estimates of those business entertainment expenses not allowable as a deduction (in computing taxable profits) have been subtracted from the Inland Revenue profits estimates for industrial and commercial companies (SM 7.62).

From the 1988 Blue Book, profits earned abroad by branches of UK companies are deducted from the Inland Revenue profits estimates for industrial and commercial companies. The deduction uses balance of payments estimates (SM 7.62 (vii)).

The financial charges adjustment to the Inland Revenue profits data for industrial and commercial companies includes certain costs associated with takeover activity (SM 7.62 (iv)). As from the 1989 Blue Book, those takeover costs that are not allowable as a deduction in computing taxable profits, and are not already included in the financial charges adjustment, have been subtracted from the Inland Revenue profits estimates. This new adjustment includes publicity, advertising, printing, opinion survey costs and consultants' fees.

From the 1988 Blue Book, profits and net interest receipts of banks are derived from returns made to the Bank of England. The figures now fully reflect the end-1981 coverage changes to the sector (SM 7.65 (i)).

From 1984, finance leasing companies' profits are based on returns made to the Bank of England (SM 7.65 (v)). From the 1991 Blue Book, assets on finance leases are recorded on a "user" basis rather than an "owner" basis for periods since 1978. This change reduced trading profits of finance leasing companies and increased their non-trading income with equal and opposite effects on the estimates for the lessee sectors.

From the 1988 Blue Book, the profits of general insurance companies have been based on returns made to the Office for National Statistics. They have been calculated as premiums less claims, commissions, management expenses and additions to technical reserves. The calculation of profits was revised for the 1994 Blue Book to lift the EC's reservation on the UK Gross National Product in respect of net accident insurance premiums. The calculation of the additions to general business technical reserve now excludes changes in some components of this reserve.

From the 1992 Blue Book, the estimates of the gross trading profits of industrial and commercial companies include specific adjustments to convert the Inland Revenue data from financial to calendar years (SM 7.56) From 1991 the former Quarterly Profits Enquiry conducted by the Inland Revenue has been replaced by an inquiry conducted by the Office for National Statistics. This inquiry covers about 1600 large company groups. From the 1994 edition the inquiry is used to estimate the sum of profits and rent.

From the 1994 Blue Book, the service earnings of banks' foreign exchange transactions have been included within gross trading profits. This change is made to bring the estimates of banks' gross trading profits into line with international standards.

Rent (Tables 5.1, 5.2 and 5.4). From the 1985 Blue Book, the figures of rent income are based on information provided by Inland Revenue - see notes on Table 2.6 (SM 7.68).

UK taxes on income (Tables 5.1 and 5.2). From the 1985 Blue Book, these series include the Independent Broadcasting Association levy (SM 7.33). In 1993 the levy was replaced by franchise payments to the Independent Television Commission (ITC).

Miscellaneous current transfers (Tables 5.1, 5.2 and 5.4), first shown in the 1989 Blue Book, comprise fees paid to OFTEL, OFGAS, the SIB and Companies House.

Capital transfers (Tables 5.2 and 5.4). From the 1992 Blue Book, this series includes contributions by contractors to capital expenditure by general government, as well as payments to public corporations.

Royalties and licence fees on oil and gas production (Tables 5.1 and 5.4). From 1990, royalties are recorded on a payments basis. For earlier years they were on an accruals basis (SM 7.42-44).

ITC franchise payments (Tables 5.1 and 5.4). These started in 1993 replacing the Independent Broadcasting Association levy (see above).

Table 5.3 : Industrial and commercial companies transactions in financial assets and liabilities

First published in the 1987 Blue Book, is a regrouping of the figures in Table 11.3.

Table 5.5: Companies and financial institutions transactions in financial assets and liabilities

First published in the 1988 edition, consolidates the data in Tables 11.4 and 11.5 and presents them in summary form.

Chapter 6: Public corporations.

Transactions have been revised back to the second quarter of 1992.

The public corporations in existence at 31 December 1995 are listed below. Those which have left the public corporations sector since the end of 1983 are also shown, while those in existence in earlier years are given in *Sources and Methods* (Chapter 8, Annex 1).

A. Institutions classified to the public corporation sector and in existence at 31 December 1995.

Name of corporation	Commencing or vesting date
Angle Train Contracts Ltd	August 1995
Audit Commission	April 1983
British Broadcasting Corporation	1927
British Coal[1]	January 1947
British Nuclear Fuels plc[2]	April 1971
British Railways Board	January 1963
British Waterways Board	January 1963

Caledonian Macbrayne Ltd[3]	April 1990
Channel Four Television Company Ltd[3]	December 1980
Civil Aviation Authority	April 1972
Commonwealth Development Corporation	February 1948
Covent Garden Market Authority	October 1961
Crown Agents and Crown Agents Holding and Realisation Board	January 1980
Development Board for Rural Wales	April 1977
European Passenger Services Ltd[3]	May 1994
Evershott leasing Ltd[3]	August 1995
Her Majesty's Stationery Office	April 1980
Highlands and Islands Airports[3]	April 1995
Highlands and Islands Enterprise[1]	November 1965
Housing Action Trusts	July 1991 to July 1994
Laganside Corporation[3]	April 1989
Land Authority for Wales	April 1976
Local authority airports	April 1987
Local authority bus companies	October 1986
London Regional Transport[1]	January 1970
National Health Service Trusts	April 1991
New Town Development Corporations and Commission	December 1946 and various later dates
Northern Ireland Housing Executive	May 1971
Northern Ireland Transport Holding Company	April 1968
Nuclear Electric plc[3]	April 1989
Oil and Pipelines Agency	December 1985
Passenger Transport Executives	October 1969 and various later dates
Porterbrook Leasing[3]	August 1995
Post Office	April 1961
Royal Mint	April 1975
Scottish Enterprise[1]	December 1975
Scottish Homes[1]	1937
Scottish Nuclear plc[3]	April 1989
Trust Ports in Northern Ireland	April 1974
Union Railways[3]	April 1995
United Kingdom Atomic Energy Authority	April 1986
United Kingdom Nares Ltd	July 1982
Urban Development Corporations	March 1981, May and December 1987, June 1988
Urban Regeneration Agency	November 1993
Welsh Development Agency	January 1976
Welsh Fourth Channel Authority	January 1981

1 Name changed. British Coal was formerly the National Coal Board; London Regional Transport was formerly London Transport Executive. Highlands and Islands Enterprise was formerly Highlands and Islands Development Board; Scottish Enterprise was formerly Scottish Development Agency and Scottish Homes was formerly Scottish Special Housing Association.

2 As of the 1994 Blue Book, British Nuclear Fuels plc has been reclassified to the public sector for statistical purposes. Data underlying annual estimates for income, expenditure and financial transactions.

3 Nuclear Electric plc was part of the former Central Electricity Board; Caledonian Macbrayne Ltd was part of the Scottish Transport Group; Channel Four Television Company Ltd was part of the Independent Television Commission; Scottish Nuclear plc was part of the former South of Scotland Electricity Board. Railtrack plc was part of the British Railways Board; European Passenger Services Ltd was part of the British Railways Board. Highlands and Islands Airports were part of the Civil Aviation Authority. Angel Train Contracts Ltd, Everest Leasing Ltd, Porterbrook Leasing Ltd and Union Railways were part of the British Railways Board.

B. Publicly owned institutions not classified to the public corporations sector for statistical purposes.

Institution	Classified to
Bank of England Banking Department	financial institutions
Girobank until end 1990	financial institutions
International Military Services (ceased trading July 1991)	industrial and commercial companies

C. Corporations reclassified to the private sector since end 1983.

Enterprise Oil Ltd in June 1984

British Telecom in November 1984

British Shipbuilders (warship yards) and other companies from July 1984

Trust Ports in Great Britain from end-March 1985

British Gas plc in December 1986

British Airways plc in February 1987

Royal Ordnance plc in April 1987

BAA plc in July 1987

National Bus Company by April 1988

Twenty-seven Local Authority bus companies from October 1988 to March 1994

British Steel in December 1988

General Practice Finance Corporation in March 1989

Regional Water Authorities in England, Welsh Water Authority and Water Authorities Association in December 1989

Liverpool Airport in June 1990

Girobank plc in July 1990

Scottish Transport Group subsidiary bus companies from August 1990 to October 1991

Regional Electricity Companies and National Grid Company in December 1990

National Power plc and PowerGen plc in March 1991

Scottish Hydroelectric plc and ScottishPower plc in June 1991

Supplementary information

British Technology Group in April 1992

Northern Ireland Electricity Service in June 1993

East Midlands International Airport in August 1993

Southend Airport March 1994

Belfast International Airport July 1994

British Coal - coal mines in December 1994

London Regional Transport - ten subsidiary bus companies during 1994

Railtrack plc 3 April 1994

Cardiff - Wales Airport April 1994

Bournemouth International Airport April 1995

D. Corporations dissolved

National Film Finance Corporation, in December 1985, being replaced in the private sector by the British Screen Finance Consortium British National Oil Corporation, in March 1986, being replaced by the Oil and Pipelines Agency

National Dock Labour Board in July 1989

Electricity Council in March 1990, being replaced in the private sector by the Electricity Association.

Crown Suppliers in March 1991

Pilotage Commission in April 1991

Six Local Authority Bus Companies from April 1989 to November 1994

E. Other changes.

The Housing Corporation was reclassified in the 1987 Blue Book as a central government trading body and the data were revised back to 1974. The Independent Television Commission (other than Channel Four) was reclassified to the central government sector from October 1991. The Urban Regeneration Agency was established from November 1993, and incorporated the former English Industrial Estates Corporation from April 1994, trading as English Partnership. Letchworth Garden City Corporation became Letchwoth Garden City Heritage Foundation, a private charity from October 1995.

For statistical purposes within the National Accounts, the income and expenditure transactions of the Bank of England Banking Department have been reclassified from the 1993 Blue Book to the financial sector. Data have been revised back to 1984. There has been a similar reclassification of the Girobank transactions from 1984 to its privatisation in July 1990. Previously, only their financial transactions have been included in this sector.

From the 1993 Blue Book the fossil fuel levy on electricity distribution is now separately identified as a capital grant within the public corporation accounts. Until this Blue Book income generated was included in gross trading surplus. See chapter 7.

Debt written-off. The entry for 1980 in *Sources and Methods* Chapter 8 Annex 2 is revised to read:

1980 The write-off of £320 million comprising:

(i) £100 million outstanding debt of the National Freight Corporation under the Transport Act 1980;

(ii) £160 million of government loan debt of the British Airways Board under the Civil Aviation Act 1980;

(iii) £60 million of public dividend capital of British Aerospace under the British Aerospace Act 1980.

The write-off of £40 million in 1984 represents the net effect of replacing £2,790 million of debt owed to the National Loans Fund by British Telecommunications plc with £2,750 million of debentures under the Telecommunications Act 1984.

The write-off of £1,624 million in 1986 comprises:

(i) £1,591 million outstanding debt of certain New Town Development Corporations - Milton Keynes, Telford, Peterborough, and Warrington and Runcorn - under the New Towns and Urban Development Corporation Act 1985;

(ii) £33 million outstanding debt of the Development Board for Rural Wales under the Development of Rural Wales Act 1976.

The write-off of £3,980 million in 1988 is attributed to British Steel; it comprises £500 million Public Dividend Capital and £3,480 million under the Iron and Steel Act 1975.

The write-off of £5,028 million in 1989 comprises loans to Regional Water PLCs from the National Loans Fund (£4,973 million) and from the Public Works Loan Board (£55 million).

The write-off of £1,734 million in 1990 comprises:

(i) £1,368 million outstanding debt of Scottish Nuclear plc under the Electricity Act 1989;

(ii) £366 million outstanding debt of the Northern Ireland Housing Executive, agreed by the Department of Finance, Northern Ireland.

The write-off of £418 million in 1991 comprises:

(i) the net effect of replacing £509 million of debt owed to the National Loan Fund by ScottishPower plc with £393.9 million of debentures;

(ii) the net effect of replacing £534.9 million of debt owed to the National Loans by Scottish Hydroelectric plc with £232 million of debentures.

In March 1995 £1,598 of debt was written-off under the Coal Industry Act 1994 (British Coal Corporation) Extinguishment of Loans Order 1995.

Table 6.1: Operating account

Subsidies. From the 1986 Blue Book, the total has been divided to show those subsidies which are included in the calculation of the *Gross trading surplus* and those which are included in income from *Rent* (SM 8.30-31).

Table 6.4: Transactions in financial assets and liabilities

From the 1986 Blue Book the item formerly shown as 'Other identified transactions in financial liabilities (net)' has been split into two components, 'Trade creditors' and 'Other liabilities', comprising compensation payments by regional water authorities to local authorities arising from the transfer of fixed assets to the former in 1974 (SM 8.70).

The item formerly shown as 'Other identified transactions in financial assets (net)' now appears as its separate components, 'Trade debtors' and 'Other assets', comprising: credit extended by gas (up to end 1986) and electricity showrooms (up to the end of 1990); advance and progress payments on imports; and compensation payments in respect of repayment of debt associated with the transfer in 1978 of some New Town Corporations' assets to local authorities (SM 8.75).

Chapter 7: Central government, including Social Security funds.

Social security contributions (tables 7.1, 7.2 and 7.4). This term has been adopted from the 1986 Blue Book, in place of the previous usage 'National insurance, etc contributions'. It is now consistent with the conventions of international organisations (SM 9.68).

Table 7.1: Summary account

For a description of miscellaneous current transfers included before the 1985 Blue Book in taxes on expenditure, see notes to Table 7.2.

For consistency with international terminology, the heading 'National Insurance etc contributions' has been replaced by 'Social security contributions' (SM 9.68, 9.150).

Table 7.2: Current account

Taxes on income. The Independent Broadcasting Authority levy was reclassified, from the 1985 Blue Book, from taxes on expenditure to taxes on income because it is a tax on excess profits (SM 9.64). With effect from 1993 this has been replaced by the series ITC franchise payments, which appears under **rent, dividends and interest, etc**.

Taxes on expenditure. From the 1993 Blue Book the fossil fuel levy on electricity distribution is included. The distribution of the levy is included in *capital grants*. From the 1985 Blue Book, separate figures are shown for the *sugar levy*, which is collected from sugar producers to offset the costs of storage, refunds and other costs and penalties, and for the *European Coal and Steel Community levy* which was formerly included in miscellaneous taxes on expenditure. Equivalent amounts are passed on to the European Communities (SM 9.66).

Figures for Customs and Excise revenue on *hydrocarbon oils* are, from the 1985 Blue Book, shown net of export rebates, shipbuilders' relief and bus fuel rebates. The separate detail of these rebates is no longer shown. *Motor vehicle duties* are shown after excluding receipts from driving licences and after deducting shipbuilders' relief. Driving licences are, from the 1985 Blue Book, included in a new item *Miscellaneous current transfers*. Other items formerly included as taxes on expenditure which (from the 1985 Blue Book) form part of miscellaneous current transfers are: fines and penalties, passport fees, public service and heavy goods vehicle drivers licence fees and certain other fees imposed by central government. From the 1985 Blue Book, accruals of Northern Ireland rates include estimates of rate arrears (SM 9.56-66).

Figures for Customs and Excise revenue on *tobacco, beer, wines, cider, perry and spirits, customs duties, agricultural levies* and *hydrocarbon oils* have been included on an accrued basis since 1979. They are now recorded when duty falls due rather than when customs records the receipt of duty. The differences between receipts and accruals are shown in the accruals adjustments on Table 7.4 (SM 9.56).

From the 1995 Blue Book, insurance premium tax and air passenger duty were included under Customs and Excise revenue.

From the 1986 Blue Book, a new tax, *London regional transport levy*, is included (SM 9.66, 9.67).

National non-domestic rates (NNDR), which replaced non-domestic local authority rates in Great Britain in April 1990, are part of central government taxes and are classified as taxes on expenditure. The accruals adjustment represents the difference between accruals and receipts from local authorities and other sources.

Proceeds from the Lottery paid to the *Lottery Distribution Fund* are included here from the 1995 Blue Book.

Gross trading surplus. The management expenses of the National Savings Bank Ordinary accounts are, from the 1985 Blue Book, treated as current expenditure on goods and services and the NSB ordinary account is no longer regarded as a trading body (SM 9.71).

Rent, dividends and interest, etc. From the 1986 Blue Book, royalty figures are no longer included with licence fees on oil and gas production, but are shown as a separate item (SM 9.76). This now includes ITC franchise payments.

Dividends and interest. From the 1988 Blue Book, receipts of interest arising from the shipbuilding credit scheme and the export credit scheme are included here, and are not treated as offsets to payments under the schemes and recorded net under subsidies (SM 9.77).

Miscellaneous current transfers. This was a new item in the 1985 Blue Book. It comprises receipts from driving licences, public service vehicle licence fees, heavy goods vehicle licence fees, passport fees, dog and gun licences, and fines and penalties in Magistrates' and Scottish courts (SM 9.66).

Final consumption. From the 1993 Blue Book, current payments (other than scholarships or maintenance grants) by central government to private sector educational institutions - universities, polytechnics (from April 1989) and grant maintained schools (from April 1990) - are treated as final consumption. In previous Blue Books, these payments to universities and polytechnics were treated as grants to persons financing consumers' expenditure, and grants to grant maintained schools were recorded as current grants to local authorities financing local authorities final consumption. Consumers' expenditure and local authorities final consumption are reduced correspondingly.

The functional analysis is now shown in Table 7.5.

The management expenses of the National Savings Bank ordinary account are, from the 1985 Blue Book, included as an item of current expenditure on goods and services (SM 9.83).

The Community Industry Scheme is, from the 1986 Blue Book, included as final consumption, but it was formerly classified to grants to non-profit-making bodies serving persons. See also entries below on other employment measures under *Subsidies* and *Current grants to local authorities* (SM 9.80, 9.90, 9.92).

Subsidies. This includes net interest support costs formerly included in interest payments. The new series is shown separately. The interest due to ECGD is included in interest receipts from the 1988 Blue Book. The functional analysis now appears in Table 7.5.

The Community Programme Scheme (which was wound up in 1988) was classified, from the 1986 Blue Book, as current grants to local authorities and to non-profit-making bodies serving persons. The local authority element was classified to *Community amenities* in the COFOG analysis. The Youth Training Scheme is being recorded variously as grants to persons, final consumption and subsidies, whereas it was included previously as grants to non-profit-making bodies serving persons. These treatments are still under review and may be amended in due course. See also entries on other employment measures under *Final consumption* above and *Current grants to local authorities* below (SM 9.80, 9.88- 92).

From the 1987 Blue Book, launch aid is classified as lending to the private sector except for expenditure on support for the Concorde aircraft which has been reclassified to final consumption.

Current grants to personal sector. Family benefits comprise child benefit, one parent benefit, family income supplement and maternity grants. Lump sum payments to pensioners (Christmas bonuses) other than those paid under the National Insurance scheme are included from

the 1985 Blue Book in *Other social security benefits* which in addition comprises old persons' pensions, attendance allowance, invalid care allowance and invalidity pension (SM 9.90).

Current grants to personal sector. Grants to universities and colleges These no longer include payments to universities (see *final consumption* above).

Current grants to local authorities. These no longer include payments to grant maintained schools (see *final consumption* above). Two employment measures (technical and vocational education initiative, and work-related non-advanced further education initiative) are included as grants to local authorities, from the 1986 Blue Book. They are classified to *Education* in the COFOG analysis. See also entries above on other employment measures under *Final consumption and Subsidies* (SM 9.92). From April 1990 these grants include National non-domestic rates (NNDR) distribution to local authorities.

Current grants paid abroad. Credits from and debits to the European Union are shown separately. Pensions paid to former government employees are regarded from the 1985 Blue Book as private sector transfer payments (SM 9.93-96).

Debt interest. From the 1985 Blue Book, interest support costs are classified as a subsidy (SM 9.99). Payments to local authorities, public corporations and other sectors are now shown separately.

Table 7.3: Capital account
Gross domestic fixed capital formation. The functional analysis now appears in Table 7.5. From the 1991 Blue Book the capital value of finance leased assets is included in GDFCF.

Value of physical increase in stocks. From the 1988 Blue Book Intervention Board for Agricultural Produce (IBAP) stocks are recorded on an accrual basis (SM 9.107).

Capital transfers. Details of investment grants and regional development grants are, from the 1985 Blue Book, no longer shown separately but are combined in the figures for transfers to the company sector. Other grants to the personal sector are shown as a separate item (SM 9.109) from the 1985 Blue Book.

Capital grants to public corporation and companies From the 1993 Blue Book these include the distribution of the fossil fuel levy.

Capital grants to local authorities In 1992 these include £5 billion commutation grant to finance the repayment of debt, almost entirely to central government.

Table 7.4: Transactions in financial assets and liabilities
Borrowing requirement. From the 1985 Blue Book, the borrowing requirement was re-ordered to show liabilities and assets separately.

However net indebtedness to Bank of England Banking department is shown net of public sector deposits (an asset). Additional detail of British Government foreign currency bonds is shown (SM 9.122-148).

From the 1986 Blue Book, 'Borrowing requirement' includes details on HMG $2.5 billion floating rate note issue. 'Miscellaneous direct borrowing (net) from overseas governments and institutions' less 'Capital subscriptions to the IMF' are no longer shown separately but are combined to form 'Miscellaneous direct official borrowing from overseas'. For compatibility with other publications (Pink Book) the subhead 'Overseas official financing' has been deleted. The entries related to this subhead are not affected. Transactions in ECGD backed promissory notes are now included in 'Commercial bills' (SM 9.122-148).

Net lending to private sector, from the 1987 Blue Book, includes launch aid for the RB 211 engine, V2500 engine, Westland 30 helicopter, EH101 helicopter and the A320 aircraft. Commercial exploitation receipts are counted as repayment of lending. This is included in net lending to other industry and trade (SM 9.151).

Lending by the Housing Corporation is now included in lending for house purchase (SM 9.152).

Accruals adjustments. The accruals adjustment for final consumption in respect of defence expenditure is now included with trade debtors and creditors in other identified financial liabilities (net) up to 1983 (SM 9.118). An accruals adjustment for Value of physical increase in stocks has been included for the 1988 Blue Book. Other customs and excise duties have now been split into the same level of detail as shown in Table 7.2. From the 1996 Blue Book, National Lottery accruals adjustments are also shown.

Transactions in financial assets (net). For consistency with international returns, the heading 'National Insurance etc contributions' has, from the 1986 Blue Book, been replaced by 'Social security contributions' (SM 9.150).

Cash expenditure on company securities. Purchases and sales of securities are shown separately, from the 1985 Blue Book (SM 9.163).

Table 7.5

This table presents a functional analysis of central government expenditure in the same level of detail as Table 9.4. It includes current and capital grants together with net lending to local authorities, items which disappear on consolidation in the general government expenditure analysis.

Table 7.6: Social security funds: current account and financial transactions account

This table now embraces all social security funds i.e. the National Insurance Funds, Redundancy and Maternity Funds for Great Britain and Northern Ireland as well as National Health Service contributions and transfers to the NHS. In addition to the current account the table includes a summary financial account. Contributions from abroad are now identified in receipts. In Table 7.2 these overseas contributions are netted off from social security benefits paid abroad. Contributions from employers includes imputed contributions in respect of Statutory Sick Pay (see glossary comment) (SM 9.165). Separate information for contributions in respect of HM Forces is, from the 1985 Blue Book, no longer given (SM 9.165).

Chapter 8: Local authorities

The estimates for local authorities given in this Blue Book incorporate information supplied for *Local Government Financial Statistics (England) no.6 1995*, for the years up to 1994/95, and corresponding information for Wales, Scotland and Northern Ireland. From the 1985 Blue Book, the functional analysis of *Current expenditure on goods and services* (Table 8.2) and of *Gross domestic fixed capital formation* (Table 8.3) is consistent with the analysis shown in Table 9.4. This is based on the international classification of the functions of government (COFOG) which is designed to standardise classifications and improve international comparisons. Further details are given in the notes to Table 9.4. The functional analyses of current grants (Table 8.2) and capital grants (Table 8.3) from central government are now shown in the central government expenditure Table 7.5. `

The following are the main methodological changes to the local authorities' account:

From the 1986 Blue Book:

(i) Housing benefit administration has been reclassified from Housing to Social security and welfare.

(ii) Other trading subsidies are recorded gross of any transfers from trading funds to the rate fund, which are now included in gross trading surplus.

(iii) Certain advances and grants for industrial and commercial enterprises have been reclassified from current expenditure on goods and services to subsidies.

(iv) The accruals adjustment on local authorities' payments of value added tax has been deleted (SM 10.47).

Subsequently:

(v) Approximately one half of the cost of the Community Programme was recorded from the 1986 Blue Book, as local authority current expenditure on goods and services, financed by central government current grants to local authorities. From October 1988, this scheme was replaced by the Adult Training Programme, expenditure on which is treated as Central government grants to persons. See also notes on Central government (Section 7, entry in 'subsidies').

(vi) The Community Charge replaced domestic rates in Scotland from April 1989 and in England and Wales from April 1990. National

F   Total wages, salaries and employers' contributions paid by general government

£ million

		1985	1986	1987	1988	1989	1990	1991	1992	1993	1994	1995
Central government												
Included in expenditure on goods and services	GILN	22 656	23 971	26 131	28 105	30 698	33 777	35 951	36 989	34 421	28 954	27 094
of which: Teachers' pension increase payments	GILO	431	449	483	505	547	617	733	802	849	863	890
In trading services	GILP	74	84	77	63	73	93	44	19	19	11	31
Charged to capital account	GILQ	87	84	103	95	119	134	129	56	33	33	30
Financed by grants	GILR	34	43	50	47	43	46	48	50	55	57	55
Local authorities												
Included in expenditure on goods and services	CSBN	20 696	22 695	24 787	27 034	28 132	30 246	32 601	35 032	34 123	34 445	36 124
In trading services	CFFV	1 929	2 024	2 055	2 482	2 981	3 547	4 316	4 595	4 758	4 927	5 104
Charged to capital account	CFFW	234	219	202	179	175	129	159	171	177	185	191
Total	GILV	45 753	49 120	53 405	58 005	62 221	67 972	73 248	76 912	73 586	68 692	68 629

non-domestic rates (NNDR), classified as a central government tax, replaced non-domestic local authority rates in Great Britain in April 1990. Rate receipts from the second quarter of 1990 relate only to district councils in Northern Ireland. Distributions from the NNDR pool to local authorities are recorded under central government grants (SM10.17).

(vii) Following the establishment of the Polytechnics and Colleges Funding Council in April 1989 (classified to the private sector) expenditure of polytechnics in England is excluded (SM 10.5). From April 1993 they have become Universities with the establishment of the Higher Education Funding Council.

(viii) Land drainage payments to regional water authorities are included as local authority final consumption until August 1989. From September 1989, when the National Rivers Authority assumed responsibility for these functions, payments made by local authorities to the National Rivers Authority (a central government body) are deducted from central government grants to local authorities.

(ix) From the 1992 Blue Book miscellaneous capital receipts include private sector contributions to local authority capital expenditure.

(x) From their inception in September 1989, expenditure by grant maintained schools has been excluded (SM 10.26).

(xi) The Council Tax replaced the Community Charge from April 1993.

(xii) Further education and sixth form colleges were reclassified to the private sector from April 1993, following the establishment of the Further Education Funding Council.

Chapter 9: General government

Table 9.1: Summary account

From the 1985 Blue Book this table includes certain central government

receipts classified as **Miscellaneous current transfers**. For details see notes to Table 7.2.

Social security contributions. This term has been adopted, from the 1986 Blue Book, in place of the previous usage 'National insurance, etc contributions'. It is now consistent with the conventions of international organisations (SM 11.7-9).

Footnote 1. Royalties are included, from the 1986 Blue Book, in the total revenue figure (SM 11.9).

Table 9.4: Analysis of total expenditure

This table shows a functional analysis of the consolidated expenditure of central and local government, sub-divided by economic category. From the 1985 Blue Book a new analysis of expenditure has been used called the 'classification of the functions of government' (COFOG). This classification has been agreed for the purposes of international statistics and details of the new system are to be found in the United Nations publication produced by the Department of International Economic and Social Affairs, Statistical Office: **Statistical Papers, Series M, No. 70, Classification of the Functions of Government**.

The classification contains three levels of detail; (i) 14 major groups (01 to 14); (ii) groups (denoted by a third digit) and (iii) sub-groups (denoted by a fourth digit). The major groups may be thought of as broad objectives of government, while the groups and sub-groups detail the means by which these broad objectives are achieved. There are 14 major groups, 61 groups and 127 sub-groups.

The United Kingdom accounts are published only at the major group level although some sub-group totals are shown in order to help for comparison with the previous analysis. A lower level of disaggregation is not available since complete consistency with COFOG at the detailed level is not possible.

The functions performed by Government fall under four main headings: (a) General government services (major groups 01-03); (b) Community and social services (major groups 04-08); (c) Economic services (major groups 09 - 13); and (d) Other functions (major group 14).

(a)   General government services comprise:

01   General public services
Executive and legislative organs, financial and fiscal affairs, external affairs, economic aid, fundamental research and general services.

02   Defence
Military and civil defence, foreign military aid.

03   Public order and safety
Police and fire protection, law courts and prisons.

(b)   Community and social affairs comprise:

04   Education.

05   Health
National Health Service and Public health.

06   Social security and welfare.

07   Housing and community amenity.
Housing and community development, water supply, sanitary affairs, street lighting.

08   Recreational and cultural.

(c)   Economic services comprise:

09   Fuel and energy
Coal mining, petroleum and natural gas, nuclear fuel and electricity.

10   Agriculture, forestry and fishing.

11   Mining and mineral resources (other than fuels), manufacturing and construction (including consumer protection).

12   Transport and communications
Road, rail, air and water transport, pipelines and communications.

13   Other economic affairs and services
Distributive trades , hotels and restaurants, tourism, multipurpose development projects, general economic and commercial affairs, general labour services.

(d)   Other functions comprise:

14   Other expenditure not classified by major group
Public debt transactions, interest etc.

Further details are to be found in the United Nations publication referred to above (SM 11.31-205).

Where there is an organisational change within government no change in classification is apparent.

The table (on the previous page) gives details of central government and local authorities' total expenditure on wages, salaries and employers' contributions to national insurance, superannuation, etc. This table may also be used to build up the income from employment figures for central

and local government in Table 2.6. In addition to the amounts included in current expenditure on goods and services, the table shows the amounts included in trading services, financed by grants, and charged to capital accounts.

Education Grants to Universities, polytechnics and grant maintained schools, formerly in **current grants to the personal sector** are now in **final consumption** (see notes to table 7.2).

Health. Reimbursement of costs of medical treatment and subscriptions to international organisations are included, from the 1986 Blue Book, as a new item under 'Current grants abroad' (SM 11.136-139 and 11.177-182).

Fuel and energy. Capital grants to the private sector and to public corporations now include distribution of the fossil fuel levy.

Table 9.5: Taxes on expenditure and subsidies: allocation by sector and by type of expenditure

From the 1987 Blue Book, the previous Table 4.10 has been combined with this table to show the allocation of taxes and subsidies by sector and type of expenditure. This table was also expanded to give more detail of the sectoral allocation of taxes and subsidies on expenditure. In more recent editions, the sectoral analysis of subsidies has been omitted. It must be noted that the figures in Table 9.5 must be taken only as a broad indication of the allocation of taxes on expenditure between the sectors (SM 6.664-667, 11.21 and 11.22).

Table 9.6: Allocation of taxes by sector, type of income and property

Income tax: Wages and salaries: Dividends, interest, rent and trading incomes. For years before the present schemes, tax relief on life assurance premiums and on mortgage interest was given through the PAYE code or through the tax assessment. The estimated amounts of relief given against tax deducted from wages and salaries and from trading income were as follows:

	Life assurance premiums		Mortgage interest	
	Wages and salaries	Trading incomes	Wages and salaries	Trading incomes
1978	230	15	979	57
1979	58	14	1 246	63
1980			1 745	77
1981			1 850	100
1982			2 132	120
1983			554	108

£ million

For rough comparison with the later years' figures given in Table 9.6, account should be taken of relief given since 1983 in addition to Mortgage Interest Relief at source (MIRAS). Such other relief is given at higher rates, or where the loan is outside the MIRAS scheme. From April 1979, relief for life assurance premiums has been given directly by deduction from the premium paid to the Life Office, which then claims reimbursement from the Inland Revenue. From April 1983 the similar MIRAS scheme has operated for mortgage interest relief (SM 11.28).

Social security benefits

Estimates of tax deducted from statutory sick pay paid by the employer are included in this item from the 1985 Blue Book as payments were financed by general government. From April 1994 most employers ceased to be reimbursed by government for statutory sick payments they had made. Where statutory sick pay is not reimbursed any tax paid on it is counted as taxes on wages and salaries from that date.

Chapter 10: International transactions.

This chapter was new from the 1989 edition. It summarises entries in *United Kingdom Balance of Payments*, 1996 edition. See note to Table 3.4 above.

Chapter 11: Sector financial accounts.

From the 1989 edition, this Chapter has been renumbered. It was formerly Chapter 10, superseding the earlier *Section 13: Financial accounts*. From the 1987 Blue Book, the data formerly given in Table 13.1: *Financial surplus or deficit: Summary analysis by sector*, are given in Tables 3.5 and 3.6.

Table 11.1: Sector summary

This gives data for the latest 5 years, shows how financial accounts link to the rest of the national accounts via the sector financial surpluses/deficits and sector capital accounts. The remaining tables in this chapter, which give time series for financial transactions of individual sectors, can be linked to the long run of sector summary capital accounts in Tables 3.5 and 3.6.

From the 1994 Blue Book, deposits with banks and building societies have been further sub-divided in to ordinary deposits and money market instruments (commercial paper, certificates of deposit, other short-term paper for both sterling and foreign currency. The split between sight and time deposits with banks is not shown.

From the 1994 Blue Book, deposits with other financial institutions are no longer shown. Only banks and building societies have been permitted to take deposits since 1982. Data for 1981 and earlier are available on request.

From the 1989 Blue Book, the term 'monetary sector' has been replaced by 'banks'. This reflects the fact that liabilities of these institutions became less dominant in the definitions of monetary aggregates. Similarly, in this chapter, building societies have been detached from other financial institutions because of the importance of their liabilities in the monetary aggregates. They are shown combined with banks in Table 11.1 and separately in Table 11.6 (SM 14.5-15).

Estimates have not been compiled for the saving, the financial surplus/

deficit, or the sector balancing item for banks, building societies, life assurance and pension funds or the remaining financial institutions. Consequently, these entries in Tables 11.5, 11.6, 11.7 and 11.8 are shown as 'not available'.

Partial estimates only have been included for some financial institutions which either do not report their financial activity or are not fully integrated into the system of financial returns.

From the 1991 Blue Book, the figures for 'other lending by financial institutions' include lending (net of repayments) in the form finance leases.

From the 1996 Blue Book, UK company securities has been sub-divided into three separate financial instruments: quoted ordinary shares; unquoted ordinary shares; and bonds and preference shares in the tables in this Chapter. The individual components are shown in Table 11.16. This revised methodology has led to substantial revisions for some sectors in some years. Revised data have been compiled going back to 1990 but not earlier because of limitations in the data source. The estimate for bonds and preference shares exclude bonds and notes with an initial maturity of 1-5 years issued by banks and building societies. Transactions in these securities appear under bank and building society sterling and foreign currency money market instruments.

The methodology used to compile the estimates of bank and building society money market instruments has also been revised. Among the changes has been to move overseas sector's transactions in bonds and notes with an initial maturity of 1-5 years from UK company securities into bank and building society money market instruments. This brings the presentation of the overseas sector's transactions in these securities into line with that for the domestic sector.

Table 11.7: Life assurance and pension funds

An accruals adjustment line has been introduced into this table. This follows a recommendation of a recent consultancy report into methodological issues within this account. It is counterparted to the personal sector.

Two new lines have been introduced into this table, for transactions in building society sterling and foreign currency money market instruments, as a result of the methodological reviews of these financial instruments and UK company securities. The transactions included in these new lines had previously been included under UK company securities.

For information about the financial accounts, an alternative source to *Sources and Methods* is Section 8 of the *Financial, Statistics Explanatory Handbook* along with the supplementary information in *Financial Statistics* which notifies changes between issues of this handbook.

Chapter 12: National and sector balance sheets.

From the 1989 edition, this Chapter was renumbered. It was formerly Chapter 11.

The tables show tangible assets analysed under the same broad headings as elsewhere in the national accounts and (since the 1989 edition) they show financial assets and liabilities in the categories used in the financial transactions accounts. National external financial assets and liabilities are consistent with those published in the United Kingdom Balance of Payments.

In general, the balance sheets are at current market value, so the changes they show from one time to another are not necessarily the same as transactions in the same interval. Price and other changes can also affect the outcome. Where there is no market valuation, the nearest available approximation is used. The data on direct investment, in particular, are only at book value, which can be substantially different from market value.

A general description of national and sector balance sheets including the sources and methods for the financial items was also given in the November 1980 issue of *Economic Trends* (No 325). Some further information on the financial data is given in the *Financial Statistics Explanatory Handbook*, Section 14.

Balance sheet estimates of UK company securities and bank and building society money market instruments have been revised in a similar way to transactions in these securities, referred to above in the notes to Chapter 11. The new estimates of levels for the three component financial instruments of UK company securities are shown in Table 12.13. The new methodology has resulted in substantial revisions to previous estimates for UK company securities for some sectors since 1990 and introduced some discontinuities at the end of 1989.

Table 12.2 Personal sector
A new line has been included in this table under financial liabilities, for UK company securities, as a result of the methodological review of this financial instrument. This series reflects issues of bonds by universities and housing associations.

Table 12.7 Life assurance and pension funds
This table has been changed to include the balance sheet equivalents of the new lines referred to under the notes for Table 11.7.

SECTION FOUR: Capital formation and capital stock.

Chapter 13: Gross domestic fixed capital formation.
From the 1989 edition, this Chapter has been renumbered. It was formerly Chapter 12.

The industrial analyses in Tables 13.6 to 13.8 are based on SIC(92). See page 148 for further details.

Estimates for 1988 and later years. Estimates of total fixed capital formation have traditionally been compiled using data collected from various annual and quarterly surveys of business expenditure. From the most recent years however, a need to supplement the survey-based estimates has been shown by studies of their apparent shortfall when compared with estimates of the supply of capital goods based on production and trade data. Accordingly the estimates from 1988 of total fixed capital formation, as well as the analyses by sector, industry and type of asset, all take due account of the available estimates of the supply of capital goods to the domestic market. The process of supplementing the survey based estimates for 1988 and later years is least well based in the case of the analysis by industry of gross domestic fixed capital formation. No comprehensive industrial analysis of the supply of capital goods is available, so the analysis of fixed capital formation by industry relies on broad assessments of the quality of the available survey estimates. In tables 13.6 to 13.8, it has been decided so to adjust the estimates of fixed capital formation for: Communication; Banking, finance and insurance; Business services, etc; and Miscellaneous services.

For 1996, estimates of total fixed capital formation have been compiled using the same approach as for preceding years. However, the results of the annual benchmark surveys of business expenditure for 1996 are not available to help the industrial analysis. In their absence, estimates based on the statutory quarterly surveys have been used. These estimates are more robust than those based on the voluntary quarterly surveys of the past so more detail is given than in earlier years' Blue Books. Once the annual survey results are available the full range of industrial estimates will be shown.

G Gross domestic fixed capital formation 1994: Analysis by industry and sector

£ million

	Private sector	Public sector		Total
		Public corporation	General government	
Agriculture, hunting, forestry and fishing	838	–	92	930
Mining and quarrying including oil and gas extraction	3 726	91	–	3 817
Manufacturing (Revised definition)	13 184	322	28	13 534
Electricity , gas and water supply	4 729	347	149	5 225
Construction	727	–	–	727
Wholesale and retail trade:repairs; hotels and restaurants	8 263	–	–	8 263
Transport,storage and communication	9 928	2 422	209	12 559
Financial intermediation, real estate, renting and business activities	11 512	380	300	12 192
Other services	4 471	1 643	10 925	17 039
Dwellings	18 147	245	2 732	21 124
Land and existing buildings	6 487	–535	–2 145	3 807
Total	82 012	4 915	12 290	99 217

Table G

Supplementary information

Analysis by industry and sector. A cross-classification by industry and sector of the estimates for 1993 is given in the table on the previous page. This table, and Tables 13.6 to 13.8 are based on the SIC(92). See page 148 for further details.

Certain detailed industrial estimates of GDFCF inclusive of finance leased assets are not available for years up to 1988. Such information as is available, exclusive of finance leased assets for years up to and including 1988, will be supplied by the ONS on request.

Airline industry. From the 1986 Blue Book, fixed capital formation in aircraft has been estimated from the Civil Aviation Authority inquiry into the balance of payments and capital transactions of UK airlines (SM 12.76-77).

Railway industry. Before 1980 expenditure on continuous welded rail is classified to capital formation rather than current expenditure, where it is classified now. This expenditure amounted to £72 million in 1979. These estimates also take no account of various other changes in British Rail's definition of railways investment (SM 12.71).

Dwellings. Revised series for stocks of uncompleted dwellings together with stocks of completed but unsold dwellings (see note on Chapter 14 below) are, from the 1985 Blue Book, used in calculating fixed capital formation in new private dwellings (SM 12.90).

Revaluation at constant prices. From the 1985 Blue Book the range of output price indices used to deflate expenditure on new building and works was extended to enable a finer deflation of public sector works, in particular distinguishing price trends for building and civil engineering projects. (SM 12.98).

Chapter 14: Capital consumption and stock of fixed capital.

From the 1989 edition, this Chapter has been renumbered. It was formerly Chapter 13.

General. The estimates of capital stock and of capital consumption published here ought to be regarded as less reliable than most estimates published in the national accounts. For the most part, they have been calculated using the perpetual inventory method. As such, they depend to a great extent on assumptions about the asset lives for different categories of asset; there is very little hard information available to support these assumptions. Some of the capital stock estimates may not be reliable to within 20 per cent. More information on the methodology used and on reliability may be found in *Sources and Methods* (paragraphs 12.104-124).

The industrial analysis in tables in this chapter is based on the SIC(92). See page 148 for further details.

Leased assets. From the 1991 Blue Book, assets on finance leases have been recorded on a "user" basis for periods from 1978.

Detailed estimates of the use of finance leased assets within the manufacturing industries are not available for the years 1978 to 1987. The analysis of gross capital stock within manufacturing, published as table 14.10 in the 1990 Blue Book, has therefore been discontinued. Such estimates as are available, exclusive of finance leased assets for years before 1988, will be supplied by the ONS on request.

Capital consumption. As described in *Sources and Methods* (paragraphs 12.105-112) depreciation is estimated using the straight line method. From the 1985 Blue Book, the asset life assumptions used in the calculations have been revised in relation to the energy and water industries.

Chapter 15: Change in the book value of stocks.

From the 1989 edition, this Chapter has been renumbered. It was formerly Chapter 14.

The industrial analysis in Tables 15.1-15.3 is based on the SIC(92). See page 148 for further details. Due to reclassification from SIC80 to SIC92, for the years 1989 to 1991, there are small differences between the industry breakdowns of stock appreciation shown in table 2.2 and the figures used to produce table 15.2.

Construction. From the 1985 Blue Book, changes in stocks of materials on site have been taken into account. Also, stock appreciation has been calculated in respect of materials on site; private sector work in progress on uncompleted dwellings; private dwellings completed but not yet sold; and land banks of private house builders. It has not (from the 1985 Blue Book) been calculated for work in progress, other than on dwellings, by the private sector (SM 13.48-50).

Stocks held abroad. From the 1985 Blue Book, where stocks held abroad by UK-based enterprises can be identified separately from other stocks, they are excluded from the estimates of stock changes (SM 13.13). *Other industries*: From the 1988 edition, stock appreciation has been calculated on silver stocks and other metals and this appreciation allocated to industrial and commercial companies (SM 13.56).

Central government. From the 1988 edition, estimates of stockbuilding by the Intervention Board for Agricultural Produce (IBAP) are calculated directly from the figures of IBAP ownership of physical stocks (SM 13.59).

SECTION FIVE: Other analyses and derived statistics.

Chapter 16: Percentage distributions and growth rates.

From the 1989 edition, this Chapter has been renumbered. It was formerly Chapter 15.

Tables 16.1 to 16.7: percentages and proportions

From the 1989 edition, these proportions are each rounded individually, so that they may not add precisely to totals and subtotals in the table.

Table 16.8: Rates of change in GDP at current market prices

This presentation is introduced from the 1990 edition.

Tables 16.9 to 16.14: Rates of change

From the 1986 Blue Book, the growth rates have been calculated at annual compound rates. Previously the calculation used an average of annual year-on-year growth rates. The results may differ by about 0.1 to 0.2 per cent from those given by the previous method; but in most instances they are the same (SM 4.61).

Chapter 17: Production, population and employment.

Table 17.1: Population and employment. Mid-year estimates

From the 1989 edition, this Chapter has been renumbered. It was formerly Chapter 16.

Local authorities' employment included approximately one-half of total employment under the Community Programme during the schemes operation from 1983 to 1988. The numbers involved in 1983 were 27,000 and in 1988, 67,000.

The reclassification of former polytechnics and higher education colleges in England to the private sector from April 1989 resulted in a fall of around 60,000 in local authority employment. The establishment of NHS trusts from April 1991, resulted in the reclassification of the staff of these trusts from the central government to the public corporations sector. At mid 1991 total employment in NHS trusts was 124,000, and 314,000 and 655,000 at mid 1992 and 1993 respectively.

Further education and sixth-form college funding transferred from local authority control from April 1993 resulting in a fall of around 160,000 in local authority employment.

Revisions since the 1995 edition

The table on the following page shows the revisions since the 1995 Blue Book to the estimates of the expenditure and income components of gross domestic product and to estimates of the main aggregates, including the estimate of Gross national product. Some of the revisions were made in the quarterly articles on national accounts published in the January and April issues of *"UK Economic Accounts - A Quarterly Supplement to Economic Trends"*. Estimates of GDP are subject to revisions as more information becomes available. Early estimates (that is, those for the most recent period of account) are particularly uncertain.

Years before 1986. In this edition of the Blue Book the years prior to 1986 have not been reopened to incorporate revisions. There have been no revisions to overall GDP for years prior to 1991.

REV
Revisions since CSO Blue Book, 1995 Edition

£ million

	1984	1985	1986	1987	1988	1989	1990	1991	1992	1993	1994
Expenditure components at current prices (Table 1.2)											
Consumers' expenditure	–	–	–	–	–	–	–	497	1 775	937	–808
General government final consumption	–	–	–	–	–	–	–	–	–	116	30
Gross domestic fixed capital formation	–	–	–	–	–	–	–	–	–	–351	–858
Value of physical increase in stocks and work in progress	–	–	–	–	–	–	–	–	–	–	429
Exports	–	–	–	–	–	–	–	55	298	610	2 140
less Imports[1]	–	–	–	–	–	–	–	199	399	861	1 420
less Taxes on expenditure[1]	–	–	–	–	–	–	–	–	–	–1 090	–812
Subsidies	–	–	–	–	–	–	–	–	–	–249	–164
Statistical discrepancy (expenditure adjustment)	–	–	–	–	–	–	–	–	–	–	–124
Expenditure components at constant 1990 prices (Table 1.3)											
Consumers' expenditure	–	–	–	–	–	–	–	122	115	–432	–1 969
General government final consumption	–	–	–	–	–	–	–	–	–	–57	–168
Gross domestic fixed capital formation	–	–	–	–	–	–	–	–	–	48	–664
Value of physical increase in stocks and work in progress	–	–	–	–	–	–	–	–	–	–	164
Exports	–	–	–	–	–	–	–	69	248	442	1 887
less Imports[1]	–	–	–	–	–	–	–	191	363	643	–424
less Adjustment to factor cost[1]	–	–	–	–	–	–	–	–	–	–821	–1 090
Statistical discrepancy (expenditure adjustment)	–	–	–	–	–	–	–	–	–	–	–106
Income components at current prices (Table 1.4)											
Income from employment	–	–	–	15	280	285	712	308	–500	–188	2 188
Gross trading profits of companies	–	–	–	385	280	280	192	–	328	–734	–4 721
Gross trading surplus of public corporations	–	–	–	–	–	–	–	–	–	–31	–299
Gross trading surplus of general government enterprises	–	–	–	–	–	–	–	–	–	–	4
Other income	–	–	–	–400	–560	–565	–904	45	1 846	2 245	2 578
Total domestic income	–	–	–	–	–	–	–	353	1 674	1 292	–250
less Stock appreciation[1]	–	–	–	–	–	–	–	–	–	–	154
Statistical discrepancy (income adjustment)	–	–	–	–	–	–	–	–	–	–	441
Output components index at constant factor cost (Table 1.6)											
Agriculture, hunting, forestry and fishing	–	–	–	–	–	–	–	–	–	–2.4	–5.1
Mining and quarrying	–	–	–	–	–	–	–	–	–	–	0.1
Manufacturing	–	–	–	–	–	–	–	–	–	0.2	0.2
Electricity, gas and water supply	–	–	–	–	–	–	–	–	–	–	–0.3
Construction	–	–	–	–	–	–	–	–	–	–	–0.1
Distribution, hotels and catering	–0.2	–0.3	–0.3	0.4	0.9	0.4	–	–	–	2.0	1.7
Transport, storage and communication	0.2	0.3	0.3	0.3	0.4	0.1	–	–	–	0.8	0.5
Other	–0.1	–0.1	–0.2	–0.3	–0.5	–0.3	–	–	–	–0.3	0.1
GDP at current factor cost	–	–	–	–	–	–	–	353	1 674	1 292	37
GDP at current market prices	–	–	–	–	–	–	–	353	1 674	451	–611
GNP at current factor cost	–	–	–	–	–	–	546	1 077	1 104	1 599	–1 791
GNP at current market prices	–	–	–	–	–	–	546	1 077	1 104	758	–2 439
GDP at 1990 factor cost	–	–	–	–	–	–	–	–	–	179	658
GDP at 1990 market prices	–	–	–	–	–	–	–	–	–	–642	–432
GNP at 1990 factor cost	–	–	–	–	–	–	546	722	–570	460	–1 074
GNP at 1990 market prices	–	–	–	–	–	–	546	722	–570	–361	–2 164

1 Estimates of imports of goods and services and taxes on expenditure (which is the main part of the adjustment to factor cost) are deducted in arriving at gross domestic product at factor cost. The effect of revisions to these estimates on the total therefore involves reversing the sign. A similar situation applies in the case of stock appreciation and the income components of gross domestic product.

INDEX

Figures indicate Table numbers. The letter "G" indicates that the item appears in the Glossary. The letter "I" indicates that the item is discussed in the section introductions and the appropriate paragraph number is given in brackets.

Index

Index

Index